THE BATTERED WOMAN SYNDROME

D1523232

Lenore E. A. Walker, EdD, is a professor at Nova Southeastern University (NSU) College of Psychology, where she is also a coordinator of the clinical forensic psychology doctoral concentration and director of the master's in forensic psychology program. She is also in the independent practice of forensic psychology, where she specializes in work with victims of interpersonal gender violence, particularly battered women and abused children. Dr. Walker earned her undergraduate degree in 1962 from City University of New York (CUNY) Hunter College, her master of science in 1967 from CUNY City College, and her EdD in psychology in 1972 from Rutgers, the State University of New Jersey. In 2004, she received a postdoctoral master's degree in clinical psychopharmacology at NSU. She has been elected as a member of American Psychological Association (APA) governance since the mid-1980s, having served several terms on the APA Council of Representatives; on the board of directors; as the president of several divisions, including Division 35, the Society for the Psychology of Women, Division 42, Independent Practice, and Division 46, Media Psychology; and on boards and committees such as the Committee on Legal Issues (COLI) and the Committee on International Relations in Psychology (CIRP).

She has worked on high-publicity (and thus high-risk) cases such as battered women who kill their abusive partners in self-defense, and has testified on behalf of protective mothers who are being challenged for custody by abusive fathers. She lectures and does training workshops all over the world about prevention, psychotherapy, legal cases, and public policy initiatives for abused women and children. Dr. Walker has authored numerous professional articles and 15 books, including *The Battered Woman* (1979), *The Battered Woman Syndrome* (1984/2000), *Terrifying Love: Why Battered Women Kill and How Society Responds* (1989), *Abused Women and Survivor Therapy* (1994), *Introduction to Forensic Psychology* (2004, coauthored with David Shapiro), *Abortion Counseling: A Clinician's Guide to Psychology, Legislation, Politics, and Competency* (2007, coauthored with Rachel Needle), *First Responder's Guide to Abnormal Psychology* (2007, coauthored with William Dorfman), and *A Clinician's Guide to Forensic Psychology* (2016, coauthored with David Shapiro).

THE BATTERED WOMAN SYNDROME

Fourth Edition

Lenore E. A. Walker, EdD

SPRINGER PUBLISHING COMPANY

NEW YORK

Springer Publishing Company, LLC
11 West 42nd Street
New York, NY 10036
www.springerpub.com

Acquisitions Editor: Sheri W. Sussman
Compositor: Westchester Publishing Services

ISBN: 9780826170989
e-book ISBN: 9780826170996

16 17 18 19 20 / 5 4 3 2 1

The author and the publisher of this Work have made every effort to use sources believed to be reliable to provide information that is accurate and compatible with the standards generally accepted at the time of publication. The author and publisher shall not be liable for any special, consequential, or exemplary damages resulting, in whole or in part, from the readers' use of, or reliance on, the information contained in this book. The publisher has no responsibility for the persistence or accuracy of URLs for external or third-party Internet websites referred to in this publication and does not guarantee that any content on such websites is, or will remain, accurate or appropriate.

Library of Congress Cataloging-in-Publication Data

Names: Walker, Lenore E., author.
Title: The battered woman syndrome / Lenore E. A. Walker, EdD.
Description: Fourth Edition. | New York : Springer Publishing Company, 2016. | Revised edition of the author's The battered woman syndrome, 2009. | Includes index.
Identifiers: LCCN 2016020159 | ISBN 9780826170989
Subjects: LCSH: Wife abuse—United States. | Abused wives—United States—Psychology.
Classification: LCC HV6626.2 .W33 2016 | DDC 362.82/92—dc23 LC record available at https://lccn.loc.gov/2016020159

Special discounts on bulk quantities of our books are available to corporations, professional associations, pharmaceutical companies, health care organizations, and other qualifying groups. If you are interested in a custom book, including chapters from more than one of our titles, we can provide that service as well.

For details, please contact:
Special Sales Department, Springer Publishing Company, LLC
11 West 42nd Street, 15th Floor, New York, NY 10036-8002
Phone: 877-687-7476 or 212-431-4370; Fax: 212-941-7842
E-mail: sales@springerpub.com

Printed in the United States of America by Gasch Printing.

CONTENTS

PREFACE

This new, fourth edition of *The Battered Woman Syndrome* has been a joy for me to write given the enormous amount of new research and practice that has arisen within the almost 40 years since the first edition was written in the early 1980s. The first edition contained the results of the initial research study that was funded by the U.S. National Institute of Mental Health from 1977 through 1981. It was the first time a psychologist had studied the impact of over 400 women experiencing domestic violence. The amount of data collected was enormous and the first edition contained numerous tables and figures to help explain the findings. Initially, some of the information was used to inform policy makers, especially in helping the criminal justice field become more sensitive to the needs of battered women so they could be better protected. The data were there for the use of new researchers, a process that is used in advancing scientific knowledge.

In the second edition, published in 2000, I integrated the new research that had been published in the almost 20 years since the original data were collected and disseminated. It was exciting to see how the field of study had grown; where it changed and where it stayed pretty much the same. Laws had changed and were enforced. More women were better protected. Political discourse about what to call domestic violence became a challenge, with advocates wanting to use the term "intimate partner abuse/violence" rather than "domestic violence" or even "battered women." The links and boundaries with child abuse and other family violence were established. The commonalities with other forms of gender violence such as rape, sexual assault, exploitation, and harassment were clarified. Calls for more policy changes, especially to better protect children and mothers going through divorces, were issued. The data were there, but the time was not right to make the necessary changes in family court laws and presumptions to better protect abused women and children, despite the fact that the issues in domestic violence were similar around the world. During this time period, the United Nations and World Health

Organization became involved and collected and disseminated information to encourage all countries to make policy changes.

By 2009, when the third edition of *The Battered Woman Syndrome* was published, I had moved to Nova Southeastern University and began collecting data again. It was exciting to see that the original information that was learned from the first study was still relevant. This made it possible to look in more depth at some of the areas that seemed to be difficult for battered women in their attempts to heal from the abuse. The research team culled through the original Battered Woman Syndrome Questionnaire (BWSQ) assessment instrument and began the task of eliminating questions that did not yield useful information and add others that we hoped would give us the data we needed. As we began to analyze the old and new data, we were able to develop the framework for how to measure the battered woman syndrome. This was important because battered woman advocates and some other researchers did not like the term, for several reasons. First, they believed that labeling a syndrome would continue to victimize women by focusing on their mental health. Second, they believed that there were other explanations for the dynamics of intimate partner abuse that would better explain the situational as well as psychological variables noted. For example, a focus on the violation of the woman's civil rights was preferred to the focus on health and mental health.

While the members of our research team accepted that their concerns were valid, we still believed that there were significant health and mental health consequences from being abused that could respond to efforts by psychologists to assist in their healing and empowerment. In the third edition, the actual psychological variables were listed that were considered part of the battered woman syndrome.

Our research team continued the data collection and analysis and these new results are integrated here in this fourth edition. In addition, we have included new chapters that highlight some of the other forms of violence against women, to demonstrate the close relationship of all forms of gender violence and its impact. In this edition, the focus is on the psychological and physical damage to children raised in homes where their fathers abuse their mothers. Three chapters dealing with the psychological effects on children living in domestic violence homes have been included, with more details on impact from coercive control, child abuse, and sex trafficking. We emphasize how our data are similar to the large-scale study conducted by Felitti and his colleagues (1998) on adverse childhood experiences (ACEs). A fourth chapter included in this edition emphasizes the high risk to divorcing moms who lose the ability to properly parent and protect their children when the family courts force shared parenting without understanding the dynamics of coercive control used by the batterer to continue his dominance and abuse. This risk extends to murder and suicide cases studied by the research team, where we found the highest risk when the domestic violence family was separated and involved with the family court. A chapter discussing these findings on murder–suicide has been added to this edition. Information on identifying the lethality potential with some risk assessment instruments was added to the chapter on risk assessment.

Although battered women are better understood in the criminal justice system, we looked at the numbers of women who are serving time in prison because they gave a false confession about their roles in the death of someone. We have been following the work of the Innocence Project that has exonerated over 200 men, many of whom falsely confessed, and are attempting to design methodology for better identifying women, especially battered women, who falsely confess for a variety of reasons described in the new chapter on false confessions. Given our concerns with health and mental health consequences, we added discussions on these issues, as well as reviewed the advances made in trauma-informed psychotherapy. We have analyzed the data from over 500 people who have been involved with our evidence-based STEP program in the jails and have slightly revised the program, developed new materials, and created a manual to assist in its administration. Although we knew the program was not the same as typical group psychotherapy, we now better understand that it is still a form of psychotherapy that includes psychoeducation and skill building along with time to process the new information. This program is ideal for working within the constraints of jails and other confined detention facilities as well as in clinics and independent practitioners' offices.

We plan to take the research to the next level by validating the BWSQ instrument statistically and attempting to streamline it so that it will be a useful assessment tool for all who are working with battered women or survivors of any form of intimate partner violence. The model we have developed and are beginning to test will involve scaling the data collected into areas of preabuse conditions, adding the frequency and severity from the abuse itself, and then testing to see if the seven factors we have identified so far as the battered woman syndrome will continue to hold up statistically.

Lenore E. A. Walker, EdD

REFERENCE

Felitti, V. J., Anda, R. F., Nordenberg, D., Williamson, D. F., Spitz, A. M., Edwards, V., . . . Marks, J. S. (1998). Relationship of childhood abuse and household dysfunction to many of the leading causes of death in adults: The Adverse Childhood Experiences (ACE) Study. *American Journal of Preventive Medicine, 14*(4), 245–258.

ACKNOWLEDGMENTS

All of the four editions of *The Battered Woman Syndrome*—or "the book" as we like to call it in our research laboratory at Nova Southeastern University College of Psychology—have been a labor of love for all the graduate psychology students who have joined our research team in the past 14 years. As we have had over 30 students per year, there are too many to name individually. However, each of their contributions has been important to gathering and analyzing the data reported in the book. Most learned how to administer the Battered Woman Syndrome Questionnaire (BWSQ) to the hundreds of courageous women who volunteered to participate in our study. Some spent the many hours looking up and reviewing the latest research in our library system, now mostly on the Internet data collections. Others drew the flyers that we passed out in the community to gain as representative a sample as possible. They helped fill out the myriad of forms needed to get institutional review board permissions each year for the studies. They made copies of materials, stapled them together, and then removed all staples from those that were brought into the jails. They sat at the computer and tediously entered the data. They helped analyze the results, but only some were able to present at conferences. We all laughed and cried when we would get together to share the stories told by the courageous women who participated in the study. I sincerely thank each and every one of the research assistants who worked together with us over these years.

There are a few of these researchers and now psychologists whom I want to single out, as they were driving forces behind the rest of us. Dr. Kate Richmond was one of the major sources of energy to help me revise the original research on battered woman syndrome (BWS) when she was a student at Nova Southeastern University College of Psychology. She brought Dr. Rachel Needle into the group as she graduated and Dr. Needle continues to work with us as an adjunct professor, now on the sexuality and body image areas. Dr. Needle and I took a side path together to publish

Abortion Counseling (Springer Publishing Company, 2007) while we were working on this research, as we realized that many of the few women who had emotional difficulties after an abortion were abuse victims. This book presents a clear view of the politics and psychological research for mental health professionals.

After Dr. Richmond graduated, Dr. Rachel Duros took over organizing the data analysis and demonstrated how BWS was empirically a part of posttraumatic stress disorder. Aleah Nathan coordinated data analysis when Dr. Duros graduated. Dr. Heidi Ardern organized the data collection section and when she graduated, Allison Tome continued her work. Gretchen Lamendola and Ron Dahl assisted in developing the reference list. Rebecca Brosch has been our research link with the women in the jail, while Kelley Gill, Crystal Carrio, Gillespie Stedding, and the rest of the women in the forensic practicum have organized the STEP program that has added such richness to our knowledge of the psychological impact of intimate partner violence on women. Cassandra Groth and then Vera Lopez Klinoff took over the management of the BWSQ, and together with the current coordinator, Lauren Schumacher, trained the researchers of the next few years.

In addition to the graduate students, there were a number of professors on our faculty who have been of enormous help in conceptualizing and operationalizing the research program. Dr. Vincent Van Hasselt has been a good friend and colleague whose knowledge about violence has been invaluable in understanding both our methodology and data analysis. Dr. Steven Gold, a superb traumatologist who has his own amazing research program, has also been available to share ideas. Dr. Tara Jungersen, who came on the faculty as an assistant professor wanting research experience, has become a strong member of our team, adding the counseling perspective to our work especially in analyzing and revising the STEP program. Her work with the local domestic violence council and Women in Distress battered women shelter has been invaluable in adding another group of volunteer participants to our data. Dr. Ryan Black, an incredible statistician, has provided the exact data analysis conceptual and operational backup to the project after the untimely death of Dr. Al Sellers who had helped us revise the BWSQ initially. Dr. Timothy Ludwig and Dr. Michelle Sanchez, psychologists at the Broward Sheriff's Organization's detention centers, were extraordinarily helpful in facilitating our work in the jails. Dean Karen Grosby has been more than generous in giving me the time necessary during crunch periods to make this research work.

The international friends who have been a part of my life remain some of my closest confidantes. Dr. Christina Antonopoulou, a Greek psychologist, whom I met at a victimology meeting in Il Ciocco, Italy, over 20 years ago, remains one of my best friends. She is the director of the Domestic Violence Institute of Greece and works on collecting data and training new psychologists there. We have traveled the world together. I have been friends with Dr. Patricia Villavicencio, a psychologist in Spain, since we met at a meeting of feminist psychologists in Amsterdam over 20 years ago. Dr. Villavicencio has also contributed to my thinking, and some of her work with her colleagues is discussed in this book. Drs. Carmen Delgado and Mark Beymach from the University of Salamanca and the Catholic University in Salamanca, where I have been teaching in their gender violence program, Dr. Jesus Melia from the University of Granada, and others in Spain have all contributed to our new understanding of the commonalities found in battered women in other countries. My good friend, the Honorable Saviona Rotlevy, a now-retired judge from Israel whom we met at a meeting in Rome over 15 years ago, helped rewrite the laws to reflect children's rights there and has helped keep me informed about the progress that the International Association of Women Judges has been making in helping develop worldwide initiatives to keep women and children safe. Dr. Josepha Steiner, a social worker and good friend from Israel, has gathered data on battered women in that war-torn country where PTSD abounds. These are just a few of the fabulous people working to make life better for women and children all over the world.

The professional friends whom I have met along this fantastic journey have filled my life with riches. I learn so much from the others I meet at each of the many conferences I have attended in the United States as well as all over the world. My women's writer group, W2W, a group of seven women who all have been strong leaders in psychology, has helped me shape my own thinking over the years. Dorothy Cantor, Carol Goodheart, Sandra Haber, Norine Johnson, Alice Rubenstein, Karen Zager, and I spend time together percolating ideas for our books on psychology each year in wonderful places. Our first book together, *Finding Your Voice: A Woman's Guide to Using Self-Talk for Fulfilling Relationships, Work, and Life* (2004), did not earn us a million dollars in money, but working on it together certainly did create a million-dollar bond of friendship. We tried our luck at the Kentucky Derby a few years later, but alas, although we had a fabulous time with the Kentucky Colonels, we won just a few dollars on the horses. We all love our chosen careers in psychology and the ability to help our clients and other professionals make a better world. Unfortunately, Norine Johnson has passed away and we all miss her presence a lot.

I thank my wonderful friend and editor, Sheri W. Sussman, who has been with me since the first edition of the book published by Springer. We grew up together over these past 35 years, laughing and crying with friends who are no longer with us, such as Lillian Schein, who was my first editor at Springer. Sheri has been so patient with my delays and the million excuses I have had that postponed the completion of the book. Through it all her vision has helped shape the manuscript, although any errors are wholly my own.

The incredible work of my dear friend, The Honorable Ginger Lerner-Wren, the first judge appointed to head the first U.S. mental health court, which opened in Broward County over 15 years ago, has taught me so much about the intersection between mental health issues and domestic violence. She has taught us all about keeping the respect and dignity for those who have emotional problems and helping them take responsibility for their recovery. We need not be afraid of stigmatizing battered women by using the language of psychology, especially talking about PTSD and BWS, where it is appropriate. Instead, we must be vigilant against victim-blaming and infantilization of women who can heal from the terrors of domestic violence. Many years ago, The Honorable Richard Price from New York City began the arduous task of training judges to better understand battered women who come before them, and he continues this important work today.

And I have saved the best for last in thanking my dear life partner, Dr. David Shapiro, who has helped nurture me while I pulled together all this information and wrote all the chapters. He has been a source of strength and I love him dearly for all that we have built together as a dual-career couple. Our children and grandchildren, who keep expanding and bringing new partners and babies into our lives, have been a source of joy and inspiration. My fabulous daughter, Karen Walker Gottesfeld, and her fantastic husband, Stephen Gottesfeld, together with their sons, my incredible grandsons, Max Walker Gottesfeld, Benjamin Mar Gottesfeld, and Oliver Gabriel Gottesfeld, fill my life with joy. My brother, Joel Auerbach, and his children, David, Jocelyn, and Rebecca, add to our joy, as does our entire family, which is too large to mention all by name here. And finally, the biggest thank you and kiss for my wonderful 99-year-young mother, Pearl Moncher Auerbach, who helped shape my values and tenacity in working in difficult places. Although she passed away this year, she is with me in spirit, always.

Lenore E. A. Walker

PART ONE

MYTHS AND SCIENCE OF DOMESTIC VIOLENCE

CHAPTER ONE

THE BATTERED WOMAN SYNDROME STUDY OVERVIEW

WHAT IS THE BATTERED WOMAN SYNDROME?

The research over the past 40 years reported in this book has led to the validation that living in a domestic violence family can produce psychological effects called the *battered woman syndrome* (BWS). The research team of professors and graduate students that I head at Nova Southeastern University's College of Psychology has been analyzing the data we have been collecting to determine if there is a group of psychological signs and symptoms called "BWS." The answer is, "yes." BWS is identified with seven factors:

1. Reexperiencing the trauma events intrusively
2. High levels of arousal and anxiety
3. High levels of avoidance and numbing of emotions
4. Cognitive difficulties
5. Disruption in interpersonal relationships
6. Physical health and body image problems
7. Sexual and intimacy issues

The first four factors are the clinical categories from the posttraumatic stress disorder (PTSD) diagnostic category. So it is said that BWS is a subcategory of PTSD. The second three factors are specific to what the women in our research told us.

The model we are using to statistically verify BWS from our data includes: childhood and preexisting situational conditions that interact with the severity and frequency of the abuse to create the seven factors of BWS in an individual.

We are entering the next phase of the research by identification of all the variables that will statistically validate the model and then hopefully will be able to develop an assessment tool to help identify and ameliorate the effects from violence.

In this edition of *The Battered Woman Syndrome*, the data that are being used to build the model are presented. Data from the previous research are included as they are being used in the creation of the model. Hopefully, it will encourage other investigators to look carefully at where these data take us.

WHAT IS THE SCOPE OF THE PROBLEM?

On September 16, 2015, all domestic violence programs in the United States were asked by the National Network to End Domestic Violence to report a census of services provided in a 24-hour period. The figures are both alarming and satisfying in the high number of battered women, over 70,000, who needed and received services during that day. At the same time, these agencies (almost 2,000 of them or 93% of known agencies reporting) had to turn down over 12,000 other requests for services, including emergency shelter, housing, transportation, child care, and legal representation because of lack of resources. Agencies reported answering over 25,000 hotline calls, averaging more than 14 hotline calls per minute, that day. The National Domestic Violence Hotline answered an additional 953 calls on the survey day. The services provided included:

- Individual support or advocacy
- Children's support or advocacy
- Emergency shelter
- Transportation
- Court advocacy/legal accompaniment
- Group support or advocacy

That is the good news. *But*, it was also reported that over 1,200 staff positions were eliminated in the past year and most of them were direct service providers.

This is just in the United States. All the other countries, most of which responded to the United Nations' calls to document services to all gender violence victims, make it clear that violence against women impacts everyone. Hopefully the research reported in this edition of *The Battered*

Woman Syndrome will make an impact on reducing or eliminating all forms of gender violence, including intimate partner abuse.

RESEARCH METHODOLOGY

Over the years, it has been found that the best way to understand violence in the home comes from listening to the descriptions obtained from those who experience it: victims, perpetrators, children, or observers. Until the first large-sized empirical study reported in the first edition of this book, in 1984, accurate descriptions of the violence had been difficult to obtain from women as well as men, partly due to the effects of the abuse experience as well as feelings of shame and fear of further harm. This particular study pioneered in using methods that were rarely used by researchers 30 years ago, although these methods are quite common today. I learned these techniques from my earlier exploratory study published in a book for the general public, *The Battered Woman* (Walker, 1979). Women were given the opportunity to fully describe their experiences in context, using what researchers today call *mixed method* with an "open-ended" technique combined together with "forced-choice" responses that prompted their memories and went beyond the denial and minimization that were the typical first responses. As a result, with a grant from the U.S. government, the study collected groundbreaking data that had never before been totally heard by anyone, including mental health and health professionals.

After almost 30 years, I published the second edition as it seemed like it was time to revisit the information collected in the original study in 1978 to 1981. In 2002, with a Presidential Scholar Grant from the President of Nova Southeastern University, where I have been a professor, the main assessment instrument, called the "Battered Woman Syndrome Questionnaire" (BWSQ), that was used in the first study was modified. A team of graduate students worked together with me, discarding some of the questions that yielded less information and strengthening those questions that appeared to assist women in remembering their experiences with an abuser. One of the most important areas in the original study was whether or not there was an identifiable collection of signs and symptoms that constituted the BWS. New questions that were specifically designed to assess for BWS were added to the BWSQ as were several standardized instruments measuring trauma that were developed by others during the intervening years. The questions were developed with the understanding of battered women gained from observations and interventions with them over all these years. The attention paid to multicultural and other diversity issues in all aspects of psychology has increased during these years, so the new sample has included women from other countries who either live in their country of origin or in the United States.

The understanding of domestic violence reported in the third edition was learned from the perceptions of the courageous battered women who were willing to share intimate details of their lives. That study suggests that even though trauma and victimization are more widely studied today, it is still difficult for women to talk about their experiences, just as it was during the late 1970s and early 1980s when we first started collecting this information. The data from all our research indicated that events that occurred in a woman's childhood as well as other factors in her life interacted with the violence she experienced by the batterer, and together they impacted upon the woman to produce her current mental state, which has been called "BWS." The research demonstrated that psychologists could reliably identify these various events and relationship factors and then measure their impact on the woman's current psychological status. These results could then be utilized to formulate treatment plans or present as testimony in court cases involving criminal, civil, family, juvenile, or other matters where the person's state of mind was at issue. Although the data we obtained supported the theories that I proposed at the time, it has become even more relevant today, almost 40 years later, to recognize the robust nature of these findings that continue to be reaffirmed in subsequent research.

After analyzing reported details about past and present feelings, thoughts, and actions of the women and the violent and nonviolent men, the data led me to conclude that there are no specific personality traits that would suggest a victim-prone personality for the women (see also Brown, 1992; Root, 1992), although there may be an identifiable violence-prone personality for the abusive men (Dutton, 1995; Holtzworth-Monroe & Stuart, 1994; Jacobson & Gottman, 1998; Kellen, Brooks, & Walker, 2005; Sonkin, 1995). From the woman's point of view, the batterer initiated the violence pattern that occurred in the relationship because of his inability to control his behavior when he got angry. There is still an ongoing debate in the field about whether the batterer is really unable to control his anger, as was perceived by the woman, or if he chooses to abuse her and therefore is very much in control of where and when he uses violence. The women's reports of the men's previous life experiences indicated that engaging in such violent behavior had been learned and rewarded over a long period of time. The women in the first study who reported details contrasting the batterer's behavior with their experience with a nonviolent man further supported this view. Information about the batterer's childhood and his other life experiences follow the psychological principles consistent with him having learned to respond to emotionally distressing cues with anger and violent behavior. The high incidence of other violent behavior correlates, such as child abuse, violence toward others, destruction of property, and a high percentage of arrests and convictions, support a learning theory explanation for domestic violence.

These data compelled me to conclude then, as well as now, that from the woman's point of view, the initiation of the violence pattern in the battering relationships studied came from the man's learned violent behavior. The connections between violence against women, violence against children, violence against the elderly, and street/community violence have been demonstrated in the subsequent research (American Psychological Association [APA], 1996; Cling, 2004; Walker, 1994, 2015). Patterns of one form of violence in the home create a high-risk factor for other abuse. Alcohol and other drugs appear to exacerbate the risk for greater injury or death. Men continue to use physical, sexual, and psychological abuse to obtain and maintain power and control over women and children, because they can. Violence works to get them what they want, quickly and with few if any consequences. Recent analysis of data from batterer treatment programs gives a very dismal picture of efforts to help offenders stop their abusive behavior (Fields, 2008). Thus, we must continue to study the impact of violence on women in the total context of our lives, to better understand its social and interpersonal etiology as an aid to prevent and stop violence. If this mostly male-to-female violence is learned behavior, and all the psychological research to date supports this view (APA, 1996; Koss et al., 1994), we must understand how men learn to use violence, what maintains it despite social, financial, and legal consequences, and how to help them unlearn the behavior.

NEW BWS RESEARCH

Since the original BWS research was completed in 1982, the field has been most often studied by social policy experts, health and mental health scientists, students, and professionals. In 1994, I was asked by the then-president of the APA, Dr. Ron Fox, to convene a special task force composed of some of the most respected psychology experts in the area of family violence to review the research and clinical programs to determine what psychology has contributed to the understanding of violence and the family, including battered women. Our goal was to prepare materials for policy makers to aid them as they created social policy to stop and prevent all forms of interpersonal violence. This antiviolence initiative is still ongoing in the Public Interest Directorate of the APA, continuing to publish materials (APA, 1995, 1996, 1997). In fact, the 2008 APA President, Dr. Alan Kazdin, chose violence against women and especially domestic violence as one of the topic areas on which to focus in a presidential initiative. Dr. Bob Geffner has gone on to form other organizations such as the Institute on Violence, Abuse and Trauma (IVAT) for educational purposes and the National Institute to End Intimate Partner Violence (NIEIPV) to support policy development.

Although we have much more data on the topic today, in fact the conclusions I reached and stated in the 1984, 2000, and 2009 editions of *The Battered Woman Syndrome* still hold up today, almost 40 years after I first proposed them in 1977. "Intimate partner violence" (IPV), as battering of women, wives, or other intimate relationships is sometimes called, is still considered learned behavior that is used mostly by men to obtain and maintain power and control over women. Those who identify as lesbians, gay men, bisexual, transgender, and others who are nonconforming also engage in violence against their partners, but the limited available research suggests that, while there may be some differences in same-sex violence from male-to-female heterosexual violence, its use to coercively obtain power and control over one's partner is still primary. In particular, research has found less physical harm in lesbian relationships (Lobel, 1986; Renzetti, 1992) and more physical harm in brief but not long-term gay male relationships (Island & Letelier, 1991). There is no reported research on violence in partners with the other groups. Our findings were that, although racial and cultural issues might impact the availability of resources for the victim, they do not determine incidence or prevalence of domestic violence (Browne, 1993; Browne & Williams, 1989; Gelles & Straus, 1988). New research looks more carefully at other cultural groups including African and Caribbean American women (Shakes-Malone & Van Hasselt, 2005) and is reported in a later chapter. Many factors appear to interact that determine the level of violence experienced and the access to resources and other help to end the violence. Although there are some who have designed intervention programs to help save the relationship while still stopping the violence, it remains a daunting and difficult task with only limited success (Fields, 2008; Harrell, 1991; Hart & Klein, 2013).

BATTERER INTERVENTION PROGRAMS

One of the most important facts we have learned about domestic violence is that it not only cuts across every demographic group we study, but also that both batterers and battered women are very different when they first come into the relationship than when they leave. Although there are "risk markers" for both men and women, increasing the probability of each group becoming involved in a violent relationship, the most common risk marker is still the same one that the BWS research study found: for men it is the exposure to violence in their childhood home (Hotaling & Sugarman, 1986), and for women, it is simply being a woman (APA, 1996). Other studies have found that poverty, immigration status, and prior abuse are also risk factors for women to become battered, although they are not predictive (Walker, 1994). We decided to conduct the same research with women who have come to live in the United States and were battered in their countries of origin in this latest round of data collection to help determine the relationship between the women's immigrant status in the United States and the abuse by her intimate partner.

New research on batterers suggests that there are several types of abusers. Most common is the "power and control" batterer who uses violence against his partner in order to get her to do what he wants without regard for her rights in the situation. Much has been written about this type of batterer as he fits the theoretical descriptions that feminist analysis supports (Lindsey, McBride, & Platt, 1992; Pence & Paymar, 1993). However, most of the data that support this analysis come from those who have been court ordered into treatment programs and actually attend them, which is estimated to be only a small percentage of the total number of batterers by others (Dutton, 1995; Hamberger, 1997; Walker, 1999). Recently, the dynamics of how power and control are used to terrorize and control women and children by men have been studied. O'Leary (1993) suggested that psychological control methods are separate but an important part of domestic violence, while Stark (2007) has found that the psychological techniques used by abusive men are similar when it comes to coercion whether or not physical and sexual abuse are actually present.

The second most common type is the mentally ill batterer, who may also have distorted power and control needs but his mental illness interacts with his aggressive behavior (Dutton, 1995; Dutton & Sonkin, 2003). Those with an abuse disorder may also have coexisting paranoid and schizophrenic disorders, affective disorders including bipolar types and depression, borderline personality traits, obsessive-compulsive disorders. Also, those with substance abuse disorders may have a coexisting abuse disorder (Sonkin, 1995). Multiple disorders make it necessary to treat each one in order for the violent behavior to stop. As the intervention methods may be different and possibly incompatible, it is an individual decision whether to treat them simultaneously or one at a time. Usually, different types of treatment programs are necessary for maximum benefit whether or not the intervention occurs at the same time.

A third type of batterer is the "antisocial personality disordered" abuser who displays what used to be called "psychopathic character flaws" that are difficult to change. Many of these men commit other criminal acts including violence against other people, making them dangerous to treat unless they are incarcerated. Dutton and Sonkin (2003) suggest that this type of batterer is a variant of men with an attachment disorder that produces borderline personality traits. Jacobson and Gottman (1998) suggest that there are actually two subtypes within this group. They call them "pit bulls" and "cobras." Pit bulls are the more common type who demonstrate the typical signs of rage as they become more angry. Cobras, on the other hand, become more calm, lower their heart rates, and actually appear to be more deliberate in their extremely dangerous actions. Women whose partners exhibit cobra-like behavior are less likely to be taken seriously as their partners do not appear to others to be as dangerous.

Understanding the motivation of the batterer appears to be quite complex, especially when consequences do not appear to stop his abusive behavior. Information gained from new research suggests that there may well be structural changes in the midbrain areas from the biochemicals that the autonomic nervous system secretes when a person is in danger or other high levels of stress. Fascinating studies of "cell memories" (Goleman, 1996; van der Kolk, 1988, 1994, 2015), changes in the noradrenalin and adrenalin levels, glucocorticoids, and serotonin levels (Charney, Deutch, Krystal, Southwick, & Davis, 1993; Rossman, 1998) all may mediate emotions and subsequent interpersonal relationships. The precise impact of these biochemicals on the developing brain of the child who is exposed to violence in his or her home has yet to be definitely studied. Obviously, this research is critical to our understanding of the etiology of violence and aggression.

HIGH-RISK FACTORS

Some reported events in the battered women's past occurred with sufficient regularity to warrant further study as they point to a possible susceptibility factor that interferes with their ability to successfully stop the batterers' violence toward them once they initiate it. It was originally postulated that such a susceptibility potential could come from rigid sex-role socialization patterns that leave adult women with a sense of "learned helplessness" so that they do not develop appropriate skills to escape from being further battered. This theory does not negate the important coping skills that battered women do develop that protect most of them from being more seriously harmed and killed. However, it does demonstrate the psychological pattern that the impact from experiencing abuse can take and helps understand how some situations do escalate without intervention. While our data supported this hypothesis, it appears to be more complicated than originally viewed. This viewpoint also assumes that there are appropriate skills to be learned that can stop the battering, other than terminating the relationship. In fact, the data from the study did not support the theory that doing anything other than leaving would be effective, and in some cases, the women must leave town and hide from the men in order to be safe. Later, it was found that even leaving did not protect many women from further abuse. Many men used the legal system to continue abusing the women by forcing them into court and continuing to maintain control over their finances and children.

LEARNED HELPLESSNESS AND POSITIVE PSYCHOLOGY

The concept of learned helplessness, one of the cornerstone theories in the original research, has continued to be refined through this and other research, despite its controversial name. As we have learned, and these studies confirm, battered women are not helpless at all. Rather, they are extremely successful in staying alive and minimizing their physical and psychological injuries in a brutal environment. However, in order to maintain their core self, they must give something up. The theory of learned helplessness suggests that they give up the belief that they can escape from the batterer in order to develop sophisticated coping strategies. Learned helplessness theory explains how they stop believing that their actions will have a predictable outcome. It is not that they cannot still use their skills to get away from the batterer, stop the abuse at times, or even defend themselves, but rather, they cannot predict that what they do will have the desired outcome. Sometimes they use force that might seem excessive to nonbattered women in order to protect themselves or their children.

In the intervening years since Seligman (1975) first formulated the theory of learned helplessness, his work has moved toward finding ways to prevent it from developing. He has concentrated his research in the area of positive psychology, teaching children and adults what he has called "learned optimism" (Seligman, 1990). In this era of empirically supported interventions, Seligman and his colleagues have provided new understanding of human resilience and the ability to survive such horrible traumatic experiences as family violence, terrorism and torture, wars, and catastrophic environmental disasters such as hurricanes, floods, tsunamis, and earthquakes (Seligman, 2002).

SEX-ROLE SOCIALIZATION

It was expected that battered women who were overly influenced by the sex-role demands associated with being a woman would be traditional in their own attitudes toward the roles of women. Instead, the original data surprisingly indicated that the women in our study perceived themselves as more liberal than most in such attitudes. They did perceive their batterers held very traditional attitudes toward women, which probably produced some of the disparity and conflict in the man's or woman's set of expectations for their respective roles in their relationship. The women saw their batterer's and their father's attitudes toward women as similar, their mother's and nonbatterer's attitudes as more liberal than the others but less so than their own. The limitation of an attitude measure is that we still do not know how they actually behaved despite these attitudes. It is probably safe to assume that the batterers' control forced the battered women to behave in a more traditional way than they state they would prefer. From a psychologist's viewpoint, this removes power and control from the woman and gives it to the man, causing the woman to perceive herself as a victim. It also can create a dependency in both the woman and the man, so that neither of them feels empowered to take care of himself or herself.

One area for further study is the relationship between the political climate in the woman's country where she currently lives and the frequency of severity and impact from domestic violence. If women continue to hold more liberal attitudes toward women's roles and men become more conservative, it would be interesting to know if a conservative political climate would put women at higher risk for being abused. It is known from other studies (Chesler, 2005) that women's behavior is more controlled by men in countries where there is state-sponsored violence or where fundamentalist religious values are the norm. It is difficult to tell if women have bruises under their burkas and veils and long modesty dresses.

There are arguments from both sides about whether women in these countries, particularly those that subscribe to the Muslim faith, actually are free to make their own life choices, as they state, or if they comply because they have to obey if they choose to stay within the community. More recent analysis of Muslim terrorist actions indicates that women have been trained to use violence along with men, perhaps because they are less likely to be detected. It is possible that women in these countries have taken a way out of being controlled by men by assuming the terrorist role themselves. Not enough information is known about how much power these women actually do have. However, some analysis of terrorist actions, such as the bombing of a government building in San Bernardino, California, appears to have been led by a radicalized woman terrorist who married an American and radicalized him also. She appeared willing to die for "the cause" despite the fact that she had an infant child, defying many stereotypes about women's behavior.

PHYSICAL AND SEXUAL ABUSE AS CHILDREN

Other events reported by the women that put them at high risk included early and repeated sexual molestation and assault, high levels of violence by members in their childhood families, perceptions of critical or uncontrollable events in childhood, and the experience of other conditions that placed them at high risk for depression. These are discussed in greater detail in the following chapters. At the time of the original research, we were surprised at the high percentage of women in the study who reported prior sexual molestation or abuse. Although the impact of having experienced sexual assault and molestation was consistent with reports of other studies, we, like other investigators at the time, tended to view victims by the event that we learned had victimized them, rather than look at the impact of the entire experience of various forms of abuse. Since that time it is clear that there is a common thread among the various forms of violence against women, especially when studying the commonality of the psychological impact on women (Cling, 2004; Koss et al., 1994; Walker, 1994).

Finkelhor's (1979) and Gold's (2000) caution that seriousness of impact of sexual abuse on the child cannot be determined by only evaluating the actual sex act performed was supported by our data. Trauma symptoms were reportedly caused by many different reported sex acts, attempted or completed, that then negatively influenced the woman's later sexuality, and perhaps influenced her perceptions of her own vulnerability to continued abuse. Incest victims learned how to gain the love and affection they needed through sexual activity (Butler, 1978). Perhaps some of our battered women did, too (Thyfault, 1980a, 1980b). Gold (2000) has found that the impact of the other family patterns has equal if not greater impact on the effects of the sexual abuse on the child. These findings were consistent with reports of battering in dating couples studied on college campuses (Levy, 1991). The critical factor reported for those cases was the level of sexual intimacy that had begun in the dating couples. At the very least, the fear of losing parental affection and disruption of their home-life status quo seen in sexually abused children (MacFarlane, 1977–1978) was similar to a battered woman's fears of loss of the batterer's affection and disruption of their relationship's status quo (Janoff-Bulman, 1985).

The impact of physical abuse reported in the women's childhoods was not clear from these data. Part of this difficulty was due to definitional problems that remain a barrier to better understanding of violence in the family. The women in this study were required to conform to our definitions of what constituted battering behavior, so we know that their responses about the impact of the violence were based on that definition. But, we do not know the specific details of more than four of the battering incidents they experienced. This makes it difficult to compare our results with other researchers such as Straus, Gelles, and Steinmetz (1980) who used different definitions of conflict behavior without putting events into the context in which they occurred. However, we do have details of over 1,600 battering incidents, four for each woman in the first sample and many more in the new samples reported in this book. Our data indicated the women perceived male family members as more likely to engage in battering behavior that is directed against women. They perceived the highest level of whatever behavior they defined as battering to have occurred in the batterer's home (often their own home, too), and the least amount of abuse to have occurred in the nonbatterer's home, in the first study. Interestingly, if the other man really was nonviolent, then the relationship should have had no abuse reported, not just the comparatively lower amount. This type of confound supports the need to be extremely precise in collecting details of what women consider abusive or battering acts.

The opportunity for modeling effective responses to cope with surviving the violent attacks but not for either terminating or escaping them occurred in those homes where the women described witnessing or experiencing abusive behavior. Certainly, the institutionalized acceptance of violence against women further reinforced this learned response of acceptance of a certain level of battering, provided it was defined as occurring for socially acceptable reasons, like punishment. Even today, those who work with batterers report that the men who do take responsibility for their violent behavior often rationalize their abuse as being done in the name of teaching their women a "lesson" (Dutton, 1995; Dutton & Sonkin, 2003; Ewing, Lindsey, & Pomerantz, 1984; Jacobson & Gottman, 1998; Sonkin & Durphy, 1982; Sonkin, Martin, & Walker, 1985). This is dangerously close to the message that parents give children when they physically punish them "for their own good" or to "teach them a lesson." In fact, although the psychological data are clear that spanking children does more harm than good, the fact that it remains a popular method of discipline is one of the more interesting dilemmas (APA, 1995).

ALCOHOL AND OTHER DRUG ABUSE

The abuse of alcohol and perhaps some drugs is another area that would predict higher risk for violent behavior. They are similar forms of addiction-type behavior, with the resulting family problems that can arise from them. The clue to observe is the increase in alcohol consumption. The more the drinking continues, the more likely it seems violence will escalate. Yet, the pattern is not consistent for most of our sample, with only 20% reportedly abusing alcohol across all four acute battering incidents. It is important to note that the women who reported the heaviest drinking patterns for themselves were in relationships with men who also abused alcohol. Thus, while there is not a cause and effect between alcohol abuse and violence, this relationship needs more careful study. We have begun looking at these details in the new research program. When looking at alcohol and other drug-abusing women, there is a high relationship with a history of abuse. Kilpatrick (1990) suggests that prior abuse is the single most important predictive factor in women who later have substance abuse problems. Our work with women who have been arrested and found to have co-occurring disorders, who attend a mandatory residential facility, indicate that their treatment plan must include intervention for their substance abuse, for whatever mental health issues they may have, and for trauma. Without the trauma component, they will risk relapse. Mothers who abuse substances, especially during pregnancy, are almost all abuse victims (Walker, 1991). They too have not been receiving trauma-specific intervention even when they do attend substance abuse and mental health treatment programs.

PROBLEMS WITH THE LEARNED HELPLESSNESS THEORY

Learned helplessness theory predicts that the ability to perceive one's effectiveness in being able to control what happens to oneself can be damaged by some aversive experiences that occur with trauma. This then is a high risk for motivation problems. The perception of lack of self-efficacy can be learned during childhood from experiences of uncontrollability or noncontingency between response and outcome. Critical events that were perceived as occurring without their control were reported by the battered women and were found to have had an impact upon the women's currently measured state. Other factors such as a large family size may also be predictive of less perception of control. It seemed reasonable to conclude that the perception of learned helplessness could be reversed and that the greater the strengths the women gained from their childhood experiences, the more resilient they were in reversing the effects from their battering, after termination of the relationship.

Those who have developed learned helplessness have a reduced ability to predict that their actions will produce a result that can protect them from adversity. As the learned helplessness is developing, the person (a woman in the case of battered women) is motivated to choose responses to the perceived danger that are most likely to work to reduce the pain from trauma. Sometimes those responses become stereotyped and repetitive, foregoing the possibility of finding more effective responses. In classical learned helplessness theory, motivation to respond is impacted by the perception of global and specific attitudes that may also guide their behavior. It is important to recognize that their perceptions of danger are accurate; however, the more pessimistic they are, the less likely they will choose an effective response, should such a response be available. One of the criticisms of learned helplessness theory, in addition to the name of the theory that is not very specific to how battered women really behave with coping responses, is that there are very few effective responses available to the woman that will protect her and her children from the batterer's nonnegotiable demands. As it is detailed in the chapter on family courts, women are often better able to protect their children from their fathers' abusive behavior by staying in the marriage rather than looking to family court for protection.

As was stated earlier, psychologist Martin Seligman, who first studied learned helplessness in the laboratory (1975), has now looked at the resiliency factor of "learned optimism" as a possible prevention for development of depression and other mental disorders (1991, 1994). When I first used the construct of learned helplessness to help explain the psychological state of mind of the battered woman, it was with the understanding that what had been learned could be unlearned. Many advocates who worked with battered women did not like the implications of the term "learned helplessness," because they felt it suggested that battered women were helpless and passive and therefore, invalidated all the many brave and protective actions they do take to cope as best they can with the man's violent behavior (Gondolf, 1999). However, once the concept of learned helplessness is really understood, the battered women themselves and others see the usefulness of it. It makes good sense to train high-risk children and adults to become more optimistic as a way to resist the detrimental psychological impact from exposure to trauma. It is also important to recognize that many battered women who become so desperate that they kill their abusers in self-defense have developed learned helplessness, too. They reach for a gun (or, sometimes it is placed in their hands by the batterer) because they cannot be certain that any lesser action will really protect themselves from being killed by the batterer.

Although certain childhood experiences seemed to leave the woman with a potential to be susceptible to experiencing the maximum effects from a violent relationship, this did not necessarily affect areas of the battered woman's life other than her family life. Many of the women interviewed were intelligent, well-educated, competent people, some of whom also held responsible jobs. Approximately one quarter of them were in professional occupations. In fact, they were quite successful in appearing to be just like other people, when the batterers' possessiveness and need for control were contained. Once we got to know them, we learned how to recognize the signs that this outward appearance was being maintained with great psychological cost. But battered women adopt behaviors in order to cover up the violence in their lives. The women who had terminated the relationship and were not still being harassed by the batterer spoke of the sense of relief and peacefulness in their lives now that he was gone. The others still faced the high-tension situations on a regular basis. For most it seemed that severing the batterer's influence was one of the most difficult tasks for them to do. Unfortunately, separation and divorce usually did not end the man's attempts at continued power, control, and influence over the woman. In fact, the most dangerous point in the domestic violence relationship is at the point of separation.

The sense of danger from the batterer seems to have a long life even after separation. In some cases the women are so terrified that they take the blame for criminal behavior of the batterer, often willing to get themselves in trouble with the law, rather than face the batterer's wrath. I detail the cases of women who falsely confess to killing someone out of that fear. In one case, a woman whose infant son was killed by her abusive husband did not admit to the domestic violence in their relationship until after she was convicted of the homicide. Only when she was safely in a jail cell, away from him, was she able to tell the truth of what happened in their relationship. Some women give up relationships with their children, their valued property, and sometimes all they have lived and worked for in friendships and family, to escape from the batterer, breaking the learned helplessness bonds, if they ever had been trapped by them.

VIOLENCE-PRONE PERSONALITY OF MEN WHO BATTER

Although the patriarchal organization of society facilitates and may even reward wife abuse, some men live up to their violent potential while others do not. Violence does not come from the interaction of the partners in the relationship, nor from provocation caused by possibly irritating personality traits of the battered women; rather, the violence comes from the batterers' learned behavioral responses. We attempted to find perceived characteristics that would make the occurrence of such violence more predictable. While a number of such perceived characteristics were identified, the best prediction of future violence was a history of past violent behavior. This included witnessing, receiving, and committing violent acts in their childhood home; violent acts toward pets, inanimate objects, other people; previous criminal record; longer time in the military service; and previous expression of aggressive behavior toward women. If these items are added to a man's history of temper tantrums, insecurity, need to keep the environment stable, easily threatened by minor upsets, jealousy, possessiveness, and the ability to be charming, manipulative, and seductive to get what he wants, and hostile, nasty, and mean when he does not succeed, the risk for battering becomes very high. If alcohol abuse problems are included, the pattern becomes classic.

Many of the men were reported to have experienced similar patterns of discipline in their childhood home in the earlier study. The most commonly reported pattern was a strict father and an inconsistent mother. The mother was said to have alternated between being lenient—sometimes in a collusive way to avoid upsetting her own potentially violent husband—and strict in applying her own standards of discipline. Although we did not collect such data, it is reasonable to speculate that if we had, it could have revealed a pattern of the batterer's mother's smoothing everything over for the batterer so as to make up for or protect him from his father's potential brutality. Like the battered woman, the batterer's mother before her may have inadvertently conditioned him to expect someone else to make his life less stressful. Thus, batterers rarely learn how to soothe themselves when emotionally upset. Often they are unable to differentiate between different negative emotions. Feeling bad, sad, upset, hurt, rejected, and so on gets perceived as the same and quickly changes into anger and then triggers abusive behavior (Ganley, 1981; Sonkin, 1992, 1995). The impact of the strict, punitive, and violent father is better known today—exposure to him creates the greatest risk for a boy to use violence as an adult. Although we called for further study into these areas with the batterers and their fathers themselves over 25 years ago, such research is still not available.

RELATIONSHIP ISSUES

There seem to be certain combinations of factors that would strongly indicate a high-risk potential for battering to occur in a relationship. One factor that has been mentioned by other researchers (Berk, Berk, Loeske, & Rauma, 1983; Straus et al., 1980) is the difference on sociodemographic variables between the batterers and the battered women. Batterers in some studies are less educated than their wives, from a lower socioeconomic class, and from a different ethnic, religious, or racial group. In this study, while there was some indication that the batterer's earning level was not consistent and was below his potential, we felt that factor was not as important a variable as others in domestic violence relationships. We looked at the different earning abilities between men and women, but since we did not account for the difference in value of dollar income for different years, these data could not be statistically evaluated. We concluded that it is probable that these issues are other measures reflective of the fundamental sexist biases in these men that indicated their inability to tolerate a disparity in status between themselves and their wives. Perhaps they used violence as a way to lower the perceived status difference.

Marrying a man who is much more traditional than the woman in his attitudes toward women's roles is also a high risk for future abuse in the relationship. Traditional attitudes go along with the patriarchal sex-role stereotyped patterns that rigidly assign tasks according to gender. These men seem to evaluate women's feelings for them by how well they fulfill these traditional expectations. Thus, if she does not have his dinner on the table when he returns home from work, even if she also has worked outside the home, he believes she does not care for him. Women who perceive themselves as liberal in their attitudes toward women's roles clash with men who cling to the traditional sex-role stereotyped values. They want to be evaluated by various ways in which they express their love and affection, not just if they keep the house clean. If the man also has a violence-prone personality pattern, the conflict raised by the different sex-role expectations may well be expressed by wife abuse.

Men who are insecure often need a great amount of nurturance and are very possessive of the women's time. These men are at high risk for violence, especially if they report a history of other abusive incidents. Most of the women in this study reported enjoying the extra attention they received initially, only to resent the intrusiveness that it eventually became. Uncontrollable jealousy by the batterer was reported by almost all of the battered women, suggesting this is another critical risk factor. Again, enjoyment of the extra attention and flattery masked these early warning signs for many women. There is a kind of bonding during the courtship period that was reported, which has not yet been quantified. The frequency with which the women, men, and professionals report this bonding phenomenon leads me to speculate that it is a critical factor. Each does have an uncanny ability to know how the other would think or feel about many things. The women need to pay close attention to the batterer's emotional cues to protect themselves against another beating. Batterers benefit from the women's ability to be sensitive to cues in the environment. At the same time they view the battered women as highly suggestible and fear outside influence that may support removal of their own influence and control over the women's lives.

Another factor that has a negative impact on relationships and increases the violence risk is sexual intimacy early in relationships. Batterers are reported to be seductive and charming, when they are not being violent, and the women fall for their short-lived but sincere promises. It seemed unusual to have one third of the sample pregnant at the time of their marriage to the batterer, although we had no comparison data then. We did not control for pre- and postliberalization of abortion to determine how battered women felt about the alternatives to marriage, including abortion or giving the child up for adoption. Thus, then as now, we were unable to analyze these data further. However, in this new round of data collection, we have added several scales to measure sexual satisfaction, intimacy, and body image. The earlier research has suggested that sexual abuse victims have greater difficulties with their body image after the assault. We are in the process of assessing these factors to see how they relate to psychological impact after domestic violence.

ARE THERE DIFFERENT DOMESTIC
VIOLENCE TYPOLOGIES?

Although the earlier research seemed to point to different typologies in the types of the men who used violence against women, as mentioned earlier in this chapter, more recently there have been proponents putting forth the perspective that there are different typologies of domestic violence with some being less dangerous than others. Dr. Dan O'Leary (1988) first proposed the notion that some domestic violence relationships that have only psychological coercion and maltreatment will not naturally escalate to physical abuse without something pushing them over that point. In fact, when interviewing battered women with our methodology, we found that in many of those relationships that originally were classified as psychological abuse only, there were incidents of physical or sexual abuse, but because there were no serious injuries, the relationships were not reported as physically abusive. In other cases, what appeared to be low-level abuse quickly escalated to physical abuse without any warning. And, in some cases where there had been physical abuse, there was the ability to stay with coercive control in frightening acute battering incidents without escalation to physical abuse. A good example of this is from the highly publicized trial of O. J. Simpson, the famous football player accused of killing his wife, Nicole, and her friend Ron Goldman in 1995. In one incident when O. J. was angry with Nicole, it was reported that he ran into the house, yelling and smashing objects. She ran upstairs and hid in a bedroom behind a locked door. He pounded on the door and continued yelling while she was calling the police, but did not smash down the door or physically abuse her. He then left the house.

I cite this case and refer to others where it is simply impossible to predict where it will go next. The prudent action to take is always whatever will afford the best protection so further harm does not occur. Yet, there are those who do not study the large numbers of domestic violence cases, are willing to take the risk, and place children in harm's way. The damage done to children's self esteem and confidence, their learning ability, and their ability to reach their fullest potential in the name of protecting the father–child relationship, is probably the biggest mistake in this country's policy. It leads to the continuance of domestic violence and other forms of violence from generation to generation. Children need to be protected from the coercive control methods used by abusive men and the defensive strategies sometimes used by their mothers trying to protect themselves and their families. I begin and end the edition of this book by calling for family court reform that affords children and mothers protection from abusive fathers.

DOES PSYCHOTHERAPY HELP?

As a psychologist, I often wonder how people can reject psychotherapy as a tool to assist in healing from wounds of many kinds. I understand the fears and shame of being labeled as mentally ill and the misery and mistreatment that this labeling has caused so many people. Yet, as a psychotherapist who has helped people heal using trauma methods that are much more developed today, I find it sad that so many people continue to suffer from the effects of abuse. Most of these people were abused through no fault of their own; rather, they have the misfortune to be born or entered into an abusive family. They often suffered in silence, knowing that to speak out might cause them further pain. Some made bad decisions that affected their lives or others' lives. Some sit in jails and prisons today having committed acts that were a product of their difficult lives. Some have created their own prisons in their minds or homes. All could be helped in some way, today. New medication, new trauma-focused and specific therapies could make a difference. I write about both preventive mental health to stop the downward spiral and psychotherapy techniques like the Survivor Therapy Empowerment Program (STEP) that will make a difference in the lives of women, children, and men who have lived with domestic violence.

SUMMARY

The book begins with a description of what the research here calls the "BWS." Although there are those who would prefer not to use a term that denotes psychological consequences from living with domestic violence, in fact, abuse negatively affects all those in the family. The impact is not only in the emotions of those affected but also in how they live their lives. It affects everyone in their family, in their community, and in some cases, spills over to indirectly affect innocent people they do not know. We can and must stop the epidemic destroying people and families. Hopefully using this research can help move policy makers to make a difference.

It is interesting that we reported the findings from this study as "risk factors" long before the recent categorization of family violence in similar terms. Once it was established that family violence and violence against women were at epidemic or even pandemic proportions by U.S. Surgeon General C. Everett Koop (1986), violence began to be conceptualized as a public health problem that would be best understood through epidemiological community standards. Planning intervention and prevention programs could use the criteria of "risk" and "resiliency" factors rather than thinking in more pathological terms of "illness" and "cure." One of the most interesting analogies comes from the public health initiative to eradicate malaria.

It was found that people would be less likely to become sick from exposure to malaria if they were given quinine as a preventive measure. So, strengthening the potential victims by prescribing quinine tablets was an important way to keep safe those who could not stay out of the malaria-infested area. Once it was learned that diseased mosquitoes carried the malaria germs, it became possible to kill the mosquito. However, unless the swamps that bred the malaria germs that infected the mosquito were drained and cleaned up, all the work in strengthening the host and killing the germ carrier would not have eliminated malaria—it would have returned!

So, too, for domestic violence. We can strengthen girls and women so they are more resistant to the effects of the abusive behavior directed toward them and we can change the attitudes of known batterers so they stop beating women. However, unless we also change the social conditions that breed, facilitate, and maintain all forms of violence against women, we will not eradicate domestic and other violence—it will return!

Our data support the demand for a "war against violence inside and outside of the home." The United Nations has placed this goal as one of the highest priorities for its member nations in order to foster the full development of women and children around the world (Walker, 1999). It is a goal worthy of the attention of all who read this book today.

REFERENCES

American Psychological Association. (1995). Issues and dilemmas in family violence. *Report of the American Psychological Association Presidential Task Force on Violence and the Family.* Washington, DC: Author.

American Psychological Association. (1996). *Report of the American Psychological Association Presidential Task Force on Violence and the Family.* Washington, DC: Author.

American Psychological Association. (1997). Potential problems for psychologists working with the area of interpersonal violence. *Report of the Ad Hoc Committee on Legal and Ethical Issues in the Treatment of Interpersonal Violence.* Washington, DC: Author.

Berk, R. A., Berk, S. F., Loeske, D., & Rauma, D. (1983). Mutual combat and other family violence myths. In D. Finkelhor, R. Gelles, C. Hotaling, & M. Straus (Eds.), *The dark side of families* (pp. 119–130). Beverly Hills, CA: Sage.

Brown, L. S. (1992). The feminist critique of personality disorders. In L. S. Brown & M. Ballou (Eds.), *Personality and psychopathology: Feminist reappraisals.* New York, NY: Guilford Press.

Browne, A. (1993). Violence against women by male partners. *American Psychologist, 48,* 1077–1087.

Browne, A., & Williams, K. R. (1989). Exploring the effect of resource availability and the likelihood of female-perpetrated homicides. *Law and Society Review, 23,* 75–94.

Butler, S. (1978). *Conspiracy of silence: The trauma of incest.* San Francisco, CA: Bantam Books.

Charney, D. S., Deutch, A. Y., Krystal, J. H., Southwick, S. M., & Davis, M. (1993). Psychobiological mechanisms of post-traumatic stress disorder. *Archives of General Psychiatry, 50,* 294–305.

Chesler, P. (2005). *The new anti-Semitism: The current crisis and what we must do about it.* San Francisco, CA: Jossey-Bass.

Cling, B. J. (Ed.). (2004). *Sexualized violence against women and children.* New York, NY: Guilford Press.

Dutton, D. G. (1995). *The batterer: A psychological profile.* New York, NY: Basic Books.

Dutton, D. G., & Sonkin, D. J. (2003). *Intimate violence: Contemporary treatment innovations.* Binghamton, NY: Haworth Press.

Ewing, W., Lindsey, M., & Pomertantz, J. (1984). *Battering: An AMEND manual for helpers.* Denver, CO: AMEND (Abusive Men Exploring New Directions).

Fields, M. D. (2008). Getting beyond "what did she do to provoke him?". *Violence Against Women, 14*(1), 93–99.

Finkelhor, D. (1979). *Sexually victimized children.* New York, NY: Free Press.

Ganley, A. (1981). *Participant's and trainer's manual for working with men who batter.* Washington, DC: Center for Women's Policy Studies.

Gelles, R. J., & Straus, M. A. (1988). *Intimate violence*. New York, NY: Simon & Schuster.

Gold, S. N. (2000). *Not trauma alone: Therapy for child abuse survivors in family and social context*. Philadelphia, PA: Brunner-Routledge.

Goleman, D. (1996). *Emotional intelligence*. New York, NY: Bantam Books.

Gondolf, E. W. (1999). A comparison of reassault rates in four batterer programs: Do court referral, program length and services matter? *Journal of Interpersonal Violence, 14*, 41–61.

Hamberger, L. K. (1997). Research concerning wife abuse: Implications for physician training. *Journal of Aggression, Maltreatment, and Trauma, 1*, 81–96.

Harrell, A. (1991). *Evaluation of court-ordered treatment for domestic violence offenders*. Washington, DC: The Urban Institute.

Hart, B., & Klein, A. F. (2013). *Practical implications of current intimate partner violence research for victim advocates and service providers*. Washington, DC: U.S. Department of Justice.

Holtzworth-Monroe, A., & Stuart, G. L. (1994). Typologies of male batterers: Three subtypes and the differences among them. *Psychological Bulletin, 116*, 476–497.

Hotaling, G. T., & Sugarman, D. B. (1986). An analysis of risk markers in husband to wife violence: The current state of the knowledge. *Violence and Victims, 1*, 101–124.

Island, D., & Letelier, P. (1991). *Men who beat the men who love them: Battered gay men and domestic violence*. Binghamton, NY: Haworth Press.

Jacobson, N. S., & Gottman, J. M. (1998). *When men batter women: New insights into ending abusive relationships*. New York, NY: Simon & Schuster.

Janoff-Bulman, R. (1985). The aftermath of victimization: Rebuilding shattered assumptions. In C. Figley (Ed.), *Trauma and its wake* (pp. 15–35). New York, NY: Brunner/Mazel.

Kellen, M. J., Brooks, J. S., & Walker, L. E. A. (2005, August). Batterers intervention: Typology, efficacy & treatment issues. In L. E. A. Walker (Chair), *Forensics for the Independent Practitioner*. Symposium conducted at the meeting of the American Psychological Association, Washington, DC.

Kilpatrick, D. G. (1990, August). *Violence as a precursor of women's substance abuse: The rest of the drugs-violence story*. Symposium conducted at the 98th Annual Convention of the American Psychological Association, Boston, MA.

Koop, C. E. (1986). *Surgeon General's conference on violence and the family*. Washington, DC: National Institutes of Health.

Koss, M. P., Goodman, L. A., Browne, A., Fitzgerald, L. F., Keita, G. P., & Russo, N. F. (1994). *No safe haven: Male violence against women at home, at work, and in the community*. Washington, DC: American Psychological Association.

Levy, B. (1991). *Dating violence: Young women in danger*. Seattle, WA: Seal Press.

Lindsey, M., McBride, R., & Platt, C. (1992). *AMEND: Philosophy and curriculum for treating batterers*. Denver, CO: McBride.

Lobel, K. (Ed.). (1986). *Naming the violence: Speaking out against lesbian battering.* Seattle, WA: Seal Press.

MacFarlane, K. (1977–1978). Sexual abuse of children. In J. R. Chapman & M. Gates (Eds.), *The victimization of women* (pp. 81–109). Beverly Hills, CA: Sage.

O'Leary, K. D. (1988). Physical aggression between spouses: A social learning theory perspective. In V. B. Van Hasselt, R. L. Morrison, A. S. Bellack, & M. Hersen (Eds.), *Handbook of family violence.* New York, NY: Springer Science+Business Media.

O'Leary, K. D. (1993). Through a psychological lens: Personality traits, personality disorders, and levels of violence. In R. J. Gelles & D. R. Loeske (Eds.), *Current controversies on family violence* (pp. 7–30). Newbury Park, CA: Sage.

Pence, E., & Paymar, M. (1993). *Education groups for men who batter: The Duluth model.* New York, NY: Springer Publishing Company.

Renzetti, C. M. (1992). *Violent betrayal: Partner abuse in lesbian relationships.* Newbury Park, CA: Sage.

Root, M. P. P. (1992). Reconstructing the impact of trauma on personality. In L. S. Brown & M. Ballou (Eds.), *Personality and psychopathology: Feminist reappraisals.* New York, NY: Guilford Press.

Rossman, B. B. R. (1998). Descartes' error and post-traumatic stress disorder: Cognition and emotion in children who are exposed to parental violence. In G. W. Holden, R. Geffner, & E. N. Jouriles (Eds.), *Children exposed to marital violence: Theory, research, and applied issues* (pp. 223–256). Washington, DC: American Psychological Association.

Seligman, M. E. P. (1975). *Helplessness: On depression, development, and death.* San Francisco, CA: W. H. Freeman.

Seligman, M. E. P. (1990). *Learned optimism: How to change your mind and your life.* New York, NY: Simon & Schuster.

Seligman, M. E. P. (1991). *Learned optimism.* New York, NY: Alfred A. Knopf.

Seligman, M. E. P. (1994). *What you can change and what you can't: The complete guide to successful self-improvement.* New York, NY: Alfred A. Knopf.

Seligman, M. E. P. (2002). *Authentic happiness: Using the new positive psychology to realize your potential for lasting fulfillment.* New York, NY: Simon & Schuster.

Shakes-Malone, L. S., & Van Hasselt, V. B. (2005, August). Racial disparities in help seeking behaviors of women in abusive relationships. In L. E. Walker (Chairperson), *Battered woman syndrome after 30 years.* Symposium presented at the 113th Annual Meeting of the American Psychological Association, Washington, DC.

Sonkin, D. J. (1992). *Wounded boys heroic men: A man's guide to recovering from childhood abuse.* Stamford, CT: Long Meadow Press.

Sonkin, D. J. (1995). *Counselor's guide to learning to live without violence.* Volcano, CA: Volcano Press.

Sonkin, D. J., & Durphy, M. (1982). *Learning to live without violence: A book for men.* Volcano, CA: Volcano Press.

Sonkin, D. J., Martin, D., & Walker, L. E. (1985). *The male batterer: A treatment approach.* New York, NY: Springer Publishing Company.

Stark, E. (2007). *Coercive control: How men entrap women in personal life.* New York, NY: Oxford University Press.

Straus, M. A., Gelles, R. J., & Steinmetz. S. K. (1980). *Behind closed doors: Violence in the American family.* Garden City, NY: Anchor/Doubleday.

Thyfault, R. (1980a, April). *Sexual abuse in the battering relationship.* Paper presented at the annual meeting of the Rocky Mountain Psychological Conference, Tucson, AZ.

Thyfault, R. (1980b, October). *Childhood sexual abuse, marital rape, and battered women: Implications for mental health workers.* Paper presented at the annual meeting of the Colorado Mental Health Conference, Keystone, CO.

van der Kolk, B. (1988). The trauma spectrum: The interactions of biological and social events in the genesis of the trauma response. *Journal of Traumatic Stress, 1,* 273–290.

van der Kolk, B. (1994). The body keeps score: Memory and the evolving psychobiology of posttraumatic stress. *Harvard Review of Psychiatry, 1,* 253–265.

van der Kolk, B. (2015). *The body keeps the score: Brain, mind, and body in the healing of trauma.* New York, NY: Penguin Books.

Walker, L. E. (1979). *The battered woman.* New York, NY: Harper & Row.

Walker, L. E. (2015). Who is the real witch in the hunt for truth about child sexual abuse: Review of Cheit's, The Witch-Hunt Narrative. *PsycCritiques, 60*(14). doi:10.1037/a0038946

Walker, L. E. A. (1991, January 19–20). Abused women, infants, and substance abuse: Psychological consequences of failure to protect. In P. R. McGrab & D. M. Doherty (Eds.), *Mothers, infants, and substance abuse.* Proceedings of the APA Division 12, Midwinter Meeting, Scottsdale, AZ.

Walker, L. E. A. (1994). *Abused women and survivor therapy: A practical guide for the psychotherapist.* Washington, DC: American Psychological Association.

Walker, L. E. A. (1999). Domestic violence around the world. *American Psychologist, 54,* 21–29.

CHAPTER TWO

HISTORY

*I*dentification of battered women and protection of women and their families from all forms of men's violence had risen to a priority in the new women's movement beginning around the mid-1960s in the United States of America and other Western European countries. Beginning in the 1970s, the United Nations (UN) focused on the eradication of all forms of violence against women in the world as one of the most important strategies for women to achieve equality with men. Sexual abuse, rape, sexual harassment in the workplace and the academy, sexual exploitation by men in authority and power positions, as well as violence against women and children in their own homes were the major topics that were discussed. Conferences were held, scientific papers were written, and by the 1995 Fourth UN Conference on Women held in Beijing, all member nations were required to present the results of their studies on the eradication of violence against women in their nations. Yet, despite the knowledge that all forms of woman abuse create the atmosphere that damages women's self-esteem and prevents them from reaching their full potential and equality with men, we still have not been able to stop men from abusing women.

BATTERED WOMAN SHELTERS

In the early 1970s, a British woman Erin Pizzey (1974) began the first known refuge or battered woman's shelter in Chiswick, England. Following the psychiatric beliefs of the times, Pizzey theorized that women liked the excitement and chaos that intimate partner violence (IPV) caused in their lives. Although today's research, presented later in this book, does find that some women have issues with attachment to violent intimate partners, it is better understood as a result of the abuse they previously experienced and the rewards for staying in the relationship rather than a personality trait. An article by Pizzey, published in *Ms. Magazine* describing her book, *Scream Quietly or the Neighbors Will Hear,* caught the attention of many in the United States and around the world who were trying to understand why men battered women and how best to stop it. Battered woman shelters began to spring up all over the world, giving the message to men that if they abused their intimate partners, then the community would protect and give them shelter. Although the early shelters, such as Pizzey's refuge, were more of a long-term residential therapeutic community model than today's shelters that permit only a short-term stay, each country began to develop methods of protecting women that were consistent with their own culture. The backlash began almost immediately from those who attacked the advocates as being against traditional values and wanting to break up families and from feminists who believed focusing on the woman further victimized and blamed the victim for being battered.

Today, around 40 years later, the battered woman shelter remains the cornerstone of the movement to protect women and children from IPV. Feminist psychologists and other health professionals began to work together with advocates who were providing services at the shelter. Many mental health professionals helped begin shelters and services in their communities and served on advisory boards. Groups were formed for women who were not in residence but still needed the assistance of others to normalize their experiences, safely leave the relationship, and remain violence free. Nurses developed protocols for identification and protection of battered women who sought medical help either in hospitals or in doctor's offices. Social workers, psychologists, and other mental health professionals around the world began to identify battered women and the concept of *masochism*, implying that women somehow felt they deserved and therefore, liked being abused, was exchanged for more relevant explanations of why women stayed in abusive relationships.

Although it was learned that men who abuse women do not let them go and are most likely to seriously harm or kill the women if they try to leave, the most asked question continues to remain, "Why don't they leave?" Interestingly, we now know that leaving the relationship does not stop the abuse, as most batterers will continue to stalk and harass the women throughout their lives. The family courts encourage and facilitate the continued abuse by insisting that batterers can appropriately share parenting of children despite the data that demonstrate the emotional and sometimes physical and sexual harm to the children. Barbara Hart, a legal advocate for battered women, has been studying why battered women leave and return to the relationship, sometimes even marrying the man again, after divorce. Evan Stark's analysis of coercive control in battering relationships found that the control actually increases during periods of separation, which propels women back into the relationship where they may actually be safer than when trying to leave (Stark, 2007).

One of the earliest analyses of IPV was done by Del Martin, a feminist who was a strong force in organizing the feminist reforms during the 1970s. Her voice at the Houston National Conference for Women in 1976 made sure that men's violence against women received top priority on the women's agenda that resulted from that conference. Her book, *Battered Wives*, was one of the first to alert the general public to the plight of women trapped in abusive relationships (Martin, 1976). Along with Martin's work, two other feminists' books had a major impact on the work that followed; Susan Brownmiller, a social historian, wrote her seminal work on rape, which was published in 1975, *Against Our Will: Men, Women and Rape*, and historian Ann Jones published her seminal work on abused women in *Women Who Kill* in 1981. Brownmiller (1988) went on to publish *Waverly Place*, which questioned the role of abuse in the famous Hedda Nussbaum–Joel Steinberg relationship that resulted in the death of their illegally adopted daughter, Lisa Steinberg, for which Steinberg served time in prison. Jones (1994) went on to publish other books in the field, including *Next Time She'll Be Dead: Battering and How to Stop It.*

These women's important historical works, which greatly influenced my own thinking about women abuse, were also built on the feminist psychology put forth by Phyllis Chesler, one of the most important and prolific authors in the psychology of women who is still publishing books, articles, and now has a blog on the web (www.PhyllisChesler.com). Chesler's (1972) seminal book, *Women and Madness*, detailed the societal abuse of women, many by their intimate partners and then by their doctors who kept women psychiatrically mummified with psychotropic medications that reduced their need and ability to complain. Broverman, Broverman, Clarkson, Rosencrantz, and Vogel (1970) had published their research demonstrating how women were placed in a no-win situation by the majority of mental health professionals who believed that the healthy man had the same characteristics as the healthy person, but those same characteristics indicated mental health problems for the woman.

Interestingly, Chesler (2003) has published a book, *Woman's Inhumanity to Woman*, detailing the abuse women do to each other, which she claims is at least as dangerous as that which men do to women, although it is more emotional abuse than physical or sexual in nature. Most of us who have worked in the feminist battered women's movement during this time understand that the Achilles' heel of this movement is the insistence of a few that everyone subscribe to the exact same views, often dubbed as being "politically correct." When women disagree with some supposed truth or politically correct way of acting, they are personally "trashed" or told that none of their views are important any more. This nasty behavior often drives women away from the feminist movement, rather than keeping them in and debating the contradictory issues. This occurred when I myself worked on the O. J. Simpson case. I became persona non grata, speaking contracts were cancelled, and positions on advisory boards of various groups, such as the National Domestic Violence Hotline, were rescinded. This phenomenon is discussed further later in this chapter. Considering the fact that we have not made much progress in stopping men's violence against women and the fact that many women talk about similar experiences when they did not walk the party line, it seems that it is time to reexamine the so-called "feminist battered women's movement" and begin to determine if there are better ways of dealing with opposing opinions.

There were many topics on the feminist agenda almost 40 years ago that have yet to be resolved. These include the right of women to control their own bodies and if and when they reproduce children, equality of women and men in the workforce with equal pay for equal work, removal of the so-called "glass ceiling" in the corporate world that permits only a few women to rise to the top, and freedom from violence in the community and in the home. When I wrote the third edition of this book, U.S. voters had the choice that was not even thinkable in the 1970s when the topic was just being studied. Race and gender were being pitted together again in 2009 as they had been in the 1800s when women gave up their chance at getting the right to vote so that African American men could get those rights with the 14th Amendment to the U.S. Constitution. It took until the early 1900s for women to finally be recognized as having the same citizen rights as men to vote, but equality in other areas is still being debated. Today, as I write this fourth edition, race and gender still dominate the political conversation and none of these agenda items have been resolved toward equality between women and men. All of them have links back to men's violence against women. I coauthored a book, *Abortion Counseling: A Clinician's Guide to Psychology, Legislation, Politics, and Competency* (Needle & Walker, 2007), to challenge the misinformation that is put out to the public by those who are opposed to women controlling their own bodies. While doing the research for the book, not surprisingly I found that the few women who are at highest risk to have psychological issues postabortion are those who are trauma victims and particularly those who have been abused by their intimate partners or in their families of origin.

BATTERED WOMAN ADVOCATES

In the United States in the 1980s, the battered women advocates attempted to take control of what loosely was called "the battered woman's movement" away from the professionals. Several reasons prompted this move, including the proposal of financing the shelters through state and federal block-grant funding rather than through mental health funding, which they had learned diverted monies designated for rape crisis counseling to other mental health needs in the community mental health center funding bills during the 1970s. Rape victims were not given priority treatment as was the original purpose in the community mental health legislation. Another reason was the desire by the government, supported by the feminist battered woman's movement at the time, to use the criminal justice system as the gatekeeper for intervention with batterers rather than focus on the woman who was the victim (Schechter, 1982). While this focus was appropriate in getting law enforcement and the criminal justice system involved in protection of women, it prioritized a focus on physical violence against women and minimized the impact from the psychological and sexual violence, which continue to remain a major problem for women who are abused by intimate partners. Using the legal system also created the need to overcome many of the sexist barriers still there. Schafran (1990) and more recently Weisberg (2012), along with others, has documented the extent of gender bias throughout the courts that is still pervasive, although sometimes not as visibly impacting protection from gender violence. In some countries where the public health system rather than the criminal justice system is the gatekeeper to all services, the psychologically abused woman gets more attention.

The psychological results of domestic violence have been the primary discussion in all prior editions of *The Battered Woman Syndrome,* and this one, even though the injuries from physical and sexual abuse of women remain a major detriment to women leading a full and satisfactory life. Interestingly, the Centers for Disease Control and Prevention's (2008) recent survey of the adverse conditions and health risk behaviors associated with IPV found that IPV causes 1,200 deaths and 2 million injuries among women and nearly 600,000 injuries among men according to a 2005 Behavioral Risk Factor Surveillance System survey. Unfortunately, many of the feminist advocate centers in the United States still refuse to acknowledge that battered women may benefit from psychotherapy that is trauma-oriented and not pathologizing as was true in earlier years. As a clinical and forensic psychologist, my research, clinical work, and experience in the courts have led to my concluding that abuse is traumatic for women and therefore, some women may develop reactions that are consistent with the aftermath of trauma or posttraumatic stress reactions and disorders. I called these signs and symptoms "battered woman syndrome" (BWS) almost 40 years ago. Although feminist politics sometimes still takes issue with BWS, in fact the research data presented here continue to be present in many women who are abused by their intimate partners. Some lucky women who have a strong support system in their community may heal from abuse on their own, but my own philosophy is that all battered women deserve access to the best treatment available should they wish to participate.

Unfortunately, battered women advocates and mental health professionals have not had a smooth relationship over the years. Advocates have been suspicious of professionally trained researchers and clinicians, often causing disruption of conferences such as occurred during the 1980s with the advocates displeased with the research presented at the New Hampshire conferences with Straus, Gelles, and their colleagues. Advocates quickly label a professional who does not agree with their positions as unfriendly and disinvite them from participating in conferences or even serving on their publicly funded advisory boards, as was mentioned earlier. Many professionals who have worked in the battered woman's movement have described being "trashed," which is a term used in the feminist movement when the person and not his or her work is so targeted. For example, after 1995, when advocates were angry with my participation in the O. J. Simpson trial, I was dismissed from a position on the national crisis helpline advisory board of directors, my theories were openly denigrated without appropriate scientific criticisms, and I was disinvited or not invited to participate in many conferences with funding from the same government sources that previously invited me along with others who continued to participate.

Although I tried to explain that forensic psychology called for reporting objectively, which could only help the cause of battered women, the emotional dislike for O. J. Simpson and belief that he had killed Nicole Brown and her friend, Ron Goldman, outweighed any rational discussion. This is a common phenomenon when working in the violence against women arena; the danger from abuse is so pervasive and the resources for protecting women are so limited that there is no room for debate about what are the best courses of action to take. Unfortunately, this behavior on the part of advocates continues their suspiciousness and often lonely positions. On the other hand, their behavior often protects battered women from the often thoughtless decisions that place them in harm's way. Considering the fact that men's violence against women is so pervasive and has such a long history, I believe we need every voice as an advocate and dismissing people who could be helpful in one area even though they may not agree in other areas seems foolish and counterproductive to the main goal, which is to stop men's violence against women.

More recently, in the work with protecting victims of sex trafficking, it has become clear that some women are assisting the usually male sex trafficker in keeping women in his group obedient to his demands. These women, sometimes called "bottom girls" because they are holding up the foundation of the sex trafficking organization, do so as they gain favorite status with the men. Working in this area has assisted the feminist advocates to look more carefully at women's abuse and violence toward other women. Although still a much smaller percentage of women use violence, the same system of rewarding desired behavior can be applied as an analysis to better understand how abuse can become learned behavior. Others such as sociologist Murray Straus (2010) have tried to broaden the family violence prevention movement to discuss the abusive behavior of women in the family, but it remains a theoretical struggle to make sense out of cause-and-effect behavior given all the politics, including funding priorities. In this book, we attempt to provide whatever little data we have on women's use of violence as a strategy with the understanding that it remains a controversial area needing more study.

Interestingly, many advocates for battered women who work in shelters or on task forces ultimately come to the opinion that they need more training in psychology to really be effective and they become professionals themselves. But, the next group of advocates, usually young women eager to be helpful, does not trust them anymore than the former advocates trusted the group that came before them and went on to graduate school in mental health areas. Unfortunately, this schism between advocates and professionals makes it difficult for the professional psychologist to also be an advocate, as if there might not be room for both types of activities in one's professional life. I believe that it is the fertilization between the various viewpoints that helps better address the enormous problem domestic violence causes in people's lives.

U.S.-FUNDED AND CONGRESSIONAL ACTIONS

In 1978, the U.S. Department of Health and Human Services funded a meeting of 10 battered women shelters that was held in Denver, Colorado, hosted by the interdisciplinary task force that formed the original National Coalition Against Domestic Violence the following year. The purpose was to identify models of protecting battered women that could be replicated elsewhere. Shelter advocates and government officials came together to plan a national strategy. U.S. Congress called for testimony that year to determine the direction of services to battered women. It was determined that the model for intervention should be primarily grassroots support with local programs encouraged to develop using funds set aside for training and employment opportunities. Advocates not counselors were encouraged to provide services to battered women. The goal was not to further victimize battered women by pathologizing them. While this was an important policy decision, in fact those battered women who needed competent mental health services did not always receive them.

The following year, similar funding brought Erin Pizzey to the United States, and a large national conference was held in Denver where the National Coalition Against Domestic Violence was formed. This organization continues to provide information and resources about ending domestic violence. Also, in 1979, the U.S. Civil Rights organization held a major conference in Washington, DC, and another congressional committee took more testimony to assist the new Reagan government that was about to take office in planning its initiative to assist battered women. A federal committee that coordinated activities between the various governmental departments was also formed during that year. In the early

1980s, there was more federal activity with Congress encouraging both research and services to battered women. A conference in Belmont, Maryland, to which leading theorists and researchers into male offenders and violence against women were invited, set the stage for the development of "offender-specific" intervention programs for batterers that were funded through the Department of Justice. Interestingly, treatment for one type of batterer was encouraged as a pre- or postadjudication diversion for men who battered women. However, the intervention was conceived as a psychoeducational program to change men's attitudes toward women, which was thought to then result in a change in their abusive behavior. Over the years, it has proven to be an effective first step but not enough to get most men to completely stop their abusive behavior toward women. Harrell (1991) found that some men who went through these short, usually 6- to 12-week, programs actually became more effective at using psychological abuse when their physical abuse was stopped. Recent literature that is reported in Chapter 20 suggests that these offender-specific intervention programs may not always be as helpful as was originally thought they would be. However, Barbara Hart has reanalyzed data from shelters all over the country and in her analysis found that women were better protected and better able to make their own decisions if the batterer was court-ordered into offender-specific treatment.

Later in the 1980s and 1990s, congressional action encouraged major changes in the legal system to further protect battered women and their children. Laws were changed that facilitated women obtaining temporary and permanent protective orders that restrained their partners from making contact with them (Hart, 1988). Criminal prosecution of batterers was encouraged by providing law enforcement officers with training in the proper response to domestic violence calls and in adopting pro-arrest policies without the need for the victim to sign an arrest warrant or even testify against the batterer who may well be engaged in loving behavior by the time the case is set for trial. Victim-witness advocates were hired by prosecutors' offices across the country as it was learned that with support many more victims would testify against their abusers provided the batterers were offered the option of diversion into batterer's treatment programs. Prosecutors' offices were redesigned for "vertical prosecutions," meaning one assistant prosecutor handled a case from start to finish rather than switching from intake to litigation prosecutors.

At the same time, battered women who killed their abusive partners in self-defense were legally able to obtain a fair trial with expert witness testimony to educate lay juries and judges as to the reasonableness of their fear of imminent danger when they defended themselves against the often escalating aggression from the batterer (Browne, 1987; Ewing, 1987; Walker, 1989). State by state, testimony on BWS was permitted, often after appellate decisions defined BWS as including both the signs and symptoms of the psychological effects from abuse as well as the dynamics of the abusive relationship that included the cycle theory of violence and the learned helplessness theory in some states. These cases are further discussed in Chapters 12 and 21. Women who did not get the benefit of this testimony at trial and were serving long sentences, often life without parole, in state prisons were reexamined and clemency petitions filed with the governors and parole committees in many states. Those women who have been released have gone on to live productive lives, proving the testimony that they were not murderers but rather killed to save their own or their children's lives.

SEX-ROLE STEREOTYPES AND MENTAL HEALTH

At the same time that interest was focused on domestic violence and other types of violence against women, mental health professionals were also examining the biases that sex-role stereotyping introduced into the scientific research. As was stated earlier, in the early 1970s, the Broverman et al. (1970) research on attitudes toward women demonstrated that professionals placed women in a double bind by finding that the healthy man but not the healthy woman was the same as the healthy person. Chesler's (1972) book, *Women and Madness,* documented a different kind of abuse that mostly male mental health professionals engaged in to keep uppity women in their place, often by hospitalizing and overprescribing the then-new psychotropic medications. Although less common today, some women continue to abuse these and other newer medications in order to bear the abuse in their homes.

The American Psychological Association (APA) and other mental health organizations began to identify the biases that occurred because of sex-role socialization patterns during the 1980s and 1990s. The Association for Women in Psychology was founded in the early 1970s, leading to the founding of the APA Division 35, Psychology for Women, which is now the Society for the Study of Psychology of Women. In 1980, the Feminist Therapy Institute was founded as a place where mental health professionals could obtain advanced training in feminist therapy. Adoption of one of the slogans from the feminist movement, "the personal is political" occurred, which reminded members that if one woman remains abused, all women are abused.

In 1985, when the American Psychiatric Association was about to revise the third edition of the *Diagnostic and Statistical Manual of Mental Disorders (DSM)*, it became clear that the task force was considering two diagnoses that were filled with stereotyped bias: "masochistic personality disorder" and "premenstrual dysphoric disorder." In neither case were there sufficient scientific data to support these diagnoses. After organized protests, both of these diagnoses were eventually dropped from the revised third edition (*DSM-III-R*; American Psychiatric Association, 1987), fourth edition (*DSM-IV*; American Psychiatric Association, 1994), and fifth edition (*DSM-5*; American Psychiatric Association, 2013), but not without a great deal of controversy. Meanwhile, the categories of "posttraumatic stress disorder" (PTSD) and later on "acute stress reaction" (ASR) were added to the *DSM* where it became possible to diagnose women who demonstrated evidence of BWS as having a subcategory of PTSD. This is further discussed in Chapters 14 and 16.

PSYCHOTHERAPY FOR BATTERED WOMEN

In the 1980s, it was determined that many of the battered women who were identified, especially those who obtained protective orders and those who came to shelters, were able to heal and get on with their lives with the help of a good support system. Often, advocate-facilitated groups run by the task forces and shelters were sufficient to help women normalize their experiences and reconnect with family and friends whose relationships were disrupted by the power and control and sometimes isolation from the batterers. However, some of those women who already have been identified with a mental disorder that is exacerbated by the abuse or those who develop BWS and PTSD from the abuse itself may need some psychotherapy to help them heal and move on with their lives.

The most popular models that have emerged include those supported by the feminist advocates, such as the prevention of IPV by encouraging the empowerment of women model, advocacy for social equality of women and men, and understanding that the responsibility for use of violence must be placed totally on the man because of his abuse of power and need for control over the woman. The nonfeminist advocates support a social services model that emphasizes assistance to women and children without attempting to destroy the family structure. This is most often favored by religious groups who advocate for the violence to stop without breaking up the family. The feminist mental health professionals also support empowerment of women and responsibility placed on the batterers to change their abusive behaviors. However, they add a PTSD and BWS treatment focus. Nonfeminist mental health professionals may support the feminist models but also focus on various other mental health diagnoses such as depression, borderline personality disorder, bipolar disorders and engage in some intentional or nonintentional victim-blaming by their focus which suggests if the woman only would change, the abuse would stop.

Feminist politics have caused some mental health professionals to abandon the PTSD and BWS models in favor of an ecological model that emphasizes the societal contributions to the IPV (Dutton, 1992, 1993). As trauma treatment begins to more clearly define itself (Briere & Scott, 2007/2015; Walker, 2017) it becomes evident that a combination of feminist and trauma theories are needed to adequately address the psychological problems that battered women may face. Since many battered women have other concurrent problems such as having experienced rape and sexual abuse, substance abuse, organic brain syndromes, poverty and its deprivations, medical issues, and the like, it is important to provide them with the appropriate interventions to help them heal.

APA has developed a series of videos where feminist therapy techniques can be viewed, as has Newbridge Communications and Brunner/Mazel. In Chapter 17, the revised Survivor Therapy Empowerment Program (STEP 2) is presented as one such evidence-based intervention that can be adapted for individual or group work.

CHILD CUSTODY AND ACCESS TO CHILDREN

At the same time all these things were happening to try to better protect women from men's abuse, the family law courts at the urging of fathers' rights groups were lobbying to change the laws to permit them equal access to parenting their children. Unfortunately, many of these fathers' rights groups were led by men who lost their parental rights because of allegations that they were abusing their intimate partners and/or their children. The research data suggest that between 40% and 60% of men who abuse their intimate partners also physically, sexually, and psychologically abuse their children (Holden, Geffner, & Jouriles, 1998). Many of these men were demanding unsupervised access to their children, often as a way to avoid paying child support if they have equal parenting time with the children's mothers. Unfortunately, this is occurring across the world with little recognition by the legal system that there are serious flaws in protecting "the best interests of the child" as is required by the law.

Perusal of the Internet today will yield many such groups with hostile and angry messages against their children's mothers as well as advocates for protection of children. In fact, there are groups opposing attempts to protect children from abusive fathers who target mental health professionals and file grievances against them in what is currently called a "mobbing" or "targeting" technique. That is, they get together and purposely target an individual so as to stop that person from providing testimony against them. Although this is clearly witness tampering that is illegal, the legal authorities have yet to identify and stop them. In a hearing before the Maryland licensing board, they issued an apology to a psychologist who had six grievances filed against her, some by men whose children she had never even seen. Earlier, the board had attempted to sanction this psychologist who refused to accept their findings that she did not follow the appropriate guidelines and violated the rules and regulations of the board. Instead, she took the case to trial and proved to the satisfaction of the hearing officer that she had been *targeted* by these individuals when she tried to protect the children from further sexual abuse. Another psychologist lost her license to practice in a different state after a father in a custody dispute filed a grievance against her. At her hearing, the administrative law judge chose to listen to a non–child psychologist, rather than child trauma specialists and ethicists, who opined that her treatment was appropriate and not a forensic evaluation. These battles are constantly being fought out in the courts and licensing boards while children and abused women are not being protected. Organizations of protected moms, the most active of which is located in California, are trying to educate the courts and mental health professionals to recognize the danger to unprotected moms and children.

The issue of protective mothers has been an important one as mothers are losing custody of their children when judges do not believe that the children are in danger from abusive fathers. The issue seems to be focused on allegations of sexual abuse of children as it is often difficult to gather evidence other than reports of the child. Many of these children are too young to withstand the cross-examination by attorneys, and methods of protecting the children while preserving their testimony seem to be conflicting with the accused persons' right to confront their accusers. Meanwhile, protective mothers are punished by family courts that become angry when they do not obtain sufficient evidence to legally prove their cases. In some cases, protective mothers appear to overstate their cases or manipulate the children into making statements that lead family courts to mistrust their credibility. While this occasionally may occur, in fact most of the time these mothers are simply not listened to because most people do not want to believe that a father could do such terrible things to his own child. As a result, these children go unprotected and their attachment and relationships with both parents become damaged by the court.

Mothers are often forced to continue a relationship with the batterer by the family court that does not permit them to relocate with the children so that they are all protected from the father's stalking and use of the children to continue his surveillance and abuse of the mother. Shared parenting plans with children forced to negotiate two totally dissimilar parenting styles do not benefit them. The presumptions of joint custody in the law today keep battered women from being able to move on with their lives (Saccuzzo & Johnson, 2004; Saunders, 2007). The Leadership Council (www.leadershipcouncil.org) along with other organizations maintains information on their website to educate those who provide assistance to the courts so that professionals could take advantage and become informed. The Cummings Foundation held a 2-day conference with invited speakers in 2012 in Scottsdale, Arizona, and published a book with the proceedings, *Our Broken Family Court* (Walker, Cummings, Cummings, & Waller, 2012). The APA and the American Bar Association held a conference in 2015 where invited speakers addressed these issues. Unfortunately, not much has been done to improve the situation since then.

TEEN VIOLENCE

Another issue that has been raised over the years without adequate intervention is the role teen violence plays in perpetuating domestic violence into the homes of the next generation. Straus et al.'s (1980) research data demonstrated how boys who were exposed to domestic violence in their homes were 700 times more likely than those who were not so exposed to use violence in their own homes, while boys who were also abused themselves were 1,000 times more likely to be abusive than those who were not abused themselves (Kalmuss, 1984). Yet, as mentioned previously, courts continue to place children with batterers despite the problems with their power and control issues that negatively impact parenting (Saunders, 2007).

It should be no surprise, then, that "physical dating violence" (PDV) has been found to impact almost one in every 11 adolescents according to the 2005 National Youth Risk Behavior Study (Masho & Hamm, 2007). Over 12,000 youth, about evenly divided between males and females, were surveyed with approximately 10% of each group reporting being victims of PDV. This rise in the violence used by girls as well as the violence used by boys in dating relationships is comparable to the rise in violence used by girls found in teens arrested and placed in detention centers. As described later, a study in one detention center found high scores on assessment measures of PTSD and family violence, although these girls did not report exposure to violence in their homes during clinical interviews. In the 2005 National Youth Risk Behavior Study, both boys and girls who engaged in current sexual activity, alcohol use, physical fighting, sexual victimization, and suicidal thoughts were at higher risk to be engaged in a PDV relationship while boys who used illicit drugs and girls who had a poor body image were also at higher risk.

Unfortunately, the intervention with teens does not seem to be age appropriate, as it often includes severe legal punishment that can prevent these youth from being admitted to colleges or even continue to work toward a career if they get intervention and stop their abusive behavior. Further, in some cases these children's brains are not well formed in both social and impulsive areas, so they are still very amenable to change. Others, however, have had a life of abuse and trauma and they need a different intervention, but again, not necessarily legal punishment.

SEX TRAFFICKING

The link between sex trafficking and domestic violence has also become much better known within the last 10 years. One of the high-risk vulnerabilities for youth to be groomed and then trafficked is coming from a home where there is domestic violence. These young teenagers are vulnerable to the charms and love given to them by their trafficker; only after they are "captured" do they realize that the love and gifts last only as long as they perform sex with the trafficker and his friends and customers. Children who have been abused by one or both parents who fail to protect them are also at high risk to become "sex slaves," one of the new terms for what used to be called "child prostitution." Safe houses have been set up in high-trafficking areas and newer trauma techniques are being used to help these girls and boys heal. More is discussed about this area and its close relationship to domestic violence and other forms of rape, sexual assault, and sexual exploitation by those in authority positions in Chapter 8.

SUMMARY

The history of society's newest interest in the eradication of violence against women and children demonstrates both the intricacies of the problem and the difficulties in dealing with it. Although shelters do provide safety for only a small number of women and children, their presence in a community sends a message about zero tolerance for such abuse. Expensive to run, shelters and advocates must continue to battle for funding from politicians in national and local positions along with other worthy causes. The attempt to professionalize the interventions for battered women has included changes in both legal and psychological delivery systems. However, advocates and professionals still do not regularly work well together, especially when there are political or personal differences.

The problems yet to be solved include the following:

- Some battered women are harmed by the abuse and want or need psychotherapy.
- Treatment goals become fuzzy and feminist therapy models are rarely used.
- Psychotherapy and forensic evaluations are often mistakenly classified by state licensing boards that are not well educated on domestic violence issues.
- Forensic testimony is not accepted within the criminal, civil, family, and juvenile courts without a diagnosis and sometimes rejected or ignored even with a diagnosis.

- Many battered women are losing custody of their children when they attempt to protect them from exposure to a coercive controlling and abusive parent.
- Constant battles occur with other diagnoses without empirical support being offered and accepted by the uninformed courts such as parental alienation syndrome or psychological Munchausen by proxy.
- Advocates working in shelters and other programs are entering into graduate schools wanting more information about psychological theories, and feminism is not as attractive to them as is the lure of psychodynamic and other theories.
- There is less support in the mental health community for the feminist model, perhaps because of the feminist "trashing" of professionals who teach and supervise students.
- There is a lack of clear feminist principles in the trauma model.
- There is a growing distance between advocates and professionals rather than a coming together to solve the common problems.
- The focus on sex trafficking needs to incorporate an understanding of the relationship to domestic violence, rape, sexual assault, and sexual exploitation.

REFERENCES

American Psychiatric Association. (1987). *Diagnostic and statistical manual of mental disorders* (3rd ed., rev.). Washington, DC: Author.

American Psychiatric Association. (1994). *Diagnostic and statistical manual of mental disorders* (4th ed.). Washington, DC: Author.

American Psychiatric Association. (2013). *Diagnostic and statistical manual of mental disorders* (5th ed.). Arlington, VA: American Psychiatric Publishing.

Briere, J., & Scott, C. (2015). *Principles of trauma therapy: A guide to symptoms, evaluation, and treatment* (2nd ed., DSM-5 update). Thousand Oaks, CA: Sage. (Original work published 2007)

Broverman, I. K., Broverman, D., Clarkson, F., Rosencrantz, P., & Vogel, S. (1970). Sex role stereotypes and clinical judgments of mental health. *Journal of Consulting and Clinical Psychology, 34*, 1–7.

Browne, A. (1987). *When battered women kill.* New York, NY: Free Press.

Brownmiller, S. (1975). *Against our will: Men, women, and rape.* New York, NY: Simon & Schuster.

Brownmiller, S. (1988). *Waverly Place.* New York, NY: Simon & Schuster.

Centers for Disease Control and Prevention. (2008). Adverse health conditions and health risk behaviors associated with intimate partner violence—United

States, 2005. *Morbidity and Mortality Weekly Report, 57*(5), 113–117. Retrieved from http://www.cdc.gov/mmwr/pdf/wk/mm5705.pdf

Chesler, P. (1972). *Women and madness.* Garden City, NY: Doubleday.

Chesler, P. (2003). *Woman's inhumanity to woman.* New York, NY: Plume.

Dutton, M. A. (1992). *Empowering and healing the battered woman: A model for assessment and intervention.* New York, NY: Springer Publishing Company.

Dutton, M. A. (1993). Understanding women's responses to domestic violence: A redefinition of battered woman syndrome. *Hofstra Law Review, 21*(4), 1191–1242.

Ewing, C. P. (1987). *Battered women who kill.* Lexington, MA: Lexington Books.

Harrell, A. (1991). *Evaluation of court-ordered treatment for domestic violence offenders.* Washington, DC: The Urban Institute.

Hart, B. (1988). *Safety for women: Monitoring batterers' programs.* Harrisburg, PA: Pennsylvania Coalition Against Domestic Violence.

Holden, G. W., Geffner, R., & Jouriles, E. N. (Eds.). (1998). *Children exposed to marital violence: Theory, research, and applied issues.* Washington, DC: American Psychological Association.

Jones, A. (1994). *Next she will be dead: Battering and how to stop it.* Boston, MA: Beacon Press.

Kalmuss, D. S. (1984). The intergenerational transmission of marital aggression. *Journal of Marriage and the Family, 48,* 113–120.

Martin, D. (1976). *Battered wives.* San Francisco, CA: Glide.

Masho, S., & Hamm, C. M. (2007, November). *Male and female adolescents equally victims of physical dating violence.* Presented at the American Public Health Association (APHA) 135th Annual Meeting, Washington, DC.

Needle, R. B., & Walker, L. E. A. (2007). *Abortion counseling: A clinician's guide to psychology, legislation, politics, and competency.* New York, NY: Springer Publishing.

Pizzey, E. (1974). *Scream quietly or the neighbors will hear.* London, UK: Penguin.

Saccuzzo, D. P., & Johnson, N. E. (2004). Child custody mediation's failure to protect: Why should the criminal justice system care? *NIJ Journal, 251.* Retrieved from https://www.ncjrs.gov/pdffiles1/jr000251f.pdf

Saunders, D. (2007, October). *Child custody and visitation decisions in domestic violence cases: Legal trends, risk factors, and safety concerns.* Harrisburg, PA: VAWnet, a project of the National Resource Center on Domestic Violence/ Pennsylvania Coalition Against Domestic Violence. Retrieved from http:// www.vawnet.org

Schafran, L. H. (1990). Overwhelming evidence: Reports on gender bias in the courts. *Trial, 26,* 28–35.

Schechter, S. (1982). *Women and male violence: The visions and struggles of the battered women's movement.* Boston, MA: South End Press.

Stark, E. (2007). *Coercive control: How men entrap women in personal life.* New York, NY: Oxford University Press.

Straus, M. A. (2010). Thirty years of denying the evidence on gender symmetry in partner violence: Implications for prevention and treatment. *Partner Abuse, 1*(3), 332–362.

Straus, M. A., Gelles, R. J., & Steinmetz., S. K. (1980). *Behind closed doors: Violence in the American family*. Garden City, NY: Anchor/Doubleday.

Walker, L. E. (1989). Psychology and violence against women. *American Psychologist, 44*, 695–702.

Walker, L. E. A. (2017). Trauma practice: Historical overview. In Gold et al. (Eds.), *Handbook of trauma practice: Vol. 2. Trauma practice*. Washington, DC: American Psychological Association.

Walker, L. E., Cummings, D. M., Cummings, N. A., & Waller, G. (2012). *Our broken family court system*. Dryden, NY: Ithaca Press.

Weisberg, D. K. (2012). *Domestic violence: Legal and social realities*. New York, NY: Aspen.

CHAPTER THREE

WHAT IS THE BATTERED WOMAN SYNDROME?[1]

The term "battered woman syndrome" (BWS) was first used in 1977 as the title to the U.S. National Institute of Mental Health (NIMH)–funded research grant that collected data on over 400 self-referred women who met the definition of a battered woman, which formed the basis for this original research. The details of the original study were reported in the previous editions of this book and only a summary is repeated here (Walker, 1984, 2000, 2009). Although the term BWS appeared prior to the addition of the diagnostic category "posttraumatic stress disorder" (PTSD) in the *Diagnostic and Statistical Manual of Mental Disorders* (3rd ed.; *DSM-III*; American Psychiatric Association [APA], 1980), the theoretical basis upon which the BWS was developed was similar to what later became known as PTSD. Over the years since then, BWS has been used in the psychological literature as a subcategory of PTSD, but, until the BWS research study, it was never empirically demonstrated to have the same or similar criteria. Despite its popularity in clinical and forensic psychology, and its similarity to trauma theory, until now BWS had not been subjected to the scientific analysis provided by this research. The lack of testable hypotheses permitted a small group of advocates, who feared the stigmatization that may accompany labeling, to raise questions about the existence of BWS as a syndrome or collection of psychological signs and symptoms that often occur from the same cause (APA, 1980, 2000).

BWS, as it was originally conceived, consisted of the pattern of the signs and symptoms that have been found to occur after a woman has been

[1]This chapter includes data that were collected by faculty and students at Nova Southeastern University's College of Psychology, including Rachel Duros, Heidi Ardern, Rachel Needle, Kate Richmond, Lauren Schumacher, Vera Lopez, Dr. Tara Jungersen, and Cassie Groth. Dr. Ryan Black worked with us on validating the BWSQ assessment instrument on which the data were collected.

physically, sexually, and/or psychologically abused in an intimate relationship, when the partner (usually, but not always, a man) exerted power and control over the woman to coerce her into doing whatever he wanted, without regard for her rights or feelings. As there are significant differences between the theory underlying the construct of BWS, and to date there are no empirically supported data, it has not yet been applied to battered men. Therefore, the term used is BWS rather than a gender-neutral battered person syndrome (BPS) or even battered man syndrome (BMS). Of course, men are abused by women, but the psychological impact on the man does not appear to be consistent with trauma in most cases. This is further discussed in Chapter 12.

The research has now demonstrated that BWS has seven groups of criteria that have been tested scientifically and can be said to identify the syndrome. The first four groups of symptoms are the same as for the *DSM-5* (APA, 2013) criteria for PTSD, while the additional three criteria groups are present in victims of intimate partner violence (IPV). They are:

1. Intrusive recollections of the trauma event(s)
2. Hyperarousal and high levels of anxiety
3. Avoidance behavior and emotional numbing usually expressed as depression, dissociation, minimization, repression, and denial
4. Negative alterations in mood and cognition[2]
5. Disrupted interpersonal relationships from batterer's power and control measures
6. Body image distortion and/or somatic or physical complaints
7. Sexual intimacy issues

These seven areas are more fully described later in this chapter.

POSTTRAUMATIC STRESS DISORDER

Although all forms of trauma are identified by the same four groups of signs and symptoms using the *DSM-5* (APA, 2013) or *ICD-10* (World Health Organization, 1992) criteria, in fact, there are differences between

---

[2]Although this criterion is a new group of symptoms clustered together, the actual symptoms previously were found under the other three criteria in earlier versions of the *DSM*.

the different types of trauma that occur. For example, traumatic events that only occur one time, such as environmental catastrophes like the tsunami in the Far East, Hurricane Katrina in New Orleans and the Gulf Coast of the United States, or the major earthquake in Pakistan, or disasters such as the terrorist attacks of 9/11 when airplanes crashed into the towers of the World Trade Center in New York City and a part of the Pentagon in Washington, DC (causing the buildings to collapse and killing thousands of people and injuring thousands more), an airplane crash killing hundreds, or the terrorist attacks in a Paris concert hall, stadium, and restaurant, all produce similar psychological effects in people who have experienced some part of the event even if they were not at the site when the disaster occurred. The event is usually experienced as unexpected, out of the person's control, and causes disruption to how a person may think, feel, or act. One-time traumatic events such as physical or sexual assault by strangers may also produce similar psychological impact. Repeated traumatic events, such as soldiers who are at combat sites in Iraq, children who are physically or sexually abused by people who love them, and those who are battered by intimate partners, also experience similar psychological impact, although those who know who the enemy is, such as soldiers, do not develop the same type of coping strategies as do victims of child and intimate partner abuse.

Physical, sexual, and psychological abuse that occur in families or with intimate partners have their own special characteristics that go beyond those seen in the typical PTSD. The "fight or flight" response to danger can be seen in each of the different types of trauma responses. For example, the person taking a walk sees a lion, becomes physiologically aroused and wants to protect himself or herself, and if possible, runs away. The autonomic nervous system that controls our emotional responses becomes activated, producing sufficient cortisol, adrenalin, and other neurochemicals to help activate the nervous system so it responds to the threat of danger. The response to traumatic events is similar. We call events that can evoke this response in people "trauma triggers." The trauma triggers will have to be desensitized during trauma-informed treatment because they continue to cause the trauma response long after they were present; they are reexperienced in the person's mind with all the same emotions, as if they were reoccurring. Various forms of trauma therapy are further discussed in Chapters 14 to 16.

When domestic violence events occur and reoccur, the woman recognizes the man's escalating anger and she becomes physiologically aroused with fear that activates the autonomic nervous system to release its neurotransmitters and hormones that then produce a hyperarousal response. Then, she assesses the threat and decides whether to cope with the problem or flee, which in this case means physical or psychological escape. Women who have been abused repeatedly learn to develop good coping strategies that usually occur as a tradeoff to escape skills. Therefore, the typical fear or trauma response of the battered woman triggers her to become hyperaroused and then to psychologically escape using a variety of methods, including minimization or denial of the danger from the particular incident, depression, dissociation, or even repression and forgetting. The psychological escape, then, can include minimization or denial of the danger, reducing fear, repression, depression, dissociation, or a combination of these automatic psychological processes that are further described in the later chapters. What is important to understand here is that these are avoidance responses that protect the woman from experiencing the full-blown trauma response. The trauma responses are mediated by the autonomic nervous system and not consciously employed, at least initially. In repeated traumas, such as domestic violence or child abuse, where the person does not believe he or she can escape, a pattern is established that permits coping with a minimum of emotional pain. The lack of belief in the ability to escape is part of the "learned helplessness" response that is further discussed in Chapter 4.

DSM-5 CRITERIA FOR PTSD

There are four sets of psychological signs and symptoms that are required to make the diagnosis of PTSD using the *DSM-5* (APA, 2013). In addition, there are three threshold criteria that must be met in order to consider this diagnosis. The threshold criteria are:

1. The person must experience a traumatic event that includes fear of personal bodily safety or death (but no longer needs to have subjective fear).
2. The aftereffects of that experience must last for more than 4 weeks. If less than 4 weeks, then it is diagnosed as an "acute stress reaction."
3. The aftereffects must impact some important part of the person's life such as job performance, school, or social relationships.

As can be seen, most battered women, especially those who believe that the batterer can or will kill them, would meet the first set of criteria here. Even those women who are not physically harmed often fear that the batterer can and will hurt them worse if they do not do whatever the man demands. In some cases, the women do not feel the full extent of their fear until later, even after the relationship has been terminated. This is similar to the delayed PTSD that may be seen in soldiers who do not develop symptoms until another incident occurs that triggers the memory of the same fear they may have repressed when the first trauma occurred. This is commonly seen in child sexual abuse victims who knew what was happening to them (such as those abused by clergy) but did not experience the full PTSD symptoms until later in life when they were adults.

The second set of PTSD criteria includes four different groups of psychological signs and symptoms:

1. The person must reexperience the traumatic event(s) in a variety of ways that include intrusive memories, nightmares, night terrors, day dreams, flashbacks, and physiological responses with or without exposure to the same stimuli.
2. The person has a hyperarousal response that includes anxiety reactions, crying, sleep or eating problems, hypervigilance to further harm, exaggerated startle response, and other fearful responses.
3. The person has a numbing of emotions and wherever possible avoids making things worse. These avoidance responses may take the form of depression, dissociation, denial, minimization of fear or harm, decreased activities, isolation from people, or other indications that their lives are being controlled by another person.
4. The person has negative alterations in mood and cognitions, including an inability to remember some aspects of the trauma event(s), negative self-esteem and expectations from others and the world, often in a pervasive negative state of mind with difficulties in experiencing positive emotions, distorts self-blame, is not as interested in activities as before, and has feelings of detachment from others (*DSM-5*, APA, 2013).

A series of analyses of the data collected using the Battered Woman Syndrome Questionnaire (BWSQ) is described in the following sections.

Data Collection

In the original study, there were several different ways used to collect data about the actual abuse experienced by the women. First, a set of criteria needed to be met to establish eligibility to participate in the study. The following were the criteria used in both the original and current studies:

- Excessive possessiveness and/or jealousy
- Extreme verbal harassment and expressing comments of a derogatory nature with negative value judgments ("put-downs")
- Restriction of activity through physical or psychological means
- Nonverbal and verbal threats of future punishment and/or deprivation
- Sexual assault whether or not married
- Actual physical attack with or without injury

Although in the original study we wanted women who had at least two physical attacks, whether or not they were injured, to assess for the rise in psychological impact and learned helplessness, in the current research we were not as strict about physical abuse. It has been demonstrated that for most women the psychological abuse is the most significant part of the relationship and causes the most unforgettable painful moments. However, even realizing the devastating power of psychological maltreatment, most women do not consider themselves battered unless they have been physically harmed. This is also true for women who have experienced severe sexual abuse as we discuss in Chapters 6 to 8.

BWSQ Revisions

The BWSQ #1 that was used to collect the data analyzed in the original study was a 100-page questionnaire with forced-choice and open-ended questions that took over 6 hours to administer in a face-to-face interview with a trained interviewer and the volunteer subject. Embedded in the BWSQ #1 were questions to collect information about a nonviolent relationship that approximately half of the women reported on. Also embedded were several well-known research scales. Over 4,000 variables were available for analysis but not all could be analyzed due to restraints on time and money. Over 400 self-referred women were evaluated in a six-state region of the

United States. Details of this research and the results have been published in the first three editions of this book (Walker, 1984, 2000, 2009).

In the current research, the BWSQ #2 was developed, after several pilot data collections helped eliminate variables that did not adequately discriminate (Walker, 2009). Then, scales were developed that measured the constructs that appeared to hang together using simple regression analyses. To measure the validity of the scales (and the theories), standardized tests and other assessment instruments were embedded in the BWSQ #2 and analyses were done comparing the scales with these assessment instruments. Controls were provided by the standardized tests. The interviewers were trained and a multisite, multilingual, and multicountry data collection was begun in 2002. Each student interviewer completed a thorough standardized training prior to his or her acceptance as an interviewer and received a copy of the manual for future reference (Walker, Ardern, Tome, Bruno, & Brosch, 2006).

To assist in uniformity of data collected, a written manual for interviewers was prepared and, like the BWSQ #2, was translated into the appropriate languages. Translations were done by either professional translators or graduate students in psychology from the country in question and then they were translated back into English from the translated version so as to check on veracity. In some cases, it has been necessary to slightly change the wording of a question in order to tap the actual data in a particular country. For example, in Russia the term *substance abuse* is less frequently used, while *drug and alcohol abuse* would be the more accurate translation. In Trinidad, we changed "spanked" to "got licks" to make sure interviewees understood the questions about childhood discipline and abuse. This year we added data collected in Colombia by Dr. Eduin Caceres and his students. There are statistical techniques that have been used in some analyses to account for these slight variations in data groups as seen in the PTSD study by Duros (2007), who used a factorial invariance, and the results can be seen in Figure 3.1.

In this chapter, the validation of the theory of PTSD and BWS is discussed, and in the subsequent chapters, various analyses of other variables are described and discussed. Some analyses utilized the subjects from the four initial countries: the United States, Russia, Greece, and Spain. Other analyses utilized data that were collected from each country separately or in different comparisons. The research project is still under way with recruitment continuing and data also beginning to be collected in various other countries, as described in Chapter 12.

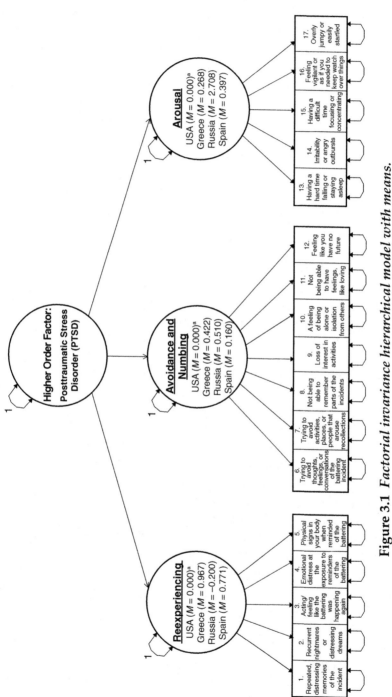

Figure 3.1 *Factorial invariance hierarchical model with means.*
[a]U.S. sample set at M = 0.000 so that it is used as the comparison group.
Reprinted with permission from Duros (2007).

Demographic Data

The two study groups were comparable on some demographic items but not on others. A beginning analysis is shown in Table 3.1.

This is to be expected for several reasons. First, the data are still being collected and therefore, those that have been evaluated were from a convenience sample without correctional factors to make sure that the sample was stratified or equal to the percentage of demographic and especially ethnic groups in the community from which they were collected, as was done in the original research. A second reason could be because the

Table 3.1 *Sociodemographic Data for Battered Women*

Demographic Variable	Original Sample N	Original Sample %	Current Sample N	Current Sample %
Racial and ethnic group				
White/Caucasian	321	80	46	43
Hispanic/Latina	3	8	9	9
Black/African	25	6	9	9
Native Indian	18	4	2	2
Asian/Pacific Islander	1	0	1	1
Other	4	1	39	37
Marital status				
Single	26	6	29	27
Married/living together	103	24	21	20
Separated/divorced	261	65	48	45
Widowed	11	3	8	8
Education				
Less than high school	66	12	29	27
High school only	99	25	42	40
Some college	160	40	17	16
College and postgrad	92	23	10	10
Mean years of education	12.7		12.11	
Mean age (years)	32.2 (Range: 18–59)		38.07 (Range: 17–69)	
Mean number of children	2.02 (Range: 0–10)		1.79 (Range: 0–8)	

sample is cross-national, from several different countries, so that these demographic groups do not make as much sense in some countries as in the United States. For example, the breakdown of racial and ethnic groups is different in other countries. This is why the "other" column contains 40% of the population studied. After we looked at these statistics, we changed the ethnic categories to better reflect the international demographics. For example, in Spain most of the "other" category included women who had immigrated to Spain from nearby countries such as Morocco and Algiers. In Greece, there was a group that had immigrated from Albania. A third reason is also due to the difficulty in comparing different national samples. Although the mean years of education are comparable (12.7 years in the original sample with 12.1 years in the current sample), in fact twice as many women in the new sample had a less than high school education, with fewer women in the international sample having at least some or completing college or postgraduate school. Access to education is different in countries other than the United States. More women called themselves "single" rather than "separated" or "divorced" in the current sample, but it is not known if they really were never married or if there was simply a misunderstanding of how the terms were to be used when translated.

Profile of Battering Incidents

In the original study, we analyzed details about the four specific battering incidents that were not reanalyzed in the current study. These include months when abuse was more likely to have occurred, days of the week, and time of day. We found that abusive incidents were pretty evenly spread out over the 12 months of the year with perhaps a slight rise in incidents in the hotter months. This is consistent with a slight rise in other crime statistics during the summer months. Weekends were the most likely days for abuse to have occurred, perhaps reflecting the amount of time spent at home and away from work. Evenings were the most likely time for a battering incident to have occurred, again perhaps reflecting the time couples spend with each other.

Battering incidents were most likely to start and stop at home, often starting in the living room, kitchen, or bedroom and ending in the same room in which they started. Interestingly, if the incident did not start at home, the most likely place was a public setting or someone else's home. This corresponds both with some women's descriptions of fights that start because of the men's jealousy of attention the women paid to others or some who describe picking a fight with the batterer in front of other people to minimize the harm from his angry explosion because others are around. These women know that the tension is so high that the acute battering incident will occur no matter what they do and they have learned the best protective behaviors. These responses were intuitive, corroborated by police reports and other research, and so, we felt that they did not need continued investigation in the current study.

Details of Four Battering Incidents

As in the original study, the interviewers collected details about four specific battering incidents that the women could remember. These included the first incident they could remember, the last battering incident before they were interviewed, the worst or one of the worst incidents if the last one was the worst, and a typical battering incident. Data were collected using both open-ended and forced-choice questions. This method was found to yield the most useful information about battering incidents in the original study and continued in the current study to provide the richness of information expected. Ardern (2005) analyzed some of the open-ended responses using qualitative methodology while Duros (2007) analyzed the data gathered from the forced-choice responses together with the PTSD checklist and Briere's Trauma Symptom Inventory (TSI; Briere, 1995).

PTSD ANALYSIS

The initial data from the current study, using the BWSQ #2, were subjected to analysis to determine if the women reported signs and symptoms consistent with the diagnosis of PTSD using the criteria from the *DSM-IV-TR* (APA, 2000), which was in effect at the time. Duros (2007) compared 68 women's responses on the details of the psychological, sexual, and physical abuse from the four battering incidents reported, their responses on the PTSD checklist, and their results on the standardized test, TSI (Briere, 1995) that was embedded within the BWSQ #2. In the more recent version, the Detailed Assessment of Posttraumatic Stress (DAPS), also developed by Briere (2009), is also included as this test actually gives a PTSD score in addition to measuring the various components of PTSD from specific incidents reported. The TSI measures the clinical scales that make up the

PTSD diagnosis in general. For this analysis, Duros (2007) utilized the scales that measured anxious arousal, depression, intrusive experiences, defensive avoidance, dissociation, tension reduction behavior, and impaired self-reference. As their titles suggest, these scales are consistent with the PTSD criteria used to make the diagnosis.

Using a standardized linear regression analysis between the total number of PTSD symptoms endorsed and the four battering incidents and followed by a logistic regression analysis to assess prediction of endorsement of necessary PTSD criteria based on the psychological, physical, and sexual abuse present in the four battering incidents, Duros (2007) found PTSD in the linear and logistic regression results. An interesting statistical technique utilized in the analysis was a *factorial invariance*, which is designed for multigroup comparisons, in order to ensure that a given construct, in this case PTSD, is measured in exactly the same way across different groups. Figure 3.1 provides a pictorial view of the procedure.

The procedure does this by accounting for and assuming an error, such as translation or adaptation issues in the different versions of the BWSQ. With this procedure, a higher confidence level is established that potential differences between groups (or in the case of the present study, lack thereof) can be interpreted as a truly reflective measure of variability in PTSD. The results can be seen in Tables 3.2 and 3.3.

In general, the criteria that would require a diagnosis of PTSD were found in the samples used. No significant difference in PTSD was found among the samples of battered women from the United States, Greece, Russia, and Spain. This is consistent with other research, including Keane, Marshall, and Taft (2006) who also found equivalent presentation of PTSD symptoms cross-nationally in the general population. Interestingly, Keane et al. found that being a woman increased the probability of developing PTSD around the globe. Given the high frequency and prevalence of violence against women around the world, this is not surprising.

These analyses gave some interesting and clarifying information about the development of PTSD, especially since not every woman who is battered will develop it, nor will all battered women, with or without PTSD, develop BWS. However, the use of a trauma model to help explain and perhaps even predict who might develop PTSD symptoms can assist in both prevention and intervention efforts by strengthening those who might be most likely to develop the psychological sequelae. This could include building women's resilience through extra community or familial support or even through administration of certain medications immediately

Table 3.2 *Standard Linear Regression Summary*

Predictors	R^2	F	p	B	t	p	Size[a]
First episode	.223	2.770	.059	—	—	—	M–L
fPsych	—	—	—	.112	.518	.609	S
fPhysic	—	—	—	.250	1.145	.261	S–M
fSexual	—	—	—	.209	1.101	.280	S–M
Most recent episode	.413	6.560	.002	—	—	—	L
mrPsych	—	—	—	.056	.251	.804	—
mrPhysic	—	—	—	.269	1.427	.165	S–M
mrSexual	—	—	—	.413	2.025	.053	M–L
Worst episode	.208	2.366	.093	—	—	—	M–L
wPsych	—	—	—	−.068	−.246	.808	—
wPhysic	—	—	—	.445	1.861	.074	M–L
wSexual	—	—	—	.099	.459	.650	S
Typical episode	.247	3.724	.020	—	—	—	L
tPsych	—	—	—	−.012	−.045	.964	—
tPhysic	—	—	—	.424	1.824	.077	M–L
tSexual	—	—	—	.137	.678	.502	S

[a]Descriptor of effect size per Cohen (1988): R^2 (small = .01; medium = .09; large = .25); B (small = .10; medium = .30; large = .5).

L, large; M, medium; S, small.

Reprinted with permission from Duros (2007).

postassault. For example, there have been some reports that administration of drugs such as selective serotonin reuptake inhibitors at the time of the trauma may prevent or reduce the fear response from developing trauma triggers that maintain the trauma response even after the person is safe. Unfortunately, it is unusual for a battered woman to report the first battering incident that occurs. Rather, it is not until there have been at least two to four battering incidents before she tells anyone. Duros (2007), in her analysis, found that the amount of physical and sexual violence in the incidents was associated with the severity of reported symptoms, particularly in the most recent incident reported and the most typical incident described.

While it is understandable that the most recent incident would generate a large effect size for PTSD because of temporal proximity to the traumatic event, it was surprising that the typical rather than the worst incident also generated such a large amount of PTSD symptoms endorsed.

Table 3.3 *Logistic Regression Analyses of PTSD as a Function of Battering Incidents*

Variable	B	Wald	Odds Ratio	95% Confidence Interval for Odds Ratio
Overall R^2 = .182				
fPsych	.342	.301	1.407	.415–4.771
fPhysic	.512	.486	1.668	.396–7.029
fSexual	1.050	.832	2.859	.299–27.297
Constant	−.256	.146	.774	
Overall R^2 = .492				
mrPsych	−4.69	.314	.625	.121–3.231
mrPhysic	.644	1.133	1.905	.581–6.240
mrSexual	−8.316	1.826	4089.33	.024–7.1E+008
Constant	−.293	.114	.746	
Overall R^2 = .195				
wPsych	−.400	.385	.670	.190–2.370
wPhysic	1.237	3.059	3.445	.861–13.782
wSexual	.254	.126	1.289	.318–5.232
Constant	−.145	.046	.865	
Overall R^2 = .182				
tPsych	−.036	.003	.964	.266–3.491
tPhysic	.834	1.910	2.302	.706–7.508
tSexual	.190	.112	1.209	.398–3.675
Constant	−.169	.055	.844	

Reprinted with permission from Duros (2007).

The *DSM-IV-TR* (APA, 2000), for example, states that the more intense the trauma, the stronger the likelihood of developing PTSD. On the other hand, the typical abuse incident may well be repeated any number of times, which of course, is what made it typical to the woman, and so, that might be experienced as more intense than one single incident, no matter how awful it is, and that may account for the PTSD symptoms it generated. Battered women also describe the totality of the abuse in the relationship as most traumatic, so the typical incident may represent the entire battering relationship to these women. In addition, the theory that the psychological effects from battering incidents increase geometrically rather than additively over time would predict that the impact from the most recent event would include the totality of the battering experience up until that event, rather than simply measuring the impact from one single event. This result lends support to the feminist jurisprudence scholars who have called for domestic violence to be considered as a continuing tort in the law, rather than considering each incident independently.

It was also interesting that the amount of physical abuse that was described during the typical incident was related to the prediction of PTSD symptoms. As Ardern (2005) and others found in their analysis of battered women's descriptions of the battering incidents themselves, it is the psychological abuse and coercive control by the batterers that seem to be the most troublesome for the women to deal with. However, results in the present study did not reflect a difference between physical and sexual abuse and psychological abuse alone in producing PTSD symptomatology. These data suggest that physical abuse together with the anticipation of further abuse is what the typical incident measured in this study.

Further logistic regressions were performed by Duros (2007) to determine if the categorical PTSD status of the woman would be related to the physical, sexual, and psychological incidents rather than the continuous number of PTSD symptoms endorsed. That is, no matter how many PTSD symptoms endorsed, if the woman had a sufficient number to reach the diagnostic threshold, would the type of trauma be predictive of whether or not PTSD would occur? In this analysis, the most recent and the worst incidents were most predictive as the theories would expect. However, when an odds ratio was calculated, it became clear that the presence of sexual abuse played a much stronger role in the development of PTSD than did psychological or physical abuse alone. For example, if the first incident recalled by the woman involved sexual coercion or abuse, the odds ratio suggested the woman would be more likely to develop PTSD. So too for sexual abuse or coercion reported in the most recent incident. Physical abuse was implicated in raising the odds of a higher PTSD score if it occurred in the typical and worst incidents.

DOES THE TSI ASSESS FOR PTSD IN BATTERED WOMEN?

An earlier analysis of 56 of the women in the same cross-national sample developed the checklist of PTSD symptoms from the data collected with the various clinical scales on the TSI (Duros & Walker, 2006). Table 3.4

indicates the specific PTSD symptoms reported by this sample to better illustrate how the aggregate group accounts for the required number of symptoms.

A distribution of the standard scores on the TSI clinical scales was then compared for a smaller number of the sample. These results are shown in Figures 3.2 to 3.9. As can be seen in each of these figures, the average scores for each of the scales on the TSI were either just below or at the 65 level above which would signify clinical significance.

In Figure 3.9, trauma scales as reported on Briere's TSI, all the women were at least one standard deviation above the mean ($M = 50$, $SD = 10$) and approaching the clinical significance of 65 or higher scores. With a larger sample, it is anticipated that these scores will reach significance for the group. Obviously, individual women already have reached a sufficient level of significance to be considered being diagnosed with PTSD.

Further analysis of an earlier sample of women from the United States, Russia, Spain, and Greece looked at the three groups of PTSD symptoms from the data collected. These included reexperiencing the

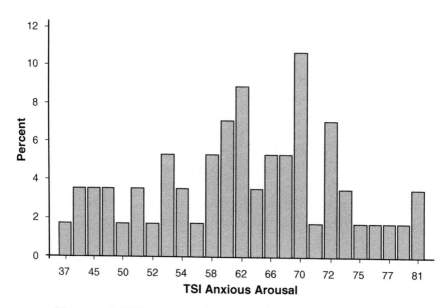

Figure 3.2 *TSI anxious arousal distribution of scores.*
TSI, Trauma Symptom Inventory.
Source: Duros and Walker (2006).

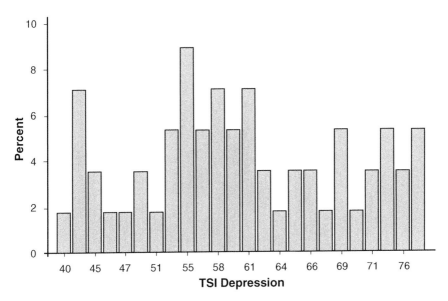

Figure 3.3 *TSI depression distribution of scores.*
TSI, Trauma Symptom Inventory.
Source: Duros and Walker (2006).

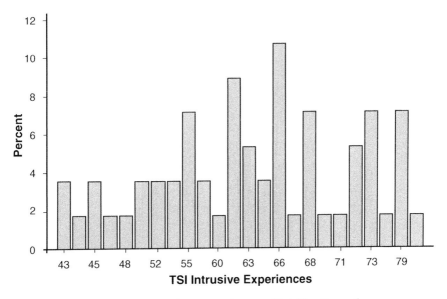

Figure 3.4 *TSI intrusive experiences distribution of scores.*
TSI, Trauma Symptom Inventory.
Source: Duros and Walker (2006).

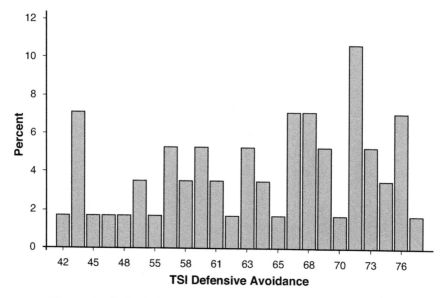

Figure 3.5 *TSI defensive avoidance distribution of scores.*
TSI, Trauma Symptom Inventory.
Source: Duros and Walker (2006).

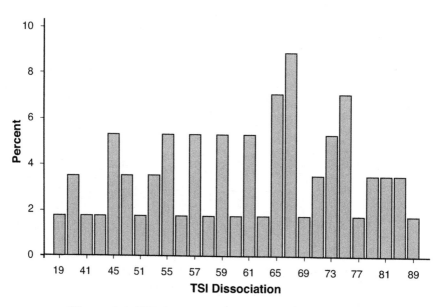

Figure 3.6 *TSI dissociation distribution of scores.*
TSI, Trauma Symptom Inventory.
Source: Duros and Walker (2006).

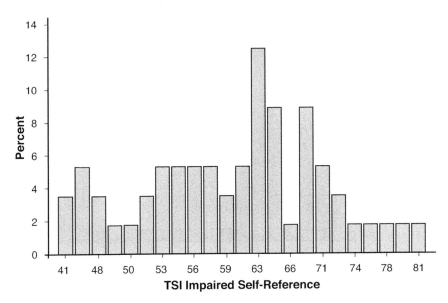

Figure 3.7 *TSI impaired self-reference distribution of scores.*
TSI, Trauma Symptom Inventory.
Source: Duros and Walker (2006).

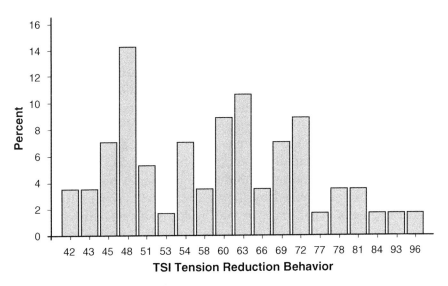

Figure 3.8 *TSI tension reduction behavior distribution of scores.*
TSI, Trauma Symptom Inventory.
Source: Duros and Walker (2006).

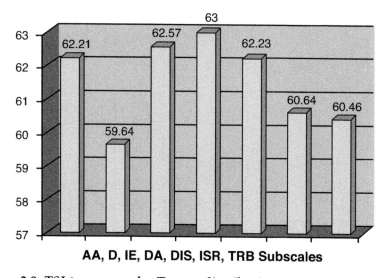

Figure 3.9 *TSI trauma scales T-score distribution.*
AA, anxious arousal; D, depression; DA, defensive avoidance; DIS, dissociation; IE, intrusive experiences; ISR, impaired self-reference; TRB, tension reduction behavior; TSI, Trauma Symptom Inventory.
Source: Duros and Walker (2006).

trauma, avoidance and numbing, and hyperarousal symptoms. Table 3.4 shows that while the women from different countries had different PTSD scores, all the groups were above the required criteria for diagnosis. The Russian women were more likely to use avoidance behaviors, including emotional numbing, to deal with trauma, not unlike their political and cultural history, while the Spanish women were more anxious than the other three groups. The Greek women experienced the most PTSD symptoms from their abuse and continue to reexperience the trauma even after they are safe from it actually reoccurring. Interestingly, the Greek women reexperienced more trauma than did the Russian women but were less likely to be hyperaroused by their experiences. Perhaps there was a higher degree of expectancy for the Greek men to act abusively toward them. The women in the U.S. sample were the least likely to develop severe PTSD as compared to the other groups, although they also met the criteria for the diagnosis.

These results are the first empirical confirmation of the theory predicting that IPV is experienced as a trauma and is predictive of the woman developing PTSD following the traumatic events. The likelihood

Table 3.4 *PTSD Symptoms*

	Reexperiencing (Mean; *SD*)	Avoidance/Numbing (Mean; *SD*)	Hyperarousal (Mean; *SD*)
Overall	3.04; 1.41[a]	4.21; 2.90[a]	3.23; 1.32[a]
United States	3.00; 1.48	3.87; 2.08	3.03; 1.52
Colombia	3.00; 1.87	3.00; 2.00	3.20; 1.30
Russia	3.10; 1.25	5.05; 1.19[a]	3.55; 1.32
Caucasian	2.60; 1.35	3.60; 2.14	2.60; 1.43
Hispanic	2.50; 2.07	2.50; 2.17	2.83; 1.47
African American	4.50; 0.58[a]	3.75; 0.96	4.25; 0.96[a]
Asian (*n* = 1)	4.00; –	7.00; –	5.00; –
Other ethnicity	3.24; 1.23	5.08; 1.15[a]	3.23; 1.32
Outpatient (*n* = 1)	4.00; –	4.00; –	3.00; –
Mental health	2.22; 1.86	2.33; 2.00	2.33; 1.50
Prison	3.37; 1.30	5.03; 1.43[a]	3.73; 0.98
Advertisement	2.83; 1.03	3.67; 1.83	2.75; 1.42
Other	2.75; 1.89	4.00; 2.16[a]	3.00; 1.83

[a]Observations referenced in chapter discussion.

SD, standard deviation.

Source: Duros and Walker (2006).

of PTSD being the response continues to occur over the course of the relationship, as is measured by the four battering incidents in the research. The scale developed to assess for PTSD symptoms were found to be as good as the TSI in assessing whether or not sufficient PTSD symptoms were present to make the diagnosis. Further, the experience of IPV can cause PTSD for women who live in different countries and cultures in the world, particularly in Spain, Russia, Greece, and the United States.

There are limitations to the generalizability of these results. Obviously, this was not a random sample but rather a convenience sample so there may be untold numbers of biases that were not controlled. For example, it may be that the women who volunteered to be interviewed for the study were different from other battered women or maybe there were no differences with other women in that particular demographic group. However, these women were similar in demographics from the battered women who volunteered to participate in the original study. Although we do not assess for the veracity of the women's reports of violence, it is assumed that large sample sizes will eliminate the individual variances in self-report data. This analysis is with a small sample and needs replication with larger and stratified samples of women from these countries as well as the additional countries from where the research is being conducted. Nonetheless, it is an important step forward to know that there is some empirical support for the theories that have been around for over 30 years now.

BWS RESULTS

The analyses in the PTSD Analysis section measure the first three criteria that were in the definition of BWS. The three additional criteria include the disruption in interpersonal relationships from the abuse of power and control and isolation of the woman, the difficulties with body image and somatic symptoms, and the sexual intimacy issues.

Disruption in Interpersonal Relationships

Ardern (2005) analyzed the power and control theme across all the battering incidents described by the Spanish, Russian, and U.S. women in the new sample. She found similar methods as were seen in the original study. In addition to physical violence and sexual coercion, a batterer uses many forms of manipulation, including isolation, following his rules, sex, degradation, jealousy, unpredictability, and direct and indirect threats of more violence.

Isolation, which was common across all cultural groups, included being treated as a possession, controlling when and if she saw family and friends, accompanying her to and from her job, restricting her time if she was allowed to go out by herself, frequent telephone contact, and the like. Sonkin has a detailed list of all the different common techniques batterers used to isolate women on his website (www.Daniel-Sonkin.com; domestic violence assessment software, including risk assessment and violence inventory). One Russian interviewee gave as an example,

"If I wanted to go somewhere, he would take a knife and threaten to kill my dog or people I cared about."

Women described many different types of *manipulation* such as threatening to kill himself if she leaves, threatening to break up with her if she does not move in with him, telling a pregnant wife that he will not buy food if she does not do outside chores, or other ways of "molding me to his way" as one woman put it. *Degrading comments* were more commonly reported in the U.S. group such as:

"He could do everything and I was made to feel like I could do nothing."
"He scolds me like a child, inadequate, inferior, stupid."

But the Russian women also reported typical degradation:

"He almost managed to persuade me that I'm nobody. Not worth a human life."
"He did everything to make me feel that I needed him and couldn't live without him."

Some of the manipulation included *unpredictable behavior* especially in the U.S. group. For example:

"I was fast asleep. He came home from the bar and was mad because there was no supper. I woke up to him dragging me by my hair down three flights of stairs. I was frightened and confused. I was asleep, what could I possibly have done wrong?"

But the Spanish women also described typical incidents:

"There was no argument. I returned to his house and without a word he hit me. I asked him, 'Why do you hit me?' He said, 'Because you are a woman.'"

Men used fear and threats in all the groups to force them into compliance. Typical threats included accusations that the woman was crazy, that he would take away their children and she would never find them, and that he would call the immigration or other authorities. In some cases, the man actually called the police first, and reported the woman for domestic violence knowing full well that she had hit him only in self-defense during the fight that he started. One Russian woman told of a terrorizing night when "he took an axe, put it under the pillow, and then told me that I should go to bed." She reported a sleepless night.

These types of incidents made it difficult for the woman to continue relationships with her family and friends partly for fear that the batterer will make good his threats to harm her and partly to keep him calm so he hurts her less often.

Sexual Intimacy Issues

A consistent theme in the battering incidents reported by the cross-national samples of women was the amount of jealousy in the relationships. Talking with other men, regardless of the context, or spending time with other people besides the batterer, resulted in an acute battering incident. Even tending to babies or older children's needs could precipitate the batterer's jealousy and a beating would follow. One woman said her partner's favorite expression was:

"Either you will be mine or you won't be at all."

Sex was used as a way for the batterer to mark the woman as his possession. He controlled whether the couple would have loving sex or abusive sex. Some women reported that the man would insist that she provide sex for his friends or prostitute herself to earn them money. As long as it was impersonal and rough sex, the man was not jealous. However, if the other men or the woman showed any emotions toward each other, then the woman would get beaten. In a small minority of cases, the batterer would not touch the woman sexually, making her feel as if she was flawed as a woman. These men often displayed cold anger and rarely showed warmth or love in their behavior. Most of the women reported that the man would insist upon having sex right after beating her whether or not she was ready. In fact, few women reported that sex was satisfactory for them.

The inability to be intimate was another theme throughout the descriptions of the relationships. It appeared that once domestic violence began, the ability to attach to others was lost. Dutton and Sonkin (2003) have found that some types of batterers actually have attachment disorders that stem from childhood. It is unknown if they find women who also have problems with attachment or if living with an abusive partner actually creates attachment problems for women. Further analysis of this area can be found in Chapter 12.

SUMMARY

In this chapter, we have discussed the analysis of how the construct of BWS was validated from the various analyses of data collected over the past 40 years. Our team is in the process of validating the BWSQ to be sure that it empirically measures the BWS. Again, the seven criteria for BWS are:

1. Reexperiencing the trauma
2. Hyperarousal of physical and mental symptoms
3. Avoidance symptoms such as depression, denial, dissociation
4. Cognitive disturbance and attention problems
5. Disruption in interpersonal relationships
6. Physical health and somatic symptoms
7. Sexual dysfunction

REFERENCES

American Psychiatric Association. (1980). *Diagnostic and statistical manual of mental disorders* (3rd ed.). Washington, DC: Author.

American Psychiatric Association. (2000). *Diagnostic and statistical manual of mental disorders* (4th ed., text rev.). Washington, DC: Author.

American Psychiatric Association. (2013). *Diagnostic and statistical manual of mental disorders* (5th ed.). Arlington, VA: American Psychiatric Publishing.

Ardern, H. (2005, August). Qualitative descriptions of battering incidents: A cross cultural comparison. In L. E. A. Walker (Chair), *BWS over 30 years.* Symposium conducted at the 113th Annual Meeting of American Psychological Association, Washington, DC.

Briere, J. (1995). *Trauma Symptom Inventory manual.* Odessa, FL: Psychological Assessment Resources.

Duros, R., & Walker, L. E. A. (2006, August). Battered woman syndrome, PTSD, and implications for treatment recommendations. In L. E. A. Walker & D. L. Shapiro (Chairs), *Forensic psychology for the independent practitioner.* Symposium presented at the 114th Annual Meeting of the American Psychological Association, New Orleans, LA.

Duros, R. L. (2007). *Posttraumatic stress and cross-national presentation in a battered women sample* (Doctoral dissertation, Nova Southeastern University). Retrieved from http://search.proquest.com/docview/304717890

Dutton, D. G., & Sonkin, D. J. (2003). *Intimate violence: Contemporary treatment innovations.* Binghamton, NY: Haworth Press.

Keane, T. M., Marshall, A. D., & Taft, C. T. (2006). Posttraumatic stress disorder: Etiology, epidemiology, and treatment outcome. *Annual Review of Clinical Psychology, 2,* 161–197.

Walker, L. E. (Ed.). (1984). *Women and mental health policy.* Beverly Hills, CA: Sage.

Walker, L. E. A. (1984). *The battered woman syndrome.* New York, NY: Springer Publishing Company.

Walker, L. E. A. (2000). *The battered woman syndrome* (2nd ed.). New York, NY: Springer Publishing Company.

Walker, L. E. A. (2009). *The battered woman syndrome* (3rd ed.). New York, NY: Springer Publishing Company.

Walker, L. E. A., Ardern, H., Tome, A., Bruno, J., & Brosch, R. (2006). *Battered Woman Syndrome Questionnaire: Training manual for interviewers.* Unpublished manuscript.

World Health Organization. (1992). *International statistical classification of diseases and related health problems* (10th revision). Geneva, Switzerland: Author.

CHAPTER FOUR

LEARNED HELPLESSNESS, LEARNED OPTIMISM, AND BATTERED WOMEN

When I first proposed using the theoretical construct of *learned helplessness* to help explain why women found it difficult to escape a battering relationship (Walker, 1978, 1979), I received support from other scientists (e.g., Barnett & LaViolette, 1993) and criticism from the feminist battered women's community (Bowker, 1993; Gondolf & Fisher, 1988). Learned helplessness was confused with being helpless, and not its original intended meaning of *having lost the ability to predict that what you do will make a particular outcome occur* or in scientific terms *loss of contingency between response and outcome*. At first, I was puzzled by the harsh criticism, as I saw learned helplessness as a theoretical, not political concept. I saw learned helplessness as accounting for how the aversive stimulation in the battering incidents themselves became paired in an identifiable pattern with reinforcements, such as the positive parts of the relationship. A learning theory explanation of the effects that are so easily observed in battered women's coping behavior meant that what was learned could be unlearned, an important finding for developing future intervention strategies. The theory provided a coherent and reasonable counterexplanation to the prevailing theory of the times—masochism or more permanent personality traits in battered women that caused them to provoke their abuse, enjoy the chaos, and stay in violent relationships (Shainess, 1979, 1985). Learned helplessness is a research-based theory; it is simple and elegant, and furthermore gives direction for prevention as well as intervention. It is used by psychologists all over the world as a paradigm to explain animal as well as human behavior (Cándido, Maldonado, Megías, & Catena, 1992), including responses to psychopharmacological interventions (Torres, Morales, Megías, Cándido, & Maldonado, 1994).

The criticism then was a good lesson in battered women's feminist politics, the subject of which could fill another book. I must say I was disappointed that there could not be a good scientific data-based debate with its critics, primarily because they did not understand the theory. Rather they were reacting to the name that contained the word "helplessness," a concept that advocates were working very hard to deconstruct from the image of a battered woman. Eventually even those colleagues who understood the concept of learned helplessness began to reject it in favor of posttraumatic stress theory, which was first introduced in the late 1970s and appeared for the first time in the 1980 version of the *Diagnostic and Statistical Manual of Mental Disorders* (3rd ed., *DSM-III*; American Psychiatric Association, 1980). Interestingly, even the posttraumatic stress disorder (PTSD) theory has been rejected by some of its original supporters in favor of an ecological system explanation that was seen as less likely to be misused against individual battered women to pathologize them (e.g., Dutton, 1993).

Today, the debate over the misinterpretation of the term "learned helplessness" is less important, particularly since the originator of the theory, Martin Seligman, has looked at the less controversial flip side, *learned optimism*. Instead of concentrating on the negative, Seligman has used the same concepts and made them more politically correct by renaming them in a more positive direction (Seligman, 1991, 1994). And while battered woman syndrome has been similarly criticized for making it easier to continue to pathologize battered women, it is my opinion that as a subcategory of PTSD, it is the most useful diagnostic category to use for battered women when it is necessary to use a diagnostic formulation. In any case, the discussion about the theories of learned helplessness and learned optimism is relevant to finding a theory that many can embrace that helps explain the complex relationships found in domestic violence.

HISTORY OF LEARNED HELPLESSNESS RESEARCH

The theoretical concept of learned helplessness was adapted in this research to help explain why women who could develop such intricate and life-saving coping strategies found it so difficult to escape a battering relationship (Walker, 1978, 1979). Seligman and his colleagues discovered that when laboratory animals (usually dogs, in their early experiments) were repeatedly and noncontingently shocked, they became unable to escape from a painful situation, even when escape was quite possible and readily apparent to animals that had not undergone helplessness training. Seligman (1975) likened what he labeled, *learned helplessness,* to a kind of human depression, and showed that it had cognitive, motivational, and behavioral components. The inability to predict the success of one's actions was considered responsible for the resulting perceptual distortions. Although not tested in this study, Seligman's theory was further refined and reformulated, based on later laboratory trials with human subjects (Abramson, Seligman, & Teasdale, 1978), to determine how attributional styles and expectancies were connected and how hopelessness related to the original theory of helplessness (Abramson, Metalsky, & Alloy, 1989).

For example, depressed humans were found to have negative, pessimistic beliefs about the efficacy of their actions and the likelihood of obtaining future rewards; helpless animals acted as if they held similar beliefs. Both depressed humans and helpless animals exhibited motivational deficits in the laboratory. Both showed signs of emotional distress with illness, phobias, sleep disturbances, and other such symptoms similar to those described as part of the battered woman syndrome as a subcategory of PTSD. A review of the learned helplessness literature, including the reformulations with the attributional style, can be found in Peterson, Maier, and Seligman (1993).

LEARNED HELPLESSNESS HYPOTHESIS RESEARCH STUDY

On the basis of clinical work with battered women, it was hypothesized that the women's experiences of the noncontingent nature of their attempts to control the violence would, over time, produce learned helplessness and depression as the "repeated batterings, like electrical shocks, diminish the woman's motivation to respond" (Walker, 1979). If a woman is to escape such a relationship, she must overcome the tendency to learned helplessness survival techniques—by, for example, becoming angry rather than depressed and self-blaming; active rather than passive; and more realistic about the likelihood of the relationship continuing on its aversive course rather than improving. She must learn to use escape skills compatible to the survival behaviors already adopted.

In order to test the hypothesis that women in a battering relationship would show more signs of learned helplessness than women who had managed to escape such a relationship, each woman in our initial sample was asked a series of questions about her reactions to the four specific battering incidents: the first, second, last, and "one of the worst." With the exception of the "worst" incident, these provided a sketch of the battering relationship as it developed over time. If learned helplessness occurs in battering relationships and must be overcome if a battered woman is to escape, women whose "last" battering incident marked the end of a relationship should have become, over time, more angry, disgusted, and willing to seek intervention; and less fearful, anxious, and depressed. Also, these women's reactions to the "last" battering incident should indicate less learned helplessness than the reactions of women who are still in the battering relationship, for whom the "last" incident was the most recent but not necessarily the last in the relationship. Of course, since it took some initiative to come to our interview, the women in our sample who were still in battering relationships may not have been as "helpless" as women who heard about the study but took no action to participate. This factor may decrease the size of the differences between women we are referring to as "in" or "out" of battering relationships. However, the "ins" reached a higher level of unpleasant emotions such as fear, anxiety, and depression across the three battering incidents than the "outs," especially at the second time point.

The curves for anger, disgust, and hostility increase for both "ins" and "outs," but the level for outs was higher, especially at the "last" time point. For both groups, a measure of "resigned acceptance" was also administered. Both showed a rise at the second time point. Combining these results, it appears that "outs" reached a high point of fear/anxiety/depression and then became less fearful and depressed as they approached a peak of anger/disgust/hostility. At the same time, their resigned acceptance decreased. Perhaps the "ins" had not yet reached the peak of fear and depression, and their level of anger, while rising, had not reached the anger level of the "outs" when the "outs" decided to leave the relationship. Coming to our interview might have been a small step toward leaving, since anger was increasing and resigned acceptance was declining.

These results are compatible with learned helplessness theory. However, they do not indicate why some women become disgusted and angry enough to leave a relationship and others do not. Analysis of the cost–benefit ratio, or specifically the relationship between positive and negative reinforcement, which is discussed in Chapter 5 on the Walker Cycle Theory of Violence, may prove more illuminating. Also possible is the reaction of their abusive partners to the women's attempts to leave the relationship. As was later found, many men stalk women and increase the danger when they start to leave (Sonkin, 1995; Walker & Meloy, 1998), while others are so cunning and controlling that the women are too fearful and paralyzed to even try to leave (Jacobson & Gottman, 1998). No matter how good a woman's coping strategies are, she needs a different set of skills to be able to terminate her relationship with these types of batterers despite what Bowker (1993) and others suggest. Bowker, for example, argues that the extraordinarily capable coping responses of battered women prove that they are capable of escape as well as coping, and they are simply waiting for a less dangerous time to get away from the batterers. Our research argues that the women trade away their escape skills in order to develop the good coping strategies and, until they are able to regain the belief that they can safely escape, breaking the learned helplessness, they will not be able to leave the relationship psychologically.

IMPLICATIONS OF SEX-ROLE SOCIALIZATION TO DEVELOPMENT OF LEARNED HELPLESSNESS

It has also been suggested that "being a woman, more specifically a married woman, automatically creates a situation of powerlessness" (Walker, 1979, p. 51) and that women are taught sex-role stereotyping, which encourages passivity and dependency even as little girls (Dweck, Goetz, & Strauss, 1980; Radloff & Rae, 1979, 1981). While most women do not perceive themselves as powerless in all situations, it is more likely that a battered woman who has not gotten community or family support will come to believe that the man holds more power in domestic violence situations even if only by his greater physical strength. Seligman's research indicated that the experience of noncontingency between response and outcome early in an animal's development increased that animal's vulnerability to learned helplessness later in life. He hypothesized that the same principles apply in human child-raising practices and his recent research into positive psychology applies his work further to all people (Seligman, 1975, 1997, 2002). To the extent that animal and human helplessness are similar, childhood experiences of non-contingency between response and outcome, including socialization practices that encourage passivity and dependency, should increase a woman's vulnerability to developing learned helplessness in a battering relationship. Palker-Corell and Marcus (2004) examined battered women in shelters and found that their sample did indeed develop the belief that they are powerless against batterers. Further, this attribution contributed to development of depression and trauma, but not necessarily to the development of more learned helplessness than the average woman might develop.

ORIGINAL LEARNED HELPLESSNESS RESEARCH

In order to further explore the possibility that women who were abused as children will be at higher risk to develop learned helplessness than women who were abused only by adult partners, many questions were asked in our original interview concerning childhood experiences, parental attitudes, and family dynamics. Answers to these questions were combined into scales (e.g., childhood health, mothers' and fathers' attitudes toward women's roles, sexual abuse during childhood) and the scales were intercorrelated to see whether they could be combined to form a single measure of childhood contributors to learned helplessness. For short, we called the resulting measure "Child Learned Helplessness (LH)." The following scales were standardized and summed to form the Child LH measure (which has an internal consistency reliability alpha = .57):

1. The number of critical life events that occurred before age 18. "Critical events" included such things as divorce, death of a family member, sexual assault, moving—events that might make life seem relatively uncontrollable.
2. Mother's attitude toward women score, based on Spence, Helmreich, and Stapp's (1973) short form, as completed by the woman being interviewed when instructed to recall what her mother's attitudes were like "when you were growing up." (Coefficient alpha for this 25-item scale was .91.)
3. Father's attitude toward women score. (Alpha = .93.)
4. Number of battering relationships in the woman's childhood home (e.g., father battering mother, mother or father battering the subject or siblings).
5. Subject's relationship with mother during childhood and adolescence. This measure was based on 17 items concerning discipline, communication, affection shown, and parental expectations and values. (Coefficient alpha for this 17-item measure was .83.)
6. Subject's relationship with father during childhood and adolescence. Also a 17-item measure, using the same items as mentioned previously. (Coefficient alpha = .84.)
7. Childhood health scale, based on 11 items covering such things as migraine headaches, eating problems, hospitalization, allergies, and serious injuries. (Alpha = .73.)

8. A measure of childhood sex acts, based on questions about forced fondling, oral sex, or intercourse. These acts were weighted equally in determining a total score because recent literature suggested that impact is determined less by the act itself than by degree of force, perpetrator, and so on.

Although alpha for the combined Child LH measure is not as high as we would have liked (alpha = .57), its components are generally reliable, and the SPSS program we used to compute reliabilities indicated that alpha would not have been higher if any component scale had been dropped. Further, it seemed wise to use a broad measure of possible childhood antecedents of learned helplessness in this initial exploration.

A similar procedure was followed to develop a tentative measure of learned helplessness within the battering relationship. Theoretically plausible indicators were intercorrelated and only those with Pearson product moment coefficients significant at the .05 level of significance were retained. Fifteen indices met this criterion. When standardized and summed, they yielded a scale with a reliability coefficient of .67. The components of this scale are as follows:

1. The frequency of battering incidents
2. The number of abusive acts within a typical battering incident
3–8. The number of injuries within each of six injury categories, averaged across four batterings described in detail during the interview
9. The frequency with which the woman was forced by her batterer to have sex
10. Whether or not the woman thought the batterer might kill her
11. The extent to which the woman thought she could control the batterer or influence his actions
12. The extent to which the woman adopted a placating stance toward the batterer in everyday life
13. The woman's emotional reaction to the typical battering incident, summing across "fear," "depression," and so on (Coefficient alpha = .90.)
14. The interviewer's rating of the woman's activity–passivity after each of the four reported incidents, averaged across incidents

The combination of these variables was called "Rel LH," or "learned helplessness during the battering relationship." While a better measure of this construct could be designed for future studies, analyses indicated that reliability would not have been increased by dropping any of the components, and we wished to retain as broad a concept as possible for our initial investigations of learned helplessness.

In addition to measures of Child LH and Rel LH, we wanted to assess each woman's current state on the same indices that might be related to learned helplessness. The following current state measures were considered: depression (Radloff's Center for Epidemiologic Studies Depression [CES-D] scale), attributional style (Levenson's internality, chance, and powerful others scales), anomie (a four-item version of Srole's [1956] scale), self-esteem (a 20-item scale created for this study), current health (an 11-item scale, parallel to the one designed to measure childhood health), and the subject's current attitudes toward women's roles (Spence et al.'s full-length scale, 55 items). Reliabilities for these measures ranged from .49 to .94; only Levenson's internal scale (.49) was below .70. Each correlated with every other beyond the .05 significance level. It seemed reasonable, for preliminary analyses at least, to combine them into a single Current State measure by standardizing and summing the components. Current State yielded an alpha of .76.

In order to see whether Child LH is a determinant of Rel LH, and whether either of these is a determinant of Current State, a series of path analyses was conducted. In the first one, as shown, the entire sample was included. Results indicate that both Child LH and Rel LH influence current state and that the childhood measure is actually a bit more influential than the relationship measure. (For the final multiple regression analysis upon which the path diagram is based, $F(2,400) = 22.56$, $p < .001$.) Contrary to the hypothesis that childhood experiences cause a woman to be more or less vulnerable to helplessness in a battering relationship, there is essentially no relationship between Child LH and Rel LH. Thus, learned helplessness has equal potential to develop at either time in the battered woman's life.

Because the path diagram might differ for women still in an abusive relationship compared with women who have left such a relationship, we recomputed the path analysis for each of these groups separately. Surprisingly, there was not much difference, despite the fact that the current state of women who are no longer in a battering relationship might be expected to be less influenced by Child LH or, especially, by Rel LH. Even when we looked only at women who have been out of the battering relationship for more than a year, the path coefficients remain the same. This suggests that either the influence of Child LH and Rel LH persists, almost regardless of later experiences, or subjects who selected themselves for our interviews at various distances from battering experiences were still troubled by them.

In order to explore this matter further, we performed an analysis of variance on each of the learned helplessness scores (Child LH, Rel LH, and Current State) with the independent variable being whether the woman was, at the time of the interview, (a) still in the battering relationship, (b) out less than 1 year, or (c) out more than 1 year. If large differences were discovered, it might mean that these three groups differed in ways that render the path analyses invalid or misleading. In fact, none of the tested differences were significant. The means revealed some interesting trends, however. Women who are still in the relationship report worse (more "helpless") childhoods and fewer current problems with learned helplessness. If this is true, it might help explain why they are still in a battering relationship. Perhaps they did have somewhat more "training" for learned helplessness during childhood than women who have left a battering relationship, and either their battering experiences are not as severe or they do not yet see them as so severe. In the discussion of results related to the cycle theory that follows in Chapter 5, the point is made that women still in a battering relationship did not report as great a level of tension-building before the last reported incident of violence. Since the differences in the last analysis are nonsignificant, we cannot be sure they are meaningful. Nevertheless, the pattern shown would be worth following up in future studies using more refined measures.

EXPERT WITNESS TESTIMONY

The concept of learned helplessness has been quite useful in expert witness testimony to help jurors understand how difficult it is for women to leave the relationship and why some women become so desperate that they must arm themselves against the batterers. While it is only one part of the explanation, jurors who have been interviewed following a trial suggest that it was an important factor in voting to acquit the woman on the grounds of self-defense. In addition to explaining the concept of learned helplessness using animal and student research as an example, I have also presented charts that describe how the woman fits into the learned helplessness factors based on this research. To describe childhood factors leading to Child LH, I use the following:

1. Exposure to physical abuse during childhood
2. Sexual molestation
3. Critical periods of loss of their power and control
4. Traditional sex-role socialization activities
5. Health problems

To describe relationship factors leading to Rel LH, I use the following:

1. Pattern of abuse
   a. Cycle of violence
   b. Frequency and severity of violence
2. Sexual abuse
3. Power and control factors
   a. Isolation
   b. Jealousy
   c. Intrusiveness
   d. Overpossessiveness
4. Threats to kill
   a. Direct threats against the woman
   b. Indirect threats against the woman
   c. Direct or indirect threats against family and friends
5. Psychological abuse
   a. Amnesty International definition of psychological abuse
6. Violence correlates
   a. Her knowledge of his violence against other people
   b. Child abuse
   c. Abuse of pets
   d. Destruction of objects
7. Alcohol and other drug abuse

The data for all of these factors come from the Battered Woman Syndrome Questionnaire (BWSQ). However, it can also be obtained in a standard clinical interview if the clinician asks the appropriate questions. The questions we used in the BWSQ can be found in Table 4.1.

Table 4.1 *Women's Reports on Controls on Behavior in Battering Relationships*

Variable	Original Sample N	Original Sample %	Current Sample N	Current Sample %
How often did he know where you were when you were not together?				
Never	3	1	6	6
Occasionally	23	6	11	10
Frequently	376	94	89	84
How often did you know where he was when you were not together?				
Never	44	11	22	21
Occasionally	180	45	42	40
Frequently	179	45	39	38
Were there places you wanted to go, but did not because of him?				
Never	51	13	15	14
Occasionally	129	32	37	35
Frequently	223	56	50	47
Did you generally do what he asked?				
Never	0	0	1	1
Occasionally	44	11	20	19
Frequently	359	89	87	81
Did you emotionally withdraw to get what you wanted?				
Never	82	21	33	31
Occasionally	233	58	53	50
Frequently	85	21	21	20
Did you restrict his freedom to get what you wanted?				
Never	293	74	82	77
Occasionally	94	24	18	17
Frequently	11	3	6	6

(continued)

Table 4.1 *Women's Reports on Controls on Behavior in Battering Relationships (continued)*

Variable	Original Sample N	Original Sample %	Current Sample N	Current Sample %
Did you stop having sex to get what you wanted?				
Never	215	54	47	44
Occasionally	142	36	37	35
Frequently	43	11	23	22
Did you threaten to leave to get what you wanted?				
Never	105	26	29	27
Occasionally	211	52	38	36
Frequently	84	21	40	37
Did you use physical force to get what you wanted?				
Never	304	77	79	75
Occasionally	91	23	19	18
Frequently	2	1	7	7
Did you say or do something nice to get what you wanted?				
Never	37	9	12	11
Occasionally	180	45	38	36
Frequently	184	46	57	53
Who wins major disagreements?				
Always him	159	40	40	37
Usually him	130	33	21	20
Equal	37	9	14	13
Usually her	29	7	4	4
Always her	0	0	2	2
Other (e.g., unresolved)	45	11	26	24
How woman shows her anger: (May choose more than one response)				
Curses or shouts	198	52	71	66
Sulks, no speaking	279	73	78	73
Directed at children or pets	63	16	14	13
Directed at objects	132	35	43	41
Physical violence toward him	58	15	26	25

Table 4.2 *Women's Reports of Social Isolation*

Demographic Variable	Original Sample N	Original Sample %	Current Sample N	Current Sample %
Frequency of women reporting they did not have access to:				
Checking account	134	34	34	36
Charge accounts	204	51	36	39
Cash	108	27	28	30
Automobiles	89	22	36	40
Public transportation	116	30	24	26
Phone	–	–	10	12

Most interesting is the disparity in knowing where their partners are when they are not together. The women reported that almost all of the men frequently knew where they were when they were not together. Less than half of the women knew where their partners were. Over 80% of the women in both samples said that they frequently did what the batterers wanted them to do and almost half of them said that they did not go places they wanted to go because of the batterers. Other forms of social isolation including access to financial resources are presented in Table 4.2.

IF LEARNED HELPLESSNESS EXISTS IN BATTERED WOMEN, WHAT CAN REVERSE IT?

If battered women do develop learned helplessness from childhood abuse or from the actual battering relationship, what would that mean for psychological prevention and intervention strategies? First, it would suggest that prevention strategies would be possible to protect girls from developing learned helplessness should they be exposed to such abuse. Learning to focus on the positive side of experiences rather than on the negative side is one such strategy to use when raising a child. Another strategy is to help promote the strengths in each child as he or she grows up in order to develop feelings of self-efficacy and self-confidence. A third strategy would be helping people develop flexibility in solving problems so that when one way does not work, they can turn to other methods. Teaching boys and girls ways to resolve conflicts without using mental coercion and physical force is another strategy. This last one is the most difficult as we live in a world that appears to reward those who fight their way to the top of whatever area they wish to conquer. Psychologist Albert Bandura (1973) has developed behavioral strategies that can be used in classrooms, other group activities, as well as counseling techniques to model positive behaviors that teach children how to feel competent in their work.

Once the social psychology construct of learned helplessness has begun to develop, it is possible to reverse it by purposely using positive behavioral strategies to feel better about oneself. The goal is to encourage self-efficacy and overcome feelings of paralysis or inability to accomplish what the person sets out to do. For women and children exposed to man's violence, it may require the support of others to help them learn new ways to live violence free. For example, most battered women's shelters have "no-hitting" rules for mothers when disciplining children. The goal is to learn new ways of appropriate and respectful discipline of their children. Using other types of consequences and rewarding positive behavior help reverse the negative impact from living with unpredictable abuse and physical punishment. We discuss specific intervention programs later in this book. The important point to be made here is that learned helplessness, if it begins to develop, is reversible.

SUMMARY

Although these results support the theory of learned helplessness being one of the factors that keeps battered women in abusive relationships, it has been so controversial among those who provide services to battered women that the theory has not been utilized to its fullest psychological potential. Nonetheless, it is a theory that does have some empirical support and can be integrated into other treatment theories and strategies without even using its name. It is not the construct of helplessness that is the key here, but rather the understanding that random and negative behavior toward a person can produce the belief that the person's natural way of fighting such abuse will not succeed in stopping it. Thus, the person stops trying to put an end to the abuse and rather develops coping strategies to live safely with the possibility that he or she will continue to be abused. It is the motivation to keep trying to escape from violence that is lost and must be regained. There is great potential for developing new and positive child-raising strategies in order to be a protective factor for children who do become exposed to family violence, even if it is not possible to prevent all forms of domestic violence at this time.

REFERENCES

Abramson, L. Y., Metalsky, F. I., & Alloy, L. B. (1989). Hopelessness depression: A theory based subtype of depression. *Psychological Review, 96*(2), 358–372.

Abramson, L. Y., Seligman, M. E. P., & Teasdale, J. D. (1978). Learned helplessness in humans: Critique and reformulations. *Journal of Abnormal Psychology, 87,* 49–74.

American Psychiatric Association. (1980). *Diagnostic and statistical manual of mental disorders* (3rd ed.). Washington, DC: Author.

Bandura, A. (1973). *Aggression: A social learning analysis.* Englewood, NJ: Prentice Hall.

Barnett, O. W., & LaViolette, A. (1993). *It could happen to anyone: Why battered women stay.* Newbury Park, CA: Sage.

Bowker, L. (1993). A battered woman's problems are social, not psychological. In R. J. Gelles & D. R. Loeske (Eds.), *Current controversies on family violence.* Newbury Park, CA: Sage.

Cándido, A., Maldonado, A., Megías, J. L., & Catena, A. (1992). Successive negative contrast in one-way avoidance learning in rats. *The Quarterly Journal of Experimental Psychology, 45*(1), 15–32.

Dutton, M. A. (1993). Understanding women's responses to domestic violence: A redefinition of battered woman syndrome. *Hofstra Law Review, 21*(4), 1191–1242.

Dweck, C. S., Goetz, T. E., & Strauss, N. L. (1980). Sex differences in learned helplessness. *Journal of Personality and Social Psychology, 38*(3), 441–452.

Gondolf, E. W., & Fisher, E. R. (1988). *Battered women as survivors: An alternative to treating learned helplessness.* Boston, MA: Lexington.

Jacobson, N. S., & Gottman, J. M. (1998). *When men batter women: New insights into ending abusive relationships.* New York, NY: Simon & Schuster.

Palker-Corell, A., & Marcus, D. K. (2004). Partner abuse, learned helplessness, and trauma symptoms. *Journal of Social and Clinical Psychology, 23*(4), 445–462.

Peterson, C., Maier, S. F., & Seligman, M. E. P. (1993). *Learned helplessness.* New York, NY: Oxford University Press.

Radloff, L. S., & Rae, D. S. (1979). Susceptibility and precipitating factors in depression: Sex differences and similarities. *Journal of Abnormal Psychology, 88*(2), 174–181.

Radloff, L. S., & Rae, D. S. (1981). Components of the sex difference in depression. *Research on Community Mental Health, 2,* 111–137.

Seligman, M. E. P. (1975). *Helplessness: On depression, development, and death*. San Francisco, CA: W. H. Freeman.

Seligman, M. E. P. (1991). *Learned optimism*. New York, NY: Alfred A. Knopf.

Seligman, M. E. P. (1994). *What you can change and what you can't: The complete guide to successful self-improvement*. New York, NY: Alfred A. Knopf.

Seligman, M. E. P. (1997). Raising optimistic children. *The Futurist, 31,* 52–53.

Seligman, M. E. P. (2002). *Authentic happiness: Using the new positive psychology to realize your potential for lasting fulfillment*. New York, NY: Simon & Schuster.

Shainess, N. (1979). Vulnerability to violence: Masochism as a process. *American Journal of Psychotherapy, 33,* 174–189.

Shainess, N. (1985). *Sweet suffering: Woman as victim*. New York, NY: Pocket Books.

Sonkin, D. J. (1995). *Counselor's guide to learning to live without violence*. Volcano, CA: Volcano Press.

Spence, J. T., Helmreich, R., & Stapp, J. (1973). A short version of the Attitudes toward Women Scale (AWS). *Bulletin of the Psychonomic Society, 2*(4), 219–220.

Srole, L. (1956). Social integration and certain corollaries. *American View, 21,* 709–716.

Torres, M. C., Morales, A., Megías, J. L., Cándido, A., & Maldonado, A. (1994). Flumazenil antagonizes the effect of diazepam on negative contrast in one-way avoidance learning. *Behavioural Pharmacology, 5*(6), 637–641.

Walker, L. E. (1978). Treatment alternative for battered women. In J. R. Chapman & M. Gates (Eds.), *The victimization of women; Sage Yearbooks in Women's Policy Studies* (Vol. 3). Beverly Hills, CA: Sage.

Walker, L. E. (1979). *The battered woman*. New York, NY: Harper & Row.

Walker, L. E. A., & Meloy, J. R. (1998). Stalking and domestic violence. In J. R. Meloy (Ed.), *The psychology of stalking: Clinical and forensic perspectives*. San Diego, CA: Academic Press.

CHAPTER FIVE

DESCRIPTIONS OF VIOLENCE
AND THE CYCLE OF VIOLENCE

One of the most important findings from the original battered woman syndrome (BWS) research was the existence of a three-phase cycle of violence that could be described and measured through careful questioning of the battered woman. Most women who experience intimate partner violence have experienced the three phases in the cycle, at least some of the time. Once a woman's own cycle is plotted on a graph, or sometimes just giving her help in identifying the three phases, it is possible for the woman to break the cycle of violence and no longer be under the abuser's control. In this chapter, we describe the cycle, update it by adding information from the courtship period, and divide the third phase into several different sections where appropriate so that there may not be any loving contrition or even respites from the abuse at times during the relationship.

DESCRIPTIONS OF VIOLENCE

Sample Demographics in the Current Sample

We interviewed battered women who were recruited from prison and jails (44%), from advertising (32%), from mental health facilities (10%), and from outpatient family centers (2%). We used other sources to recruit battered women as well (12%). Figure 5.1 depicts the referral location. The sample is approximately equal between women in jail and those who come from the community.

Childhood History of Abuse

Frequency analysis indicated that 68% of the battered women reported that they were exposed to battering in their childhood home, as compared

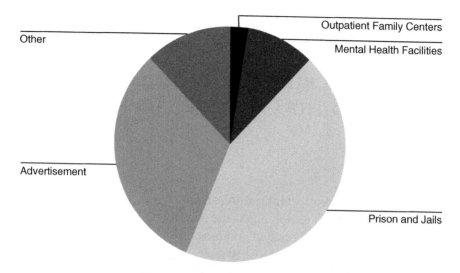

Figure 5.1 *Referral location.*

to 22% who were not so exposed and 10% who did not report. This is seen in Figure 5.2. Further descriptive statistics revealed that 93% of the sample was spanked before 12 years of age, and 54% reported that they were hit with an object. Regarding sexual abuse, 66% of the sample indicated that they were inappropriately touched, as compared to 34% who reported no inappropriate touching as a child. This is similar to the original research that indicated a large proportion of the women battered in an intimate partner relationship also had been exposed to battering in their childhood homes.

Adult History of Abuse

Figure 5.3 depicts the significant areas of adult psychological and physical abuse that the women reported in the current research. It is clear that in the psychological domain, the significant portion of battered women experienced being cursed at, humiliated, and having controlling partners. With respect to physical abuse, more battered women reported being pushed, shaken, grabbed, and slapped. The most common psychological abuse tactics used by the batterers were cursing at the women, humiliating them, constant disapproval, and trying to control their behavior. It was also reported that the men's use of jealousy was used frequently, often to justify further abuse. These psychological tactics are similar to those reported in the first study.

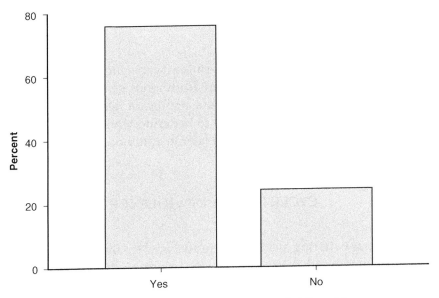

Figure 5.2 *Exposure to battering in childhood home.*

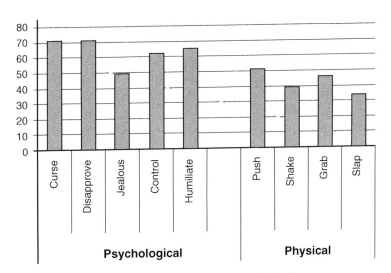

Figure 5.3 *Relevant areas of adult abuse.*

The Relationship Between Childhood History of Abuse and Adult Experiences

A test analysis was conducted to determine if exposure to battering while growing up led to physical abuse in adulthood. Results are shown in Table 5.1 and indicate that there was a significant relationship between battered women who were exposed to battering while growing up and those who were shaken and grabbed later in adulthood by intimate male partners ($p < .05$).

CYCLE THEORY OF VIOLENCE

Once the four battering incidents were analyzed for the different types of violence experienced, these data from the second study were subjected to analysis of the second major theory that was tested in the original research project, Walker Cycle Theory of Violence (Walker, 1979). This is a tension-reduction theory that states there are three distinct phases associated with a recurring battering cycle: (a) tension-building accompanied with rising sense of danger, (b) the acute battering incident, and (c) loving contrition. The cycle usually begins after a courtship period that is often described as having a lot of interest from the batterer in the woman's life and usually filled with loving behavior. Some women describe that this behavior from the batterer turns into stalking and surveillance after a while. But by the time this occurs, the woman has already made a commitment to the man and does not have the energy and often the desire to break off the relationship. Further, many of these women report that they tell themselves that once they are married, the men will feel more secure in their love, and will not have the need to continue the surveillance behavior. Unfortunately, this rarely occurs and instead, the first two phases of the cycle of violence begin with the third phase of loving behavior in the relationship similar to the good parts of the courtship period. Figure 5.4 shows different cycle patterns that can be developed and used in treatment or court hearings.

Phase I

During the first phase, there is a gradual escalation of tension displayed by discrete acts causing increased friction such as name-calling, other mean intentional behaviors, and/or physical abuse. The batterer expresses

Table 5.1 *Independent Samples Test of Women Exposed to Domestic Violence as a Child and Battered by an Intimate Partner as an Adult*

		Levene's Test for Equality of Variances		t Test for Equality of Means					95% Confidence Interval of the Difference	
		F	Significance	t	df	Significance (Two-Tailed)	Mean Difference	Standard Error Difference	Lower	Upper
Push	Equal variances assumed	2.781	.108	1.812	24	.083	.3609	.19921	-.05025	.77206
	Equal variances not assumed			1.613	8.870	.142	.3609	.22372	-.14631	.86812
Shake	Equal variances assumed	4.328	.048	2.693	24	.013	.5414	.20105	.12641	.95630
	Equal variances not assumed			3.007	13.569	.010	.5414	.18003	.15407	.92864
Grab	Equal variances assumed	.047	.831	2.211	24	.037	.4511	.20407	.02994	.87231
	Equal variances not assumed			2.132	10.066	.059	.4511	.21163	-.01999	.92225
Slapping with open palm	Equal variances assumed	3.646	.068	1.074	24	.294	.2406	.22410	-.22191	.70312
	Equal variances not assumed			1.100	11.259	.294	.2406	.21878	-.23958	.72078

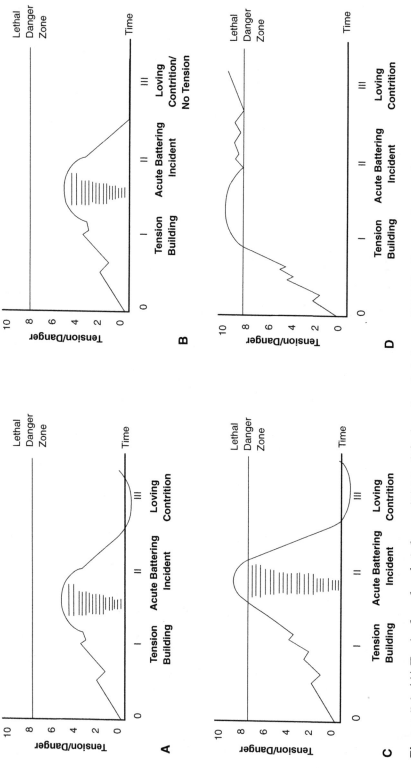

Figure 5.4 (A) Typical cycle of violence. (B) Modified cycle of violence. (C) Life-threatening cycle. (D) Life-threatening cycle in which the woman believes she could die at any time.

dissatisfaction and hostility but not in an extreme or maximally explosive form. The woman attempts to placate the batterer, doing what she thinks might please him, calm him down, or at least, what will not further aggravate him. She tries not to respond to his hostile actions and uses general anger reduction techniques. Often she succeeds for a little while, which reinforces her unrealistic belief that she can control this man. It also becomes part of the unpredictable noncontingency response/outcome pattern that creates the *learned helplessness*.

Phase II

The tension continues to escalate, the woman becomes more fearful of impending danger, and eventually she is unable to continue controlling his angry response pattern.

"Exhausted from the constant stress, she usually withdraws from the batterer, fearing she will inadvertently set off an explosion. He begins to move more oppressively toward her as he observes her withdrawal. . . . Tension between the two becomes unbearable" (Walker, 1979, p. 59).

The second phase, the acute battering incident, becomes inevitable without intervention. Sometimes, she precipitates the inevitable explosion so as to control where and when it occurs, allowing her to take better precautions to minimize her injuries and pain. Over time she may learn to predict the point in the cycle where there is a period of inevitability—after that point is reached, there is no escape for the women unless the man permits it.

"Phase two is characterized by the uncontrollable discharge of the tensions that have built up during phase one" (Walker, 1979, p. 59). The batterer typically unleashes a barrage of verbal and physical aggression that can leave the woman severely shaken and injured. The woman does her best to protect herself often covering parts of her face and body to block some of the blows. In fact, when injuries do occur they usually happen during this second phase. It is also the time police become involved, if they are called at all. The acute battering phase is concluded when the batterer stops, usually bringing with its cessation a sharp physiological reduction in tension. This in itself is naturally reinforcing. Violence often succeeds because it works.

Phase III

In Phase III that follows, the batterer may apologize profusely, try to assist his victim, show kindness and remorse, and shower her with gifts and/or promises. The batterer himself may believe at this point that he will never allow himself to be violent again. The woman wants to believe the batterer and, early in the relationship at least, may renew her hope in his ability to change. This third phase provides the positive reinforcement for the woman for remaining in the relationship. Many of the acts that he did when she fell in love with him during the courtship period occur again here. Our research results demonstrated that Phase III could also be characterized by an absence of tension or violence, with no observable loving-contrition behavior, and still be reinforcing for the woman. Sometimes the perception of tension and danger remains very high and does not return to the baseline or loving-contrition level. This is a sign that the risk of a lethal incident is very high.

Assessment of the Cycle of Violence

In our original interviews with battered women, we asked for detailed descriptions of four battering incidents: the first, the second, one of the worst, and the last (or last prior to the interview). The first two and the last incident, taken together, reflect the temporal course of a stream of acute battering incidents. Each of these is an example of "Phase II" in the cycle theory.

After the description of each incident, basing her judgment on both the open-ended description and a series of closed-ended questions concerning the batterer's behavior before the event ("Would you call it ... irritable, provocative, aggressive, hostile, threatening"—each on a 1–5 scale) and after the event ("nice, loving, contrite"), the interviewer recorded whether or not there was "evidence of tension building and/or loving contrition." Comparisons between interviewers' responses indicated a high level of agreement.

In 65% of all cases (including three battering incidents for each woman who reported three), there was evidence of a tension-building phase prior to the battering. In 58% of all cases, there was evidence of loving contrition afterward. In general, then, there is support for the cycle theory of violence in a majority of the battering incidents described by our sample.

For first incidents, the proportion showing evidence of a tension-building phase is 56%; the proportion showing evidence of loving contrition is 69%. Over time, these proportions changed drastically. By the last incident, tension building preceded 71% of battering incidents, but loving contrition followed only 42%. In other words, over time in a battering relationship, tension building becomes more common (or more evident) and loving contrite behavior declines. Since our sample included 24% of women who were still in the battering relationship, it is possible that there was a difference in the pattern between those who were in the relationship and those who had left the relationship by the time of the interview. The former group may not yet have experienced the truly final battering incident as they were asked about the last incident prior to their coming to the research study.

When we separate the two groups, both show the same decline of loving contrition, but the patterns of tension building are different. Women still in a battering relationship report less evidence of tension building preceding the last incident before our interview. This may be a valid indication of a difference between battering incidents that cause a woman to leave the relationship and battering incidents other than the final one. Or it may indicate a defensive bias on the part of women who choose to remain in the relationship. Our data do not allow us to distinguish between these two possibilities.

It is clear, however, that our data support the existence of the Walker Cycle Theory of Violence. Furthermore, over the course of a battering relationship, tension building before battering becomes more common (or evident) and loving contrition declines. Thus, results strongly suggest further investigation into the psychological costs and rewards in these relationships.

Theoretical Implications

Most battered women in our original sample perceived three different levels of control over their lives. They scored significantly higher than the norms on the Levenson IPC Locus of Control Subscales of Internal, Powerful Others, and Chance. These findings suggest that the internal–external locus of control dichotomy does not fully explain battered women's attributions. Women still in a violent relationship did not report powerful others as being in any more control of their lives than themselves. Perhaps a battered woman cannot begin to terminate her marriage while there is this lack of realization that her batterer really is in control of her everyday activities and of her life.

Seligman's (1978) reformulation of learned helplessness theory would suggest an attributional style of assigning causality for successful experiences to external and specific factors, and failures to internal and global ones. Thus, women with an external attribution might think that their success was due to luck and a particular combination of things that day, whereas their getting a beating was because they failed to keep their mouths shut and did not pay enough attention to their batterers. Our measurement of attributional style was not designed to test this reformulation as our study was designed prior to its publication. Therefore, our sample's perception of both internal and external causation may not be unusual in light of this reformulation of learned helplessness theory.

Self-Esteem

In the original research, the woman's self-esteem was measured by use of a typical Likkert style semantic differential scale. It was predicted that battered women's self-esteem would be quite low and our results, surprisingly, show the opposite. They perceived themselves as stronger, more independent, and more sensitive than other women or men. It is possible that battered women develop a positive sense of self from having survived in a violent relationship, which causes them to believe they are equal to or better than others. However, there is incompatibility between these high self-esteem findings and the reports of depression and other learned helplessness measures. Given these conflicting results, more careful study into the mental health of battered women is recommended.

Depression in the original sample was measured by the Center for Epidemiologic Studies Depression (CES-D) scale (Radloff, 1977). Our subjects scored higher than the high-risk-for-depression cutoff score. Younger women in the sample were more likely to be depressed than older ones, as were those who were unemployed. An interesting but surprising finding was that women out of the relationship were more likely to be more depressed than those still in it. They were also not consistent in demonstrating the negative cognition and moods we would have expected in other indices within the questionnaire.

Depression

Lewinsohn's behavioral reinforcement theory of depression might explain some of our findings on depression (Lewinsohn, 1975; Lewinsohn, Steinmetz, Larson, & Franklin, 1981). It postulates that depression occurs when there is a sharp reduction in the amount of positive reinforcement received by people. A lower rate of rewards would result in a lower response rate or passivity, which then spirals downward into a depressed state. Cognitive or affective disturbances occur simultaneously to the downward spiral or are a consequence of the lowered reinforcement rate. This is similar to the learned helplessness theory, which postulates the lowered behavioral response rate or passivity as learned response to uncontrollable trauma. It also postulates distorted perceptions in the cognitive and affective domains. While the learned helplessness theory did not specify when these cognitive and affective perceptions occurred, the reformulations suggest an attributional style that serves as a cognitive set for a depressive state to develop.

Learned Helplessness

The finding of a set of factors that could result in childhood learned helplessness, and another, responsible for development of learned helplessness in the relationship, supports the application of this theory to battered women. Unfortunately, actual learned helplessness is usually directly measured in a laboratory setting under experimentally controlled conditions. Our research attempted to identify its presence from variables that cause it to develop as predicted by the literature. Although our results are positive, it is strongly recommended that a controlled laboratory setting be constructed to test if learned helplessness can be easily induced in a sample of battered women comparable to this one. Such direct measurement is necessary to confirm the theoretical application to battered women.

WALKER CYCLE THEORY OF VIOLENCE FROM THE RESEARCH

The Walker Cycle Theory of Violence (Walker, 1979) was also confirmed by our data. Sufficient evidence supports the three phases in battering relationships that occur in a cycle. Over time, the first phase of tension building becomes more common, and loving contrition, or the third phase, declines. Our results also show that Phase III could be characterized by an absence of tension or violence and no observable loving-contrition behavior and still be reinforcing for the woman. In those cases, it is the relationship interactions themselves that propel the cycle and not just the three distinct phases with their corresponding behaviors.

Lewis (1981a) has tested the cycle theory in the laboratory to match its compatibility with the anxiety arousal model of the delay of punishment paradigm. This paradigm has been found to have three phases of anxiety arousal: increase during the anticipatory period; asymptote at the moment of stimulus delivery; and then, relief with a return to baseline levels. People have been found to prefer the immediate delivery of a negative stimulus in order to avoid a prolonged anticipatory period. Thus, the experimental model parallels the cycle theory derived from battered women's descriptions of the battering incidents. Lewis (1981b) attempted to measure the differences between battered and nonbattered women's responses on a classic delay of punishment paradigm and compare these results to the cycle theory. The description of the cycle theory used came from her independent reading of published work (Walker, 1978, 1979) and not through direct contact with this project. Nevertheless, the results are interesting in that they extend the descriptive work to experimental laboratory analogues.

Lewis (1981b) hypothesized that battered women have learned the probability of receiving a beating by recognizing specific predictive cues emitted by the batterers in Phase I of the cycle. These predictive cues result in a high level of anxiety arousal, which the battered women may attempt to reduce through several different means, one of which is to avoid delaying the beating any longer. She hypothesized that battered women would be more likely to avoid delay of punishment in the experimental analogue she constructed. Using the Conflicts Tactics Scale (CTS) developed by Straus, Gelles, and Steinmetz (1980), she measured battering behavior and found that it was not useful in identifying an adequate sample of battered women. However, she did generate a sample with a variety of marital conflicts and found that the cycle theory held for couples' less violent disputes, also.

Thus, her results support her hypothesis that women may elect to receive a brief aversive stimulus immediately and yet also prefer to delay a somewhat longer aversive event. This research offers promising insights into why battered women chose various tactics to respond to the batterers' behaviors, particularly during Phase I of the cycle. For example, a woman may choose a delay tactic, such as withdrawing or doing something to calm the batterer, or she may choose to get the beating over with immediately, depending on her perception of the intensity and probability of the predicted battering incident. The commonalties between the anxiety arousal model of marital dispute cycles demonstrated in the laboratory and the cycle theory of violence, which developed from battered women's descriptions, were supported in this analogue study.

Cost–Benefit Models

The analysis of lower reinforcement rates presented with the results of the Walker Cycle Theory of Violence demonstrates that women who left the battering relationship left after the ratio between the tension-building and loving-contrition phases sharply diverged. Women still in the battering relationship reported more positive reinforcement (loving contrition) following the last battering incident they discussed. Thus, women who were less depressed while still in the relationship may have still been receiving some rewards from it despite the violence. Once the cost–benefit ratio changes, however, and the rate of reinforcement decreases, the women may be more inclined to leave the relationship, but subsequently become depressed as a result of the separation. Further investigation into the psychological cost and benefits in these relationships is still necessary.

It is interesting that other family violence researchers are also examining the costs and benefits of battering relationships. Gelles (1983) presented an exchange/social control theory of intrafamily violence in which he attempted to construct a multidimensional causal model to account for all forms of family abuse, including child abuse, spouse abuse, and sexual abuse. Although Gelles does not use a social learning theory paradigm, he suggests that human behavior follows the pursuit of rewards and avoidance of punishment (Gelles, 1983, p. 11). As a sociologist, it is understandable that he utilized traditional exchange theory (Blau, 1964) rather than the reciprocal contingency contracting models developed by behavioral psychologists (Patterson, 1982; Weiss, Hops, & Patterson, 1973). If the discipline vocabulary can be set aside, it is apparent that there are similarities between this approach and the one suggested by our data.

Gelles (1983) suggests that a multidimensional causal model needs to be explored—a concept these data certainly support. Inequality between men and women is one area that we both agree must be a part of that model. Our results indicate that sex-role stereotyping is a primary cause for men battering women. Gelles also suggests that such unequal gender socialization patterns are causal in other forms of family violence, specifically sexual assault and child abuse. He states that the privacy of the family reduces accessibility to outside agencies of social control. Our results support this concept, as the social isolation measures were the highest for women living with their batterers.

Once the cost of living in a violent relationship begins to escalate, paralleling the escalation of the seriousness of the abusiveness and injuries, women's help-seeking behavior breaks through the privacy of the home, if they perceive actual help is available. Gelles also included the cost of loss of status because the label "wife" or "child beater" is less a factor in subcultures where aggressive behavior is held in high esteem. Perceived status of the men was not measured in either of our studies. However, our data suggest that this factor is probably significant so long as it does not approach the risk of the man losing his wife and family, which would then result in a loss of status in many subcultures. This analysis is consistent with the behavior seen by the man's mother toward his wife. The mother-in-law is often the most supportive to help the woman heal from an acute battering incident until the time comes when the woman is ready to leave the relationship. Women described being shocked at the immediate change in their mothers-in-law's behavior toward them should they decide to leave the family.

While he goes on to describe other factors in his model, Gelles's primary thesis is that men abuse women because they can, and suggests changing the contingencies so that the costs become too high. Gelles does not discuss the key principle of learning theory; that is, people will repeat behavior that is positively rewarded especially if reinforced with social approval. Aversive stimulation or punishment will stop negative behavior initially but it will return at even higher base rates if the external control (in this case, higher costs) is removed. While none of our results would be incompatible with this view, it is seen as not being comprehensive enough. For example, our data suggest behavioral patterns in men and women that are associated with violence. We argue that these are temporary-state–like characteristics related to the situation of being battered, for the women, and either temporary-state–like learned behaviors or perhaps more stable personality traits seen in the men. Battered women seem more likely to respond to the batterers' behavior than batterers do to women's behavior.

Although the concept of mutual reciprocity cannot be disproved, the striking differences we found between the woman's perceptions of her behavior with the batterer and a nonbatterer lend strong support to this belief in her reactive behavior. Measurement of the tactics used by couples that do not take such inequality into account, such as the CTS, may well obscure the field rather than add to the knowledge base. It emphasizes the violent nature of all of society, while our results would place the greatest emphasis on the position of women in a society where they are the predominant victims of such violence.

CYCLE THEORY AND INTERVENTIONS

When I first began collecting data from individuals and using the information to plot their individual cycle graphs, it became clear that once the code for the individual's own personal cycle is broken, it becomes necessary for the woman to begin to protect herself and her children more vigorously. Although battered women are quite sensitive to the rise of tension and perception of danger, they often shut off their intuitive feelings while trying to calm down the batterer. Rarely do they connect the quiet during the aftermath of the violent incident with a constant repetitive cycle. Nor are they consciously aware of how similar the behavior the batterer displays is to the behavior they saw during their courtship period. Rather, they associate the Phase III behavior with who they believed their batterer really is. They reason that they were able to smooth the world for the batterer and so the *real man* emerged once again. This became a powerful message for the woman, fitting right into the sex-role socialization that teaches women to believe that they are responsible for the health, well-being, and psychological stability of their husbands! Thus, it becomes important to teach battered women their cycle of violence so they can choose to stop being held captive by their belief that the person they see during the third phase is the *real man* and somehow, if the behavior he displays during Phases I and II disappears, then they will be left with the person with whom they fell in love. Only when they see the inevitability of the recurring cycle and understand that their partner has the ability to be both loving and cruel will they be able to better protect themselves and their children.

In battered woman shelters, support groups, and psychotherapy sessions, battered women are being encouraged to graph their own cycle of violence. It is important to gather data on at least four battering cycles. Usually, the woman is encouraged to remember the first time she was hurt by the batterer. Sometimes this includes a physically abusive act during Phase I or II, other times it is some act that humiliated the woman and hurt her feelings. Most women remember the incident that made them first realize that this man was able to hurt them in ways they never dreamed of. By asking her to remember and recount the details of what happened before and led up to it, what happened during the acute battering incident part, and what happened afterward, it is possible to get an idea of how to rate the seriousness of the incident, what level of tension the woman felt, and how much danger she perceived herself to be in at the time.

I suggest using a graph such as shown in Figure 5.4 rather than the circle that many other battered woman center facilitators suggest because it is possible to demonstrate more easily the escalation and repetitiveness of the cycle. I try to get materials to the woman from the actual project. On the vertical axis of the graph put the measurement of tension and perception of danger. Use the scale from 0 to 10 with anything over an 8 considered life-threatening violence. On the horizontal axis place the three phases of the cycle over time. By drawing the incidents on this graph, it makes a powerful statement that the abuse is escalating and that the woman is becoming more frightened of the dangerousness of her situation.

If I want to measure the rapidity of the escalation of violence in a relationship, I often ask for the details of the next (second) incident she can remember. This helps get data about how frequent and how serious the acute battering incidents are initially as compared to later on in the relationship. I then draw that incident as continuous to the first on the graph. The next incident that I ask about is the last one before the woman has come in to see me. Sometimes this is quite recent but in other clients who do not come for treatment until after she has terminated the relationship, it might be quite some time ago. This becomes the anchor on the other side of the graph. Sometimes the loving contrition in the third phase is still present; more often it has decreased or disappeared entirely. Then I ask for a third (or fourth by now) incident that the woman describes as the worst one, unless the last one is the worst, and then it is one of the worst that she picks out to discuss. Although this incident frequently deals with humiliation and not necessarily physical injuries, it is important to diagram it attached to the others. The final incident that I request is a typical battering scene. Often more than one incident gets put together here but again, it is important to see how the woman perceives the abuse in general, on a day-to-day basis rather than just when there are more dramatic incidents occurring. In long-term relationships, there might be more than one typical incident. When there is sexual abuse in the relationship and the woman is willing to talk about it, those incidents are often reported in this section.

It is interesting to see how quickly most battered women catch on to the graphing of these battering incidents. In a film that I made about therapy with abused women, I demonstrate this technique in connection with the development of a safety plan (Walker, 1996). Most battered women cannot leave the house when an acute battering incident is beginning because they wait too long and the batterer is in too much of an angry, controlling state to let her go. However, if women can be taught to recognize the signals that the tension is building and an acute battering incident is approaching a threshold before exploding, it may be possible for her to get out then. During the development of a crisis plan, battered women are often taught when to leave and that they can decide if they want to tell the batterer that they intend to leave. They can say that they are scared his violence will escalate, but they will come back to discuss it later when he calms down.

Just knowing there is a cycle to the violence and that it is repetitive helps the woman better assess her situation. It also helps the man understand that he no longer will be able to manipulate the woman by his behavior during the third phase. Sometimes what seemed to be so loving in one context actually seemed a continuation of the controlling and over-possessive behavior of the batterer. For example, in the film, Sara tells the therapist that after one battering incident, her husband filled the dining room with lilac bushes, so when she came downstairs that was all she saw. Then they spent the entire day planting those bushes. Sara liked that sequence, especially the attention that Dan, her husband, gave her as they planted the bushes that day. However, he gave her no choice but to be with him planting bushes even though she might have made other plans that did not include him. Not until the therapist pointed it out did Sara realize that her husband's supposedly nice gesture was an example of the third phase of their cycle that also had secondary benefits for his needs to keep her as close to him as possible.

SUMMARY

This chapter describes the violence that the women in our study reported occurred during the courtship period, the four specific battering incidents, and the loving contrition or absence of violence that they experienced. The cycle of violence that measures the magnitude of the woman's perception of danger and feelings of tension over the time that it took for the four incidents they reported was also described. Teaching the woman how her perception of tension and danger rises to an acute battering incident after which she experiences feelings of relief and then gets seduced back into the relationship by the batterer's loving behavior, often similar to what she experienced during the courtship period, has been found to be helpful in breaking the cycle of violence that keeps the woman in the relationship.

REFERENCES

Blau, P. M. (1964). *Exchange and power in social life*. New York, NY: Wiley.

Gelles, R. J. (1983). An exchange/social control theory of intrafamily violence. In D. Finkelhor, R. Gelles, G. Hotaling, & M. Straus (Eds.), *The dark side of families*. Beverly Hills, CA: Sage.

Lewinsohn, P. M. (1975). The behavioral study and treatment of depression. In M. Hersen, M. Eider, & P. M. Miller (Eds.), *Progress in behavioral modification* (Vol. 1). New York, NY: Academic Press.

Lewinsohn, P. M., Steinmetz, J. L., Larson, D. W., & Franklin, J. (1981). Depression and related cognitions: Antecedent or consequence? *Journal of Psychology, 90*, 213–219.

Lewis, E. M. (1981a). *An experimental analogue of the spouse abuse cycle*. Paper presented at the National Conference for Family Violence Researcher, University of New Hampshire, Durham.

Lewis, E. M. (1981b). The effects of intensity and probability on the preference for immediate versus delayed aversive stimuli in women with various levels of interspousal conflict (Doctoral Dissertation, University of Illinois at Chicago Circle, 1980). *Dissertation Abstracts International, 41*(10), 3897-B.

Patterson, G. R. (1982). *Coercive family process*. Eugene, OR: Castalia Press.

Radloff, L. S. (1977). The CES-D Scale: A self-report depression scale for research in the general population. *Applied Psychological Measurement, 1*(3), 385–401.

Seligman, M. E. P. (1978). Comment and integration. *Journal of Abnormal Psychology, 87*, 165–179.

Straus, M. A., Gelles, R. J., & Steinmetz, S. K. (1980). *Behind closed doors: Violence in the American family*. Garden City, NY: Anchor/Doubleday.

Walker, L. E. (1978). Treatment alternative for battered women. In J. R. Chapman & M. Gates (Eds.), *The victimization of women; Sage Yearbooks in Women's Policy Studies* (Vol. 3). Beverly Hills, CA: Sage.

Walker, L. E. (1979). *The battered woman*. New York, NY: Harper & Row.

Walker, L. E. A. (1996). *Survivor therapy with abused women video series*. New York, NY: Newbridge Communications.

Weiss, R. L., Hops, H., & Patterson, C. R. (1973). A framework for conceptualizing marital conflict, technology for altering it, and some data for evaluating it. In L. A. Hamerlynck, L. C. Handy, & E. J. Mash (Eds.), *Behavior change: Methodology, concepts, and practice*. Champaign, IL: Research Press.

PART TWO

INTERACTION OF INTIMATE PARTNER VIOLENCE AND OTHER FAMILY VIOLENCE

CHAPTER SIX

IMPACT OF VIOLENCE IN THE HOME ON CHILDREN

*T*he impact of exposure to violence in the home on children has been found to have a most detrimental effect on them, even more signifi-cant than being raised in a single parent home. It would be a rare person who would argue that children would not be better off raised in a home with two loving and nonviolent parents. However, the data are clear; chil-dren who are exposed to violence have a significant risk for using violence themselves, becoming delinquent, demonstrating school and behavioral problems, and having serious and lifelong mental health problems, includ-ing depression, anxiety, and posttraumatic stress disorder (PTSD) symp-tomatology (Kendall-Tackett, 2013; Walker, 2010). In fact, some have suggested that an exposure to both domestic violence and violence in the community may be the most toxic combination for negative outcomes for both children and their parents (Jaffe, Wolfe, & Wilson, 1990; Prothrow-Stith & Spivak, 2005).

Wolak and Finkelhor (1998) reviewed four large-scale surveys and estimated that approximately 11% to 20% of children lived with parents where domestic violence had occurred during a 1-year period. Childhood prevalence rates were high; close to one third of all children have been exposed to fathers battering their mothers. Using a population of school children, Singer, Anglin, Song, and Lunghofer (1995) found that between one quarter to one half of them reported seeing a family member slapped, hit, or punched during the past year and one third reported witnessing someone being beaten up in their home. In some of these cases, it was siblings who were physically harmed in the home. There are also other ways besides directly observing domestic violence that children can be exposed. These include overhearing verbal conflicts, becoming a target of the violence or attempting to intervene in it, and observing the aftermath while not the actual conflict itself (Edleson, 1999). Studies have reported major discrepancies between what parents think and what children state they are exposed to when there is violent conflict in their homes (O'Brien, John, Margolin, & Erel, 1994). Based on these estimates, however, most would agree that somewhere between 10 and 17 million children who live in the United States are exposed to intimate partner violence (IPV) each year. If we include the children who are exposed to violence around the world, the numbers would be staggering.

In the 40 years since the original battered woman syndrome (BWS) research, there has been a plethora of data collected about children who have been exposed to domestic violence, particularly by their fathers or father-like substitutes abusing their mothers. Along with the physical and psychological damage done to these children, even if they are never physically abused themselves, it is clear that they are in danger of being killed along with their mothers by their unstable fathers who are unable to tolerate separation from their families. The attitude, "If I can't have you, no one will," is still widely quoted by the women we have studied. Typical are the news reports of homicide of all family members and then suicide by the father. This problem has not been seriously addressed by communities or the courts that still insist that shared parental custody is healthy for children, even if the father is a batterer. In the following chapter on murder–suicide in domestic violence homes, the devastating toll on families, especially those going through separation and divorce, is further explored.

Those of us who work with battered women and support their protection of their children believe that these senseless deaths can be prevented. We can also prevent living with this fear if mothers are permitted to protect their children from angry and often mentally unstable batterers. However, the courts around the world will have to change their attitude and use their powers to empower mothers to make decisions about the best interests of their children themselves, instead of forcing shared parental responsibility. I have been preaching against the harmful family court procedures in ignoring and minimizing the psychological devastation caused by the family court system for many years now. Later in this book, I write about what this research has taught me about the courts' failure to protect women and children or even preserve the relationship with the abusive dads in a chapter on family courts. Unless abusers must prove to the courts that they can stop their controlling behavior and they can parent appropriately, they should not be given the ability to gain their parental responsibilities. Legally, this means putting the burden of proof on a batterer to show his appropriate parenting skills, not requiring the victim to prove the perpetrator is not a fit parent.

In this chapter, some of the negative effects on children when exposed to violence against their mothers by batterers are addressed. We have added a section on teenagers as more data have become available about teens, delinquency, and violence in their homes. We have also added a section on child custody issues as this appears to be one of the most significant areas of controversy among mental health professionals, many of whom do not pay sufficient attention to the dangers of not protecting children from the rampant power and control issues to which batterers subject them, especially when using them as pawns against their mothers for control or revenge.

MODELING AGGRESSIVE BEHAVIOR RESEARCH

The probability that IPV, like all forms of violence in the family, has a profound influence on children who are exposed to it during their early years was found to be consistent with most psychological theories popular at the time of our original research. Social learning theory would predict its significance for future violence as typified by Bandura's (1973) and Berkowitz's (1962) early writings on the learned aspects of aggressive behavior. Eron and colleagues have detailed the role of parenting in the learning of aggression (Eron, Huesman, & Zilli, 1991). Gelles and Straus (1988) have theorized about the connection between wife abuse and child abuse using data from the Family Violence Research Center at the University of New Hampshire. Straus has gone on to demonstrate the detrimental effects to children whether it is the mother or father who uses physical punishment and violence.

More recently, although still almost 20 years ago, Cummings (1998) reviewed the data on conceptual and theoretical directions and discussed the interaction factors that occur from the different ways conflict and violence are expressed together with constructive parenting behaviors in a particular family. He found that children respond emotionally to adults' disputes by a variety of behaviors and those responses may be aggravated by some factors such as comorbidity of alcoholism in one or more parents, parental depression, and the meaning given to marital conflict by the children. On the other hand, Cummings also found that constructive conflict resolution may mediate the effects of children's exposure to destructive conflict and prepare them to develop better coping strategies for future exposure. Graham-Bermann (1998) found that although only 13%

of the children from families where there was domestic violence that she studied met all the criteria for a PTSD diagnosis, more than half of the children were reexperiencing the battering incidents to which they had been exposed, 42% experienced arousal symptoms, and fewer children experienced avoidance symptoms that are part of the criteria for the PTSD diagnosis. Others have also found PTSD in children who have been exposed to domestic violence in their homes (Goodwin, 1988; Hughes, 1997; Pynoos, 1994; Rossman & Rosenberg, 1998; Terr, 1990).

Rosenberg and Rossman (1990) suggest the impact of exposure to domestic violence on children has ranged from minimal to placing severe limitations on personality development and cognition. Further, most child abuse experts agree that the next generation of abusers will come from those who have been abused themselves (Garbarino, 1999, 2007; Garbarino, Guttermen, & Seeley, 1986; Garbarino, Kostelny, & Dubrow, 1991; Geffner, Sorenson, & Lundberg-Love, 1997; Gil, 1970; Helfer & Kempe, 1974; Holden, Geffner, & Jouriles, 1998; Jaffe, Wolfe, & Wilson, 1990; Peled, Jaffe, & Edleson, 1995; Rossman & Rosenberg, 1998). Carlson (2000) reviewed the research on children exposed to violence by intimate partners in their homes and found that there were factors that moderated the distress experienced by the children. These moderators included the nature of the violence, the child's age, gender, exposure to other forms of maltreatment, and social supports that protected the child or served as a "buffer" (Carlson, 2000, p. 321).

Patterson's Coercion Theory of Aggression

Psychologist Gerald Patterson's (1982) studies of aggressive boys, based on learning theory, assume that all social interactions are learned from what is directly or indirectly modeled by other persons. Given the high rate of aggressive behaviors to which all children are exposed, and therefore learn, the question becomes: Why do some perform aggressive acts at higher rates and in different patterns than others? The coercion theory developed to answer this question came from methodical observations of the interaction of behaviors emitted by family members studied in a variety of environmental conditions. Patterson made a list of fairly typical aggressive and positive interactions usually seen in families and sent graduate students into the homes of reportedly aggressive 9-year-old boys to see how many of these behaviors could be coded in a specified period of time. They also went into the homes of nonaggressive 9-year-old boys who reportedly had other problems, and into the homes of "normal" children where no unusually aggressive or problematic behavior was reported. In the homes of the nonaggressive and aggressive children, Patterson found aggressive and coercive behaviors reported more often than positive interactions toward family members than in the "normal" children's homes where there were more positive interactions noted among family members. However, what differentiated the aggressive boys' aggressive, negative, and coercive behavior was how it was directed against their sisters and mothers, rather than the other males in the household. Further, the behaviors occurred in a particular pattern, with the groups of aggressive interactions followed by groups of positive behaviors directed at the opposite gender in their homes.

The implication of coercion theory is that if modeling takes place in interactive, conditioning relationships, then children raised in violent homes are at high risk to develop those same violent patterns whether or not they are themselves deliberately abused. Interestingly, Patterson's research on coercion theory in families with an aggressive boy has found the same cross-gender abusive behaviors among the family members that our study has found associated with domestic violence and in a pattern similar to the cycle of violence where the tension building and acute battering incidents were followed by more loving types of behavior (Patterson, 1982).

Stress Theories

Other theories, such as stress and coping perspective by Lazarus and Folkman (1984) and the trauma perspective given the PTSD responses prevalent in the children (Briere & Scott, 2007; Silvern & Kaersvang, 1989), have also been used to explain how children respond to the violence as a stressor. There is some research that documents how earlier exposure to violence as a child creates brain dysfunction and diseases (Ellsberg, Jansen, Heise, Watts, & Garcia-Moreno, 2008) in adults. We discuss some of these diseases in the later chapter on battered women's health and on body image concerns. Carrion, Weems, and Reiss (2007), working at the Stanford University School of Medicine's Packard Children's Hospital, looked at the brain function of severely traumatized children with functional MRI (fMRI) and found that these children were more impulsive, agitated, hyperactive, and that they engaged in avoidance behaviors. Many children with PTSD from exposure to violence in their homes and on the streets are misdiagnosed with attention deficit hyperactive disorder or other learning problems and placed on medication that is inappropriate for their problems. In many cases that we evaluate through our forensic clinic, we find children diagnosed with a variety of different disorders who have PTSD after being removed from an extremely abusive family home and placed in one or more foster homes. These children are very aggressive or very avoidant, have attachment problems, and do not function well in a learning environment or with other children.

Interestingly, boys are not alone in the escalation of violence. From 1999 to 2004, we studied teenage girls who were arrested, charged with delinquency, and held in the detention center. Although more than half of them denied exposure to abuse in their families when asked directly, over 85% of them scored in the PTSD range on standardized tests that measure the impact of abuse on children's psychological functioning. Reports from other psychologists who work with the juvenile justice population also mention an increase in girls' violent behavior. Although the movies and other media that portray this violence (Wedding, Boyd, & Niemiec, 2005) suggest that it may be due to changes in women's social roles, in fact it appears that these girls are acting out the impact from the abuse they have received themselves.

Adverse Childhood Experiences (ACEs) Study

In 2000, child abuse experts began a study funded by the U.S. Centers for Disease Control and Prevention (CDC) to retrospectively assess for the relationship between adverse childhood events and lifetime prevalence of health concerns (Felitti et al., 1998). The study originally wanted to see if health risks could be related to exposure to traumatic events as well as psychological and behavioral difficulties in childhood and later on in adulthood. It was a large-scale study surveying the health records of a cohort of almost 20,000 families using a health maintenance organization for their physical and psychological health needs. There are now over 60 publications detailing various findings from this study, including a book, *Treating the Lifetime Health Effects of Childhood Victimization*, written by psychologist Kathleen Kendall-Tackett in 2013.

The ACEs studied in this research included several areas in which we were interested in comparing our study outcomes. These included childhood abuse and neglect, including physical abuse, sexual abuse, verbal abuse, physical neglect, and emotional maltreatment. They also included domestic violence and IPV in the child's home, suicide or attempted suicide of a parent, a family member who was incarcerated, a family member who engaged in alcohol or other substance abuse, and death of a parent or parental separation or divorce. ACE-related disorders and health-risk problems were consistent with alcoholism and alcohol abuse, chronic obstructive pulmonary disease (COPD), depression, fetal death, health-related quality of life, illicit drug abuse, ischemic heart disease, liver disease, risk for IPV, multiple sexual partners, sexually transmitted diseases (STDs), smoking, suicide attempts, unintended pregnancies, early initiation of smoking, early initiation of sexual activity, and adolescent pregnancy. These and others are discussed in other chapters in this book as it is the first comprehensive study to connect the risks of traumatic events to later negative health and behavioral outcomes.

One of the most interesting findings with forensic implications is the relationship of the number of different traumatic and adverse events to negative behavioral outcomes such as being arrested and held in jail or prison. Although this is discussed further in the later chapter on our research on battered women in jails and prisons, it is important to state here how the number of ACEs and the negative outcomes are what is said to be "dose" related. That is, the more ACEs in a person's childhood history, the more adverse was his or her lifetime outcome. In the total sample, about one third of both men and women reported no ACEs. Another one quarter reported one ACE and another one quarter reported two or three, again fairly equally distributed between men and women. However, there were almost twice as many men than women who reported four or more ACEs during childhood and the higher the number, the more adverse their outcomes, both for health and behavior. Not surprisingly, psychologist Steven Gold, who studies trauma in those who commit homicides where the prosecution is seeking the death penalty, has found high numbers of ACEs in this population.

EMPIRICAL DATA ON CHILD-RAISING PATTERNS FROM THE BWS STUDY

Reports from battered women shelters support the learning theory of aggression. Male and female children, some as young as 2 years old, model "daddy hitting mommy" to get what they want from their mothers

(Hughes & Marshall, 1995). Shelters, in order to give mothers and children an opportunity to learn new ways of communicating with each other, have almost universally adopted "no-hitting rules." Washburne (1983) found that mothers are more likely to abuse their children when they are the major caretaker with few other supportive people in their lives. This is consistent with our finding that mothers are more likely to abuse children when they are living in a violent situation. Some women report using more controlling parenting techniques out of fear that the batterer will use even more harsh discipline should the child continue to misbehave. Despite some of the difficulties in shelter living, including crowded conditions, even abusive mothers are able to learn and use new nonabusive, nonphysical discipline techniques (Hughes & Marshall, 1995).

For the families surveyed in the Straus, Gelles, and Steinmetz (1980) study, the rate of marital violence increased in direct proportion to the amount of physical punishment experienced as children. Thus, the frequency and type of physical punishment of children need to be carefully evaluated. Early learning history of whether frustration and other negative emotions are linked with aggression can be of importance. Social factors can mediate the learned responses, both inhibiting and facilitating the display of aggressive behavior when experiencing frustration or other such emotions.

The battered women in our original study reported that two thirds of batterers' fathers battered their mothers while almost one half of their fathers and one quarter of the nonbatterers' fathers battered their mothers. Three times as many fathers of batterers than nonbatterers battered sisters and brothers when they were growing up. A smaller number of mothers of batterers were reported to batter their children but, again, it was more than the mothers of battered women or nonviolent men.

Discipline, Punishment, and Positive Comments

In addition to asking our interviewees about the perception of being battered as a child, we also directly asked about discipline methods used by their parents in the original study. We found that almost all of our subjects (89%) had been spanked as a young child at age 6 or younger, while 83% had continued to be spanked when older. Even more surprising was the report that over three quarters of the women (78%) had been hit by an object. About half of the batterers were reported to have received "strict" discipline while the other half received "lenient" discipline from their mothers. "Lenient" and "strict" were subjectively rated by the responders. But, nonviolent men were reportedly divided into approximately thirds: one third experiencing "strict" discipline, one third "lenient," and the remainder reporting "fair" discipline from their mothers.

While more fathers were rated as administering "strict" discipline than mothers (for batterers), one and one-half times as many more nonbatterers' fathers were perceived as "strict." Four times as many nonbatterers were reported to have received "fair" discipline from fathers. Approximately one quarter of batterers' and nonbatterers' fathers reportedly were "lenient," which could also have been the catch-all category for noninvolvement in their children's upbringing.

Personality Development

Another measure of child-raising patterns, albeit indirect, is the perception of whether or not separation and individuation from parents have been completed. The observation of the extreme dependency abused children have on their mothers and fathers to the point of protecting them by refusal to cooperate with social service investigations has been well documented (Helfer & Kempe, 1974; Lystadt, 1975). Such dependency is also seen in battering relationships (Dutton, 1980, 1995; Giles-Sims, 1983). Giles-Sims discusses the bonds that a closed system such as an abusive family can foster. Often, this pattern of intimacy gets carried over into children's own marriages and families. In our questionnaire, we asked about dependency on mothers and fathers and found that twice as many batterers as nonbatterers were said to still be dependent on their mothers and fathers as adults. Over half of the violent men reportedly had unresolved dependency issues, which were seen as being perpetuated in their dependency on their wives and children too. Direct measures of dependency on their children would be warranted as a next step in investigating how this dependency is developed.

Another way of looking at dependency relationships is analyzing the attachment issues in relationships with people. In Chapter 9, we describe attachment issues we found in the current research. Children exposed to IPV have not been studied as a group to determine if their attachment issues come from before or after exposure to the abuse. Aleah Nathan compared attachment styles between battered women who also were abused during childhood and those whose only abuse was in the adult intimate relationship. Interestingly, she did not find any significant difference between the two groups, supporting the research that suggests attachment styles set as children can be modified by traumatic experiences as adults.

Hughes attempted to measure the psychological functioning of children who came to an Arkansas battered woman's shelter using several standardized anxiety and self-esteem measures. She found the children displayed the characteristics of jumpiness, nervousness, withdrawal, fright, and impaired academic performance (Hughes & Marshall, 1995). Pizzey (1974) found fear, poor academic performance, confusion, reticence in discussing violence, and fantasizing about a different home life in the children seen at Chiswick Women's Aid refuge in London. Only one fifth of Labell's (1979) sample of 521 battered women with 682 children reported emotional, behavioral, or physical problems. This is a much lower figure than would have been expected from a mental health professional's observations. Perhaps the abused women who were interviewed while in crisis and at a shelter could not identify their children's problems until they themselves were out of crisis. Rarely do studies look at long-term impact on the child's personality from exposure to IPV. In Carlson's review (2000), she found that most studies used problem checklists such as the Child Behavior Checklist (CBCL) (Achenbach & Edlebrok, 1983) and, although they have found that most children score in the clinically significant range, it is not known if this has a permanent impact on their personalities.

The Hughes study actually measured the children's personality development. It found that preschool children's development was the most disrupted by violence in their homes and often showed signs of obvious developmental delay. Boys' self-concept tended to be more negative than girls', who had more anxiety, worry, and oversensitivity. As would be expected from all other reports, boys demonstrated more aggressive behavior than girls at every age. And, not surprisingly, mothers rated boys more negatively on conduct and personality problems than girls. Yet, all the children viewed physical punishment as the primary mode of parental discipline. Interestingly, a bimodal split occurred in mothers' discipline preferences. After a short stay in the shelter, one half of the mothers reported preferring nonphysical discipline while the other group continued to use physical punishment. Giles-Sims (1983) also found a drop in the number of previously violent families continuing to use physical punishment after a shelter experience. Considering the Straus et al. (1980) survey findings of widespread acceptance of physical punishment as a discipline technique, it is heartening that so many shelter mothers are adopting the no-hitting rule for their families.

Garbarino et al. (1986) have measured the impact of psychological abuse on children who are maltreated and found that in many cases it has a more detrimental effect over a longer period of time. Children are able to communicate in their own way when they are distressed by the danger to which they are exposed (Garbarino et al., 1991). Garbarino's later work ties together child abuse with later use of violence in both girls (Garbarino, 2007) and boys (Garbarino, 1999), including those who kill other people. Cummings suggests that if parents resolve the conflict so that the child is aware of the peaceful resolution, it might mitigate some of the psychological impact (Cummings & Davies, 1994). Others have suggested intervention programs that remediate the damage (Peled et al., 1995). However, it is important to note that the newer studies that suggest the very structure of the brain is altered by the biochemical changes from chronic posttraumatic stress reactions, and the studies of attachment styles described earlier in this book, strongly suggest that there is a more lasting impact on these children's personalities.

Cummings (1998) observed children's emotional responses to simulated conflict situations and found a great deal of distress, including discomfort, anxiety, concern, anger, fear, sadness, guilt, shame, and worry, when exposed to audiotaped conflict situations with actors posing as parents fighting. Laumakis, Margolin, and John (1998) also used similar vignettes to assess children's emotional responses to conflict. They found more negative responses to the scenarios with threats to leave as well as physical aggression compared to benign scenarios, especially with boys who had been exposed to similar situations in their own homes. These analogue studies are the closest measures to what really happens to children as they are being exposed to parental anger and violence. It is the aftermath that is more often studied.

The most troublesome behaviors reported in children exposed to domestic violence are those that can be seen by others—or externalizing behaviors. These include aggression, disobedience, noncompliance, hostility, and oppositional behavior. However, it is difficult to separate the impact from the domestic violence in the home and the aftermath from being forced to live in two different homes with two different sets of rules and expectations after parents separate and divorce. Unfortunately, courts have been counseled by well-meaning professionals who do not understand these effects of exposure to domestic violence, to keep the children in constant contact with both parents so the children are constantly in the middle of the power struggles and attempts to protect them.

In one family with which we have been working closely, we found that, in the 2-year period since the parents divorced, the now 6-year-old child has gone from a happy, easy-to-care-for child to a defiant, aggressive, and hostile child who has become seriously overweight, such that he cannot engage in athletics with other boys his own age. He has been expelled from school for aggression against other children. The court has ordered that the father be permitted to telephone this child and speak for 30 minutes every evening before he goes to bed so that the mother never has the opportunity to develop her own bedtime routines uninterrupted from the father. This child was not exposed to physical abuse, although he hears horrible screaming and yelling as his father tries to control his mother even after they have been divorced and the father has remarried. However, the consequences for him are no different than we see in another case, a 4-year-old boy who also has been expelled from school because he stuck a pencil in another child's eye. This child witnessed his father kill his mother after being exposed to domestic violence for over 1 year.

PHYSIOLOGICAL CHANGES FROM PTSD

Charney, Deutch, Krystal, Southwick, and Davis (1993) have found changes in the levels of some neurotransmitters associated with PTSD. This includes elevations in adrenalin and noradrenalin that raise the heart rate and blood flow and prepare the body and muscles for quick action in the "fight or flight" reaction to danger that occurs in such traumatic situations. Focus is narrowed and agitation increased, which probably is associated with the difficulties in concentration and attention reported by victims. Greater levels of glucocorticoids help the body deal with injury by reducing inflammation but also impact the memory functions of the hippocampus. Memory may also be interfered with by the high levels of endogenous opiates that also reduce the perception of pain. High levels of dopamine in the frontal cortex stimulate thought processes but may also facilitate the intrusive memories and reexperiencing of the trauma. Serotonin levels have also been found to be lowered, which may interfere with regulating emotional arousal that is also associated with PTSD.

Rossman (1998) describes these physiological changes and suggests that the prolonged threat to survival may leave the individual in a dysregulated state where perception, cognition, and emotional systems are attempting to compensate for the changes being experienced. Children who experience prolonged traumatic stress may well experience permanent and irreversible physiological responses. Goleman (1996) suggests that the new field of psychoneuroimmunology (PNI) can help account for some of the cognitive, emotional, and behavioral changes seen in children exposed to abuse in their homes. One of the most critical areas of emotion controlled by this midbrain system is the social interaction between the child and peers, including the lack of development of ability to experience empathy for others. We further describe these issues in Chapter 7 and later in Chapter 14 where medication issues are discussed.

ISSUES COMMONLY FOUND IN CHILDREN EXPOSED TO ABUSE

Children tend to model and identify with powerful adults so that they, too, can feel safe and powerful. While children are young, many batterers are reported to be very nurturing fathers. They care for their sons and daughters and, when not angry, show genuine concern over their upbringing. Many battering incidents reportedly occurred over fights about who had a better method of taking care of the child. Yet, as children grow older and become more independent, these men are less able to tolerate the separation and individuation necessary for the child's healthy development. They often become as possessive and intrusive into their child's life as into their partner's. If they take too much control over the child's life, then self-esteem and feelings of self-worth are less likely to develop in the child, and can result in learned helplessness when the child does not perceive personal power.

Children who grow up in violent homes show its effects in their overall socialization process as well as in mental health symptoms. The areas most likely to be affected are affectional relationships, anger, sexuality, stress-coping techniques, and communication problems. They often develop certain skill deficits, including an inability to deal effectively with confrontation and aggression, and have greater confusion about interpersonal relationships. Some children are developmentally delayed while others develop so rapidly that they miss major parts of their childhood.

Learning to cope with angry confrontations and aggressive behavior is one of the critical areas for these children as reported in my clinical practice. Some adapt to the seemingly limitless anger expressed in their homes by withdrawing, both emotionally and physically. Unresponsiveness and failure to thrive is noted in some during infancy. Many learn to use television or the stereo as a way to shut out the loud yelling. This is one of the more popular tactics still visible when I visit battered women's shelters. As these children grow older, they are more likely to leave the house when the fights begin. Many continue this withdrawal pattern through the use of drugs and alcohol. Others react to anger in more aggressive ways themselves. Two- and 3-year-old boys and girls have been forced to join their fathers in actually beating their mothers. When their daddy is not present they become his surrogate and help keep their battered mommy in line. No doubt many of these children do commit parent abuse and "granny bashing" as they become older, although there are insufficient studies on these cases. They also become aggressive with peers and perhaps repeat their violent behavior in their own adult homes. This finding gave way to the admonition of the APA Task Force on Violence and the Family to always look for other forms of interpersonal violence when one form of violence is found in a family (American Psychological Association, 1996).

Anger

Children who live in violence are exposed to more uncontrolled angry feelings than most. At the worst times, such anger can be displaced onto the children by parents who are too preoccupied with their own survival to adequately parent them. Other times, the parenting they receive is quite appropriate. Most of them learn how to control their parents' anger through manipulative tactics. They learn to expect unpredictable criticism, abuse, and neglect and cope as best they can, terrified of being abandoned. When they are young, they become confused that they are the cause of their parents' anger and believe that if they behave better, then the violence will cease. Thus, they become like other victims, accepting the responsibility for causing their own predicament, but feeling frustrated, depressed, angry, and so on when they cannot stop the aggression. When they are successful in getting the violence to stop, they develop feelings of omnipotence, which only encourage them to try harder for harmony at home. The association with unlimited violence causes them to fear anyone's expression of anger. As they grow older, they are more likely to give in on little things than take a chance of unleashing such rage. Yet, should the rage be unleashed, some become the aggressor in order to handle it by covering up their fear.

Overparentified Children

Many of the children reportedly become so extra-sensitive to cues in their environment that they cease behaving like a child and become *overparentified*, or begin to take care of their parents, so they can reduce the tension. They may try to stop the violence but they fear making a mistake as their errors are measured in pain. These children are similar to those who take care of alcoholic parents and there has been literature describing them as "children of alcoholic parents." In many ways the experiences of both these types of children are similar. They never know if they are waking up or coming home to a calm or chaotic situation. Overparentified children are always anxious and try hard to keep things calm and stable as best they can. They are the ones who clean up the mess after an acute battering incident. If they are the oldest child with siblings, they help raise the younger ones, making sure they are fed and safe. Some of these children choose not to marry and raise their own families, stating that they have already raised one family and cannot do it again. Some end up as battered women in their own homes, caring for dependent men who cannot take care of themselves.

Alienated Child Syndrome

As children exposed to domestic violence grow older, many stop trying to please and drop out of productive society. Some of them begin using alcohol and other drugs early, often while in middle or high school. I have labeled these children with "alienated child syndrome" and we sometimes see them in the juvenile detention centers. They are not leaders and rarely plan antisocial events, but rather go along with others in a loose social group, and may get in trouble.

These youth can be easily persuaded to accompany others on a variety of missions ranging from a benign searching for companionship for an evening to "wilding" or going out and killing another person. These teens appear to have lost the capacity for empathy for another person and appear to have no visible emotions or connections to societal norms. They are different from teens who join gangs and adopt the gang norms rather than those of their culture. They seem to be alienated in a manner similar to those described in a popular book, *The Lord of the Flies* (Golding, 1959). I have worked with some of these teens after they are arrested for participating with others in heinous crimes, some of which appear to be senseless. Traumatized while very young, these teens do not subscribe to any cultural norms. Nor do they have any connections with other people or groups to help give them guidance. Rather, they agree to go out with a spontaneously put together group of others, most of whom they do not know beyond acquaintanceship. Some of them might be homeless and drifting from one city to another, while others might be from local homes, appearing seemingly normal from the outside, like Eric Harris and Dylan Klebold, who gunned down and killed 13 others and themselves during the 1999 Columbine High School massacre in Colorado. There is usually one charismatic leader and one or more "enforcers," who are chosen by the leader to carry out the job of keeping control over the others. In the 1999 Columbine High School case, it appears that Eric Harris was the leader and managed to get help from several others besides Klebold despite his "weird" and "scary" fringe-type behavior.

For example, there were several boys and girls who participated in the killing of Bobby Kent in a deserted sand pit near Fort Lauderdale, Florida, some years ago. One girl in particular was present at the several meetings where killing this high school student was discussed as well as at the scene of the homicide. She had also been present at the previous attempt on his life about a week prior to the actual homicide. During the initial evaluation, this teen described events in an almost emotionless manner. She was totally disconnected from her feelings as she talked about her entire life that was filled with different forms of trauma, including exposure to domestic violence. When asked why she went along with the other kids, if she thought they might kill someone, she shrugged her shoulders and said that she did not have anything else to do when they invited her to come along. It sounded like she put the invitation in the same category as I might if asked to go to the movies with a friend.

Some of these youth have left abusive homes and live with other teenagers wandering around the world in unstable groups. Once they drop into this culture, they learn where the safe places are and travel there with very little in material things. For example, there has been a group of them who live under a bridge in downtown Portland, Oregon, and steal money and food to survive. In Fort Lauderdale, Florida, a group of four boys roamed the deserted streets in the middle of the night, and beat up and killed several homeless men who were sleeping on the streets. When asked why they did it, one of the followers repeated his father's stereotyped bigotry. Further evaluation revealed his mother was suffering from PTSD and BWS, unable to supervise her teenage son, and his father was hostile and derogatory toward women. He was quick to criticize any behavior that did not conform to his own rules and used violence in the family to maintain his power and control.

While exposure to IPV in their homes is not the only behavior that results in producing an alienated child, there is a pattern that I have noted in these forensic cases. Occasionally, a very charismatic and charming man, usually in his 20s, comes along and energizes some of them into a loosely formed group and persuades them to engage in antisocial and violent activities. This charismatic leader usually picks on another teenager or someone in his 20s, who is very angry and willing to use violence to win the leader's attention. Both often come from homes where they were exposed to severe parental conflict. The teen then becomes the leader's enforcer, making sure the others in the group go along with what is being planned. The kids drift in and out of these groups, with some going on to become part of the invisible homeless population in the United States, others spending a long time in detention centers or prison for their antisocial actions, and others cleaning up and dropping back into society. As might be expected, they often need psychotherapy to help them learn to feel and express emotions and make important connections with interpersonal relationships.

Gangs and Cults

Some children exposed to violence in their homes continue to look toward peers for comfort and support, albeit with gangs and cults, or through sexual exploitation and other antisocial group norms. Unlike the alienated youth, these children actually believe in the norms of the gang or the cult and do have good interpersonal relationships, albeit with a group that often espouses antisocial ideas and engages in similar behaviors. Interestingly, the gang kids are the easiest to help back into society once they become motivated to do so as they often have good interpersonal skills and can express a range of emotions despite their antisocial behavior. It is the motivation that is the problem as they fear being killed or seriously harmed if they go against the gang norms and betray the other members. Many of the youth who belong to gangs become intricately involved in the culture and engage in selling and distributing drugs, sex trafficking, and other antisocial activities to maintain the gang. This is a major problem in some of the large cities in the United States. The gang membership extends to the jails and prisons when they are arrested, with other members welcoming them into their new housing and rules of life there. Like on the outside, power and control is maintained by the dominant members using violence and threats to establish fear-based control.

Premature Sexualization

Another area reportedly affected by the home environment is learning to use sexuality as a means of winning approval. Little toddlers can learn to smile cutely, and tell mommy or daddy, "I love you," as seductively as their parental models, to reduce tension and avert an acute battering incident. Sexual expressions can then be substituted for intimate love. The men take advantage of less powerful children by reinforcing and encouraging such behavior. This is called "grooming" behavior. The rate of incest between batterers and their children is much higher than ever suspected. These children, normally girls though in some cases, boys, too, have learned how to manipulate other men using their sexuality. For those who become involved in sex trafficking, the lifestyle can be more of a comfortable and familiar choice rather than a reflection of the rebellion professionals used to assume it was. The demand for child sex partners continues around the world with exposés of illegal child trafficking frequently publicized. Attempts to put them out of business frequently fail, especially because of the use of the Internet to procure these children's services. Many of these children earn more money and live better than they did in their family homes. In other countries, parents may actually sell their young children to pimps who manage brothels where providing child sex partners may be legal or simply ignored. The amount of money and the corruption it brings are extreme and lead to such abuses. Unfortunately, many of these children are exploited and abused in this lifestyle. I discuss the work we have begun to do in this area of sex trafficking in Chapter 8 as so many of the children involved describe growing up in dysfunctional and abusive homes.

Substance Abuse and Domestic Violence Issues

There are several studies of the family backgrounds of teenagers who show up at drug treatment centers and drop-in centers around the country. Most report a history of abusive family behavior (Freudenberger, 1979). In an interesting study, King and Straus (1981) evaluate the retraining procedures in nonviolence for residents of Odyssey House, a New Hampshire residential drug treatment center. They found that the structured encounter groups along with a strictly enforced prohibition against violent behavior were quite successful in helping individuals use nonviolent and noncoercive problem-solving techniques. The typical home pattern reported for teenage girls who enter into the prostitution and pornography industry is one filled with physical, psychological, and sexual violence according to James's (1978), Farley and Barkan's (1998), and Farley's (2004) research. Barry (1979) describes the abuse that many of the prostitutes have experienced throughout their lives. All in all, adolescence is the time when children (and parents) need the most strength to cope with pressures. Those who have lived with violence at home seem to be more vulnerable to succumbing to those negative pressures. Yet, not all do. Examination of the mediating factors that can protect these vulnerable children is an important next step in research.

Children Exposed to Other Traumatic Experiences

Much has been learned about how children are impacted by trauma given some of the large-scale traumatic events that have occurred around the world from rescue workers in countries where earthquakes, tsunamis, and hurricanes have devastated the populations. Psychologist Annette LaGreca and her colleagues have studied children's reactions to these disasters (LaGreca, Sevin, & Sevin, 2005). One of the most important lessons for first responders to learn was the total disorganizing features of these traumas especially on children who already have been exposed to domestic violence and other traumatic experiences. Depending on the age of the child, they have been found to lose all ability to communicate with the world or to even become part of a gang that steals from others in forced confinement because homes have been damaged. Training in domestic violence and other trauma is important for all rescue workers (Dorfman & Walker, 2007).

ADOLESCENT DEVELOPMENTAL ISSUES

Teen-aged children exposed to domestic violence are reported by others to become withdrawn and passive like their mothers, or else, violent like their fathers. It often depends on who has the money and power. It is commonplace to see teenagers in the family choose one or the other parent with whom to identify rather than the norm of identifying with both parents. Davidson (1979) cites the tendency of teenage girls to identify with their fathers and like them, also abuse their mothers, at least verbally. Of course, teenagers are often verbally abusive to anyone who tries to control them or deny them the privileges they demand. Pizzey (1974) describes her British teenagers in sex-stereotyped terms; girls are seen as passive, clinging, anxious, with many psychosomatic complaints, while boys were seen as disruptive and aggressive. In many of those families, the girls, especially if they were older, had to do more than the usual child care functions. Hilberman and Munson (1978) report similar findings in their rural Appalachian sample. There is more likelihood of fathers abusing teen-aged children than of mothers committing such abuse (Martin, 1982) and some researchers have suggested that abuse during adolescence is a high-risk factor for later emotional and behavioral disturbance.

CHILD CUSTODY, VISITATION, AND REMOVAL ISSUES

In the earlier editions of reports of this BWS research, I hesitated to add a section on child custody, visitation, and removal issues for fear of being unable to do justice given the enormity of the topic. If there is any area that impacts women and children the most, it is the inability of family courts to take seriously their fears of further abuse and need for protection. Rather than focus on the danger to children and women, the courts and legislators, with the approval of many mental health professionals who do not understand the issues of domestic violence, focus on the right of equal parental access to children. In order to justify this misguided focus, they make claims that it is in *the best interests of the child* (the standard that must be met when a child custody decision is made) to have a relationship with both parents. However, this is a belief that is based on theory, religion, and custom and is not supported by the literature.

Prior to the adoption of the best interests test, legislators had issued laws, rules, regulations, and guidelines to the courts to follow what was then called the *Tender Years Doctrine,* which permitted children to live with mothers as long as necessary. Although fathers were granted visitation rights, they often abdicated their parental responsibilities, including not paying to support their children. In the early 1970s, along with the feminist movement in the United States to expand women's right to enter the workplace and enjoy careers besides motherhood, legislators were persuaded to pass laws that would hold fathers more accountable to their children. This led to the *Best Interests Doctrine.* As child support payments were based on the amount of time mothers or fathers spent with the child, it became popular for fathers to demand equal time so they could limit the amount of money they had to give their children's mothers. But, it is not always in the best interests of children exposed to domestic violence to be equally shared by their fathers. In fact, our research shows that most batterers continue to abuse their power and control against the children and their mothers when such custody arrangements are ordered by the court (Bancroft & Silverman, 2002; Holden et al., 1998).

This is a highly controversial area with very heated emotions from fathers' rights groups on the Internet soliciting others to harm the careers of psychologists and lawyers they do not like (Shapiro, Walker, Manosevitz, Peterson, & Williams, 2008), to heated emotions from domestic violence and child abuse advocates who demand that mental health professionals get out of the child custody evaluation business. Numerous websites, listservs, and blogs exist, each with a different idea about how to handle this difficult problem. Mothers who run away with their children, fearing that disappearing is the only way to protect them from an abusive father, are frequently caught and brought back to the United States. They are prosecuted to the fullest extent of the law despite their pleas that this is their first offense and they only did it to protect their children. Even more frightening, the courts are so angry with these women that they punish them by giving sole custody to the abusers.

If the mother attempts to overcome the presumption of shared parental responsibility, it is an uphill battle even when the child provides direct evidence that physical or sexual abuse has occurred. Vulnerable, special needs children are forced into shared custody when they desperately need one safe home with no conflict to grow and thrive. Court-appointed psychologists use psychological tests that are not meant to determine custody and do not address the legal issues (Otto, Edens, & Barcus, 2000). Guardians-Ad-Litem (GAL) either like or do not like the mothers and base their recommendations on their own preconceived biases rather than a realistic appraisal of the situation and how to best meet the children's needs.

Battered Women's Loss of Power in Child Raising When Divorced

The truth is that battered women lose the ability to properly raise their children when they file for divorce. They will be forced into shared parental custody as that is the presumption in almost every state. This means they cannot choose the school their child will attend, what medical doctor they will see when ill, what religious service to take them to if it is their turn to have them when services are held, or even where to live without permission of the man who has physically, sexually, and/or psychologically abused and controlled them. Even if they wish to remarry and move, the batterer can withhold permission. The courts give the man even more control over the woman and the children than he had before the separation. In most homes where domestic violence has occurred, the batterer accepts the socialized norms and gives the woman a lot of freedom in making the decisions on how to raise the children, especially when they are well behaved and conform to his rules. He may spend very little time with the children alone; most of the time is spent with other family members present. That all changes the minute a separation occurs and the batterer is thrust into taking care of the children on his own, especially if he does not have a mother around to help him out.

If the battered woman does not terminate the relationship with the batterer, social services may step in and remove the children from her custody, especially if they are found to be harmed by the abuse in the home. If she gets them back and leaves him, she then will be controlled by the state child abuse authorities as well as the batterer. There is no question that the data demonstrate the harm to children exposed to domestic violence with both parents in the home, but the continued harm to them when they must negotiate between two homes where high conflict continues because the batterer's power and control needs have not been addressed has not been studied.

This is a no-win situation for the battered woman. Together with the batterer, she has a better chance of raising the children who are harmed by being in the middle of the abusive atmosphere. But, separated, they all have a greater chance of being harmed worse and even killed. And if they survive the separation, the woman will lose the ability to protect the children from an abusive father.

Protection From Legal Abuse?

What, if anything, can be done to protect the woman and the children from this fate? In other countries, such as Israel and Australia, the laws impacting children have been reformed to give children their own right to legal standing in the court. This means that children themselves can be heard, either by themselves if old enough or by an attorney. Voicing their opinions is empowering and hopefully will impact many judges when they hear repeatedly what horrible situations they have been forcing children into with shared parental responsibility orders. Children can be represented legally by real attorneys who must take their wishes into consideration and not GALs who supposedly act in the best interests of the child but rarely have studied child development, do not know what children need at different ages, and may not have even spent more time with the children they represent than they spend with their parents. Although there is a small movement toward children's rights in the United States, it is dwarfed by those who fear giving children some power will somehow take away their own power and legal rights. In fact, the U.S. government has not signed the United Nations Declaration of the Rights of Children despite the fact that many other countries have ratified the document.

I have recommended that children harmed by exposure to a batterer have a time-out from contact with their father. Usually this lasts for 1 year, giving the child time to develop normally, be available for learning in school once freed from worry and fear, and live a simple and more normal life. I suggest to the court that the batterer should prove his adequacy as a father by attending offender-specific treatment and the child should be permitted to attend trauma-specific therapy where trauma triggers are addressed. The battered woman should choose a child therapist with whom she can work effectively to assist the child to heal. However, there are times when children need to stop therapy, especially if they have been attending sessions without much benefit. This should be determined by the mother and the child, taking into account such factors as the age of the child, his or her developmental needs, school performance, behavior of the child, and the ability of the mother and child to further develop their own relationship. Fathers should be required to contribute to the therapy financially as well as continue their support of the child. Further comments on the dreadful state of affairs with the family court can be found in Chapter 19 where I go into greater detail on how the family court is broken for battered women and their families.

SUMMARY AND IMPLICATIONS FOR PARENTS IN RAISING CHILDREN

Perhaps a most important first step is to reexamine our child-raising practices, especially discipline methods. Straus et al. (1980) say the marriage license is a hitting license. They are right. We must also recognize that when we hit a child to teach that child a lesson, we also send the message that the person who loves you the most has the right to physically hurt you in the name of discipline. When we teach children rigid sex-role stereotypes delineating how women and men must perform in society, we also teach them to be insecure if their expectations are not met by the other person. Such sexism combined with violence training surely creates the atmosphere necessary to raise a batterer and a battered woman. To eradicate domestic violence and violence in the community, we must stop modeling both sexist and violent behavior. And, we must change the divorce laws to empower children and abused women so they are no longer victimized by the abusers.

REFERENCES

Achenbach, T. M., & Edelbrock, C. (1983). *Manual for the Child Behavior Checklist and Revised Child Behavior Profile*. Burlington: University of Vermont Department of Psychology.

American Psychological Association. (1996). *Report from the Presidential Task Force on Violence and the Family*. Washington, DC: Author.

Bancroft, L., & Silverman, J. G. (2002). *The batterer as a parent: Addressing the impact of domestic violence on family dynamics*. Thousand Oaks, CA: Sage.

Bandura, A. (1973). *Aggression: A social learning analysis*. Englewood, NJ: Prentice Hall.

Barry, K. (1979). *Female sexual slavery*. New York: New York University Press.

Berkowitz, L. (1962). *Aggression: A social psychological analysis*. New York, NY: McGraw-Hill.

Briere, J., & Scott, C. (2007/2015). *Principles of trauma therapy: A guide to symptoms, evaluation, and treatment*. Thousand Oaks, CA: Sage.

Carlson, B. E. (2000). Children exposed to intimate partner violence: Research findings and implications for intervention. *Trauma, Violence, & Abuse, 1*(4), 321–342.

Carrion, V. G., Weems, C. F., & Reiss, A. L. (2007). Stress predicts brain changes in children: A pilot longitudinal study on youth stress, posttraumatic stress disorder, and the hippocampus. *Pediatrics, 119*(3), 509–516.

Charney, D. S., Deutch, A. Y., Krystal, J. H., Southwick, S. M., & Davis, M. (1993). Psychobiological mechanisms of post-traumatic stress disorder. *Archives of General Psychiatry, 50*, 294–305.

Cummings, E. M. (1998). Children exposed to marital conflict and violence: Conceptual and theoretical directions. In G. W. Holden, R. Geffner, & E. N. Jouriles (Eds.), *Children exposed to marital violence: Theory, research, and applied issues* (pp. 55–93). Washington, DC: American Psychological Association.

Cummings, E. M., & Davies, P. T. (1994). Emotional security as a regulatory process in normal development and the development of pathology. *Development and Psychopathology, 8*, 123–139.

Davidson, T. (1979). *Conjugal crime: Understanding and changing the wife-beating pattern*. New York, NY: Hawthorne.

Dorfman, W. I., & Walker, L. E. (2007). *First responder's guide to abnormal psychology: Applications for police, firefighters and rescue personnel*. New York, NY: Springer.

Dutton, D. G. (1980). *Traumatic bonding*. Unpublished manuscript. University of British Columbia, Vancouver, Canada.

Dutton, D. G. (1995). *The batterer: A psychological profile*. New York, NY: Basic Books.

Edleson, J. L. (1999). The overlap between child maltreatment and woman battering. *Violence Against Women, 5*(2), 134–154.

Ellsberg, M., Jansen H. A., Heise, L., Watts, C. H., & Garcia-Moreno, C. (2008). Intimate partner violence and women's physical and mental health in the WHO multi-country study on women's health and domestic violence: An observational study. *Lancet, 371*, 1165–1172.

Eron, L. D., Huesman, L. R., & Zilli, A. (1991). The role of parental variables in the learning of aggression. In D. J. Pepler & H. Rubin (Eds.), *The development and treatment of child aggression* (pp. 169–188). Hillsdale, NJ: Erlbaum.

Farley, M. (Ed.). (2004). *Prostitution, trafficking, and traumatic stress*. Binghamton, NY: Haworth Press.

Farley, M., & Barkan, H. (1998). Prostitution, violence and posttraumatic stress disorder. *Women and Health, 27*(3), 37–49.

Felitti, V. J., Anda, R. F., Nordenberg, D., Williamson, D. F., Spitz, A. M., Edwards, V., . . . Marks, J. S. (1998). Relationship of childhood abuse and household dysfunction to many of the leading causes of death in adults: The Adverse Childhood Experiences (ACE) Study. *American Journal of Preventive Medicine, 14*(4), 245–258.

Freudenberger, H. (1979, September). *Children as victims: Prostitution and pornography.* Symposium presented at the annual meeting of the American Psychological Association, New York, NY.

Garbarino, J. (1999). *Lost boys: Why our sons turn violent and how we can save them.* New York, NY: Free Press.

Garbarino, J. (2007). *See Jane hit: Why girls are growing more violent and what we can do about it.* New York, NY: Penguin.

Garbarino, J., Guttermen, E., & Seeley, J. W. (1986). *The psychologically battered child: Strategies for identification, assessment, and intervention.* San Francisco, CA: Jossey-Bass.

Garbarino, J., Kostelny, K., & Dubrow, N. (1991). What children can tell us about living in danger. *American Psychologist, 46,* 376–383.

Geffner, R., Sorenson, S. B., & Lundberg-Love, P. K. (Eds.). (1997). *Violence and sexual abuse at home: Current issues, interventions, and research in spousal battering and child maltreatment.* Binghamton, NY: Haworth Maltreatment & Trauma Press.

Gelles, R. J., & Straus, M. A. (1988). *Intimate violence.* New York, NY: Simon & Schuster.

Gil, D. G. (1970). *Violence against children.* Cambridge, MA: Harvard University Press.

Giles-Sims, J. (1983). *Wife battering: A systems theory approach.* New York, NY: Guilford Press.

Golding, W. (1959). *The lord of the flies.* New York, NY: Putnam.

Goleman, D. (1996). *Emotional intelligence.* New York, NY: Bantam Books.

Goodwin, J. (1988). Post-traumatic symptoms in abused children. *Journal of Traumatic Stress, 1,* 475–488.

Graham-Bermann, S. A. (1998). The impact of woman abuse on children's social development: Research and theoretical perspectives. In G. Holden, R. Geffner, & E. Jouriles (Eds.), *Children exposed to marital violence* (pp. 21–54). Washington, DC: American Psychological Association.

Helfer, E. R., & Kempe, C. H. (1974). *The battered child* (2nd ed.). Chicago, IL: University of Chicago Press.

Hilberman, E., & Munson, L. (1978). Sixty battered women. *Victimology: An International Journal, 2*(3–4), 460–471.

Holden, G. W., Geffner, R., & Jouriles, E. N. (Eds.). (1998). *Children exposed to marital violence: Theory, research, and applied issues.* Washington, DC: American Psychological Association.

Hughes, H. M. (1997). Research concerning children of battered women: Clinical implications. In R. Geffner, S. B. Sorenson, & P. K. Lundberg-Love (Eds.), *Violence and sexual abuse at home: Current issues, interventions, and research in spousal battering and child maltreatment* (pp. 225–244). Binghamton, NY: Haworth Maltreatment & Trauma Press.

Hughes, H. M., & Marshall, M. (1995). Advocacy for children of domestic violence: Helping the battered women with non-sexist childrearing. In E. Peled, P. G. Jaffe, & J. L. Edleson (Eds.), *Ending the cycle of violence: Community responses to children of battered women* (pp. 97–105). Newbury Park, CA: Sage.

Jaffe, P. G., Wolfe, D. A., & Wilson, S. K. (1990). *Children of battered women.* Newbury Park, CA: Sage.

James, J. (1978). The prostitute as victim. In J. R. Chapman & M. Gates (Eds.), *The victimization of women* (pp. 175–201). Beverly Hills, CA: Sage.

Kendall-Tackett, K. (2013). *Treating the lifetime health effects of childhood victimization* (2nd ed.). Kingston, NJ: Civic Research Institute.

King, D. F., & Straus, M. A. (1981, August). *When prohibition works: Alternatives to violence in the Odyssey House Youth program and in the family.* Paper presented at the annual meeting of the American Sociological Association, Toronto, Ontario, Canada.

Labell, L. S. (1979). Wife abuser: A sociological study of battered women and their mates. *Victimology, 4,* 258–267.

LaGreca, A. M., Sevin, S. W., & Sevin, E. L. (2005). *After the storm: A guide to help children cope with the psychological effects of a hurricane.* Coral Gables, FL: 7-Dippity.

Laumakis, M. A., Margolin, G., & John, R. S. (1998). The emotional, cognitive, and coping responses of preadolescent children to different dimensions of marital conflict. In G. W. Holden, R. Geffner, & E. N. Jouriles (Eds.), *Children exposed to family violence* (pp. 257–288). Washington, DC: American Psychological Association.

Lazarus, R. S., & Folkman, S. (1984). *Stress, appraisal, and coping.* New York, NY: Springer Publishing Company.

Lystadt, M. H. (1975). Violence at home: A review of the literature. *American Journal of Orthopsychiatry, 45*(3), 328–345.

Martin, V. (1982). Wife-beating. A product of socio sexual development. In M. Kirkpatrick (Ed.), *Women's sexual experiences: Explorations of the dark continent* (pp. 247–261). New York, NY: Plenum Press.

O'Brien, M., John, R. S., Margolin, G., & Erel, O. (1994). Reliability and diagnostic efficacy of parents' reports to assess children's exposure to interparental aggression. *Violence and Victims, 9,* 45–62.

Otto, R. K., Edens, J. F., & Barcus, E. H. (2000). The use of psychological testing in child custody evaluations. *Family Court Review, 38*(3), 312–340.

Patterson, G. R. (1982). *Coercive family process.* Eugene, OR: Castalia Press.

Peled, E., Jaffe, P. G., & Edleson, J. L. (Eds.). (1995). *Ending the cycle of violence: Community responses to children of battered women.* Newbury Park, CA: Sage.

Pizzey, E. (1974). *Scream quietly or the neighbors will hear.* London, UK: Penguin.

Prothrow-Stith D., & Spivak, H. (2005). *Sugar and spice and no longer nice: Preventing violence among girls.* San Francisco, CA: Jossey-Bass.

Pynoos, R. S. (1994). Traumatic stress and developmental psychopathology in children and adolescents. In R. S. Pynoos (Ed.), *Posttraumatic stress disorder: A clinical review* (pp. 65–98). Lutherville, MD: Sidran Press.

Rosenberg, M. S., & Rossman, B. B. R. (1990). The child witness to marital violence. In R. T. Ammerman & M. Hersen (Eds.), *Treatment of family violence* (pp. 183–210). New York, NY: Wiley.

Rossman, B. B. R. (1998). Descartes' error and post-traumatic stress disorder: Cognition and emotion in children who are exposed to parental violence. In G. W. Holden, R. Geffner, & E. N. Jouriles (Eds.), *Children exposed to marital violence: Theory, research, and applied issues* (pp. 223–256). Washington, DC: American Psychological Association.

Rossman, B. B. R., & Rosenberg, M. S. (1998). *The multiple victimization of children: Conceptual, developmental, research, and clinical issues.* Binghamton, NY: Haworth Press.

Shapiro, D., Walker, L., Manosevitz, M., Peterson, M., & Williams, M. (2008). *Surviving a licensing board complaint: What to do, what not to do.* Phoenix, AZ: Zeig, Tucker, & Theisen.

Silvern, L., & Kaersvang, L. (1989). The traumatized children of violent marriages. *Child Welfare, 68*(4), 421–436.

Singer, M. I., Anglin, T. M., Song, L. Y., & Lunghofer, L. (1995). Adolescents' exposure to violence and associated symptoms of psychological trauma. *Journal of the American Medical Association, 273,* 477–482.

Straus, M. A., Gelles, R. J., & Steinmetz, S. K. (1980). *Behind closed doors: Violence in the American family.* Garden City, NY: Anchor/Doubleday.

Terr, L. (1990). *Too scared to cry.* New York, NY: Harper & Row.

Walker, L. E. A. (2010). Child physical abuse and maltreatment. In J. C. Thomas & M. Hersen (Eds.), *Handbook of clinical psychology competencies.* New York, NY: Springer.

Washburne, C. K. (1983). A feminist analysis of child abuse and neglect. In D. Finkelhor, R. J. Gelles, C. Hotaling, & M. Straus (Eds.), *The dark side of families* (pp. 289–292). Beverly Hills, CA: Sage.

Wedding, D., Boyd, M., & Niemiec, R. M. (2005). *Movies & mental illness: Using films to understand psychopathology* (2nd ed.). Cambridge, MA: Hogrefe & Huber.

Wolak, J., & Finkelhor, D. (1998). Children exposed to partner violence. In J. L. Jasinski & L. M. Williams (Eds.), *Partner violence: A comprehensive review of 20 years of research* (pp. 73–112). Thousand Oaks, CA: Sage.

CHAPTER SEVEN

CHILD ABUSE AND DOMESTIC VIOLENCE

*A*ssessment of the impact of child abuse on children, especially those who are also exposed to parental violence, has been difficult to obtain partly because children are not believed nor are their mothers. Rather, equal time is given to the accused abusers who deny, blame others, and accuse mothers of lying and causing their children to become alienated from them. Collecting accurate data is difficult given these biases even when incontrovertible evidence is presented. There are many reasons for this, including the variable definitions of what actually constitutes child abuse and lack of understanding of the impact of trauma and abuse on the developing child's brain and other functions. Funding difficulties of the child protection service agencies and dependency courts make it easier to simply follow the legislative mandates toward the policy of reunification of the family despite its destructiveness for the child's future. Some of these issues are discussed in this chapter.

Despite the problems, the empirical evidence about the exact nature of the impact on children of witnessing or experiencing family violence has grown during the past 40 years. Our data have added a little more to the still small knowledge base. While we asked some direct questions concerning child development, most of our data are inferred from open-ended responses and thus must be cautiously interpreted. However, it is important to add these data to the knowledge base as they are from a more heterogeneous sample, while most of the other studies come from homogeneous samples of children who are in shelters or under state care and have been exposed to the most serious forms of abuse. In the original study, we dealt with ethical and legal issues that forced us to deliberately sacrifice the ability to question our subjects directly about present or potential child abuse because of the difficulty posed by Colorado's mandatory child abuse reporting law. If you remember, this study was conducted predominantly in Denver. However, we are aware that most studies on child abuse indicate that in more than half of them, abuse of their mothers has also occurred, usually by the same perpetrator (American Psychological Association [APA], 1996).

As a licensed psychologist and principal investigator of the original research grant, too, I was in the category of professionals who must report any *suspicion* of harm to a child. In some states, the law requires some actual *knowledge* or *belief* of harm, a different standard. *Willful nonreport* of suspected abuse would have been grounds for removal of my license to practice psychology and criminal prosecution. As the principal investigator, all project staff were under my supervision, which also made me liable for reporting any evidence they *suspected* or *uncovered* during the interviews. The widespread community publicity announcing our original project caused several Colorado juvenile court judges at that time to assure us that we were going to be held responsible to report any disclosures relevant to *potential, suspected,* or *current* child abuse. Failure to report, we were told, would result in immediate prosecution despite our protests that accuracy of our data could be compromised if we were forced to report past or suspicions of child abuse. Nor would the U.S. Department of Justice's Certificate of Confidentiality, which was intended to protect our data from being subpoenaed in a court action, suffice to protect the project. Today, these issues have been taken care of in research projects looking directly at child abuse, but back in the late 1970s this was the first project to directly assess for the impact of domestic violence on the family.

This unexpected difficulty caused us to revise our original intent to collect data on perceived child abuse in homes where women were being battered. Instead, we compromised by asking about past child abuse and discipline procedures. We also agreed we would make a formal report if we inadvertently uncovered any current instances of child abuse. Since our research was designed to measure women's perceptions of events, there was no way to verify the accuracy of their self-reported data. Therefore, unlike in clinical interviews, potential risk for child abuse could not be directly ascertained from the questions we asked, and thus, could not be considered "willful nonreport" as the statute demanded. The resolution satisfied the Colorado legal community, the National Institute of Mental Health (NIMH) funders, and did not compromise the project goals.

As a result of our dilemma, NIMH and the Department of Justice have negotiated a new agreement that extends the certificate of confidentiality to protect research projects needing to collect such sensitive child abuse data without being subject to the numerous states' mandatory report laws. There are also newer statistical techniques that allow for systematic sampling that can overcome this problem. We found that establishing personal contact with understanding child protective services caseworkers guarded against possible punitive responses toward those few women for whom we did file a report, with their knowledge and cooperation.

A SHORT HISTORY OF CHILD ABUSE LAWS

Although it seems difficult to believe, the mandatory reporting of child abuse and neglect began only in the mid-1960s with pediatricians Henry Kempe (Kempe & Helfer, 1972) at the University of Colorado and David Gil (1970) at Brandeis University each writing a book detailing their research results that found far more incidents of child abuse and neglect than had ever before been suspected. By the early 1970s, most states had passed child abuse reporting laws and began to collect data of reported cases. The National Center on Child Abuse and Neglect (NCAN) and its statistics branch (National Child Abuse and Neglect Data System [NCANDS]) were established within the executive branch of the U.S. government in 1974 with the Child Abuse Prevention and Treatment Act (CAPTA; PL-93-247) that provided for uniform definition of the different forms of child maltreatment. By 2003, there were 2.9 million referrals regarding over 1 million children made to child protective services (CPS) around the United States with approximately one third subsequently being substantiated. During that year 1,500 children reportedly died from child abuse or neglect. Most of the reports made to CPS agencies are for neglect rather than physical abuse. Reports that cannot be substantiated but still might be legitimate abuse are called "unfounded" and the rest are considered as not being reportable abuse (U.S. Department of Health and Human Services [USDHHS], 2005). Psychologists and other mental health professionals are asked to work closely with the judicial and executive branches of government in order to properly assess and treat many of these children and their families.

Interestingly, child abuse and neglect are treated as serious problems all over the world, although there are cross-cultural differences in definitions of "abuse" and "neglect" that are most likely related to the amount of resources a particular country can provide to children in general as well as when identified as "at risk" (Bottoms & Goodman, 1996). The Convention on the Rights of the Child (CRC) was developed by the United Nations over a 10-year period to protect the human rights of the child by banning discrimination against children and affirming special protection and rights appropriate to minors. Specifically, children have the right to survival, to develop to their fullest, to be protected from harm including abuse and exploitation, and to participate fully in family, cultural, and social life. Guidelines also govern health care, education, legal, civil, and social services. All member nations have signed the document except for the United States and Somalia (UNICEF, 1989). The United States claims it will ratify the document as soon as it determines it is not in conflict with any of the myriad of laws that impact children (Schwartz & McCauley, 2007). But meanwhile, children have no legal rights in the United States, which I believe adds to the problem of their lack of sufficient protection by the courts.

What Is Child Abuse?

In 1974, the U.S. Congress passed what is called the "CAPTA law" (Child Abuse Prevention and Treatment Act) where child abuse and neglect were defined in broad terms that described injuries to the child and harm to the child's welfare. Over the years, the definitions have been clarified and in 1996, the U.S. Congress changed the definitions to:

> [T]he term "child abuse and neglect" means, at a minimum, any recent act or failure to act on the part of a parent or caretaker, which results in death, serious physical or emotional harm, sexual abuse or exploitation, or an act or failure to act which presents an imminent risk of serious harm. (Federal Child Abuse Prevention and Treatment Act, 1999)

The International Society for the Prevention of Child Abuse and Neglect (ISPCAN) has collected research throughout the world and behaviorally defined abuse and neglect (ISPCAN, 2008). Although most countries define child physical abuse as any nonaccidental injuries inflicted upon the child or placing the child in harm such as allowing children to live on the streets or be forced into sex trafficking, the definition of neglect may have more differences based on regional, cultural, and religious values. It has also been stated that these data reveal that more-developed countries with resources for services for children may have broader definitions of neglect that those countries with fewer available services (Schwartz & McCauley, 2007). This is also true when there are jurisdictional issues such as cases filed in both dependency court for abuse and family court for dissolution of marriage. The bottom line is that those with authority do not want to believe that child abuse is as rampant as it actually is.

Kleinman and Kaplan (2015) in a recent article criticized the child protection field and specifically attorneys and judges for citing unproven statistics that exaggerate the number of false allegations of child abuse. They call for more science in order to better protect children. In Chapter 19, our research substantiates their claims that children are both intentionally and unintentionally left unprotected because of the biases both implicit and explicit against believing fathers who batter the child's mother also abuse the child.

CHILD ABUSE CORRELATES IN THE ORIGINAL RESEARCH

Despite the difficulties in data collection described previously and our subsequent compromises, our results on child abuse in our sample are consistent with other researchers in this area. It is interesting to note that 87% of the women reported that the children were aware of the violence in their homes even if they did not directly witness it. Most field workers now believe that closer to 100% of children who live in domestic violence homes are aware of their fathers' abuse against their mothers despite a parent's attempt to cover it up, even if they do not discuss their perceptions with anyone, including their mothers. The APA Task Force on Violence and the Family (1996) considered treating the abuse of children exposed to domestic violence as a form of nonphysical child abuse because of the similarity of the psychological effects that also occur with other forms of child abuse. The damage to children from trauma and subsequent posttraumatic stress disorder (PTSD) includes neurobiological changes in brain development (see Research on Impact of Child Abuse and Maltreatment section). Many child protective services agencies in different states now require the reporting of children living in homes where intimate partner violence (IPV) is occurring, even though most states do not require reporting domestic violence itself.

These results also point to the inadequacy of understanding this form of child abuse and neglect in the previous, more medically oriented child abuse literature such as is represented by Helfer and Kempe (1974) that stress can physically injure children. Often, their condemnation of the mother for not protecting her child overlooked the possibility that she might have been without the ability to control the man's violent behavior against herself or her children. Perhaps the most visible case where this was dramatically seen was with Hedda Nussbaum who could not protect her 6-year-old daughter, Lisa Steinberg, from her husband's abuse of the child because she too was being abused by him.

Hedda Nussbaum was an author and editor for a major New York publishing firm while her common-law husband, Joel Steinberg, was a successful lawyer. However, he battered her and the children, sometimes while under the influence of cocaine, and eventually killed 6-year-old Lisa. Steinberg was found guilty of manslaughter and sentenced to prison. Hedda Nussbaum was not arrested but was condemned by the public for failure to protect Lisa and her younger brother who was not physically abused (Brownmiller, 1988). I suggested that perhaps any other intervention she might have done could have made things worse, perhaps even getting them all killed (Walker, 1989). Nussbaum has spent many years recovering from her own mental health and substance abuse issues and today speaks against domestic violence around the world.

In the legal cases in which we have consulted there have been other cases where the mother has been blamed for the father's abusive behavior, resulting in the death of a child. Most recently, I was involved in an appeal for a California woman who had already spent 20 years in prison for not stopping her husband from starving their son who died from malnutrition, surely a form of child abuse under any definition. However, the extenuating circumstances that were not permitted to be testified to at her trial were the inability of either his parents or hers to stop him despite the fact that they knew he abused her and that child, locking both in their rooms, and closely monitoring the food they could eat. Barely 16 years old when this child was born, she had three more babies quickly, and was unable to parent all of them in the abusive home in which she lived. Escape seemed impossible to her as it is for many battered women and, although she was diagnosed as depressed with PTSD at the time of her trial, the court and jury did not pay attention to how her mental condition impacted her inability to protect her son.

In other cases where mothers have been in dangerous abusive relationships where they have been unable to protect their children, they too have been charged with first-degree murder or even a capital crime requesting the death penalty. In some of these cases, the woman has falsely confessed to being the abuser in order to protect her partner who actually committed the abuse leading to the child's death. I discuss some of these issues further in a later chapter on false confessions.

Can Battered Women Protect Their Children?

Our original research found a high overlap between partner and child abuse. While living together in a battering relationship, over one half (53%) of the men who abused their partners reportedly also abused their children. This result compares favorably with other research that suggests as high as a 60% overlap between child and woman abuse. Further, one third of the batterers also threatened to physically harm the children whether they did it or not. This compares with about a quarter of the women (28%) who said they abused their children when living in a violent home, and 6% who threatened to abuse the children. Clearly, in our sample, children were at greater risk of being hurt by the batterers, although not out of harm's way from a quarter of their mothers who were being abused themselves.

One of the more popular myths about child abuse and family violence is that the man beats the woman, the woman beats the child, and the child beats the dog. It is so common that even nursery rhymes tell of such a hierarchy. Given its popularity, we tried to measure whether or not the woman abused her children when angry with the batterer. We found that 5% of the women said they did use physical violence against the children when angry with the batterer. But, only 0.6% of the women said they did so when living in a nonviolent relationship. This supports the notion that anger begets more anger. Violence begets more violence. Some newer research is suggesting that it is not just abuse that creates the psychological harm to children but also the environment within which abuse takes place. For example, Gold (1997) has found that the impact from child sexual abuse can be moderated or buffered by some positive social supports in the family environment. However, his research also found that most homes where incest has occurred had a very dysfunctional environment in addition to the sexually inappropriate behavior that occurred.

Our mothers said they were eight times more likely to hurt their children while they were being battered than when they felt safe from violence. Less than 1% said they occasionally used physical force against the children to get something from the batterer. Thus, from our data, it can be concluded that the level of reported child abuse by the women was low enough to disprove the pecking order myth. The alternate possibility, which is that men who beat their wives also beat their children, has much more support from these data. However, although many of these mothers were unable to totally protect their children from the batterer's psychological power and control abuses, they were better able to protect them when living with the batterer than when they tried to terminate the relationship. We discuss the reasons for this more fully in the later chapter on family court and its inability to protect these children when parents divorce.

Can Society Really Protect Our Children?

In analyzing why mothers seem to get so much of child protective services caseworkers' and child abuse experts' wrath, the most plausible explanation seems to be the prevailing view that women are expected to take care of their children and prevent them from harm no matter what the cost to themselves. In families with a high risk of incest, the presence of a strong mother reportedly does prevent serious child abuse (APA, 1996). Positive parenting by mothers can moderate against damages from exposure to abuse. Thus, the focus of some child abuse treatment programs has been to help women become better wives and mothers, often without realization that these women were also victims of terrible intimate partner abuse. Others, such as children's programs in battered women shelters, focus on cognitively restructuring the family to define it as a mother–child bond without the inclusion of the father. Unfortunately, the divorce courts do not accept this model and often perpetuate the abusive environment by failing to protect either the mother or the child from the abuser. Forensic mental health experts who specialize in child custody evaluations come more from the perspective of child protection and rarely understand how to support and reempower the mother who has been abused. Rather, they often mistake the mother's behavior as causing alienation and estrangement of the child toward the father, instead of accepting that children exposed to parental domestic violence may be frightened of the father because of his controlling and often psychologically abusive behavior rarely seen by the evaluation instruments used by these forensic evaluators. The controversy about parental alienation syndrome and other similar so-called mental illnesses perpetuates further abuse of children.

Although the long-term consequences on the child's mental health when redefining the family unit have not yet been established, the critics have attacked this model as being evidence of women's vindictiveness and labeled it as *parental alienation syndrome* using old models of the two-parent home as needing to be extended to the child's equal contact with two parents. Gardner (1987, 1992), who was one of the loudest critics, stated that he exempted domestic violence cases from his model, but then he redefined domestic violence in his own way often excluding cases that had police evidence of physical abuse if they did not meet his idiosyncratic criteria. These issues are further discussed in what follows.

Washburne (1983) examined how child welfare programs reinforce traditional female role patterns rather than help women develop skills to strengthen their ability to be independent and strong. She cites examples of how a woman who wants her children returned from foster care placement is often required to clean up her home and improve her appearance. One of our subjects was in serious jeopardy of losing her children in a custody fight because, when the assigned caseworker made an unannounced home visit, she was feeding the children dinner from MacDonald's restaurants! It would be more beneficial to parents and children to teach them nonsexist parenting skills in treatment programs than perpetuating stereotyped roles that are no longer valid in our lives.

Interestingly, many abusive men are now using the child welfare system to retaliate against women who accuse them of being batterers. Forced to coparent children, they call the child abuse hotline if they see a bruise on the child, refusing to accept the mother's explanation of how it occurred. Public Advocate Betsy Gotbaum was so concerned about the increase in these false calls that she prepared a report for her supervisors in New York City (Gotbaum, 2008). Given the concern about the malicious use of the city's child abuse reporting laws, they established a program to monitor these calls and developed ways to prosecute offenders. In Fort Lauderdale, Florida, the Broward Sheriff Organization has developed guidelines to assess a batterer for harassment by using cell phone text messages from the batterer to the woman. Telephone and text messages as frequent as 50 or more per day have been seen, especially when the woman has parenting time with a child. Continued use of the telephone, e-mails, social media, or text messaging from and to cell phones is a newer form of harassment and a way to continue power and control over the woman by the man with the use of technology.

Modeling Nonviolent Behavior

Modeling learned behavior of parents is probably the most powerful way that violence as a strategy gets passed down to the next generation. In a 25-year longitudinal study, Miller and Challas (1981) found that men who were abused as children were almost two times more likely to become abusive parents than were women. While they do not look at the natural reinforcement of male aggression in a sexist society, their conclusions certainly support such a concept. In the original research, we attempted to measure the differences between men and women on their attitudes toward the role of women. Our results indicated that there were widespread differences, consistent with sex-role conditioning. Given the consistency of most of the literature on the gender issues in violent relationships, we did not continue to measure it in the new research.

RESEARCH ON IMPACT OF CHILD ABUSE AND MALTREATMENT

The research on the impact of trauma such as child abuse and maltreatment of children demonstrates that many areas of their lives are negatively affected in a variety of different ways. Most important is the Adverse Childhood Experiences (ACEs) Study described in the previous chapter of this book where the lifelong health and mental health consequences of adverse childhood experiences disprove the old adage that children will forget and grow up "just fine" if abuse and trauma are not discussed. Many children do learn to accommodate and do "just fine" but imagine what their potential could have been. Let us look at a few areas described in the following sections.

Neurological Development

The research on the development of children's brains and nervous systems has grown significantly in the past 20 years given the new imaging techniques that can measure cell activity in the various brain structures. Psychiatrist Bessel van der Kolk has been studying the impact on the brain and body from abuse for most of his career. Earlier he formulated the theory that the body remembers the bruises even when the brain forgets. Most recently in his 2014 book, *The Body Keeps the Score: Brain, Mind, and Body in the Healing of Trauma,* van der Kolk details the findings from the new brain scans that suggest that violence changes everything. Comparing data from combat soldiers and children's experiences of PTSD, it becomes possible to better understand how abuse impacts the entire nervous system. In young children, trauma from abuse actually changes the structure as well as the function of the nervous system.

In a review of the neurobiological aspects of PTSD, Painter and Scannapieco (2013) describe some of the life-changing effects on the child when abuse occurs during the critical times of brain development. Trauma can negatively impact cognitive, behavioral, social and affective functioning as well as result in personality changes and other mental health disorders. As we know, the brain is made up of millions of cells called "neurons" that group together in systems for various functions. The structures in the brain that develop in a child include the brain stem that regulates most of the autonomic nervous system (ANS) functions that keep us breathing, our heart pumping, and alive. The limbic system actually is located in the midbrain area and is made up of structures that regulate our emotions and formulation of memories, particularly trauma memories that eventually may get stored in the cortex or thinking center of the brain, the central nervous system (CNS). In the limbic system is located the reticular activating system (RAS) that is involved in arousal, anxiety, and modulation of limbic and cortical processing.

In the limbic system are several other structures such as the hypothalamus, hippocampus, amygdala, and locus coeruleus, all of which have specific functions. For example, the hypothalamus regulates the ability to control anger and aggressive behavior as well as physical things such as hunger, pleasure, sexual satisfaction, and the ANS. The hippocampus works with the ANS and stores trauma memories that often have all the emotions as well as other senses attached and stored as they occurred. Unlike the cognitive memory storage system in the cortex of the brain, memories in the hippocampus cannot be retrieved easily since many do not have verbal labels on them. It is also believed that the hippocampus plays a role in regulating socially appropriate behaviors and is involved in learning. If there are too many noradrenergic influences from stress, it is thought that the hippocampus is involved in anxiety and panic attacks. PTSD is known to cause damage to both the development of and function of the neurons in the hippocampus, including damaging dendrites where the electrical nerve impulses originate. It is also believed that the hippo-campus may be where dissociative symptoms originate.

Although it is not known exactly how the amygdala and hippocam-pus work together, it is thought that the cognitive aspects of the memory storage are more likely to occur in the hippocampus and the emotional aspects are stored in the amygdala. It is most sensitive to *kindling*, which is the spontaneous electrical discharges resulting in long-term alterations in neuronal excitability that then can impact behavior. The amygdala also plays a role in emotional memory processing, interpreting and integrat-ing emotional functions, fear conditioning, and control of aggressive, oral, and sexual behavior. It is also involved in motor behavior, the ANS, and neuroendocrine areas of the CNS and is important to help us recognize threats if they appear. Damage to the amygdala, however, can play a role in reliving the traumatic experience by recognizing similarity with a threat.

Why go into all this detail about neurological functioning, you may be asking? It is important to understand that exposure to child abuse and other trauma can and does interfere with the development of these and other significant brain structures and functions that are then responsible for some of the trauma symptoms seen in children and adults. When sub-ject to such extreme stressors, such as abuse and violence, we respond by releasing hormones such as cortisol and adrenaline, which are also known to damage neurological structures and functions. These and other bio-chemicals change the brain and other body systems such as cardiovascu-lar, respiratory, and muscular in fundamental ways. We know more about how these changes impact the adult nervous system than we do about chil-dren. But, those studies that are available point to the changes in structure and biochemical output that then change how the system reacts.

For example, in normal brain functioning, memories stored in the limbic system are thought to be processed and moved into the thinking area or brain cortex. But children who have experienced violence and abuse may remain in a state of constant hyperarousal or even a dissocia-tive state, where they focus on less painful stimuli and have fragmented memories of the abuse. These memories may not be moved automatically into the cognitive memory system and need to be assisted such as during trauma-specific psychotherapy. The high levels of stress can produce irre-versible changes in all the neurological activation systems without treat-ment. They may automatically overreact to stimuli that nonabused children would not find threatening. Prompts in the environment that are called "trauma triggers" may set off fear and anxiety responses. These triggers can continue to dominate in the child's life and even later in life if they encounter similar situations.

Interesting, the younger the child is when exposed to abuse, the more likely the child will respond with a dissociative response. This is due to the limited resources young children have to find other ways of protection when their caregivers on whom they depend become the abusers. We discuss the damage to personality and ability to attach securely in other interpersonal relationships as they get older in a later chapter on attachment and other disorders from abuse. There is not a lot of research on children who dissociate, although it is known that they are more likely to be daydreamers, fantasize a lot, or exhibit depersonalization and derealization symptoms. In the new diagnostic manual, dissociation is now considered a part of PTSD. Extreme forms of dissociation can lead to a personality disorder called "dissociative identity disorder" (DID) where they may have split off parts of their personality and ascribe it to others, called "alters." This is a serious disorder and needs intensive psychotherapy to heal. Psychologist Joyanna Silberg's 2013 book, *The Child Survivor: Healing Developmental Trauma and Dissociation,* is an excellent resource for those working with these children. Psychologist Elaine Ducharme's 2015 book is another excellent resource for those working with adults who have been diagnosed with DID.

Emotional Regulation

Children who have experienced child abuse have been known to struggle with the ability to regulate their emotions in several ways. First, they are prone to extremes in emotions where their feelings about things are either more emotional or more withdrawn than others might be. When they get angry about something, they cannot modify or release the angry feelings easily or quickly. So, they stay angry longer. If they have been conditioned to certain strong feelings when confronted with a problem, those feelings may be triggered by other similar problems whereas nonabused children might not tie together two different things. These children grow up always expecting something bad to happen so they are hypervigilant and quick to use self-protection. For example, if someone raises his or her hand to stretch, the abused child may quickly react as if there will be a slap coming next.

Always fearing what may come next, usually because there is little stability in their young lives, these children often become pleasers; that is, they try to keep the abusive parent calm by doing whatever it is that the parent will respond to. Those who have watched their abused mothers calm down their abusive fathers may repeat what the mothers do. This behavior is more commonly seen in girls, although boys also engage in keeping the abusers calm. There are gender differences reported in the literature with girls becoming more withdrawn and turning their feelings inwardly while boys are more likely to act out aggressively. High levels of mood disorders such as fear, anxiety, and depression are commonly seen in these children. As we know, depression in children is often seen in "acting out" behavior rather than symptoms seen in adults. These children often turn to substances to numb the extreme emotions that they cannot regulate in normal ways. We discuss substance abuse further in a later chapter.

PTSD is the most commonly diagnosed disorder in abused children, although some of the symptoms are not easily seen in young children who often show dysregulation of their body functions. Children who are sexually abused are often conflicted emotionally; on one hand, they may appreciate the extra attention from the abusive parent's grooming behaviors, but on the other hand, they dislike the abuse itself and the demands that are made on them. Many become alienated from one or the other parent as trying to please both becomes too difficult. Some simply walk away from the family, understanding that nothing they can do will make it all right for them.

Lucy was a 15-year-old girl when I first met her as she was referred for a psychological evaluation to determine if she was capable of being legally emancipated from her parents and family. Lucy had been sexually abused by her 3-year older brother since she was 9 years old. Her parents found out after Lucy had a seizure in school at age 13 and was taken to the hospital where she disclosed the sexual abuse. Her parents, who fought with each other all the time, became angry with her when her 16-year-old brother was arrested by the police and placed in a juvenile detention center. Eventually he was sent to live with a grandparent and Lucy was permitted to go home. However, her parents kept blaming her for "ruining her brother's life" and begged her to recant her story. Previously an A student, her grades began to drop and she was in danger of failing some classes. In psychotherapy and on psychotropic medication, Lucy refused to recant, and angry with her parents for not supporting her, she ran away from home.

This is not an atypical story for runaway children, most of whom fail to get parental support when they disclose the abuse, particularly the sexual abuse, by another family member. Unlike those who often get picked up by sex traffickers, as described in the next chapter, Lucy got picked up by security and taken to a juvenile shelter where she met Andrea. They became girlfriends and were physically intimate very quickly, each needing the other for emotional support. When I saw her she had obtained her general equivalency diploma (GED) from high school and, instead of going to college, she wanted to get a job, move out of the shelter, get an apartment with Andrea, and never see her parents or family again. Her test results indicated that despite some of the effects of PTSD on her cognition; her intellectual abilities were still very high and she would probably succeed in a college program rather than getting a job with which she might grow bored within a short period of time.

If Lucy remained in state custody at least until she was 18 years old, she could receive state support to go to college provided she got good grades. If she were emancipated, then she would lose those benefits and maybe others, too. A better resolution for Lucy would be to apply and be accepted to a local college if she wanted to remain with Andrea and move into the dorms there with state support. The difficulty was to make it clear that until Lucy was ready, even if it was never, she should not be forced to be reunified with her parents whose betrayal of trust was a fundamental breach in their previously dysfunctional relationship. This turned out to be more complicated than expected, although with a strong lawyer and a judge who really listened to the best interests of the child and did not try to compromise with the parents' interests, things worked out for Lucy in the end.

Cognitive Functioning and School Learning

The 2013 edition of the *Diagnostic and Statistical Manual of Mental Disorders* (5th ed.; *DSM-5*; American Psychiatric Association, 2013) added a new category to the criteria needed to make the diagnosis of PTSD that included cognitive confusion, poor concentration, and attention disorders. The symptoms were already accounted for across the other three groups of PTSD criteria as discussed in the earlier chapter, but it emphasized the impact on intellectual functioning, judgment, impulsivity, and learning skills. Many of these abused children have learning disabilities; sometimes because they have inconsistent school attendance due to parental difficulties and other times because they are not mentally available to pay attention and learn the required information presented at school. They may be hungry from poor eating habits or even lack access to proper nutrition. They may be tired after being kept up all night listening to parents fighting.

Abused children have damaged self-esteem and loss of belief in their own efficacy, so they do not try to do anything that seems difficult to them. They often have negative self-evaluation and guilt feelings especially if they are unable to protect their mothers or siblings from their fathers' anger. They do not trust others to be able to help and fear that another person will just make the situation worse. In and out of the child protection system, these children feel more comfortable on their own than in a foster home. Although many foster homes are friendly, warm, positive experiences for many children, some are very abusive and only cause further damage to the children's self-esteem and lack of ability to cope with the aftermath of the trauma.

Social and Interpersonal Functioning

Some believe that the idealization of what life *should* be like and the reality of what it really *is* like is an important part of the disillusionment that comes with being an abused child in the system. One of the most significantly impacted areas of the abused child's life is difficulty in social functioning and interpersonal relationships. They are impulsive and go from receptivity to reactivity in a nanosecond with little or no separation between their impulse and their action. Their entire system is on alert all the time, which impacts their social behavior and interpersonal functioning. The children who heal from child abuse are those who can make friends with other children and people. Because they are constantly misinterpreting others' behavior toward them, they often confront another person who is trying to be friendly and cause that person to move away. They are mistrustful of the intentions of others and often seem paranoid as they are always blaming or anticipating something terrible will happen.

WHAT CAN WE DO?

Can the CPS System Be Fixed?

It is important to think about whether the CPS system can be fixed to really protect children and their families. I believe that some children, maybe many children, are still alive because of CPS intervention. The

NCANDS data from 2013, the latest year analyzed, indicate 23,000 fewer children died that year than the year before.

But of the huge numbers of children who are abused each year all over the world, very few are actually reported. In the United States in 2013, CPS agencies in each state reported that there were over 3 million calls with only 60% acted upon in some way. It is unclear why 40% of the calls get screened out. Most of the alleged perpetrators are family members with more women being accused of child maltreatment than men who are more likely to be accused of physical and sexual abuse. In fact, almost 80% of all reported cases are for neglect while 18% are for physical abuse and 9% for sexual abuse. Given the difficulties in assessment for sexual abuse of children, these numbers appear to be extremely low. So too for those children who are caught in the middle of their parents' divorce, especially when there has been domestic violence.

Of the 60% of calls screened in, there are several known risk factors. Perhaps most important is the risk of poverty. One quarter of the cases involved people who were receiving public assistance, with another 10% who claimed to have financial problems. This means one third of the families where a child has reportedly been abused or neglected might be prevented if medical or psychological services were available without being tied to finances. Further, if there were more services available for families, including caseworkers with lower case loads and more training to deal with complex situations, other children might also be protected. But as the current system is structured, it does not seem likely that abuse can be prevented.

Daniel Pollack, a social work professor who is critical of how CPS functions, states that the coercion and bias that is shown during their investigations of child abuse may also keep people from using the system. He and others such as attorney Toby Kleinman have claimed in their 2015 book, *Social Work and the Courts: A Casebook,* that CPS is a coercive system couched in a helping wrapper. They give example after example of where mistakes were made that, had the intervention been appropriate, children would be saved. Psychological maltreatment, which is the category in which children exposed to domestic violence would most likely be classified, is reported in less than 10% of all the cases with which CPS deals.

In most countries, including the United States, it is difficult for people to permit the authorities into their homes voluntarily. Privacy of our family is especially prized in the United States and it is difficult to let anyone look inside. Even when other family members or close friends notice something is wrong, they rarely believe it is their responsibility to help the family fix their problems. In some countries where labor is cheap, it is possible to send child care workers into the homes where abuse or neglect has been reported. In other countries where the extended family forms a kinship network, other members of the family take responsibility when a child is in danger. This system works well when those responsible are not also abusive toward the child. In the United States, it is not unusual for CPS to place children in the home of relatives for what they term "kinship care." However, those relatives are not properly vetted to see how the children are getting along there. We hear stories of children who are left in the unsupervised contact with an abusive parent, a grandparent who has her or his own substance abuse problems, or family members who have so many children to care for that none get the attention they so desperately need.

Can Psychotherapy Help?

Newer psychotherapy strategies called "trauma-specific treatment" may help children who have been abused heal from the trauma. I discuss them in a later chapter on trauma-informed and specific psychotherapy. Psychologist Ricky Greenwald has developed treatment techniques that include accurate assessment and treatment strategies when trauma occurs. There are also new strategies using medication if it is administered immediately after the trauma has occurred to prevent the development of the traumatic memories that continue to trigger the PTSD symptoms. As it has not been approved for children, it is still in an experimental phase. Play therapy, the standard treatment for helping children heal from trauma, has a variety of additions that attempt to rebuild trust relationships as well as reduce anxiety, depression, dissociation, and other symptoms. But, treatment of children is fraught with problems, including keeping parents, especially those who have been abusive, involved in the child's healing when the child is ready to begin working on reunification, not when the court orders it. Far too many cases of neglect deal with parents who have substance abuse issues and trauma symptoms of their own, which do not permit them to put their child first. Removing the child from the home and placing them in foster care homes may seem like a good idea, but it cannot substitute for the child's need for the parents' love and attention.

States have tried to normalize the lives of children whose parents are unable to complete their own treatment plans and become responsible parents for their children by instituting relinquishment proceedings. Many of these mothers and fathers are trauma survivors themselves who have not had trauma treatment even though they may have had numerous rounds of substance abuse therapy and other psychotherapy. Relapses are common if the underlying trauma reactions are not dealt with also. Termination of parental rights does allow permanency planning for the child so they can be adopted, usually by a foster family where they have bonded or a relative who is willing to take on the responsibility. Although this helps the child have a secure home, it does not help the longing for the idealized parent who will love them. It is not unusual for these children, like others who are adopted for different reasons, to search for their parent(s) once they age out of the system. In some cases, it may undo all the positive gains the child has made, throwing them back into a negative and abusive home. We can do better for these children and their families.

SUMMARY

The complex relationship between child abuse and domestic violence has been addressed in this chapter. The exact overlap between children who are being abused in families where their mothers are also being abused by their fathers or stepfathers is not known, although child abuse is thought to be occurring in at least half of the homes. However, if psychological abuse that occurs from all the turmoil, chaos, and psychological maltreatment is counted as part of child abuse, which the data from several major studies show is an important precursor to negative health and criminal justice issues, then all children in homes where domestic violence occurs should be considered abused also. Obviously the child protective services system in the United States and other countries could not handle this number of referrals, so other remedies should be explored. Most important is the legal and psychological empowerment of the children exposed to violence and the availability of services wherever needed.

REFERENCES

American Psychiatric Association. (2013). *Diagnostic and statistical manual of mental disorders* (5th ed.). Arlington, VA: American Psychiatric Publishing.

American Psychological Association. (1996). *Report from the Presidential Task Force on Violence and the Family.* Washington, DC: Author.

Bottoms, B. L., & Goodman, G. S. (Eds.). (1996). *International perspectives on child abuse and children's testimony: Psychological research and law.* Newbury Park, CA: Sage.

Brownmiller, S. (1988). *Waverly Place.* New York, NY: Simon & Schuster.

Ducharme, E. (2015). *Assessment and treatment of dissociative identity disorder.* Camp Hill, PA: The Practice Institute.

Federal Child Abuse Prevention and Treatment Act (CAPTA), 42 U.S.C. § 5106g(2) (1999).

Gardner, R. (1987). *The parental alienation syndrome and the differentiation between fabrication and genuine child abuse.* Creskill, NJ: Creative Therapeutics.

Gardner, R. (1992). *True and false accusations of child sex abuse.* Creskill, NJ: Creative Therapeutics.

Gil, D. G. (1970). *Violence against children.* Cambridge, MA: Harvard University Press.

Gold, S. N. (1997). Training professional psychologists to treat survivors of childhood sexual abuse. *Psychotherapy, 34,* 365–374.

Gotbaum, B. (2008). *Calling in abuse: How domestic violence perpetrators are using the child welfare system to continue their abuse.* A report by Public Advocate of New York City. Retrieved from www.pubadvocate.nyc.gov

Helfer, E. R., & Kempe, C. H. (1974). *The battered child* (2nd ed.). Chicago, IL: University of Chicago Press.

International Society for Prevention of Child Abuse and Neglect. (2008). *World perspectives on child abuse* (8th ed.). Retrieved from https://c.ymcdn.com/sites/www.ispcan.org/resource/resmgr/world_perspectives/world_persp_2008_-_final.pdf

Kempe, C. H., & Helfer, R. E. (Eds.). (1972). *Helping the battered child and his family.* Philadelphia, PA: Lippincott.

Kleinman, T., & Kaplan, P. (2016). Relaxation of rules for science detrimental for children. *Journal of Child Custody, 13*(1), 72–87.

Miller, D., & Challas, D. (1981, July). *Abused children as adult parents: A twenty-five year longitudinal study.* Paper presented at the National Conference of Family Violence Researchers, University of New Hampshire, Durham.

Painter, K., & Scannapieco, M. (2013). Child maltreatment: The neurobiological aspects of posttraumatic stress disorder. *Journal of Evidence-Based Social Work, 10*(4), 276–284.

Schwartz, B. M., & McCauley, M. (2007). Child abuse: A global perspective. In N. A. Jackson (Ed.), *Encyclopedia of domestic violence* (pp. 119–23). New York, NY: Routledge.

Silberg, J. L. (2013). *The child survivor: Healing developmental trauma and dissociation.* New York, NY: Routledge.

UNICEF. (1989). *Convention on the rights of the child (CRC).* Retrieved from http://www.unicef.org/crc

U.S. Department of Health and Human Services. (2005). *Child maltreatment 2005.* Washington, DC: Author. Retrieved from http://archive.acf.hhs.gov/programs/cb/pubs/cm05/cm05.pdf

Walker, L. E. (1989). *Terrifying love: Why battered women kill and how society responds.* New York, NY: Harper & Row.

Washburne, C. K. (1983). A feminist analysis of child abuse and neglect. In D. Finkelhor, R. J. Gelles, C. Hotaling, & M. Straus (Eds.), *The dark side of families* (pp. 289–292). Beverly Hills, CA: Sage.

CHAPTER EIGHT

SEX TRAFFICKING OF CHILDREN

Why have a chapter on sex and labor trafficking in a book about domestic violence? Easy. The relationship between both forms of exploitation have many commonalities, although there are differences, of course. Estimates range from 20 to 27 million victims of human trafficking in the world. In a 2014 Urban Institute Report, it was estimated that the underground sex economy ranged from $39.9 million just in Denver, Colorado, and $290 million in Atlanta, Georgia. Others estimate that human trafficking is a $150 billion industry globally. Sex trafficking is said to be the second most lucrative crime other than involvement in illegal drug trafficking.

The worldwide movement to stop the international trafficking of people began in the 1990s and it became clear that the belief that many persons engaging in what was then called "prostitution" or the "sex trade" were not doing so voluntarily. Similar issues were raised with the trafficking of people for a new form of slave labor, where people were treated like indentured slaves brought to a new country and exploited by keeping them in debt to the traffickers. As we began to study all forms of human trafficking, the links among the various forms of gender violence became clear. Children exposed to trauma in their homes are the most vulnerable to be lured into a life of exploitation with drugs, promises of fast money, and love. Not until they have been successfully seduced for some time do many of these children realize they may have traded one horrible situation for another. Some families actually sell their children or bring them into the family business so to speak. We call it "survival sex" in some of these cases. Boys and girls, lesbian, gay, bisexual, transgender, and in question (LGBTQ), and other gender nonconforming children all can be victims, but we know more about girls and young women in the sex trafficking industry as they are more likely to seek help as they get older.

While sex trafficking is a global problem, in this chapter we focus more on domestic forms as they relate to our work on domestic violence. A group of faculty and students became interested in studying the problem for several reasons. First the identifying conditions in homes where trafficking occurs often have underlying domestic violence. Second, the attachment of the victim/survivor is similar to the attachment of the battered woman to her batterer. Both love and fear coexist. Third, there are similarities to other forms of child abuse, both intrafamilial and exploitation by coaches, the religious, and other authority figures. Fourth, the predominant psychological symptoms are similar to other trauma survivors with posttraumatic stress disorder (PTSD), depression, and anxiety, and sometimes complex PTSD, and should respond to trauma-specific treatment such as the Survivor Therapy Empowerment Program (STEP). What we did not know until we began working with survivors, but surmised, was the resiliency that many of these survivors showed. We also had to face the fact that some of the female victims became victimizers, some to curry special favors from traffickers and others to use their own power and control needs with others.

WHO ARE THE TRAFFICKING VICTIMS/SURVIVORS?

The statistics are enormous. The U.S. State Department estimates that 600,000 to 800,000 victims are trafficked across international borders each year and that over half of them are children. Like other abused children, they are at higher risk for experiencing long-term physical and mental health conditions. The younger they are, the more likely they will have adverse effects on their neurobiological development such as deficits in emotional regulation, attachment issues, poor self-esteem causing loss of self-confidence and self-efficacy, and impaired cognitive abilities, including educational deficits. Many have developmental delays, language deficits, and poor memory skills that prevent them from escaping their captives. According to the Trafficking in Persons Report (U.S. Department of State, 2007), victims of trafficking in the United States often come from Latin America and the Caribbean, Asia, Europe, and the Pacific Islands. There are known places in Mexico where victims are taken and then distributed throughout the United States. In Europe, the Balkan Countries and Eastern Europe have large numbers of trafficked persons that then are distributed through the wealthier European countries. The recent Syrian refuges have brought with them large numbers of trafficked persons, many of whom have been saved from death by being forced into another form of living death. The need to understand the impact of cultural as well as psychological difficulties for these survivors is enormous. Some members of our research team are involved in a transnational feminist project from which a book, *Sex Trafficking: A Transnational Feminist Perspective,* is being written with contributions from victims/survivors, advocates, and psychologists around the world.

The Polaris Project (www.polarisproject.org) provides information about domestic trafficking victims/survivors in the United States. The National Human Trafficking Resource Center (NHTRC) is located at the Polaris Project where there is a 24-hour trafficking hotline and website where victims can find assistance to become free from trafficking. Others can use the hotline, text, and e-mail resources to make reports or can go online to learn more about safety for trafficking victims/survivors. In 2015, the NHTRC received over 16,000 calls or signals as they count the various contacts and was involved with almost 5,000 victims themselves using text messaging and e-mail. Safe homes have been set up in most states where trafficking victims can go to receive assistance. Arrests for prostitution became rare as it became understood that these young people were not voluntarily selling their bodies; rather, most were being supervised and regulated by their traffickers. Instead, the FBI and Homeland Security began to arrest the traffickers rather than the victims/survivors.

The U.S. government has been active in preventing trafficking, especially with vulnerable children. In 2012, the National Center for Victims of Crime held a roundtable of national, state, and local stakeholders who were active in identification and intervention issues. The child welfare system was identified as a primary source where victims were recruited in the United States. In 2014, an estimated one of six runaways in the United States that were reported to the National Center for Missing and Exploited Children were likely sex trafficking victims. Of these, over two thirds (68%) were in the care of social services or foster care when they ran. Many of these child victims came from homes where child abuse and domestic violence were present. Often they were removed from their homes and placed in foster care where abuse and maltreatment too often followed them. There were recommendations made for changes in policy, legislation, research, training, access to resources, and better legal representation for children in the child welfare system. Professionals began to work together; law enforcement became partners with child welfare staff and mental health workers. In 2015, the U.S. Department of Health and Human Services (DHHS) began a series of stakeholder meetings in different regions of the country with the goal to provide identification, intervention, and prevention by training allied professionals in high sex-trafficking areas. Others who were likely to have contact with these children, such as flight attendants or bus terminal supervisors, were also included. Special units in local police departments were trained to work collaboratively with Homeland Security and the FBI since trafficked victims were often taken beyond the borders of a country.

IDENTIFICATION OF A TRAFFICKED CHILD

Although the Polaris Project mentioned previously has been able to get some small number of trafficking victims to self-identify, this does not happen regularly. Rather, it is more likely that someone or group notes that something is not right and makes a report to child protective services or another community provider. Children then get identified and offered services. As we describe later, working with these children, particularly teenagers, is very difficult especially if they have developed a bond with their trafficker or do not want to give up the money and other benefits from the lifestyle. Many of the identifiers of these children are similar to those who identify a physically or sexually abused or psychologically maltreated child. They often will not speak on their own behalf even if they do know English. Some are no longer in school while others have spotty attendance records. Most have engaged in numerous commercial sex acts and will not cooperate in locating their traffickers. Some live at their workplace with many others in crowded conditions or somewhere else where they are controlled by the traffickers or their appointed lieutenants. Most work unusually long hours and are in a constant state of debility and tired all the time. They often have a heightened sense of fear and distrust of authority.

RECRUITMENT

Vulnerabilities

As mentioned earlier, children who grow up in homes where there is domestic violence and other forms of family dysfunction and abuse are vulnerable to being lured into the sex-trafficking industry. Middle schools are frequently a recruitment site but so are shopping malls and other places where young teens congregate. Girls are often asked to help recruit their friends or at least identify those who are having a difficult time for some reason. The trafficker takes over from there by using seduction and other lures to meet a new girl's needs, give her what she wants, and make her think she is special. Recruiters with others in their trafficked group take their time and use very subtle techniques before they introduce the idea of commercial sex. Many have sex with the girl themselves, first. Some LGBTQ youth who are questioning their own sexuality may also be lured into trafficking without realizing how difficult it might be to get out.

Some traffickers hang out at bus or train stations where they can pick up runaways. These traffickers may use a place to sleep and drugs to entice and keep them, as well as other lures such as a pretty sweater or even the latest color in nail polish. Listening to the stories of those who were trafficked and got out demonstrates the numerous techniques, strategies, and creativity of the traffickers and how they play on the vulnerabilities of those who are chosen.

Lures With Schemes

In one case in which I was asked by the prosecutor's office to testify, the trafficker allegedly stood outside a local jail and watched the girls being released. He would offer those who did not have anyone there to pick them up the opportunity to be trained as a female wrestler and provided a home with other girls in training along with food, clothing, and whatever else they wanted. He would get the other girls to help the new one adjust and once she became comfortable, he would coerce or force her to have sex with him. Sometimes he would tell her that it was to make her more comfortable with her body being touched in different places. For others, he would come into their room when they were sleeping and rape them. Next, he would take a new girl to a party with one or two other girls, where he would tell her she would meet men who could get her good wrestling jobs if she was nice to them.

Most of the girls said they had no idea they were going to be required to have sex with these men. Several women described horrible rapes that occurred when they resisted the men's sexual advances. Other women described how they were supposed to calm down the new victim and help her realize the benefits of being in this man's group. The trafficker then paid the girl a weekly salary but instead of giving her the money directly, he wrote it down in his ledger book, deducting the amount he charged her for rent and wrestling-training activities. At the time of his arrest, none of the girls had wrestling careers as they were too busy being forced into commercial sex activity.

In another case, the trafficker allegedly visited college campuses and picked out attractive but vulnerable young women. He would seduce them with a modeling contract, showing them pictures of other women whom he claimed to have represented to various legitimate modeling agencies. He would lend the girls money to fix themselves up to take glamour photos, and part of the contract was for them to repay the loans once they got the jobs. Then, he would take them to sex parties where they were initially unaware that they would be forced into sex. Once into debt and fearful and embarrassed about their victimization, many of the girls remained under his control, even though they did not live in the same house as he did.

Lures With Gangs

Although gangs have been part of various cultures for as long as we have written history, there is no one definition of what a "gang" is. In the 1970s in the United States and Central and South America, gangs began to expand beyond large cities until they became entrenched in suburban and even rural areas. Today it is known that gangs run massage parlors and have legitimate fronts for all their activities. This development not only increased the number of people who join the various gangs but also expanded gang activity. Many gangs are involved in illegal activity such as those portrayed in the media as the "mafia" or youth gangs such as the "bloods" and "crips." Gangs have also become involved in sex trafficking, which in some gangs has replaced drugs as a major income stream. They have learned that drugs are expendable commodities while trafficking in sex continues to bring in money to support the gang's other activities. Some reports indicate that gangs consider sex trafficking, especially with girls, as a renewable resource that can bring in anywhere between $1,000 and $14,000 a day.

One of the most important activities for some gangs that engage in sex trafficking is their recruitment strategies. Taking advantage of most people's need for affiliation, they persuade others to join them and participate in their activities. Traditionally male-dominated street gangs now recruit girls to join them, demanding sexual activity as part of their membership. The members are encouraged to seek out vulnerable girls who are enticed at first by easy money or drugs. Many of them come from domestic violence homes. As with other recruiters, there is the accumulation of debt or exchange of sexual activity for money or other valuable goods such as clothing, food, shelter, and the sense of belonging. Rarely is force used in recruitment, although drugs are often a powerful tool in keeping the trafficked persons engaged with the gang for their supply. However, it is the affiliation and friendship bonds that are the most important according to those who are survivors.

Is Trafficking Free Choice?

There are some in the trafficking life who insist that they choose this lifestyle freely. For some, they believe in sexual liberalism, where sex is a commodity that is for sale just like other services that people provide. This argument has been made before in the movement to legalize prostitution and indeed has some benefits as is seen in the Netherlands and other countries where prostitutes can obtain free medical care, drug addiction treatment, and safety measures provided by the social welfare state's safety net. There are fewer juvenile runaways, less rape, assault and murder rates, and greater gender equality reported. Nonetheless, the questions remain: Is it really free choice? Are there traffickers, usually male, involved? Can the trafficked person stop the work at any time?

WHY DO MEN BUY SEX?

Part of the movement to eliminate sex trafficking has been to look at those who buy sex, almost all of whom are men, and try to change their behavior. There are many different needs that buyers say they get fulfilled from paying for sex, almost all dealing with access to a sex partner and exerting their own power. Perhaps mentioned most often is their need for sex without commitment or no-strings-attached sex. They can ask for what they want, enjoy it without any obligation or emotional complications. For some men, it may bolster their ideas about masculinity, and for others allow them to act out their fantasies, sometimes abusing the woman or man. Sex does relieve anxiety and other negative emotions and in many cases, the trafficked person makes the man feel like he is the most wonderful person in the world. Many of these men need to feel that they exercise control over their environment, including during sex. They do not see it as a mutual experience nor are they interested in making their partners feel good, despite the fact that some of the buyers are sexually skilled and like to make the women reach orgasm. Some buyers are dissatisfied with their relationships with others and believe that there is a genuine relationship with someone whom they pay for having sex. Others like showing off in front of other men at sex parties where women are brought in for their entertainment. Interestingly, the buyers of sex often talk about heterosexual sex with women, not men, although it is known that the market for young boys is very active, too.

Prevention activities have reached out to change the attitudes of boys and young men to reduce their demand for buying sex in the future. One way is to help them realize how they are exploiting women and children to satisfy needs that they were socialized to believe were important to fulfill. This is done by using examples challenging those sex-role stereotypes of masculinity such as the importance of paying for sex as a rite of passage or why sex without intimacy is considered part of a "real" man's self-esteem. Another strategy used is to personalize the women and children who are being trafficked; put a name and face on them and describe the exploitation and their inability to control their own lives. It is difficult to pretend a woman is enjoying her encounter after being made aware of how she may have been lured and forced into becoming a victim.

DRUGS AND SEX

Actor Charlie Sheen, who announced he had contracted HIV from his years of sexually exploiting women and using drugs, could well be a poster person for the face of prevention activities. Once heralded for his "bad boy" attitude, he now faces the rest of his life with a debilitating disease that will impact how he lives his life. Why do drugs and sexual exploitation go together? Looking at both activities when they occur together shows how one supports the other; both keep the users from dealing with their real feelings.

Studies of trafficking victims reveal their high drug use; in some cases over 50% of those interviewed said they had a substance abuse or dependence disorder. Some use drugs to numb themselves while performing sex acts while others calm down their anxieties and other trauma symptoms. Some traffickers are also involved in selling drugs and supplying them to their victims, creating even more dependency. The victims then use their participation in sex to support their drug habit. Some were dependent on drugs even before their involvement with a trafficker and several studies found that becoming involved with sex trafficking was an intentional behavior to fund their need for drugs. However, when drug use comes before their entrance into trafficking, the trafficker continues to exploit their drug dependency and entraps them by giving them their drugs based on their engaging in commercial sex.

Cocaine powder and crack cocaine have been a favorite drug for trafficking victims, as it acts as a stimulant and provides a sense of euphoria that can keep them performing with one person after another in an evening. They have a higher risk of infection, especially if they share needles and injecting equipment with others. For these victims/survivors, they will need substance abuse treatment in addition to trauma treatment and other forms of health care to rebuild their resiliency and health wherever possible.

REBUILDING HEALTHY LIFESTYLES

One of the more promising programs for teenager survivors of sex trafficking is the CHANCE (Citrus Helping Adolescents Negatively Impacted by Commercial Exploitation) program in Miami, Florida, in 2013. Working together in partnership with a community health center, state department of children and families, law enforcement, and the local government, the program provides a variety of services, including a community response team that deals with assessment, home-based services, and crisis intervention; a system of specialized foster homes where the youth may be placed; and an in-patient psychiatric unit for girls who need more intensive care. In its third year as I write this, the program has found that rebuilding the ability to trust may be the most important foundational step before most other services can be utilized. Without trust, the girls simply cannot engage with the services in a meaningful way and they often quit or elope from their homes, which makes bonding and trust building even more difficult. Psychologists and other mental health providers are available to provide individual psychotherapy two to four times a week, group therapy, family therapy where possible, and life skills coaching, and behavioral intervention experts all participate working as a team.

At present, we are adding a component for working with survivors of sex trafficking to the STEP intervention program described later in the book. Here we deal with the bond to the trafficker that is often seen in both domestic violence survivors and those who have survived sexual exploitation by those in authority positions. While they are all displeased by the power and control and abusive treatment from these men, they also still have some loving feelings or at least attachment to them that makes them not want to hurt them.

SUMMARY

The recent focus on global human and sex trafficking has demonstrated the close connection between the recruitment of disaffected and alienated youth into trafficking and homes where child abuse and domestic violence have occurred. Identification of these youth and prevention actions may help protect them from abuse both by their own families and by the traffickers who prey on them. Sex trafficking is big business for many groups and as such is difficult to stop. Domestic violence homes are important places to introduce prevention actions to better protect these youth.

REFERENCE

U.S. Department of State. (2007, June). *Trafficking in persons report*. Retrieved from http://www.state.gov/documents/organization/82902.pdf

CHAPTER NINE

BATTERED WOMEN'S ATTACHMENT STYLE, SEXUALITY, AND INTERPERSONAL FUNCTIONING

T he initial research provided a glimpse into several areas that were negatively impacted by intimate partner violence (IPV) previously not associated with domestic violence and posttraumatic stress disorder (PTSD). These included the negative body image developed by the women as well as various sexual issues that were reported. As we began to analyze our data around these initial issues, it became clear that the impact of living in a home where domestic violence occurred caused major interpersonal disruption, usually because of the isolation and coercive control and abuse of power from the batterer. However, we also noticed that in some cases, the women themselves either had previously held or began to develop attachment issues of their own that interfered in how they functioned with other people. Although we initially attributed these attachment issues as stemming from living with their abusive partners, in some cases it appeared that they may have had interpersonal attachment issues even earlier.

ATTACHMENT THEORY

Attachment theory provides a rich conceptual framework for understanding issues that arise in IPV that have not been well studied in adults previously. It has been politically sensitive within the battered women's community to discuss possible problems that battered women may have within the relationship for fear of reinforcing the old victim-blaming attitudes. Nonetheless, intimacy issues have been an important theme when analyzing the data from this project and it seemed important to try to better understand them from a feminist perspective. For example, women who have recently left their abusers often exhibit patterns closely associated with what has been called an "anxious" or "ambivalent" attachment style. While both styles tend to characterize women who are no longer in an abusive relationship, their effect on future relationships may be tremendous. This may be one reason why so many of the women in our study do not go into another relationship with a man. A woman characterized by a fearful attachment style has a conscious need for social contact but is held back in doing so, as she fears the consequences of establishing and maintaining social interaction. As a result, she feels as though she cannot obtain or even recognize the love and support that distinguishes positive intimate relationships. After years of abuse, she may even believe she does not deserve it.

On the other hand, a dismissing approach lends the woman to become defensive in denying the need for social contact. These women then have a tendency to minimize their personal distress and need for relationships as they hold on to a positive model of the self, which only serves to continue their cycle of rejecting future relationships. Bartholomew (1990) and his colleagues have found that overall, fearful and dismissing attachment styles are both forms of avoidance. However, each style differs in approaching intimacy—fearful women have a strong dependency on others to maintain positive self-regard, whereas dismissing women rely heavily on themselves, opposing others' acceptance, in order to maintain a positive self-image (Bartholomew & Horowitz, 1991).

Bowlby's Attachment Theory

Bowlby (1973) originally proposed the attachment theory on the premise that a child's early relationship with his or her primary caregiver serves as a template for future relationships (Karen, 1994; Klein, 1975). Attachment was initially conceived as a neurobiological-based need for the purpose of safety and survival. The theory stated that all humans are innately driven to seek attachments or close enduring emotional bonds with others in a relationship. Moreover, through the attachment process individuals develop an internalized set of beliefs about the self and others, otherwise known as "internal working models" (Bowlby, 1973, 1988). The internal working model of self influences one's perceptions about his or her self-worth, competence, and lovability, whereas the working model of others is responsible for expectations about the availability and trustworthiness of others. This begins in infancy and continues through childhood as the neural pathways are forming. However, today we believe that the development of healthy attachment continues throughout the life span.

Subsequently, an individual's relationship formation is influenced by his or her internal representation of attachment. These structures of the self and others are unique, as they are both distinct and interrelated and they become implicit action strategies when an individual feels threatened or violated (Lopez & Brennan, 2000). Additionally, Bowlby (1973) proposed that an individual's representation of attachment, and in turn the internal working model, is activated in stressful, unpredictable, and unstable situations. Thus, attachment to others will assist in learning about regulation of emotion or "affect" as it is sometimes called. Jean Baker Miller and her associates at the Stone Center at Wellesley College have studied the gender variables that impact attachment and how attachment fosters building relationships. Although not applied to domestic violence or other forms of negative attachment styles, their work has helped understand what a woman needs to develop interpersonal social skills as she develops and grows as an adult.

More recently, psychologist Dan Siegel has translated the attachment theory to practical parenting skills. In his book, *Parenting from the Inside Out*, he talks about how children develop aggressive and violent attachment styles or what has been called the "disorganized" attachment style. He shows that there are two major ways children learn social relationships: (a) they mirror their parents' reactions to fear and terror and (b) they develop their own fear response from abuse. He adds that this fear also develops from being subjected to harassment and humiliating behavior, not just from physical or sexual abuse itself. The child then is in a no-win situation if something happens where he or she needs the support of a loving parent. First, the child moves toward the attachment figure but then, when fearful, moves away. This causes several different kinds of reactions. First, the child does not know whether or not the parent or attachment figure will react lovingly or angrily. So the child's emotional development is seriously compromised and not easily regulated. There is no separation between feeling disappointed and angry and the resulting actions taken.

Second, the child develops an inability to understand other people and misinterprets people's feelings and actions. Mirroring people's behavior teaches children how to interpret what meaning to give people's actions toward them. They learn whether it is safe or unsafe and then can react properly to it. Those with disorganized attachment often feel hopeless and helpless and may freeze or they interpret the behavior as being extraordinarily dangerous to themselves, or they may begin a fight response almost immediately. So, those with disorganized attachment can go from receptivity to reactivity almost immediately. They are impulsive with no separation between impulse and action. Their whole system is on alert all the time. Daniel Sonkin in his work with men who batter women has applied the attachment theory to his clients and finds it important to teach them how to relax, be less impulsive and reactive, and learn how to interpret people's true intentions.

Most researchers state that there are three levels of attachment style functioning: the first level, attachment security, is described as the healthy orientation found in most people. In the second level, attachment functions are organized, but considered flawed, as they are considered insecure. Insecure attachment forms two models that are able to predict individual differences in behavior—attachment avoidance and attachment anxiety. Consequently, research supports the conceptualization of secondary attachment operating as two dimensions, or functions (Brennan, Clark, & Shaver, 1998; Lopez & Brennan, 2000). The third level is the disorganized attachment as described previously.

The first dimension, attachment avoidance, is characterized by a pervasive discomfort with intimate closeness and a strong orientation toward self-reliant and counterdependent relationship behavior. The second dimension, attachment anxiety, is represented by low self-esteem and dependent relationship behavior. Whereas the avoidant dimension is closely related with a negative model of the self, the second style is associated with anxious attachment. Although the third level, disorganization, was initially thought to be rare, later research has shown it to be more common than previously thought. It is suggestive of extreme interpersonal problems. Interestingly, as stated earlier, Dutton and Sonkin (2003) suggested that some batterers demonstrate disorganized attachment patterns. More recent research has found that attachment issues can be determined from adult relationships as well as during childhood as was the original belief.

Adult Attachment

In adult relationships, attachment processes are activated by way of a cognitive–affective–behavioral triad. An individual is first cognitively aware of a perceived threat or danger, which then leads to the activation of his or her attachment system. In turn, anxiety is felt in response to the perceived threat, leading to behavioral avoidance. Since this cognitive triad is part of the cognitive behavioral theory, treatment for attachment disorders may need to cross both relationship and cognitive therapies, stressing the newer affect regulation techniques.

Sonkin (www.daniel.sonkin.com) suggests that attachment in batterers is governed by the three important principles first postulated by Bowlby as an innate or neurobiological attachment behavioral system.

First, a stressor activates an alarm to the individual that he or she is in need of emotional soothing. This releases biochemicals that alert the emotional system (remember the autonomic nervous system [ANS] described in earlier chapters) and help support the cognitive awareness of a perceived problem or threat. Emotional soothing can come from a variety of sources but most commonly, it is from the soothing behavior of the attachment figure. In infants, only physical contact with the attachment figure will provide the soothing needed to turn off the alarm. Therefore, the child engages in behaviors designed to get the attention of the attachment figure: visually checking for her or him, signaling in some way to try to reestablish contact, calling, pleading, and moving toward the person. In children raised in homes where parents or caretakers are inconsistent, they may become confused and become unable to establish a useful routine to soothe their anxiety. In adults, there are a variety of ways to reduce the tension produced, some more self-destructive than others. Alcohol and other drug use, cutting behavior, and hostile abusiveness are several negative features. Relaxation, meditation, reading a good book, playing computer games, and engaging in other pleasurable activities may be more positive ways of calming down.

Second, when the system has been activated for a long time without soothing and shutting down the alarms, the person becomes angry. Here the infant screams and cries, sometimes without the ability to shut off the alarm easily even if physical contact does arrive. Sonkin suggests that anger is an attempt to recapture the person who can soothe the child's tension and distress before the child can do so alone. It also tells the attachment figure that he or she is wanted or needed. But, anger can become dysfunctional and actually distance the person who could have provided soothing behavior from the person needing it instead of bringing him or her closer. This is what often occurs in the early and middle stages of dependency relationships such as domestic violence.

Third, if soothing and protection are consistently not found, the child's attachment capabilities become suppressed or disorganized. These children tend to be disinterested in whether or not the caretaker is present or absent. However, some studies suggest that they really purposely engage in avoidant behavior to reduce their anxiety. They are called *anxious-avoidant*.

If the attachment behavioral system is inconsistently modulated, then the signaling behaviors become stronger and the child becomes preoccupied with the attachment figure's availability. This is seen in hypervigilance and anxious behavior, perhaps even phobic responses or panic attacks. They are called *anxious-ambivalent* because they become very distressed when the parent leaves the room, and even if the attachment figure does return, this will not soothe these infants or children.

There is a third group that originally was not understood by Bowlby and his colleagues, but later other researchers such as Main and Solomon found a common denominator and called it *disorganized attachment*. These children would approach the attachment figure when it reappeared but then stop and turn away. This approach and avoidant behavior seemed to demonstrate what researchers called a "collapse of the strategies in managing distress." There is no organized strategy for obtaining their attachment needs.

The continuum of attachment goes from *secure* when the person's anxieties and emotions can be regulated to *insecure* when they are not. The insecure may be resistant and ambivalent, avoidant and dismissing, or disorganized and unresolved. The secure may signal and get their needs met; the resistant may cling but still not be soothed; and the avoidant may ignore the attachment figure and not be soothed. Interestingly, Main and Hesse found that the disorganized children were more often being abused by their caretakers and suggested that they were experiencing fear without solution. Other caretakers themselves had been abused and the effects had not been resolved for them, preventing them from being able to attach to their children. These parents became frightened when their children needed protection or soothing and thus were unable to provide it.

These same factors have been found to develop in the women and men involved in domestic violence relationships. This is consistent with other research indicating that attachment is closely related to an adult's ability to regulate his or her emotions, creating unusual dependency in relations. Feminists suggest that women are more in need of attachment with others than are men. For example, studies published by researchers at the Stone Center at Wellesley University have indicated these gender differences. How gender, biology, and environment interact together is now being studied by psychologists. However, there are some areas that are well understood.

Interpersonal Functioning

Given the development of attachment, it is not surprising that other researchers have found that battered women are likely to demonstrate increased dependency on others and less able to function independently (Henderson, Bartholomew, & Dutton, 1997). Studies also indicate that battered women with low self-esteem and dysphoria have an inclination to employ high perceived control over their current abusers and exhibit greater use of substances, behavioral disengagement, denial, and self-blame as coping mechanisms. Similar to the fearful and dismissing styles, these women carry their coping mechanisms to future relationships. On the other hand, Clements, Sabourin, and Spiby (2004) found that women who believed they could control their futures in abusive relationships, primarily exhibited lower dysphoria and hopelessness, in addition to increased self-esteem. While not totally validated by the investigators, attachment style seems to play a monumental role in all coping mechanisms discussed. In addition, there is evidence to suggest that battered women's depressive symptoms increased while reported self-esteem decreased as a result of the number, type, severity, incremental quality, and consequence of intimate partner abuse (Cascardi & O'Leary, 1992).

STUDY OF BATTERED WOMEN'S ATTACHMENT STYLE

The data gathered in Battered Woman Syndrome Questionnaire (BWSQ) #2 began an investigation of battered women attachment styles along the dimensions of secure, avoidant, and anxious-ambivalent. Based on the attachment theory, (a) we expected battered women to be at an elevated risk for avoidant and/or anxious-ambivalent attachment styles, and less likely to exhibit secure attachment styles; (b) we expected battered women to exhibit high levels of interpersonal functioning difficulties; and (c) we expected that attachment style would be implicated in interpersonal functioning difficulties. Unfortunately, our data could not permit determining when attachment difficulties might have begun, either before, during, or after the battering relationship.

Methodology

Participants

The sample consisted of 32 women who reported a history of domestic violence. Their ethnic composition was as follows: 64.5% Caucasian, 12.9% African American, 6.5% Hispanic, 3.2% Asian American, and 12.9% of "other" minorities. Participants' ages ranged from 18 to 69 years, with a mean age of 42.56 years ($SD = 13.10$). Their level of education ranged from 6 to 16 years, with a mean of 13.38 years ($SD = 2.55$). The majority of the participants were recruited from advertisements in the community or from forensic settings.

Measures

In addition to selected questions from the BWSQ #2, the Revised Adult Attachment Scale (RAAS) was used to assess for attachment style in adults. The RAAS (Collins, 1996) is a self-report questionnaire that assesses adult attachment style in adult relationships. The 18-item scale was first proposed by Hazan and Shaver (1987) who categorized three dimensions of attachment styles from the questionnaire: the capacity to be close (close), the capacity to depend on others (depend), and the anxiety over relationships (anxiety). Collins (1996) later undertook an extensive statistical analysis of these categories and found that there were merits to identifying the categories as nominal variables, namely secure, avoidant, and anxious-ambivalent. Participants score each of the 18 items using a five-point Likert scale ranging from "not at all characteristic of me" to "very characteristic of me." In this study, the RAAS has valuable psychometric properties yielding a Cronbach's alpha of .629.

Results

Results confirm the hypothesis that battered women are at an elevated risk for avoidant and/or anxious-ambivalent attachment styles, and less likely to exhibit secure attachment styles. Indeed, results indicate that the participants predominantly exhibited an avoidant attachment style.

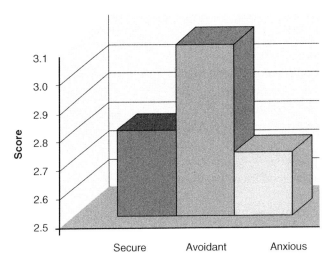

Adult Attachment Scale

Figure 9.1 *Attachment style.*

However, fewer exhibited an anxious attachment style, even when compared to secure attachment. See Figure 9.1.

Frequency results confirm the hypothesis that battered women experienced interpersonal functioning difficulties. Some of the more striking interpersonal issues can be seen in Table 9.1. By collapsing the rarely/occasionally and often/always categories, approximately half or more of the women in the study include feeling dependent on others (47%), feeling trapped in a relationship (60%), having no real friends (47%), feeling lonely (65%), feeling afraid to form close relationships (69%), and being treated like a thing (53%). Also noteworthy is the women's report that they become good friends quickly (88%). It would be interesting to compare their responses to those women who claim never to have been battered. Perhaps as we collect more data, we will be able to break down these data into cross-national and cross-cultural groups for comparisons.

Further Statistical Analysis

A standard multiple regression analysis was performed between reported interpersonal difficulties as the dependent variable (as measured by the BWSQ), and the three attachment styles, including secure, avoidant, and anxious as independent variables (as measured by the RAAS), using the

Table 9.1 *Frequencies*

How Often Do You Feel . . .	Never (%)	Rarely/ Occasionally (%)	Often/ Always (%)
. . . dependent on others	38	41	6
. . . you have difficulty making friends	25	22	13
. . . trapped in a relationship	22	44	16
. . . you have no real friends	25	34	13
. . . you need to control your relationships	22	41	9
. . . lonely	25	56	9
. . . people love you	–	38	44
. . . you become good friends with someone quickly	6	60	28
. . . afraid to form close relationships	25	56	13
. . . people treat you like a thing	25	50	3

SPSS program. Overall, results supported the hypothesis that a significant relationship would be observed between interpersonal difficulties and attachment style. More specifically, results suggest that approximately 42% of the variance in interpersonal functioning difficulties can be accounted for by attachment style ($R^2 = .415$), with statistically significant analysis of variance (ANOVA) results ($F = 6.623$; $p = .002$). According to Cohen's (1988), R^2 effect size classification, large effect size was evidenced for the overall regression. As for the individual components of the regression equation, results yielded small to medium effect size for secure ($B = -.276$), avoidant ($B = .210$), and anxious-ambivalent ($B = .363$). See Table 9.2.

The Relationship Between Battered Women and Attachment Style

Overall our results confirmed the hypothesis that battered women are at an elevated risk for avoidant and/or anxious-ambivalent attachment styles, and are less likely to exhibit secure attachment styles. More specifically, results generated from our frequency analysis indicated that battered women are more likely to have an avoidant attachment style when compared to anxious and secure attachment styles. This finding is consistent with the literature, which states that battered women have an

Table 9.2 *Linear Regression Summary*

Predictors	R^2	F	p	B	t	p	Size[a]
Attachment style	.415	6.623	.002	–	–	–	L
Secure	–	–	–	–.276	–1.746	.092	M
Avoidant	–	–	–	.210	1.183	.247	S–M
Anxious	–	–	–	.363	2.197	.036	M

[a]Descriptor of effect size as per Cohen (1988): R^2 (small = .01; medium = .09; large = .25); B (small = .10; medium = .30; large = .5).

L, large; M, medium; S, small.

increased tendency to be less secure in their intimate relationships. There are several possible explanations.

The first that is consistent with the literature on the effects of the inconsistent attachment in an adult relationship would be expected to result in either anxious-avoidant or anxious-ambivalent attachment style as described previously. From the literature, we extrapolated that battered women report histories that include risk factors for poor attachment, such as exposure to trauma from residing in domestically violent households and experiencing the personal trauma of being abused in their intimate relationships. Therefore, the women's life experiences alone may have exposed them to insecure forms of attachment. Indeed, it is probable that relational trauma is a precursor for their avoidant attachment style.

On the other hand, the attachment literature is also replete with data that these attachment styles come from insecurities developed during childhood. Examination of the women's childhood experiences does not suggest that this group had reported being exposed to more risk factors than others according to the National Violence Survey (Straus & Gelles, 1990). Hotaling and Sugarman (1986) found that there were no risk markers to becoming a battered woman in the epidemiological survey except for being a woman.

Furthermore, in light of Bowlby's (1973) attachment theory, it appears battered women developed an internal working model that is associated with them having an overly pessimistic self-representation pertaining to their self-worth, competence, and lovability. This can also largely account for battered women not being secure in their intimate relationships or, once that relationship is terminated, avoiding other intimate relationships. Additionally, our view of battered women's avoidance is consistent with

Lopez and Brennan (2000) who proposed that when placed in a threatening situation, one's attachment response is activated and that the person will progressively develop a behavioral avoidance pattern to minimize fear.

The Relationship Between Battered Women and Interpersonal Functioning

Results generated from the frequency analysis revealed that the battered women in our sample continued to experience interpersonal functioning difficulties at the time of their participation in the study. This finding is consistent with our hypothesis that batterers train battered women into dependency relationships. The statement "becoming close friends with others too easily" received the highest endorsement (88%). It may be an indication of the battered women's neediness and hasty decision making as well as their potentially indiscriminant behavior when selecting interpersonal relationships. It is possible that battered women possess a higher level of dependence on individuals with whom they come in contact, while failing to weigh their needs and wants with what the persons are actually able and/or willing to provide. A part of their internal working model may include feeling that whatever their partners do, even if it includes violent behavior against them, is justifiable and interpreted by the women as something they deserve. There is a possibility that battered women have low self-esteem and may devalue themselves as well as think of themselves as undeserving of someone who will respect and love them without being violent. On the other hand, it could also be a result of the enforced isolation imposed on the women by the batterers so that once out of the relationship, they are eager to make new friends. Or, it could be a combination of both of those reasons.

Interestingly, fear of forming close relationships was the second highest frequency statistic. While this could be contradictory to the first statement, with most of the women saying they make friends easily, this finding appears most closely related to the predominance of avoidant attachment style endorsed by battered women in this sample. Based on the attachment theory, avoidant individuals desire an intimate relationship but are fearful of forming an attachment of that nature. Such fear may stem from past and/or current relationships where they have either witnessed or experienced domestic violence. Furthermore, their social milieu likely taught them that the world is unsafe, thereby leading the women to prematurely withdraw from relationships and/or maintain more superficial and therefore less dependable interpersonal relations. In summary, the conditioned perception of an environment that is untrustworthy and devoid of stable and nurturing qualities may very well lead to inconsistent and avoidant behavior toward that environment.

All remaining interpersonal functioning statements confirm that battered women experienced interpersonal functioning difficulties. For example, they reported feeling trapped and dependent on others, signaling that the women may lack autonomy and/or self-reliance. Consequently, when involved in abusive intimate relationships they feel as though they lack the skills and resources to leave their male partners. This finding is consistent with the existing literature on battered women's increased sense of dependency (Henderson et al., 1997). However, these results should not be interpreted as an indication that a battered woman is innately more dependent than the average woman. Indeed, the present study did not have the capacity to establish the women's dispositions prior to their first abusive episode/relationship. On the other hand, there is more established evidence that the women's power and control limitations during their involvement in abusive relationships foster more dependence.

The Relationship Between Attachment Styles and Interpersonal Difficulties in Battered Women

In an effort to determine the implication of attachment style on interpersonal functioning, we performed the multiple regression analysis between interpersonal functioning as the dependent variable and attachment styles as the predictor, as seen in Table 9.2. It should be noted that although avoidant attachment was the predominant style reported by the women in our sample, we were surprised that more participants endorsed items depicting secure attachment style when compared to anxious attachment style. On the other hand, secure attachment was negatively correlated with interpersonal difficulties, indicating that the more secure the women, the less interpersonal difficulties they experienced and vice versa.

As expected, our results indicated that interpersonal functioning difficulties are significantly implicated in attachment styles. More specifically, results suggest that approximately 42% of the variance in interpersonal functioning difficulties can be accounted for by attachment style. Whether the women's insecure attachment style was formed in childhood and/ or formed or exacerbated by abusive intimate relationships in adulthood, it is reasonable to conclude that, consistent with the literature (Karen,1994; Klein,1975), the attachment style formed in past experiences may have set the template for future behavior and consequent interpersonal difficulties.

Attachment Behavior and Perpetrators

Psychologist Donald Dutton (1995) has put forward a classification system suggesting that there are three types of batterers, each of whom developed a different attachment style. His research on batterers who were court ordered or voluntarily sought psychotherapy to stop their domestic violence divided them into those who were the *psychopathic batterer* who committed antisocial behavior and violence both inside and outside of the home, *borderline batterers* who demonstrated the cyclical pattern of abuse with high levels of jealousy, and *overcontrolled* or *preoccupied batterers* who appear jovial and avoid conflict but mask high levels of hostility. When Dutton applied the attachment theory to these three groups, he found that the psychopathic batterer had a *dismissing* attachment style, the borderline batterer had a *fearful and disorganized* attachment style, and the overcontrolled batterer had a *preoccupied* or *avoidant* attachment style.

Further analysis demonstrated that those with a dismissing attachment style were more cold and distant and managed their vulnerabilities by devaluing their partners. They sound similar to Jacobson and Gottman's (1998) *cobras* who used carefully controlled and deliberate attacks against their partners. Those batterers with a preoccupied or avoidant attachment style learned to manage their emotional vulnerabilities by keeping their distance. Some even learned to soothe themselves to the exclusion of any dependence on a relationship. Not surprisingly, the group that demonstrated a disorganized attachment style was more confused and depressed without a consistent strategy to regulate the emotional distress of its members. Most of them also had histories of unresolved trauma as children and learned to use an approach and avoidance style when they felt emotionally vulnerable.

When understanding the batterers' behaviors through the attachment behavior analysis, it becomes clear that one type of batterers' treatment program will not be adequate to meet the needs of these men. At a minimum they will need treatment plans that address their attachment issues. But, even then, they will need more specific and individualized treatment as within each group there are factors that interact such as substance abuse and other mental health diagnoses. The interaction of insecure men with insecure women appears to be a high risk for an abusive relationship to develop between them and there are negative implications for any children they may attempt to parent together.

Children in these homes may also exhibit varying attachment styles. For those who are most impacted by their fathers' abuse of their mothers, it is anticipated that they will demonstrate certain characteristics. These include (a) difficulty with behavior and emotions that negatively impact their relationships with others, (b) attempts to control their caretakers to make it more predictable whether or not they will get their needs met, and (c) tendency to dissociate from relationships and form more avoidant attachment types. Although these behavioral patterns are not enough to diagnose children who are observed to have them, they are a signal that the children are in distress and need some intervention, especially a consistent firm but loving parent.

SEXUALITY ISSUES

Analysis of the attachment issues for battered women seemed to us to be closely related to the attachment styles described previously. It is difficult to have a positive intimate and sexual relationship with someone who is as inconsistent as are the reports of batterers' behaviors. Sometimes they are very loving and other times described as mean terrorists. Even when they do not inflict sexual abuse on their partners, the inability of battered women to know whether they will be loved in a gentle and kind way or in a rough and distant manner has to affect how they approach intimacy.

The definition of a battering relationship has always included sexual jealousy and abuse as part of IPV. However, until the data from this research were collected, it was not known precisely how the sexual abuse in the battering relationship differed from other forms of sexual abuse. Perhaps the most significant fact was the realization that sexual abuse in intimate relationships is more like incest than stranger rape, which has more physical violence than the psychological coercion noted in the domestic violence cases. The women in this research reported that it was not unusual for batterers to use sexual coercion to shame and humiliate the women, making it easier for them to gain their desired psychological control. Battered women often use sex to barter for their safety—they think that if they give in to sex, even when they do not desire it, then perhaps they will not be as badly physically or psychologically harmed. Therefore, one of the interesting areas that we studied in the original research was the impact of repeated sexual coercion and assault by someone who is capable of tender lovemaking at other times (Finkelhor & Yllo, 1983; Walker, 1979, 1994).

In the new research we expanded our studies into the impact of abuse on the woman's sexual satisfaction in general (Duros & Walker, 2006; Needle et al., 2007). In addition, our researchers, like others (Russo & Denious, 2001), found that many of the small number of women who develop mental health issues after an abortion to terminate an unintended pregnancy have previously experienced abuse in their lives (Needle & Walker, 2007). This is an important finding as those few women who do have negative reactions to an abortion could be counseled about abuse and trauma rather than just mental health issues alone, so as to prevent these problems from exacerbating.

Marital Rape

Rape within marriage or marriage-like relationships has been found to occur far more frequently than previously estimated (Laura X, 1998; Martin, 1982; Russell, 1975, 1982). Part of the difficulty in measuring incidence and prevalence rates is that of confusing definitions. Since marital partners are presumed to engage in sexual relations, and such consent is thought to be given automatically along with the marriage vows by some, it is difficult for many to conceive of either partner having the right to say "no." Sexual assault statutes used to exclude marital rape but, due mostly to the untiring work of Laura X at the National Clearinghouse on Marital Rape, all states in the United States now permit some form of criminal prosecution (Laura X, 1998).

However, as long as the couple is living together, unless the forced sex includes physical assault that can be prosecuted under the regular assault or domestic violence laws, it may not be considered criminal behavior and its effects are usually discounted. Even when they are no longer living together, it is difficult to persuade prosecutors to take on these cases.

Occasionally a civil tort action may be filed for damages from sexual abuse within the intimate relationship but unless the damage is obvious and severe, such as transmitting a sexual disease or preventing the ability to bear a child, it is difficult to persuade others of the damage.

Some cases have been successful, however, such as *Curtis v. Curtis*, a 1988 Idaho case. In this case, Sandra Curtis claimed that her common law husband, Carl Curtis, had sexually abused her during the 10 years they lived together by using cocaine and coercing her into all-night sex that included pornography. Mr. Curtis attempted to show videotapes that he took during sex to prove that Ms. Curtis was enjoying herself. Ms. Curtis countered by stating she perceived more danger if she did not give in to his demands. The jury agreed and she won $1.2 million in actual and punitive damages. Mr. Curtis appealed both the decision and the amount of the award, but the Idaho Supreme Court affirmed both. In a Colorado case, the amount won by another woman was considerably less, but the precedent was set. The facts in the Colorado case have been used for a mock trial conducted by University of Colorado law school professors teaching future lawyers the important issues of both personal injury torts and battered woman syndrome.

Given the difficulties in reaching a common definition of marital rape, our first research project decided to measure the woman's perception of her entire sexual relationship with the abusive partner. Questions about sexual abuse were embedded in the section that asked other questions about sex. We decided to use a broad definition of "sexual abuse" that included any kind of forced oral, anal, or vaginal penetration. Washburne and Frieze (1980) found that women were more likely to discuss sexual abuse in their relationships if they were asked in a more indirect way. They found that they gained more reliable and valid information by asking questions like, "Is sex with your batterer ever unpleasant for you?" and then giving her several answers from which to choose, such as, "Yes, because he forces me to have sex when I don't want to." A more direct question, and perhaps more threatening one for the women, would be, "Did he ever force you to have sex?" We included some questions worded the same way as Frieze and her colleagues (1980) did as well as some that asked for the information in a more direct way. This also helped us better understand the contradictions often seen when battered women answer questions differently from one interviewer to another.

SEXUAL ISSUES AND DOMESTIC VIOLENCE RESEARCH

Original Study

We did not use the term "rape" in the questions we asked as other research-ers had reported that it is such an emotionally loaded term that women will be less likely to use it to describe what their husbands do to them (Doron, 1980; Russell, 1982). This is interesting as more recently there have been articles appearing in the news that judges in rape cases are prohibit-ing victims from using the term "rape" to describe what happened to them, finding it is so pejorative that the term itself would likely prejudice the defendant from getting a fair trial. That was not why we did not use the term "rape." Rather, we were concerned that women would not connect the term with sex with their husbands even if it was not consensual.

In the original research, the questions regarding sexual abuse were placed at different parts of the interview rather than in just one section to both reduce the stress around these emotionally charged questions and provide a reliability check. While many of our questions required a forced-choice response, some allowed the woman to respond with open-ended answers. An entire set of questions was asked about the woman's rela-tionship with both a batterer and a nonbatterer in the 200 cases where such data were collected. The specific incidents described supported the contention that sex can and is used as a way to dominate, control, and hurt a woman even if there is no physical abuse. Table 9.3 presents the results from both the original sample and the current one. Forty years later, with a totally different sample of women, the responses were pretty similar.

Of our sample, 59% said that they were forced to have sex with the batterer as compared to 7% with the nonbatterer. Of course, the men who were described by those 7% were not actually "nonbatterers" by definition of the behavior described here, but the women perceived them as such, obviously not defining "forced sex" as battering behavior by itself. With the batterer, 41% were asked to perform what they described as unusual sex acts, as compared to 5% of the nonbatterer. Women reported being forced to insert objects in their vaginas, engage in group sex, have sex with ani-mals, and partake in bondage and various other sadomasochistic activi-ties. A large variety of uncommon sexual practices were reported similar to that told to me during my previous research (Walker, 1979).

Table 9.3 *Women's Report on Sexual Relationship With Batterers*

Variable	Original Sample N	Original Sample %	Current Sample N	Current Sample %
Who initiates sex?				
Neither	1	0	0	0
Man	257	64	67	63
Both	115	29	30	28
Woman	29	7	9	9
Sex unpleasant for the woman?				
Never	59	15	24	23
Occasionally	186	46	43	41
Frequently	155	38	39	37
Sex unpleasant for the man?				
Never	200	53	73	72
Occasionally	122	32	21	21
Frequently	50	13	7	8
How often are you jealous of his affairs?				
Never	128	32	36	34
Occasionally	163	40	47	44
Frequently	112	27	23	22
How often is he jealous of you having affairs with other men?				
Never	26	6	11	10
Occasionally	101	25	21	20
Frequently	275	68	74	70

When asked if sex was unpleasant, 85% said "yes" with the batterers and 29% with the nonbatterers. Of those who found sex unpleasant with the batterer, 43% of them said that sex was unpleasant because he forced her when she did not want it. Interestingly, about one half thought that sex with her was unpleasant for the batterer but only 12% thought it was unpleasant for the nonbatterer. As we see later, a large number of battered women were also incest survivors for whom any sex may have been seen as traumatic. This may also explain those who reported sex with nonbatterers as unpleasant.

Almost two thirds of the women reported that batterers almost always initiated their sex, while both initiated sex with one half of the nonbatterers. This is an important finding to refute the often-held notion that battered women are frigid and cause their marriages to fail (Snell, Rosenwald, & Robey, 1964). Two times as many women felt guilt and shame about the sex that they had with the batterer than with the nonbatterer. No specific questions were asked to determine how many women perceived nonviolent sex as rape, although they were clear that they did not want it at the time. The open-ended responses to the question of why sex was unpleasant indicated (for those 85% who said it was) that they gave in to the batterer's coercive demands so that it would calm him down. These women believed the men were in total control of their sexual interactions. Some of the reasons given were as follows: initiating sex to avoid a beating; having sex after a beating to calm him down; having sex after he beat the baby for fear he would do it again. For some women, refusing sex meant they did not get money for groceries or other essentials for their survival.

Couples in an abusive relationship often withheld sex from one another as a means of getting what they wanted. Forty-six percent (46%) of the women said they had stopped having sex with the batterers to get what they wanted from them. Forty-five percent (45%) of them said the men stopped having sex with them. In contrast, 16% of the women said they stopped having sex with the nonbatterers and 11% of the nonbatterers did the same. Although these percentages are similar to those who said that sex with the batterers was unpleasant for them, our analysis did not permit us to see if they were the same responders. A small number of women said that the batterers refused to have sex with them, especially as the violence escalated. These women were psychologically devastated by this rejection and felt that the pain experienced from the psychological humiliation and cold anger demonstrated by these men was as cruel and abusive as were the other psychological and physical abuses they experienced. Jacobson and Gottman (1998) in their study found this behavior was consistent with the type of batterer they called a "cobra." They found this type of batterer used a lack of sexual passion and withholding of sex as a deliberate control technique.

New Study Results

From the earlier data we created a scale to assess for satisfaction with sexuality for the 2005 BWSQ. At present, we are attempting to refine the scale using the preliminary cross-cultural data. The initial scale using these questions can be found in Table 9.4.

Table 9.4 *Frequency Results From the BWSQ's Sexuality Section*

Question Asked	Never/ Rarely (%)	Occasionally (%)	Often/ Always (%)
How often do you find yourself interested in sexual activity?	32.2	38.7	29
How often do you find yourself satisfied with your arousal during sexual activity?	33.4	30	36.7
How often do you find your partner satisfied with your arousal during sexual activity?	46.7	23.3	30
How often do you achieve orgasm?	45.2	19.4	35.5
In general, how satisfied are you with your sex life?	43.3	30	26.6
How often do you experience pain during sexual activity?	65.5	31	3.4
How often do you have sexual thoughts or fantasies?	50	26.7	23.3
In general, how often are sexual activities enjoyable for you?	40	23.3	36.7
How often do you find yourself sexually excited?	53.4	30	16.7
How often do you experience pleasure during sexual activity?	30	27.6	41.4

Pearson's two-tailed correlations were done between the BWSQ and the Trauma Symptom Inventory's (TSI) *sexual concerns* (SC) and *dysfunctional sexual behavior* (DSB) scales. The results indicated no significant relationship ($r = .299$, $p = .103$ for SC; $r = .055$, $p = .770$ for DSB), based on results from the 31 women participants.

Furthermore, Pearson's two-tailed correlation was computed between the BWSQ and each scale of the Derogatis Interview for Sexual Functioning–Self-Report (DISF-SR). The results revealed no significant relationship, and there does not appear to be a relationship between the TSI sexuality scales and the scales of the DISF-SR either, based on the 15 participants who completed all three measures (see Table 9.5).

Results generated from the TSI's SC and DSB scales revealed respective means of 57.06 ($SD = 14.713$) and $M = 56.97$ ($SD = 15.398$). Although these means fall short of the cutoff score for clinical significance (i.e., minimum T-score of 65), they are somewhat elevated.

Table 9.5 *Two-Tailed Pearson Correlation for the BWSQ's Sexuality Section, the TSI's SC and DSB Scales, and the DISF-SR Scales*

		Correlations						
		TSI_SC	TSI_DSB	Sexual Cognition/Fantasy Score	Sexual Arousal Score	Sexual Behavior/Experience	Orgasm Score	Sexual Drive/Relationship Score
TSI_SC	Pearson correlation	1	.783[a]	-.030	-.066	.382	-.037	-.079
	Sig. (two-tailed)		.001	.916	.823	.160	.897	.788
	N	15	15	15	14	15	15	14
TSI_DSB	Pearson correlation	.783[a]	1	.046	-.005	.327	-.261[b]	-.400
	Sig. (two-tailed)	.001		.871	.988	.234	.348	.157
	N	15	15	15	14	15	15	14
Sexual cognition/ fantasy score	Pearson correlation	-.030	.046	1	.575[b]	.432	.307	.320
	Sig. (two-tailed)	.916	.871		.032	.108	.266	.264
	N	15	15	15	14	15	15	14
Sexual arousal score	Pearson correlation	-.066	-.005	.575[b]	1	.739[a]	.772[a]	.595[b]
	Sig. (two-tailed)	.823	.988	.032		.003	.001	.032
	N	14	14	14	14	14	14	13

Sexual behavior/ experience	Pearson correlation	.382	.327	.432	.739[a]	1	.713[a]	.454
	Sig. (two-tailed)	.160	.234	.108	.003		.003	.103
	N	15	15	15	14	15	15	14
Orgasm score	Pearson correlation	-.037	-.261	.307	.772[a]	.713[a]	1	.717[b]
	Sig. (two-tailed)	.897	.348	.266	.001	.003		.004
	N	15	15	15	14	15	15	14
Sexual drive/ relationship score	Pearson correlation	-.079	-.400	.320	.595[b]	.454	.717[a]	1
	Sig. (two-tailed)	.788	.157	.264	.032	.103	.004	
	N	14	14	14	13	14	14	14
Sex total	Pearson correlation			-.360	-.433	-.285	-.381	-.118
	Sig. (two-tailed)			.188	.122	.303	.161	.688
	N			15	14	15	15	14

[a]Correlation is significant at the 0.01 level (two-tailed). [b]Correlation is significant at the 0.05 level (two-tailed).

Sig., significance; TSI_DSB, Trauma Symptom Inventory_ Dysfunctional Sexual Behavior; TSI_SC, Trauma Symptom Inventory_ Sexual Concerns.

A total score on the DISF-SR that is below a standardized score of 40 is considered clinically significant. The mean total scores generated from our sample fell well beyond clinical significance on all of the DISF-SR scales (sexual cognition/fantasy $M=15.80$, $SD=9.63$; sexual arousal $M=8.50$, $SD=7.50$; sexual behavior/experience $M=10.13$, $SD=9.83$; orgasm score $M=8.87$, $SD=7.86$; sexual drive/relationship score $M=10.50$, $SD=5.389$).

These questions were utilized in the first analysis of the factors contributing to PTSD and BWS and it was found that sexual issues were a separate factor that made up BWS, as described in Chapter 3. In the Duros analysis of PTSD, she found that the most recent battering incidents reporting sexual abuse produced the most severe PTSD symptoms in the women who made these reports. This is understandable and consistent with the literature on temporal proximity as a significant factor in the development of PTSD symptomatology. In addition, she found that sexual abuse in the first battering incident increased the woman's likelihood of developing PTSD nearly three times.

As we learned more about the negative impact of sexual abuse in battering relationships, we also decided to use the Derogatis (1978) Sexual Satisfaction Inventory, an already developed questionnaire about sex in intimate partner relationships that is now included in the new BWSQ. These results will be analyzed and published separately. It is interesting that in our Greek sample we have a group of Albanian women who were kidnapped and kept in sex slavery by international groups. They had been set free and placed in a shelter for battered women to help them heal from their ordeal (Antonopoulou, 1999). We are analyzing their data separately to see what common factors there might be between them and other women held hostage by their intimate partners.

DISCUSSION OF OUR RESEARCH WITH OTHER RESEARCHERS

Much research has been devoted to exploring the consequences of sexual victimization, in addition to the association with emotional problems such as depression, anxiety (Bartoi, Kinder, & Tomianovic, 2000), and posttraumatic stress disorder (PTSD; Janoff-Bulman, 1985; Walker, 1994). The impact of such trauma can be found to change attitudes and cognitions related to sexuality (Dutton, Brughardt, Perrin, Chrestman, & Halle, 1994; Finkelhor et al., 1988), and sexual functioning and relationships (Finkelhor et al., 1988; Merrill, Guimond, Thomsen, & Milner, 2003; Sarwer & Durlak, 1996). Additionally, victims of childhood sexual abuse (CSA) have been found to be less satisfied in their sexual relationships, more likely to experience marital disruption (Finkelhor et al., 1988), more dissatisfied with their relationships, and to experience more interpersonal problems (Bartoi & Kinder, 1998; Greenwald, Leitenberg, Cado, & Tarran, 1990) than nonvictims.

Victims of rape, domestic violence, and battery are at risk of developing PTSD (American Psychiatric Association, 2013) and other symptoms related to it such as depression (d'Ardenne & Balakrishna, 2001; Dutton et al., 1994; van Berlo & Ensink, 2000; Walker, 1994, 2007). Similar to victims of CSA, adult sexual victimization has been found to be associated with sexual desire disorders, vaginismus, anorgasmia, polarized sexual activity frequency, and other sexual difficulties (Bartoi & Kinder, 1998; d'Ardenne & Balakrishna, 2001; van Berlo & Ensink, 2000). Regardless of sexual abuse history, similar to those with histories of sexual abuse, battered women had poor body image, decreased sexual satisfaction, and increased sexual dysfunction. These results are more fully discussed in Chapters 13 and 14.

Our finding that over half of the battered women in the earlier research study reported forced sex is consistent with that of other researchers on violence against women. Frieze and Knoble (1980) found that 34% of the battered women in her sample were victims of at least one incident of marital rape with 11% stating it occurred several times or often. Finkelhor and Yllo (1985) report that Spektor's study of 10 Minneapolis battered women shelters found that 36% of the women (and Pagelow's 1982 study found 37% of the women) said their husbands or cohabiting partners raped them. This compares to 59% in our sample, a figure that is almost twice as high as the others. None of these studies used a random sampling technique due to the difficulties in obtaining a sufficiently large population of women who had experienced only partner abuse. One explanation for our larger number is that our questions were more carefully worded due to the experience of underreporting that the other researchers had previously reported.

Diana Russell (1982) surveyed a large-sized (930) random sample of women in the San Francisco area to learn more about their experiences with various forms of sexual assault. Of the approximately two thirds who were married, 12% said that they had been sexually assaulted by their husbands at least one time. She found that sexual assaults by marital partners were twice as common as sexual assaults by strangers. Interestingly, she used a conservative definition of "marital rape" that included "forced intercourse with penetration." If these data can be generalized to the population at large, then battered women have three to five times the risk of being sexually assaulted by their partners than do nonbattered women.

Yllo (1981) discusses two types of marital rape in addition to the violent type that she found in her research. They were (a) those that occur in what she defines as relationships with little or no physical abuse and (b) those that occur in relationships where the man is apparently obsessed with sex. Our data did not support such distinct categories, although my clinical evaluations of battered women who are involved in litigation do. It is interesting to speculate on whether marital rape and acquaintance rape produce the same or different psychological impacts given the literature that suggests that the person's expectations and attributions about what constitutes a rape will modulate the influence of situational factors (Frese, Moya, & Megias, 2004).

In fact, it is not unusual for men obsessed with sex, demanding vaginal intercourse, oral and anal sex several times daily, to also physically and psychologically abuse their partners. A subsection of these men also have a history of abusing other women and children. These men often demand shared parental custody of their children and when their partners attempt to protect the children from their seductive and grooming behaviors, these men make allegations of parental alienation and other spurious charges against the women. They rarely understand the impact of their inappropriate or even abusive behavior on the child. Whether this is a subtype of batterer or a combination of a batterer and a sex offender is not clear at this time.

Our findings are consistent with Yllo's conclusions that forced sex occurs more frequently as a form of violent power and control rather than the more common stereotype of the sexually deprived husband who must use force to get his sexual needs met. Her women report, as do ours, that they would be delighted to engage in warm, tender, lovemaking with their partners who are more frequently hostile than lustful, interested in their own pleasure!

SEXUAL JEALOUSY

Sexual jealousy is one of the most frequently reported features of violent relationships (Browne, 1993; Dutton & Goodman, 1994; Frieze & Knoble, 1980; Hilberman & Munson, 1978; Koss et al., 1994; Martin, 1976; Pagelow,

1982; Roy, 1978; Straus, Gelles, & Steinmetz, 1980; Walker, 1979). This earlier finding was confirmed by our data and continues to be found in later research. When asked if the batterer was ever jealous of her having an affair with another man, almost every woman said "yes" with over half saying such jealousy "always" occurred. Of those women reporting on a nonviolent relationship, about one quarter said the batterer was sometimes jealous, and only 6% said it "always" occurred. Almost one quarter of the sample said the batterer was also jealous of her having an affair with another woman as compared to 3% of the nonbatterers. As we did not inquire if the woman was actually having an affair, these findings cannot be analyzed for accuracy of his jealous perceptions. In most cases, the women described battering incidents that were triggered by unfounded jealous accusations. Women said they had learned to walk with their eyes downcast, to not speak to others in public, to not smile too much, or to not dance too long with others at a party. Sometimes jealousy was responsible for them being kept as prisoners in their own homes, resulting in further social isolation.

The women reported on their own feelings of jealousy with batterers and nonbatterers. In 67% of the cases, the women were jealous of the man having an affair with another woman and in 12%, with another man. This contrasts with one half of them being jealous of the nonbatterers having an affair with another woman and 1% with another man. About one half of the women said the men actually had an affair at least once to their knowledge and another 14% suspected it but were not sure. These data support our conclusions that sexual jealousy is often part of the battering relationship and like sexual assault is part of the battered woman syndrome. In essence, what we have observed is a breach in the kind of trust and the boundaries expected in an intimate relationship. Insecurity about the relationship was apparent no matter how the woman tried to reassure the batterer.

ABUSE DURING PREGNANCY

A large number of women stated they became romantically involved with their batterers rather quickly. This involvement usually involved sexual intimacy and over one third of the women were not married when they first became pregnant. Our subjects had an average of two pregnancies and 1.53 children while in the battering relationship. Battering took place in each of the three trimesters. It is probably accurate to assume that many of those pregnancies that ended in a miscarriage were terminated by the batterers' violent acts.

Our sample, like Gelles's (1975), reported that a high degree of battering occurred during each pregnancy with 59% reporting that battering occurred during the first pregnancy, 63% during the second, and 55% during the third pregnancy. These data were further analyzed to see if there was a difference in which time period during the pregnancy the woman was battered, and the results indicated that if battering occurred, it was likely to happen across all three trimesters. Over 50% of the batterers reportedly were happy about the pregnancy, at least initially, even though the women were later battered, so the women did not perceive the men's unhappiness about the pregnancy as the violence trigger.

We looked for differences in birth control methods in battering and nonbattering relationships, but no major differences were seen. In about two thirds of the cases, the women assumed responsibility for the use of birth control, with the most popular methods being the pill and the IUD. Surprisingly, about one fifth of the women used no birth control at all. Most of the women did not report religious reasons, but just that the batterers would not permit them to use any birth control. Although we did not inquire in this study, because it was too early to be aware of the dangers, it has later been shown that batterers also do not permit women to protect themselves from the possibility of HIV transmission by making them use condoms so that they are at high risk for the transmission of the virus that causes AIDS (Seligson & Bernas, 1997).

In many cases, the batterer kept detailed records of the woman's menstrual cycle and may have known more about her body than she did. The women did not regularly report abortion as a birth control option. However, it must be remembered that this study was conducted a few years after *Roe v. Wade* became the law in 1972, and women first became able to obtain safe and financially possible abortions. One quarter of the women interviewed had no pregnancies, and there was a relatively small number of pregnancies and live births for the rest. Again, this may be explained by the battering relationships, as many women said they did not want to bring a child into a domestic violence family, but it would not explain the nonbatterers' relationships. However, some women may have been beyond the childbearing years and others may not have been in a relationship with a nonbatterer long enough to have a child with him.

Issues Around Abortion

One area of psychology that is extremely controversial is that of whether or not having an abortion should be considered a trauma that causes long-lasting emotional consequences. The term "postabortion syndrome" (PAS) has been used by antichoice activists, despite a lack of scientific data to support it (Needle & Walker, 2007). Charles Everett Koop, who served as the Surgeon General of the United States from 1982 to 1989 under Ronald Reagan's presidency, issued a report confirming that abortions alone do not cause physical or emotional harm. He did this despite his personal opposition to abortion. According to more recent studies, women who have emotional problems following an abortion are likely to have had them prior to the abortion. There remains no scientific validity supporting PAS. Unfortunately, those few women who do experience some psychological problems after having an abortion tend to misattribute these problems to the abortion rather than to other factors such as life experiences, biochemical changes during pregnancy, and expectations set up by misinformation and scare tactics used by abortion protestors (Needle & Walker, 2007). The most common factors found to impact emotional adjustment after terminating a pregnancy are preexisting psychiatric conditions and a history of physical and sexual abuse.

It is important to control certain factors when doing research on the psychological sequelae to abortion. In order to gain an accurate understanding of what may cause undesirable effects after a woman has had an abortion, trauma variables have played an important part. For example, Russo and Denious (2001) at first found greater depressive symptoms, diminished life satisfaction, and a greater likelihood of experiencing rape, child physical or sexual abuse, and partner violence when they compared a sample of women who had experienced abortion ($n = 324$) with a sample of women who had not ($n = 2,201$). But after controlling for all aspects of the women's violence histories, they found that the abortion itself had no effect on the women's mental health variables. Other researchers also found that a history of violence may be related to postabortion, distress-related moderating factors such as social support and unstable relationships (Coleman, Maxey, Rue, & Coyle, 2005). However, their analysis has been criticized as methodologically flawed because they did not control for variables lost by excluding certain groups of subjects from the study initially. Additionally, "interpersonal pressure," which could be another way to label "controlling behavior," from a male partner has been found to significantly predict continuous postabortion distress at both 6 months and 2 years after an abortion (Broen, Torbjorn, Bodtker, & Ekeberg, 2005).

Although it seems obvious when studying the literature on domestic violence and controlling partners that they would be more likely to cause the woman's emotional distress rather than the misattribution to the abortion, this is rarely stated due to abortion politics where antiabortion supporters wish to emphasize the possible negative effects of the abortion itself. Most importantly, there are trauma-specific techniques that mental health professionals can use to work with those few women who do have emotional distress from abuse issues that rise to the surface after an abortion. Needle and Walker (2007) present them in their recent book on the topic.

SEXUAL ABUSE OF CHILDREN

The two areas of sexual abuse of children that were studied here included the sexual abuse of the children living in the home with the batterer and the prior sexual abuse of the battered women interviewed when they were children. Although we had to compromise the data we collected on sexual abuse of children living in the home because of the conflict with the mandatory child abuse report laws in Colorado at the time of the original study, we were able to get information that supported the findings of other researchers who were specifically studying child sexual abuse, and we report these results in Chapter 7, which discusses the negative effects on children. Moreover, the frequency with which incest occurred in homes where other forms of family violence existed was much higher than expected. We report the frequencies of various child sexual abuse acts in Table 9.6 and the racial and ethnic composition of those who engaged in child molestation in Table 9.7. As is evident from these data, like other forms of family violence, child sexual abuse within homes where mothers are battered by fathers cuts across all demographic lines.

Reports on child sexual assault by victims of battering in their adult homes are quite different from the typical rape victim report because of the complicated nature of the relationship between the father and the child. Most of the sexual assaults were incest committed by fathers against daughters, although some were brothers, uncles, and other family members.

Table 9.6 *Frequency of Childhood Sexual Assault Acts*

Sexual Assault Acts	Original % Attempted	Current % Attempted	Original % Single Incident	Current % Single Incident	Original % Several Times	Current % Several Times
Child fondled						
By father	.5	0	3	4	12	9
By sibling	4	5	7	0	12	2
By relative	7	2	11	3	27	15
By other	5	4	19	13	23	24
Child fondled						
By father	.5	0	1	0	2	5
By sibling	2	2	.5	0	5	0
By relative	0	2	2.5	0	10	8
By other	3	2	2	6	5	9
Oral sex						
By father	1	2	0	0	.5	0
By sibling	1	0	0	0	2	0
By relative	2	0	1	2	5	5
By other	3	0	3	3	3	5

(continued)

Table 9.6 Frequency of Childhood Sexual Assault Acts (continued)

Sexual Assault Acts	Original % Attempted	Current % Attempted	Original % Single Incident	Current % Single Incident	Original % Several Times	Current % Several Times
Sexual intercourse						
By father	2	2	1	0	0	0
By sibling	4	0	2	0	2	0
By relative	3	0	3	0	5	5
By other	6	1	11	9	6	13
Watch sex acts						
By father	0	0	.5	3	1	7
By sibling	1	0	1	2	.5	2
By relative	.5	0	2	2	3.5	11
By other	1	0	3	13	2	16
Other abuse						
By father	—	0	—	0	—	2
By sibling	—	0	—	2	—	2
By relative	—	0	—	0	—	8
By other	2	0	6	2	4	2

Table 9.7 *Racial and Ethnic Backgrounds of Women Reporting Childhood Sexual Assault*

	Original Sample N	Original Sample %	Current Sample N	Current Sample %
Total sample				
White/Caucasian	321	80	46	43
Hispanic/Latina	3	8	9	9
Black/African	25	6	9	9
Native Indian	18	4	2	2
Asian/Pacific Islander	1	0	1	1
Other	4	1	39	37
Women reporting childhood sexual assault				
White/Caucasian	144	45	10	42
Hispanic/Latina	23	68	2	8
Black/African	14	56	3	12
Native Indian	8	44	0	–
Asian/Pacific Islander	1	100	0	–
Other	2	50	9	37

Incest is more similar to marital rape and sexual coercion not only because of the complicated relationship with the perpetrator but also because the goal is to gain affection from the child even using coercion and force. It is dissimilar to physical child abuse in that it includes some kind of genital behavior and its primary goal is usually not to inflict pain on the victim. Rather, most incest perpetrators begin with what is called "grooming" behavior, where the father slowly engages the child and prepares her for further sexual behavior by giving her rewards of affection and sometimes special privileges to comply with his demands. It is dissimilar to other forms of coerced genital behavior as the young victim often perceives the perpetrator as needing love and affection from her as she does from him. Obviously, incest—whether or not overt violence is involved—has serious psychological ramifications for the victim. Although we suggested that our results be interpreted cautiously at the time they were first collected 30 years ago, we realize today that we only touched the tip of the iceberg. It is clear that incest occurs far more often than previously thought, in battering homes especially, and the impact is more far reaching than we suspected (Goodman et al., 1993; Herman, 1992; Koss et al., 1994; Walker, 1994).

It is interesting to speculate on the relationship between being molested as a child and subsequent physical and sexual abuse later in life as an adult. As previously described, almost one half of these battered women reported they had been repeatedly sexually victimized as children. This is two and a half times the number expected from other survey data available at the time of our study (Finkelhor, 1979). In his study of 795 college students, Finkelhor found that 19% of college women reported such early sexual victimization. He was also surprised to find that 9% of the college men reported childhood sexual experiences. In almost all cases, the aggressor was an adult male in the family—similar to our data. Finkelhor concluded from his data that the vulnerability for such sexual experiences could be created in the family, particularly where there are unhappy marriages. Our data suggest that the risk for sexual victimization of children increases if there is also violence in these families with poor boundaries between its members.

The knowledge of the impact on the child of early sexual molestation, with or without physical violence as part of the coercion, has expanded over the past 15 years. Most believe that such behavior is always coercive because of the adult's greater size, strength, and position of power over the child. However, there have always been some who question the actual harm to a child, especially if there is no physical violence or if there is fondling and no genital penetration. It is true that definitions keep changing even since our research. We were less conservative than Diana Russell who used the classic definition of rape that includes only penile–vaginal penetration with our definition of a broader array of sexual behaviors. In fact, no reports of child sexual abuse are totally free from the emotions of the reporter. It is abhorrent to think of an adult having sex with a child for most people, even its defenders. That may be why today it is more common for the general public to not want to believe that child sexual abuse, and particularly incest, really happens.

There is an entire industry that has sprung up to deny the existence of sexual abuse reports by claiming that there are many mental health professionals whose business depends on the epidemic of child sexual abuse reports (Loftus, 1993) or the mother is using false reports to alienate the child from the father (Gardner, 1987, 1992). Pope (1996, 1997) has demonstrated that using little relevant empirical data advocates for a false memory syndrome and obscures the clinical field so that children who may report truthfully are disbelieved. Unfortunately, this group of alarmists includes many of the former defenders of child sexual abuse who used to claim that it was not harmful to the child if it was done with loving intentions on the part of the perpetrator. Information countering their information can be found on the website of The Leadership Council, an interdisciplinary group whose purpose is to make accurate and scientific information on child abuse available (www.leadershipcouncil.org).

Courtois (1999) among others has demonstrated that the memory of adults who experienced sexual abuse as children is far more stable than otherwise believed, although from time to time certain facts are remembered and forgotten. Freyd (1994, 1996) suggests that the betrayal of the parent is a significant cognitive trauma that also must be assessed along with the actual physical, sexual, and other psychological behavior. Obviously, this debate makes the understanding of child sexual abuse even more complex than it already has been.

Children who experience early sexual molestation have been found to develop certain personality characteristics that assist their adaptation to an uncontrollable and frightening situation (Brown, 1992; Butler, 1978; Courtois, 1999; Finkelhor, 1979; Herman, 1992; Leidig, 1981; MacFarlane, 1978; Walker, 1994). Little girls learn they can control their mothers and fathers by being seductive and cute especially since this behavior is reinforced and rewarded. They also learn how important it is for them to keep this behavior a secret (Walker, 1988). Most incest survivors learn to equate sexuality with intimacy as they never fully experience the developmental stages of adolescence that encourage the growth of psychological intimacy. Their need for secrecy gets in the way of developing close friendships with girls in early adolescence. They also perceive, perhaps accurately, that other girls may not understand their feelings about boys and sex. Some report that they view nonsexually experienced girls as more naïve and less mature than themselves. These feelings are similar to our sample of battered women, at least as measured by their responses on the self-esteem scales. In essence, they report they missed out on teenage companionship and fun, but they also report they feel more experienced in other areas of their lives, particularly in sexual matters. Monica Lewinsky, the woman who had a sexual affair with President Clinton that almost brought down the Clinton White House, is a good example of such a person. Some incest victims report that they develop a sexual relationship with a boy closer to their own age, often as a way of terminating the sexual molestation. They rarely report platonic friendships with adolescent boys. This may promote different social skills that can leave the woman more isolated than if she had been able to develop more variety in her friendships during adolescence.

Terminating incest is usually accomplished by the victims, often during middle adolescence, by using a variety of methods (Finkelhor, 1979). Usually they seek assistance indirectly from a supportive peer or adult; that is, they do not ask directly for help but they do give enough hints or actually talk about the sexual molestation so that help is received. Sometimes they threaten the offender that they will disclose if it does not stop immediately. Depending on the offender, this may be sufficient to stop it, which helps reempower the girl. Victims hint that they might have dropped hints to their mothers but rarely do they tell them openly, perhaps recognizing their mothers' own vulnerability to the batterers' abuse.

The whole issue of complicity in mothers in permitting incest to continue has been one that has been given much attention in feminist analysis (Cammaert, 1988; Yllo, 1993). Given women's lack of power in some marital relationships, they may not have the ability to protect their daughters. In incest families where there is also spouse abuse, the girls perceive their mothers' inability to deal with the violence against themselves, too. While some girls harbor deep resentment against their mothers, usually for not being strong enough to protect them, they also report that they protected their mothers from the knowledge and they believed that giving in to their fathers' demands protected their mothers and the rest of the family from the fathers' violent behavior. This is an interesting perception as it includes some sense of power and purpose for these young women that may provide them with some resilience to a more severe impact from the abuse.

Some specialists in incest and child abuse have blamed the mother for encouraging the father's incestuous behavior as a way to escape from what they named as the mother's own obligations and "wifely duties" (Helfer & Kempe, 1974). Using this analysis, however, does not permit the man's sexual misconduct to be accurately understood. The data indicate that he is more likely to be attracted to the daughter precisely because she is a young girl who can be more easily coerced. Abel et al. (1981) have found that despite reports to the contrary, the incest fathers they evaluated demonstrated physiological arousal patterns in the laboratory similar to other child molesters. This occurred when they viewed slides of young girls and adult women in erotic poses. A penile-tumescence–measuring device recorded the respondents' sexual arousal to the pictures of young girls. Thus, it appears that many family members who molest young children are more sexually aroused by children than by adult women. This empirical evidence certainly supports the victims' and their mothers' retrospective incest accounts. It has serious implications for reevaluating family treatment modalities and creating new treatment programs for offenders that follow the protocols that have been developed for other pedophiles (Becker, 1990).

The impact of child sexual abuse (including incest), like battering and other interpersonal trauma, seems to be based on a multidimensional model that includes intervening contextual or mediating variables together with the acts that occurred, who did them, and over what time span. Finkelhor (1979), for example, found that some reported long-term and repeated occurrences had the same psychological impact as did some short-term behavior. Some reported encounters that involved exhibitionism and/or fondling as equally traumatic as some where intercourse was completed. These findings have been responsible for the broadening of the definition of child sexual abuse so that it is understood that the impact must be studied from the child's perspective and not just the arbitrary assignment of the severity of acts committed by the perpetrator. Father–daughter incest was reported as the most devastating for the child, perhaps because it robs the child of her right to have a father and a mother in her life. Sex with other family members was seen as devastating as sex with a stranger in our population. Finkelhor's study, like ours, found that sexual abuse accompanied with violent force reportedly produced the most serious psychological trauma. Some of these children run away from home at an early age and become caught up in a life of drugs, sex, and violence (James, 1978). In our sample, over half left home before the age of 17. Obviously, it is critical to try to prevent the toll that this kind of violence takes on the family and especially the future lives of these children.

BATTERED WOMEN, SEX, AND INTIMACY

Many of the behaviors described by our battered women were similarly described by those who work with sexually molested children, which is why I have placed the discussion around the sexual abuse of children in this chapter rather than the earlier one on child abuse. The behaviors include "manipulativeness" that is important to help "keep the peace," the unrealistic sense of power achieved through the use of seduction, the intense concentration on self-survival, the willingness to become dependent on a man who can be both loving and violent at times, the fear of attempting survival alone, the knowledge of how to decrease a man's violence by demonstrating love to him, and the joy from experiencing intense intimacy. It is quite possible that early exposure to sexual abuse, with or without accompanying violence, creates a dependency on the positive aspects of the intense intimacy experienced prior to the beginning of the battering behavior and maintained throughout the third phase of loving contrition.

This raises some questions about these battered women's ability to make distinctions between sexual and emotional intimacy. It seems as if both the violent man and the battered woman confuse their need for emotional intimacy with sex, thinking they have met both needs through their intensely sexual relationships. However, the men cannot sustain such intimacy without becoming intensely frightened of their growing dependency on the women; the women become frightened by their dependency on the men also, and both begin to pull away from each other. Then, needing the intimacy to lessen the violence, both come back together again. Although the women do not need or like the violence that is part of this cycle, they often accept it as part of what they have to put up with in order get all the other benefits of the relationship. Only when the costs of the relationship outweigh the benefits will a battered woman take steps to terminate it. If the man permits her to leave, then it is over like so many other relationships. But if his dependency needs, possessiveness, and vindictiveness get in the way, he will not let her go even after the ties may be legally severed.

Stalking and continued harassment of battered women by their current and former abusive partners are better understood now than 15 years ago (Burgess et al., 1997; Walker & Meloy, 1998). Some of the reports we had during the research are similar to the attachment theories proposed by Meloy (1998); and for those where there is also sexual abuse, Meloy's construct of *erotomania* may also apply. Erotomania, considered part of a psychotic delusional disorder, occurs when persons fall in love with someone without any evidence that the other person has any feelings of affection or love toward them. Some people diagnosed with erotomania have never even met the object of their intense love, such as movie or television stars. They may follow their love object around, stalk them, sneak into their homes, write them love notes, and find other ways of attempting to make a reciprocal relationship. Of course, the issue of stalking in domestic relationships is broader, as described in Chapter 12, but in relationships where sexual abuse is a featured component, it is important to assess for these issues, too.

BATTERED WOMEN AND SEXUALLY TRANSMITTED DISEASES

HIV and AIDS

Although this research asked many different questions about sexuality, we did not inquire into the issue of sexually transmitted diseases, especially HIV and AIDS. However, new data since our study show that there is a higher risk for battered women to be unprotected during sexual intercourse with abusive partners (American Psychological Association [APA], 1996; Koss et al., 1994; Koss & Haslet, 1992; Seligson & Bernas, 1997). Both the coercive nature of the sexual relationship and the need for the batterer to have control over the woman make it difficult if not impossible for her to demand that her partner use condoms and other protection during sex. Women who have been sexually abused previously are also known to be more likely to have unprotected sex (APA, 1996) although it is not known if it is a lack of assertiveness especially around sexual matters or a naïve belief that their partners are not sexual with anyone else unless they tell them so. It is interesting that battered women shelters do not ask for this information while women live in shelter, perhaps because they would not know what to do with the women should they turn out to be HIV positive. Therefore, they are exposing the other women and children to high risk when taking simple precautions would permit an HIV-positive woman to live in the communal home.

Those who engage in the commercial sex industry also have a much higher risk of contracting a sexually transmitted disease, including HIV and AIDS. Although many young women who have escaped from abusive homes may engage in survival sex for a short period of time, often to support drug habits they have developed, if they do not use protection during sexual contact, they may not be able to get out of that life as they often plan to do. In any case, the need for good education and training for professionals as well as battered women in this area is critical (Dalla, Xia, & Kennedy, 2000).

PORNOGRAPHY

The issue of pornography and sexual abuse is one that has divided feminists for many years, not in their collective understanding that there is a relationship with those who frequently use pornography, particularly to stimulate themselves to orgasms, but rather, in what to do about it (MacKinnon, 1989). Many feminists, particularly those who have contributed to the scholarship in feminist psychology (Brown, 1994; Farley, 2004) and feminist jurisprudence (MacKinnon, 1983), debate the civil rights issue of freedom of speech and other First Amendment arguments while acknowledging the inherent dangers of access to the brutal violent images of defiled women often seen in popular pornography. Men interested in changing gender-role stereotypes believe that pornography contributes to the "macho-man" image (Brooks, 1996; Levant, 1997; Levant & Pollack, 1993).

Lederer (1980), Rave (1985), and others have written about how pornography is a negative leveler by men against women, permitting them to see women as sex objects. Brooks (1996, 1998) supports this feminist position and details how men permit themselves to shut off their real feelings and violate women by numbing themselves to the full range of sexual expression while focusing on pornographic and centerfold images. These men are much less likely to feel empathy, sympathy, or support for women who then can more easily become their victims. Many of these men engage in frequent masturbation, sometimes as much as hourly during each day. Obviously, these men have learned to self-soothe their anxiety and other unpleasant emotions using sexual stimulation and relief. We still do not know if there is a direct behavioral connection between frequent masturbation, frequent viewing of pornography, and attachment issues and violence, although the studies point to trends in that direction. However, recent studies have demonstrated that men who use pornography are significantly more likely to sexually abuse as well as physically abuse their intimate partners and those who also use alcohol with the pornography increase the odds of a battered woman being sexually abused (Shope, 2004).

An interesting phenomenon that ties use of pornography on the Internet together with the sexual abuse of women and children has been found in the legal community. This is especially common in treatment centers for pedophiles. These men will molest anywhere around several hundred victims, most of whom are too frightened into not making disclosures. Some of the most difficult child custody cases involve men who molest children copying the images they have downloaded on their computers or rented from adult video stores. In fact, it is common for divorce attorneys to subpoena the family computers and learn what websites have been entered to view or even interact with pornography and chat rooms.

DATING VIOLENCE

Young women have been found to be at risk for abuse in their dating relationships especially if they become sexually active when young teens (Levy, 1991). Studies have shown that maybe as many as 25% of teens are abused by their boyfriends on a regular basis (Makepeace, 1981). Often these girls come from homes where they have witnessed abuse of their mothers by their fathers. It is not unusual for the abuse to begin after sexual intimacy occurs in a battering relationship, often starting with jealousy, possessiveness, and attempts to isolate the woman. Many teenage girls who want the security of a boyfriend are uncomfortable with an abuser's attempts to isolate her from high school activities and other friends. Monopolizing her perceptions before she has a chance to learn how to think for herself is a typical way dating violence starts.

In a number of cases, the women reported that the first sexual encounter was really a battering incident and a rape where the men refused to stop sex when they asked them. The women stated that they thought they were just kissing and fooling around with no intentions of having sexual intercourse when all of a sudden, they realized the men were gratifying themselves without communicating with or showing concern for the women. Sometimes the young women went on to marry the men hoping that this would prove to them that they really loved them and wanted the relationship to work out. Some of the women described themselves as very religious or from other cultures where their virginity was essential to getting a good husband. These women felt that they had no choice but to marry these men, speaking as though there was now no going back!

We asked women to describe the different types of intimate relationships that they had during their lives. On average they had 2.1 intimate relationships, with one half married to one of the men and one half in significant relationships with other living arrangements. Interestingly, they had been dating less than 6 months when they moved in or married the batterers. The average age of the women in our sample when the battering relationship became intimate was 22 years old for battering and 24 years old for nonbattering relationships. Our data suggest that sexual intimacy may occur sooner in the dating period of battering than nonbattering relationships. No apparent differences were found if the battering relationship came first, second, or in another sequence in their life history relationship.

Sex and Aggression

Researchers have postulated a connection between sex and aggression in some individuals, usually men, that appears to have been conditioned in an earlier stage of development (Abel, Becker, & Skinner, 1980; Donnerstein, 1982; Feshback & Malamuth, 1978; Malamuth & Donnerstein, 1982). In several studies, average male college students were exposed to movies that depicted sexual aggression and then given a situation to discuss concerning their potential to take sexual advantage of a young woman. Interestingly, the more aggression associated with the sex in the movie, the greater the proclivity to rape found in their responses. Although the researchers did not collect data on the exposure of the males to violence in their childhood homes or their current sexual behavior if they were dating, our results would predict that these attitudes would result in greater use of violence in their homes. However, Donnerstein (1982) and Malamuth and Donnerstein (1982) found that debriefing the subjects carefully in a discussion group that talked about the feelings that were aroused right after the movies lowered the proclivity to rape to even lower levels than the baseline levels collected prior to exposure to the sex and aggression movies. This is important information for prevention programs for those children who are at high risk for developing such attitudes and behavior pairing sex and aggression when they become adolescents. Talking about their feelings or psychotherapy may well be an important prevention tool.

SUMMARY

Attachment theory is proposed as a theoretical framework within which to examine the disrupted interpersonal issues found as one of the areas in BWS. Whether the disruption occurred earlier than the battering relationship or from the relationship itself could not be answered from this research. However, it poses several interesting issues to continue to study especially since almost half of the original sample had been sexually abused as children. It is known that such early sexualization of children may cause interpersonal difficulties that may make it more difficult to recognize the cycle of violence engaged in by the batterer.

The research project that we conducted found support for other research that links sexual abuse to other forms of violence in the relationship. Several points stand out and need further clarification. What role does early sexualization of a relationship play in later sexual violence that occurs? Obviously to answer this question, we would have to follow women over a long period of time to see what happens in their lives and, once we appear as permanent or even semipermanent parts of their lives, we will change the outcome. After all, we have learned that the less isolation and more supportive presence of others are there in the woman's life, the greater are the chances of stopping the abuse or at least mitigating against serious effects! We also need more information about the interrelationship between child sexual abuse, specifically incest, and later sexual abuse in the relationship, and then, sexual abuse of the woman's children by the adult abuser. To collect the data in this area is more difficult given the interrelatedness of several legal systems (family, criminal, and juvenile) and the involvement of child protective services. However, it is not impossible to do so, in the other chapters on children. Finally, it would be interesting to know more about the battered woman's perceptions of emotional and sexual intimacy and how that impacts on her during the time she is in the relationship. Comparing these data to women who are sexually abused as children but not as adults will help us gain more knowledge in this area.

REFERENCES

Abel, G. G., Becker, J. V., Murphy, W. D., & Flanagan, B. (1981). Identifying dangerous child molesters. In R. B. Stuart (Ed.), *Violent behavior: Social learning approaches to prediction, management, and treatment* (pp. 116–137). New York, NY: Brunner/Mazel.

Abel, G. G., Becker, J. V., & Skinner, L. J. (1980). Aggressive behavior and sex. *Psychiatric Clinics of North America, 3*(1), 133–151.

American Psychiatric Association. (2013). *Diagnostic and statistical manual of mental disorders* (5th ed.). Arlington, VA: American Psychiatric Publishing.

American Psychological Association. (1996). *Report from the Presidential Task Force on Violence and the Family.* Washington, DC: Author.

Antonopoulou, C. (1999). Domestic violence in Greece. *American Psychologist, 54,* 63–64.

Bartholomew, K. (1990). Adult avoidance of intimacy: An attachment perspective. *Journal of Social and Personal Relationships, 7,* 147–178.

Bartholomew, K., & Horowitz, L. M. (1991). Attachment styles among young adults: A test of a four category model. *Journal of Personality and Social Psychology, 61,* 226–244.

Bartoi, M. G., & Kinder, B. N. (1998). Effects of child and adult sexual abuse on adult sexuality. *Journal of Sex & Marital Therapy, 24,* 75–90.

Bartoi, M. G., Kinder, B. N., & Tomianovic, D. (2000). Interaction effects of emotional status and sexual abuse and adult sexuality. *Journal of Sex & Marital Therapy, 26,* 1–23.

Becker, J. M. (1990). Treating adolescent sex offenders. *Professional Psychology: Research and Practice, 21,* 362–365.

Bowlby, J. (1973). *Attachment and loss: Volume 2. Separation: Anxiety and anger.* New York, NY: Basic Books.

Brennan, K. A., Clark, C. L., & Shaver, P. R. (1998). Self-report measurement of adult romantic attachment: An integrative overview. In J. A. Simpson & W. S. Rholes (Eds.), *Attachment theory and close relationships* (pp. 46–76). New York, NY: Guilford Press.

Broen, A. N., Torbjorn, M., Bodtker, A. S., & Ekeberg, O. (2005). The course of mental health after miscarriage and induced abortion: A five year follow-up study. *BMC Medicine, 3*(18). Retrieved from https://bmcmedicine.biomedcentral.com/articles/10.1186/1741-7015-3-18

Brooks, G. (1996). *The centerfold psychology.* San Francisco, CA: Jossey-Bass.

Brooks, G. (1998). *A new psychotherapy for traditional men.* San Francisco, CA: Jossey-Bass.

Brown, L. S. (1992). The feminist critique of personality disorders. In L. S. Brown & M. Ballou (Eds.), *Personality and psychopathology: Feminist reappraisals.* New York, NY: Guilford Press.

Brown, L. S. (1994). *Subversive dialogues: Theory in feminist therapy.* New York, NY: Basic Books.

Browne, A. (1993). Violence against women by male partners. *American Psychologist, 48,* 1077–1087.

Burgess, A. W., Baker, T., Greening, D., Hartman, C. R., Burgess, A. G., Douglas, J. E., & Halloran, R. (1997). Stalking behaviors within domestic violence. *Journal of Family Violence, 12,* 389–403.

Butler, S. (1978). *Conspiracy of silence: The trauma of incest.* San Francisco, CA: Bantam Books.

Cammaert, L. (1988). Non-offending mothers: A new conceptualization. In L. E. A. Walker (Ed.), *Handbook on sexual abuse of children* (pp. 309–325). New York, NY: Springer Publishing Company.

Cascardi, M., & O'Leary, K. D. (1992). Depressive symptomatology, self-esteem, and self-blame in battered women. *Journal of Family Violence, 7*(4), 249–259.

Clements, C. M., Sabourin, C. M., & Spiby, L. (2004). Dysphoria and hopelessness following battering: The role of perceived control, coping, and self-esteem. *Journal of Family Violence, 19*(1), 25–36.

Cohen, J. (1988). *Statistical power analysis for the behavioral sciences* (2nd ed.). Hillsdale, NJ: Erlbaum.

Coleman, P. K., Maxey, C. D., Rue, V. M., & Coyle, C. T. (2005). Associations between voluntary and involuntary forms of perinatal loss and child maltreatment among low-income mothers. *Acta Paediatrica, 94*(10), 1476–1483.

Courtois, C. A. (1999). *Recollections of sexual abuse: Treatment principles and guidelines.* New York, NY: W. W. Norton.

d'Ardenne, P., & Balakrishna, J. (2001). Domestic violence and intimacy: What the relationship therapist needs to know. *Sexual and Relationship Therapy, 16*(3), 229–246.

Dalla, R. I., Xia, V., & Kennedy, H. (2000). "You just give them what they want and pray that they don't kill you." *Violence Against Women, 9,* 1367–1394.

Derogatis, L. R. (1978). *Derogatis Sexual Functioning Inventory.* Baltimore, MD: Clinical Psychometrics Research.

Donnerstein, E. (1982). Aggressive-erotica and violence against women. *Journal of Personality and Social Psychology, 39,* 269–277.

Doron, J. (1980). *Conflict and violence in intimate relationships: Focus on marital rape.* New York, NY: American Sociological Association.

Duros, R., & Walker, L. E. A. (2006, August). Battered woman syndrome, PTSD, and implications for treatment recommendations. In L. E. A. Walker & D. L. Shapiro (Chairs), *Forensic psychology for the independent practitioner.* Symposium presented at the 114th Annual Meeting of the American Psychological Association, New Orleans, LA.

Dutton, D. G. (1995). *The batterer: A psychological profile.* New York, NY: Basic Books.

Dutton, D. G., & Sonkin, D. J. (2003). *Intimate violence: Contemporary treatment innovations.* Binghamton, NY: Haworth Press.

Dutton, M. A., Brughardt, K. J., Perrin, S. G., Chrestman, K. R., & Halle, P. M. (1994). Battered women's cognitive schemata. *Journal of Traumatic Stress, 7*(2), 237–255.

Dutton, M. A., & Goodman, L. S. (1994). Posttraumatic stress disorder among battered women: Analysis of legal implications. *Behavioral Sciences and the Law, 12,* 215–234.

Farley, M. (Ed.). (2004). *Prostitution, trafficking, and traumatic stress.* Binghamton, NY: Haworth Press.

Feshback, S. & Malamuth, N. M. (1978). Sex and aggression: Proving the link. *Psychology Today, 12*(6), 111–122.

Finkelhor, D. (1979). *Sexually victimized children.* New York, NY: Free Press.

Finkelhor, D., Williams, L. M., & Burns, N. (1988). *Nursery crimes: Sexual abuse in day care.* Newbury Park, CA: Sage.

Finkelhor, D., & Yllo, K. (1983). Rape in marriage: A sociological view. In D. Finkelhor, R. J. Gelles, G. T. Hotaling, & M. A. Straus (Eds.), *The dark side of families* (pp. 119–130). Beverly Hills, CA: Sage.

Finkelhor, D., & Yllo, K. (1985). *License to rape: Sexual abuse of wives.* New York, NY: Holt, Rinehart, & Winston.

Frese, B., Moya, M., & Megias, J. I. (2004). Social perception of rape: How rape myth acceptance modulates the influence of situational factors. *Journal of Interpersonal Violence, 19,* 143–161.

Freyd, J. (1994). Betrayal-trauma: Traumatic amnesia as an adaptive response to childhood abuse. *Ethics and Behavior, 4,* 304–309.

Freyd, J. J. (1996). *Betrayal-trauma: The logic of forgetting child abuse.* Cambridge, MA: Harvard University Press.

Frieze, I. H., & Knoble, J. (1980, September). *The effects of alcohol on marital violence.* Paper presented at the 88th Annual Convention of the American Psychological Association, Montreal, Quebec, Canada.

Gardner, R. (1987). *The parental alienation syndrome and the differentiation between fabrication and genuine child abuse.* Creskill, NJ: Creative Therapeutics.

Gardner, R. (1992). *True and false accusations of child sex abuse.* Creskill, NJ: Creative Therapeutics.

Gelles, R. J. (1975). Violence and pregnancy: A note on the extent of the problem and needed services. *Family Coordinator, 24,* 81–86.

Goodman, L., Koss, M. P., Browne, A., Fitzgerald, L., Russo, N. F., Biden, J. R., & Keita, G. P. (1993). Psychology in the public forum. Male violence against women: Current research and future directions. *American Psychologist, 48,* 1054–1087.

Greenwald, E., Leitenberg, H., Cado, S., & Tarran, M. J. (1990). Childhood sexual abuse: Long-term effects on psychological and sexual functioning in a non-clinical and nonstudent sample of adult women. *Child Abuse & Neglect, 14*(4), 503–513.

Hazan, C., & Shaver, P. R. (1987). Romantic love conceptualized as an attachment process. *Journal of Personality and Social Psychology, 52,* 511–524.

Helfer, E. R., & Kempe, C. H. (1974). *The battered child* (2nd ed.). Chicago, IL: University of Chicago Press.

Henderson, A., Bartholomew, K., & Dutton, D. G. (1997). He loves me; he loves me not: Attachment and separation resolution of abused women. *Journal of Family Violence, 12,* 169–191.

Herman, J. L. (1992). *Trauma and recovery.* New York, NY: Basic Books.

Hilberman, E., & Munson, L. (1978). Sixty battered women. *Victimology: An International Journal, 2*(3–4), 460–471.

Hotaling, G. T., & Sugarman, D. B. (1986). An analysis of risk markers in husband to wife violence: The current state of the knowledge. *Violence and Victims, 1,* 101–124.

Jacobson, N. S., & Gottman, J. M. (1998). *When men batter women: New insights into ending abusive relationships.* New York, NY: Simon & Schuster.

James, J. (1978). The prostitute as victim. In J. R. Chapman & M. Gates (Eds.), *The victimization of women* (pp. 175–201). Beverly Hills, CA: Sage.

Janoff-Bulman, R. (1985). The aftermath of victimization: Rebuilding shattered assumptions. In C. Figley (Ed.), *Trauma and its wake* (pp. 15–35). New York, NY: Brunner/Mazel.

Karen, R. (1994). *Becoming attached: First relationships and how they shape our capacity to love.* New York, NY: Oxford University Press.

Klein, M. (1975). *The psychoanalysis of children.* New York, NY: Free Press.

Koss, M. P., Goodman, L. A., Browne, A., Fitzgerald, L. F., Keita, G. P., & Russo, N. F. (1994). *No safe haven: Male violence against women at home, at work, and in the community.* Washington, DC: American Psychological Association.

Koss, M. P., & Haslet, L. (1992). Somatic consequences of violence against women. *Archives of Family Medicine, 1,* 53–59.

Laura X. (1998). National Clearinghouse on Marital Rape. Berkeley, CA: Women's History Research Center.

Lederer, L. (Ed.). (1980). *Take back the night: Women on pornography.* New York, NY: William Morrow.

Leidig, M. W. (1981). Violence against women: A feminist-psychological analysis. In S. Cox (Ed.), *Female psychology: The emerging self* (2nd ed., pp. 190–205). New York, NY: St. Martin's Press.

Levant, R. F. (1997). Nonrelational sexuality in men. In R. F. Levant & G. R. Brooks (Eds.), *Men and sex: New psychological perspectives* (pp. 9–27). New York, NY: Wiley.

Levant, K. S., & Pollack, W. S. (1993). *A new psychology of men.* New York, NY: Basic Books.

Levy, B. (1991). *Dating violence: Young women in danger.* Seattle, WA: Seal Press.

Loftus, E. F. (1993). The reality of repressed memories. *American Psychologist, 48,* 518–537.

Lopez, F. G., & Brennan, K. (2000). Dynamic processes underlying adult attachment organization: Toward an attachment theoretical perspective on the healthy and effective self. *Journal of Counseling Psychology, 47,* 283–300.

MacFarlane, K. (1978). Sexual abuse of children. In J. R. Chapman & M. Gates (Eds.), *The victimization of women. Sage Yearbooks in Women's Policy Studies* (Vol. 3). Beverly Hills, CA: Sage.

MacKinnon, C. A. (1983). Feminism, Marxism, method, and the state: Toward feminist jurisprudence. *Signs, 8*(4), 635–658.

MacKinnon, C. A. (1989). Sexuality, pornography, and method: Pleasure under patriarchy. *Ethics, 99*(2), 314–346.

Makepeace, J. (1981). Courtship: Violence among college students. *Family Relations, 30,* 97–102.

Malamuth, N. M., & Donnerstein, E. (1982). The effects of aggressive-pornographic mass media stimuli. *Advances in Experimental Social Psychology, 15,* 103–136.

Martin, D. (1976). *Battered wives.* San Francisco, CA: Glide.

Martin, V. (1982). Wife-beating: A product of socio-sexual development. In M. Kirkpatrick (Ed.), *Women's sexual experiences: Explorations of the dark continent* (pp. 247–261). New York, NY: Plenum Press.

Meloy, J. R. (Ed.). (1998). *The psychology of stalking.* San Diego, CA: Academic Press.

Merrill, L. L., Guimond, J. M., Thomsen, C. J., & Milner, J. S. (2003). Child sexual abuse and number of sexual partners in young women: The role of abuse severity, coping style, and sexual functioning. *Journal of Consulting and Clinical Psychology, 71,* 987–996.

Needle, R., Walker, L., Duros, R., Darby, S., Tang, J., & Tome, A. (2007, August). *Traumatic effects of battered woman syndrome: Sexuality, body image, and the battered woman syndrome.* Symposium presented at the annual meeting of the American Psychological Association, San Francisco, CA.

Needle, R. B., & Walker, L. E. A. (2007). *Abortion counseling: A clinician's guide to psychology, legislation, politics, and competency.* New York, NY: Springer Publishing Company.

Pagelow, M. D. (1982). *Woman battering: Victims and their experiences.* Beverly Hills, CA: Sage.

Pope, K. S. (1996). Memory, abuse, and science: Questioning claims about the false memory syndrome epidemic. *American Psychologist, 51*(9), 957–974.

Pope, K. S. (1997). Science as careful questioning: Are claims of a false memory syndrome epidemic based on empirical evidence? *American Psychologist, 52*(9), 997–1006.

Rave, E. (1985). Pornography: The leveler of women. In *Feminist Therapy: A coming of age.* Selected proceedings from the Advanced Feminist Therapy Institute, Vail, CO, April 1982.

Roy, M. (1978). *Battered women: A psychological study.* New York, NY: Van Nostrand.

Russell, D. E. H. (1975). *The politics of rape.* New York, NY: Stein & Day.

Russell, D. E. H. (1982). *Rape in marriage.* New York, NY: Macmillan.

Russo, N. F., & Denious, J. E. (2001). Violence in the lives of women having abortions: Implications for practice and public policy. *Professional Psychology: Research and Practice, 32*(2), 142.

Sarwer, D. B., & Durlak, J. A. (1996). Childhood sexual abuse as a predictor of adult female sexual dysfunction: A study of couples seeking sex therapy. *Child Abuse & Neglect, 20,* 963–972.

Seligson, M. R., & Bernas, R. J. (1997). Battered women and AIDS: Assessment and treatment from a psychosocial-educational perspective. *Psychotherapy, 34,* 509–515.

Shope, J. H. (2004). When words are not enough: The search for the effect of pornography on abused women. *Violence Against Women, 10,* 56–72.

Snell, J. E., Rosenwald, R. J., & Robey A. (1964). The wifebeater's wife: A study of family interaction. *Archives of General Psychiatry, 2,* 107–112.

Straus, M. A., & Gelles, R. J. (1990). *Physical violence in American families: Risk factors and adaptations to violence in 8,145 families.* New Brunswick, NJ: Transaction Press.

Straus, M. A., Gelles, R. J., & Steinmetz, S. K. (1980). *Behind closed doors: Violence in the American family.* Garden City, NY: Anchor/Doubleday.

van Berlo, W., & Ensink, B. (2000). Problems with sexuality after sexual assault. *Annual Review of Sex Research, 11*(1), 235–257.

Walker, L. E. (1979). *The battered woman.* New York, NY: Harper & Row.

Walker, L. E. (Ed.). (1988). *Handbook on sexual abuse of children.* New York, NY: Springer Publishing Company.

Walker, L. E. A. (1994). *Abused women and survivor therapy: A practical guide for the psychotherapist.* Washington, DC: American Psychological Association.

Walker, L. E. A. (2007, August). *Traumatic effects of BWS.* Presented at the 115th Annual Meeting of the American Psychological Association, San Francisco, CA.

Walker, L. E. A., & Meloy, J. R. (1998). Stalking and domestic violence. In J. R. Meloy (Ed.), *The psychology of stalking: Clinical and forensic perspectives.* San Diego, CA: Academic Press.

Washburne, C., & Frieze, I. H. (1980, March). *Methodological issues in studying battered women.* Paper presented at the meeting of the Association for Women in Psychology, Santa Monica, CA.

Yllo, K. (1981, July). *Types of martial rape: Three case studies.* Paper presented at the National Conference for Family Violence Researchers, University of New Hampshire, Durham.

Yllo, K. (1993). Through a feminist lens: Gender, power, and violence. In R. J. Gelles & D. R. Loeske (Eds.), *Current controversies on family violence* (pp. 47–62). Newbury Park, CA: Sage.

CHAPTER TEN

MURDER–SUICIDES AND SELF-DEFENSE

MURDER, SUICIDE, AND SELF-DEFENSE

Florida, where I live and work, is known as the murder–suicide capital of the world, and South Florida, particularly the Miami–Fort Lauderdale–Palm Beach area tops the list. Several students working on our research teams decided to look at why there were so many reports in the newspapers of women being killed by their intimate partners. Although there are not a lot of studies about families where one person kills the other person and then kills himself or herself, those that are available are pretty clear that Florida simply has more of what is found in other areas. For example, the Violence Policy Center in 2008 found that Florida goes back and forth within the top three states in the United States during the past 10 years with two to four times as many murder–suicides as in other regions. Further, other studies such as those using data from the National Violent Death Reporting System (NVDRS) show that like in other areas that send in their data, it is a man who kills the woman and then himself in 95% of the cases. In cases where the woman commits homicide, it is usually against the children and then she kills herself. Further, in close to three quarters of the cases, there had been intimate partner violence reported of the man toward the woman prior to the homicide–suicide, especially if he also killed the children as well as his partner and himself.

Dr. Thomas Joiner, a psychologist at Florida State University, has been trying to understand murder–suicides culminating in his book in 2014, *The Perversion of Virtue*. Having studied suicides for many years, he believes that most murder–suicides are really suicides by persons who have premeditated suicide and then, in a perverted mission to protect the people who might be left to deal with their absence, kill them also. While this may be true for some murder–suicides such as mercy killings or even those who believe that life is too horrible for their family members to live,

I do not believe it applies to the murder–suicides where a batterer kills his partner and maybe also their children. Rather, I believe he wishes to murder his partner and kills himself to avoid facing the consequences or to remain together in "heaven" if he truly is a believer. This behavior of the batterer appears to stem from a desire to kill the person who has rejected him and make her suffer by watching him kill their children. In almost all these cases, the murder–suicide occurs during the separation period, not while they are together. He tortures his victim by threatening to do exactly what he ends up doing. Fortunately, not all untreated batterers who make these threats actually kill their victims. Some do commit suicide while others go on to abuse another partner.

We attempted to analyze the murder–suicide cases we found through a review of the newspaper reports of murder–suicides in the five major regions of the state of Florida to see if we could identify common risk factors. What we found paralleled what is reported in other areas. The typical risk factors are: a 30- to 50-year-old man who has had some depression, some intimate partner violence including psychological power and control needs, separations, and reunions in the relationship, may use alcohol or other drugs, and has a history of being dependent on the woman to meet his emotional needs. The man is said to have morbid jealousy, delusions, and paranoia, often accusing the woman of having other affairs and making verbal threats to harm her or others. Although the man may be seen by others as being very assertive, underneath he is fragile and cannot tolerate any rejection. The homicide–suicide trigger is the separation and if there are children, then a custody dispute in family court may set him off. The man often blames others for his problems and fears losing his control over the woman.

Guns in the home are the predominant weapons used in the murder–suicides in the United States. In fact, there is a study by Casey Gwinn, a long-time prosecutor in San Diego, who found that guns kept in the home are most likely used to threaten women by men who engage in intimate partner battering. In countries where guns are not as accessible in the home, such as Great Britain, there is a lower murder and suicide rate. When murder–suicides occur in those countries, it is more likely by sharp objects or strangulation. Jacqueline Campbell and her colleagues found in a multisite study of femicide in abusive relationships that lack of employment and education by the man, the presence of a child in the home who was not his biological child, and use of illicit drugs were additional risk factors.

Given the frequency with which guns are easily accessible for police officers, it was not surprising in our research to find that a high number of police are involved in murder–suicide cases in their own homes (Klinoff et al., 2015). In some of these cases, there was known domestic violence that had been reported previously. In others, the domestic violence was learned about afterward, usually through investigation or family members. Most of the cases we uncovered were of a man who killed the woman and then himself; although in one police case, it appeared that the woman shot him first and then killed herself.

The finding that the family court process can serve as a trigger for some murder–suicides is important especially since Florida keeps passing new legislation to force families into shared parenting arrangements that continuously fail to meet the needs of children and their parents. It is not in the best interests of these children, as discussed in the other chapters on child abuse and custody and access issues, to have to move back and forth between the homes of parents when there has been domestic violence. Nor is it in their best interests for their fathers to transfer their unmet dependency needs to them instead of finding other people in their lives with whom they can form new relationships. Protective moms, as we have said before, are in constant danger from their former batterers who continue their psychological abuse even if they stop the physical harm. Unfortunately, neither the courts nor custody evaluators pay sufficient attention to the dangers that occur when a batterer, especially one with a serious mental illness, is given access to the children and his partner.

Ed and Linda

In one murder–suicide case in which I was involved, the man, let us call him Ed, was about 20 years older than the woman, Linda, whom he married when she was still a teenager. Having survived her own abusive childhood, Linda was happy to have Ed be her protector and did not find his behavior controlling until he stopped permitting her to leave their apartment when he was not there by locking her inside without a phone or other way to make contact with outsiders. Ed's own work habits were sporadic and even after they had two children, he would pack up their things on what seemed to be a whim to her, and they would all travel to different places in the country, basically isolating her and the children. When the children were 4 and 6 years old, he drove them to a recreational vehicle

(RV) park and while they were in the car, he got out and knocked on the door of an occupied RV. When the man answered the door, Ed shot and killed him. The woman fled from the house as Ed motioned for Linda and the children, who were both shocked and terrified, to join him in the RV. They remained secluded in the RV for hours, during which time Ed shot each of the boys forcing Linda to watch, then shot Linda, and then shot and killed himself. One of the boys and Linda barely survived and were able to tell the story. After Linda healed from her wounds, sadly she was arrested and charged with the death and attempted death of the children. This is not unusual in cases where the man murders the child or children and then himself. Their mothers are held responsible for failing to protect them despite the failure of the court system itself.

SELF-DEFENSE CASES

The statistics for homicide are not much better for battered women whether or not the abuser kills himself. Domestic violence is definitely not good for a woman's health nor for longevity. More women are killed by men than are men killed by women. In fact, a man is less likely to be killed by a woman if they live in an area where there are services available for battered women. The homicide rate is down for men dying but not so for women being killed by abusive partners. In addition to being murdered, Jacqueline Campbell suggests that domestic violence is implicated in premature deaths of women from aggravated health conditions such as strokes, heart attacks, and other major illnesses that occur after being choked or strangled, resulting in some anoxia even for a short time. So what is a woman to do?

Some women take matters in their own hands and attempt to protect themselves by killing the abuser. But these cases do not always end well for the woman, either. The cases are not new but not always understood at attempts at self-defense. Let us look at a few in the following sections.

Nellie Mae Madison

In 1934, Nellie Mae Madison shot and killed her husband by shooting him as he was raising his hand with a knife in it and coming toward her in a threatening manner. Nellie Mae was not your typical 1930s woman; she smoked, had been married and divorced previously, and did not have any children. She was quite glamorous and often hung out with a Hollywood movie crowd. In fact she was dubbed the "enigmatic woman." She had bought the gun she used to shoot him shortly before, later claiming it was to defend herself due to his violence getting worse. But no one who knew her would have expected her to kill her husband. After she was found and arrested, she refused to speak and actually denied that the man whose body was found in her apartment was her husband. She was convicted of first-degree murder and sentenced to die, a rarity in California in 1934. However, a newspaper reporter took an interest in the story and Nellie Mae agreed to speak with her after she was convicted. The story she told was similar to other battered women who ended up killing their abusers in self-defense. He had beaten Nellie Mae previously and had also beaten a former wife of his, who came to Nellie Mae's defense, and the death penalty was overturned. After serving 9 years in prison, Nellie Mae was released and pardoned by the governor. She married again and supposedly lived happily ever after until she died.

Nancy Kissell

Nancy Kissell is still in prison after killing her husband, Robert, by striking him on the head with a metal statue that she picked up to defend herself as he came after her, attempting to force her into having sex with him, again. Nancy might have been able to persuade a jury in the United States that she acted in self-defense, but she and her husband were living as expatriates in Hong Kong, China, where domestic violence was not readily talked about in the English-speaking population. Prior to the homicide, Nancy had visited several doctors who noted her worsening depression and complaints of domestic violence and child abuse by her husband who was frequently out of town on business. Due to the SARS epidemic in China, Nancy had been living in their home in the United States for a few months with their three children where she had an affair with a repair person and her husband found out. Robert had sent her there and remained in Hong Kong to work, visiting the family occasionally. Although Nancy returned to Hong Kong with Robert at his insistence, his controlling abuse worsened and she began to make plans to end the marriage. As she began emotionally pulling out of the marriage, Robert became more controlling, causing Nancy to become more depressed and anxious. She went to see several doctors who prescribed medication and despite her internal chaos, she continued to function at her children's school where she provided fund-raising expertise with other expatriate mothers who were not permitted to work in Hong Kong despite their education, training, and skills.

The day the homicide occurred, the family went to a family-oriented program with members of another family who lived in their luxury building. When they returned home, the children had milk shakes. The police later believed she put sleeping medicine in the milk shakes because the children, her husband, and another child's parent drank them and took a nap afterward. Nancy denied it and said that her husband used Ambien, a well-known medication to assist sleep, on his own. Nonetheless, this so-called evidence was admitted at her trial without any laboratory evidence that there was such medication in the drink and the headlines called her the "milk shake murderer." When her husband awoke from his nap later in the evening, he continued his threats to harm her and she picked up a metal statue and put it next to the bed just in case he made good on the threats. As he began to sexually assault her, she reached for the statue and hit him with it several times. She became frightened when she saw all the blood splattered in the room and he wasn't moving. Not knowing what to do, she left the house and then came back and proceeded to wrap his body in a rug and went to sleep. The next morning, she drove the children to school like she always did and purchased new linens to clean up the bedroom.

She slept with the body in the room for 3 days, mentally decompensating as his body was physically decomposing. Like before, however, she rotely did what she needed to do, such as getting the children ready for school and shopping. Finally, when she spoke with her father, she asked him to come from the United States to Hong Kong as her husband was missing. She told others that Robert was away on a business trip, which was common for him anyhow. When her father arrived, he helped her go to the police and file a missing person report. She also hired several maintenance workers from the building in which they lived to carry the old carpet, in which Robert's body was rolled up, into a storage room and put a new rug down. Robert's coworkers, however, knew he was not on a business trip and they notified the police about his missing status, also. By the next day, the police came to the house, opened up the storage room, and found her husband's decomposing body. Her mental state totally unraveled at this point, and she was so distraught that she was taken to the hospital where the doctors transferred her to the state psychiatric hospital. She remained there for almost 1 year under the care of a psychiatrist trained in working with people with severe depression and posttraumatic stress disorder (PTSD). After she was released, she was arrested and charged with her husband's murder. She was kept under house arrest until her trial with her many friends coming daily to make sure she was all right.

Her first trial did not permit any evidence admitted about the husband's abuse toward her or toward the children and she was found guilty and sentenced to life in prison in Hong Kong. She wrote to me and asked if I would perform an evaluation that she might be able to use for her appeal. As one of my students was going home to Hong Kong to visit family during the holidays, I arranged for her to conduct an evaluation and bring me back the data for my analysis. Given all the findings were consistent with Nancy being a battered woman who killed her husband in self-defense, I wrote a report for her attorneys. She won a new trial and this time I was first sent to Hong Kong to perform the evaluation myself and then spent almost 1 month sitting in the defense part of her trial in the Hong Kong court.

What an experience! Although the Hong Kong justice system is based on British common law with some differences based on Chinese law and customs, it was very different from the U.S. adaptation of British common law. First, the barristers and the judge all wear wigs and robes while the solicitors who prepare the information for the barristers dress in business clothes. Although all rise when the judge enters the courtroom in most venues, in Hong Kong, all must also bow to the judge and call him "m'lord." The defendant sits in a wooden cage in the back of the courtroom while all the action goes on in front of the judge and jurors. Myself as the forensic psychologist and the forensic psychiatrist (who also treated her while in the hospital and jail) were required to sit in a front row seat. Evidence was permitted that would have been called *hearsay* and kept out of trials in the United States. A Chinese jury that understood and spoke English was seated. They were chosen from the small minority of Hong Kong citizens who were fluent in English and the trial was conducted in English, not either of the Mandarin or Cantonese Chinese languages. Obviously this was not a jury of Nancy's peers.

During my evaluation, Nancy was able to give a good chronology of her marriage that paralleled histories of abuse and of a major depressive disorder. However, she would decompensate mentally when asked questions about her husband's abuse of the children. One child had a broken arm after another witness said she saw Nancy's husband hurting the child. The youngest child had a digestive illness but her husband would not permit her to take him to a specialist in the United States recommended by the Hong Kong doctor. Not surprisingly, during the trial, every time there were questions or testimony about her children, Nancy would decompensate into rocking back and forth, mumbling while looking at the pages of a bible in her lap, and then breaking into loud sobs and moaning. She would fall on the floor and ended up in a fetal position, rocking back and forth and screaming. Only her mother could bring her out of these states toward the end of the trial. Often the jury would be excused but they did get to see some of these episodes.

Meanwhile her children were first placed with her husband's brother rather than her father, whom she had directed them to go to, because of threats by the husband's family toward her father and his family. However, the court did permit the management of the children's money to be with Nancy's father. Within the year, the husband's brother, who was under federal indictment for financial fraud, was shot to death and the children were transferred to the husband's sister. Nancy was not allowed to have any contact with these children throughout these years.

The second trial ended less badly as the first one did with the jury convicting her of manslaughter this time, but the penalty is the same in Hong Kong, life in prison. I made contact with the U.S. Bureau of Prisons to see if they could accept her as an inmate at one of our federal prisons since she remains a U.S. citizen. Then, she could receive the physical and mental treatment that she needed while serving her sentence. She remained in a wheelchair as she is not able to walk due to old injuries from the abuse that have not healed well and she weighed around 70 pounds. This is an incredible difference from when she was an expatriate socialite who dressed well, ran charity events for her children's private school and other activities. No family is around to visit regularly but some friends still come occasionally. So far, the U.S. Bureau of Prisons has said they would accept her but China will not let her go. She has been incarcerated somewhere since 2003.

The good news is that Hong Kong and China will now permit battered woman syndrome evaluations and trial testimony for other battered women who kill in self-defense.

Catherine Pileggi

In the United States, in Fort Lauderdale, Catherine Pileggi shot and killed her abusive partner, Ron, with whom she had lived for the past 20 years. They were both somewhere in their late 50s or early 60s and part of the Fort Lauderdale boating crowd. These are people who own or work on large boats or yachts and sail up and down the intracoastal waterway into parts of the Caribbean. Many of the boat owners have known each other over the years and often go drinking and partying together. Catherine's partner like many in that group was wealthy; in his case he earned his money from his ownership of various businesses.

Like other domestic violence relationships that end in homicide or suicide, Catherine and Ron had lots of physical and psychological violence in the past punctuated by separations and reunions. They lived a life of travel and luxury, both having received a pilot's license at one time for flying their own plane. Alcohol was always available at their home wherever it was located and when he was drunk, he would verbally abuse anyone around. Others who worked for Ron were always hanging around the house and often saw him physically abuse Catherine but never did anything to intervene. Although she was frequently hurt, she rarely went to see a doctor although shortly before the homicide, Ron chased her as she ran away from him and injured her back and thumb. She went to see a chiropractor after waiting for hours in the emergency room. When she was sleeping he would sexually abuse her, often using rough sex to satisfy himself.

The night of the incident, Ron had been drinking with his workers who eventually went home and he began verbally abusing Catherine. He got his gun and forcing her to kneel on the floor, he pointed it at her head and yelled that she had become a problem for him so he had to get rid of her. She was so scared that she defecated in her pants. Crying she ran away from him, telling him not to kill her as she wanted to live. He came chasing after her as she ran up the stairs, similar to another fight they had a few weeks earlier when she hurt her thumb. She reached the top when she heard a loud noise, like a boom. She ran down the stairs and found him lying on the bottom, having fallen down. She helped him up and brought him to the bedroom after he refused to get medical help and then went back upstairs to change her clothes.

When she came downstairs, she remembered being angry and scared when she went into room where he was lying down. She did not remember picking up his gun, nor aiming or firing it. She just remembered being on the floor kneeling and holding the gun, pointing it across the bed in his direction. She remembered thinking she had to be quiet so as not to wake him up because he was going to kill her. She must have gone into the kitchen because she got a knife and cut his throat and his chest, but she has no memory of doing it. She cleaned up the room, put new sheets on the bed, and everything else in trash bags, as she always would get beaten if she left a mess. She knew he was dependent on her to keep everything perfect for him. After that she passed out, woke up, and cleaned up her vomit, and then lay down in the bed next to him and went to sleep. As she described these events, she recited it as an automaton, which is what would be expected if she had been in a dissociative state due to her fear of being killed. Her behavior was on automatic pilot to survive.

When she awoke the next morning, she called the handyman to come to the house. When he came she told him Ron had fallen down the stairs and died. They both cried. Together they planned to put Ron's body in a container and bury him at sea, since that was always his wish. Ron's two other coworkers came to the house and were told that Ron had died after falling down the steps. They called the police. Catherine was arrested and went to trial. Despite testimony on domestic violence, how scared she was and her fear that Ron was about to kill her, she was convicted and sentenced to spend the rest of her life in prison.

IS IT SELF-DEFENSE?

Did Nancy and Catherine save their own lives just to end up spending them in prison? Are there tools that can identify the risks that battered women who stay in the relationship face as opposed to the risks when leaving the relationship? Aaron Kivisto, a psychologist in Indianapolis, attempted to develop a typology from a review of the literature that included four types of men who committed intimate partner homicide: the mentally ill, the undercontrolled/dysregulated, the chronic batterer, and the overcontrolled/catathymic subtypes. Like the risk factors mentioned earlier for murder–suicide perpetrators, those men who committed intimate partner homicide were about 10 years older than the typical nondomestic homicide partner. The old adage that older men are less dangerous than younger men does not hold up in domestic violence homicides. In fact, these men were more likely to also threaten to commit suicide at some point, making it clear that the line between homicide and suicide may be very unclear in domestic violence perpetrators.

A recent study in Chicago offered some new information about the neuropsychological profile of men who killed an intimate partner as compared to those who kill others. A striking proportion (almost 85%) of those in the study sample had a history of head injury with almost half having been diagnosed with hyperactivity disorder or learning problems needing special education. Almost half of the sample had a serious psychological diagnosis: psychotic spectrum disorders, mood disorders, and personality disorders. They were prescribed psychotropic medication. Over 40% had a history of physical or sexual abuse during their lifetimes. Almost 80% gave a lifetime history of substance abuse with over one quarter having used alcohol or other drugs during the commission of the homicide. Most important, the overall pattern of neurocognitive test performance showed serious deficits in their IQ scores, language, attentional functions, executive functions, and memory. Although these deficits are not unusual in other studies of homicide offenders, they do represent a higher proportion in those men who killed spontaneously in a domestic argument. So too did the presence of psychotic disorders. The researchers further suggested that the use of alcohol or other drugs may further weaken the already low inhibitory controls. Obviously, more research is needed especially to see if there are differences with nonlethal batterers. At that point, perhaps actuarial models can be developed to add to the risk prevention literature.

REFERENCES

Klinoff, V. A., Van Hasselt, V. B., & Black, R. A. (2015). Homicide-suicide in police families: An analysis of cases from 2007–2014. *Journal of Forensic Practice, 17*(2), 101–116.

Violence Policy Center. (2008). *American roulette: Murder-suicide in the United States.* Retrieved from http://www.vpc.org/studies/amroul2008.pdf

CHAPTER ELEVEN

CROSS-CULTURAL AND CROSS-NATIONAL ISSUES IN DOMESTIC VIOLENCE

U nderstanding different cultures has become one of the most important variables to analyze when studying issues that are found in all societies, such as intimate partner violence (IPV). National surveys on domestic violence estimated that 1.5 million women each year experience physical or sexual violence from a current or former intimate partner in the United States (Tjaden & Thoennes, 2000). These statistics have not gone down very much in the 16 years since Tjaden and Thoennes conducted their survey. The National Network to End Domestic Violence takes a census during 24 hours each year of battered women in shelters and services, the most recent one being in 2015. Most agree these numbers are an underestimate of the problem especially since definitions of what is considered IPV or domestic violence differ. Battered women come from all demographic groups. As I have suggested throughout this book, domestic violence is an enormous social problem in the United States as well as in other countries around the world. The United Nations Beijing Conference on Women held in China in 1995 required all member nations to bring statistics on all forms of violence against women in their countries, which demonstrated the perniciousness of the problem. These data support the need to better understand how domestic violence impacts across cultures within the United States and internationally.

The attention from the UN stimulated new research that is being collected in many countries around the world and therefore, more information is accessible, especially to English-speaking and English-reading scholars. Malley-Morrison's (2004) authors sampled countries in various parts of the world such as Western, Central, and Southern Europe, the Middle East, Africa, Asia and the Pacific, and North and South America. Like our project, they found similar issues being raised everywhere, although each country and culture has its own specific problems. Erez and Laster (2000) put together an anthology of global responses to domestic violence in various countries from a feminist perspective and also found issues similar to those raised in our study. In Cling's (2004) collection of articles on sexual violence against women and children, she found common psychological and legal perspectives with overlapping issues raised by IPV. I attended a large conference on domestic violence in Buenos Aires, Argentina (November 1, 2007) where over 1,500 attendees came from most countries in Central and South America (some from Spain and Portugal, also) and brought literature published in Spanish, Portuguese, Catalan, and indigenous languages citing studies done in their own countries and cultures. This past year I was invited to speak at conferences in Vienna, Austria, and Bucharest, Romania. I visited Kenya where the problem is difficult to address given the different tribes and extreme poverty in the slums. In Israel, much progress is being made despite the intifada with the neighboring countries. The rest of the Middle East is dealing with kidnapping of girls by Islamic State of Iraq and al-Sham (ISIS), domestic violence, and other atrocities that are unimaginable to those of us in the Western world. Despite all the attention and focus on domestic violence, the pervasiveness of men's violence against women is still glaring.

Definitions of what constitutes IPV differ from country to country and cross-culturally, on individual and institutional levels, but it is clear that the experience of women who are abused is similar. From the feminist perspective, "male violence against women is used to maintain women's disadvantaged social and political status" wherever we find it (Russo, Koss, & Goodman, 1995).

Culture is not a cause of domestic violence, but it can have an impact on the level of tolerance of the violence and how the violence is expressed.

COMMONALITIES ACROSS CULTURES

What are the commonalities found when we look at IPV across cultures and nations? Most important for this chapter is the commonality between domestic violence and other forms of violence against women. Sexual assault, rape, sex trafficking, harassment, and exploitation by those in positions of power all have a similar impact on women. The link is the use of power by men to force women into submission to the men's will and desires. Brownmiller (1975) called rapists the "shock troops" who coerced women into monogamous relationships through shame and violence. Jones (1980) added that batterers were the "home guard" who kept women in their place at home. My dear friend, colleague, and author, Phyllis Chesler (2015), has written about the use of culture to subjugate women especially in Afghanistan where she lived for a while as a child bride. Many cultures are based on subjugation of women by men, interweaving religion or other forms of authoritarianism into their social mores. If so, then the goal of equality between women and men is a definite threat to the maintenance of that culture. This simple fact may well be a major reason why it has been so difficult to achieve both equality and eliminate violence against women these past 30 years.

Understanding these issues, our researchers decided to look at cultural issues both in the U.S. sample and in data from women in several countries. Psychologist La Toya Shakes Malone analyzed some of our data together with data from psychologist Vincent Van Hasselt's sample of American women who sought services in the family violence clinic at our university when she worked with us during her postdoctoral year in residence. I present her findings in the Study 1 section in this chapter, as they demonstrate that the types, frequencies, and severity of the violence experienced by African and Caribbean American women were not different from other racial and cultural groups even though the ability to seek assistance was more limited.

The original researchers on this second research program, that is myself, Kate Richmond, Kristin David, Julie Johnson, and Amber Lyda initially chose three countries to study as they provided a convenience sample: Greece as Greek psychologist Christina Antonopoulou from the University of Athens worked with us on the project; Spain because psychologist Patricia Villavicencio from the Complutense University in Madrid worked with us and Kate Richmond went to Spain to collect the data with her from battered women in Villavicencio's hospital treatment group; and Russia because psychologist Amber Lyda spent several weeks in Russia, including a visit to a maximum security prison, to collect the data. Later, we added Colombia because then-doctoral student in psychology, Sandra Jimenez, was from that country. Graduate students in psychology are still collecting data that have not yet been analyzed from Indian women because Tarmeen Sahni was Indian American, Trinidad because Brenda Jeffers gathered data for her master's thesis there, and Haitian women because Beverly Jean-Jacques is from that country. Shatha

Atiya analyzed posttraumatic stress disorder (PTSD) in Iraqi Americans at the start of the Gulf War and continues gathering data from this population, and Rachel Duros analyzed PTSD across the original four groups, as was reported in Chapter 3. We have limited data from Hong Kong, but we do not know how generalizable it is to either Hong Kong or the rest of China. The Battered Woman Syndrome Questionnaire (BWSQ) is currently being translated to other languages so we can begin data collection in countries where these languages are spoken. We remain open to data collection in other countries to see if our model holds up there, also.

Cultural Issues in the United States

There are at least two major types of cultural issues that need to be understood in the United States by researchers and service providers: first, the cultural issues of those with less access to resources and the dominant cultural privileges, and second, the cultural issues of those who have emigrated to the United States from other countries, whether legally or illegally. Obviously, illegal immigrants try to remain more invisible because of the danger of being sent back to their original countries. Unfortunately, the current U.S. policies make it more advantageous for others who object to immigrants who violate immigration policies to identify these people so they can be returned to their native countries regardless of whether they face more beatings and other punishment. Fortunately, the U.S. Violence Against Women Act (VAWA) protects women who are in danger of further abuse and upon legal proof, permits them residency in the United States. Others have found that women who emigrate to a new country or even other moves resulting in isolation from family and friends are at higher risk to be abused by a partner. I discuss evaluations with immigrant women in a later chapter as they are at higher risk for abuse than those in a more stable community network.

African Americans

The unfortunate legacy of slavery and other horrible and demeaning conditions for African Americans in the United States remains a strong force in all of our society today, especially in the U.S. family. African American families are known to be matriarchal-focused with strong women heading up households that are often absent of men, sometimes because they are in prison or sometimes for many other reasons. When abusive men are part of these families, women find it difficult to call the police and use the criminal justice system for protection because they believe that the African American man will not be treated fairly by the system (Hampton, 1987). The disproportionate numbers of poor men of African and Caribbean descent in prison today suggests they are not wrong. This is also true for Black women who attempted or actually killed their abusive husbands.

Earlier, I analyzed 100 cases of women who had killed their abusive partners in what they claimed was self-defense and found that African American women were two times more likely to be convicted on higher charges than were Caucasian or Latina women, many because they were reluctant to damage the reputations of the African American men any further (Walker, 1989). The prosecutors in the O. J. Simpson murder trial learned from the African American women on that jury that they were more reluctant to identify with being a woman instead of their race and culture when they insisted that the domestic violence was not relevant and acquitted Simpson of murder. Some analysts suggest that the use of BWS is somehow to blame for the unfortunate lack of justice for Black women (Allard, 2005) partly because many African and Caribbean American women do not fit the stereotype of the passive, weak, fearful, helpless battered woman suggested by others who were not familiar with our data. However, even if that is true, it is the socialization into these stereotypes and not BWS per se that is responsible for the lack of justice.

Despite the increase in research concerning domestic violence, there are still few empirical studies reported on African or Caribbean American men. In fact, rarely are these two groups separated even though there are both racial and cultural differences between the two groups (Anyalon & Young, 2005; Coley & Beckett, 1988; Walker, 1999).

Given the attention to cultural diversity issues in providing clinical services, there is a body of literature that deals with how these services, particularly medical and psychological treatments, must accommodate to cultural differences. Some suggest that the racial differences in help-seeking behavior may be due to different beliefs in internal control and attribution of psychological symptoms (Anyalon & Young, 2005). Other researchers (Coley & Beckett, 1988) suggest that women of color in domestic violence relationships are less likely to seek help from mental health professionals because they perceive the helpers as insensitive to the racial and cultural context of their lives.

STUDY 1

Shakes-Malone and Van Hasselt (2005) compared the help-seeking behavior of 547 battered women who sought services at the family violence clinic at the mental health center at our university. Only 10% (55) of these women were designated as Black, with 13% (73) as Hispanic, and 60% (379) as White. See Table 11.1 for more information about demographic data for the participants. As this clinic adopted culturally sensitive treatment methods recommended by the literature, an analysis of their data may help us better understand if we are meeting their needs.

Study of Racial Disparities of Help-Seeking Behavior

As mentioned previously, Shakes-Malone and Van Hasselt (2005) studied 547 U.S. women who sought services in a special treatment clinic for those who experienced family violence for a 10-year period of 1994 through 2005. As the clinic is associated with a university, research data were collected from participants. Table 11.1 lists the demographic data for these women demonstrating that Black women (including African American and Caribbean American women) were 10% of the participants.

They were about equally divided between those who were never married, still married, separated, and divorced. Approximately two thirds of them were high school graduates or had some college but two thirds of them (66%) stated their own income was less than $10,000 per year. However, one quarter of them stated that their entire family income was also below $10,000 per year while another quarter of the women disclosed their family income was over $40,000.

When comparing racial disparities in help-seeking behavior, it was found that the main sample was most likely to seek help because of psychological distress, while the sample of Black women was most likely to seek help because they were court-ordered, either by a child protection agency or while on probation for some unknown criminal acts. Table 11.2 shows the statistical analysis for these findings.

The women were asked about physical and psychological abuse during intake prior to receiving services. Table 11.3 demonstrates the analysis between the groups. It was found that there was no significant difference between them even though they sought help for different reasons.

Table 11.1 *Sociodemographic Data for Study Participants*

Demographic Variable	Current Sample N	Current Sample %
Racial and ethnic groups		
White/Caucasian	379	69
Hispanic/Latina	73	13
Black/African	55	10
Other	39	7
Total sample	547	–
Marital status		
Single	156	29
Married/living together	137	25
Separated/divorce pending	116	21
Divorced	126	23
Widowed	11	2
Education		
Below seventh grade	8	1
Junior high school	35	6
Partial high school	72	13
High school graduate	178	33
Partial college	181	34
College graduate or/and graduate school	70	13
Participant income		
Less than 10K	347	66
11K–20K	105	20
21K–35K	60	11
36K–40K	7	1
More than 40K	7	1
Family income		
Less than 10K	119	26
11K–20K	91	19
21K–35K	114	24
36K–40K	38	8
More than 40K	104	22

Table 11.2 *Racial Disparities in Seeking Help From Mental Health Professions*

	SS	MS	$F(3,530)$
Abuse from partner increasing			
Between groups	.44	.15	.67
Within groups	115.80	.22	
Abuse toward partner increasing			
Between groups	.45	.15	1.92
Within groups	41.59	.08	
Psychological distress			
Between groups	4.82	1.61	7.82**
Within groups	108.82	.21	
Children at risk from partner			
Between groups	.39	.13	1.54
Within groups	44.93	.09	
Children at risk from self			
Between groups	.04	.01	.42
Within groups	18.28	.03	
Required by Human Service Agency			
Between groups	1.08	.36	4.22*
Within groups	45.05	.08	
Required by court upon probation			
Between groups	.79	.26	4.14*
Within groups	33.64	.06	
Required by court upon parole			
Between groups	.00	.00	.15
Within groups	.99	.00	
Partner requested/demanded			
Between groups	.11	.04	1.21
Within groups	13.35	.03	

$*p < .01.$ $** p < .001.$

MS, mean square; SS, sum of squares.

Table 11.3 *Racial Difference in Physical and Psychological Abuse at Intake*

	SS	MS	F(3,457)
Physical abuse index			
Between groups	13.79	4.60	.07
Within groups	30828.39	70.22	
Psychological abuse index			
Between groups	358.93	114.64	.73
Within groups	74442.07	162.89	

MS, mean square; SS, sum of squares.

This study found that Black women who experienced the same type of IPV did not voluntarily seek mental health services as did Caucasian women, further supporting the literature that suggests African American women view services as more beneficial to others than to themselves. However, once they are in treatment, it appears that they utilized the services and they were appropriate to their needs. The study further suggests the need for more detailed studies of how to motivate women to seek services without waiting for the courts to mandate they do so, especially since culturally sensitive mental health treatment appears to be beneficial.

Some studies have found possible differences in severity of violence across different racial groups (Dutton, Kaltman, Goodman, Weinfurt, & Vankos, 2005). In their study they found that the greater the severity of the violence, the greater the impact on mental health, including PTSD and depressive symptomatology. This was especially true for women who also experienced sexual violence and for those who had continued contact with the batterers, especially those who were forced to do so because of access to children. In the Shakes-Malone and Van Hasselt study, they found that there was no difference in severity of violence across the different racial and cultural groups studied. Figure 11.1 demonstrates the frequency and severity of the different types of abuse surveyed.

These data are more consistent with studies that compared African American and Caucasians and found no major difference in the nature and extent of domestic violence (Joseph, 1997). The categories we used were similar to those analyzed by others and included pushing and shoving, restraining the woman (both of which were the highest categories in

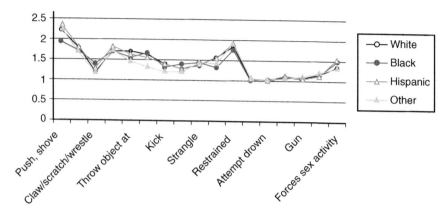

Figure 11.1 *Incidence of physical abuse experienced in the past 12 months.*

our sample but not by very much), clawing/scratching/wrestling, throwing an object at the woman, kicking, strangling or choking, attempting to drown, using of a gun, knife, or other weapon, and forcing sexual activity. However, further analysis suggests that African and Caribbean American women in particular fight back more often, which may partially explain why more of them are arrested and serve time in jail.

INTERNATIONAL PERSPECTIVES

It has also been suggested that culture makes a difference in how long abuse may be tolerated. For those reasons, we decided to explore the same questions with women who were still living in their countries of origin. Comparisons of cross-national research have been difficult because of the different social constructions of domestic violence in the United States and other countries, particularly in Europe where research has been taking place. In most countries, there are myths that dominate and shape the development of services designed mostly to rescue and save these women from their horrible fates (Davies, Lyon, & Monti-Catania, 1998). These myths include the belief that battered women are pure victims often without any of their own resources, that they are totally dependent on their abusive husbands or are housewives with numerous children whom they must care for, that they are women with little or no education or career opportunities, and that they are unable to do anything about their unfortunate situations.

The Beijing Declaration and Platform for Action (UN, 1995) and the subsequent report by the Committee on the Elimination of Discrimination against Women (CEDAW; UN, 2004) following the Beijing conference where all member nations were required to bring reports of what was being done to improve women's lives in their countries, defined IPV as a part of gender violence rather than subsume it as a part of family violence, making the social connections between being a woman and being subjected to many different forms of violence by men the focus. Nonetheless, the ability to change social institutions, particularly in countries where the family is regarded as sacrosanct because of sociopolitical mores and religious values, has been extremely difficult, although changing the ability to receive treatment for victims and sometimes perpetrators has been easier. Given my personal focus on removing the barriers to adequate psychological and legal treatment for battered women, these are the areas that I have concentrated on while acknowledging the difficult and often unrewarding work of others in different parts of this all encompassing problem.

STUDY 2

Therefore, we began to look at European countries, where IPV was seen as part of gender violence against women rather than family violence as is more common in the United States, to see if there were differences in the psychological impact on women victims. Spain, Greece, and Russia were our first cross-national studies as the political and social systems were so very different and we had contacts with researchers who were in these three countries.

Spain

Given the high numbers of Hispanic women in the United States, we decided to accept the opportunity we were offered to go to Spain and collect data from Hispanic women living there. Psychologist Patricia Villavicencio, part of a group of clinical psychologists and researchers in Madrid, worked with our researchers and especially psychologist Kate Richmond, for three summers (2002–2005) while studying the research and interventions for battered women here in the United States. Villavicencio was one of several therapists who conducted individual and group therapy for women who were seriously mentally ill and hospitalized in one of the hospitals associated with the Complutense University in Madrid (Valiente & Villavicencio, 2002). As this was a different population from those women we were evaluating in the United States, it seemed like a golden opportunity to learn what, if any, impact serious mental illness made when coupled with domestic violence. As might be expected, many of their women also had childhood sexual abuse histories, so the picture was complex.

In 2004, after the election of a socialist political party, new laws protecting women from gender violence were instituted in Spain, changing a history of oppression against women from the Franco dictatorship years (1939–1975) when married women were not allowed to open a bank account, receive a salary, or sign a contract on their own. During the first 13 years post-Franco, the new government tried to pass laws for women to gain equality but the conservative Catholic Church and the long tradition of *machismo* were blamed for making the road to equality extremely difficult (Sciolino, 2004). When the socialist party was elected in 2004, it made a commitment to a liberal campaign to change the divorce laws and to enact other laws designed to protect battered women and sexual assault victims. A vigorous education campaign was instituted to help change attitudes and behaviors of health practitioners, those in social service agencies, and legal staff (Pires & Lasheras, 2004). Battered women shelters and outpatient services for victims of intimate partner abuse can now be found throughout the country with local authorities and state-run ministries supporting the development of services with money and social awareness publicity. However, like in the United States and other countries, the new laws are difficult to enforce and the family courts have made it more difficult by insisting on shared parental custody of children when parents divorce, even when domestic violence is present. Since 2004, I have been teaching in various universities and programs in Spain permitting the training of service providers to assess and treat victims of domestic and other forms of gender violence. Therefore, our sample has women from the areas surrounding Granada, Madrid, Salamanca, and Barcelona at this time, although not all participants' responses have been analyzed yet.

Interestingly, IPV has been considered part of the campaign to end all forms of gender violence against women. It is clearly stated in the Spanish Organic Act 1/2004 of 28 December (Official State Gazette, 2004) that: "It is violence against women for the mere fact of being women; considered by their aggressors, as lacking the most basic rights of freedom, respect and power of decision." Using a very public incident where a battered woman, Ana Orantes, was murdered by her ex-husband after she had publicly accused him of domestic violence on a regional television show, the media began an accompanying campaign to educate and change attitudes so that IPV would no longer remain invisible. Had the risk factors been analyzed, Orantes's death, like so many other battered women's deaths, would have been predictable (Campbell et al., 2003). The Spanish section of Amnesty International (2003) also described women's fears of public disclosure, but despite the knowledge among women leaders, it took a very violent and predictable death to motivate reform in the Spanish institutions, especially in health care.

Several national surveys on IPV in Spain have been published in Spanish publications (Pires & Lasheras, 2004; Villavicencio, Bustelo, & Valiente, 2007) with a recent summary in English (Medina-Ariza & Barberet, 2003). Using the Conflict Tactics Scale 2 (CTS2; Straus, Hamby, Boney-McCoy, & Sugarman, 1996) along with several other measures, women were contacted and a final sample of 90 women was interviewed across Spain about experiences with IPV. The authors discuss the limitations of using the CTS2, including the inability of this instrument to assess for low levels of psychological abuse and controlling behavior. Because abusive acts are taken out of context, data collected from men and women using the CTS2 create the misimpression that male violence against women is the same as female violence against men, which other studies have found not to be true (Dobash, Dobash, Wilson, & Daly, 1992).

Interestingly, the Medina-Ariza and Barberet (2003) Spanish sample had a high prevalence of severe sexual abuse that was almost as high as serious physical abuse. As we discussed in Chapter 3, our findings indicated that the women in our sample did not want to discuss sexual abuse as compared to the United States, Greek, and Russian women. Their data support our suggestion that perhaps the Spanish women are less able to discuss sexual abuse within their intimate relationships, but nonetheless it is occurring with frequencies similar to other groups. Their traditional Catholic culture may well block their ability to even conceptualize forced or coerced sex within a marriage as abuse. These findings would also be consistent with those found by Villavicencio and her colleagues in a more recent study. Another interesting finding from other studies in Spain has been the difference in defining who the marginalized women in society are.

In the United States, it is often seen that women of color are more marginalized than others, while in Spain it is the immigrants from North Africa. However, our BWSQ research did not pick up this group as we were not sufficiently aware of their prominence in the interventions for domestic violence groups.

Bosch Fiol and Ferrer Perez (2004) suggest that although it is estimated that 12% of women in Spain are battered by male partners, less than 4% will report it due to cultural imperatives not to speak about it. Even so, our study, the Villavicencio et al. study, and the Medina-Ariza and Barberet study all found that IPV was as prevalent and serious in Spain as it was in other countries despite the methodological and cultural differences. Further, it was also found in the research into the psychological impact from IPV that BWS and PTSD are present as were more serious psychological disorders, including depression and even complex PTSD. Given the more recent economic downturn in Spain, it is hypothesized that there is at least as much or more domestic violence and other forms of gender violence than these earlier studies show. Economic problems seem to bring out more violence rather than less in most countries. Unfortunately, the Spanish Psychological Association has also approved the use of parental alienation syndrome in child custody cases, forcing children to continue contact with abusive fathers and sometimes placing them in grave danger.

Russia

In September 2006, I was unexpectedly invited to be part of a group from the Institute for Russian American Behavioral Studies traveling to St. Petersburg, Russia, on a faculty exchange program for a 1-week meeting with scholars and professionals in law and psychology associated with the University of St. Petersburg and St. Petersburg State University. Russia was beginning to study domestic violence and had already formed several task forces to serve women, although they were all part of other women's services and not specific to abused women. Our researcher, psychologist Amber Lyda went into a woman's prison and collected data with the BWSQ (translated into Russian) from women there. According to Amnesty International (2005), violence against women has been treated more as an internal, domestic, or social problem in Russia, often associated with the high alcoholism rate, and not as a gendered human rights violation as in other parts of Europe. Nonetheless, it is estimated that at least 36,000 Russian women are beaten daily, with one woman dying every 40 minutes from a domestic violence incident. The Russian government's report to the UN Committee on the Elimination of Discrimination Against Women (UN, 2004) stated,

> Sociological studies show that 30 percent of married women are regularly subjected to physical violence. The situation is exacerbated by the lack of statistics and indeed by the attitude of the agencies of law and order to this problem, for they view such violence not as a crime but as "a private matter between the spouses" (as quoted in Amnesty International, 2005).

Horne (1999) describes that throughout Russian history women were considered sinful and needed the dominance and discipline of men. She describes common customs such as the passing of a whip from a bride's father to her new husband during a wedding ceremony taking place until the late 19th century. Other customs have remained unchanged and old proverbs remain in use such as, "If he beats you, it means he loves you" (Horne, 1999, p. 58).

Others have concluded that women's rights have been on a roller coaster in Russia with a declaration of equality that followed the 1917 revolution and attempted to include all women in the Russian workforce. However, women were also expected to fulfill their expected gender-socialized roles such as caring for the children, cooking, and other household chores in difficult circumstances, especially since scarce housing often forced two or more families to share a small apartment. Even so, men were still given preferential treatment in jobs so that women ended up with the low-paying and often unfulfilling ones (Horne, 1999; Levant et al., 2003). A return to traditional women's roles began in the 1970s and by the time of Perestroika in 1991, with the collapse of the Soviet state, the gender-role socialization patterns that underlay power imbalances between men and women were again part of the oppression and coercion of women in Russia. A nongovernmental organization, Stop Violence, recently attempted to form crisis shelters throughout Russia, but as we learned during our visit, most of these crisis centers were underfunded and overwhelmed with the large numbers of social problems that women presented, despite the Russian cultural value of keeping family matters private. In 2001, according to Amnesty International, over 65,000 women came to crisis shelters for help. These crisis shelters, however, did not deal directly with issues from living with domestic violence given the large number of other social problems needing attention.

In addition to the collapse of the Soviet government in 1991, Russia became more democratic with less dependence on the society to provide economically. This has caused a shift in the culture as people must depend on themselves partly and also still partly on the government to provide jobs, housing, and other necessities of life. With the fall of communism, the country became more open to interactions with the Western world, bringing with it a demand for more goods and services. The Russian women's movement began to catch up to others around the world and more has become known about the violence that women have experienced both within their homes and in Russian society in general. As Hemment (2004) suggests, this cultural paradigm shift is still occurring and the fact that violence against women is now being discussed is an indication that its previous invisibility is changing. Our research indicates that Russian women are talking about gender violence. Their years of being economically self-sufficient have also helped them believe that they have more power and control in their relationships. These results differ from the responses of women from the United States, Spanish, and Greek samples, as can be seen in Chapter 3.

Greece

In 1975, the new Greek Constitution declared that "Greek men and women have equal rights and equal obligations" (Greek Helsinki Monitor and World Organization Against Torture, 2002, p. 11). However, Greek society mores still subscribe to traditional socialization with Greek women in the child-raising and homemaker roles and men as the financial providers. Marriage is still vital to Greek society and is the only way for women to get social approval and respect (Chatzifotiou & Dobash, 2001). This means getting a divorce, even if a woman is beaten by her husband, is not accepted. Perhaps even more important, children must have both parents listed on the birth certificate in order to enjoy full privileges in Greek society (Antonopoulou, 1999). An old proverb still thriving in Greece, "It's better to have my eye taken away, than to take away my good name," indicates the woman's plight in Greece even today (Chatzifotiou & Dobash, 2001).

An analysis of the status of women in the Greek workforce has found that there is still flagrant discrimination against women with a disparity in wages as well as access to higher-level jobs. In 2002, a study conducted by the Greek National Center for Social Research revealed that 88% of Greek men are employed compared to only 45% of Greek women. Similarly, the Minister for Labor and Social Security stated that female unemployment at 12.9% was almost three times that of males at 4.7% (as cited in Greek Helsinski Monitor and World Organization Against Torture, 2002). In fact, their report indicates that as high as 83% of Greek women have experienced one or more forms of victimization in their homes with 16% having experienced physical, sexual, and psychological abuse collectively. However, most Greek women do not press charges even if they do report the domestic violence, keeping their experiences private for fear of being blamed for their victimization. Although there are battered women shelters in Athens and several other cities in Greece, most battered women do not use them. Interviews with those who have sought services indicate that they did not seek help until they were exhausted, lost hope of preserving their marriage, and they could not tolerate any more abuse. In some cases, they overcame their fear because of concern for the safety of their children (Chatzifotiou & Dobash, 2001).

In her 1999 study, psychologist Christina Antonopoulou found that over one third of the almost 700 people she surveyed admitted a history of domestic violence in their childhood homes. Even more astounding, a majority of men believed that gender equality had been achieved in Greece and that women were to blame for domestic violence because of their demands for equality. One third of the men also demanded obedience from their wives while 90% of the women surveyed believed that this clause in the Greek marriage contract no longer mattered. Antonopoulou concluded that without a change in the Greek social attitudes, neither equality for women with men or ending violence against women would be possible (Antonopoulou, 1999). During this research, she administered the BWSQ with a group of Greek battered women in a battered woman's shelter outside of Athens. As shown earlier, the Greek women's results were similar to those of women from Spain, Russia, and the United States.

Additional Countries

Our research began to look at battered women who had immigrated to the United States both because the literature was suggesting these women were the most vulnerable and because of our experiences in Spain and

Greece with immigrant women (Rogler, 1994). South Florida was an ideal place to find women who fit this description as there were numerous legal and illegal immigrants within different cultures and different immigration policies. The two largest groups were those who emigrated from Cuba and those who came from Haiti. The major influx of Cubans occurred many years earlier, and today the United States has a policy that permits people from Cuba to seek legal status if they arrive safely on our soil, even if they arrive without documentation. This is in direct contrast to those who arrive illegally on boats from Haiti, who are sent back if caught. Many others who emigrate from Central and South American countries without documentation may pay large sums of money to gangs that smuggle them into the United States. Desperate to escape with just their lives that are often in danger in their countries of origin, many of the women and children cling to hope that life will be better for them in the United States. Sometimes life for them is better in the United States, but other times some of these women meet up with abusive men who continue the cycle of abuse, creating multiple stressors that contribute to their BWS and PTSD (Levinson, 1989).

Haiti

The tiny island of Haiti has one of the lowest economic and social conditions in Central America and in the world. Over 60% of the population lives in poverty without any access to services (UN Development Program, 1999). Unemployment is around 70% and half of the population cannot read or write in any language. Many Haitians escape to the United States both legally and illegally, often leaving families behind while they come to earn sufficient money to send back to those at home. Thus, the migration back and forth to Haiti is constant, keeping people rooted in the Haitian culture whether they live in the United States or in Haiti. Most young people who emigrate to the United States learn to speak and write the Haitian language, which is a combination of French and Creole dialects as well as English once they arrive in the United States. Older Haitians read and write French but also speak Creole. The Haitians' ability in English directly determines their success in finding and keeping jobs and therefore, many of them are unskilled workers, often hired as caretakers of the infirm and elderly or are hired as manual day laborers.

Haiti has a long history of the use of violence in its society. Sexual violence was used during the Duvalier political regimes as recently as the early 1990s as an instrument of political repression (Fuller, 1999). There has been little information on the prevalence of domestic violence in Haiti, although in 1996 one investigation revealed that seven out of 10 women revealed experiencing abuse, mostly sexual, with over half from their husbands (CHREPROF, 1996). The study also found that 80% of the men interviewed believed that their violence toward the women was justified, usually because the women were behaving badly (rowdy, extravagant) or nonobedient. It is not known if their attitudes toward using violence to control women will change if they emigrate to the United States.

Although Haiti has been a party to the CEDAW since 1981, it has not lived up to its commitment to make regular reports. The UN found that there are no laws to protect women from domestic violence in Haiti. All forms of violence against women fall under assault and battery laws, which depend on the degree of injury and circumstances of the attack (Fuller, 1999). A qualified police force is not in place and therefore it is not surprising that incidents of domestic violence are rarely reported to the police. This is especially true in the rural areas outside of Port-au-Prince where there are gangs that are often uncontrolled by the rule of law. In one case on which I worked, a 60-year-old woman whose husband was organizing farm-labor workers was violently raped and beaten as were their teenage children. She escaped to the United States and obtained amnesty but, last heard, her husband remained in hiding in Haiti, terrified that if he even tried to leave the country, he would be killed. To save her own life, she had to give up her life with her husband and children.

Haitians pursue their migration to the United States to escape the climates of terror and upheaval generated by the economic and political crisis in Haiti. However, when they arrive in the United States, they must undergo a transition period of acculturation, which impacts their ability to follow the rules and mores of a different society. Further, many more women migrate than do men, often taking jobs in the United States and sending money back home to support their families. It is common for a married woman to leave her husband and children in Haiti with her family, although, given the increasingly dire situation in Haiti, more families are also migrating together.

Most immigrants, including Haitians, will undergo the acculturation process, which includes changing behaviors and attitudes. This occurs at different rates for individual family members. Language, socioeconomic status, level of education, immigration status, and number of family members in the new country all figure into assessing the level of acculturation of any group. If the immigrants have many ties with their original country and can go back and forth freely, acculturation to the new country takes more time, if at all. This is also true if the immigrants live in a sheltered area and relate mostly to others from their country. For Haitian immigrants, acculturation will mean giving up ways of violence that were acceptable in their own country. This includes IPV. There are some data to suggest that low-acculturated groups are less prone to seek health services (Gil, Vega, & Dimas, 1994) as well as less able to benefit from educational, social, and economic opportunities (Miranda, Frevert, & Kern, 1998). Perhaps it is not surprising that highly acculturated women are younger and better educated than their less acculturated counterparts (Kranau, Greene, & Valencia-Weber, 1982). But little is known about their attitudes toward IPV or if their way of family life changes when they come to the United States.

Our researcher, psychologist Beverly Jean-Jacques, has studied the acculturation patterns of Haitian Americans in Miami as she herself comes from a Haitian family. She has begun an investigation of attitudes toward aggression, attitudes toward domestic violence, and relationship to acculturation levels, and is attempting to find if there is a relationship with incidence, prevalence, and tolerance of domestic violence among Haitian immigrants. Key variables used include level of education, length of time in the United States, level of acculturation as measured by the Short Acculturation Scale (Marin, Otero-Sabogal, & Perez-Stable, 1987) and the Attitudes Toward Aggression (ATA) Scale (Herzberger & Rucckert, 1997). The measure of acculturation that was originally designed for Hispanics will be adjusted to fit the Haitian experience. The ATA Scale is a modified version of the inventory of beliefs about wife beating that originated from psychologist Dan Saunders's work when he was a researcher at the New Hampshire domestic violence laboratories (Saunders, Lynch, Grayson, & Linz, 1987). These data are in the process of being collected and analysis is not yet completed.

One of the most interesting issues that has been raised by the Haitian women who are here in the United States is the degree of both poverty and violence they have experienced while living in Haiti. Many of them who lived in poor, rural areas in Haiti were illiterate when they came to the United States as children and were not usually sent to school. Some did not even know how old they were or how to read or write anything but their name. However, they were good business women, often learning how to go to one market to purchase some supplies needed in their towns and then selling them out of their homes to local people. Homes are often open with cooking for meals as a communal activity outside of the house. The police are ineffective in stopping violence by gangs of men who retaliate against families of those who support the people rather than the government. Women are raped and beaten as a lesson to their husbands or fathers to stop their political activity. Religion sustains many of these women and they take their prayers to God seriously. It is a colorful and emotional relationship with God, one with lots of shouting, singing, praying out loud, and touching each other as they move to their own inner thoughts. Some have also been influenced by Voodoo and may appear to be mentally ill to those who are unaware of this part of the Haitian culture. These cultural issues must be understood when analyzing the data obtained about domestic violence.

India

Acculturation patterns of Indian Americans who have emigrated from India to the United States are another interesting group that our research group decided to study as one of our graduate students, Tarmeen Sahni, comes from such a family. When most Indian families emigrate, they often come together or shortly after arrival focus on bringing other family members left behind to the United States. It is a long and expensive trip back and forth from India to the United States, so unlike some Haitians who are able to go back and forth once or twice a year, it takes many years for the Indian American to make such a trip. However, when Indian families arrive in the United States, they try to find housing and jobs in communities where there are other Indian families, so their level of acculturation is slower than if they were totally assimilated into American society.

The Indian culture continues to hold patriarchal values that shamelessly believe in the inferiority of women. This is not inconsistent with the strong caste system that also remains in Indian culture where different levels of social class bring with it privileges or penalties. Specifically, in India, sexism is present within different social classes, religions, cultures, and regions. Nonetheless, there have been tremendous changes in women's ability to obtain freedoms that were not previously part of the laws so that women now have the right to vote, own land in their own name, are not considered a man's property, and are protected by the law against intimate partner and family violence. However, the laws are not always followed nor are there always consequences to the violations. Men and women are still being raised with different ideas of what their value is in the world and societal expectations are based primarily on gender (Niaz, 2003). Males are raised to become the primary providers for the family and their birth is celebrated by the family. Females are considered to fulfill the role of a wife and seen as a burden to the family. Women must be taught to obey and provide for men. Even midwives receive a lower fee if they bring a girl into the world (Moor, 1998).

When girls become women and are married, they are required to go to live in their husband's family home. Traditionally, their families choose their husbands, and the choice is often regulated by the bride price they are able to afford. Some second-generation Indian Americans are permitted to choose a suitable husband themselves, but he must be approved by their parents based on various factors, including caste, status, religion, and family (Bhattacharya, 2004). Women are trained as children to obey their parents' wishes and they continue to be controlled by their parents, their husbands, and/or their husbands' parents. For some, refusal to obey can bring with it death, as the family cannot tolerate the shame that disobedience from a woman brings. A survey conducted by Bhattacharya (2004) in the major Indian cities of Delhi, Chennai, Bhopal, Lucknow, and Thiruvananthapuram showed that in urban regions, physical violence was reported in at least one quarter (26%) of the homes surveyed, with psychological abuse reported in almost one half (45%) of the Indian homes. In rural regions, there was a little less physical abuse reported (20%) while psychological abuse was a little above one half (51%) of the time.

Similar rates were reported in Uttar Pradesh (Koenig, Stephenson, Ahmed, Jejeebhoy, & Campbell, 2006) with 30% also reporting sexual abuse within their homes in the last year. Like in other countries and the United States, this study found that there was a lower rate of physical violence reported if husbands and wives were educated over 7 years in school as well as those who reported higher socioeconomic status. Conversely, when examining individual variables, longer length of marriage, a lack of children, extramarital affairs, and the husband's previous exposure to violence in his family were associated with higher levels of physical violence. Certain contextual variables such as high murder rates of women in a town and community attitudes toward domestic violence were predictive of significantly higher rates of physical violence within the year but not associated with the rates of sexual violence in the home.

The Indian government has passed laws forbidding the practice of *sati,* which was the requirement of women to throw themselves on their husband's funeral pyre so they died with him; *dowry deaths,* which was the husband's family causing the woman to die if her dowry was not paid or was insufficient; and *custodial rapes* in an attempt to better protect women, but unfortunately, most claim it is not sufficient, is flawed (Adaval, 2006; Bhattacharya, 2004), and is usually ignored. Before the Protection of Women from Domestic Violence Act in 2005, there was a dearth of laws that protected women against domestic violence. After much discourse among the government and activist groups in regard to the proposed domestic violence laws in India, the law that finally passed continues to be debated due to its overall elusiveness, unclear use of terminology, and difficulty in implementation. Although this law was put into effect in September 2005, for years women and activist groups had been pushing for the bill to pass, but problems in regard to the ambiguity in defining domestic violence, prosecuting only a "habitual assaulter," and the right to use violence against women under the excuse of self-defense were seen to thwart the success of the proposed bill (Bhattacharya, 2004; De Sarkar, 2005; "Protection of Women," 2005).

Like in many other countries, there was an emphasis on the importance of family preservation instead of women's safety. In May 2004, a new government led by the Congress party adopted new regulations to increase the reverence of human rights in India (Human Rights Watch, 2005). The law not only protects against wife abuse, but also expands to include other females in the house, including sisters, mothers, and other women living with the abuser ("Protection of Women," 2005). Since this law was passed recently, it is hard to predict how well the Indian judicial system and law enforcement will be in executing it. However, the new law alone cannot help fight the battle against domestic violence. Rather change needs to take place within Indian society and its existing mores. According to Pandey (2005), a survey by the International Institute for Population Studies reported that 56% of women in India stated that wife beating was acceptable in some situations. Furthermore, cases that are reported to the police seem to rarely make it to court as a result of bribes the police are willing to accept or the lack of importance law enforcement places on the subject of abuse against women (Narasimhan, 2000). Thus, the negative attitudes toward women continue to exist. These negative attitudes may also be present among Indian immigrants who continue to believe that abuse is tolerable due to the unfair treatment they have observed or experienced as well as sexist traditions such as arranged marriages and dowries, which are still very much a part of Indian society.

Domestic violence in India is usually perpetrated on newlywed women. Unlike the cycle of violence portrayed in the United States (i.e., Walker, 1989), Indian women often experience the abuse at the beginning of a relationship. Through arranged marriage, women leave their families and are brought to live in unfamiliar environments, a stranger's home to take on the role of a wife. The Indian culture has been one in which arranged marriages are a normal way of life. The parents choose their son's or daughter's life partner as they see fit, and the burden of a daughter is considered to be transferred from the parents' household to the husband and his family. To some extent, there is a spillover of arranged marriages seen in second-generation Indian American families that have brought their traditions over from India. Usually both families take an active role in deciding on whether the marriage would be a suitable one. There is a "viewing" of the bride-to-be, and the male is asked whether or not he finds the woman to his liking. The woman has little or no say in regard to her future, and if she wants to voice her opinion against it, she is discouraged from doing so.

While handing over the burden of the daughter, the parents also practice in a ritual of gift giving, the dowry system. According to Natarajan (1995), "the amount of the dowry is determined by the groom's family status, level of education, and occupation or income." The marriage "kanyadan," which literally means the act of donating a virgin to the groom (Natarajan, 1995), is required to be accompanied with gifts to compensate the husband's family for the responsibility of the daughter. Dowry usually includes materialistic gifts such as gold, jewelry, and any retail gifts that may be purchased. The dowry is also considered to be the daughter's share in the family's property (Fernandez, 1997). It is considered to increase the daughter's self-worth when compared to the husband. According to Teays (1991), since the daughter is "viewed as an economic liability, the dowry system acts to balance the added burden" along with "forming part of the wife's conjugal estate." Interestingly, there is also a dowry system in Kenya with the Kikuya tribe requiring payment of food, clothing, housewares, and money that gets distributed to the needy in the community if there is a marriage where the couple's family has wealth. This type of dowry system seems to avoid the sexism associated with some of the other cultures that still utilize the dowry like India, where there is still a very strong caste system.

When the promised gifts are not paid fully, due to either the inability of the parents' financial state or the lack of resources available after the wedding, the bridegroom and his parents according to Natarajan (1995) "may humiliate, harass, and physically abuse the bride." The threat of violence along with actual physical abuse may also be used to obtain more money from the family. Thus, violence becomes a "bargaining tool" for the husband and his family, and more violence may be exhibited toward women who come from affluent families in order to gain more riches (Bloch & Rao, 2002). Many dowry disputes have been speculated to end with the bride's death or with her suicide (Prasad & Vijayalakshmi, 1988).

According to a study by Fernandez (1997), family members contribute to the violence displayed by husbands against their new wives. Although husbands may use violence to discipline and punish their wives, there is a difference in the course domestic violence takes within Indian society when compared to typical domestic violence in the United States. It is used by the husband and his family as a way to castigate the wife for any "inappropriate behaviors." The abuse can start as soon as the wedding day and the trigger factors can vary from jealousy to wanting more dowry, to accusations of not performing wifely duties well. The family members can indirectly or directly contribute to the abuse. They may either encourage the husband to commit violent acts against the bride by fabricating stories (i.e., accusing the bride of inappropriate looks or advances toward other men) or they may partake directly in physically beating the bride. According to Fernandez (1997), "husbands were considered the primary oppressors, but there was a significant participation of violence from the husband's family members, in particular the mother-in-law and in some cases the sister-in-law." If the extended family includes an increased number of the husband's siblings, the probability of conflict may increase (Natarajan, 1995).

Research has shown that Asian Indian immigrants tend to adapt to their new environment, but hold on to the gender roles they acquired in their home country in order to preserve their ethnic identity (Agarwal, 1991). This may lead to traditional Indian practices in the United States and explain why there may be more acceptance of domestic violence within the Indian community in America as well as the hesitancy in reporting abuse. Also, previous research shows that Asian Indian immigrant parents and children hold similar attitudes toward women's societal roles, but U.S.-born Indian children are more liberal in their views of women's roles than children born in India (Dasgupta, 1998). Furthermore, immigrant parents of marginalized and separated acculturated Indians were said to have a positive association with family conflict in relation to American-born Indian adolescents (Farver, Narang, & Bhadha, 2002). In order to assess whether Indian traditions and values influence domestic violence, it is important to examine if acculturation of Indian immigrants has an effect on the rates of reported domestic violence among Indians in the United States. Moreover, it is important to examine how or whether tradition and customs will interplay with acculturation.

Our researcher, psychologist Tarmeen Sahni (2008), has looked at the problem of domestic violence against Indian women living in the United States as they have shown increased rates in reporting domestic violence. Organizations such as All India Democratic Women's Association intervenes on an average 50,000 cases of women in distress through its justice centers in different states a year (*The Times of India* as cited in Bhattacharya, 2004). Furthermore, many organizations have been specifically established in the United States to provide services for Indian women who are suffering from domestic violence (e.g., SAKHI in New York, Apna Ghar in Chicago), answering 581 calls in 2004 ("SAKHI Statistics," n.d.) and serving over 5,400 domestic violence victims since January 1990 (Apna Ghar, n.d.). Many of these newly married women have been brought over from India by the husbands' parents so they can marry a traditional Indian bride. Within a short time, these women report being subjugated into a kind of slavery and without any help from family who do not live within the United States; the women end up beaten and depressed.

Sahni proposed that the rate of acculturation in an Indian family will have a relationship to those women who will be beaten by their husbands. Sahni suggests that the more traditional the family, the more traditional the marriage, then the more likely the woman will be subjected to IPV. Although she is still collecting data for her research at this time, it is expected that the Indian American associations will assist her in gathering a sufficient sample so as to answer some of these questions, and in particular, how strong is culture in keeping the negative as well as positive aspects that contribute to wife-beating.

Colombia

The influx of families from various Latin American and South American countries is a major contribution to the culture in South Florida as well as the rest of the United States. Although they all speak Spanish or Portuguese, the many dialogues that are spoken provide a glimpse into the richness of the cultural potpourri. When our researcher, psychologist Sandra Jimenez was a graduate student, she translated the BWSQ and went to visit her family in Bogota, the capital of Colombia. In addition to her father's work as a businessman with numerous factories there, he also supports several centers that provide social services to the people of the community. Many of the women who utilize the services are battered by their partners and provided a rich sample of life in this South American city. Psychologist Dr. Eduin Caceres, a professor at the Catholic University in Bogota, has also collected data about domestic violence using our methodology more recently (Caceres & Espinola, 2013).

The culture of Colombia is different from other South American countries due to the political structure of the government and its close relationship with the United States. Once ruled by drug lords, especially in the mountain regions, Bogota is now a major city with commerce and trade all over the world. However, like most South American countries, there is only a very small middle class population, with the majority of the people being very poor and a small minority being very rich. The experiences of both the poor and the rich are so different, it is as if they live in two different worlds—which they do. Those who are considered rich by Colombian standards are educated, have jobs, often have maids to assist women with the care of their homes, and live in comfortable homes. However, most of these people would be considered middle class if they were living in a country such as the United States. As might be expected, people in each of the two major socioeconomic classes in Colombia have different values that impact upon their responses to the BWSQ, so it is important to know from which culture the women come in the sample. Street violence is more common in the lower socioeconomic classes while political violence is more common in the cities. Nonetheless, domestic violence occurs in each class.

Culturally, the justification for violence evolves from gender norms, that is, social norms about men's and women's roles and responsibilities. Typically, men are given control as long as they financially provide for the family. At the same time, women are expected to take care of house chores, raise their children, and show submission and respect to their husbands. Many cultures hold that men have the right to control and punish their wives, and women who do not behave as expected or those who challenge men's rights over them could be battered. Consequently, a man might react violently if he perceives that his wife has somehow failed in her role, stepped beyond her boundaries, or challenged his rights (Heise, Ellsberg, & Gottemoeller, 1999).

As well as in several countries around the world, domestic violence constitutes one of the social problems of greatest incidence in Colombian families. According to the Colombian Service of Communication, domestic violence and its effects are the primary causes of death in women from 15 to 44 years old. While Colombia's Constitution (Article 42) declares domestic violence destructive and orders its penalization, Law 294 of 1996 requests authorities to assist the victims in order to prevent further abuse. However, these laws seem to fall short of fulfilling the system's commitment to eradicate domestic violence because of the unavailability of shelters for battered women and the lack of governmental legal aid services.

A study conducted (Profamilia, 2000) with 7,602 Colombian women indicated that 66% were objects of psychological abuse and 41% were victims of physical aggressions from whom 54% had physical injuries and 15% suffered severe wounds. The results revealed that 37% of women were prevented from having contact with their families and friends, and 11% were sexually abused by their partners. The study also indicates that although 91.2% of the female population is victimized by some type of abuse, only 5% of women reported the incidents to official entities. However, the significant increase in cases filed during the past years has alarmed both governmental and social entities.

The most common form of domestic violence in Colombia is conjugal abuse as it happens in 62% of all cases of domestic violence; furthermore, women are the victims of this type of violence in 91% of the cases. According to the National Institute of Legal Medicine and Forensic Science, in 2002, domestic violence was the reason for 64,979 reports of personal injuries. Nevertheless, 62% of battered women did nothing to seek out help. The Colombian Institute of Family Welfare (ICBF) estimates that 95% of all abuse cases are not reported. National and international organizations draw attention to the problem of domestic violence in Colombia. The Human Rights' report for 1999 to 2000 described domestic violence in Colombia as an "increasing problem."

A survey conducted in 2005 by the ICBF and Profamilia reported that 39% of women across the country were abused by their partners while the percentage in the capital city (Bogota) rose to 47%. Physical violence included pushing (40%), beating with hands (35%), hitting with objects (11%), threatening with firearms (8%), and attempting strangulation or burns (5%). This study also revealed that when faced with attacks, Colombian women responded with aggression as well (64%).

In 2005, Profamila conducted a national demographic and health survey that included 37,211 families, 38,143 women from 15 to 49 years old, and 9,756 women from 50 to 69 years old. The results of the study indicated that 66% of the participants felt controlled by their partners, while 37% were victims of other forms of psychological abuse. Thirty-nine percent were victims of physical abuse, from which 85% presented physical injuries. The study also revealed that 13% of women were raped by their partners or ex-partners.

During 1994, the Institute of Legal Medicine reported an average of 93 cases of domestic violence per day. The same institution indicated that the number of cases increased by 40% in 1997. The National Institute of Legal Medicine and Forensic Sciences of Colombia reported approximately 33,000 cases of domestic violence against women during 2006. However, it pointed out that only a small percentage of cases were reported to the institution. Even though there is legislation that criminalizes violence within the family, domestic violence is generally perceived and managed as a "private" issue. Consequently, many women do not report abuse and those who do report it might not press legal charges. According to the Colombian Institute of Forensic Medicine, every 6 days a woman dies as a consequence of her partner's abuse.

According to Greek Helsinki Monitor and the World Organization Against Torture (OMCT), the report Violence Against Women in Colombia was submitted to the Committee Against Torture, as a result of the concern at reports of violence against Colombian women at the hands of both private individuals and state officials. The report states,

Discrimination against women in Colombia persists and this discrimination often manifests itself as gender-based violence. Women's main role is that of mother and caretaker, and they are often viewed as sex objects, taught to be submissive from a very early age. In Colombia, women especially experience gender-based violence in their families. With respect to domestic violence as many as 41% of women are victims of violence at the hands of their husbands or partners. (Greek Helsinki Monitor and the World Organization Against Torture, 2002)

The government of Colombia has taken different actions to condemn violence against women. Currently, family laws in Colombia require that the government provide victims of domestic violence access to shelters and immediate protection from physical or psychological abuse. Therefore, official entities, in some instances, are required to remove the abuser from the household and request him to attend therapy or reeducation. The law also includes sentences such as prison time if the abuser causes severe harm to his victim or is involved in recurrent abuse. On the other hand, the ICBF is intended to provide safe houses and counseling for victims. Nevertheless, its services are insufficient for the magnitude of this problem. The lack of resources and the government's deficient commitment to enforcing the family violence laws leave the victims vulnerable to revictimization.

With reference to sexual offenses, in 2000, 11% of women reported having been sexually abused by their partners or ex-partners, while the number increased to 13% in 2005 (Profamilia, 2000, 2005). Only since 1996, Colombian law on family violence criminalized spousal rape and provided legal recourse for victims of domestic violence. Although the laws related to the prevention of, and protection against, rape and sexual violence have improved, their enforcement remains inadequate. The penalization of sexual violence against women depends on the judge's subjective judgments about the "reputation" of the victim who is frequently considered a "noncredible witness." Consequently, the injustice against women still is pervasive while the perpetrators enjoy a culture of impunity.

Among the effects of domestic violence, previous studies conducted by Profamilia (2000, 2005) revealed severe traumatic injuries, sexually transmitted diseases, burns, high-risk pregnancies, abortions, and ultimately deaths. The results also showed significant psychological effects such as anxiety, depression, PTSD, substance abuse, suicide attempts, somatoform disorders, and sexual dysfunction. Furthermore, the effects of domestic violence not only affected the abused women but also their children. Women who were victims of domestic violence reported displacement of violence toward their children.

Although the number of Colombian women who reported physical and psychological abuse is considerable, the number of women who take measures to prevent further abuse is extremely low. Battered women in Colombia not only rarely report the abusive incidents but also normally maintain the relationships with the abusers. Previous studies conducted in Colombia revealed significant rates of domestic violence. The present study seeks to explore the relation between domestic violence and PTSD in Colombian women using the BWSQ (Walker, 1978), and the Trauma Symptom Inventory (TSI; Briere, 1995). Participants will eventually include 40 volunteer women who will be required to meet the same inclusive criteria; volunteers are accepted if they are adults and have experienced at least two physical, sexual, and psychological battering incidents. The interviews will be conducted in Spanish using the Spanish version of the BWSQ and the TSI (Jimenez, 2008).

Jimenez analyzed data for the first eight women who have been interviewed to see if they were similar to those of the other countries studied using the BWSQ. Although the sample was not large enough to reliably perform the same statistical analyses, we found that the Colombian women had elevations on the scales that measured PTSD and factors that measured BWS. The results also indicated an elevated endorsement on questions related with the experience of psychological, physical, and sexual abuse occurring during a general battering incident. The women in this sample endorsed several items related to their exposure to psychological abuse; however, the more predominant among all were being cursed at or called names, publicly humiliated, and controlled by their partners. Regarding physical abuse, the participants reported they were frequently hit with objects, slapped or hit with an open palm, and threatened with a weapon. The women in this sample also endorsed items regarding sexual abuse, such as being victims of unwanted sexual advances, unwanted or rough touching of genitals, and forced or coerced sex, among many others. As more Colombian women are added to the sample, we anticipate that the results will continue to follow these trends.

The study by Jimenez has been followed up by a larger study conducted by Professor Eduin Caceres and his graduate psychology students at the university in Bogota. They provided services to victims of domestic violence and child abuse using the BWSQ. We are in the process of analyzing these data and comparing them to what is happening in other countries.

Trinidad, Grand Cayman, the Bahamas, and the Caribbean

Here in South Florida we are close to the Caribbean countries where a lot of domestic violence is reported by students who come to our university for an education and then go back home to work to improve their own countries. We have been collecting data from Trinidad and have projects moving forward in the Grand Cayman and the Bahamas. These are countries where English is the first language spoken. Like many of the Caribbean countries, the people from Trinidad, Grand Cayman, and the Bahamas are mostly poor, although there is a growing middle class similar to that in Colombia and other South American countries.

Arab American Women

Our researcher, psychologist Shatha Atiya, studied the impact of the current American war against Iraq on Arab Americans who lived in the United States. Although she originally attempted to gather a population of Arab American women who experienced domestic violence, like some of the others, she found it difficult to get people to participate in the BWSQ study even though they were willing to speak about their reactions to the violence from the unrest and wars in the Middle East. As she was a graduate student at the time, Atiya decided to collect the data using the TSI and some questions she had generated for her study (Atiya, 2008). Interestingly, she found that these participants did experience PTSD vicariously, by watching television accounts of the war or speaking directly with family members who still lived in Iraq or other countries in the Middle East. However, the type of PTSD experienced included more physical symptoms than the psychological ones more often associated with PTSD.

They reported lack of concentration, difficulty conducting daily routines, sleep problems, fatigue, disinterest in engaging in fun or entertaining activities, and a sense of helplessness. In addition to worrying about their loved ones in their homeland, Americans of Iraqi heritage and Arab Americans watched in terror, anger, and much frustration the robbing, "raping," and destruction of their museums and old libraries that housed thousands-of-years-old treasures, artifacts, and irreplaceable books. They reported a sense of loss of the history and heritage that Arab Americans are so proud of.

Throughout this ordeal, the Arab Americans had to deal with additional extraordinary burdens. Most Americans of Iraqi heritage, in addition to many of Arabic heritage, were contacted and visited by the FBI more than once. They reported feeling that the freedom every American is entitled to enjoying, the very reason they migrated to this country, was violated. Arab Americans reported their phones being tapped and their conversations being listened to. However, they could not voice their opinions freely. Unfortunately, the Arab Americans are stereotyped and discriminated upon just because of their racial background and looks. Several of them reported harassment at their workplaces, loss of jobs, and their children being discriminated upon in their schools or in their applications to schools or jobs. They have to somehow deal with the stigma of "Arab terrorists" that the media portrayed so intelligently. The two words have somehow become synonymous.

Since September 11, the Americans of Arab heritage not only had to worry, like everyone else, about their safety and children's well-being, they had the extra burden and tension of dealing with the stigma and the stereotypes associated with being of an Arabic heritage, or having a Middle Eastern name or look. Many lost their jobs, were harassed, visited by the FBI, and even jailed till proven innocent. These circumstances changed many Arab Americans' outlooks on their rights as American citizens, their safety, their children's future and limitations in the United States. The war in Iraq has revived several of these concerns and more. Americans of Arab descent reported worrying about their stability in the United States, confiscation of their assets, increased discrimination, and being deported. Many reported avoiding gatherings or places of worship in fear of ignorant retaliation. This is also true during the unrest in Syria and the rise of violent gangs such as Al Qaida and ISIS that are openly recruiting young Americans to fight against the United States and the Western culture. Therefore, the threat is real, existing, and a precursor to several posttraumatic stress disorders symptomatology.

Given this background information about the Arab American population, it was interesting to evaluate those who had been interviewed. Rather than the typical PTSD symptom pattern, they demonstrated a pattern identified by Briere (1997), who noted the similarity to PTSD of several culture-bound syndromes that involve dissociation, somatization, and anxiety-related stress responses. These are listed in the appendix of the fifth edition of the *Diagnostic and Statistical Manual of Mental Disorders* (*DSM-5*; American Psychiatric Association, 2013). Each of these is found among Hispanic, Asian, Western Pacific, Inuit, and Native American societies. They all appear to have significant dissociative features. These syndromes are *ataque de nervios, nervios,* and *susto.*

Ataque de nervios seems to be triggered by stress such as accidents, funerals, natural disasters, or hearing of or observing the death of a family member. Typical symptoms of this disorder are crying, trembling, heart palpitations, intense heat rising from the chest to the head, followed by, in some cases, shouting or physical aggression, convulsions, and loss of consciousness. Amnesia for the *ataques* is typically reported (Briere, 1997).

Nervios typically include a much wider, but potentially less extreme group of symptoms. It used to refer to an individual's general tendency to respond to stressors with anxiety and somatization. The stressors are thought to produce less acute reaction than with *ataques* and manifest themselves in chronic family dysfunction. Some etiologies of this response may not be related to stressful events. In other cases, *nervios* appears to reflect chronic anxiety, dissociation, and somatization that arise from an acute stressor. Wider range symptoms of emotional distress may include somatic disturbances and inability to function. Common symptoms include sleep difficulties, nervousness, easy tearfulness, inability to concentrate, trembling, tingling sensations, headaches, irritability, stomach disturbances, and mareos (dizziness with occasional vertigolike exacerbations; American Psychological Association [APA], 1994; Briere, 1997).

Susto (translated as "soul loss"), most typically found in Mexico, Central America, and South America, is often precipitated by a frightening or life-threatening event thought to cause the soul to leave the body. Typical symptoms are anxiety, hyperarousal, appetite loss, sleep disturbance, frequent startle responses, and constant worrying. Depressive symptoms include chronic sadness, decreased motivation, and decreased self-worth. Somatic complaints that include headaches, muscles aches, stomachaches, and diarrhea may be present too (APA, 1994; Briere, 1997).

Atiya and others have been in the process of collecting BWSQ data from Arab American battered women that will be analyzed and compared with the samples from other countries and cultures. These data will also help identify whether or not the *ataques de nervios* are consistent with BWS or if they are a different form of psychological or physical disorders that impact women's health and lives.

SUMMARY

The attempt to understand the psychological impact of domestic violence using a culturally competent approach has brought new richness to our knowledge. Yet, despite the many differences between people from different countries, the experiences of domestic violence appear similar. As long as patriarchal values prevail and sex roles are assigned by the culture, women are treated as less important than men. In some countries, such as India, the discrimination starts with paying midwives less who deliver female babies while others are more sophisticated but still discriminate against women. As the world organizations have declared, women must be treated as equals with men before violence against them by men will stop. An important question raised by these different studies is whether it is possible to keep a culture and stop the abuse against women, especially when IPV is so ingrained within the other cultural values. There is a feminist phrase that sums it up: "The personal is political." If one woman remains battered, all women are in danger of being abused. Cultures within the United States as well as cultures within each of the countries we have studied suggest that our differences as well as our similarities must be celebrated, while at the same time stopping the parts of the culture that support violence against women.

REFERENCES

Adaval, N. (2006, April 2). Indian women and the law. *Hindustan Times.*

Agarwal, P. (1991). *Passage from India: Post 1965 Indian immigrants and their children: Conflicts, concerns, and solutions.* Palos Verdes, CA: Yuvati.

Allard, S. A. (2005). Rethinking battered woman syndrome: A Black feminist perspective. In N. J. Sokoloff & C. Pratt (Eds.), *Domestic violence at the margins: Readings on the race, class, gender and culture.* Rutgers, NJ: Rutgers University Press.

American Psychiatric Association. (2013). *Diagnostic and statistical manual of mental disorders* (5th ed.). Arlington, VA: American Psychiatric Publishing.

American Psychological Association. (1994). Guidelines for child custody evaluations in divorce. *American Psychologist, 49*(7), 677–680.

Amnesty International. (2003). *Amnesty International Report 2003—Spain.* Retrieved from http://www.refworld.org/docid/3edb47d52.html

Amnesty International. (2005). *Russian federation: Nowhere to turn to—Violence against women in the family.* Retrieved from http://www.amnestyinternational .be/IMG/pdf/russia20051214_svaw_report.pdf

Antonopoulou, C. (1999). Domestic violence in Greece. *American Psychologist, 54,* 63–64.

Anyalon, L., & Young, M. (2005). Racial group differences in help-seeking behaviors. *Journal of Social Psychology, 145,* 391–403.

Apna Ghar. (n.d.). Retrieved from http://www.apnaghar.org

Atiya, S. (2008). *Current war stresses in the Arab and Arab American population who live in the United States.* Unpublished paper.

Bhattacharya, R. (Ed.). (2004). *Behind closed doors.* New Delhi, India: Sage.

Bloch, F., & Rao, V. (2002, September). Terror as a bargaining instrument: A case study of dowry violence in rural India. *American Economic Review, 92*(4), 1029–1043.

Bosch Fiol, E., & Ferrer Perez, V. A. (2004). Battered women: Analysis of demographic, relationship and domestic violence characteristics. *Psychology in Spain, 8*(1), 3–15.

Briere, J. (1995). *Trauma Symptom Inventory Manual.* Odessa, FL: Psychological Assessment Resources.

Briere, J. (1997). *Psychological assessment of adult posttraumatic states.* Washington, DC: American Psychological Association.

Brownmiller, S. (1975). *Against our will: Men, women, and rape.* New York, NY: Simon & Schuster.

Caceres, E., & Espinola, M. (2013). Domestic violence in Latin America. In L. Finley (Ed.), *Encyclopedia of domestic abuse.* Santa Barbara, CA: ABC-CLIO.

Campbell, J. C., Webster, D., Koziol-McLain, J., Block, C., Campbell, D., Curry, M. A., . . . Sharps, P. (2003). Risk factors for femicide in abusive relationships: Results from a multisite case control study. *American Journal of Public Health, 93*(7), 1089–1097.

Chatzifotiou, S., & Dobash, R. (2001). Seeking informal support: Marital violence against women in Greece. *Violence Against Women, 7,* 1024–1050.

Chesler, P. (2015). *Muslim women.* Retrieved from https://phyllis-chesler.com/ category/muslim-women

CHREPROF. (1996). *Violence exercee sur les femmes et les filles en Haiti* [Forms of violence performed against women and girls in Haiti]. Port-au Prince, Haiti: Centre de Rescherches et d'Actions Pour la Promotion Feminine.

Cling, B. J. (Ed.). (2004). *Sexualized violence against women and children.* New York, NY: Guilford Press.

Coley, S. M., & Beckett, J. O. (1988). Black battered women: A review of empirical literature. *Journal of Counseling & Development, 66*(6), 266–270.

Dasgupta, S. D. (1998). Gender roles and cultural continuity in the Asian Indian immigrant community in the US. *Sex Roles, 38*(11–12), 953–974.

Davies, J., Lyon, E., & Monti-Catania, D. (1998). *Safety planning with battered women: Complex lives/difficult choices* (Vol. 7). Thousand Oaks, CA: Sage.

De Sarkar, B. (2005, July 3). How the bill was won, *Telegraph*, p. 3.

Dobash, R. P., Dobash, R. E., Wilson, M., & Daly, M. (1992). The myth of sexual symmetry in marital violence. *Social Problems, 39*(1), 71–91.

Dutton, M. A., Kaltman, S., Goodman, L. A., Weinfurt, K., & Vankos, N. (2005). Patterns of intimate partner violence: Correlates and outcomes. *Violence and Victims, 20*(5), 483–497.

Erez, E., & Laster, K. (Eds.). (2000). *Domestic violence: Global responses.* Oxfordshire, UK: A B Academics.

Farver, J. A. M., Narang, S. K., & Bhadha, B. R. (2002). East meets west: Ethnic identity, acculturation, and conflict in Asian Indian families. *Journal of Family Psychology, 16*(3), 338–350.

Fernandez, M. (1997). Domestic violence by extended family members in India: Interplay of gender and generation. *Journal of Interpersonal Violence, 12*(3), 433–456.

Fuller, A. (1999). Challenging violence: Haitian women unite women's rights and human rights. *Bulletin of the Association of Concerned African Scholars, 55*, 55–56.

Gil, A. G., Vega, W. A., & Dimas, J. M. (1994). Acculturation stress and personal adjustment among Hispanic adolescent boys. *Journal of Community Psychology, 22*, 43–54.

Greek Helsinki Monitor and the World Organization Against Torture. (2002, August). *Violence against women in Greece: Report prepared for the Committee on the Elimination of Discrimination Against Women.* Retrieved from http://www.refworld.org/docid/46c1906d0.html

Hampton, R. L. (Ed.). (1987). *Violence in the Black family: Correlates and consequences.* Lexington, MA: Lexington Books.

Heise, L., Ellsberg, M., & Gottemoeller, M. (1999). Ending violence against women. *Population Reports,* Series L, No. 11. Baltimore, MD: Johns Hopkins University School of Public Health, Population Information Program.

Hemment, J. (2004). Global civil society and the local costs of belonging: Defining violence against women in Russia. *Signs, 29*(3), 815–840.

Herzberger, S. D., & Rucckert, Q. H. (1997). Attitudes as explanations for aggression against family members. In G. K. Kantor & J. L. Kaminski (Eds.), *Out of the darkness: Contemporary perspectives on family violence.* Thousand Oaks, CA: Sage.

Horne, S. (1999). Domestic violence in Russia. *American Psychologist, 54*, 55–61.

Human Rights Watch. (2005). *World report 2005.* Retrieved from https://www.hrw.org/legacy/wr2k5/wr2005.pdf

Jimenez, S. (2008). *Domestic violence and its psychological effects among battered Colombian women.* Unpublished directed study. Nova Southeastern University, Fort Lauderdale, FL.

Jones, A. (1980). *Women who kill.* New York, NY: Holt, Rinehart, & Winston.

Joseph, J. (1997). Women battering: A comparative analysis of Black and White women. In G. K. Cantor & J. L. Janinski (Eds.), *Out of the darkness: Contemporary perspectives in family violence* (pp. 161–169). Thousand Oaks, CA: Sage.

Koenig, M. A., Stephenson, R., Ahmed, S., Jejeebhoy, S. J., & Campbell, J. (2006). Individual and contextual determinants of domestic violence in North India. *American Journal of Public Health, 96*(1), 132–138.

Kranau, E. J., Green, V., & Valencia-Weber, G. (1982). Acculturation and the Hispanic woman: Attitudes toward women, sex-role attribution, sex-role behavior, and demographics. *Hispanic Journal of Behavioral Sciences, 4*(1), 21–40.

Levant, R. F., Cuthbert, A., Richmond, K., Sellers, A., Matveev, A., Mitina, O., . . . Heesacker, M. (2003). Masculinity ideology among Russian and U.S. young men and women and its relationship to unhealthy lifestyle habits among young Russian men. *Psychology of Men & Masculinity, 4*, 26–36.

Levinson, D. (1989). *Family violence in cross-cultural perspective.* Newbury Park, CA: Sage.

Malley-Morrison, K. (Ed.). (2004). *International perspectives on family violence and abuse: A cognitive ecological approach.* Mahwah, NJ: Erlbaum.

Marin, B. V., Otero-Sabogal, R., & Perez-Stable, E. J. (1987). Development of a short acculturation scale for Hispanics. *Hispanic Journal of Behavioral Sciences, 9*, 183–205.

Medina-Ariza, J., & Barberet, R. (2003). Intimate partner violence in Spain: Findings from a national survey. *Violence Against Women, 9*, 302–322.

Miranda, A. O., Frevert, V. S., & Kern, R. M. (1998). Life-style differences between bicultural, and low and high acculturation level Latinos. *Individual Psychology, 54*, 119–134.

Moor, E. P. (1998). *Gender, law, and resistance in India.* Tucson: University of Arizona Press.

Narasimhan, S. (2000). A married woman's right to live. *Ms. Magazine, 10*(6), 76–81.

Natarajan, M. (1995). Victimization of women: A theoretical perspective on dowry deaths in India. *International Review of Victimology, 3*, 297–308.

Niaz, U. (2003). Violence against women in south Asian countries. *Archives of Women's Mental Health, 6*, 173–184.

Official State Gazette. (2004). *Organic Act 1/2004 of 28 December on integrated protection measures against gender violence.* Retrieved from http://www.isotita .gr/var/uploads/NOMOTHESIA/VIOLENCE/SPANISH%20LAW%20 Organic%20Act%201_28-12-04%20on%20Violence.pdf

Pandey, G. (2005, August 24). India backs domestic abuse bill. *BBC News.* Retrieved from http://news.bbc.co.uk/2/hi/south_asia/4181574.stm

Pires, M., & Lasheras, L. (2004). *La violencia de pareja contra las mujeres y los servicios de Salud* [Gender violence against women and health services]. Madrid, Spain: Instituto de Salud Publica.

Prasad, B. D., & Vijayalakshmi, B. (1988). Dowry-related violence towards women: Some issues. *Indian Journal of Social Work, 49*(3), 271–280.

Profamilia. (2000). Encuesta Nacional de Demografía y Salud. Violencia Contra las Mujeres y los Niños Capitulo XII, pp. 169–188. Retrieved from http://www .profamilia.org.co

Profamilia. (2005). Encuesta Nacional de Demografía y Salud. Violencia Contra las Mujeres y los Niños Capitulo XIII, pp. 313–342. Retrieved from http://www .profamilia.org.co

Protection of women from domestic violence bill welcomed. (2005, September). *The Hindu.* Retrieved from http://www.thehindu.com/2005/09/07/stories/ 2005090702520200.htm

Rogler, L. H. (1994). International migrations: A framework for directing research. *American Psychologist, 49,* 701–708.

Russo, N. F., Koss, M. P., & Goodman, L. (1995). Male violence against women: A global health and development issue. In L. L. Adler & F. L. Denmark (Eds.), *Violence and the prevention of violence* (pp. 121–127). Westport, CT: Praeger/Greenwood.

Sahni, T. K. (2008). *Domestic violence within Asian-Indian immigrant communities in the United States: Does acculturation affect the rate of reported domestic violence?* Dissertation proposal submitted to Nova Southeastern University College of Psychology. Fort Lauderdale, FL.

SAKHI for South Asian Women. (n.d.). SAKHI statistics. Retrieved from http:// www.sakhi.org

Saunders, D. G., Lynch, A. B., Grayson, M., & Linz, D. (1987). The inventory of beliefs about wife beating: The construction and initial validation of a measure of beliefs and attitudes. *Violence and Victims, 2,* 39–55.

Sciolino, E. (2004, July 14). Spain mobilizes against the scourge of Machismo. *New York Times.* Retrieved from www.nytimes.com

Shakes-Malone, L. S., & Van Hasselt, V. B. (2005, August). Racial disparities in help-seeking behaviors of women in abusive relationships. In L. E. Walker (Chairperson), *Battered woman syndrome after 30 years.* Symposium presented at the 113th Annual Meeting of the American Psychological Association, Washington, DC.

Straus, M. A., Hamby, S. L., Boney-McCoy, S., & Sugarman, D. B. (1996). The Revised Conflict Tactics Scales (CTS2) development and preliminary psychometric data. *Journal of Family Issues, 17*(3), 283–316.

Teays, W. (1991). The burning bride: The dowry problem in India. *Journal of Feminist Studies in Religion, 7*(2), 29–52.

Tjaden, P., & Thoennes, N. (2000). *Full report of the prevalence, incidence, and consequences of violence against women* (NCJ 183781). Washington, DC: National Institute of Justice, Office of Justice Programs.

United Nations. (1995). *Beijing declaration and platform for action.* Retrieved from http://www.unwomen.org/~/media/headquarters/attachments/sections/ csw/pfa_e_final_web.pdf

United Nations. (1999). *The human development report 1999.* New York, NY: United Nations Development Programme.

United Nations. (2004). *Report by the CEDAW Committee* (Report No. A/59/38). *Committee on the Elimination of Discrimination Against Women.* New York, NY: Author. Retrieved from http:www.un.org/womenwatch/daw/cedaw/31sess.htm

Valiente, C., & Villavicencio, P. (2002). Predictores de ajuste psicosocial de mujeres victimas de malostratos [Predictors of psychosocial adjustment of women victims of violence]. *Proyecto de investigacion del instituto de la mujer.* Exp No: 22/98.

Villavicencio, P., Bustelo, M., & Valiente, C. (2007). *Domestic violence in Spain.* Unpublished manuscript.

Walker, L. E. (1978). Treatment alternative for battered women. In J. R. Chapman & M. Gates (Eds.), *The victimization of women: Sage Yearbooks in Women's Policy Studies* (Vol. 3). Beverly Hills, CA: Sage.

Walker, L. E. (1989). Psychology and violence against women. *American Psychologist, 44,* 695–702.

Walker, L. E. A. (1999). Domestic violence around the world. *American Psychologist, 54,* 21–29.

PART THREE

INTERVENTION STRATEGIES

CHAPTER TWELVE

RISK ASSESSMENT AND LETHAL POTENTIAL

*T*he amount of violent behavior expressed in abusive families is enormous. Those of us in the project over the past 40 years have been continuously surprised by what we have heard and we have never habituated to the high level of brutality. Instead, our amazement and respect keeps growing for the battered woman's strength, which has permitted her to survive such terrifying abuse. Today, the amount of violence in these relationships is less shocking to the general public than 40 years ago, especially since we now know that most of the reported homicide–suicides often occur in domestic violence families, as discussed in an earlier chapter. Most of the reported kidnappings of children occur in families where there has been domestic violence, either protective moms escaping from abusive judicial orders to place their children in harm or abusive dads trying to get control of their children without sharing with their former partners. We are much more aware of the fact that from the point of separation to about 2 years afterward is the most dangerous time in a battering relationship. But, despite all we have learned and all the steps we have taken to help society's institutions and agencies be more supportive toward battered women, we still have difficulty in protecting women and their children from men's abuse.

WOMEN'S PERCEPTIONS OF DANGER

At the time we collected our original research data, it seemed as if either the man or woman or both of them could have died any number of times, given the lethal level of some of the acts and threats against her. We wondered if the women knew how close to death they actually were. Women were asked directly about their perception of danger with the batterers. Their responses are reported in Table 12.1.

Table 12.1 *Women's Perceptions of Danger With the Batterer*

Variable	Original Sample N	Original Sample %	Current Sample	Current Sample %
Did you think he ever would or could kill you?				
Never	32	8	12	22
Maybe	22	6	0	0
Yes, accidentally	46	12	7	13
Yes, if mad enough	99	26	14	26
Yes	184	48	21	39
Did you think you ever would or could kill him?				
Never	181	45	32	63
Maybe	37	9	0	0
Yes, accidentally	14	4	2	4
Yes, if mad enough	75	19	4	8
Yes, only in self-defense	–	–	8	16
Yes	92	23	5	10
If someone were to die during a battering, who would it be?				
Neither	14	4	0	0
Him	24	6	2	4
Me	341	87	43	86
Both	10	3	2	4

These results indicate the women's perception of the high risk of lethality, or of someone dying in battering relationships. The women believed the batterers could or would kill them in three quarters of those relationships, and in almost half, that they might kill the batterers. Only 11% said they had ever tried to kill the batterers, and 87% believed that they (the women) would be the one to die if someone was killed. Half of the batterers and about one third of the women had threatened to commit suicide. We did not ask if either had made an actual suicide attempt. However, from the literature on suicide, we can assume the likelihood that actual attempts followed at least some of the threats in a number of these high-risk relationships. Jens (1980) points out the ease with which batterers move from being suicidal to homicidal in violent relationships, as does

Boyd (1978), Ganley (1981), Jacobson and Gottman (1998), Kaslow (1997), Sonkin and Durphy (1982), Walker (1979, 1989b), and others. From this we assume that suicide threats by the batterers should be taken as a warning of homicidal tendencies, also.

A study in Washington state by the Domestic Violence Fatality Review Board examined 113 domestic violence deaths occurring between July 2004 and June 2006 and found that the man rarely committed just suicide. Rather, in almost one half of those cases examined, the man shot his current or former partner and then committed suicide. This is similar to the reports in our murder–suicide study reported earlier. Another quarter attempted to kill their partners before killing themselves, and 10 children were also killed. When expanding its research, it was found that almost one third of the 320 abusers who committed homicides between January 1997 and June 2006 committed homicide–suicides with an additional 12 abusers killing themselves after attempting to kill their woman partners. In many of the cases examined where the man did not kill or physically harm the partner, he did psychologically manipulate her into believing that it was her fault for not saving him from death (Washington State Coalition Against Domestic Violence, 2006).

Other studies have supported our findings that the woman herself can provide a good assessment of the man's dangerousness. Eisikowitz, Winstock, and Gelles (2002) examined escalation from nonviolence to violence in couples' relationships and found that there were at least five junctures that they could identify where the women perceived that the abuse could have escalated. Interestingly, the batterers perceived their use of aggression as a way to solve a problem with the women, while the women perceived it as the batterers intensifying their use of aggression if the women did not do what they required. Although Eisikowitz and her colleagues attempted to use these different perceptions as a call for revising the terms *victim* and *aggressor* in favor of understanding the reciprocal process going on, in fact years of marital therapy using this model seemed only to increase the level of aggression if the woman did not give in to the batterer's demands. This is not new and has proved not helpful in lowering aggression especially where the woman is the victim of physical injury.

O'Leary and his colleagues have also studied the escalation of the man's aggression toward the woman and have found several points where the abuse went from psychological to physical violence and then lethal violence (Arias & O'Leary, 1988; O'Leary, 1988). Their analysis indicated that there were interventions that psychotherapists could make that would prevent this escalation and may even stop the aggressiveness in the relationship. However, they acknowledged the difficulties of such interventions, preferring to work with couples where the abuse had not escalated into physical abuse. Some have called this period *domestic discord* rather than "battering" or "domestic violence." Although Eisikowitz et al. found that some of their couples could return to a nonviolent level, most other researchers have found that once the violence turns physical, it is extremely difficult if not impossible to return to a violence-free relationship.

Jacobson and Gottman (1998) also studied the violent couple and found that there were at least two types of batterers whom they termed the *pit bull* and the *cobra*. The pit bull is the type of batterer who will not let go of the woman. His anger escalates and is visible in his physiological signs such as heart pounding, blood rushing to the head, and heavy breathing accompanying his rising aggressiveness. The cobra gets calmer as he gets angrier and appears to be under very tight control, often physiologically shutting down with a slower heart rate and more deliberate actions. These terms have been found to be quite helpful in getting judges to recognize that even when the man is well dressed and well spoken, he can be extremely dangerous.

The researchers in the Jacobson and Gottman (1998) study found that a woman in a relationship with a cobra has a much more difficult time leaving the relationship due to fear that he will continue to stalk and harass her, using all kinds of verbal threats and surveillance techniques to keep her under his control. The cobra's aggressiveness is usually well thought through while the pit bull is more impulsive and reactive to what the woman does or does not do. Jacobson and Gottman also have designed several scales to assist in measuring psychological abuse techniques, particularly isolation and denigration and humiliation of the woman.

Interestingly, the recent discussion over whether or not there are typologies of different types of battering relationships has attempted to minimize the escalation of violence that is seen in almost all the descriptions of violence. As described earlier in the book, there are different ways the violence may start or even progress, such as psychological, physical, or sexual abuse in different patterns, but eventually it all gets to the high risk of lethality stage.

Although we are working on a paradigm to try to understand how it might escalate to lethal levels and then measure those factors, in fact that is not only not possible now but also dangerous.

In the original Battered Woman Syndrome Questionnaire (BWSQ) study, 60% of the original sample reported that they never felt that they really had control over the batterers' behavior; over three quarters believed batterers would continue to be batterers, and four fifths believed the batterer would batter other women. What is even more surprising is that despite the women's perception of danger, 17% still believed the batterers would eventually change, and not batter any longer. Perhaps they were in the group that was still living with the batterers at the time of the interview and still in denial about the seriousness of the violence. Power and control issues in the current study were discussed further in Chapter 3 as they contribute to the fifth factor in the battered woman syndrome (BWS) criteria.

BATTERER'S VIOLENCE-PRONE PERSONALITY PATTERNS

In the original research it became clear that the women's reports of their batterers' personalities suggested they all went to the same *school* to learn the lessons of violent behavior. The attitudes and behavioral patterns in the men reported by the women strongly suggest the men have a violence-prone personality, although it is not known if this is learned or genetically determined. While I previously estimated that only about 20% of the population of batterers exhibited other forms of violent behavior (Walker, 1979), the data from the first study caused me to reverse those statistics and estimate that only 20% limit their abusive behavior as just toward their wives. The other 80% may also engage in abusive behavior directed against other targets, such as child and parent abuse, incest, hurting pets and other animals, destroying inanimate objects, and responding abusively to other people. The high number of arrests (71%) and convictions (44%) as compared to 34% arrests and 19% convictions for nonbatterers in the first study also indicated a generalized pattern of violence-prone behaviors.

Abuse in Their Childhood Homes

The women reported that many of these men have always lived in an atmosphere of violence in their families. This can be seen in Table 12.2. Spouse or child abuse occurred in 81% of the batterers' childhood homes as compared to 24% of the nonviolent men's homes. In 63% of the men's families, their fathers beat their mothers. This is in contrast to abuse in

Table 12.2 *Battering History*

Variable	Original Sample N	Original Sample %	Current Sample	Current Sample %
Battering in childhood home	267	67	67	66
Battered by mother	147	41	43	50
Battered by father	144	44	45	51
Father battered mother	156	44	56	62
Mother battered father	104	29	21	26
Mother battered sister(s)	62	21	22	29
Mother battered brother(s)	61	20	19	26
Father battered sister(s)	85	29	13	18
Father battered brother(s)	97	32	25	23
Spanked as young child	353	89	87	82
Spanked as older child	332	83	46	44
Hit with an object	317	78	52	62

only 27% of the nonbatterers' homes. In 61% of the men's childhood homes, they told the women that their fathers battered them, and in 44%, they told the women that they were battered by their mothers. In some cases, they were battered by both. These data become even more significant when compared to the 23% of nonbatterers beaten by their fathers and 13% beaten by their mothers. And, perpetuating the high level of violence in the family, over one half of the batterers (53%) reportedly battered their children. This is consistent with Hotaling and Sugarman's (1986) study that the highest risk marker to predict if a man will use violence in his relationship is if he was exposed to abuse in his childhood home.

Although the women reported these data about the men in the original sample, other research and clinical reports indicate they are still accurate [see, for example, Brewster (2003) and Mohandie, Meloy, McGowan, & Williams (2006) on stalking and increased dangerousness of batterers]. Clinical experience has shown that batterers will volunteer little detailed information about the violent acts that they commit. However, once in effective offender-specific treatment programs, the men's information corroborates the women's reports of their dangerousness (Dutton, 1995; Hamberger, 1997; Jacobson & Gottman, 1998; Lindsey, McBride, & Platt, 1993; Sonkin & Durphy, 1982). Orders of protection were sought by over one third of the women when living with batterers as compared to 1%

when with nonbatterers. The issue of the effectiveness of restraining orders will be discussed later. In any event, battered women feel stronger if they are armed with such an order and the police are more likely to offer protection when it is produced.

These findings are consistent with other research. In one of the few studies at the time of our original research that actually questioned the batterers, Hanneke and Shields (1981) found they exhibited three general patterns of violence. The three groups were: (a) men who were violent against family members only, (b) men who were violent against nonfamily members only, and (c) men who were generally violent against both family and nonfamily members. They found that men in groups 2 and 3 used the most severe forms of violent behavior and showed more similar characteristics than men in group 1 who were violent only with family members. Yet, despite important differences between these three groups, including groups 2 and 3 using violence as a general interpersonal strategy, they found no significant differences between them in use of life-threatening behaviors against the women they battered. This is supported by our data indicating that almost all of our subjects thought the batterers were capable of killing them.

Psychopathology or Learned Behavior?

While others, such as Adrienne Raine (2013), have looked to some form of biological psychopathology to predispose men to become batterers, most of the literature suggests that they learn to be violent because such coercive behavior works. They usually get what they want with very few negative consequences. Exposure as a child to the use of violence as an interpersonal strategy seems to be a common pattern for batterers as found in our study and by Fagan, Stewart, and Hansen (1983), Frieze and Knoble (1980), Gelles (1983), Hanneke and Shields (1981), Hilberman (1980), Patterson (1982), Reid, Taplin, and Lorber (1981), Straus, Gelles, and Steinmetz (1980), and others. However, such socialization alone is not enough to create a batterer. Certain environmental situations must also occur and the combination then creates a man who uses coercion (physical, sexual, or psychological) as his primary means to obtain his needs.

Hanneke and Shields (1981) suggested that all three of their groups of violent men started out being generally violent as adolescents, perhaps similar to Patterson's (1982) and Reid et al.'s (1981) aggressive children. Their group 1 men, who were violent only in their families, tended to have higher educational levels and careers. They were more law-abiding in general than men in groups 2 and 3. Hanneke and Shields suggest that the more middle class the man, the more likely his violent behavior will remain in the family only. This serves to keep his violent behavior invisible and does not threaten his social status.

But, at the same time, they found that about one half of the group of men were never violent toward family members despite their generally deviant lifestyle. Hanneke and Shields suggest that perhaps there are some factors in those relationships that stopped them. Our data suggest that the men themselves may set such limits, and they can keep them only if they never do express physical violence directly toward their wives.

Reinforcement of violence as a strategy occurs at all levels in our society. It is particularly evident in some of our child-raising practices. When we teach children that it is appropriate to hit them for disciplinary purposes, we also teach them that the people who love them the most have the right to physically hurt them if they do something wrong. It should not be a surprise, then, that the men say they have the right to physically hit the women they love if they do something wrong. The women accept such minor abuse in the name of discipline. However, unlike most cases of child discipline, physically punishing an adult woman rapidly escalates into violent abuse. Considering that there are many more effective methods of disciplining children, such as time-out procedures, I strongly urge adopting no-hitting rules for all members in families.

Men's dominance over women in a patriarchal society is an important factor in spouse abuse, as discussed in this book. Our data—and that of Berk, Berk, Loeske, and Rauma (1983), Fagan et al. (1983), and Straus et al. (1980)—all demonstrate that in homes where the man is more dominant, the woman is more likely to suffer serious battery. The Berk study found that White men married to Hispanic women tended to be the most brutal in their sample. Martin (1976) has found that Asian women married to American servicemen tend to be brutally beaten. However, our research indicates that in general, race and ethnicity do not determine dangerousness.

Attachment Disorders of Batterers

Psychologist Daniel Sonkin (www.daniel-sonkin.com) has been treating and studying batterers for the past 30 years. He has found that there are very high insecure attachment rates among both perpetrators and victims of abuse. I discuss the concept of attachment in Chapter 9. Sonkin's work has examined the ability of both the men and women who live in domestic violence relationships to regulate their feelings or their *effect* as feelings are sometimes called in psychology terms. Attachment theory states that all organisms need soothing behaviors from a figure with whom they will attach, especially if they cannot do so themselves. If the attachment figure does not take care of their needs and provide the soothing needed to make them comfortable, then they may get angry. This anger motivates the needy person to try to get those needs met somehow, usually by trying to get the attention of some attachment figure, even if it is negative attention. If they do find some way to feel better, then the neurobiological alarm that went off will shut off. In some people, the anger does not dissipate and instead keeps festering, especially if there are long periods of feeling unsatisfied. Research has suggested that these neural pathways are formed by late adolescence or early adulthood, but if the person is subjected to high levels of certain biochemicals such as cortisol, which is released during fear and other uncontrolled emotions, then the pathways may not form properly. Thus, the capacity for attachment may be altered by both biology and environment, which means attachment disorders may be amenable to psychotherapy and good relationships (Dutton & Sonkin, 2003). The role of attachment issues is further discussed in Chapter 9.

Social Class

It is also interesting that in the many countries where I have traveled, the domestic violence problem is always ascribed to whatever group occupies the lowest status there. For example, in Israel, at first it was those who immigrated from Arab lands, then Ethiopian immigrants, and then the Russian immigrants who supposedly had the most violent relationships; in China, it was those who lived in the rural countryside; in England, it was the Indians and Pakistanis; in Latin America, the poor, unmarried women; in Africa, the tribal cultures; and in the United States, poor people of color. While most of the women who use the battered woman shelters are indeed economically disadvantaged minority women, often with young children, in my travels I have met battered women from all social strata. Battering is not a class issue, although access to resources and safety may be. But, again, like the middle-class men reported by Hanneke and Shields (1981), violence in the family can more easily remain invisible in the dominant class.

This is important information for other researchers to pay attention to. When studying domestic violence, it is of critical importance to the findings to carefully select the place from which the population is to be gathered. If the sample to be studied is gathered from the criminal justice population only, it will skew the data toward the overrepresentation of the poor and marginalized classes. If social service or battered woman shelter populations are studied, data will also be skewed, as these groups are overrepresented using these services. On the other hand, in university clinics and counseling centers, mental health centers and private practice populations, more of the so-called advantaged or educated populations will be found. Divorcing populations would probably give a good cross-section from which to sample, although many states that do not require a reason for divorce other than "irreconcilable differences" would not provide access to large numbers of those who seek dissolution of their marriages and thus, only those with problems will become known to the court.

WOMEN'S VIOLENCE TOWARD MEN

Despite the opportunity men have had to report domestic violence by their female intimate partners, the rates of woman to man intimate partner violence has not changed much since statistics were first collected (Walker, 1984, 2000). Analyses of Straus et al.'s (1980) first survey of family violence indicated that women used physical abuse against men (Steinmetz, 1978). However, it was later found that they extrapolated large numbers from the reports of six men in a small part of the study. A reanalysis by Steinmetz (1978) of Straus et al.'s (1980) first survey has continued to claim that women are as violent toward men as are men to women, but men are too well socialized into not reporting it.

Hamel (2005) has made one of the most cogent arguments based on clinical data he has gathered from court-ordered batterer's intervention groups, but even his work has been critiqued by researchers for many of the same arguments that have surfaced over the past 30 years. For example, social worker Ila Schonberg (2005) suggested that Hamel's misinterpretation of data, particularly from the Straus and Gelles (1990) National Family Violence Surveys of 1975 and 1985, is fueled by a backlash against women's fighting back against being abused. Although Hamel presents data from his study of several California batterers' treatment programs demonstrating that less than one third of the men court ordered to attend the program claimed to have physically battered their intimate partners, it is unclear whether these men are responding to another definition of battering behavior, which Hamel proposed, or if they were simply in denial of their behavior. Unfortunately, imprecision in the definition of terms used within this field of study has hampered the ability to compare data from one study to another.

Joan Zorza (2005) who is an attorney who produces the Domestic Violence and Sexual Assault Report and director of Domestic Violence Legal Empowerment and Appeals Project (DV LEAP) likens the backlash in family violence to when Galileo risked torture and death when he dared to report the scientific findings from his telescope. The continued reports that women are equally violent as are men make it even more difficult for agencies, particularly the courts, to believe women's perceptions of danger from further violence; this, then, leaves women more vulnerable to further abuse. However, the argument raised by Hamel is one that can be answered only by examining both the efficacy of batterer treatment programs, not just in Contra Costa County, California, but in general and by reevaluating the way batterers are treated in programs. Straus (2010) continues to remind us that women do have a high rate of using certain types of violence using the Conflict Tactics Scale (CTS) to assess it. However, the CTS does not measure the pattern of violence nor does it account for what happens before or after the physical assault, so the results are skewed to physical abuse, which may not leave the most serious effect from domestic violence. As Harway (2004) reminded us, not all batterers are alike, and many need different types of treatment programs rather than the one-size-fits-all that currently occurs. Some would be better served in psychiatric hospitals, others while incarcerated, and still others while in drug rehabilitation centers rather than in community-based offender-specific treatment groups.

The question of women's violence against men has also been investigated when women and men are dually arrested for domestic violence. In heterosexual couples, it has been found that women are arrested for two types of violence: one type is for self-defense and the other type is using violence instrumentally, or to get something they want. In one recent study, these two types of behavior seem to be confused or, perhaps it is not confusion, rather the police are using dual arrests to thwart the legislative intent of proarrest policies when on a domestic violence call. Henning and Feder (2004) found that almost five times as many women were arrested in a dual-arrest situation in comparison to their male counterparts. While it is possible that these women were both victims and perpetrators of domestic violence, it is not consistent with the gendered model seen in other research such as the National Crime Victimization Survey (NCVS) where 85% of reported domestic violence victims are women. Most national studies have found that women were much more likely to report being abused by their current or former intimate partners than were men (22% vs. 7%, respectively; Tjaden & Thoennes, 2000).

Critics of the gendered approach to reports of domestic violence suggested that there may be an offender effect where both male and female offenders underreport their violence relative to reports from their victims (Arias & Beach, 1987). Self-help books such as *Men Are From Mars and Women Are From Venus* (Gray, 1993) have popularized the knowledge gained from social psychology research that women more often describe events in context rather than one event at a time. This has been found to be true in domestic violence research also (Walker, 1989a). Currie (1998) found that both men and women underreported men's violence directed toward women, but men overreported women's violence toward them. Others have found that women's violence against men was more often used as self-defense (Cascardi & Vivian, 1995; Henning & Feder, 2004; Saunders, 1998). In fact, the only researchers who seem to favor the explanation that women are equally as violent as men are those who have used the CTS to collect their data or have attempted to interpret parts of the Straus and Gelles data.

Nonetheless, there is a dearth of information about women offenders who have been arrested for domestic violence. Much of what is known supports the self-defense argument. However, there are increasing numbers of women who are arrested for other problems but who also have been victims of domestic violence. In Chapters 16, 17, and 21, several programs for women in jail, including the application of the Survivor Therapy Empowerment Program (STEP) by psychology students in jail, are described. Feder and Henning (2005) studied 317 dually arrested men and women, with 80% African American and 20% Caucasian. Their ages were similar to those in our current study, but 72% of the couples were unmarried and dating partners, and almost two thirds of the women had children living in their homes at the time of the offense. Their results indicated that obtaining data just from the criminal justice records did not match what the women and men described in the clinical interviews. For example, the criminal justice arrests recorded that women-only were only

5% of all the domestic violence cases while women together with men were dually arrested in one third of the arrests. Slightly more than one third of the arrests involved a weapon and about one fifth of the injuries required medical attention. Alcohol or other drug use was noted in over one third of the arrests.

No significant differences were noted between men and women when arrested. However, when men and women were interviewed, there were major differences noted. Women were more likely to use a weapon against their partner, while men were more likely to have abused alcohol or drugs. But, dually arrested men were more likely to have physically assaulted their partners in an escalating pattern of violence causing injuries than did dually arrested women. Even more interesting, almost 80% of the women reported that the batterers had used physical violence on them prior to the incident for which they were being arrested with one half having threatened to kill them. Thus, many of the crimes that women have been arrested for may well be associated in some way with their violent relationship. Two thirds of the women had called the police previously. Obviously these differences between male and female arrestees are significant to the argument that female violence against males is not the same as male violence against women.

DOMESTIC VIOLENCE TREATMENT PROGRAMS

When first designed as an alternative to incarceration for batterers who were motivated to change their abusive behavior, domestic violence or offender-specific treatment programs were hailed as an important strategy in stopping violence against women. However, a review of 30 years of providing special treatment programs has suggested that it has not fulfilled its promise. More battered women have cooperated with the criminal justice system when there is a treatment program for their batterers. But, the effects of the program have been limited and account for only a minimal impact on reducing recidivism beyond the actual arrest and overnight incarceration. In trying to understand why these programs have such a minimal effect on getting batterers to change their behavior there are two major reasons. First, these programs are not psychotherapy but rather psychoeducational in nature and are too short to be of much value even when therapists are well trained in the area. Second, all batterers do not need the same type of intervention and these types of programs are designed to be manualized, meaning the therapists must follow the same steps for all those who attend the groups. For example, although the literature suggests that psychopaths get worse with psychotherapy and it is believed that at least 20% of batterers who are arrested have psychopathic traits or tendencies, they are grouped together with other types of batterers.

Far too many batterers have other untreated mental health and substance abuse problems in addition to their propensity to use violence when angry. These groups do not deal with either the mental illness or substance abuse problems, leaving these men without adequate treatment to foster and maintain behavioral change. Most of the psychoeducational treatment programs that accept court-ordered men do not pretend to do psychotherapy. In fact, one popular model, called the "Duluth" model because it originated in that city, claims to be strictly looking to change attitudes, which will then change behavior. However, it is lacking focus on the most important ingredient in any behavioral change program, which is the therapeutic relationship to the therapist. In fact, therapists are encouraged to be in contact with both the victims and the court so that the usual confidentiality that accompanies the psychotherapy relationship is not afforded these participants. It is not known if any of these factors actually account for the lack of success, or if getting violent men to change their behavior is just too complex and difficult to expect will happen with psychotherapy or psychoeducational groups. Treatment providers are inconsistent in providing an answer to this dilemma while courts continue to depend on batterers to stop their abusive behavior when they order them into treatment. I discuss some of these programs further in Chapter 20 on domestic violence courts.

RISK ASSESSMENT

Although it has great promise to identify those batterers who might be helped by treatment and those who are too dangerous to be near their families, the relatively new forensic psychology field of risk assessment of potential or further violence has not been adequately studied, nor has it utilized the population of those families involved in domestic violence as part of its basis. This is partly due to a debate in the field with some

(Hart, 1988) insisting that the woman's predictions of severity is the best risk assessment, others believing that clinicians working with the woman can best predict escalation and severity of changes over time (see Harris, Rice, & Quinsey, 1993), and still others favoring a more statistical analysis (Campbell, 1995; Monahan, 1981). Hart's analysis from shelter data claimed that the women themselves are the best predictors of risk as they know the batterers best. Given the inexact assessment of violence, our data suggest she is probably most correct. However, those women who have made accommodations with the abuse, using denial and minimization in order to be able to stay in the relationship, may not recognize or communicate the rising levels of danger even if they perceive it. Some women actually perceive the rising danger but doubt themselves because the batterers have called them "crazy" or have used other words designed to make them more under the batterers' control (Dutton & Dionne, 1991). Monahan (1981) and his colleagues working on the 15-year MacArthur studies have demonstrated that even clinicians have difficulties in recognizing and reporting high-risk situations without the assistance of risk-assessment materials.

Risk-Assessment Studies in Domestic Violence

Much of the previous research on risk assessment has been conducted with mental patients or adjudicated violent criminals, not those committing domestic violence, most of whom do not get arrested or go into mental health treatment on their own. This is problematic for many reasons; perhaps the most important is that there is some evidence that batterers who use the most severe physical abuse during the relationship might be different from those who escalate their physical violence during the threat of separation (Holtzworth-Munroe & Stuart, 1994; Jacobson & Gottman, 1998). There have been several attempts to develop risk-assessment instruments for use by clinicians and researchers. Millar, Code, and Ha (2009/2013) have authored the *Inventory of Spousal Violence Risk Assessment Tools Used in Canada* available from the Research and Statistics Division of the Canadian Department of Justice that gives a thorough list of numerous instruments, some validated and some not, that are used across Canada.

We discuss some of the more popular instruments used around the world in the following sections.

Conflict Tactics Scale (CTS)

The first to be developed for research was the CTS (Straus, 1979) mentioned previously but its inability to measure abuse within context, emphasis on physical abuse, dependence on adding numbers of violent behaviors and not using the multiplicative effects of continuous abuse, and frequent misinterpretation of the data does not permit clinicians to have confidence in its ability to predict risk of dangerousness (Walker, 1989a). Even today with several different versions of the CTS available, the results are not always very meaningful. When discussing additive violent behaviors, it is meant to signify research that simply counts how many times the batterer hits, kicks, bites, throws, chokes, and otherwise harms the woman using physical force. However, all slaps, kicks, and other physical acts are not the same. Some are more frightening than others, especially if accompanied with a certain look on the man's face that signals to the woman that he is out of control. Others are qualitatively different in the type of slap, the length of time the choke hold is held, or other differences in an act described by the classification into which it fits. The effect on the woman of each type of act will impact her behavior that may influence the next act inflicted by the man. This could have a multiplicative effect; in other words, the quality of the act will increase its impact beyond the expectation of its frequency.

One of the most damaging results from research using the CTS is the insistence by some analysts that the data from the instrument proves that women use violence as often as do men and sometimes they are even more violent. This misinterpretation most easily occurs when using an instrument that strips the context from the events. For example, one slap by the woman becomes equivalent to one slap by the man, even if it is the first slap she has used while it is the 1,000th slap from him to her (Hamel, 2005). Sonkin (www.daniel-sonkin.com) has developed an assessment instrument to be used on the Internet that calculates risk from the number of times various physical, sexual, and psychological events occurred. This measure is dependent on the woman's or the man's memory of behaviors that occurred and when. Aside from figuring in the extent of the damage from the abuse itself, it is also important to recognize that who might escalate to violence in an argument first is rarely an accurate way to determine who is the primary abuser. While there are relationships where mutual violence does occur, in fact most of these relationships start out with the man abusing the woman and eventually the woman escalates it either to try to equalize the violence, a form of psychological protection, or to protect herself from further physical harm. Attempts to confront the myth that women are as violent as men were discussed earlier in this chapter.

Spousal Assault Risk Assessment (SARA)

The SARA has some known validity with certain groups but has not been empirically validated for prediction of danger (Kropp, Hart, Webster, & Eaves, 1999). As the SARA is basically a checklist of factors and domains used in the violence risk actuarials that are based on empirical data, it should not be too difficult to empirically validate the SARA, especially since many battered women shelters and programs embed its items into their data collection. Interestingly, in an analysis of the 1985 National Family Violence Survey, Straus (1996) found that three or more assaultive incidents within a year along with three or more criteria from a list of 18, including police involvement, drug abuse, extreme male dominance, abuse of a child, violence outside of the family, and frequent verbal aggression, were also predictive of increasing aggression. Most of these items are surveyed in the SARA.

Danger Assessment Scale (DAS)

Campbell (1986, 1995) and colleagues (Campbell et al., 2003) have been statistically developing a risk-assessment instrument, DAS, to measure the danger of homicide. The assessment scale is used by researchers and clinicians working with domestic violence victims and perpetrators. In a recent study, with multiple sites across 11 cities where femicides occurred, Campbell compared these women's danger signs using proxies with others in the same city. Not surprisingly, she found that 79% of the femicide victims had been physically abused prior to their deaths by the same intimate partners who killed them. They found that two risk markers for femicide accompanied the models: The first was the presence of the batterer's children in the victim's home and the second was the attempt at separation of the couple (Campbell et al., 2003).

Their models for their study demonstrated that the other factors also expected to be risk markers held up with availability of guns owned by the abusers and the victims as highly predictive of a fatality. If the woman is about to leave the batterer for another partner, this also increases the danger, even more than if she leaves for other reasons. In a small percentage, 5% of the women in this study who lived apart from their intimate partners owned a gun, but there was no evidence that the ownership of the gun was a protective factor. However, never having lived with the batterer was a protective factor. Interestingly, previous arrests were also a protective factor against intimate partner femicide in the final models, but all of the cities in the study did have coordinated community responses when such arrests were made. Campbell suggested that practitioners should make reports to the police as a protective factor if the women they are treating wish them to do so. Browne and Williams (1989) had found that women who expected the community responses to work, but they did not, were more vulnerable to being killed. So it is not just prior arrests but also the follow-up that accompanies the arrest that protects women from being killed. It is unclear that clinicians working with battered women have sufficient knowledge about community responses to determine whether or not a report is truly a protection for the woman.

Saunders (1995) reviewed many of the risk assessments available prior to the development and refinement of the current assessment of violence used in the general forensic psychology field today. In a more recent study, Weisz, Tolman, and Saunders (2000) attempted to undertake an actuarial investigation of the domains of domestic violence risk markers using the data generated by Harrell's (1991) study of treatment outcomes from batterers' offender-specific treatment programs. This permitted comparison of the survivors' general rating of risk markers, a statistical approach similar to Campbell's Danger Assessment instrument, and a combination of both approaches. The authors defined "severe violence" as threats to kill and threats with a knife or gun as they both usually precede or accompany the death of the victim. Using bivariate and multivariate analyses, they found that the risk markers alone were not strong predictors of further violence alone, but with the addition of the women's predictions of danger of repeated violence, the risk rose to a higher level of dangerousness and lethality. Still, the ability to predict risk of further violence was weak for a 4-month period.

Other studies have attempted to use longer periods, such as 15 months in the Heckert and Gondolf (2004) study. A history of repeated violence between court dates was perhaps the most significant risk marker in the Weisz et al. (2000) study while the Heckert and Gondolf study found several other risk markers using a different statistical design.

Not surprisingly, they found that if the woman felt *uncertain* if the man would repeat the violence, he usually did repeat, but her report of feeling safe was not necessarily accurate. For example, they found that the woman's assessment of feeling *somewhat safe* as compared to *very safe* was the best predictor of repeated violence. There were also limitations to the risk-assessment instruments that were used by Hecker and Gondolf, including the Campbell DAS and the *SARA* discussed previously. Interestingly, the predictive value of these risk-assessment instruments was enhanced by the addition of the woman's own predictions of danger. Although the limitations in both of these studies may have introduced bias, for example, the woman gave both the self-report for the repeated violence as well as the prediction of further violence, albeit at different times, it is still important to emphasize that both predictions are an important part of risk assessment. Unfortunately, as a rule, the courts do not respect a woman's predictions and in fact, often penalize the woman and accuse her of exacting revenge against the man, or when children are involved and the woman attempts to protect them, label her as causing "parental alienation" or having other mental health diagnoses.

In a review of the studies of homicides, Sonkin, Martin, and Walker (1985) indicated that there were approximately 15 factors that stood out as adding to the high risk:

Lethality Checklist

- ☐ Frequency of violent incidents escalating
- ☐ Frequency of severity of violence escalating
- ☐ Man threatens to kill woman or others
- ☐ Frequency of alcohol and other drug abuse increasing
- ☐ Man threatens to kidnap or harm children
- ☐ Man forced or threatened sex acts
- ☐ Suicide attempts
- ☐ Weapons at home or easily accessible
- ☐ Psychiatric impairment of man or woman
- ☐ Close to each other at work and at home (stalking and surveillance)
- ☐ Man's need for control around children
- ☐ Current life stresses
- ☐ Man's prior criminal history
- ☐ Man's attitude toward violence
- ☐ New relationship for man or woman

FORENSIC PSYCHOLOGY AND RISK ASSESSMENT

Courts have traditionally asked mental health professionals for predictions of dangerousness. Although battered women advocates and researchers have demonstrated that the woman's perceptions of dangerousness are better than the risk-assessment tools alone, and enhance the models of prediction of further danger, they are not being used in the same way as the general violence risk assessment. Recent research from the MacArthur Foundation has challenged the assumption that there is a unitary concept called "dangerousness." Rather, the research suggests that what mental health professionals can do best is to reframe the question of dangerousness into one of risk assessment. Instead of a dichotomous statement (danger, yes or no), the risk-assessment research suggests that we can identify relevant risk factors, evaluate a given individual to see on which risk factors there is loading, modify those risk markers in terms of various contextual factors, and then provide a probability estimate of the likelihood of future violent behavior. Even in the larger forensic field, there has been a great deal of controversy regarding what kinds of assessments would be most appropriate, ranging all the way from a purely clinical to a purely actuarial approach. Since in assessing for general dangerousness there is usually not one repeated victim, like in domestic violence, so the victim's predictions of future dangerousness has not been seen as an option to add to the models generated.

The tendency in the field at the present time is to use some kind of structured interview format, in which the areas of inquiry are fixed, based on the extant research in a particular area. This is referred to as a "structured clinical approach," and is the basis for instruments such as the Historical, Clinical, Risk Factors (HCR-20), Sexual Violence Risk (SVR-20), and Psychopathy Checklist, Revised (PCL-R). The BWSQ was developed using these principles. Once there is an estimate of the potential for violence, given a certain context, various intervention strategies can be devised to address the specific risk. For the most part, however, as suggested earlier, most of this major research has not studied, as a separate entity, domestic violence. Even the risk-assessment instruments that show some promise, with similar structured interview formats (such as the SARA and DAS discussed previously), appear to be lagging behind studies of more generalized forms of violence.

In doing any kind of risk assessment, the examiner needs to specify what the referral question is. For example, what kind of violence are we trying to assess? What does the empirical data regarding base rates show for a given population? Are there idiographic factors that make a particular individual more or less like the hypothetical person described by the actuarial data? What contextual factors further modify this assessment? How should that information be communicated? and What intervention strategies may be effective in lowering the risk of further violence?

Actuarial Approach to Risk

Let us now look at some of the specific assessment instruments used in violence risk assessment to see if there is applicability to the field of domestic violence risk assessment. As noted earlier, at one extreme is the pure actuarial approach, where various static variables, such as age, number of years of education, family structure, number of previous offenses, and substance abuse are plugged into a formula. What emerges is a likelihood of recidivism percentage. Proponents of this approach maintain that since it does not rely at all on clinical judgment, it is "pure" and not influenced by variability among clinicians. Proponents of this approach further maintain that attempting to modify or adjust the actuarial equation with clinical input actually reduces the accuracy of the prediction. Some examples of these instruments are the Violence Risk Appraisal Guide (VRAG), Sexual Offense Risk Assessment Guide (SORAG), Rapid Risk Assessment of Sexual Offense Recidivism (RRASOR), STATIC 99, and Minnesota Sex Offender Screening Tool, Revised (MNSOST-R).

On the opposite extreme are the purely clinical approaches, in which an individual clinician, guided by her or his own theoretical orientation regarding the etiology of violence, asks a series of questions that are supposed to elicit answers helpful in determining the potential for recidivism. There are no standardized questions or tests used here, since the interview approach of one clinician may differ from another. The middle ground is occupied by those assessments described as "structured clinical approaches." Here, a body of research, such as the MacArthur Foundation, may be surveyed to determine the primary risk factors to be considered in an assessment of violent behavior. These factors are then used to structure the interview; as long as the clinician covers all of the risk factors, how she or he goes about doing the interview is left up to the individual. As noted previously, the HCR-20 and the SVR-20 are examples of these assessments.

The MacArthur research has identified approximately 30 "domains" or risk factors that need to go into a comprehensive risk assessment. These are presented in Table 12.3. Some of these are "collapsed" into other factors, as seen in the 20 factors of the HCR-20 presented in Table 12.4. As mentioned earlier, the HCR-20 is the only risk assessment that uses clinician report as well as static variables in the MacArthur group. While there is some variability, generally the examiner looks for various demographic variables that "anchor" the assessment, and then looks at psychological, sociological, biological, and contextual variables.

Of some interest is that a risk factor that weighs heavily in virtually all of the risk assessments noted, both clinical and actuarial, is the dimension of "psychopathy." As described by psychologist Robert Hare (1996), psychopathy is a constellation of affective and behavioral characteristics including not only antisocial behavior, but also impulsivity, irresponsibility, a grandiose sense of self, a callousness in interpersonal relations, a tendency to externalize all responsibility, and pathological lying. Table 12.5 lists some of these variables.

Table 12.3 *MacArthur Variables*

Demographic variables
   Age range, sex, SES

Sociological variables
   Peers and family support violence
   Economic instability
   Familiarity and skill with weapons
   Size of potential victim pool
      Particular pattern or random

Biological variables
   History of head injury
   Soft neurological signs
   Abnormal neuropsychological findings

Psychological variables
   Mental disorders
   Substance abuse (most powerful predictor)
   Poor impulse control
   Low intelligence

Table 12.4 HCR-20 Variables

Historical items
  Age at first battering—younger = higher risk
  Early maladjustment
  Other relationships with abuse
  Employment problems
  Substance abuse problems
  Major mental illness
  Personality disorder
    Psychopathy

Clinical items
  Lack of insight
  Negative attitudes
    Violence justification
  Active symptoms of major mental illness
  Impulsivity
  Unresponsive to treatment

Risk management items
  Plans lack feasibility
  Exposure to destabilizers
  Lack of personal support
  Stress

There does appear to be some overlap between the psychopath as described by Hare and some types of batterers, particularly the cobra, as described by Jacobson and Gottman, but this has not been researched at the present time. Using Straus's (1996) list of risk markers together with Campbell et al. (2003), Saunders (1996), Sonkin (www.daniel-sonkin.com), and Weisz et al. (2000), as described previously, it is possible to develop a risk-assessment instrument that would include all of these variables.

Homicide

Occasionally, the violence between the man and the woman escalates out of control and someone dies. Most of the time, it is the woman; her batterer either kills her or she commits suicide as a result of his abusive

Table 12.5 PCL-R Variables

Glibness/superficial charm
    Does he have Dr. Jekyll–Mr. Hyde lability?
Grandiose sense of self-worth
    Narcissism
Need for stimulation/boredom
    Fear of being alone
Pathological lying
    Conning/manipulative
Lack of remorse or guilt
    Blames others or is always feeling guilty
Shallow affect
    Very affectionate or shallow affect
Callous/lack of empathy
    Overconcern or no empathy
Parasitic lifestyle
    Overinvested in power job
Poor behavior controls
    Poor boundaries or over control
Promiscuous sexual behavior
Early behavioral problems
Lack of realistic, long-term goals
Impulsivity
Irresponsibility
Failure to accept responsibility for actions
    Blames others or situations
Many short-term relationships
Juvenile delinquency—adult criminality
Revocation of conditional release

behavior. Sometimes they both die; he kills her and then himself. And, in a smaller number of cases, the woman strikes back with a deadly blow and kills the batterer. While statistics vary, just reading the newspaper gives a good estimate of the number of such deaths. The 1994 FBI Uniform Crime Report indicated that approximately one quarter of all homicides in the United States occur within the family. Wolfgang (1968), studying homicides in Philadelphia, found that one quarter of those homicides occurred within the family and one half of those were between spouses. Of those, only 11% of the homicides were committed by women.

Campbell (1981), in her study of homicides in Dayton, Ohio, found that 91% of the murderers of women during an 11-year period (1968–1979) were men. She also reports that in 1977, of the 2,740 American female homicide victims, 2,447 of the perpetrators were men. Of the 8,565 male victims, 1,780 of the offenders (21%) were women. In her Dayton sample, 19% of the perpetrators who killed men were women.

Steadman (1986) notes that the homicide rate in the United States occurs at a base rate of nine in 100,000 and the homicide rate where there is known family violence is 16,000 in 100,000. Another way to look at the risk is in percentages; the Bureau of Justice Statistics (Catalano, Smith, Snyder, & Rand, 2009) indicated that the majority of women are killed by someone they know (64% by an intimate partner or family member, 25% by a friend/acquaintance, and 10% by a stranger). Men are more likely than women to be killed by a stranger (16% by an intimate partner or family member, 54% by a friend/acquaintance, 29% by a stranger). The rate of being killed by an intimate partner was twice as high for women (1.07 per 100,000) as for men (0.47 per 100,000). It would be interesting to know how many of those women had told others that they knew their batterers would not seriously harm or kill them. In family murders, 45% of those killed were women but only 18% of those killed were women in nonfamily murders. Campbell (1981) concluded that the predominance of men killing women results from the misogyny created by our patriarchal society. Certainly, it does not appear to be accidental.

Ann Jones (1980) has found that, historically, the rate of women committing homicide against anyone has remained around 15%. However, today we know that it is more likely that the women who kill men are doing so in self-defense after a period of having been the victims of their violence. An Italian psychiatrist, who studied 30 men in prison for killing their wives, found that almost all had been seriously abusing the women prior to their deaths (Alesandro Neschi, personal communication, 1981). Charles Ewing's (1987) studies have similar findings. However, although 74% of all defendants on trial for murder had prior criminal records of arrest or conviction for a crime, a substantial percentage of victims (44%) also had prior criminal records. Only 19% of family murder victims had prior criminal records as compared to 51% of nonfamily murder victims, and only 56% of family murder defendants as compared to 77% of other murder defendants had prior criminal records (Bureau of Justice Statistics [BJS], 1994b).

Interspousal homicide is rarely unexpected. Battered women in our sample recognized the potential for lethality, even though they often denied it would really happen. Almost all of the women (92%) believed that the batterers could or would kill them and 87% of the women believed if someone would die during a battering incident, they would be the one. About one half said they could never kill a batterer, no matter what the circumstances, while the other half said they possibly could. Only 11% said they had tried to kill the batterers and nine women out of the original sample of 403 actually had been successful. Several men had killed themselves while their women were involved with our project and others had done so earlier. Relationships that have a high risk for lethality can be recognized, albeit retrospectively, although prediction is still difficult given the large number of high-risk battering relationships that do not result in homicide. In fact, the number of women who are killed by men with whom they have been in a violent relationship is about the same as those who do not have any earlier abuse history.

The latest National Crime Victimization Survey reports indicate that these figures break down into 40% of women who live in suburbia and 60% who live in urban areas are killed by former or present partners (BJS, 1994a). Angela Browne (1987) analyzed the data from the original research study for lethality patterns and found that there were a number of high-risk factors to look for when attempting to protect women from being killed. Some characteristics of relationships at high risk for interspousal homicide include an intense level of attachment and involvement between the two parties, a history of physical and psychological battering, and threats of further violence, or even death. Pathological jealousy, sexual assault, violence correlates such as child abuse, injury to pets and animals, threats and actual violence against others, and alcohol and/or drug abuse are also part of the highly lethal relationship.

In Chimbos's (1978) study of Canadian spousal homicides, 70% reported repeated physical abuse and 83% reported a physical fight within 4 months of the fatal incident. In many of our cases, there is also a longer period of loving-contrition behavior, as described in Chapter 5 as the third phase of the cycle of violence, and then a gradual escalation of the abuse again. In the Chimbos study, over half of the survivors reported threats to kill made either by the offender or victim, prior to the fatal incident. The threat, which had occurred many times before, was taken or given more seriously this last time, and someone died. These data have continued to hold steady in more recent studies as well (American Psychological Association, 1996). A Kansas City study found that there had been a domestic disturbance call at least one time prior to the homicide in 85% of the cases, and in 50% the police had been involved at least five times (Gates, 1978). It was not uncommon for the women in our study to report that neither the police nor others they had told took the threats of further violence or death seriously. The problem caused by the police officers' inability to understand the high risk of lethality in responding to domestic disturbance calls will be discussed later. However, in the intervening years, there have been significant changes in how police respond to domestic violence calls helping to keep women safe.

Several factors are more common in the life histories of individuals where an abusive relationship ends in the death of one or both partners. Some of these factors, such as a high degree of social isolation, long-standing battering histories, use of coercion as the major form of communication in resolving interpersonal conflicts, and a high degree of withdrawal through the abuse of alcohol and drugs have been confirmed by the major researchers in this field, to date (Berk et al., 1983; Chimbos, 1978; Fagan et al., 1983; Gelles, 1972; Jones, 1980; Straus et al., 1980; Totman, 1978).

Women Who Kill in Self-Defense

In our work at Walker and associates since the original research project, we have had the opportunity to evaluate over 400 battered women who killed their abusive partners in what they claimed was self-defense. The data on the first 100 cases were reported in another book, *Terrifying Love: Why Women Kill and How Society Responds* (Walker, 1989b). These interviews, similar to those done with over 500 women in the research projects, have provided a rare glimpse into the escalation of violent behavior to its ultimate conclusion, death and destruction of human lives. In each case, there were numerous points when some intervention might have prevented the tragic outcome. The women felt that no one took them seriously, that they alone had to protect themselves against brutal attacks, and that they knew by observable changes in the men's physical or mental state that this time they really would kill them. Most of the time the women killed the men with a gun, usually one of several that belonged to them. Many of the men actually dared or demanded the woman use the gun on him first, or else he said he would kill her with it. Others seemed to set up their own deaths in other ways, similar to the group Wolfgang (1968) studied.

Some women, who had made suicide attempts previously, at the last second before attempting to kill themselves again, turned their rage against their tormentors. Most women who killed their batterers have little memory of any cognitive processes other than an intense focus on their own survival. Although, retrospectively, it can be seen where the women's defenses against denial of their anger at being abuse victims are unraveling, the women do not have any conscious awareness of those feelings. Their descriptions of the final incident indicate that they separate those angry feelings by the psychological process of a dissociative state and thus, do not perceive them. This desperate attempt at remaining unaware of their own unacceptable feelings is a measure of just how dangerous they perceive their situation. They fear showing anger will cause their own deaths, and indeed it could, as batterers cannot tolerate women's expressions of anger.

In less lethal situations, the battered woman might deal with the high level of appropriate anger at being abused in other ways. Our data showed that going "crazy," becoming physically ill, abusing prescription drugs and alcohol, becoming passive and servile, and expressing anger in safe, public situations all helped lower the immediate risk of homicide or suicide, but only for a time. The women all told of ways they learned to keep control of their own minds, recognizing that the batterers had the ability to control their bodies. They let the batterers think they were stupid or suggestible and appeared to conform to their wishes. Sometimes, despite these efforts at only making believe, the batterers' mind control techniques were successful. For some of the women who kill, however, their violence is a desperate attempt to keep the batterers from gaining total control of their minds, too. For example, several told us of how the men managed to convince doctors to prescribe major psychotropic drugs for the women and began supervising their taking them.

Desperation

Although our data indicate the women kill their abusers for different reasons, they all resorted to using such violence as their last attempt at protecting themselves from further physical and mental harm. These findings are similar to others who have also concluded that women do not kill unless it is their last resort (Browne, 1987; Ewing, 1987; Jones, 1980; Walker, 1989b). They do not want the batterers to die, but rather, they just want them to stop hurting them. Thus, to predict the risk of lethality, it is important to assess the level of the victim's coping skills. If she is feeling terrified, overwhelmed, angry, or trapped, and perceives a high level of dangerousness in his behavior, then, in certain situations, she could respond in self-defense with deadly force.

Children

Children in the home add to the stress and opportunity for more violent behavior, although their presence is not sufficient to add to the risk factor unless they are involved in the violence. This involvement can include protection of their mother from abuse or the woman's attempt at protection of the children from the father's abuse. Several women shot their husbands rather than let them physically or sexually abuse their children. Others acted with adolescent or adult children for protection with one or the other or both administering a fatal blow to the men who had abused them. In several cases, the presence of adult children in the home served as a deterrent; once they left, the batterers' violent behavior escalated.

Threat to Kill

Another high-risk situation that increases the potential for a lethal incident is the occurrence of threats to kill made by the batterer. In the original research sample, over half of the women (57%) reported that the batterer had threatened to kill someone else besides herself, and half reported that he had threatened to commit suicide. Women who killed in self-defense recognized that something changed in the final incident and believed that the batterers were going to act out their threats this time. Only 11% of the women studied said they had ever threatened to kill anyone other than themselves. Very few of the women who actually killed the batterers had threatened to do so earlier, although overzealous prosecutors often try to use a general kind of statement, like, "I'm gonna kill him for that," as evidence of premeditation. This is consistent with the Bende (1980), Browne (1987), Ewing (1987), Jones (1980), and Pleck (1979) reports of actual homicides committed by women.

Suicide Ideation and Attempts

Over one third of the women told us about having made suicide attempts while living with a batterer. There is no way to know how many women who successfully commit suicide were driven to it by abusive men. We do know from suicide studies that the threat of death from a terminal illness raises the likelihood that a person will choose to die at his or her own hands. Perhaps battered women believe that batterers will inevitably kill them and choose to kill themselves instead. Since the original study, clinical reports indicate that many women feel that the only way to take back control over their lives is to choose when to end them, especially if they believe that they have a foreshortened future, as is common in trauma victims.

Presence of Weapons

The presence of weapons in the home also seems to increase the risk for a lethal incident to occur. While about 10% of the battered women in the research study reported being threatened by a dangerous weapon during an acute battering incident, many more indicated that the presence of guns in their homes constituted a constant threat to their lives. In contrast, in the sample of 50 women who did kill their batterers, almost all of the men reportedly seemed fascinated by weapons and frequently threatened the women with a weapon during abusive incidents. For that sample, of the 38 women who killed the batterers with a gun, 76% used the same weapon with which the batterers had previously threatened them. Each of them believed he was prepared to make good on his threat to use it against her. In the later samples, we found a similar proportion of homicides committed with the same gun that the batterers had used when threatening to kill the women.

Isolation

Threats of retaliation made by the batterer also raise the risk for lethality. Women commonly reported phrases such as, "If I can't have you, no one will"; "If you leave, I'll find you wherever you go"; "Just do that and you'll see how mean I can really be." Threats of bodily mutilation such as cutting up her face, sewing up her vagina, breaking her kneecaps, and knocking her unconscious also served to terrify women and confirm their fears of receiving lethal blows. They often isolate themselves from family and friends who could help because of the batterers' threats to hurt, mutilate, and/or kill them, too. Many of the women said that they learned not to let a batterer know how much someone meant to them, simply to protect that person from being threatened by the batterer. The more isolation, however, the higher the risk for a lethal incident to occur. In fact, one of the main hints for families and friends of battered women is to keep hanging in with contact as the more the isolation can be broken, the more likely the women will be rescued from serious or fatal injuries.

Jealousy

The presence of the man's excessive jealously has been described as a major component in battering relationships. Campbell (1981) cites data to support jealousy as the predominant reason given by men who kill their wives or lovers. Hilberman and Munson (1978) found pathological jealousy to be a cornerstone to homicidal rage in their study of family violence in North Carolina. Based on our data, this jealousy is most often unfounded; the abused women in our research were not that interested in another sexual relationship. However, the batterers' need to control their women leads them to be suspicious and intrusive. Sometimes their very possessiveness drives some women briefly to another man. But, more often, it is the batterers who are involved in other sexual liaisons. Some of the battered women were unable to control their jealous feelings, especially when the men flaunted the other women. A few of the women killed the batterers when they set up a situation to be "caught." For these women, the defenses to control their anger were no longer adequate, and their rage exploded. The jealousy seems to be used as a catalyst for the women while it provides the entire rationale for the men who kill. Nevertheless, despite the differences in men and women, the presence of excessive jealousy is a high-risk factor for prediction of lethality.

Substance Abuse

Alcohol and drug abuse is another high-risk factor for potential lethality. While the exact relationship between alcohol intoxication and battering is not clear, excessive drinking is often present in those relationships in which there is a fatality. None of the research to date, including ours, finds a direct cause-and-effect relationship between chemical substance abuse and aggressive behavior. Nonetheless, it cannot be ignored that 88% of the men and 48% of the women were frequently intoxicated in the 50 homicide cases, as compared to 67% of the men and 20% of the women in the research study. Although getting high or drunk is not a cause of abusive behavior, it may facilitate it. An offender may become intoxicated to excuse or escalate the violence, or the altered state of consciousness may cause poor judgment in dealing with the aggression. A full discussion on the findings concerning alcohol can be found in a later chapter.

In our study, we found that both the frequency and severity of the abuse escalated over time. Two thirds (66%) of the women said that the battering incidents became more frequent, 65% said that the physical abuse worsened, and 73% reported that the psychological abuse became more severe.

Escalation of Abuse

It is often helpful to contrast the violent acts reported in first battering incidents with more recent incidents. Higher lethality risk is predicted when the first incident starts out with life-threatening or severe violent acts or injuries. Sharp escalation rates are also a predictor. In working with battered women, it is useful to graphically demonstrate how the violence is increasing so they can recognize its dangerousness and their need for greater protection.

Was There Escalation Between Nicole Brown and O. J. Simpson?

Although the prosecutors in the O. J. Simpson murder trial claimed that his anger toward Nicole Brown was escalating and therefore this proved that he killed her, in actuality there were no data that supported this allegation. In fact, O. J. had been away playing golf and working on a film for most of the 2-week period prior to Nicole's death. The weekend before she was killed, he and his then-current girlfriend, who had been seen at a charity event, had signed a contract with a designer to redecorate his bedroom to accommodate their different tastes. The day of the murders a videotape taken by another person supported O. J.'s contention that he was in a good mood at a dance recital that they both had attended for their young daughter. Reports from people who sat next to him on the airplane to Chicago that left after the murders had occurred also reported his good mood. Although many of the domestic violence advocates wanted this case to be a poster for danger of homicide in these relationships, in fact the pattern of their past few months together was not typical of what has been found in the research where other batterers have killed their estranged partners.

MEASURING SEVERITY OF VIOLENCE:
THE BATTERING QUOTIENT

Neither the violent acts nor the resultant injuries alone can measure the severity of the battering relationship. Rather, a combination of both must be used. To predict lethality, two other factors must be included: the frequency with which the beatings occur and the total length of time in the relationship. The latter variables were measured directly in the questionnaire, while the first two variables require interpretation, since perceptions of seriousness or severity were not directly assessed.

One of the goals, following completion of the original research, was to develop a battering quotient (BQ) to assess severity and predict lethality in a battering relationship. This task was begun, with hopes of further funding, by having both battered women and shelter staff rate their perceptions of severity of injuries and violent acts on a 1 to 100 scale. The battered women living in shelters who completed these ratings turned out to be "unreliable" because they tended to give rating scores of 100 to acts or injuries they themselves had experienced, regardless of a more "objective" standard of seriousness or severity. This has become a more important finding today than we initially thought at the time because of the difficulty in identifying those women who are more likely to heal from their experiences and become survivors and those who remain caught up in a victim lifestyle. There appear to be several stages of healing that take place for those who go on to become survivors, including an intense self-focus without the ability to discriminate protective actions, which is then supplanted by a more generalized view of violence against women from which there is no effective protection and then, the development of some ability to protect from some violence even if it is not complete protection.

Consequently, in order to proceed with the development of a Battering Quotient, we had the acts and injuries rated by 20 shelter staff and project interviewers. Each act was rated under three headings: threatened but not committed, committed briefly, and committed repeatedly. The higher the score, the more serious or severe the act. The severity of injuries was also given ratings from 1 to 100; the higher the score, the more severe the injuries were thought to be, in general.

These ratings have a lower variability than would have been expected given their range of "objective" seriousness. Our raters were not able to use the bottom third of the scale for acts threatened or bottom half of the scale for rating injuries. Most of the severity ratings for the acts and injuries specified clustered in the top third of the scales. And, when the battered women rated their seriousness, almost all clustered in the top 10% of the scale. It is possible that once people are involved in understanding the extent of violence that occurs in battering relationships, there is little tolerance for any kind of abusive behavior. For example, in my work as a forensic psychologist, I am often questioned by prosecutors who trivialize slaps, punches, and bruises that do not necessitate emergency medical care. Many of those same states' attorneys have great difficulty prosecuting cases unless they have broken bones or injuries requiring stitches to repair them.

This attitude can be understood by looking at the addictions field where former victims also provide many of the services to those current victims who are trying to become survivors. Recovered alcoholics in the AA program would rate one drink with a higher seriousness than would those who have not been involved in alcohol abuse. Probably, so would alcohol counselors who have seen firsthand its destructive impact on people. Thus, a standard of battering severity or seriousness must take into account that high upper range, too. In finalizing the ranked orders of acts and injuries, it would be useful to add the opinions of those not directly involved with the syndrome. We have not done so at this time but report our work-to-date as encouragement for those who are interested in finding new directions for their own studies.

The categories of acts and injuries that we used in this preliminary exercise were taken from the acts and injuries most frequently reported and therefore measured in the interview. We planned the analysis from the data already collected in this research study. Given what we have learned from our results, I would change some of the categories if new data were being gathered. Delineating areas of the body struck and psychological acts and injuries more carefully seems to be a necessary addition if this scale is to be more useful. I would also add a measure of the Patterson (1982) and Reid et al. (1981) component of "fogging" or "chaining" of acts which our headings of "briefly" and "repeatedly" committed tried to tap. Sonkin (1998) has attempted to be more specific in his rating scale that is used by many domestic violence workers. In addition, I would add some categories that we did not measure in the research but now find important in looking at potential long-term neurological injuries that occur from head banging, head and shoulder shaking, and hair pulling, all of which are more frequently associated with closed-head injuries and neurological demyelinization disorders.

Had funds continued to be made available, we would have attempted to develop the BQ using two different methods of computation. The first method is based on standard-scale construction techniques. The four variables are intercorrelated, and the BQ is computed using either an equally weighted or factor-weighted sum, depending on the correlations obtained. The second method is one that relies more on stronger assumptions. Logically, overall battering severity would seem to be a multiplicative (rather than additive) function of duration frequency, and average severity of acts and injuries. If a woman is battered once a week for 2 years, for example, the number of incidents would be 104 (52×2); each incident (or the typical incident) can be weighted by the average severity of acts and injuries, determined as described. Therefore, the two severity variables are combined (again, in a way based on their intercorrelation) and multiplied some form of these times the duration and frequency. The relative power of these two battered women variables will determine which computation method is more accurate and useful.

The usefulness of the BQ is obvious in predicting lethality. Violent couples could learn their BQ scores, much like learning other medical high-risk factor scores, such as their blood pressure that indicates the life-threatening nature of hypertension. Perhaps translating the lethality potential of domestic violence to a numerical value might help people take it more seriously. Spouse abuse is a life-threatening disorder that is "catching." It can be prevented, by changing individual lifestyle behaviors and, thus, societal norms. But it is causing an enormous loss of life, now. Our data indicate it can be stopped.

SUMMARY

Assessment of the risk of future violence in domestic violence relationships has been one of the most difficult areas in which to obtain real data. Assessment instruments that merely count physical acts or take the violence out of the context of the entire relationship give misleading pictures of what really goes on in domestic violence relationships. Newer methods of risk assessment for dangerousness have not yet been able to account for violence in the home even though these instruments are beginning to assess for general violence in the criminal justice population and in the community. Important studies such as the MacArthur Foundation that studied violent behavior over 15 years did not assess for violence within the home. Several domestic violence researchers have begun to develop instruments that may be useful in assessing for risk of dangerousness. However, at this time, it is clear that whether objective measures such as actuarials and standardized tests or clinical assessment are used, the accuracy rate of risk of future violence is enhanced when the battered woman's own perceptions are taken into account.

REFERENCES

American Psychological Association. (1996). *Report from the Presidential Task Force on Violence and the Family.* Washington, DC: Author.

Arias, I., & Beach, S. R. H. (1987). Validity of self-reports of marital violence. *Journal of Family Violence, 2*(2), 139–149.

Arias, I., & O'Leary, K. D. (1988). Cognitive-behavioral treatment of physical aggression. In N. Epstein, S. E. Schlesinger, & W. Dryden (Eds.), *Cognitive-behavioral therapy with families* (pp. 118–150). New York, NY: Brunner/Mazel.

Bende, P. D. (1980). Prosecuting women who use force in self-defense: Investigative considerations. *Peace Officer Law Report: California Department of Justice,* 8–14.

Berk, R. A., Berk, S. F., Loeske, D., & Rauma, D. (1983). Mutual combat and other family violence myths. In D. Finkelhor, R. Gelles, C. Hotaling, & M. Straus (Eds.), *The dark side of families* (pp. 197–212). Beverly Hills, CA: Sage.

Boyd, V. D. (1978). *Domestic violence: Treatment alternatives for the male batterer.* Paper presented at the meeting of the American Psychological Association, Toronto, Ontario, Canada.

Brewster, M. (2003). Power and control dynamics in prestalking and stalking situations. *Journal of Family Violence, 18*(4), 207–217.

Browne, A. (1987). *When battered women kill.* New York, NY: Free Press.

Browne, A., & Williams, K. R. (1989). Exploring the effect of resource availability and the likelihood of female-perpetrated homicides. *Law and Society Review, 23,* 75–94.

Bureau of Justice Statistics. (1994a). *Selected findings: Violence between intimates* (NCJ 149259). Washington, DC: U.S. Department of Justice, Office of Justice

Programs, Bureau of Justice Statistics. Retrieved from http://www.bjs.gov/content/pub/pdf/vbi.pdf

Bureau of Justice Statistics. (1994b). *Special report: Murder in families.* Washington, DC: U.S. Department of Justice.

Campbell, J. C. (1981). Misogyny and homicide of women. *Advances in Nursing Science, 3*(2), 67–86.

Campbell, J. C. (1986). Assessing the risk of homicide for battered women. *Advances in Nursing Science, 8*(4), 36–51.

Campbell, J. C. (1995). *Assessing dangerousness: Violence by sex offenders, batterers, and child abusers.* Thousand Oaks, CA: Sage.

Campbell, J. C., Webster, D., Koziol-McLain, J., Block, C., Campbell, D., Curry, M. A., . . . Laughon, K. (2003). Risk factors for femicide in abusive relationships: Results from a multisite case control study. *American Journal of Public Health, 93*(7), 1089–1097.

Cascardi, M., & Vivian, D. (1995). Context for specific episodes of marital violence: Gender and severity of violence difference. *Journal of Family Violence, 10,* 265–293.

Catalano, S., Smith, E., Snyder, H., & Rand, M. (2009). *Female victims of violence* (NCJ 228356). Washington, DC: Bureau of Justice Statistics. Retrieved from http://www.bjs.gov/content/pub/pdf/fvv.pdf

Chimbos, P. D. (1978). *Marital violence: A study of interspousal homicide.* San Francisco, CA: R&E Research Associates.

Currie, D. H. (1998). Violent men or violent women? Whose definition counts? In R. K. Bergen (Ed.), *Issues in intimate partner violence* (pp. 97–111). Thousand Oaks, CA: Sage.

Dutton, D. G. (1995). *The batterer: A psychological profile.* New York, NY: Basic Books.

Dutton, D. G., & Sonkin, D. J. (2003). *Intimate violence: Contemporary treatment innovations.* Binghamton, NY: Haworth Press.

Dutton, M. A., & Dionne, D. (1991). Counseling and shelter for battered women. In M. Steinman (Ed.), *Women battering: Policy responses* (pp. 113–130). Cincinnati, OH: Anderson.

Eisikowitz, Z., Winstock, Z., & Gelles, R. (2002). Structure and dynamics from escalation from the victim's perspective. *Families in Society, 83,* 142–152.

Ewing, C. P. (1987). *Battered women who kill.* Lexington, MA: Lexington Books.

Fagan, J. A., Stewart, D. K., & Hansen, K. V. (1983). Violent men or violent husbands? Background factors and situational correlates. In D. Finkelhor, R. J. Gelles, G. Hotaling, & M. Straus (Eds.), *The dark side of families* (pp. 49–68). Beverly Hills, CA: Sage.

Feder, L., & Henning, K. (2005). A comparison of male and female dually arrested domestic violence offenders. *Violence and Victims, 20,* 153–171.

Frieze, I. H., & Knoble, J. (1980, September). *The effects of alcohol on marital violence.* Paper presented at the 88th Annual Convention of the American Psychological Association, Montreal, Quebec, Canada.

Ganley, A. (1981). *Participant's and trainer's manual for working with men who batter.* Washington, DC: Center for Women's Policy Studies.

Gates, M. (1978). Introduction. In J. R. Chapman & M. Gates (Eds.), *The victimization of women. Sage Yearbooks in Women's Policy Studies* (Vol. 3, pp. 9–28). Beverly Hills, CA: Sage.

Gelles, R. J. (1972). *The violent home: A study of the physical aggression between husbands and wives.* Beverly Hills, CA: Sage.

Gelles, R. J. (1983). An exchange/social control theory of intrafamily violence. In D. Finkelhor, R. Gelles, G. Hotaling, & M. Straus (Eds.), *The dark side of families.* Beverly Hills, CA: Sage.

Gray, J. (1993). *Men are from Mars and women are from Venus: A practical guide for improving communication and getting what you want in relationships.* New York, NY: HarperCollins.

Hamberger, L. K. (1997). Research concerning wife abuse: Implications for physician training. *Journal of Aggression, Maltreatment, and Trauma, 1,* 81–96.

Hamel, J. (2005). *Gender inclusive treatment of intimate partner abuse: A comprehensive approach.* New York, NY: Springer Publishing Company.

Hanneke, C. R., & Shields, N. M. (1981). *Patterns of family and non-family violence: An approach to the study of violent husbands.* Paper presented at National Conference of Family Violence Researchers, University of New Hampshire, Durham.

Hare, R. D. (1996). Psychopathy: A clinical construct whose time has come. *Criminal Justice and Behavior, 23,* 25–54.

Harrell, A. (1991). *Evaluation of court-ordered treatment for domestic violence offenders.* Washington, DC: The Urban Institute.

Harris, G., Rice, M., & Quinsey, V. (1993).Violent recidivism of mentally disordered offenders: The development of a statistical prediction instrument. *Criminal Justice and Behavior, 20,* 315–335.

Hart, B. (1988). *Safety for women: Monitoring batterers' programs.* Harrisburg, PA: Pennsylvania Coalition Against Domestic Violence.

Harway, M. (2004). *Handbook of couple's therapy.* Hoboken, NJ: Wiley.

Heckert, D. A., & Gondolf, E. W. (2004). Battered women's perceptions of risk factors and instruments in predicting repeat reassault. *Journal of Interpersonal Violence, 19*(7), 778–800.

Henning, K., & Feder, L. (2004). A comparison of men and women arrested for domestic violence: Who presents the greater threat? *Journal of Family Violence, 19*(2), 69–80.

Hilberman, E. (1980). Overview: The wifebeater's wife reconsidered. *American Journal of Psychiatry, 137,* 1336–1347.

Hilberman, E., & Munson, L. (1978). Sixty battered women. *Victimology: An International Journal, 2*(3–4), 460–471.

Holtzworth-Munroe, A., & Stuart, G. L. (1994). Typologies of male batterers: Three subtypes and the differences among them. *Psychological Bulletin, 116,* 476–497.

Hotaling, G. T., & Sugarman, D. B. (1986). An analysis of risk markers in husband to wife violence: The current state of the knowledge. *Violence and Victims, 1,* 101–124.

Jacobson, N. S., & Gottman, J. M. (1998). *When men batter women: New insights into ending abusive relationships.* New York, NY: Simon & Schuster.

Jens, K. (1980, April). *Depression in battered women.* Paper presented at the annual meeting of the Rocky Mountain Psychological Association, Tuscan, AZ.

Jones, A. (1980). *Women who kill.* New York, NY: Holt, Rinehart, & Winston.

Kaslow, F. (Ed.). (1997). *Handbook of relational diagnosis.* New York, NY: Wiley.

Kropp, P. R., Hart, S. D., Webster, C. D., & Eaves, D. (1999). *Spousal assault risk assessment guide: User's manual.* North Tonawanda, NY: Multi-Health Systems.

Lindsey, M., McBride, R. W., & Platt, C. M. (1993). *AMEND philosophy and curriculum for treating batterers.* Denver, CO: Gylantic.

Martin, D. (1976). *Battered wives.* San Francisco, CA: Glide.

Mohandie, K., Meloy, R., McGowan, M. G., & Williams, J. (2006). The RECON typology of stalking: Reliability and validity based upon a large sample of North American stalkers. *Journal of Forensic Science, 51*(1), 147–155.

Monahan, L. (1981). *Predicting violent behavior: An assessment of clinical techniques.* Beverly Hills, CA: Sage.

Millar, A., Code, R., & Ha, L. (2009/2013). *Inventory of spousal violence risk assessment tools used in Canada.* Department of Justice Canada. Retrieved from http://www.justice.gc.ca/eng/rp-pr/cj-jp/fv-vf/rr09_7/rr09_7.pdf

O'Leary, K. D. (1988). Physical aggression between spouses: A social learning theory perspective. In V. B. Van Hasselt, R. L. Morrison, A. S. Bellack, & M. Hersen (Eds.), *Handbook of family violence* (pp. 31–55). New York, NY: Plenum.

Patterson, G. R. (1982). *Coercive family process.* Eugene, OR: Castalia Press.

Pleck, E. (1979). Wifebeating in nineteenth-century America. *Victimology, 4*(1), 62–74.

Raine, A. (2013). *The anatomy of violence: The biological roots of crime.* New York, NY: Pantheon.

Reid, J. B., Taplin, P. S., & Lorber, R. (1981). A social interactional approach to the treatment of abusive families. In R. B. Stuart (Ed.), *Violent behavior: Social learning approaches to prediction, management, and treatment* (pp. 83–101). New York, NY: Brunner/Mazel.

Saunders, D. G. (1995). Prediction of wife assault. In J. C. Campbell (Ed.), *Assessing dangerousness: Violence by sexual offenders, batterers, and child abusers* (pp. 68–95). Thousand Oaks, CA: Sage.

Saunders, D. G. (1996). Feminist-cognitive-behavioral and process-psychodynamic treatments for men who batter: Interaction of abuser traits and treatment models. *Violence and Victims, 11*(4), 393–414.

Saunders, D. G. (1998). Child custody and visitation decisions in domestic violence cases. *Violence Against Women Online Resources.* Retrieved from www .vawnet.org

Sonkin, D. G. (1998). *Domestic violence: The perpetrator assessment handbook.* Sausalito, CA: Author.

Sonkin, D. J., & Durphy, M. (1982). *Learning to live without violence: A book for men.* Volcano, CA: Volcano Press.

Sonkin, D. J., Martin, D., & Walker, L. E. A. (1985). *The male batterer: A treatment approach.* New York, NY: Springer Publishing Company.

Steadman, H. J. (1986). Predicting violence leading to homicide. *Bulletin of the New York Academy of Medicine, 62,* 570–578.

Steinmetz, S. (1978). The battered husband syndrome. *Victimology: An International Journal, 2*(3–4), 499–509.

Straus, M. (1996). Identifying offenders in criminal justice research on domestic assault. In E. S. Buzawa & C. G. Buzawa (Eds.), *Do arrests and restraining orders work?* (pp. 14–29). Thousand Oaks, CA: Sage.

Straus, M. A. (1979). Measuring intrafamily conflict and violence: The Conflict Tactics (CT) Scales. *Journal of Marriage and Family, 41,* 75–88.

Straus, M. A. (2010). Thirty years of denying the evidence on gender symmetry in partner violence: Implications for prevention and treatment. *Partner Abuse, 1*(3), 332–362.

Straus, M. A., & Gelles, R. J. (1990). *Physical violence in American families: Risk factors and adaptations to violence in 8,145 families.* New Brunswick, NJ: Transaction.

Straus, M. A., Gelles, R. J., & Steinmetz, S. K. (1980). *Behind closed doors: Violence in the American family.* Garden City, NY: Anchor/Doubleday.

Tjaden, P., & Thoennes, N. (2000). *Full report of the prevalence, incidence, and consequences of violence against women* (NCJ 183781). Washington, DC: National Institute of Justice, Office of Justice Programs.

Totman, J. (1978). *The murderers: A psychological study of criminal homicide.* San Francisco, CA: R&E Research Associates.

Walker, L. E. (1979). *The battered woman.* New York, NY: Harper & Row.

Walker, L. E. (1984). *The battered woman syndrome.* New York, NY: Springer Publishing Company.

Walker, L. E. (1989a). Psychology and violence against women. *American Psychologist, 44,* 695–702.

Walker, L. E. (1989b). *Terrifying love: Why battered women kill and how society responds.* New York, NY: Harper & Row.

Walker, L. E. A. (2000). *The battered woman syndrome* (2nd ed.). New York, NY: Springer Publishing Company.

Washington State Coalition Against Domestic Violence. (2006). *2006 Fatality review: If I had one more day.* Retrieved from wscadv.org

Weisz, A. N., Tolman, R. M., & Saunders, D. G. (2000). Assessing the risk of severe domestic violence: The importance of survivor's predictions. *Journal of Interpersonal Violence, 15*(1), 75–90.

Wolfgang, M. E. (1968). *Studies in homicide.* New York, NY: Harper & Row.

Zorza, J. (2005). *Violence against women.* Kingston, NJ: Civic Research Institute.

CHAPTER THIRTEEN

BATTERED WOMEN'S
HEALTH CONCERNS

*I*n the original study of battered women, one of the surprises we found was how important the issue of health concerns was to the risk of development of learned helplessness. The impact of somatic symptoms on the development of learned helplessness was true for illnesses in childhood as well as adulthood in that sample. As we tried to understand our data, it made good intuitive sense as there is a lack of predictable control over the child's or woman's environment usually associated with chronic illnesses. Learned helplessness, as we described it in Chapter 4, is about the loss of the ability to predict between something that happens and its outcome, so the perception of unpredictability would be consistent. In the current study, we attempted to expand our focus beyond illnesses to broader health and body concerns. The concern for prevention of diseases either caused by or exacerbated by lifestyle has become much more focused on what we eat, where we live, and how much exercise we get. Newer research by Campbell and her colleagues (Decker et al., 2012) has focused on the health needs of women exposed to intimate partner violence (IPV) and child abuse. The Adverse Childhood Experiences (ACEs) Study, described in Chapter 6, demonstrated the impact exposure to abuse, violence, and other adverse childhood events has on later physical and mental health.

Forty years after the original study, we know much more about how our bodies work, including issues about stress and how it impacts nutrition, sleep, exercise, and lifestyle choices. Also, we now understand the association between stressors and the exacerbation or the reduction of some illnesses depending on the amount of stress to which the person is exposed. So, it makes intuitive sense that the more health concerns a battered woman has experienced as a child or as an adult will contribute to the psychological impact from the domestic violence.

HEALTH CONCERNS

Original Research

We explored the women's health and other potential stress factors while growing up. Almost 90% of the women stated that their physical health was average or above during childhood, although about one quarter reported problems with eating, menstruation, sleep, and weight, and two thirds reported suffering from depression. This inconsistency in reporting the presence of symptoms indicative of less than adequate health, yet labeling their childhood health as average or better, was a constant problem in interpreting our results. This is a case where the population needed to be asked more structured questions, with specific response choices, rather than to assume that they responded consistently to a general definition. Obviously, this is a problem with qualitative data collected in a context-specific method. While we anticipated definitional problems in many areas, we did not hypothesize the importance of prior health issues emerging as a factor in determining the impact of abuse or occurrence of battered woman syndrome.

We also looked at the frequency of critical periods in the women's childhood as a factor to produce learned helplessness. The critical periods were self-defined and included events perceived as uncontrollable like moving a lot, early parent loss from death or divorce, school failure, shame or humiliation because of poverty or other reasons, one or both parents as substance abusers, sexual assault, family disruptions, and so on. Over 91% of the women in our sample reported experiencing such critical periods, with the mean number of critical periods experienced being 2.1. This is further discussed in the learned helplessness theory section in Chapter 4. We concluded that it was the impact of the uncontrollability and unpredictability of response-outcome at an early age, rather than simply the outcome from the individual events themselves that formed the factor we measured. It was predicted that battered women and batterers came from homes where traditional attitudes toward sex roles were held and that they would also hold such traditional attitudes. Using the AWS (Attitudes Toward Women Scale) as a measure, we found that the women reported that the batterers and their fathers held very traditional values. Their own attitudes toward women's sex roles were self-reported as more liberal than 81% of the normative population, while the scores of their mothers and the nonbatterers were reported at about the average level. The implications of these results are discussed later in this chapter as we explore the impact on the women's body image (Duros, Nathan, Gill, & Needle, 2009). It is evident that the women perceived their family members as less liberal in their attitudes toward women's roles than themselves.

Medical Attention

In our sample, the need for medical attention increased from about one fifth of the women after the first incident to almost half after one of the worst incidents. Despite that need, only about two thirds of the women who needed it actually went for medical treatment. This was consistent with other reports at the time of the original study that battered women were less likely to seek the medical treatment they required (Stark, Flitcraft, & Fraiser, 1979; Walker, 1979). Others had found that even when medical treatment was sought, doctors were less likely than nurses to ask patients about the origin of their injuries. This made it even more likely that if they did seek treatment, they did not tell the doctor about the abuse. During the 1990s, the American Medical Association and other doctors' and nurses' groups began an education campaign for their members, teaching them how to ask women who appeared to be battered the appropriate questions. The most recent data suggests that battered women are more likely to talk to their doctors about the abuse they experience if they seek out treatment, although it is still unclear about how many battered women never go for medical treatment. Campbell and colleagues (Amar, Laughon, Sharps, Campbell, & AAN Expert Panel on Violence, 2013) shows that these education campaigns have been successful in that many more women will report domestic violence when they visit a health care provider. We now have data that show the toll that intimate partner abuse takes on these women's lives.

Doctors describe those women who do seek treatment as having a greater tolerance for the pain usually associated with their injuries. Two things appear to account for this observation. First, it is quite probable that, like our interviewers, they are observing the woman in a process of dissociation, whereby the battered woman perceives her mental state separate from her physical body. Descriptions and observations of the battered woman's disassociation suggest it is similar to a form of self-hypnosis with intense focus on surviving the physical and emotional trauma. The second explanation is in the more recent studies of biochemical changes in the autonomic nervous system that lower the pain threshold during the experience of trauma (Cotton, 1990; Goleman, 1995). Changes in the gluco-corticoids that are secreted in the midbrain structures lower the perception of pain at the time of the trauma. So is the release of endorphins, the body's own heroin-like substance that produces some relief from the pain of the trauma. This is obviously an adaptive response helpful to the organism for survival in crisis situations.

POSTTRAUMATIC STRESS DISORDER (PTSD) AND BRAIN CHEMISTRY

The new research mentioned previously has linked PTSD together with a breakdown in the body's capacity to fight illness and disease (Crofford, 2007). This field of study is called "psychoneuroimmunology" or PNI. The immunological system is located in the midbrain area along with the brain structures that produce and secrete the biochemicals that regulate our emotions. Many of the symptoms that make up the diagnosis of PTSD are actually produced by the autonomic nervous system that is part of our life-force involuntary responses to protect us from death or serious inju-ries. It is the perception of danger that is key, here. So, it is not surprising that human service workers who spend long hours listening to the expe-riences of trauma survivors would also develop secondary PTSD or what is also called "compassion fatigue" (e.g., Adams, Figley, & Boscarino, 2008; Figley, 2002; Pearlman & Saakvitne, 1995).

The brain perceives a stressor and it sends the message to the auto-nomic nervous system that then releases the appropriate neurotransmit-ters into the blood stream. As our nervous system needs both electrical impulses and chemicals to work properly, these neurotransmitters facili-tate the conduction of the electrical impulses throughout the body. When the danger has passed, the autonomic nervous system shuts off their production and clears the chemicals from the synapse, which is the gap between neurons that the electrical impulse must jump through in order for the message to be continuous. This is like a kitchen faucet: under stress the hormones and biochemicals that make up the neurotransmitters flood the system and when the stress is over, they recede. When battered women say they are "feeling nervous" it is usually because they are feeling the effects of so much nervous activity. The human stress response does have numerous checks and balances that are built in to make sure that it does not become overactive. However, these normal checks and balances often fail in the case of severe or chronic stress and then the person becomes vulnerable to disease. According to McEwen (2003), physiological mediators of the stress response are catecholamines, glucocorticoids, and cytokines. These chemicals also have an important role in maintaining the body through these types of changes called "allostatis."

Obviously, this has wear and tear on both the structural parts that produce and utilize these neurotransmitters as well as the body itself. This affects the immunological system that needs to respond to fighting intrusions to the integrity of the body. Newer research suggests that traumatic events produce inflammatory responses in the body that mediate the response between traumatic stressors and health problems (Kendall-Tackett, 2008, 2013). For children who are exposed to such stressors, the latest research suggests damage to the brain structures as well as the rest of the neurological system and the body, including cardiovascular disease (Batten, Aslan, Maciejewski, & Mazure, 2004; Danese, Pariante, Caspi, Taylor, & Poulton, 2007; Steinbaum, Chemtob, Boscarino, & Laraque, 2008). For adults, there is a whole host of health problems that can be associated with PTSD depending on how long and how serious the traumatic response is (Sareen, Cox, Stein, Afifi, Fleet, & Asmundson, 2007; Sutherland, Bybee, & Sullivan, 2002; Woods et al., 2005). Chronic illnesses such as cardiovascular disease, asthma, diabetes, and gastrointestinal disorders have long been associated with high levels of stress (Black & Gar-butt, 2002; Spielberger, 1991). Other somatic disorders such as fibromyalgia, chronic fatigue syndrome, temporomandibular disorder (TMD), and irritable bowel syndrome (IBS) have also been associated with high stress. One of the factors is the constant reexperiencing in the person's mind of the trauma as if it were reoccurring, causing the autonomic nervous system to secrete its neurotransmitters to deal with the extra stressors. This then causes a number of responses, including systemic inflammation, which then alters the immune system. Blood pressure rises, the person's focus narrows to deal with the perceived threat, and the rest of the body systems, such as the digestive system, take second stage to dealing with the trauma.

Although this description is a simplification of the complex reactions that PNI measures, at this time the presence of the systemic impact of PTSD is assessed only through psychological tests and not biomedical tests such as blood tests. Even more alarming, without precise assessment of the impact from the inflammation that alters the immune system when PTSD is present, it is difficult if not impossible to assess what body systems are being impacted. Thus, body reactions associated with PTSD and BWS are often misdiagnosed or ignored until it is too late to prevent chronic disease.

In some cases, it is possible to measure the amount of cortisol-releasing factor (CRF) in the blood, which is one of the major body signals to start the autonomic nervous system response to stress and danger. After exposure to a traumatic event, cortisol appears to shoot up to unusually high levels when another stressor is perceived. In some people, the resting, noncrisis response to cortisol levels is unnaturally low, which might trigger the abnormally high level of CRF when a stressor occurs. CRF can be measured easily through saliva. However, since it changes regularly over the 24-hour day, it is not possible to use it to assess for PTSD until levels are assessed throughout the time periods. Nonetheless, collecting CRF is noninvasive, inexpensive, and easy to obtain, these levels and dentists might be the perfect researchers to shed more information about how different adverse events and stressors impact the individual's body and mind. As a forensic psychologist, I think it might also be possible to demonstrate the impact stressors have on a person's state of mind when committing certain acts using CRF levels, but we are not at that point yet.

Some researchers have found that starting someone exposed to a traumatic event on medication that will quickly calm down the autonomic nervous system's stress response can prevent long-term PTSD (Pico-Alfonso, Garcia-Linares, Celda-Navarro, Herbert, & Martinez, 2004). Drugs such as alpha-2 agonists, the antidepressants, or even the atypical antipsychotic medications may help, although the most efficient would be a medication that could directly control the amount of cortisol released when faced with a stressor. We discuss the issue of psychotropic medication in another chapter when discussing intervention and treatment.

Researchers have found that PTSD is just as good an indicator of a person's long-term health status as having an elevated white blood cell count. An elevated white blood cell count can indicate a major infection or a serious blood disorder such as leukemia. The study also found a high erythrocyte sedimentation rate (ESR), which indicates inflammation. There was a similar finding for a possible indicator of serious neuroendocrine problems (Boscarino, 2008). There have been similar findings of the damage to other organs such as the heart in those with chronic long-term PTSD (Black & Garbutt, 2002) and the gastrointestinal system and its disorders (Leserman & Drossman, 2007). Kendall-Tackett (2008) suggests that the "flight or fight" response to trauma by the sympathetic nervous system, a response that releases catecholamines such as norepinephrine, epinephrine, and dopamine, signals the hypothalamic–pituitary–adrenal (HPA) axis that then releases chemicals such as the corticotrophin-releasing hormone (CRH). This causes the pituitary to release adrenocorticotropin hormone (ACTH), which causes the adrenal cortex to release cortisol, a glucocorticoid. The immune system then responds to the threat from the traumatic stressor by increasing inflammation by releasing proinflammatory cytokines that help the body fight infection and heal wounds. Researchers in PNI have been able to measure PTSD responses triggered in this way with three plasma markers: proinflammatory cytokines, C-reactive protein, and fibrinogen. So, both psychological and physiological markers can signal how the body and mind respond to both one-time and repeated traumatic events.

Behavioral Risk Factor Surveillance System (BRFSS)

The U.S. Centers for Disease Control and Prevention (CDC) has conducted studies about adverse health conditions and health risk behaviors in those who have experienced IPV. Using the 2005 BRFSS telephone survey, data were collected from over 70,000 U.S. homes with approximately 40,000 women and 30,000 men completing the optional IPV module. Questions on adverse health conditions included current use of disability equipment such as a cane, wheelchair, or special bed, and whether they were ever told they had high blood cholesterol, nongestational high blood pressure, nongestational diabetes, cardiovascular disease (heart attack, angina, coronary heart disease, or stroke), joint disease (arthritis, rheumatoid arthritis, gout, lupus, and fibromyalgia), or current asthma. In addition, the survey inquired about some high-risk health behaviors such as risk factors for HIV infection or sexually transmitted diseases (STDs). This included whether or not during the preceding year the responder had used intravenous drugs, had been treated for an STD, had given or received money for sex, or had participated in anal sex without a condom. Other health risk behaviors assessed were whether the person currently smoked and how much alcohol the person drank. For alcohol, the person was assumed to be a heavy or binge drinker if, for a man, he drank more than two drinks per day on average or if, for a woman, she drank one drink per day on average.

Further, an alcohol binge was defined as five or more drinks on one occasion during the preceding 30 days for both men and women. The final health risk was a body mass index (BMI) over 25, which is calculated by weight in kilograms over height.

Lifetime IPV prevalence estimates were calculated using age, sex, race/ethnicity, annual household income, and educational level. For women, the lifetime prevalence rate for impact from trauma was almost 30% and for men was almost 10%. Lifetime prevalence rates were higher among multiracial, non-Hispanic, and American Indian/Alaskan Native women and higher among lower-income respondents who often have poor access to good health care. Lifetime prevalence rates for IPV women were calculated separately and again, with the exception of diabetes, high blood pressure, and BMI over 25, battered women reported significantly higher numbers of health risk factors and risk behaviors than those who had never experienced abuse. Interestingly, those men who reported being victims of IPV also had higher health risk factors and risk behaviors than those who did not experience abuse. The men particularly had increased use of disability equipment, arthritis, asthma, activity limitations, stroke, risk factors for HIV infection or STDs, smoking, and heavy or binge drinking (CDC, 2006). For further information, see www.cdc.gov/ViolencePrevention/NISVS.

Childhood Abuse and IPV

The high numbers of women (and men) who report childhood abuse and IPV and receive no assistance in healing from the psychological effects obviously will be seen in medical clinics, often too late to stop a disease process that might have been prevented had their PTSD responses been dealt with earlier. As the CDC study in the previous section shows, high-risk behavioral activities coexist with those who have PTSD. Dutton, Kaltman, Goodman, Weinfurt, and Vankos (2005) describe different patterns of IPV and their correlates and outcomes. Coker et al. (2002) also detail the physical and mental health impacts for both male and female IPV victims. Eventually, it may be possible to predict what types of impact will produce certain PTSD responses in people with certain types of psychological and neurological histories. In our work, we have seen the impact of PTSD from multiple lifestyle stressors on women who have been arrested for various crimes, often substance abuse that is usually associated with their partners. We describe some programs in the jail for battered women willing to work on reducing the impact of domestic violence. However, when

PTSD co-occurs with substance abuse and other health concerns, the psychological issues are both more difficult to treat and less likely to get attention from caregivers. This suggests the need for programs to reduce the trauma responses to be more widely integrated in medical and psychological services especially for battered women.

Newer research on choking or "attempted strangulation," which is the correct health term, indicated a high prevalence in IPV, some studies finding over 50% of IPV women as compared to 10% of other abused women in actual or attempted homicides (Glass et al., 2008). Even though there may not be any visible injury from attempted strangulation, hoarseness, incontinence, internal swelling, petechiae, and marks visible under enhanced light often occur. There is an increased risk of death within 24 to 48 hours from stroke or aspiration. The risk of central nervous system distress from anoxia, memory loss, and seizures was also found in this study (Glass et al., 2008). Given the high prevalence of attempted strangulation in attempted or actual homicides, prevention may decrease the number of women killed in each year.

Ann Coker and colleagues (2010) have examined the symptoms reported in her studies, finding that neurological symptoms, including traumatic brain injuries, stroke, soft tissue damage, and falls, are consistent with IPV. Her work also highlighted the chronic pain associated with IPV, including back, abdominal, chest, and head pain. Others have reported high numbers of IPV in women seeking treatment for fibromyalgia, chronic fatigue syndrome, chronic bowel syndrome, gynecological problems such as sexually transmitted infections, urinary tract infections, infertility, and pelvic pain, leading Coker to examine other high-risk behaviors of battered women such as smoking, other substance use, unwanted and unsafe sex, less use of contraceptives resulting in more unwanted pregnancies and abortions, and high levels of stress. She also found more chronic diseases reported for these women, including cancer, diabetes, obesity, hypertension, and cerebral vascular diseases. As Coker and others remind us, however, we must also factor in the economic problems that so many of these women have with poverty, divorce, low-income jobs, inadequate health care, and higher legal and social welfare costs.

The Affordable Care Act (ACA) that is now in effect in most places in the United States may make a difference in women seeking health care, especially since they are entitled to at least one yearly visit for preventive health care where health care providers are supposed to ask them about many factors, including domestic violence specifically.

WHEN HEALTH CARE IS AVAILABLE

Even when health care is available, it is difficult for some battered women to utilize it on a consistent basis. However, battered women have used emergency rooms and urgent care centers for acute medical care even if they are unable to follow up with nonacute or even preventive medical care (Flitcraft, 1977; McLeer & Anwar, 1989; Stark et al., 1979; Ulrich et al., 2003). Kelley Gill (2006) attempted to compare battered women from six shelters in Connecticut with a similar sample of moms from a day-care center. She found that like the earlier studies, battered women were less likely to employ the services of a primary care doctor or clinic than nonbattered women. This did not appear to be due to barriers in access to treatment but rather barriers from their life situation in utilizing treatment consistently. Although they did utilize emergency rooms more often than nonbattered women for crisis intervention and they reported significantly more traumatic life events in the recent past and overall, they did not utilize the preventive health information disseminated there. Interestingly, battered women did report visiting the dentist and gynecologist as often as nonbattered women. Gill suggested that these two health care settings may be the most efficient places to distribute preventive health care information that they could not utilize from the emergency room when they are in crisis.

Although health care under the ACA will be more available for battered women, there are still many barriers for them to access the care. Ambuel and colleagues (2013) have been attempting to train health care professionals to reach out and improve their own health care response skills when a battered woman does come in for treatment. In their model, developed at the Medical College of Wisconsin, they encourage health care clinics to partner with individuals who have expertise in IPV prevention and women's advocacy organizations to better deliver services. One of the most important changes in the organizational culture of the modern health care clinic is the need to provide adequate time for the woman to relax sufficiently to be able to confide in the doctor. Unfortunately, health care clinics today are organized to move people in and out of service in the fastest and most efficient manner possible. Yet, even with posters and brochures portraying healthy relationships decorating the office and asking appropriate screening questions, Ambuel et al. found that without making the time to talk with the patient, it would be difficult for the battered woman to reveal her situation.

At Nova Southeastern University, the dental school has been experimenting with delivering health care services to battered women directly in the shelter. With portable dental clinics available, they set up a temporary dental office right in the shelter, eliminating the need for the women to go to a clinic or private office for care for themselves or their children. Students who are in a dental residency program were delivering the services, which then sensitized them to being able to provide support for battered women they would see in their own clinics or private offices. Interestingly, given the large numbers of battered women who are hit in the facial area, both their natural teeth and devices used to replace them are often broken in these assaults. Medicaid permits only one replacement of a broken device, so the woman's nutrition and self-esteem suffer when they cannot be replaced after another assault. We learned when working in this program how shaming it is for a battered woman not to be able to smile because she has so many lost teeth or repeatedly broken bones in her face and jaw. Women in the substance abuse rehabilitation program reported similar difficulties. Dentists in the community now give their time to go into the shelter and the substance abuse residential center to continue this important program.

BODY IMAGE

The discussion in this chapter indicates that all three types of domestic violence, physical, sexual, and psychological abuse all have an impact on both the psychological and physical health of the victims. One of the most negative and lasting effects of IPV on women appears to be the impact on the women's body image, which is related to their self-esteem. In the earlier work, we focused on assessment of self-esteem in battered women we studied. Although we mention body image, we did not understand the extent to which body image is affected by both physical and psychological abuse tactics used by the abusers. However, the literature on development of both body image and self-identity tie the two together (Cash & Prunzinsky, 1990). They define body image as a person's attitudinal dispositions toward the physical self and suggest that positive body image development is crucial to healthy self-esteem. There is also evidence that negative body image is associated with negative self-confidence (Cullari, Rohrer, & Bahm, 1998), social interactions (Cash & Fleming, 2002), and physical intimacy within romantic relationships (Wiederman, 2000). In addition, body dissatisfaction has been linked to eating disorders such as anorexia and bulimia nervosa (Stice & Shaw, 2002). Sexually assaulted women have been found to develop negative body image as one result of their victimization (Widman, Lustyk, & Paschane, 2005), but until recently, there has been only limited research with battered women who have reported forced sex with their partners (Campbell & Soeken, 1999).

Self-Esteem

In the first three editions of this book, I discuss the difficulty in measuring self-esteem with battered women. It is clear that self-esteem is not a unitary concept. People who have good self-esteem often express self-confidence and feel that they can accomplish the things they wish to do (self-efficacy). Most of us like some things about ourselves and do not like other things. If we have participated in psychotherapy, we often spend many hours trying to learn about ourselves and learn to give up or simply accept those things we do not like. Most of the time we are successful, at least with the most noxious things that go into making up our self-esteem that can be changed. This was true for the battered women in the original study. Interestingly, they liked themselves better than they liked other women but felt that they were not as strong in doing many things as were men.

Although low self-esteem has been associated with powerlessness (Aguilar & Nightingale, 1994) and depression (Cascardi & O'Leary, 1992) more recently, it has also been found to be a component of body image. Whether physically or emotionally abused, the more severe the abuse, the more often the battered women report symptoms associated with low self-esteem (Follingstad, Brennan, Hause, Polk, & Rutledge, 1991; Pagelow, 1984). In fact, Follingstad et al. found that different types of emotional abuse had a different impact on women, with humiliation, name-calling, and verbal harassment being the worst. However, emotional abuse that was considered isolating, restricting, and controlling also had a negative impact on battered women (Aguilar & Nightingale, 1994). Stark (2007) has developed a detailed analysis of various forms of emotional and psychological abuse, including the controlling behaviors that are so common that many dismiss their potential damage to the recipients.

More recent studies have found that the opposite is also true: that is, the more the woman is satisfied with her body, the more likely she is to have higher self-esteem. For example, Gillen, Lefkowitz, and Shearer (2006), in their cross-national study of over 400 college students, found that sexually active women who were satisfied with their body image were less likely to engage in unprotected sex and other risky behaviors. The authors noted that a positive view of their bodies provided an extra dose of confidence in the women they sampled. Further, they suggest that programs that focus on improving young women's attitudes toward their bodies could help promote healthy relationships for women. Interestingly, this was not true for the men they interviewed as those with a more positive body image were happy with how they looked and were more likely to engage in sex with multiple partners without using a condom. The authors then suggest that programs be separated by gender, with men learning more about respect for themselves, and women becoming less likely to engage in risky behaviors.

BODY IMAGE STUDY

In light of the new research connecting body image, self-esteem, and other psychological symptoms from both physical and emotional abuse in intimate relationships as well as from sexual abuse, we decided to try to measure women's satisfaction with their physical bodies in the current study. We added a number of questions in the Battered Woman Syndrome Questionnaire (BWSQ) that were specific to body image. These can be found in Table 13.1 and the analysis of their significance in Table 13.2. Further, our findings indicated the following:

- More women reported being never/rarely satisfied with their unclothed physical appearance (61.3%) as opposed to often/always being satisfied (19.4%).
- More women reported never/rarely having knowledge that their weight is appropriate (63.3%) as opposed to often/always knowing that it is appropriate (20%).
- More women reported often/always thinking their stomach is too big (67.8%) as opposed to never/rarely thinking it is too big (25.8%).
- Alarmingly, 43% of the women reported occasionally, often, or always restricting food intake.

Table 13.1 *Responses on the Objectified Body Consciousness Scale*

Objectified Body Consciousness Questions	SD/D %	Slightly Disagree %	Neutral %	Slightly Agree %	SA/A %	N/A %
I rarely think about how I look.............	75		12.5		12.5	
When I can't control my weight, I feel like something must be wrong with me...	62.5				25	12.5
I think it is more important that my clothes are comfortable than whether they look good on me..............	37.5		37.5	12.5		12.5
I think persons are pretty much stuck with the looks they are born with.............	25	50	12.5	12.5		
I feel ashamed of myself when I haven't made the effort to look my best.............	25	25	25	12.5	12.5	
A large part of being in shape is having that kind of body in the first place.............	12.5	37.5	37.5		12.5	
I think more about how my body feels than how my body looks.............	37.5	12.5	25	12.5	12.5	
I feel like I must be a bad person when I don't look as good as I could...	50	25	12.5	12.5		
I rarely compare how I look with how other people look.............	50	12.5	37.5			
I think persons can look pretty much how they want if they are willing to work at it.....		37.5	12.5	25	25	
I would be ashamed for people to know what I really weigh.............	50		12.5	25		12.5

I really don't think I have much control over how my body looks.........	50	37.5		12.5		
Even when I can't control my weight I think I'm an okay person...........	12.5		25	12.5		
During the day, I think about how I look many times......		25	25		50	
I never worry that something is wrong with me when I'm not exercising as much as I should.........	25		12.5	25	25	
I often worry about whether the clothes I am wearing make me look good.........	12.5	12.5	12.5	37.5	25	
When I'm not exercising enough, I question whether I am a good enough person...........	62.5		12.5	12.5		12.5
I rarely worry about how I look to other people.........	37.5		25		37.5	
I think a person's weight is determined mostly by the genes with which they are born...	50	12.5	25	12.5		
I am more concerned what my body can do than how it looks......	25		37.5	12.5	25	
It doesn't matter how hard I try to change my weight, it's probably always going to be about the same............	37.5			12.5	12.5	37.5
When I'm not the size I think I should be, I feel ashamed...............	25		37.5		12.5	12.5
I can weigh what I'm supposed to when I try hard enough.......	12.5		37.5		37.5	12.5
The shape you are in depends mostly on your genes.........	25	12.5	25	12.5	25	

Note. Data from eight participants from English sample.

SA/A, strongly agree/agree; SD/D, strongly disagree/disagree.

Table 13.2 *Body Image Questions*

Question Asked	Never/Rarely (%)	Occasionally (%)	Often/Always (%)
I am happy with the way I look.	29	32.3	38.7
I am aware of changes in my weight.	3.2	12.9	83.8
I am happy with the way I look with no clothes.	61.3	19.4	19.4
My body is unattractive.	35.5	29	35.6
I know that my weight is normal for my age and height.	63.3	16.7	20
If I gain a pound, I worry that I will keep gaining.	45.1	19.4	35.5
I am preoccupied with the desire to be thinner.	29.1	38.7	33.3
I think that my stomach is too big.	25.8	6.5	67.8
I exaggerate or magnify the importance of weight.	32.3	32.3	35.5
I sometimes restrict food intake as a way to lose weight.	58.1	9.7	33.3

Consistent with our hypothesis, independent sample t test results reveal that there is no significant difference between sexually abused and nonsexually abused battered women on body image ($t = .686$; $p = .498$; see Table 13.3). Therefore, our study suggests that physical, sexual, and emotional abuse all can produce distortions in body image.

We were pleased that we were able to create the Objectified Body Consciousness Scale using the questions that are seen in Table 13.1. When put together, the results can assist those working with battered women in understanding what areas of body image need to be resolved for the women's self-esteem to rise to a higher level. This is an important tool as many of the women who are in the Survivor Therapy Empowerment Program (STEP) groups, described later in Chapter 17, ask for ways to improve their self-esteem. The concept of self-esteem is difficult to assess and

Table 13.3 *Body Image Results*

		Levene's Test for Equality of Variances		*t* Test for Equality of Means				95% Confidence Interval of the Difference	
		F	Significance	*t*	*df*	Sig. (Two-Tailed)		Lower	Upper
BODTOTAL	Equal variances assumed	.495	.487	.686	29	.498		-4.54004	9.1234
	Equal variances not assumed			.689	28.808	.496		-4.50840	9.0917

Independent Samples Test

335

purposefully change, so attempting to assist the women in better understanding their own body image issues along with sexuality issues, as discussed further in Chapter 9, will provide some ways to help them heal.

Given the large numbers of battered women who have difficulties with their body image we included these variables in the analysis of what factors are found in battered woman syndrome. As stated in earlier chapters, body image distortion and somatic concerns have been found to be one of the six factors that constitute battered woman syndrome (BWS). We further discussed these issues in Chapter 9 when describing the sexual intimacy responses that battered women described in our studies.

Body Image of Women in Jail

We decided to examine the body image of women in jail and compare it to their attachment style (Lewis, Schumacher, Walker, & Schmit, in preparation). A sample of 143 women awaiting trial or in a substance abuse program in a local jail volunteered to talk about their experiences with IPV as measured with the BWSQ. They were also administered the Objective Body Concept Scale (OBCS) and the revised Adult Attachment Style Inventory (AASI). Although attachment styles, as discussed, are usually thought to originate in childhood, in part based on how well or poorly their needs are met by their parents or caretakers, the AASI also takes into account experiences that may impact attachment style from adult relationships, also.

"Secure" attachment is characterized by a positive self-model, a positive model of others, a sense of self-worth, and comfort with intimacy (Bartholomew & Shaver, 1998). Secure individuals have a sense of lovability and are comfortable with autonomy (Cash, Theriault, & Annis, 2004). The research suggests that those with secure attachment had their needs or expectations met by others in their lives and believe they are competent to take care of their own needs, too. There are several different styles of attachment that are engaged in by individuals who do not have secure attachment. "Preoccupied" attachment is characterized by a negative self-model and a lack of a sense of self-worthiness. Individuals with this style of attachment do not believe they are as able to take care of themselves as others can. They have a positive model of others and seek others' love and acceptance, often in a dependent way. Preoccupied individuals believe that security can be obtained only if others respond well to them so what others might think about their body image would be important to them.

Another attachment style by those who do not have secure attachment is "dismissing" attachment style. Dismissing attachment is characterized by a positive self-model, a negative model of others, avoidance of closeness because of negative expectations, and denial of the value of close relationships. Dismissing individuals feel that they are worthy of love but they detach from others whom they view as untrustworthy. They tend to be more aloof and pay less attention to what others might say about their body image. "Fearful" attachment is characterized by a negative self-model and a lack of a sense of lovability. Individuals with a fearful attachment avoid others and intimate interactions because they anticipate rejection (Bartholomew & Shaver, 1998; Cash et al., 2004).

In the earlier research conducted on attachment styles of battered women, we found that 88% of these women had a primarily insecure attachment pattern. In that sample, 53% had a fearful attachment pattern and 35% had a preoccupied attachment pattern (Henderson, Bartholomew, & Dutton, 1997). Another study found preoccupied attachment to be significantly linked to IPV (Henderson, Bartholomew, Trinke, & Kwong, 2005). Based on past findings, the researchers hypothesized that higher levels of anxiety on the Revised Adult Attachment Scale would be correlated with higher levels of body consciousness. An additional hypothesis was that women with a secure attachment style would have the lowest levels of self-reported body consciousness compared to women with preoccupied, dismissing, and fearful attachment styles.

Analyses of variance (ANOVAs) and a Pearson correlation were computed to determine the relationship between the scores on the OBCS scale and scores on the Revised Adult Attachment Scale (RAAS). The results indicated that 101 participants had an insecure attachment, which included 30 participants with a preoccupied attachment style, 51 participants with a dismissing attachment style, and 20 participants with a fearful attachment style. Thirty-eight participants had a secure attachment style. Mean OBC scores were significantly positively correlated with anxiety ($r = .18$, $p = .03$). Body surveillance was significantly positively correlated with anxiety ($r = .27$, $p = .001$). Body shame was significantly positively correlated with anxiety ($r = .26$, $p = .002$). Appearance control was significantly negatively correlated with anxiety ($r = -.23$, $p = .004$).

Results of a one-way ANOVA demonstrated that there was not a significant mean difference in overall body consciousness between the four attachment styles, $F(3, 135) = 0.75$, $p = .52$. There were marginally significant mean differences in body surveillance between the four attachment styles, $F(3, 135) = 2.30$, $p = .08$. Dismissive individuals had a significantly lower average level of body surveillance ($M = 3.98$, $SD = 1.36$) than preoccupied individuals ($M = 4.70$, $SD = 1.13$; $p = .02$) and had a marginally significantly lower average level of body surveillance than fearful individuals ($M = 4.60$, $SD = 1.25$; $p = .08$). There were significant mean differences in body shame between the four attachment styles, $F(3, 135) = 3.12$, $p = .03$. Dismissive individuals had a significantly lower average level of body shame ($M = 2.65$, $SD = 1.33$) than preoccupied individuals ($M = 3.53$, $SD = 1.22$; $p = .005$) and had a significantly lower average level of body shame than secure individuals ($M = 3.24$, $SD = 1.49$; $p = .040$). There were significant mean differences in appearance control beliefs between the four attachment styles, $F(3, 135) = 4.35$, $p = .006$. Preoccupied individuals had a marginally significantly lower average level of appearance control beliefs ($M = 4.27$, $SD = .826$) than secure individuals ($M = 4.78$, $SD = 1.23$; $p = .063$). Preoccupied individuals had significantly lower average level of appearance control than dismissive individuals ($M = 5.18$, $SD = 1.23$; $p = .001$) and fearful individuals ($M = 5.00$, $SD = 1.17$; $p = .025$).

These findings were very interesting in that women with a dismissing attachment style were less impacted by other people's views of their body image, even more so than women with a secure attachment style, although they too were less impacted by objectified body consciousness mores. Like predicted, women who were more dependent on others for their self-esteem were also more likely to be anxious about their own body image and what others thought about their body image. The more body satisfaction, the less likely they were to feel unloved or rejected by others. The women studied possess two risk factors, negative body image and insecure attachment style, which can lead to a myriad of negative consequences. Therefore, it is important to understand the relationship between these two areas of concern for battered women. This study indicates that the relationship between attachment and body image is also a topic of concern for incarcerated women. It is an area of study that should not be neglected due to the fact that self-objectification contributes to eating disorder behaviors and high levels of body shame and surveillance are negatively correlated with autonomy, environmental mastery, personal growth, life purpose, and self-acceptance (Grossbard, Lee, Neighbors, & Larimer, 2009; Noll & Fredrickson, 1998; Sinclair & Myers, 2004).

MEDICAL ISSUES IN THE CURRENT STUDY

We measured common physical ailments in both the original and current studies to attempt to determine if there were common somatic complaints for the women. These results can be found in Table 13.4.

Interestingly, the most frequent somatic complaints that women reported were depression (50%), sleep problems (46%), headaches (40%), and weight problems (32%). We further analyzed them and the results can be found in Table 13.5.

When asked about these responses, most women included the feelings of sadness and unhappiness when asked about what made them feel depressed. It is possible that the feelings of depression were consistent with PTSD rather than a true clinical depression but they were not asked for that clarification and we did not attempt to compare their responses on the Trauma Symptom Inventory (TSI) with this scale. The sleep problems were most often mentioned because of the partners' waking them or not letting them sleep. They reported the partners' demands that they stay up

Table 13.4 *Somatic Complaints Questions*

How Often Do You Experience the Following?	Never (%)	Rarely/ Sometimes (%)	Often/ Most Times (%)
Headaches	14	47	40
Hospitalizations	57	33	9
Eating problems	39	39	22
Depression	10	41	50
Serious injury	75	22	4
Menstrual problems	57	24	18
Serious disease	80	11	10
Weight problems	40	28	32
High blood pressure	64	16	19
Sleep	28	26	46
Allergies	63	21	17
Asthma	71	15	15
Gastrointestinal problems	67	17	16
Other	66	13	22

Table 13.5 *Independent Samples Test*

		Levene's Test for Equality of Variances		t Test for Equality of Means				95% Confidence Interval of the Difference	
		F	Significance	t	df	Sig. (Two-Tailed)		Lower	Upper
Headaches	Equal variances assumed	1.457	.230	-3.029	103	.003		-1.41088	-.29432
	Equal variances not assumed			-2.779	31.668	.009		-1.47786	-.22734
Depression	Equal variances assumed	.000	.993	-2.925	103	.004		-1.36755	-.26235
	Equal variances not assumed			-2.820	33.626	.008		-1.40258	-.22732
Weight problems	Equal variances assumed	3.314	.072	-2.587	102	.011		-1.59323	-.21031
	Equal variances not assumed			-2.858	41.599	.007		-1.53866	-.26488
Sleep	Equal variances assumed	1.368	.245	-3.233	102	.002		-1.81095	-.43382
	Equal variances not assumed			-3.454	39.259	.001		-1.77951	-.46525

with them while being harangued with the partners' negative ranting and raving, usually about whatever the partners thought they had done wrong.

SUMMARY

Our findings that body image distortions and somatic concerns are part of BWS placed an emphasis on these areas both to better understand how to help already abused women to heal and as a way to develop protective factors toward healthy relationships. The research into PTSD and PNI provide an explanation to understand how the immune system is more likely to be damaged by trauma, especially chronic abuse experienced by battered women. Studies that indicate how the actual parts of the autonomic nervous system work both to protect the body against trauma and to understand what happens when such resiliency is lost are important to help the women better understand why they have so many physical as well as emotional ailments. Although the health care system has attempted to deal with battered women, in fact both the structure and function are not set up to be helpful, especially when chronic illnesses are exacerbated by environmental stressors such as living with domestic violence. Not surprisingly, all these issues create a climate where the battered woman's self-esteem and her body image become lower than before, which provides a cyclical pattern—low self-esteem, distorted body image, psychological depression and anxiety, PTSD, physical damage to the nervous system, low self-esteem, and so on. It is difficult to rebuild self-esteem as it is made up of so many components. However, newer research demonstrates the ability of raising women's self-esteem by increasing satisfaction with their bodies. Obviously, there are many points at which intervention can be successful in helping battered women recover from IPV. Assisting in raising body image may actually help in preventing more serious damage to body organs as well as in raising self-esteem and increasing psychological functioning.

REFERENCES

Adams, R. E., Figley, C. R., & Boscarino, J. A. (2008). The compassion fatigue scale: Its use with social workers following urban disaster. *Research in Social Work Practice, 18*, 238–250.

Aguilar, R. J., & Nightingale, N. N. (1994). The impact of specific battering experiences on the self-esteem of abused women. *Journal of Family Violence, 9,* 35–45.

Amar, A., Laughon, K., Sharps, P., Campbell, J. C., & AAN Expert Panel on Violence. (2013). Screening and counseling for violence against women in primary care settings. *Nursing Outlook, 61,* 187–191.

Ambuel, B., Hamberger, L. K., Guse, C. E., Melzer-Lange, M., Phelan, M. B., & Kistner, A. (2013). Healthcare can change from within: Sustained improvement in the healthcare response to intimate partner violence. *Journal of Family Violence, 28*(8), 833–847.

Bartholomew, K., & Shaver, P. R. (1998). Methods of assessing adult attachment: Do they converge? In J. A. Simpson & W. S. Rholes (Eds.), *Attachment theory and close relationships* (pp. 25–45). New York, NY: Guilford Press.

Batten, S. V., Aslan, M., Maciejewski, P. K., & Mazure, C. M. (2004). Childhood maltreatment as a risk factor for adult cardiovascular disease and depression. *Journal of Clinical Psychiatry, 65,* 249–254.

Black, P. H., & Garbutt, L. D. (2002). Stress, inflammation, and cardiovascular disease. *Journal of Psychosomatic Research, 52,* 1–23.

Boscarino, J. A. (2008). Psychobiologic predictors of disease mortality after psychological trauma: Implications for research and clinical surveillance. *Journal of Nervous and Mental Disease, 196*(2), 100–107.

Campbell, J. C., & Soeken, K. L. (1999). Forced sex and intimate partner violence: Effects on women's risk and women's health. *Violence Against Women, 5,* 1017–1035.

Cascardi, M., & O'Leary, K. D. (1992). Depressive symptomatology, self-esteem, and self-blame in battered women. *Journal of Family Violence, 7*(4), 249–259.

Cash, T. F., & Fleming, E. C. (2002). Body image and social relations. In T. F. Cash & T. Pruzinsky (Eds.), *Body image: A handbook of theory, research and clinical practice* (pp. 277–286). New York, NY: Guilford Press.

Cash, T. F., & Pruzinsky, T. (1990). *Body images: Development, deviance, and change.* New York, NY: Guilford Press.

Cash, T. F., Theriault, J., & Annis, N. M. (2004). Body image in an interpersonal context: Adult attachment, fear of intimacy and social anxiety. *Journal of Social and Clinical Psychology, 23*(1), 89–103.

Centers for Disease Control and Prevention. (2006). *Behavioral risk factor surveillance system 2005 report.* Retrieved from http://msdh.ms.gov/brfss/brfss 2005ar.pdf

Coker, A. L., Davis, K. E., Arias, I., Desai, S., Sanderson, M., Brandt, H. M., & Smith, P. H. (2002). Physical and mental health effects of intimate partner violence for men and women. *American Journal of Preventive Medicine, 23,* 260–268.

Cotton, D. (1990). *Stress management: An integrated approach to therapy.* New York, NY: Brunner/Mazel.

Crofford, L. J. (2007). Violence, stress, and somatic syndromes. *Trauma, Violence & Abuse, 8*(3), 299–313.

Cullari, S., Rorher, J. M., & Bahm, C. (1998). Body image perceptions across sex and age groups. *Perceptual and Motor Skills, 87*, 839–847.

Danese, A., Pariante, C. M., Caspi, A., Taylor, A., & Poulton, R. (2007). Childhood maltreatment predicts adult inflammation in a life-course study. *Proceedings of the National Academy of Sciences, 104*(4), 1319–1324.

Decker, M. R., Frattaroli, S., McCaw, B., Coker, A. L., Miller, E., Sharps, P., . . . Gielen, A. (2012). Transforming the health care response to intimate partner violence and taking best practices to scale. *Journal of Women's Health, 21*(12), 1222–1229.

Duros, R., Nathan, A., Gill, K., & Needle, R. (2009). Body image and health concerns. In L. E. A. Walker, *The battered woman syndrome* (3rd ed., pp. 145–165). New York, NY: Springer Publishing Company.

Dutton, M. A., Kaltman, S., Goodman, L. A., Weinfurt, K., & Vankos, N. (2005). Patterns of intimate partner violence: Correlates and outcomes. *Violence and Victims, 20*(5), 483–497.

Figley, C. R. (2002). Compassion fatigue: Psychotherapists' chronic lack of self-care. *Journal of Clinical Psychology, 58*(11), 1433–1441.

Flitcraft, A. (1977). *Battered women: An emergency room epidemiology with a description of a clinical syndrome and critique of present therapeutics.* Unpublished doctoral dissertation. Yale University School of Medicine, New Haven, Connecticut.

Follingstad, D. R., Brennan, A. F., Hause, E. S., Polek, D. S., & Rutledge, L. L. (1991). Factors moderating physical and psychological symptoms of battered women. *Journal of Family Violence, 6*, 81–95.

Glass, N., Laughon, K., Campbell, J. C., Block, C. R., Hanson, G., Sharps, P. W., & Taliaferro, E. (2008). Non-fatal strangulation is an important risk factor for homicide of women. *Journal of Emergency Medicine, 35*, 329–335.

Gill, K. (2006). [Court model and procedure gathered from secretary chair position of the Greater New Haven Domestic Violence Task Force]. Unpublished raw data.

Gillen, M. M., Lefkowitz, E. S., & Shearer, C. L. (2006). Does body image play a role in risky sexual behavior and attitudes? *Journal of Youth and Adolescence, 35*, 230–242.

Goleman, D. (1995). *Emotional intelligence.* New York, NY: Bantam Books.

Grossbard, J. R., Lee, C. M., Neighbors, C., & Larimer, M. E. (2009). Body image concerns and contingent self-esteem in male and female college students. *Sex Roles, 60*(3–4), 198–207.

Henderson, A., Bartholomew, K., & Dutton, D. G. (1997). He loves me; He loves me not: Attachment and separation resolution of abused women. *Journal of Family Violence, 12*, 169–191.

Henderson, A. J., Bartholomew, K., Trinke, S. J., & Kwong, M. J. (2005). When loving means hurting: An exploration of attachment and intimate abuse in a community sample. *Journal of Family Violence, 20*(4), 219–230.

Kendall-Tackett, K. (2008). Inflammation and traumatic stress: A likely mechanism for chronic illness in trauma survivors. *Trauma Psychology, 3*(2), 12–14.

Kendall-Tackett, K. (2013). *Treating the lifetime health effects of childhood victimization* (2nd ed.). Kingston, NJ: Civic Research Institute.

Leserman, J., & Drossman, D. A. (2007). Relationship of abuse history to functional gastrointestinal disorders and symptoms. *Trauma, Violence & Abuse, 8,* 331–343.

Lewis, R., Schumacher, L., Walker, L., & Schmit, A. (2016). *Attachment and body consciousness in incarcerated battered women.* Manuscript in preparation.

McEwen, B. S. (2003). Mood disorders and allostatic load. *Biological Psychiatry, 54*(3), 200–207.

McLeer, S. V., & Anwar, R. (1989). A study of battered women presenting in an emergency department. *American Journal of Public Health, 79*(1), 65–66.

Noll, S. M., & Fredrickson, B. L. (1998). A mediational model linking self-objectification, body shame, and disordered eating. *Psychology of Women Quarterly, 22*(4), 623–636.

Pagelow, M. D. (1984). *Family violence.* New York, NY: Praeger.

Pearlman, L. A., & Saakvitne, K. W. (1995). *Trauma and the therapist: Countertransference and vicarious traumatization in psychotherapy with incest survivors.* New York, NY: W. W. Norton.

Pico-Alfonso, M. A., Garcia-Linares, M. I., Celda-Navarro, N., Herbert, J., & Martinez, M. (2004). Changes in cortisol and dehydroepiandrosterone in women victims of physical and psychological intimate partner violence. *Biological Psychiatry, 56*(4), 233–240.

Sareen, J., Cox, B. J., Stein, M. B., Afifi, T. O., Fleet, C., & Asmundson, G. J. (2007). Physical and mental comorbidity, disability, and suicidal behavior associated with posttraumatic stress disorder in a large community sample. *Psychosomatic Medicine, 69*(3), 242–248.

Sinclair, S. L., & Myers, J. E. (2004). The relationship between objectified body consciousness and wellness in a group of college women. *Journal of College Counseling, 7*(2), 150–161.

Stark, E. (2007). *Coercive control: How men entrap women in personal life.* New York, NY: Oxford University Press.

Spielberger, C. D. (1991). *State-Trait Anger Expression Inventory: STAXI professional manual.* Tampa, FL: Psychological Assessment Resources.

Stark, E., Flitcraft, A., & Frazier, W. (1979). Medicine and patriarchal violence: The social construction of a "private" event. *International Journal of Health Services, 9*(3), 461–493.

Steinbaum, D. P., Chemtob, C., Boscarino, J. A., & Laraque, D. (2008). Use of a psychosocial screen to detect children with symptoms of posttraumatic stress disorder: An exploratory study. *Ambulatory Pediatrics, 8*(1), 32–35.

Stice, E., & Shaw, H. E. (2002). Role of body dissatisfaction in the onset and maintenance of eating pathology: A synthesis of research findings. *Journal of Psychosomatic Research, 53,* 985–993.

Sutherland, C. A., Bybee, D. I., & Sullivan, C. M. (2002). Beyond bruises and broken bones: The joint effects of stress and injuries on battered women's health. *American Journal of Community Psychology, 30,* 609–636.

Ulrich, Y. C., Cain, K. C., Sugg, N. K., Rivara, F. P., Rubanowice, D. M., & Thompson, R. S. (2003). Medical care utilization patterns in women with diagnosed domestic violence. *American Journal of Preventive Medicine*, 24(1), 9–15.
Walker, L. E. (1979). *The battered woman.* New York, NY: Harper & Row.
Widman, M., Lustyk, M. K. B., & Paschane, A. A. (2005). Body image in sexually assaulted women: Does age at the time of the assault matter? *Family Violence & Sexual Assault Bulletin, 21*, 5–11.
Wiederman, M. W. (2000). Women's body image self-consciousness during physical intimacy with a partner. *Journal of Sex Research, 37*, 60–68.
Woods, A. B., Page, G. G., O'Campo, P., Pugh, L. C., Ford, D., & Campbell, J. C. (2005). The mediation effect of posttraumatic stress disorder symptoms on the relationship of intimate partner violence and IFN-γ levels. *American Journal of Community Psychology, 36*(1–2), 159–175.

CHAPTER FOURTEEN

MENTAL HEALTH NEEDS OF BATTERED WOMEN

To state that women who live with domestic violence have special mental health needs as a group is a controversial statement within the battered women's community but would not surprise most current or formerly battered women. Over the past 40 years, there has been much work done to demonstrate that all battered women are not mentally ill but that does not mean that they do not have serious mental health problems after living with a batterer. This should not be a difficult proposition as having emotional problems does not necessarily mean they rise to the level of a mental illness. But, battered women advocates argue that it is dangerously close to blaming the victim for her victimization and not holding the batterer responsible for his own abusive behavior. Postmodern feminism posits the argument that all women should be treated with equality and respect and when certain classes of women, like battered women, are segregated for special treatment, it weakens the movement toward equality between women and men. Perhaps this would be true if women and men have already achieved equality in their societies, but that has not yet happened. While most feminists would agree with the goal of equal opportunity for all, it is abundantly clear that we have not yet achieved it and that some classes of women are more vulnerable to not accessing equality than others. Feminists believe that the personal is political; if one woman is being battered, then all of us are in danger of being battered. In order to strengthen the vulnerable women so that they too have the opportunity to be all that they can be, we must look toward building the resiliency of all women. Psychology can assist in finding ways to accomplish this process.

The research presented in this book demonstrates that there are various psychological issues that get raised for many women who live with domestic violence. This being the case, we then believe that they deserve the best care that the mental health community can provide for them, understanding that their mental health needs will vary from person to person. Battered women themselves are terrified about being labeled with a mental illness especially since so many are threatened into silence by their batterers who tell them that everyone will think they are "crazy." While health service providers are now better trained in identification of both health and mental health needs of battered women and their children, there is still little understanding of what to do after identification. Women's continued invalidation in the courts, especially the family courts where batterers succeed in keeping control over the women through the children and through access to money, also makes discussing mental health issues frightening, as they could be used against the women to persuade judges to take away custody of the children. In Chapter 19, I describe some examples of how accurate this perception may be especially when children are in the home and exposed to domestic violence.

The international community through the UN and the WHO has declared that domestic violence is a violation of the person's human rights. This is an important declaration as it supports those commentators who believe that without women being treated as full equals to men, there can be no stopping violence against women. Sociologist Evan Stark (2007) has suggested that in most abusive relationships, men use a largely unidentified form of subjugation that more closely resembles kidnapping or indentured servitude than physical assault. He calls this pattern *coercive control*. He uses his knowledge gained from working in the domestic violence field to demonstrate how men can use coercive control to extend their dominance in ways that subvert women's autonomy, isolate them, and infiltrate what he describes as the most intimate corners of their lives. Stark has suggested that we must elevate the use of coercive control from a second-class misdemeanor in the criminal justice system (where most criminal prosecutions of domestic violence cases end up) to a human rights violation so it ceases to permit men to continue to jeopardize women's freedom in everyday life. Psychologist Gerald Patterson (1982) demonstrated how coercive control is modeled by children who learn to use aggression against their mothers by exposure to their fathers' behavior. The fact that domestic violence is always about the abuse of power and control in addition to other forms of abusive and violent behavior makes learning to assess for coercive control and manage it in relationships imperative if we are to uphold people's human rights.

Other sociologists have tied the political structure of a country together with the lack of human rights for women (Dobash & Dobash,

1981). The U.S. Violence Against Women Act (VAWA) that has once again been renewed by the U.S. Congress in 2013 clearly declares that domestic violence such as rape and other forms of discrimination is against women's civil or human rights. VAWA funds many different programs for battered women including both criminal and civil penalties for those who violate it. It permits immigrant women whose legal status in the United States is regulated by abusive husbands to apply for citizenship in their own right and it commands police officers who commit domestic violence to forgo the use of their weapons, which virtually makes it impossible for them to continue in law enforcement. Stopping all forms of violence against women is an important issue around the world, yet despite the promise to pass new laws or enforce those already legislated, the violence against women continues. Women who have experienced male violence must have access to treatment if they have issues resulting from that abuse at the same time that we continue finding ways to both prevent violence and lessen its impact on those who have experienced it.

TRANSNATIONAL FEMINIST MODEL

A new way to look at mental health issues around the world is to remove the national borders of the woman's country of origin and instead substitute the understanding of the region from which she identifies. This provides the ability to look at culture in its broadest sense given the mobility of people around the world. The model has been used in political science and sociology more than in psychology but more recently has been useful in conceptualizing interventions with victims of trafficking as they have been taken across national borders, which creates new and difficult mental health problems caused by isolation. Battered women are isolated not always by being forced to leave their homes, but sometimes by being forced to remain inside their homes without the support of family and friends. This leaves them open to hearing only the views of their batterers.

Most battered women talk about the attempts by the batterers to control their minds and force them to believe only the batterers' "truths." Helping to overcome the effects of this isolation and reintroduce the women to their own culture and personal beliefs is a major part of healing from the effects of domestic violence. This may be why the psychoeducational groups that are found in battered women shelters and out-client services are so helpful to the women. They could be said to be psychotherapeutic, not specifically psychotherapy. The Survivor Therapy Empowerment Program (STEP-2) described in Chapter 17 has been designed to provide the information that battered women need as well as skill development to overcome the battered woman syndrome (BWS) effects.

PUBLIC HEALTH MODEL

The Public Health Model for community distribution of health and mental health services may be a way to conceptualize all of the health services that battered women need to have in place for both prevention and intervention. Many countries outside of the United States have strong public health services where victims of intimate partner abuse can seek both health and mental health care without being labeled as having a disease. The public health system in the United States attempts to deal with epidemiological problems and while violence against women is considered a health problem, it is the violence research arm at the Centers for Disease Control and Prevention (CDC) that appears to drive the services available in public health. Most of these services are in primary prevention through educational programs such as encouraging people to use seat belts for car safety or campaigns to recognize when a woman has been battered and should seek help. Even so, the public health model has a more community-based focus than the traditional medical model, so that people have a way to reduce risk and build resilience to keep their health strong through prevention as well as intervention.

The model attempts to look at prevention and intervention with a tripartite division in services usually referred to as primary, secondary, and tertiary levels. Primary prevention uses methods of reaching large numbers of the general population to prevent a disease from occurring in the first place. For domestic violence, it means building resilience in girls and women (the typical victims) and lessening the motivation or ability of boys and men (the usual perpetrators) to commit violence. Secondary prevention uses early case findings to lessen the impact of the disease on those who demonstrate beginning or mild symptoms, usually in some form of treatment. This would be the outpatient psychotherapy programs for women and men. Tertiary level prevention takes persons already demonstrating more severe symptoms out of the community and helps them heal in a protected environment, usually a hospital but in the case of domestic violence, battered women shelters or jails can be used, also.

Primary Prevention Programs

Primary prevention programs are those that prevent disease or accidents and injuries from occurring by removing the elements that allow them to occur. Sometimes, like in malaria, it means that in addition to strengthening the host and spraying to kill the mosquito, we must also drain the swamps where the infected mosquitoes live. The analogy in domestic violence is that in addition to intervention programs to stop men's violence and strengthen women's resilience, we must also eliminate the sexism, racism, and classism that permits violence against women to thrive. In many primary prevention programs, the individual is never even seen alone by a health or mental health professional, but rather, the group to which the person belongs is exposed to some educational programs to build resilience and lower risk. Sometimes it is general education for everyone, like television public service announcements or news stories, and other times it is information aimed at a particular group that is known to have high risk for something.

For example, in the case of domestic violence, pregnant mothers have been considered a high-risk group, and therefore, pamphlets offering information and services for victims of intimate partner abuse might be distributed at clinics providing obstetrical services. Targeted programs have been developed for teenage girls who are at a higher risk for abusive relationships than at other ages or even for welfare mothers who are forced into the new TANF (Temporary Assistance to Needy Families) as they are required to get into the workplace within a short period (usually 5 years) whether or not the batterers approve (Saunders, Holter, Pahl, Tolman, & Kenna, 2005). Women who have physical and mental disabilities are another high-risk group and there are resources for many of them through state and local government services under the U.S. Americans with Disabilities Act (ADA).

Programs for girls and women in other countries are sponsored by the U.S. Department of State's Office to Monitor and Control Trafficking in Persons (TIP), which has been involved in partnering and funding activities in many international countries and transnational regions to "prevent, protect, prosecute, and form partnerships" to stop trafficking but it also deals with domestic violence as that is one of the high-risk factors for girls being trafficked. TIP is a member of President Obama's Interagency Task Force so activities are coordinated. In 2015, there were 27 projects funded by this agency around the world to NGOs and governments to help organize responses to child trafficking and give direct services to victims of trafficking both within countries and transnationally. Several studies were commissioned and publication of the results distributed. Given the pandemic proportions of trafficking and domestic violence, a public health approach is critical and prevention will not be successful unless the extreme poverty, violence, and hunger that exists worldwide, the need for migration in poor countries disrupted by violence, and the lucrative criminal activities are stopped.

Some interesting programs have been developed for community workers in the United States who often serve as confidantes for women, particularly hairdressers who work in beauty salons where mostly women are served. In some communities where pubs are a gathering place, bartenders have also been trained to provide accurate information about domestic violence to their customers, noting the link between violence and too much alcohol. Religious leaders, particularly in the African American community where there is a strong spiritual connection, have also been trained to provide accurate information about domestic violence. Sermons that decry domestic violence, including men's demanding too much power and control over women, can build resilience in both women and men so that abuse may be prevented from the beginning. The goal of these programs is to build resilience in the women should they become exposed to male violence and to assist men in understanding that violence is wrong and a crime that has serious consequences, including the loss of their families.

Fatalities in the workplace have been found to have a strong link with domestic violence so companies have been providing information to all workers on how to protect women should a batterer enter the premises without permission. Some studies funded by the CDC have found that over one fifth of all full-time workers have been or currently are being abused by their intimate partners and lose nearly 8 million days of work annually because they have been threatened, stalked, or assaulted by them. Major companies have begun to address the problem by offering the workers transfers to offices at other sites in an attempt to prevent the abusers from having easy access to their victims. Other companies may fire the abusive employee, but this may cause certain workers to become so destabilized and enraged that they displace their rage onto the supervisors and commit workplace violence (Mohandie, Meloy, McGowan, & Williams, 2006).

Primary Intervention Programs

In primary intervention programs, the goal is early identification of women who are either at high risk for or are already being abused but not showing any symptoms yet. Hospitals, health centers, and private doctors' offices are an important place to encourage early identification and referrals to intervention programs. Literature can be left out for women to take away and read at their leisure or doctors and nurses can talk directly with women who appear to be at risk. For example, a woman whose husband must be in the examining room with her all the time, who answers all the doctor's or nurses' questions for her, or whom she seems afraid of would be in that targeted high-risk group even though there might not be any other direct signs of abuse. It may be easier to identify the high-risk woman whose husband is argumentative with everyone, speaks rudely to her, and refuses to follow the rules but, even so, many health service providers without training in recognizing such behavior as domestic violence might not recognize its significance. Women also have been socialized to protect their men, so even when confrontation takes place, they are hesitant to admit their vulnerability. However, just like the police have been trained to give these women cards with the phone numbers of resources to use when they are ready, so can health service providers do the same along with a brief talk naming the abuse and describing its potential for further violence. The women in our research project talked about visiting doctors for other problems and taking seriously what they were told, even if they did not acknowledge it at the time.

Like other psychologists, we have provided risk assessments for corporations that want to know if taking such protective behavior is necessary and wise. For example, in one large corporation with offices in many different locations, we were asked to consult on a case where the woman did not want to move but the company wanted to keep her working for them and believed that transferring her, at least for a short period of time, would permit the batterer to cool down and get on with his life. He also worked for the company and was told that he had to stop his stalking behavior, go into offender-specific treatment, and follow the court mandates, including observing the restraining order, if he wanted to keep his job. As both of these employees' skills were valuable to the company, it was large enough and the supervisors were willing enough to take the risk of keeping them both as employees. In this case, it proved to be a good decision for the company, the family, and the community. In other cases, other recommendations have been made, such as hospitalization if necessary, considering the level of risk of escalating the violence in each case.

The legal system also contributes to the primary prevention and intervention with women who are victims of intimate partner violence. Police have been trained to respond to domestic violence calls quickly and if there is probable cause to make an arrest, then their protocol permits them to do so. In Broward County, Florida, the Broward Sheriff's Organization has a grant to assign a police officer to work with Women in Distress, the local battered woman shelter, in high-risk cases to prevent further violence. This is a major change from when law enforcement expected the victim to sign the complaint before an arrest was made. Women can obtain restraining orders more easily without having to make a decision about their relationships until they get past the crisis. Batterers are taken into custody and many jurisdictions follow the recommended protocol by taking domestic violence off the bonding schedule and detaining the alleged abuser until the next regularly scheduled court hearing. Many communities have victim witness programs where the intimate partner violence victim is seen by an advocate who can direct her to various appropriate resources. Family law attorneys and criminal defense attorneys can also help identify a woman who is battered and needs services.

As a U.S. senator, Joe Biden introduced legislation to support a plan to train 100,000 lawyers specializing in domestic violence and set up a national domestic violence attorney referral project to be managed by the American Bar Association. His legislation would coordinate with the VAWA so that the national hotline supported by VAWA would serve as a referral network. Biden's press announcement (October 18, 2007), issued while he was campaigning as candidate for president of the United States, cited statistics of women who could not afford to obtain a lawyer for civil remedies including family law disputes. It might be remembered that Biden was the author of the original VAWA that was passed by Congress in the 1990s. If this new bill passes, it calls for an initial pilot program in five states before going national. How this federal legislation would coordinate with the myriad of different laws in the 50 states has not yet been determined. Biden continued his support as vice president of the United States with access to both Congress and the executive branch of government to help efforts to eradicate domestic violence.

In the United States, the legal system is the gateway to services for battered women, while it is the public health system in other countries such as in Latin America. One major difference is that the public health system sees the problem from the victim's perspective and the legal system, especially the criminal justice system, must protect the alleged perpetrator to make sure he or she is treated fairly and according to the law. One of the major losses for the victim is the lack of attention paid to psychological abuse in the criminal justice system, which is much more focused on severe physical violence. Although stalking behavior can be charged criminally, it rarely happens until it leads to attempted murder and other highly dangerous behaviors. In the public health system, psychological abuse is given more attention because it is known that it may be impossible to separate the harm from physical, sexual, and psychological abuse even though the methods are different. Since prevention of harm is the mandate for public health systems, it is unnecessary to make the distinctions that are called for in the criminal justice system.

Nonetheless, the criminal justice system has its benefits, particularly in mobilizing law enforcement and the courts to use consequences to stop the batterer from committing abuse in the first place. Unfortunately, the consequences are not applied consistently or fairly across all people, resulting in the underserved minorities in society, those with the weakest ties to the values of the society as a whole, most likely to get punished by this system. For punishment to work as a deterrent, people must have a stake in the system. Studies of people in jails and prisons all over the world provide examples of how those incarcerated rarely share the same values as those who have power and control within their society. Reforming the criminal justice system in the United States should have priority as it is a microcosm of how those with power oppress those without power. The riots over seemingly unnecessary police shootings of minorities in the United States serve to underscore these differences in values and behaviors.

James Garbarino, a psychologist and researcher into the effects of child abuse and domestic violence on children who grow up to be killers, underscores the point of prevention by treating the trauma effects in these men as children in his book, *Listening to the Killers: Lessons Learned in My 20 Years as a Psychological Expert Witness in Murder Cases* (Garbarino, 2015). In an interview with the *Monitor on Psychology*, Garbarino (2016, p. 38) stated, "Most killers are untreated traumatized children who are controlling the actions of the scary adults they have become." He sees severe, pervasive, chronic trauma as a frontal assault on the basic processes of child development but by the time a psychologist sees the person 20 years later, it becomes a clinical diagnosis. Rather, it is important to understand how attachment, emotional regulation, and executive function have been damaged both by the violence in their homes and in their communities that have become like war zones with gangs, street violence, and chronic threats to their safety, creating high stress levels.

Secondary Prevention and Intervention

Secondary prevention programs attempt to use the early identification of domestic violence victims as a way to prevent the development of further psychological and physical injuries. Recent research demonstrated that adults with early symptoms of posttraumatic stress disorder (PTSD) who were treated within 4 weeks of the traumatic event can prevent the development of chronic PTSD (Shalev, 2007). Interestingly, the use of cognitive therapy that helped people change their harmful or unproductive thoughts and desensitization to the traumatic memories was the most effective after 3 months. Medications that control the cortisol levels in the brain during the few weeks or months after a traumatic event also have promise in preventing more severe forms of PTSD from developing as is further described later in the chapter.

Another promising program that prevents the development of more serious problems after exposure to disasters in first responders such as police, firefighters, and crisis medical workers is the Crisis Incident Stress Management (CISM) Model. These volunteers and workers are encouraged to discuss the horrible events that they witnessed with each other and facilitators provide correct factual information to help them develop a positive outlook that their distress will lessen over time. Individuals who have gone through the debriefing procedures report that it is beneficial in reducing the normal symptoms expected after experiencing trauma. It is important to remember that acute stress reactions are normal after a traumatic incident. PTSD is not diagnosed until the symptoms last for over

4 weeks. However, the newer research is demonstrating that it is too late to wait 4 weeks before instituting some interventions to prevent further symptom development.

Studies of people who have been exposed to trauma such as prisoners of war and women who have experienced physical and sexual abuse and have come through these traumas without the usual severe psychic toll from major stressors demonstrated factors that contributed to their resilience (Charney, Deutch, Krystal, Southwick, & Davis, 1993). Having an optimistic outlook on life appears to be the number one factor toward building such resilience. Seligman (1997), the psychologist who first identified learned helplessness in the laboratory discussed in Chapter 4, has also demonstrated the usefulness of optimism in preventing depression from developing even in those who have familial or genetic propensities toward depression. While Seligman suggested encouraging children to develop optimism as a primary prevention strategy, Charney et al.'s work demonstrated that it was possible to develop optimism and the other nine characteristics that were identified in these survivors at any point including during psychotherapy following the traumatic exposure. The 10 characteristics are:

1. Optimism
2. Cognitive flexibility
3. A personal moral compass or shatterproof set of beliefs
4. Altruism and willingness to help others
5. A resilient role model or mentor
6. Ability to face one's fears
7. Positive coping skills
8. Ability to establish and nurture a supportive social network
9. Physical well-being
10. A good sense of humor with the ability to laugh frequently

Secondary-level intervention strategies are the programs that attempt to fix the problems at the earliest levels possible. These may be programs in clinics and private offices of doctors or even in agencies such as battered women shelters and community task forces that conduct outpatient groups for victims of intimate partner abuse. These programs provide remediation and rehabilitation for those who have been harmed by the domestic violence. They are usually designed with the typical victim's needs in mind and some actually follow a general manual of directions while others base treatment on an individual woman's needs. The benefit of a manualized treatment program is that facilitators who are not that well trained in psychotherapy skills can assist women in healing by covering the basic areas that are known to have an impact on those who experience domestic violence. An example is provided in Chapter 17 with discussion of the STEP and in Chapter 16 with further details of how trauma therapy is integrated with a feminist therapy empowerment model. Individualized intervention programs are usually given by trained psychotherapists who understand how to treat a broader range of mental health problems in addition to those specifically caused by domestic violence. These issues can also be inserted within regular psychotherapy although most therapists are not trained to do so.

Information about current intervention programs can be obtained from a local battered women's shelter or the National Domestic Violence Hotline at 800-799-SAFE (7233) or 800-787-3224 TYY (for the deaf and hard of hearing), or online at www.ndvh.org. Programs for intimate partner violence prevention can be found in a number of websites including the CDC, the National Center for Injury Prevention and Control (NCIPC) at www.cdc.gov, the Gains Center that provides resources for women with substance abuse and domestic violence issues and those who need diversion programs from jail at www.samhsa.gov/gains-center, and the National District Attorneys Association at www.ndaa.org. Perhaps one of the most comprehensive websites is the Community Against Violence Network where resources for all forms of violence against women including those with disabilities can be found at www.cavnet2.org. Other websites are listed in the References sections but as websites and domains must be renewed each year, these sites may be good only through the publication date of this book.

Tertiary Prevention and Intervention

Programs at the tertiary level are for those who have such serious problems that they must be taken out of the community in a protected environment for intervention. Prevention programs at this level do prevent the problems from worsening, even preventing death. Intervention programs aim to slow the progress of the damage rather than try for a complete cure and the return of the person to the community as soon as possible for continued treatment conducted at the community level. The

U.S. hospital system is based on the premise that people should be stabilized and then returned to the community for the rest of treatment, when necessary. In Spain, the hospital system keeps people in inpatient treatment for longer periods of time before sending them into outpatient treatment for continuation. Psychologists Carmen Valiente, Patricia Villavicencio, and Delores Cantero work at the university-sponsored hospital in Madrid where we conducted some of our research from Spain. Women with more serious diagnoses such as bipolar disorder and borderline personality disorder, who also had developed PTSD from domestic violence, were treated there. They found that those with a more complex form of PTSD, first identified by psychiatrist Judith Herman (1992), also had dissociative symptoms and these women needed a more protected environment to begin the healing process such as what could be provided by a longer psychiatric hospitalization than merely a few weeks for stabilization (Valiente-Ots et al., 2006).

For other domestic violence victims, the equivalent of hospitalization is the battered woman shelter where women can remain with their children until they are able to make decisions about where they want to live. Again, in the United States, stays in the shelter are relatively short as compared to other countries, especially where obtaining adequate housing is an issue. While many do go back into homes with their batterers, they report feeling stronger, understanding the resources available to them, and are able to prepare themselves to make better lifestyle decisions. For some, especially those whose batterers also undergo offender-specific counseling and legal consequences including jail time, the physical abuse stops, at least for a while. For others the abuse continues to escalate and they finally do terminate the relationship sometimes after several more attempts to leave.

Battered women shelters are particularly helpful for poor women or those who have been so isolated that they do not have knowledge of or access to services for themselves and their children. In the United States, these women are assisted with applying for government financial assistance, housing, medical care for themselves and their children, food stamps, and other benefits until they can begin to support themselves. While batterers are required to financially support themselves and their families, many of these men are so destabilized by their mental health conditions and/or substance abuse that they cannot be counted on to provide adequate money. Others choose to join militant fathers' rights groups, often joining with other men who are angry that their intimate partners have left them, and spend their time obsessing over ways to get even with their partners and the system rather than focusing on rebuilding their lives in a more productive way. Their websites on the Internet are filled with their anger, which sometimes is taken out on lawyers, psychologists, and other professionals who help their partners. It is unfortunate that legitimate fathers' rights concerns have been taken over by these men who teach others how to file spurious legal complaints and demands, tying up the legal system.

Some batterers also need tertiary level care, usually in jails or prisons. In some places, there are programs for men who batter their partners or children conducted in the jails and prisons but, like services for battered women, these groups are just beginning. Rather, anger management groups or substance abuse programs have incorporated some information about domestic violence for those arrested and so charged but it is surely not sufficient especially for those batterers who also have mental health problems. In Israel, psychologist Hannah Rosenberg, under the auspices of the organization Women's International Zionist Organization (WIZO), designed a shelter for male batterers. They provide round-the-clock interventions to help men learn alternative ways of getting their needs met instead of using violence against their partners. Interestingly, although there was some opposition to spending the limited resources on the men rather than the women victims, in fact the program has been very successful. In Israel, like many other countries where housing is a problem, most of these men would have had to go back to live with their parents. Since many of those homes still have the same problems as the men were exposed to as children, this was not helpful to stop their violent behavior. Placing them in a residential living arrangement with other batterers reduces the shame, keeps the men from contacting the victims inappropriately, and helps them discover new ways of living without violence.

Battered Woman's Shelters

One of the most successful means of providing relief for battered women and their children has been the shelter or safe home concept. It began in England when Erin Pizzey opened the first refuge in 1972 (Pizzey, 1974) and rapidly spread to the United States and many other European countries (Davidson, 1979; Dobash & Dobash, 1981; Martin, 1976; Roy, 1978; Schechter, 1982; Walker, 1979). Today, we find battered woman shelters in most countries. The presence of even just one battered woman shelter, though inadequate to meet everyone's needs, is critical to give the message to the entire community that abuse against women will be not be tolerated. This is particularly important when cultural and religious messages conflict, sometimes even facilitating further abuse by sending the woman right back into the violent home when she seeks help. Of course, there are limitations to the services that battered woman shelters can provide. Although there are few policies regulating who can use the shelter, the programs are usually designed to address women who are battered by male partners and not female or other lesbian, gay, bisexual, transgender, and questioning (LGBTQ) partners. Male children over the age of 13 or 14 are rarely accepted into a shelter, partly because many have already identified with their fathers' violent behavior and partly because it is a woman-oriented experience. Rarely can pets be accommodated, necessitating making other arrangements in the middle of the crisis that usually brings the women to shelter. However, veterinarians in many communities have volunteered boarding these animals for the short time that women are in shelter.

While there have been a variety of shelter models provided, all of them meet the primary purpose of protecting women and children from violent men's immediate abuse. Most shelters are located in their own home-like building whose address is not widely known within the community, but neither is it completely hidden so as not to encourage a "hide-and-seek" type of game-playing for batterers. Usually 20 women and their children can be accommodated at any time. During peak periods, overcrowding does occur. A typical shelter costs approximately U.S. $350,000 per year to operate. Some small communities cannot financially support a separate home and, instead, use a system of trained volunteers to provide safety in their own homes. Many places have both systems in operation. Rural areas train people to drive a battered woman to safety and, in some places, a relay system of drivers can get a woman to another state within a short time. A "virtual underground railroad" exists, which can move women and children throughout the world, whenever it becomes necessary. The presence in a community, then, makes a clear statement that spouse abuse will not be tolerated, and if it occurs, the community will provide a separate home for the victim.

While there have been lots of debates concerning the correct philosophy of a battered woman's shelter, few dispute its effectiveness in a crisis. Forty years ago, most shelters in North America were developed using a feminist model. Today, most shelters have evolved into a social service model, perhaps in order to obtain government financing to survive. Loeske and Berk (1981) evaluated what battered women in the Santa Barbara shelter deemed as helpful as in an attempt to resolve the service provider/feminist organization issue. They found that stressing the immediate incident that brought about the woman's call to the crisis line was the usual entry into the shelter system itself. Almost one half called for help within 1 day of an acute battering incident. However, over 20% of their callers reported that the most recent incident had occurred a week or more prior to seeking help, indicating that fear of the future might be more of some women's concerns, which finally brought them into the shelter. The diversity that was found in what battered women said they needed and expected from a shelter indicates that no one philosophy could meet all these needs. Loeske and Berk suggest that it might be helpful if the shelter worker and client both define their goals and the nature of available help within each situation.

Some shelter models suggested that staff roles be limited to woman advocacy and not provide direct services. In West Germany, for example, Hagemann-White (1981) described the conflict surrounding professional training and pay for full-time work in the Berlin shelter and the other shelters in the Federal Republic of Germany. She made a compelling argument for promoting a microcosm of a woman-identified feminist society in the shelter to avoid being merely a Band-Aid and thus encouraging women to return to abusive homes. Shelters are seen, then, as more than a crisis haven, but also as a place to try out new social orders. In the past 20 years, battered women shelters have created a model of mothers and children developing a new family unit, free from violence. In most shelters, there are no-hitting rules forcing some mothers to learn new forms of discipline, particularly positive reinforcement strategies. This is an important way to reverse the effects of being exposed to violence in childhood and for children to be exposed to many positive experiences. The typical visitation problems that occur when both parents are forced to share parental responsibilities in homes where there has been domestic violence often perpetuate the abuse and prevent children and their mothers from healing from the trauma. At least when in shelter, women have some time and psychological space to begin to think about their goals for the rest of their lives. Being together with other battered women often helps women to stop blaming themselves, normalizes their experiences, and emphasizes their own strengths.

Rebecca and Russell Dobash (1981), American sociologists living in Scotland, argued that shelters must provide an alternative to the patriarchal structure fostered in a capitalistic society. Stark (2007; Stark & Flitcraft 1983) still agrees with the need for such a political as well as social analysis. But, while their political analysis correctly predicts class oppression, there is no direct evidence that it makes a substantial difference in the rate of spouse abuse, which is found to occur across all social classes and in all political systems. Rather, it is the way in which women and men are socialized to relate to each other that seems to be most critical.

Looking at women in Nicaragua has provided a good example of a country torn apart with political civil war that has been able to provide some services to women while rebuilding the political and economic infrastructure of the country. Not surprisingly, women who were never married during this period were found to be less depressed and to have suffered less from the trauma than those who also faced abuse within their marital homes (Ellsberg, Caldera, Herrare, Winkvist, & Kullgren, 1999). The current status of women in Russia where a socialistic order under communism was expected to provide the opportunity for more equality for women did not turn out that way (Horne, 1999). Economic rather than political organization may well be a more important variable to women's safety. We discussed these cultural issues earlier in Chapter 11.

Shelters organized around an alternative collective approach seemed to have more difficulty staying funded than those more compatible with the social service philosophy within their own countries. In the United States, there has been much concern that fear of losing funds would be used as a way to scapegoat those feminist and lesbian women who work in shelters where the community political climate became more conservative. This has happened. The original feminist philosophy that prevailed in battered woman shelters throughout the United States and Canada has been replaced in many communities by a more social services model. However, the politics of the battered woman movement has remained feminist, often causing conflicts that may impact the quality of services delivered in some places. Since there are few training resources for shelter workers outside of the university or national organizations, these tensions remain a part of providing shelter. Further, the tensions between advocates and professionally trained service workers have not been resolved, again placing battered women and their children in the middle—facing hostile husbands on one side and hostile advocates on the other. When this type of situation occurs, no one gets her needs met. However, the political climate among lawmakers and policy makers continues to be supportive of finding better ways to provide safety for battered women and their children, which does give strength to the important work of the advocates.

In Finland, Peltoniemi (1982) and Peltoniemi and Aromaa (1982) described four battered woman shelters funded by the government for a 3-year pilot period. Over 500 women and an equal number of children used these shelters during the first year. Peltoniemi told of the deliberate decision to choose a family-dynamic model instead of an alternative feminist ideology despite the Finnish socialist political system. The same occurred when Israel set up 15 centers for domestic violence around the country where social services, not shelter were offered. Even the funding source came from two different centers in the government—the women's programs and the family programs (Steiner, 1999). The arbitrary dichotomy of family versus feminist orientation is one that is unnecessary although understandable given the fear that women's demands for equality have engendered. Most shelters need to provide family support services and can still do this within a feminist ideology. The goal is to keep the women and children violence free. If to do so can occur only if there is a separation between the husband and the wife, then it may be necessary to isolate the violent man to protect the family. This is a stand that the family courts are unwilling to accept, often responding to vocal fathers' rights groups and placing women and children in danger of continued violence.

The decision of whether or not shelters should provide offender-specific treatment for the batterer has been more controversial in the shelter movement. Myers (1982) described a program for working with the abusers run by the Houston battered woman's center because the women there have requested such a service be provided. Many battered women feel that they must get help for the men to try to get them to change their behavior before they are willing to give up the dream of making this relationship work. This is particularly true when using the criminal justice system, as described in Chapter 12 on risk assessment and Chapter 20 on domestic violence courts. Battered women are more likely to testify against the batterers if they believe they will get help to stop their violent behavior, whether or not they want to keep the relationship. The better psychoeducational programs are often supervised by or run by the battered woman groups in a community, as they are careful to include changing men's socialized attitudes toward women within their treatment programs.

On the other hand, many shelters believe that any public or private funding received must go directly into programs for women and children victims. Obviously, in a system with finite resources, decisions must be made to prioritize services. Some shelters would disagree with the Houston approach, insisting as does Hagemann-White, that women must cease taking responsibility for the men's mental health. The need to make these kinds of political decisions has caused tensions that more often divide rather than unite those with different philosophies. The feminist philosophy supports the power of each woman to make her own decisions. It suggests allowing a battered woman to have the option of trying everything she needs to do before giving up a relationship that has provided her with both pleasure and pain. Yet, there is also a responsibility to demonstrate viable alternatives to the current socialized concept of intimate relationships. The dignity and courage these women demonstrate, even at their greatest point of frustration, can be appreciated when they finally choose to be safe and free from violence. Shelters, whatever their philosophy, do manage to give them that choice. Most women in shelters need some support to move forward with their lives, whether they stay out of the relationship or try to fix it so that they and their children live violence free. For some women, psychotherapy that empowers and validates them can be a means to help carry their decision out. Thus, I have spent the past 18 years training psychotherapists at Nova Southeastern University and advocates through the Domestic Violence Institute in new ways to deliver psychotherapy services that empower women to help them go from being victims to survivors. This is further described in Chapter 16 on trauma-informed and specific psychotherapy.

MENTAL HEALTH ISSUES

Whether the mental health issues that battered women experience come from the actual abuse or from their other life experiences, there are definitely issues that must be confronted for the women to be able to heal and move on with life. Many of the issues come from the lack of equality for all women and especially women of diversity in our society as described previously. Others come from living in an environment that supports violence and high stress, like the war zones described by Garbarino earlier in the chapter or the socioeconomic pressures of poverty. Still others come from the women's own internal and biological issues. Although I have stayed away from using mental health diagnostic terms in this chapter, it is important to note that some battered women come into the relationship with mental health problems that may or may not have been treated. The abusive situation, then, exacerbates whatever the mental health issue is that they might have. For example, some women have inherited a nervous system that makes them more prone to experiencing depressive episodes than others when faced with the same external circumstances. Medication and psychotherapy can be helpful in these cases but will not be sufficient if it does not deal directly with the trauma.

Keisha is a good case example. She was raised as an only child by her mother and grandmother, who also helped raise her son's two children who were much older than Keisha. Although their home was definitely supported by women, various men were in and out of their lives; some were family and some not. At age 13, Keisha was sexually assaulted by one of the family relatives. Living in a community where other violence was frequently seen, including street shootings, Keisha did not tell anyone. Her average grades went down in school and she fell behind in all activities she used to enjoy. A teacher noticed the change in Keisha and took the time to befriend her, trying to find ways to help her. A school referral resulted in Keisha being seen by a psychologist who diagnosed her with depression and suggested that her mother take her to a doctor for medication. Keisha was placed on a commonly used selective serotonin reuptake inhibitor, Prozac, and seemed to become more interested in her schoolwork. However, she still kept the sexual assault to herself, not feeling that anyone would believe her or be able to help her since it did stop. She took the Prozac for a few months and then stopped it also.

By age 15, Keisha dropped out of school and had her first baby. This was shortly followed by two more babies, each with a different father. At age 19, she came to a battered woman shelter with her three babies after having been seriously beaten by the last boyfriend. Depressed and traumatized, Keisha seemed pretty hopeless. She had few skills to work and was dependent on welfare to support herself and her children. Her grandmother, the major support figure, had developed Alzheimer's disease and became unable to take care of herself. Her mother was in jail, having been arrested for substance abuse, and Keisha had nowhere to go and no formal or informal support system. She was still depressed, which made it even more difficult for her to try to figure a way out of her dilemma.

Fortunately, the battered woman shelter was able to help Keisha get more financial assistance and adequate housing in their second-stage facility where she met some other women and developed friendships. She got treatment for her depression, which had a biochemical basis that was worsened by her life stress. Her children were accepted into day care so Keisha had some child care relief from parenting during the day. In fact, she enjoyed going to the day-care center and working with the other children there so much that she began a course to become a day-care aide. Within a year, Keisha was like a different person. She had a job and was not looking for a man to support her; she moved into nice housing of her choice. She was taking care of her children, had a supportive friendship network, and was smiling a lot.

There was a time when women were discouraged from looking at mental health needs that might warrant a diagnosis and medication as it masked the underlying social causes of their unhappiness. In fact, women were oppressed by the medical and psychiatric establishment by looking toward fixing only their biological or internal problems rather than taking a comprehensive approach as was done in Keisha's case. The battered woman shelter and other feminist interventions have called attention to the intersection of gender, race, socioeconomic class, and other discrimination from biology and other disabilities. Women should not be afraid to seek out mental health treatment when necessary but neither should they refrain from trying to better their situation in the world. This is called "empowerment" and is one of the major factors in healing from all forms of violence and abuse, especially gender violence. Feeling in charge of one's own life is the most powerful cure for depression and other negative mental health issues.

BUILDING RESILIENCE AND WELLNESS

Many trauma intervention programs go beyond healing from PTSD and other symptoms to assisting the survivors in rebuilding their resilience and moving toward wellness. It is known that victims of all traumatic events may lose resilience when faced with a new trauma. Sex offenders often state that they can recognize some women who were victimized at an earlier time by the way they look or behave. While this may be an over-statement, it is known that victims often have experienced more than one trauma. In fact, the *Diagnostic and Statistical Manual of Mental Disorders* (*DSM-5*; American Psychiatric Association, 2013) suggested that one of the results of trauma is the belief that one has a shortened life span. So, adding a component to treatment that helps survivors rebuild their resilience is an important intervention.

What Is Resilience?

"Resilience" is the process of adapting well in the face of adversity, trauma, tragedy, threats, illness, or significant sources of stress. It is not a trait that an individual has or does not have but rather, it is learned behaviors, thoughts, and accompanying feelings. It is the capacity to effectively cope with, adjust to, or recover from stress or adversity. People who are resilient can recover from trauma. They often have positive thoughts, like the glass is half full instead of half empty. They may have "hardiness," which is an unmeasurable quality that helps people survive and even thrive despite adversity and high stress levels. Even when traumatic events such as being held captive in a trafficking ring occur, someone who is resilient can heal and even experience posttraumatic growth from the ordeal. Not everyone can be resilient to every form of traumatic stressor, but it is believed that everyone can strengthen their own resilience at least a little, which will help them feel better and enjoy their world again.

Resilience is connected to the psychology of well-being or "eudaimonia," first proposed by the Greeks, further conceptualized by Aristotle, and more recently being investigated by psychologists interested in rehabilitation and wellness. Ryff (2014) proposed six components of wellness from research with people who were happy. These include: (a) the extent to which respondents felt their lives had meaning, purpose, and direction (purpose in life); (b) whether they viewed themselves to be living in accord with their own personal convictions (autonomy); (c) the extent to which they were making use of their personal talents and potential (personal growth); (d) how well they were managing their life situations (environmental mastery); (e) the depth of connection they had in ties with significant others (positive relationships); and (f) the knowledge and acceptance they had of themselves, including awareness of personal limitations (self-acceptance; Ryff, 2014, p. 11). The focus of intervention is to move beyond symptom reduction or absence of feelings of distress and on to improvements in well-being such that positive thoughts and experiences are routine and prevent relapse.

SUMMARY

Many of the mental health needs of battered women have been met by using a public health model that has primary-, secondary-, and tertiary-level prevention of any impact, or at least stopping development of further symptoms, and intervention to ameliorate any symptoms at the earliest point possible. Mental health clinicians have learned that the needs of the trauma survivor go beyond intervention to the prevention of further traumatic reactions by developing resilience and well-being.

REFERENCES

American Psychiatric Association. (2013). *Diagnostic and statistical manual of mental disorders* (5th ed.). Arlington, VA: American Psychiatric Publishing.

Charney, D. S., Deutch, A. Y., Krystal, J. H., Southwick, S. M., & Davis, M. (1993). Psychobiological mechanisms of post-traumatic stress disorder. *Archives of General Psychiatry, 50*, 294–305.

Davidson, T. (1979). *Conjugal crime: Understanding and changing the wife-beating pattern.* New York, NY: Hawthorne.

Dobash, R. E., & Dobash, R. P. (1981). *Violence against wives.* New York, NY: Macmillan.

Ellsberg, M., Caldera, T., Herrare, A., Winkvist, A., & Kullgren, G. (1999). Recommendations for working with domestic violence survivors with special attention to memory issues and posttraumatic processes. *Psychotherapy, 34*, 459–477.

Garbarino, J. (2015). *Listening to killers: Lessons learned from my 20 years as a psychological expert witness in murder cases.* Oakland: University of California Press.

Garbarino, J. (2016, February). Listening to killers. Interview by Rebecca Clay. *Monitor on Psychology, 47*, 36–39.

Hagemann-White, C. (1981, December). *Confronting violence against women in Germany.* Paper presented at the International Interdisciplinary Congress on Women, Haifa, Israel.

Herman, J. L. (1992). *Trauma and recovery.* New York, NY: Basic Books.

Horne, S. (1999). Domestic violence in Russia. *American Psychologist, 54*, 55–61.

Loeske, D. R., & Berk, S. F. (1981, July). *Defining "help": Initial encounters between battered women and shelter staff*. Paper presented at the National Conference of Family Violence Researchers, University of New Hampshire, Durham.

Martin, D. (1976). *Battered wives*. San Francisco, CA: Glide.

Mohandie, K., Meloy, R., McGowan, M. G., & Williams, J. (2006). The RECON typology of stalking: Reliability and validity based upon a large sample of North American stalkers. *Journal of Forensic Science, 51*(1), 147–155.

Myers, T. (1982, January). *Wifebeaters' group through a women's center: Why and how*. Paper presented at the International Conference on Victimology, Sicily, Italy.

Patterson, G. R. (1982). *Coercive family process*. Eugene, OR: Castalia Press.

Peltoniemi, T. (1982, January). *The first 12 months of the Finnish shelters*. Paper presented at the International Conference on Victimology, Sicily, Italy.

Peltoniemi, T., & Aromaa, K. (1982, January). *Family violence studies and victimization surveys in Finland*. Paper presented at the International Conference on Victimology, Sicily, Italy.

Pizzey, E. (1974). *Scream quietly or the neighbors will hear*. London, UK: Penguin.

Roy, M. (1978). *Battered women: A psychological study*. New York, NY: Van Nostrand.

Ryff, C. D. (2014). Psychological well-being revisited: Advances in the science and practice of eudaimonia. *Psychotherapy and Psychosomatics, 83*(1), 10–28.

Saunders, D. G., Holter, M. C., Pahl, L. C., Tolman, R. M., & Kenna, C. E. (2005). TANF workers' responses to battered women and the impact of brief worker training: What survivors report. *Violence Against Women, 11*(2), 227–254.

Schechter, S. (1982). *Women and male violence: The visions and struggles of the battered women's movement*. Boston, MA: South End Press.

Seligman, M. E. P. (1997). Raising optimistic children. *The Futurist, 31*, 52–53.

Shalev, A. Y. (2007). PTSD: A disorder of recovery? In L. J. Kirmayer, R. Lemelson, & M. Barad (Eds.), *Understanding trauma: Integrating biological, clinical and cultural perspectives* (pp. 207–223). New York, NY: Cambridge University Press.

Stark, E. (2007). *Coercive control: How men entrap women in personal life*. New York, NY: Oxford University Press.

Stark, E., & Flitcraft, A. (1983). Social knowledge, social policy, and the abuse of women: The case against patriarchal benevolence. In D. Finkelhor, R. J. Gelles, G. Hotaling, & M. Straus (Eds.), *The dark side of families* (pp. 380–348). Beverly Hills, CA: Sage.

Steiner, Y. (1999). Prevention and intervention for high risk girls in Israel and the Arab sectors. *American Psychologist, 54*(1), 64–65.

Valiente-Ots, C., Villavicencio-Carrillo, P., & Cantero-Martinez, M. D. (2006). La fenomenología de la comorbilidad del trauma y la psicosis. *Apuntes de Psicología, 24*(1–3), 111–135.

Walker, L. E. (1979). *The battered woman*. New York, NY: Harper & Row.

CHAPTER FIFTEEN

SUBSTANCE ABUSE AND DOMESTIC VIOLENCE

*T*he association of alcohol and other drugs with domestic violence is well known by those who work with victims and perpetrators. It is commonly thought that alcohol and abuse of some other drugs, particularly the amphetamines and cocaine derivatives, are directly associated with violent behavior even though there is no clear cause-and-effect relationship nor is the strength of the relationship known (Coleman & Straus, 1983; Maiden, 1997; Van Hasselt, Morrison, & Bellak, 1985). Currently, the explosion of oxycodone pills, morphine, and designer drugs such as Flakka are also being associated with violence. More recent investigators have begun to look at the additional risk substance abuse has on acute battering incidents (Lipsky, Caetano, Field, & Larkin, 2005), finding that men's alcohol use especially is associated with greater risk of injuries needing hospital emergency room attention, while no similar relationship is seen when women abuse substances. However, a recent Centers for Disease Control and Prevention (CDC) study on adverse childhood experiences (ACEs), more fully described in Chapter 13, found that women who drink one drink per day on average or binge drink often have intimate partner violence (IPV) in their history. In our earlier research, we found that women were less likely to be able to leave a domestic violence relationship if they had substance abuse problems. Given this high association, there has been a great deal of research on the nature of the relationship over the past 40 years since we originally asked women about their partners' and their own use of these substances. Even so, it still remains that there are few programs that combine treatment for both domestic violence and substance abuse problems.

DEFERRAL INTO THERAPEUTIC COURTS

Most of the research over the past 30 years has demonstrated that different treatment methods are necessary to change both violent behavior and substance abuse (American Psychological Association, 1996; Maiden, 1997), although there is still controversy whether to treat simultaneously or eliminate one behavior before the other. Complicating the issue is the co-occurrence of substance abuse and mental illness together with violent behavior, necessitating different treatment methods for all three behavioral areas (see www.samhsa.gov/gains-center for program information). Many domestic violence courts, such as the Miami/Dade County domestic violence court, order all three types of interventions for those who are willing to go for treatment as a condition of deferral or probation. However, the new mental health courts and drug courts that defer defendants into community or residential treatment programs often do not screen for prior domestic violence, although if the current arrest is for domestic violence the defendants usually get deferred into domestic violence court, and these defendants rarely get all three types of treatment at the facility to which they are sent.

Voluntary and Involuntary Intoxication

In most countries, debate still occurs concerning the role of alcoholism and other drugs in a variety of criminal offenses. In the United States, where domestic violence is considered a separate crime, some states differentiate between voluntary and involuntary substance abuse. Thus, if it can be proven that the individual's reactions under the influence of alcohol and other drugs are not under his or her control, it could be considered an involuntary drug reaction or addiction illness that can mitigate some responsibility under the law than if the drug response was controllable. This often creates a legal argument about whether or not the use of substances is under the person's control if an addiction is present (Collins & Messerschmidt, 1993). While it is generally known that alcohol abuse can increase physically violent behavior in the laboratory settings (Taylor & Gammon, 1975; Zeichner & Pihl, 1979), and lower inhibition to commit other types of criminal behavior (Powers & Kutash, 1978), some of these effects can be due to expectation of other nonphysiological effects (Goldstein, 1975; Lang, Goeckner, Adesso, & Marlatt, 1975). Gondolf and Fisher

(1988) and Jacobson and Gottman (1998) suggest that the high rate of alcoholism in the population of known batterers may play a role in their high arrest rate, also. Thus, there may be a bias in the information we receive from arrest records since many other batterers are not known. We reviewed some of the more recent studies in the following sections as the association remains complex and still not fully understood, although we do have a better idea of base rates particularly with alcohol abuse.

INTIMATE PARTNER VIOLENCE AND ALCOHOL ABUSE

Linking alcohol abuse with batterers and battered women, then, is a natural association (Bard & Zacker, 1974; Frieze & Knoble, 1980; Gelles, 1972; Richardson & Campbell, 1980; Van Hasselt et al., 1985). Some have found alcohol abuse to be a risk marker for more dangerous injuries and death (Browne, 1987; Hotaling & Sugarman, 1986). The association of violent behavior with drug abuse is less well documented, although it has been appearing in reports of posttraumatic stress disorder (PTSD) seen in war veterans (Roberts et al., 1982). Given the high expectation of a relationship between alcohol, drug abuse, and violence, we carefully measured its reported use in our research.

As mentioned earlier, research exploring the link between substance abuse and violence against women dates back over 40 years with the more rigorous studies looking at reports of substance abuse by men in batterer treatment programs, finding that more than 50% of the participants were also diagnosed as substance abusers (Gondolf, 1999; Tolman & Bennett, 1990). Studies of men in domestic violence treatment programs have reported that from 50% to over 60% of their sample participants were alcohol and/or drug abusers (White, Ackerman, & Caraveo, 2001; White, Gondolf, Robertson, Goodwin, & Caraveo, 2002). Researchers acknowledge that identifying whether these men were primarily substance abusers using violence or domestic violence offenders using substance was difficult. Studies of batterers (Stith, Crossman, & Bischof, 1991) and substance abusers (Brown, Caplan, Werk, & Seraganian, 1999) each found that there were no significant differences in their childhood histories, substance abuse and frequency, and severity of domestic violence initiated by men.

At first glance, domestic violence is closely related to substance abuse and vice versa. Acording to a meta-analysis of 22 studies examining the treatment efficacy of programs for male batterers (Babcock, Green, & Robie, 2004), most interventions generated only a minimal effect on the recidivism measure. Simultaneously, no significant differences were found when comparing the effectiveness among these treatment models. Evidence showed that alcoholic men who successfully quit drinking reported levels of partner abuse comparable to demographically similar nonalcoholic men (O'Farrell, Van Hutton, & Murphy, 1999). When reviewing this literature, the question among our researchers that arose is: Should practitioners focus on the addictive behavior of the batterers prior to treating their aggressive behavior toward their partners? This is an important question and has not been answered, partly because the practitioners in the domestic violence and in the substance abuse fields generally do not communicate with each other. In many states, practitioners in each area require different certifications to work with court-ordered clients. This results in each group staking out its own domains without integrating their work together, keeping the relationships among mental illness, battering, and substance abuse unclear. Although they appear to be correlated (meaning there is some association among them), the Kantor and Straus (1987) study found that 60% to 75% of batterers they surveyed said they were not drinking during their battering incidents. This is similar to the findings in our original study. These findings are not as contradictory as it would seem on first glance, as a batterer who is a substance abuser may well be engaged in abusive behavior while sober as well as when he is high or drunk. The assumptions are many: Either they may be in their early phase of abstinence, or they may not be able to obtain their substance of choice. In any case, the term *dry drunk* is often used to explain such behavior in substance abuse treatment programs.

Alcohol and Violence

An early prevalence study (Kantor & Strauss, 1987) estimated that physical partner assaults in a U.S. population survey was observed to be approximately three times higher for men who frequently engaged in binge drinking compared with alcohol-abstaining men. Based on the research that male partners were reported to frequently have been drinking prior to their assaults (Walker, 1979, 1984), in our original study (Battered Woman Syndrome Questionnaire [BWSQ] #1) we interviewed 400 self-identified battered women on the drinking habits of their male partners, both batterers and nonbatterers, and found that 67% of male batterers were frequently consuming alcohol (as compared to never drinking or occasionally drinking) versus 43% of nonbatterers. In one of our early analyses of the first 77 participants in this current study (BWSQ #2), we found that only 53% of the batterers were said to be frequently consuming alcohol. Whether this is really a drop in the rate of alcoholism in general or just for this small sample is not known. Frequencies comparing responses of the participants in both studies can be found in Table 15.1.

Over the years, numerous studies have found greater alcohol abuse and problem drinking patterns among batterers when compared to other groups of men, as well as higher alcohol consumption as a risk factor for partner violence among alcoholic men (Fals-Stewart, 2003; Leonard & Quigley, 1999; Murphy, Winters, O'Farrell, Fals-Stewart, & Murphy, 2005). Moreover, studies (Brookoff, O'Brien, Cook, Thompson, & Williams, 1997) have also found that heavy drinking can result in more serious injury to the victim than if the perpetrator was sober (Brecklin, 2002).

Table 15.1 *Report of Batterer's Substance Abuse During Relationships in BWSQ #1 and BWSQ #2*

Drug	Original N	Original %	Current N	Current %
Alcohol				
Never	40	10	22	29
Occasionally	92	23	14	18
Frequently	269	67	41	53
Prescription drugs				
Never	188	8	62	83
Occasionally	125	32	7	9
Frequently	81	20	6	8
Marijuana				
Never	154	40	36	51
Occasionally	143	37	4	6
Frequently	91	23	31	44
Street drugs				
Never	249	65	59	85
Occasionally	75	20	3	5
Frequently	57	15	8	10

The prevalence of alcohol consumption is related to its legitimacy, accessibility, and its "cost-effective" outcome. Studies have found high rates of domestic violence among men and women in substance abuse treatment programs. Schumacher, Fals-Stewart, and Leonard (2003) found that 44% of men perpetrated one or more acts of physical violence in the year preceding treatment. Chermack and Blow (2002) found that more than 67% of men reported perpetrating moderate or severe violence in the 12 months prior to their entering a treatment program. Brown, Werk, Caplan, Shields, and Seraganian (1998) reported almost 58% of men in alcohol or drug treatment had perpetrated physical violence or abuse toward a partner or child, and, with the inclusion of verbal threats, this figure rose to 100%.

Comparing two samples, men entering a domestic violence treatment program and domestically violent men entering an alcohol treatment program, Fals-Stewart (2003) found the odds of male-to-female physical aggression to be eight and 11 times higher, respectively, on days when men drank than on days involving no alcohol consumption. A study (Pan, Neidig, & O'Leary, 1994) employing a sample of nearly 12,000 White male military participants found that the odds that men with alcohol problems would use physical aggression against partners was 1.28 times higher than those for men without alcohol problems.

Problem-Solving Coping Style

The studies mentioned in the previous section have concurred that alcohol appears to be the highly correlated risk factor of physical aggression of male batterers, although other plausible factors cannot be ignored. Parallel to the trend of conceptualizing aggression between intimate partners as a multifaceted phenomenon, it is crucial to examine the relative importance of and causal directions among other risk factors.

The previously mentioned study (Pan et al., 1994) indicated that having an alcohol and/or drug problem uniquely increased the risk of severe physical aggression. Marital discord and depressive symptomatology further increased the odds of physical aggression. Those who were severely physically aggressive, usually earning covarying with lower incomes, were more likely to report an alcohol and/or a drug problem, and had more marital discord and depressive symptomatology. Snow and Sullivan (2006) found that men who employed inappropriate problem-solving coping styles to deal with relationship problems were characterized by abusive behavior through problem drinking. For instance, greater use of avoidance-coping strategies was more likely among problem drinkers. By contrast, men who used higher levels of problem-solving coping skills were less likely to be problem drinkers.

Alcohol Effect on Cognitive Functioning

Until recently, the impact of alcohol on various aspects of cognitive functioning was not widely investigated. The majority of studies on this relationship have only been carried out over the last 15 years. Studies suggested that acute alcohol intoxication impairs cognition, including episodic memory (Tiplady et al., 1999), verbal and spatial learning (Mungas, Ehlers, & Wall, 1994), and visuospatial attention (Post, Lott, Maddock, & Beede, 1996). The literature on substance abuse and neurology also suggested that alcohol's most pronounced effects are on the cognitive abilities associated with the prefrontal cortex (Peterson, Rothfleisch, Zelazo, & Phil, 1990). All of these studies are in agreement with neuroimaging studies that show acute intoxication reduces glucose metabolism in the prefrontal cortex (de Wit, Metz, Wagner, & Cooper, 1990; Volkow et al., 1990; Volkow, Wang, & Doria, 1995) that decreases the ability of the brain to function upon commands. These studies have shown a direct causal relationship between alcohol and an increased likelihood of interpersonal aggression. Despite the neurological data suggesting otherwise, Arbuckle and colleagues (1996) stated that homicides caused by domestic violence were less likely to involve alcohol and drugs than homicides resulting from other causes. However, domestic violence homicides involving substance abuse was still high at 54%. In an analysis of the first 100 cases where battered women killed their abusers, I found a high rate of alcohol use (Walker, 1989) as did Browne (1987).

Perception of the Batterers When Using Alcohol by the Battered Women

A qualitative study (Galvani, 2006) reiterated that the majority of women felt that alcohol alone was not enough to explain their partners' violent and abusive behavior. Instead, these women held the men responsible for their inappropriate actions. The majority of the women in this study perceived alcohol as having an impact on aggression but felt it "depended" to a greater or lesser degree on the presence of other variables. The impact of their partners' emotions prior to drinking was crucial to their post-alcoholic behavior. As a result, women often become hypervigilant about their partners' emotional state together with their alcohol intake in determining a strategy for avoiding possible violence or abuse. In addition, women evidently attempted to minimize the potential violence and abuse that might occur by mitigating their partners' "bad mood" through their own behavior. However, the resulting abuse or violence was no different than if they had made no attempt to pacify their partners. Nevertheless, some women in abusive relationships often blame themselves for "provoking" their abusers, especially when they were drunk.

LEGAL AND ILLICIT DRUGS

The relationship between substance abuse (alcohol and drugs) and aggression and/or interpersonal violence is more complex because of the pharmacological and physiological interaction of the different substances. A recent study indicated that cocaine use was significantly associated with being sexually active and used in exchange for sex (Raj, Saitz, Cheng, Winter, & Samet, 2007). Among the psychoactive substances examined, the use of alcohol and cocaine was associated with significant increases in the daily likelihood of male-to-female physical aggression (Denison, Paredes, & Booth, 1997; Fals-Stewart, Golden, & Schumacher, 2003). One study indicated that cannabis and opiates were not significantly associated with an increased likelihood of male partner violence (Fals-Stewart et al., 2003). It is, therefore, necessary to examine the effects of the various types of illicit drugs and their unique withdrawal symptoms in relation to aggression and domestic violence.

Sedatives–Hypnotics–Anxiolytics (Benzodiazepines)

In a task force report, the American Psychiatric Association (1990) recommended that benzodiazepines (well-known antianxiety medication such as Valium, Xanax, or others) be prescribed for short-term treatment only in the lowest dosage possible and for the shortest period of time. Benzodiazepines may have a heightening effect on aggression by interfering with the anxiety/threat detection system. This effect has been repeatedly demonstrated in numerous studies (Cherek, Spiga, Roache, & Cowan, 1991; Weisman, Berman, & Taylor, 1998). While this effect has been shown to be statistically significant, specific individual differences in the majority of users have been shown to be clinically insignificant. However, it has been demonstrated that men given a control dose of benzodiazepines have a more aggressive response than those taking a placebo. A moderating factor may be identified, such as a preexisting level of hostility or an expectation of increased aggression to explain the increase in aggressive responses. Other factors, including preexisting brain damage and alcohol consumption in association with benzodiazepines, have also revealed greater aggression than would normally be expected. An important variable determined by the studies is the dosage. Controlled experiments that did not show benzodiazepines-related increases in aggression involved relatively low dosages (Cherek et al., 1991).

It is important to better understand the effect of benzodiazepines on people's behavior because they are widely prescribed medications and easily available on the street market. They are also very effective in reducing anxiety responses that occur in PTSD and especially in stopping panic attacks. They also help with insomnia. However, they are dangerous when used inappropriately and are physiologically addictive, which means the dose must be increased when the person habituates to the initial dose. Even more dangerous, they can be fatal if too many pills are taken or if they are taken together with alcohol. While psychiatrists are hesitant to prescribe them for these reasons, many family doctors will and since they do not need to build up to a steady state as do antidepressants such as the selective serotonin reuptake inhibitors, people often share them with friends and family members, without realizing how dangerous they can be.

Opiates (Morphine, Heroin, and Codeine)

Similar to benzodiazepines, there is considerable confusion regarding the extent that opiates are linked to interpersonal aggression. There appears to be a complex interaction of interpersonal and pharmacological factors, including withdrawal factors, as the cause of violence initiated by opiate abusers. Studies have shown that the level of aggression by opiate users seems to be more related to individual personality traits than to the effects of the drug. There are, however, some anomalies and inconsistencies in published literature. In a study of 533 opiate addicts (Rounsaville, Weissman, Kleber, & Wilber, 1982), the comorbidity of this sample was as follows: depression (53.9%), alcoholism (34.5%), and antisocial behavior (26.5%). The National Drug Control Strategy (1997) stated that the drug itself may not cause the aggressive behavior; however, the aggression may be caused by the need minus the availability of the drug. The report highlighted that opiates have the capacity to absorb all of an individual's attention, resources, and energy that become devoted exclusively to obtaining the next dose at any cost.

Cannabis (Marijuana)

Cannibis, also known as "marijuana" or "weed," is a drug that has had such widespread use that it is now legal in a number of states for medical use and in several states for recreational use, also. The research on its safe use is controversial, although most people believe that if used in moderate amounts it is not particularly harmful, at least in the short term. In small amounts it causes relaxation, which in domestic violence cases might be useful in regulating emotions and lowering risk of physical violence. Some studies show it lessens motivation to be productive. Most people say it increases their appetite for sweets or munchies after smoking a "joint." One of the difficulties in the research is that the precise amount of tetrahydrocannabinol (TCH), the active ingredient, is not regulated in non-state-regulated drug quantities, and the higher the percentage, the more dangerous the effects. The marijuana plant can easily be grown in homes but again the amount of TCH is not regulated so the strength of the weed varies. When phencyclidine (PCP) or other drugs are added to the marijuana, they increase the potency and danger from the drug.

Although cannabis has been widely labeled a social menace, most recent research has found that cannabis users are less likely to act aggressively. However, cannabis intoxication can cause increased anxiety, paranoia, and even panic, particularly in inexperienced users (Thomas, 1993). There are no documented fatalities from cannabis overdoses (Hall, Solowij, & Lemon, 1994). Alcohol is the drug most commonly used in conjunction with cannabis and augments the level of intoxication and impairment in an additive way (Chait & Perry, 1994; Hall et al., 1994). The relationship between cannabis use and aggression is still controversial, although some studies seem to support the linkage in cannabis withdrawal syndrome (Kouri, Pope, & Lukas, 2000). There are no data to indicate its use in juveniles is safe over the long term.

Cocaine and Amphetamines

Both of these drugs and their derivatives are psychostimulants, and are usually obtained illegally. Cocaine is more expensive than its derivative crack, and therefore, it is not surprising that more wealthy abusers use powder cocaine while crack cocaine is more likely to be found in poorer communities. Although powder cocaine and crack cocaine are both illegal, the penalties for using and selling crack cocaine are much more severe than for powder cocaine. This contributes to the inequality in our prisons where more poor and minority persons are serving longer terms than those who are more affluent. We discuss the inequality in our prisons in the later chapter on battered women in jail and prison.

Methamphetamine pills can be made in the laboratory and are easily available on the street but their strength is not easily calibrated. Extensive literature concludes that both types of stimulants may generate aggression (Taylor & Hulsizer, 1998). In Warner's 1993 study, violent behavior was found to be the leading cause of death among stimulant users, with the most common forms of death being accident, suicide, and homicide. In fact, cocaine has been associated with more deaths than any other drug (National Institute on Drug Abuse, 1990). The stimulants cause acute dopaminergic stimulation of the brain's endogenous pleasure center. Users experience euphoria, heightened energy and libido, decreased appetite, hyperalertness, and bordering on overconfidence. High doses cause intensification of euphoria, accompanied by heightened alertness, volubility, repetitive behavior, and increased sexual behavior. Aggression, under these circumstances, may be due to interpersonal factors that existed prior to the psychostimulant use or aggression displayed in an effort to obtain these drugs. Behavioral changes are also part of the criteria for stimulant intoxication; these include fighting, grandiosity, hypervigilance, psychomotor agitation, impaired judgment, and impaired social functioning (Fischman & Schuster, 1982).

Several studies have associated cocaine, crack, amphetamine, and methamphetamine use with increased violence (Brody, 1990; Wright & Klee, 2001). The reasons are likely to be varied and multifaceted. First, individuals who abuse psychostimulants may be inherently aggressive, antisocial, or psychopathic sensation seekers. It has been suggested that only individuals with preexisting impulse control problems may act aggressively when under the influence of psychostimulants (Powers & Kutash, 1978). Second, an intense dependency on these drugs may make users in even mild withdrawal more aggressive. A recent study indicated that cocaine-dependent individuals were significantly more aggressive than a nondependent control group (Moeller, Steinberg, Petty, & Fulton, 1994). Third, aggression may result from a physical need to obtain the drug due to the expense and the difficulty of procurement.

Interestingly, the battered women in both the original study and the recent one attribute greater levels of violence, particularly sexual abuse, to both forms of cocaine use by the batterer. Batterers are able to stay up for days at a time when using cocaine. Although they are able to maintain an erection, unlike alcohol abusers who rarely can obtain or maintain one when intoxicated, they have more difficulty in ejaculating, so they blame the woman and keep trying through both sexual intercourse and oral sex. It is common to find forced anal sex during cocaine use, also. Many of the women in the jail sample also described their addiction to drugs as contributing to their vulnerability to being coerced into committing crimes so they could get money to buy these drugs.

Phencyclidine

As with psychostimulants, the linkage of PCP abuse and violence is not supported by empirical evidence. Violent behavior by PCP abusers may be explained by factors other than pharmacology. The literature on PCP-producing violence is at best inconsistent. Careful examination suggested that PCP does not directly induce violence in individuals who are otherwise not prone to violence (Brecher, Wang, Wong, & Morgan, 1988). Rather, it appeared that the injuries occur in the context of trying to subdue an agitated or irrational user who, by virtue of being relatively anesthetized, will not respond to typical methods of restraint and may seem to have "superhuman strength." However, McCardle and Fishbein (1989) found that personality characteristics and usage history were more accurate predictors of aggression and hostility. Very few of the women in our study discussed PCP as a drug commonly used by themselves or their batterers.

3, 4-Methylenedioxymethamphetamine (MDMA; "Ecstasy")

MDMA (Ecstasy/Molly) users usually experience a dreamy state sometimes accompanied by hallucinations and delusions, along with an increase in motor activation, stimulation, and general arousal. The duration is relatively short (Watson, Ferguson, Hinds, Skinner, & Coakley, 1993), which is why it is often used at nightclubs and/or music festivals where it is easily obtainable. In a recent study (Gerra et al., 2001), individuals with a history of MDMA use and a control group of nonusers were tested on a measure of aggression. The user group was found to be more aggressive than nonusers. It also found that the user group's aggressiveness was associated more with MDMA's pharmacological effects than with their personality traits that may be due to the possible neurotoxic effect of the substance. However, more research is needed.

Flakka and Other Designer Drugs

As the government attempts to shut down illegal sources of drugs, new ones appear on the horizon. Most of them are created in small laboratories from ingredients that are widely available, permitting them to be made and sold without much detection. Used mostly in clubs, some of these so-called designer drugs can be lethal, especially when combined with alcohol. Since they are "home grown," the exact measurement of ingredients may also vary, causing bad reactions. One of these new drugs, Flakka, has been extremely dangerous as it can cause an internal burning sensation that causes mental disturbance and feelings that the fire inside cannot be quenched. Suicides and unintended deaths are associated with these drugs.

COMMON THEMES OF ALL SUBSTANCE STUDIES

The common theme of the substance studies mentioned in the previous section is that each of the drugs themsleves, including alcohol, does not cause violence; rather, they may trigger a reaction in the individual who is predisposed to aggressive and violent behavior. Some studies have shown that alcohol or drugs disinhibit our human tendency toward aggression. For example, Pernanen (1991) found that the classical disinhibition is a psychophysiological perspective in which psychoactive substances disengage lower brain functions (i.e., sex, aggression) from higher brain control. It is commonly assumed that drugs and alcohol have a direct chemical effect on the brain, disinhibiting violence; this, however, is a myth, as no violence-inhibiting center exists in the brain. Lang et al. (1975) challenged the theory of disinhibition through experimentation. They suggested that the expectation of an alcohol-aggression effect may better predict aggressive behavior than alcohol itself. In another experiment, Cheong, Patock-Peckham, and Nagoshi (2001) demonstrated a more complicated pattern between expectancy and alcohol-related aggression. This study showed that the direct influence of the substance on domestic violence, independent of a person's cognitive processes, beliefs, and social contexts, is minimal.

ORIGINAL BWSQ #1 STUDY OF ALCOHOL AND OTHER DRUGS

In the original study, we looked at the women's reports of the batterers' use of alcohol and other drugs in general as well as their reports of both their use and their partners' use during each of the four battering incidents (the first, the most recent, the worst, and the typical incident). We also compared the batterers' use of substances with the nonbatterers' use in those who gave details about a battering and nonbattering relationship. The frequencies for BWSQ #1 as compared to BWSQ #2 for the first incident and worst incident can be found in Table 15.2. Interestingly, the women's alcohol use appears to be a little higher than the national level for alcoholics. There was a slight rise from 16% in the original group to 25% in the current group in use of alcohol during the worst incident. Other drug use also showed a rise with 7% in the original study to 22% admitting using other drugs during the current first incident and 8% during the original study to 14% in the current study. The drop in drug use from the first incident to those battering incidents later on is similar in both groups, supporting our original results that battered women use fewer drugs to cope with the increasing domestic violence from their partners.

The women's reports of the batterers' overall drinking patterns and reports of the batterers' alcohol use during these incidents in the original study were correlated at .77. The mean differences between the two groups

Table 15.2 *Women's Report of Alcohol and Drug Use During First and Worst Battering Incidents in BWSQ #1 and BWSQ #2*

Original Data	Original First Incident		Current First Incident		Original Worst Incident		Current Worst Incident	
	BW %	BP %	BW %	BP %	BW %	BP %	BW %	BP %
Alcohol								
Yes	2	0	0	1	6	6	5	1
No	8	6	2	0	3	2	6	4
Not sure	0	4	8	9	1	2	9	6
Drug use								
Yes	7	5	2	8	8	7	4	1
No	2	1	7	7	2	8	5	4
Not sure	0	4	1	6	0	5	1	5

BP, battering partner; BW, battered woman.

on the variables measured demonstrated that distinctions could be made using the variables themselves. The discriminant function coefficients show that two variables make statistically significant contributions to differences between no alcohol and excessive alcohol users.

The question of the relationship between alcohol use and the degree, severity, and number of battering incidents was explored in an analysis of the data done to meet part of the doctoral program requirements for one of the data analysts (Eberle, 1982). The discriminant results of the analysis she used are reported here. (Some of the numbers may be different from our other analysis, as these data were run using a smaller sample, $N = 390$.) A multivariate approach was used to discriminate differences between those batterers reported to abuse alcohol and those who did not use any alcohol at all. Our data permitted comparisons of multiple measures of violence, some of which were used to create composite measures.

This resulted in the creation of the following seven variables, which were used in the discriminant analysis: (a) the total number of battering incidents reported; (b) severity of injuries inflicted on the battered woman; (c) perceptions or actual violence toward the children in the family; (d) the batterer's criminal background; (e) the victim's use of alcohol; (f) the average age of the batterer for the four battering incidents reported; and

(g) the batterer's socioeconomic status. The dependent variable used was a dummy variable created by computing the batterer's alcohol use rate over the four battering incidents. Only those who either did not use alcohol at all or used it excessively through all four battering incidents were selected, decreasing the N to 131. There were 73 subjects whose batterers reportedly did not use any alcohol and 58 who used it excessively.

This procedure produced an interesting finding: The frequency distributions depict a bimodal distribution, with each battering incident having about 50% of the subjects using excessive alcohol, and the other half being sober. However, when looking at batterers' drinking patterns individually, they were not consistent in its use across the four battering incidents. For example, it was reported that the batterer could use "a lot" of alcohol during one incident, "some" during another incident, and "none" during the third. This inconsistent pattern of alcohol abuse across all the battering incidents had not been reported before, perhaps because multiple measures had not been available.

Battered women in the first study who used alcohol were more likely to be older than those who did not (.46). Three of the four violence measures that were calculated at the time contributed less significantly to the discriminant function, and the fourth, criminal behavior, was dropped from the analysis during the stepwise selection procedure. Adding other violence correlates to that variable might have given it more power. The variable that represented the degree and severity of the women's injuries was approaching significance (.26), lending some empirical support to the clinical observation that batterers who abuse alcohol inflict more serious injuries on the women. More research is still suggested in this area.

This analysis shows some support for the discriminant function of the other variables used, as they are in the predicted direction, but they still do not make a major contribution. The .25 coefficient for the variable measuring social status indicates that violent men from a low socioeconomic status may be more likely to be alcohol abusers. This finding was supported by the literature that indicated, in general, there are more drinking problems in the lower socioeconomic class. Thus, batterers may not be that different from the rest of the population when it comes to drinking problems. This is an important finding to consider, as Calahan's (1970) data indicated a 15% alcohol abuse rate for men and a 7% to 14% alcohol abuse rate for women. Our sample of batterers and battered women also falls into that range, when the consistent pattern over more than one battering incident is used as the measure.

CURRENT BWSQ #2 STUDY OF ALCOHOL
AND OTHER DRUGS

In this study, we analyzed what 98 of the battered women from five countries (United States, Russia, Spain, Greece, and Colombia) in our study described about their male partners' substance abuse and the subsequent battering incidents. This sample is different from the U.S.-only sample we analyzed in the original study. Again, we wanted to assess the types and frequencies of substance abuse and whether batterers who engaged in acute battering incidents would be more likely to be under the influence of alcohol and other drugs across all four incidents.

Questions relating to substance use in the BWSQ #2 were more carefully designed to capture the accuracy of the alcohol consumption and drug use as well as the severity of the battering incidents than in the BWSQ #1. Simultaneously, the BWSQ #2 also consists of a comprehensive substance use inventory, which is a 20-item self-report measure that is designed to assess the type of substance and its frequency of use for the batterer and the battered woman. The types of substance on the questionnaire included prescription drugs, sedatives–hypnotics–anxiolytics, opioids, stimulants, gamma-hydroxybutyrate (GHB), cannabis, alcohol, hallucinogens/PCP, and others, as described previously. All items are on a frequency scale that was coded by 1 = "never," 2 = "daily," 3 = "weekly," 4 = "monthly," and 5 = "yearly."

Results

Our frequency analysis indicated that the women described three leading substances that batterers consume: alcohol (60%), marijuana (45%), and stimulants (31%). Other substances used by the batterers included prescription drugs, sedatives, opioids, GHB, and hallucinogens. Figure 15.1 reveals the substance use frequencies of batterers as reported by the battered women.

As was consistent with the results of BWSQ #1, the women in this study also stated that alcohol was the most common drug used by the batterers. Therefore, we conducted further analysis to investigate the batterers' alcohol consumption during the battering episodes as reported by the battered women in this sample. We found that alcohol was consumed in 38% of the first battering incidents reported, in 44% of the time during the most

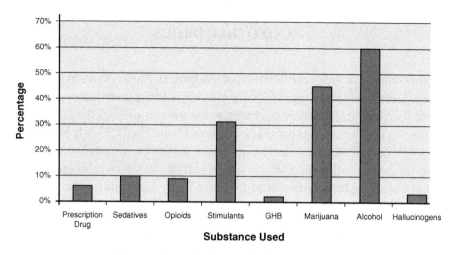

Figure 15.1 *Batterers' substance use.*

recent battering incidents reported, in 40% during the worst, and in 65% during the typical battering incidents reported. See Figure 15.2 for these results.

A standard multiple regression was performed between substance use and battering incidents. When all the substances were looked at collectively, results revealed that substance use accounted for approximately 29% of the variance in battering incidents that can be accounted for substance use ($R^2 = .287$). This was significant at the .05 level (Table 15.3).

Further analysis was conducted to determine for each substance use how badly the woman was injured by the male batterer. Overall, results indicated that of all the substances used, alcohol was the only significant predictor in how badly battered women were injured during the battering incidents ($p = .020$). See Table 15.4.

Prescription Drugs, Marijuana

Pearson correlation was performed to examine the relationship between substance use and severity of injury during the battering incident. We did analysis across all battering incidents: general, typical, most recent, first, and worst incident. Our results indicated that there was a significant relationship between alcohol consumption and degree of injury during the most recent episode. No significant relationship was found for other episodes. See Table 15.5.

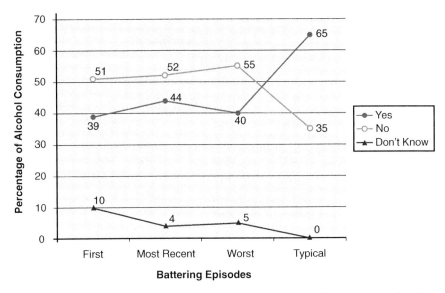

Figure 15.2 *Batterers' alcohol consumption across battering episodes.*

Table 15.3 *ANOVA Summary*

Model Summary				
Model	**R**	**R²**	**Adjusted R²**	**Standard Error of the Estimate**
1	.535ᵃ	.287	.095	.736

ᵃPredictors: (Constant), hallucinogens, opioids, stimulants, alcohol, sedatives/hypnotics, prescription drugs, marijuana.

Discussion

Overall, the results of our study confirmed the hypothesis that batterers engage in substance use during battering incidents. Based on the frequency analysis, it is evident that batterers used a range of substances including but not limited to alcohol, marijuana, stimulants, prescription drugs, hallucinogens, and opiates. This finding is similar to that of previous research reflecting that approximately 50% of batterers used substances (Gondolf, 1999, Tolman & Bennett, 1990). When taking an even closer look at the substances used, we saw that alcohol consumption was the leading drug category, indicating that this may be the drug of choice among batterers.

Table 15.4 *Substance Use and Injury During the Battering Episodes*

	Coefficients[a]				
	Unstandardized Coefficients		Standardized Coefficients		
Model	B	Standard Error	Beta	t	Significance
1 (Constant)	1.868	.252		7.420	.000
Prescription drugs	−.105	.385	−.052	−.273	.787
Sedatives/hypnotics	.043	.496	.016	.086	.932
Opioids	−.608	.819	−.135	−.743	.464
Stimulants	.638	.500	.355	1.275	.214
Marijuana	−.659	.560	−.394	−1.176	.250
Alcohol	.845	.339	.505	2.490	.020
Hallucinogens	−.402	.716	−.150	−.562	.579

[a]Dependent variable: How badly were you injured by what he did to you?

Table 15.5 *Pearson Correlation*

		Were you injured during the most recent episode?	Was he using alcohol during most recent incident?
Were you injured during the most recent episode?	Pearson correlation	1	−.330[a]
	Significance (two-tailed)		.013
	N	62	56
Was he using alcohol during most recent incident?	Pearson correlation	−.330[a]	1
	Significance (two-tailed)	.013	66
	N	56	

[a]Correlation is significant at the 0.05 level (two-tailed).

This finding provided further confirmation that alcohol was the most used drug by batterers and is consistent with the literature as well. More specifically, 60% of batterers reported engaging in alcohol consumption.

When looking at alcohol consumption across episodes, it was apparent that during the first, most recent, and worst episodes batterers were less likely to have reported drinking alcohol. This was rather surprising as we expected that batterers' alcohol consumption would have been the same or greater over time, especially since it was reported that during the typical episode, batterers reportedly drank approximately 60% of the times. One explanation is that the women are less likely to remember the use of alcohol specifically during some individual battering incidents, but can remember that the men typically drank over time. Others have also found that batterers do not consistently abuse alcohol in each battering incident, even though over time they do (Kantor & Straus, 1987). This finding has major implications for treatment as it suggests that substance abuse intervention without offender-specific treatment will not be enough to help men stop their abusive behavior.

Consistent with the literature reviewed in the chapter, our study found that alcohol abuse is a risk factor for intimate partner violence, especially among alcoholic men. From the regression analyses conducted it was evident that of all the substances used, alcohol was the only significant predictor in how badly the women were battered. As we know, alcohol intoxication impairs cognition and the possibility exists that while under the influence of alcohol, the batterers may demonstrate less judgment when "beating" their female counterpart, which may lead to a more severe degree of injury. Other studies have also corroborated that abusing alcohol increases the risk of severe physical aggression (Pan et al., 1994). Collectively, drugs are perceived to be used as a form of self-medication. It is not known if batterers' poor problem-solving skills lead them to resort to drug use to avoid dealing with their problems or if it is simply an escape. In any case, our data demonstrate how substance use is definitely associated with domestic violence. Although alcohol was the most significant predictor in physical aggression, we expected that there would have been more statistical significance across all the episodes. One limitation of this study is that the batterers' substance use is reported by the battered women; therefore the possibility exists that the figures could be over- or underreported. Additionally, as postulated by Galvani (2006), women who have been battered often feel that alcohol alone is not enough to explain their partners' violent and abusive behavior.

With regard to further research, attempts should be made to interview the batterers so that we can attain a more accurate picture of batterers' substance use. Having batterers complete the section on substance use is crucial for substance use issues. Additionally, when questioning women and men about substance use issues, a more detailed and comprehensive substance use inventory should be utilized in order to determine a wider perspective of their use of substances. In this study, the questionnaire used included only closed-ended questions and Likert scale items, which restricted the interviewees' responses. This issue is particularly relevant when considering the impact of substance use on the battered woman syndrome.

ROLE OF ALCOHOL AND OTHER DRUG ABUSE IN BATTERED WOMEN

Alcohol and drug abuse has been found to be used as a form of self-medication to block the intense emotions that are often experienced by abuse victims, particularly physical and sexual assault victims. Kilpatrick and Resnick (1993) found that the highest risk factor for alcoholism in women after a sexual assault was exposure to prior abuse. Goldberg (1995) reviewed the literature on substance-abusing women and found that although they were a diverse group, the major risk factors were not poverty or exposure to substance-abusing parents, as was common for substance-abusing men, but rather childhood physical or sexual abuse, adult victimization by domestic violence, and a partner who abuses substances. It is interesting that in the original study, too, many of the women who reported to being alcohol dependent were also living with alcohol-dependent partners. Some of those women said that they avoided further abuse by going out and drinking with their partners. It is not uncommon for women to become addicted to drugs that are supplied by their batterers who then have greater power and control over them as the batterers dispense their drugs based on how the women behave. We have not yet completed the analysis of battered women who were also substance abusers in the new study. However, we have some observations from the women in the Survivor Therapy Empowerment Program (STEP) program in jail detailed in Chapter 17.

WOMEN'S SUBSTANCE ABUSE AND PUBLIC POLICY

In the 1980s, the government began to arrest and prosecute pregnant women who potentially were harming their children through the ingestion of alcohol and other drugs. However, when a closer look was taken at these women, it became clear that over 90% of them were battered women (Walker, 1991). Research by others found that there were no treatment programs for substance-abusing, pregnant, battered women. Battered woman shelters would not take them nor would drug treatment centers. Putting them in jail was not a solution, especially since detoxification needed special techniques to protect both the mother and the fetus. Removing the baby from the mother at birth exacerbated the child's potential developmental problems, which appeared to have a direct relationship with the degree of bonding that could occur between the mother and the child. The best solution, of course, was to provide assistance to the woman to stop her substance use, for the woman to get out of the violent relationship, and to bond with her baby. Given the fact that many battered women temporarily get more depressed when they leave an abusive relationship and are in greater danger especially if the batterers stalk and find them, this is a problem without satisfactory resolution much of the time.

Substance abuse treatment programs for women need to have trauma therapy in addition to other types of intervention. In 2000 to 2002, we provided a day treatment center program for 70 women with serious mental illness who had some kind of criminal justice involvement. Most of these women also had substance abuse problems and over 85% of them were also battered in their homes and on the street. We found that without trauma-focused intervention, these women could not stop their substance abuse, even with appropriate medication management. Most important was helping these women begin to rebuild interpersonal relationships, in some cases with families of origin who had given up on their ever being sober, and in other cases with families of choice, where women worked on developing close friendships that served as family. We have found that very few programs for women who have the co-occurring disorders of severe mental illness and substance abuse include the trauma component. While this book focuses on battered women, in fact many of those women experiencing domestic violence have also experienced child physical and sexual abuse, sexual assaults, rape and harassment, head injuries causing neurological problems, sex trafficking, addictions to various substances, poverty, racism, and other forms of discrimination. These multiple problems can leave the women emotionally exhausted in trying to cope with all of them.

Intervention

Although our data show that batterers are reported to drink and use drugs more frequently than the battered women, further study of these variables in abusive relationships is needed to provide more specific information. For example, in a review of over 400 homicide and attempted homicide cases in which the abused victim becomes aggressive toward the abuser, there are frequent reports of alcohol and other drug abuse in one or both parties. The level of severity of injuries from the assaultive combat while intoxicated appears to be more serious in many of those cases. We first found this association during an analysis of the first 100 homicide cases (Walker, 1989) and over the years it appears to be fairly consistent.

The use of alcohol may start out to calm one's nerves or be a pleasant relaxant, but it quickly takes on menacing properties. So too for other drug use that also reportedly starts out as a pleasant way to overcome tensions and anxieties, but soon takes over as a way of life. In some of our cases, the women described how their entire days were spent trying to find ways to obtain sufficient prescription drugs to keep themselves and their batterers calm so they would be less likely to beat them up. These women report quickly becoming addicted. In one case, a woman told of how she allowed herself to be caught by the police for passing forged prescriptions, perhaps as a way of finding safety in jail. In other cases that escalate to homicidal or suicidal levels, it has been found that cocaine and its derivatives, particularly crack, crank, amphetamines, and methamphetamines are the drugs most likely to be used in addition to alcohol (Walker, 1989, 1994).

It is important for drug and alcohol treatment programs to recognize that violent behavior cannot be stopped through alcohol and other drug counseling. Neither will a substance-abusing battered woman gain the assistance she needs to become independent and remain violence free. Programs that appropriately deal separately with the violence and the substance abuse are crucial. Communities that have special domestic violence courts often have a drug court that is associated with them. Thus, even if an alcoholic batterer becomes sober, he will not become a nonbatterer until he goes through a process designed to teach or help batterers become nonviolent. And women who abuse substances to self-medicate from the symptoms of PTSD and battered woman syndrome (BWS) need specialized treatment for the abuse they have experienced in addition to treatment for alcohol and other drugs. We discuss treatment programs in more detail in Chapters 16 and 17.

It is important to recognize that alcohol and other substances used on a regular basis over a long period of time can lead to serious cognitive deficits. In those who have had a chronic substance abuse problem, it is often necessary to participate in a cognitive rehabilitation program similar to those used with stroke victims. This type of treatment will help retrain the brain so that the effects of chronic substance abuse will be moderated. Without such treatment it is less likely that they will be able to make use of traditional verbal psychotherapy.

SUMMARY

The relationship between substance abuse and domestic violence is clearly demonstrated in numerous studies over the past 40 years. However, the new problem-solving courts have added mental illness as a third factor that must also be investigated. Alcohol is frequently the drug of choice that is associated with intimate partner violence, although cocaine and methamphetamines are also frequently reported. Battered women are likely to use substances to self-medicate from the psychological effects of abuse. Women who have been arrested for drug offenses often have been abused by intimate partners. The latest research by Dvorak and colleagues (2013) suggests that the National Comorbidity Survey Replication indicated the lifetime prevalence of alcohol abuse is 13.2% and 5.4% for alcohol dependence. For PTSD, the lifetime prevalence is 6.8%, which seems quite low given the numbers of soldiers returning from combat zones. However, even using these figures, there is a high comorbidity for a combined alcohol and PTSD lifetime prevalence of 52% of men and 25% of women with PTSD. Cognitive rehabilitation as well as trauma treatment and drug treatment are all needed, especially for those who have been abusing substances over a long period of time.

REFERENCES

American Psychiatric Association. (1990). *Benzodiazepine dependence, toxicity and abuse.* Washington, DC: American Psychiatric Press.
American Psychological Association. (1996). *Report from the Presidential Task Force on Violence and the Family.* Washington, DC: Author.

Arbuckle, J., Olson, L., Howard, M., Brilman, J., Anctil, C., & Sklar, D. (1996). Safe at home? Domestic violence and other homicides among women in New Mexico. *Annals of Emergency Medicine, 27*, 210–215.

Babcock, J. C., Green, C. E., & Robie, C. (2004). Does batterers' treatment work? A meta-analytic review of domestic violence treatment. *Clinical Psychology Review, 23*, 1023–1053.

Bard, M., & Zacker, J. (1974). Assaultiveness and alcohol use in family disputes. *Criminology, 12*(3), 281–292.

Brecher, M., Wang, B. W., Wong, H., & Morgan, J. P. (1988). Phencyclidine and violence: Clinical and legal issues. *Journal of Clinical Psychopharmacology, 8*, 397–401.

Brecklin, L. R. (2002). The role of perpetrator alcohol use in the injury outcomes of intimate assaults. *Journal of Family Violence, 17*, 185–197.

Brody, S. L. (1990). Violence associated with acute cocaine use in patients admitted to a medical emergency department. *National Institute on Drug Abuse Research Monograph, 103*, 44–59. Retrieved from http://archives.drugabuse .gov/pdf/monographs/103.pdf#page=53

Brookoff, D., O'Brien, K. K., Cook, C. S., Thompson, T. D., & Williams, C. (1997). Characteristics of participants in domestic violence: Assessment at the scene of domestic assault. *Journal of the American Medical Association, 277*, 1369–1373.

Brown, T. G., Caplan, T., Werk, A., & Seraganian, P. (1999). The comparability of male violent substance abusers in violence or substance abuse treatment. *Journal of Family Violence, 14*, 297–314.

Brown, T. G., Werk, A., Caplan, T., Shields, N., & Seraganian, P. (1998). The incidence and characteristics of violent men in substance abuse treatment. *Addictive Behaviors, 23*, 573–586.

Browne, A. (1987). *When battered women kill.* New York, NY: Free Press.

Chait, L. D., & Perry, J. L. (1994). Acute and residual effects of alcohol and marijuana, alone and in combination, on mood and performance. *Psychopharmacology, 115*, 340–349.

Cheong, J., Patock-Peckham, J. A., & Nagoshi, C. T. (2001). Effects of alcoholic beverage, instigation, and inhibition on expectancies of aggressive behavior. *Violence and Victims, 16*, 173–184.

Cherek, D., Spiga, R., Roache, J., & Cowan, K. (1991). Effects of triazolam on human aggressive, escape, and point-maintaining responding. *Pharmacology, Biochemistry & Behavior, 40*, 835–839.

Chermack, S. T., & Blow, F. C. (2002). Violence among individuals in substance abuse treatment: The role of alcohol and cocaine consumption. *Drug and Alcohol Dependence, 66*, 29–37.

Coleman, D. H., & Straus, M. A. (1983). Alcohol abuse and family violence. In E. Gottheil, K. A. Druley, T. E. Skoloda, & H. M. Waxman (Eds.), *Alcohol, drug abuse and aggression* (pp. 104–124). Springfield, IL: C. Thomas.

Collins, J. J., & Messerschmidt, P. M. (1993). Epidemiology of alcohol-related violence. *Alcohol Research and Health, 17*(2), 93–100.

Denison, M. F., Paredes, A., & Booth, J. B. (1997). Alcohol and cocaine interactions and aggressive behaviors. In M. Galanter (Ed.), *Recent developments in alcoholism, volume 13: Alcoholism and violence: Epidemiology, neurobiology, psychology, and family issues* (pp. 283–303). New York, NY: Plenum.

de Wit, H., Metz, J., Wagner, N., & Cooper, M. (1990). Behavioral and subjective effects of ethanol: Relationship to cerebral metabolism using PET. *Alcoholism, Clinical and Experimental Research, 14*, 482–489.

Dvorak, R. D., Arens, A. M., Kuvaas, N. J., Williams, T. J., & Kilwein, T. M. (2013). Problematic alcohol use, trauma history, and PTSD symptom level: A path analysis. *Journal of Dual Diagnosis, 9*(4), 281–291.

Eberle, P. A. (1982). Alcohol users and non-users: A discriminant analysis between two subgroups of batterers. *Journal of Health and Social Behavior, 23*(3), 260–271.

Fals-Stewart, W. (2003). The occurrence of partner physical aggression on days of alcohol consumption: A longitudinal diary study. *Journal of Consulting and Clinical Psychology, 71*(1), 41.

Fals-Stewart, W., Golden, J., & Schumacher, J. A. (2003). Intimate partner violence and substance use: A longitudinal day-to-day examination. *Addictive Behaviors, 28*(9), 1555–1574.

Fischman, M. W., & Schuster, C. R. (1982). Cocaine self-administration in humans. *Federal Proceedings, 41*(2), 241–246.

Frieze, I. H., & Knoble, J. (1980, September). *The effects of alcohol on marital violence.* Paper presented at the 88th Annual Convention of the American Psychological Association, Montreal, Quebec, Canada.

Galvani, S. (2006). Alcohol and domestic violence: Women's views. *Violence Against Women, 12*(7), 641–662.

Gelles, R. J. (1972). *The violent home: A study of the physical aggression between husbands and wives.* Beverly Hills, CA: Sage.

Gerra, G., Zaimovic, A., Ampollini, R., Giusti, F., Delsignore, R., Raggi, M. A., . . . Brambilla, F. (2001). Experimentally induced aggressive behavior in subjects with 3, 4-methylenedioxy-methamphetamine ("Ecstasy") use history: Psychobiological correlates. *Journal of Substance Abuse, 13*(4), 471–491.

Goldberg, M. E. (1995). Substance-abusing women: False stereotypes and real needs. *Social Work, 40*(6), 789–798.

Goldstein, D. B. (1975). Physical dependence on alcohol in mice. *Federation Proceedings, 34*(10), 1953–1961.

Gondolf, E. W. (1999). A comparison of reassault rates in four batterer programs: Do court referral, program length and services matter? *Journal of Interpersonal Violence, 14*, 41–61.

Gondolf, E. W., & Fisher, E. R. (1988). *Battered women as survivors: An alternative to treating learned helplessness.* Boston, MA: Lexington.

Hall, W., Solowij, N., & Lemon, J. (1994). *The health and psychological consequences of cannabis use.* Canberra: Australian Government Publishing Service.

Hotaling, G. T., & Sugarman, D. B. (1986). An analysis of risk markers in husband to wife violence: The current state of the knowledge. *Violence and Victims, 1*, 101–124.

Jacobson, N. S., & Gottman, J. M. (1998). *When men batter women: New insights into ending abusive relationships.* New York, NY: Simon & Schuster.

Kantor, G., & Straus, M. A. (1987). The drunken bum theory of wife beating. *Social Problems, 34*, 213–230.

Kilpatrick, D. G., & Resnick, H. S. (1993). Posttraumatic stress disorder associated with exposure to criminal victimization in clinical and community populations. In J. R. T. Davidson & E. B. Foa (Eds.), *Posttraumatic stress disorder: DSM-IV and beyond* (pp. 113–143). Washington, DC: American Psychiatric Press.

Kouri, E. M., Pope, H. G., & Lukas, S. E. (2000). Changes in aggressive behavior during withdrawal from long-term marijuana use. *Psychopharmacology, 143*, 302–308.

Lang, A. R., Goeckner, D. J., Adesso, V. T., & Marlatt, G. A. (1975). The effects of alcohol on aggression in male social drinkers. *Journal of Abnormal Psychology, 84*, 508–518.

Leonard, K., & Quigley, B. M. (1999). Drinking and marital aggression in newly-weds: An event-based analysis of drinking and the occurrence of husband marital aggression. *Journal of Studies on Alcohol, 60*, 537–545.

Lipsky, S., Caetano, R., Field, C. A., & Larkin, G. L. (2005). Psychosocial and substance-use risk factors for intimate partner violence. *Drug and Alcohol Dependence, 78*(1), 39–47.

Maiden, R. P. (1997). Alcohol dependence and domestic violence: Incidence and treatment implications. *Alcoholism Treatment Quarterly, 15*(2), 31–50.

McCardle, L., & Fishbein, D. H. (1989). The self-reported effects of PCP on human aggression. *Addictive Behaviors, 14*, 465–472.

Moeller, F. G., Steinberg, J. L., Petty, F., & Fulton, M. (1994). Serotonin and impulsive/aggressive behavior in cocaine dependent subjects. *Progress in Neuro-Psychopharmacology & Biological Psychiatry, 18*(6), 1027–1035.

Mungas, D., Ehlers, C. L., & Wall, T. L. (1994). Effects of acute alcohol administration on verbal and spatial learning. *Alcohol and Alcoholism, 29*, 1065–1081.

Murphy, C. M., Winters, J., O'Farrell, T. J., Fals-Stewart, W., & Murphy, M. (2005). Alcohol consumption and intimate partner violence by alcoholic men: Comparing violent and nonviolent conflicts. *Psychology of Addictive Behaviors, 19*, 35–42.

National Drug Control Strategy. (1997). Washington, DC: U.S. Government Printing Office.

National Institute on Drug Abuse. (1990). *Data from the drug abuse warning network, Series 1, No. 9* (No. 90–1717). Washington, DC: Alcohol, Drug Abuse, and Mental Administration.

O'Farrell, T. J., Van Hutton, V., & Murphy, C. M. (1999). Domestic violence before and after alcoholism treatment: A two-year longitudinal study. *Journal of Studies on Alcohol, 60*, 317–321.

Pan, H. S., Neidig, P. H., & O'Leary, D. K., (1994). Predicting mild and severe husband-to-wife physical aggression. *Journal of Consulting and Clinical Psychology, 62*, 975–981.

Pernanen, K. (1991). *Alcohol in human violence*. New York, NY: Guilford Press.

Peterson, J. B., Rothfieisch, J., Zelazo, P. D., & Pihl, R. O. (1990). Acute alcohol intoxication and cognitive functioning. *Journal of Studies on Alcohol, 51*, 114–122.

Post, R. B., Lott, L. A., Maddock, R. J., & Beede, J. I. (1996). An effect of alcohol on the distribution of spatial attention. *Journal of Studies on Alcohol, 57*, 260–266.

Powers, R., & Kutash, I. (1978). Substance-induced aggression. In I. Kutash, S. Kutash, & L. Schlesinger (Eds.), *Violence: Perspective on murder and aggression* (pp. 317–342). San Francisco, CA: Jossey-Bass.

Raj, A., Saitz, R., Cheng, D. M., Winter, M., & Samet, J. H. (2007). Associations between alcohol, heroin, and cocaine use and high risk sexual behaviors among detoxification patients. *American Journal of Drug and Alcohol Abuse, 33*, 169–178.

Richardson, D. C., & Campbell, J. L. (1980). Alcohol and wife abuse: The effect of alcohol on attributions of blame for wife abuse. *Personality and Social Psychology Bulletin, 6*(1), 51–56.

Roberts, W. R., Penk, W. E., Gearing, M. L., Robinowitz, R., Dolan, M. P., & Patterson, E. T. (1982). Interpersonal problems of Vietnam combat veterans with symptoms of posttraumatic stress disorder. *Journal of Abnormal Psychology, 91*(6), 444–450.

Rounsaville, B. J., Weissman, M. M., Kleber, H. D., & Wilber, C. H. (1982). The heterogeneity of psychiatric diagnosis in treated opiate addicts. *Archives of General Psychiatry, 39*, 161–166.

Schumacher, J. A., Fals-Stewart, W., & Leonard, K. E. (2003). Domestic violence treatment referrals for men seeking alcohol treatment. *Journal of Substance Abuse Treatment, 24*, 279–283.

Snow, D. L., & Sullivan, T. P. (2006). The role of coping and problem drinking in men's abuse of female partners: Test of a Path Model. *Violence and Victims, 21*(3), 267–285.

Stith, S. M., Crossman, R. K., & Bischof, G. P. (1991). Alcoholism and marital violence: A comparative study of men in alcohol treatment programs and batterer treatment programs. *Alcoholism Treatment Quarterly, 8*, 3–20.

Taylor, S. P., & Gammon, C. B. (1975). Effects of type and dose of alcohol on human physical aggression. *Journal of Personality and Social Psychology, 32*(1), 169–175.

Taylor, S. P., & Hulsizer, M. R. (1998). Psychoactive drugs and human aggression. In R. G. Geen & E. Donnerstein (Eds.), *Human aggression: Theories, research, and implications for social policy* (pp. 139–165). San Diego, CA: Academic Press.

Thomas, H. (1993). Psychiatric symptoms in cannabis users. *British Journal of Psychiatry, 163*, 141–149.

Tiplady, B., Harding, C., McLean, D., Ortner, C., Porter, K., & Wright, P. (1999). Effects of ethanol and temazepam on episodic and semantic memory: A dose-response comparison. *Human Psychopharmacology, 14*, 263–269.

Tolman, R., & Bennett, L. (1990). A review of quantitative research on men who batter. *Journal of Interpersonal Violence, 5*(1), 87–118.

Van Hasselt, V. B., Morrison, R. L., & Bellack, A. S. (1985). Alcohol use in wife abusers and their spouses. *Addictive Behaviors, 10*(2), 127–135.

Volkow, N. D., Hitzemann, R., Wolf, A. P., Logan, J., Fowler, J. S., Christman, D., . . . Hirschowitz, J. (1990). Acute effects of ethanol on regional brain glucose metabolism and transport. *Psychiatry Research: Neuroimaging, 35*(1), 39–48.

Volkow, N. D., Wang, G., & Doria, J. (1995). Monitoring the brain's response to alcohol with positron emission tomography. *Alcohol Health and Research World, 19*, 296–299.

Walker, L. E. (1979). *The battered woman*. New York, NY: Harper & Row.

Walker, L. E. (Ed.). (1984). *Women and mental health policy*. Beverly Hills, CA: Sage.

Walker, L. E. (1989). Psychology and violence against women. *American Psychologist, 44*, 695–702.

Walker, L. E. A. (1991, January 19–20). Abused women, infants, and substance abuse: Psychological consequences of failure to protect. In P. R. McGrab & D. M. Doherty (Eds.), *Mothers, infants, and substance abuse: Proceedings of the APA Division 12, Midwinter Meeting*, Scottsdale, AZ.

Walker, L. E. A. (1994). *Abused women and survivor therapy: A practical guide for the psychotherapist*. Washington, DC: American Psychological Association.

Warner, E. A. (1993). Cocaine abuse. *Annals of Internal Medicine, 119*, 226–235.

Watson, J. D., Ferguson, C., Hinds, C. J., Skinner, R., & Coakley, J. H. (1993). Exertional heat stroke induced by amphetamine analogues. *Anaesthesia, 48*(12), 1057–1060.

Weisman, A. M., Berman, M. E., & Taylor, S. P. (1998). Effects of clorazepate, diazepam, and oxazepam on a laboratory measurement of aggression in men. *International Clinical Psychopharmacology, 13*, 183–188.

White, R. J., Ackerman, R. J., & Caraveo, L. E. (2001). Self-identified alcohol abusers in a low security federal prison: Characteristics and treatment implications. *International Journal of Offender Therapy and Comparative Criminology, 45*, 214–227.

White, R. J., Gondolf, E. W., Robertson, D. U., Goodwin, B. J., & Caraveo, L. E. (2002). Extent and characteristics of woman batterers among federal inmates. *International Journal of Offender Therapy and Comparative Criminology, 46*, 412–427.

Wright, S., & Klee, H. (2001). Violent crime, aggression and amphetamine: What are the implications for drug treatment services? *Drugs: Education, Prevention Policy, 8*, 73–90.

Zeichner, A., & Pihl, R. O. (1979). Effects of alcohol and behavior contingencies on human aggression. *Journal of Abnormal Psychology, 88*(2), 153–160.

Chapter Sixteen

Trauma-Informed Psychotherapy

CONTRIBUTIONS FROM FREUD AND PSYCHOANALYSIS

The history of trauma-informed psychotherapy began differently from other psychotherapy theories as it was not based on just one person's theory but rather was built up over the entire history of psychotherapy practice adding on piece by piece. In fact, it owes its beginnings to the earliest psychotherapists, Freud, Charcot, Breuer, and other psychodynamic theorists who uncovered the early trauma of child abuse and its impact on the development of the psyche as it was called in the late 1800s and early 1900s. While they did not understand the impact of the trauma they uncovered with their "talking cure" methods of their day, and they certainly did not understand its impact on women, they did note that trauma memories remained, sometimes hidden, and continued to impact the victim, unless treated. Freud first studied hypnosis with Charcot in France hoping to use the method to access buried trauma memories in his patients and later developed the psychoanalytic method of using primary process thinking in a stream of unconscious talking, as a way to strip the emotions from the troubling traumatic memories.

Freud might be very surprised today to learn that his theories have been supported by sophisticated brain imaging techniques that show trauma memories are stored in the hippocampus area of the midbrain with all the sensations including emotion intact. The act of processing the memories verbally can strip these memories of the actual sensations of sights, smells, emotions, and others to be consolidated and stored in the cerebrum's memory area. This makes the memories more easily accessible than in what Freud called the "unconscious." Psychotherapy, then, is the process by which these changes can occur.

CONTRIBUTIONS FROM PSYCHOTHERAPY WITH
TRAUMATIZED VETERANS

Bessel van der Kolk (2015), a psychiatrist at Harvard Medical School, described the progress from moving Freud's psychoanalytic work to the application of healing from trauma in war veterans in his book, *The Body Keeps the Score*. Initially, soldiers returning from war with mental health symptoms that today we know as "posttraumatic stress disorder" (PTSD) were diagnosed with "combat fatigue" (Figley, 1995) or what some called "traumatic neuroses" or "shell shocked" (van der Kolk, 2015). Once PTSD became an official category in the *Diagnostic and Statistical Manual of Mental Disorders* (3rd ed.; *DSM-III*; American Psychiatric Association, 1980), the literature began to be filled with stories about the psychological trauma in the Vietnam veterans and today we are dealing with multiple traumas from the Gulf War veterans who often have traumatic brain injuries from that war also (van der Kolk, 2015). It is now well accepted that the *affective state-dependent storage of memories* or parts of trauma memory is not easily accessible due to physiological changes in the brain chemistry and structure. However, much of what we do today in trauma treatment is based on others who began to develop trauma-specific treatment for veterans, such as Keane, Marshall, and Taft (2006), Figley (1995), and van der Kolk (2015) to name a few of these pioneers.

Janoff-Bulman (1985) described the psychological symptoms of those who were exposed to prolonged combat or death-defying experiences as having been impacted by the destructions of their assumptions about life due to their new feelings of vulnerability. This was accompanied by feelings of anxiety, helplessness, and the lost sense of safety and security by continuing to be preoccupied by the possible reoccurrence of the trauma. She suggested that repairing the assumptions of invulnerability of the world is part of what needs to happen in trauma therapy. Some of this is now done in rebuilding resilience and the move toward wellness.

Application of the trauma therapy designed by those who treated combat veterans began to be applied to victims of gender violence; first by Burgess and Holmstrom (1974) in their treatment of rape victims and then by Foa, Rothbaum, Riggs, and Murdock (1991) with her prolonged exposure therapy with rape victims and some battered women. Judith Herman (1992), Laura Brown (1992, 1994, 2013), Christine Courtois (1999), Steve Gold (2000), and others began to describe a form of PTSD named

"complex PTSD" (or Disorders of Extreme Stress Not Otherwise Specified [DESNOS] in the *DSM* diagnostic system) that often had its roots in
child abuse. The theories all attended to the importance in healing of
empowerment, changing negative cognitions, sometimes called "cognitive reappraisal," rebuilding support networks and reexamining attachment to others, and emotional re-regulation.

An important issue is whether different PTSD events produce the
same PTSD response in different people. This question has been difficult
to research as we found in the battered woman syndrome (BWS) research
where we had to take into account the different preexisting conditions,
situational factors, and impacts from the abuse itself that our women
experienced. Wilson, Smith, and Johnson (1985) examined PTSD from
eight different trauma events such as combat in war, rape, other life-
threatening events, divorce, death of a partner, critical or near-fatal illness of a significant other, family violence, multiple trauma events and
compared them with each other and those with no trauma-event experience. Using an Eriksonian model, they examined people at different
stages of development when the trauma event occurred, compared them
with others who may have reverted back to an earlier developmental level,
and with others who may have had psychosocially accelerated development from the trauma. It has been reported in the literature that some
people who experience crisis and trauma can not only heal but go beyond
to produce altruism, ethical behavior, and humanitarianism where it did
not exist before. Wilson and his colleagues used Lifton's psychoformative
theory model and Seligman's learned helpless model to understand the
death or near death and other adverse experiences.

They found 10 dimensions that went into their model:

1. Degree of life threat
2. Degree of bereavement
3. Speed of onset
4. Duration of trauma
5. Degree of displacement from home
6. Potential for recurrence
7. Degree of exposure to death, dying, and destruction
8. Degree of moral conflict inherent in the situation
9. Role of the person in the trauma
10. Proportion of the community impacted by the trauma
    (Wilson, Smith, & Johnson, 1985, pp. 142–172)

404   PART III   INTERVENTION STRATEGIES

In Chapter 13, some of the changes in the brain chemistry when PTSD occurs are discussed. Even the structures of the brain are known to change when exposed to prolonged stress. Medication such as antidepressants, antianxiety drugs, newer antipsychotic medications, and mood stabilizers are often prescribed for people with PTSD. Which medication is prescribed depends on the person's individual tolerance for the medication, the behavior it is supposed to change, and sadly, the economics of the situation. All drugs in the class prescribed do not have similar effects in different people. So, for example, someone could be prescribed Zoloft and another person prescribed Prozac, both in the selective serotonin reuptake inhibitor (SSRI) category, for the same problems from PTSD. Or, those who also are reexperiencing traumatic memories may need a medication from the antipsychotic group that can also calm down delusions and hallucinations even if they are real memories but things that are not actually happening at the time. Obviously, the revolution in psychotropic medications beginning in the 1950s has been important in helping some people heal from PTSD and other trauma effects.

CONTRIBUTIONS FROM FEMINIST THERAPY

My good friend and colleague, psychologist Phyllis Chesler, was one of the first authors to document the misuse of psychotherapy and medication with women who tried to break out of gender socialized roles in the early 1970s (Chesler, 1972). Women who tried to defy social traditions were called "uppity" and ridiculed as "bra-burning feminists." Many were overdosed on antianxiety medications such as Valium and encouraged to keep their trauma memories to themselves. For a period of time, feminists were leery of prescribing any medication, remembering the days when it was used for political purposes of keeping them quiet and trying to quash the feminist revolution. More recently, we have learned that psychotropic medication used appropriately can be useful in healing various forms of mental illness including PTSD.

The early feminists began to adopt a method of group intervention that was developed in China during the cultural revolution called "speaking bitterness" there but in the United States called "consciousness-raising." Speaking out about their oppression in these consciousness-raising groups became so popular that in some groups women were held to taking turns, sometimes even with being given "chips" that got spent each time they spoke. Many of the battered woman groups run in shelters and clinics have similar features today. The attempt was to develop a more egalitarian model using consensus to reach a group opinion or action. Many women in the 1970s and 1980s used these groups to become "empowered" and it became a cornerstone of feminist therapy that then became adopted by trauma therapy also.

Another good friend and colleague, psychologist Laura Brown, helped write down the tenets of feminist therapy and practice as it developed over the years (Brown, 2013). Like trauma theory, feminist therapy did not have any one person who developed it, but rather, it became accepted around the world perhaps paralleling the UN efforts during these years with the Decade for Women conferences held in the United States in 1976, in Nairobi in 1985, and in China in 1995. Having attended the first two of these conferences as a delegate, I personally observed and took part in the transformation as women moved toward self-determination and equality sharing and learning from one another. Part of self-determination was a major effort to protect women from gender violence through a variety of empowering actions including acceptance of feminist therapy that embraced the focus on power relationships between the client and the therapist as a model for self-determination. Feminist therapists were encouraged to negotiate goals together with their clients, to respect boundaries, to be transparent so the clients had choices, and to value the clients' knowledge of their own lives. Today, many of the principles of feminist therapy are considered good therapy techniques, but they were novel for much of the therapy community in the 1970s and 1980s as they were being developed by women and for women.

In 1981, a group of us who called ourselves "feminist therapists" founded the Advanced Feminist Therapy Institute that met each year to discuss and advance the topic. As there was almost no attention being paid to multicultural issues in addition to gender issues in the generic therapy theories in the mainstream of psychotherapy, we added the importance of race, culture, sexual orientation, and lesbian, gay, bisexual, transgender, and queer (LGBTQ) and gender-nonconforming issues, and those with disabilities to the feminist agenda. Working in close collaboration with other feminist research psychologists studying the impact of oppression on behavior and attempting to identify and overcome the impact of rigid sex-role socialization on women's mental health, the group continued its work over the years with new theorists and practitioners getting together and combining interests. Although the term "feminist" has been less widely used in the past decade or two, in fact the principles have always remained. Therapy today is less authoritarian; power in the therapy relationship has been curbed by ethical standards that regulate therapists' behavior (i.e., no sex between the client and the therapist or no multiple relationships that exploit the client or impair the therapist's judgment); multicultural awareness is mandated; and treatment goals are often required by third-party insurance payors.

One of the issues raised in feminist therapy was the confusion between victims of early trauma such as child abuse and later trauma reactions that looked like character changes seen in the diagnosis of borderline personality disorder (BPD). An important feature of BPD was the intense mood swings and affect toward people with whom they were in a relationship. One minute they thought a person was the greatest and the next minute, they developed equally intense feelings of anger and dislike. Both extreme feelings appeared to be out of proportion to whatever it was that the person did or did not do. However, in feminist therapy these feelings began to be attributed to the abuser or the person who failed to protect them in their early life, which made the intensity of the emotions more understandable.

Other issues often attributed to BPD were also commonly seen in survivors of severe abuse. Feminist therapists began to develop a category called "complex PTSD" to account for these various issues and have been trying to differentiate them from BPD for several reasons. First, BPD, like most personality disorders, is usually thought of as a disorder in which it is extremely difficult to help a client change his or her personality even with good motivation. Given the focus on the interpersonal relationship, those with true BPD are difficult clients as their intense mood swings and feelings often keep them from developing the type of relationship with the therapist that is needed for change. Even though those with complex trauma reactions also have intense feelings, once the trauma is identified and explored, those mood swings may become more manageable by the client. For example, the firm boundaries with clients diagnosed with BPD are more flexible with those diagnosed with complex trauma. This is due to feminist therapy's focus on power in the relationship rather than other issues. The goal in feminist therapy is always moving toward self-determination and empowerment by the client.

TRAUMA THERAPY

As described early in this chapter, the need for a treatment approach that dealt directly with trauma was noted early on in the development of psychotherapy. However, it was based mostly on situational traumas such as disasters, impact from combat during fighting wars, and child abuse. The trauma from rape and domestic violence was added later and today other traumatic situations such as victims of human trafficking have been added.

As it became more identified with healing from trauma, the interventions have dealt more with PTSD and complex PTSD and less with major depression and other mood disorders, perhaps because treatments for these disorders have already evidence-based practice guidelines. Some of the early pioneers in trauma-specific psychotherapy such as psychologists and psychiatrists Briere and Scott (2007), Christine Courtois (1999), Charles Figley (1995), Edna Foa et al. (1991), Steve Gold (2000), Judith Herman (1992), Bessel van der Kolk (2015), and Lenore Walker (1984) to name just a few began with treatment techniques and added theory later.

Trauma-informed services have a culture where all aspects of service delivery understand the prevalence of trauma, the impact of trauma, and the complex pathways to healing and recovery. Trauma-informed services specifically avoid retraumatizing both those who seek their services and those who are on the staff. They put safety first and commit to do no harm. To follow these principles, agencies and individuals offering trauma-informed treatment pay attention to safety issues, collaborate with the clients, are trustworthy, give clients choices, and focus on empowerment issues during treatment. Given the high numbers of people who have experienced trauma at some time during their lives, many agencies are offering trauma-informed services even if they are not directly dealing with healing from the trauma specifically. Harris and Follet (2001) provide guidance for agencies that are interested and willing to change their culture so that trauma victims are more likely to get their mental health needs met there.

Trauma-specific services address the trauma and its impact directly in order to facilitate recovery. Usually trauma-specific services address PTSD and its subcategories as well as other consequences of trauma. Trauma-specific services also deal with the complexities of intersecting problems such as substance abuse, serious mental health problems, social problems, and client contact with the legal system. Mental health practitioners who practice trauma-specific therapy are expected to be experts in understanding different types of trauma and their effects.

Trauma-specific treatment, which continues to evolve as evidenced by the constant changes in the criteria needed for diagnosis of PTSD, suggests that anyone can be exposed to a traumatic event that stresses and overwhelms the person's capacity to deal effectively with that event. Sometimes the event can be incorporated into the person's development, but more often it is necessary to provide some psychotherapy to assist in the healing. And the newest addition to trauma treatment is going beyond healing to rebuilding resilience and well-being, as discussed later in this chapter.

There are now four groups of criteria in the *DSM-5* (American Psychiatric Association, 2013) that need to be met for the formal diagnosis of PTSD and three additional criteria from our research that are met when someone has BWS, which is considered a subcategory of PTSD. This is further discussed in Chapter 3 but bears repeating here as I discuss the evaluation and treatment strategies in this chapter. They are:

1. Intrusive reexperiencing of the trauma
2. High levels of hyperarousal and anxiety
3. Avoidance behaviors, depression, and dissociation
4. Cognitive difficulties including negativity, attention, and concentration
5. Interpersonal disruption from isolation and coercive control by batterer
6. Health issues and body image problems
7. Sexual dysfunction and sexual satisfaction issues

These criteria can be simplified into the "fight or flight" paradigm that occurs when someone is afraid. Studies demonstrate how the person's body and mind prepare to fight using the biochemicals that are discharged by the autonomic nervous system, the body's survival system that protects the person from harm. If the danger remains after being noted, then the person may attempt to flee the situation physically. If physical escape is not possible, then psychological escape occurs. This includes behaviors that can be measured by psychologists such as anxiety, hypervigilance, exaggerated startle response, deficits in attention and cognition, depression, repression, minimization, denial, and dissociation.

Specific standardized tests assess for these reactions to trauma so that one person's responses can be compared to those on whom the tests were standardized. While these tests can measure the amount of trauma, they cannot tell what the type of trauma was that was experienced nor how many different traumatic events may be in the person's past. For that, a good clinical history is needed. If the person's ability to think and make good judgments also needs to be measured, standardized cognitive tests can be used and other standardized tests are available to assess a person's emotions and personality.

EVALUATION FOR BWS

Battered women seek psychological services for a variety of reasons—usually to provide some assistance in coping with a particularly difficult life situation. Sometimes a woman will seek out services because of the violence itself, while other times another reason gets her there. Problems with the courts, substance addiction, psychophysiological pain complaints and health issues, and school problems of children are frequent indirect reasons for seeking out someone, usually a therapist, with whom to speak. Pleading by family, friends, lawyers, shelter staff, and her own determination to stop the abuse are the usual direct reasons. Whatever brings her to a therapist's office, it is predictable that her basic lack of trust will pull her out if certain measures are not taken to convince her that the therapist will be helpful (Moore & Pepitone-Rockwell, 1979; Walker, 1994). Several assumptions made by the therapist work well to establish rapport and create the atmosphere she needs to be able to confide her story.

The first one is to believe a woman when she claims to be battered. It is rare that a woman would make up such ghastly stories, and if it should happen, inconsistencies during the interview will alert the clinician's suspicions. Many of the new strategies for detecting malingering and deception have not been normed on a population of battered women, who may have self-interest in claiming to be battered when they are not, but also may be telling as much of the truth as they can, given their long history of lying and manipulating to cover up for the abusers when they believed they could be hurt more if they exposed them and did not follow their orders. In performing an evaluation, it is always necessary to remember that what appears to be pathology in a nonabused woman may well be a coping or survival strategy for a battered woman. Whether or not she can drop that behavior when it is no longer necessary for her safety is the best test of how embedded it is in her personality structure. Obviously, this will necessitate a period of time, usually 6 months to 1 year, of her being free from violence and abuse.

History Gathering

It is suggested that at least 2 hours be allowed for the initial interview with a potential client. A longer time may be necessary if the woman appears to be in crisis. The first hour is usually spent taking a brief history and building trust. If successful, then the battered woman will begin to detail the abuse in the second hour. When I do an evaluation with someone who has not yet taken any steps to terminate the relationship, she and I explore how she might do so safely, examining the trouble spots carefully. I offer to develop a safety plan with her and listen for information in her recitation that will be helpful to do so. Active listening without giving interpretations of behavior can help validate the woman's experiences and reassure that you will not label her "crazy" as both she and her partner have feared. I also label her as a battered woman at some point in the interview so that she has a name for the symptoms she is experiencing. In addition, I give her information about BWS and PTSD, helping her understand that a normal person may be expected to respond with the PTSD and BWS symptoms in order to cope with the stressful situation. While it may initially frighten some women to be labeled as "battered," it also gives them a justification and explanation for the changes they know they have experienced in cognition, emotions, and behavior. It also gives them hope that they can be helped to feel like themselves again.

Risk Assessment in Crisis Situations

In evaluating the risk of further danger, it is most important to learn the frequency and severity of the violence both at present and in the past. There are various checklists that can be of assistance in gathering the risk of further violence in a systematic way discussed in Chapter 12 as well as with a comprehensive checklist by Daniel Sonkin (1995) and warnings about stalking by Walker and Meloy (1998). Estimating the rapidity of the violence escalation can be done by using data gathered about the first acute battering incident, a typical one, one of the worst, and the final incident, similar to what we did in this research study. This four-incident method was developed during the research project and has stood the test of time. Since many women minimize violent acts and injuries, it is important to ask specific questions about them. Inquiries are made into threats to kill, available weapons, choking and other life-threatening acts, violence potential toward others, and specific examples of psychological abuse.

While physical abuse is easy to recognize, it is often difficult for therapists to ask for specific details. Figley (1995) and Perlman and Saakvitne (1995) describe the potential effects of trauma on those who provide assistance to trauma victims where it is not unusual to develop secondary posttraumatic stress symptoms themselves. The American Psychological Association (1996) Presidential Task Force on Violence and the Family suggested that it is common for professionals who hear repeated stories of the violence to skip the details either because they felt that recounting them would be too difficult emotionally for the victim or they were unable to hear it again. Becoming too compassionate or too emotionally distant from the victim will impede the ability to be genuine and authentic in therapy and may suggest the need for a referral or consultation before proceeding. Stark's redefinition of batterers' power and control needs as coercive control behaviors may make it easier to gather information about psychological abuse to which women are subjected. It is necessary to clarify what is culturally relevant to women in a partnered relationship and what is considered coercive controlling behaviors.

Trauma theory makes it clear that it is important for victims to repeatedly talk about their experiences so that they can gain mastery over the emotions raised and learn new cognitive schemas that give the trauma a different meaning (Foa et al., 1991; Kolodny, 1998) than the initial distortions that sometimes come from retrospective guilt and memory errors. Some interventions, such as eye movement desensitization and reprocessing (EMDR; Shapiro & Forrest, 1997), are more oriented around preverbal memories and therefore, emotional responses are dealt with differently. Some of these issues are further discussed in the following sections. If the woman currently is separated from her partner, it is important to learn how frequent their contact is and what kinds of conflicts occur when they do have contact. Escalation around access to the children is an important sign of increasing danger to both the woman and the children (Sonkin,

1995; Walker & Meloy, 1998). The woman's perception of the level of the man's anger at any particular time is also important as she usually is the best judge (Walker, 1994).

Preparation for Psychotherapy

It is crucial for the woman to understand that the purpose of psychotherapy, should she decide to pursue it after the evaluation is completed, is to help her grow and regain her emotional strength and sense of self in a violence-free environment, not to terminate the relationship. At some point, she may decide that the only way for her to continue to grow is to leave the battering relationship. This is important because many batterers attempt to intrude on the therapy to make sure the treatment will not be antithetical to their interests in keeping the relationship the same. When a batterer questions the woman, which most report that the man inevitably does if he knows she is in treatment, then she can honestly report that "my therapist is not interested in whether or not we stay together, just in my staying violence-free and safe." This also minimizes any power struggles that may result from the initial phase of therapy and permits the woman to begin to develop trust in the therapeutic relationship. This may change once the woman starts to feel stronger and more assertive in the relationship and the woman must be prepared for the possibility that the batterer will react negatively to her growing strength. It is difficult for a batterer to accept any independent actions from the woman, particularly if he is dependent on her and feels anxious that she will not be there for him. Such reactions often result in a greater amount of power and control through coercion and psychological means first, and then physical abuse should he perceive that he is losing control over her.

In highly lethal situations, the clinician has a responsibility to share perceptions of danger with the woman and others, where appropriate. It is important to be honest that good therapy will help her be stronger and safer, but not always out of the way of the batterer's harm. If the batterer is in treatment and the woman is willing to give permission, it may be helpful to have some communication with his treating therapist. However, this must be done carefully so that it does not interfere with her trust of the therapist's total allegiance to her. A battered woman, like other trauma victims, does not have the ability to perceive neutrality or even objectivity. Either someone is totally on her side, or that person is perceived as being against her. Yet, at the same time, therapists cannot condemn the batterer himself or it may be seen as another power struggle for the woman. Rather, it is important to inform the woman that the battering behavior is unacceptable without passing judgment on the man himself. Examples of how to do this can be seen in training video demonstrations (Walker, 1994, 1998).

Safety Plans

Understanding the ability of a domestic violence situation to quickly escalate into a lethal incident, most health and mental health workers understand the need for crisis intervention and safety plans to be implemented before any treatment begins. It is important to begin any crisis intervention or safety plans with a good evaluation of the woman to determine if she has developed BWS or any other type of health or mental health injuries from the domestic violence. A standard clinical evaluation encompassing a mental status examination and information about the woman's history is first important to gather relevant information in order to individualize the safety plans if there is time. Otherwise, crisis intervention techniques designed to stabilize the woman must be implemented immediately.

During this first interview, I encourage a woman still living in the relationship to devise an escape plan for when the violence escalates. First, she identifies the cues she perceives as a signal for an impending battering incident. Most battered women can do this even though initially they may have difficulty verbalizing such cues. Sometimes the first cue is their own physiologically perceived anxiety—other times, it is a change in the man's facial expressions, particularly his eyes that are described as "getting darker," "no eye contact," "looking like nobody is home," and other recognizable patterns being repeated.

Then, we discuss a plan of escape including specifying strategies that must be preplanned to execute it. For example, one strategy is to locate the nearest telephone, either her personal cell phone or an additional throw-away cell phone that he cannot listen in on, or leave if possible and go to a nearby store or a neighbor's home. Other strategies are to make extra keys to the car and house and hide them, leave a change of clothes for self and the children with a neighbor, create a personal bank account or make arrangements for other access to cash, alert children to a danger signal so they know what to do if they get scared, and so on.

Finally, we rehearse the plan of escape, step by step, both orally and in writing, sometimes drawing a map, in order to estimate how much time it will take for various activities such as dressing the baby in the wintertime. We encourage women to take their children with them if they leave as the courts will not look kindly on them for leaving them with a violent dad even if they think the dad will not harm them. As we discuss in Chapter 19, the family court system does not look kindly on women, especially battered women who lose control of protecting their children when dads fight for custody.

The goal is to make safety planning an automatic and familiar response in crisis, in much the same way of routine fire drills when she went to school. It makes the therapist less anxious and frightened for the client's safety and gives the woman some hope of really being able to escape. It is important to remember that most women who have developed learned helplessness, as described in Chapter 4, have traded escape strategies for coping strategies and are unable to think that escape is even possible during a crisis. Even if this woman does return after the crisis passes, she has learned an important escape plan that may save her life next time the violence begins.

HEALTH CONCERNS

The separation of health needs from mental health needs is an artificial division that is not useful when providing treatment, especially in domestic violence cases. Continued stressors take a toll on the body as well as the mind. Therefore, it is not surprising that so many women who have been victims of men's violence develop physical illnesses including chronic pain. Studies of those women who seek out services in pain clinics indicate large percentages of them have experienced physical or sexual abuse as children or adults. Back pain, migraine headaches, and gastrointestinal and gynecological problems are common in women having experienced intimate partner violence. Some of the battered women's more common health needs are described in Chapter 13.

Interestingly, in some cultures, PTSD symptoms are largely experienced as physical symptoms such as in the Arab American community where both women and men displayed such symptoms while obsessively watching the U.S. war against Iraq on television. Studies of Cambodian women who moved to the United States after the war indicated a large number of cases of idiopathic blindness, as if their psyches were telling them that they had seen enough destruction. Other studies of torture victims, who also have experienced intimate partner and child abuse, have similar physiological and psychological findings associated with PTSD. Therefore, health and mental health professionals must encourage patients to seek out other services and permit all health service providers to communicate with each other.

PTSD AND BIOCHEMICAL CHANGES

It is not surprising that those who develop PTSD have measurable changes in the secretion of biochemicals, especially those that facilitate the nervous system. Research by Boston psychiatrist Bessel van der Kolk (1994, 2015) first demonstrated that physical injuries were remembered by the cells at the site as well as by the brain. His findings supported the memories that some women had of being abused even before they had the words to describe it. For some women, they may not demonstrate any PTSD symptoms from domestic violence for many years until they experience another trauma when all the symptoms appear. This sometimes happens when battered women are in car accidents and cannot heal from seemingly minor injuries. Or, in some cases, the years of being shaken vigorously by the shoulders, hair pulling, choking, and head banging finally produce debilitating neurological damage that appears to be far more widespread than would have been expected from a minor injury, which may have triggered the full response.

Studies by Israeli psychiatrist Arieh Shalev (2002) were some of the first to identify the variable course of PTSD together with the brain chemistry. The major changes occur along the hypothalamic–pituitary–adrenal axis in the subcortical areas of the brain that regulate our emotions. They cause the neurotransmitters and receptors that regulate the nerve impulses to change how they function in order to adapt to the high-stress situation caused by trauma. This extremely complex system is just now beginning to be understood as we are better able to measure the minute amounts of biochemicals and hormones released at different stages. The major changes in the autonomic nervous system involve elevations in adrenalin and noradrenalin that regulate our major life functions such as heart rate, blood pressure, breathing, increased glucocorticoids that are regulated by amounts of cortisol signaled by the cortisol-releasing factor (CRF), and increased amounts of endorphins that counteract physical pain from injuries. In addition, the major neurotransmitters that regulate our emotions are also impacted with dopamine being increased and serotonin being lowered. Together, these changes keep us hyperalert and focused on the crisis precipitated by the trauma while being able to ignore other parts of our lives to which we normally pay attention.

Research shows that reexperiencing the trauma memories after the incident may be the single most detrimental factor in producing severe PTSD responses. If intervention takes place within 4 to 12 weeks, it is possible to lessen the effects. Since during the first 4 weeks after a trauma normal acute stress reactions are expected, it is difficult to know who might be at high risk for more severe PTSD symptoms. Genetics, other mental health conditions, and the environment all can play a role in the severity of the PTSD response in addition to the characteristics of the trauma itself. The more destabilizing the response to the acute trauma, including agitation and nervous behavior, high levels of anxiety, sleep disturbances, aggression, and confused thinking, the greater the severity. Southwick and Charney's (2012) studies are most interesting as they used women victims of sexual and physical assault in their studies at Mt. Sinai Hospital in New York City and Yale University in Connecticut and then compared them with others who had experienced torture and imprisonment during war. Not surprisingly, they mostly fared the same.

MEDICATION FOR PTSD

Both medication and psychotherapy are useful in lessening or even eliminating the PTSD responses after trauma. The medication of choice would be *antiadrenergic agents* such as propranolol, guanfacine, and clonidine or *benzodiazepines* such as Xanax, Valium, or Ativan. For severe reactions it is possible to use antipsychotic medications such as Thorazine or injectable Haldol or some atypical agents that have fewer side effects such as Risperdal for impulsive aggression. For insomnia, it is possible to use tricyclics such as low doses of trazodone or nefazodone and for panic attacks low doses of amitriptyline. Interestingly, although SSRIs such as Prozac, Zoloft, and Lexapro are often prescribed as first-line psychotropic medications for depression, studies show that during the first 4 to 12 weeks they have little or no effect on PTSD symptoms. This is not surprising since it often takes 4 to 6 weeks for them to start working, which is too late for treating early stage PTSD. However, they do show promising results later on in treatment of some PTSD symptoms.

Benzodiazepines are often used first as they are fast acting to calm down the arousal system, help with insomnia, and have few side effects. However, the major problem is that they are dangerous especially when taken together with alcohol and they are addictive, meaning that the more they are used, the more they will have to be taken to achieve the same effect. Most health professionals prescribe them in low doses and give only a few pills at a time, especially if someone is impulsive or suicidal.

Antiadrenergic agents modulate both physical and cognitive symptoms of PTSD, control hyperarousal and intrusive memories, lower blood pressure, and reduce irritability and aggressive responses. There are some data looking at their use with alcohol and other drug users but there is little research for their use with PTSD in general. They are counterindicated for those with diabetes, high blood pressure, and heart problems and may lower blood pressure too much with inconsistent dosing. It is important to be careful of other medication combinations when these agents are prescribed and their discontinuance must be carefully moderated. Nonetheless, there is research to suggest that they may modulate CRF, which controls the levels of cortisol, implicated in chronic PTSD responses. In one study, researchers found that repeat trauma victims have lower resting cortisol levels, but when stimulated by another stressor, the cortisol levels rise way higher than normal. This study demonstrates the complexity of just one biochemical reaction to chronic stress, so imagine the complexity when several different neurotransmitters, hormones, and catalysts are involved in the response to repeated cycles of domestic violence.

Anticonvulsant agents are often used for seizure control and more recently for mood control in bipolar disorders. They have also been used as an additive for refractory PTSD. In addition to being a mood stabilizer, they often modulate the glutamatergic transmission in the hippocampus and other regions in the midbrain structures controlling emotions. Memory for emotional events gets stored in the hippocampus and only when processed verbally does it move into the cognitive memory regions in the cortex of the brain. This is what makes verbal trauma therapy so helpful in separating emotions from the events and restoring the less emotional memories in the cognitive memory center. These medications can take several days to weeks to take effect and they also have side effects that include possible liver toxicity as they are metabolized there, so blood serum levels must be checked at 3- to 4-month intervals. However, they have been found effective in those with PTSD from car accidents, child abuse, and combat veterans.

EVIDENCE-BASED TRAUMA TREATMENT

Within the past 10 years, the rise of evidence-based trauma treatment has flooded the treatment models often used by funding agencies. In order to get a program to be considered evidence based it is important to obtain data that support the claims that the treatment really does work in helping people heal from trauma or whatever the issues are that bring the person into treatment. Conducting this type of research is difficult outside of the university and especially for those seeing clients individually in independent practice. As described in Chapter 17, we have been able to measure the Survivor Therapy Empowerment Program (STEP) to demonstrate evidence-based validation. But, many evidence-based treatment protocols deal only with a few of the treatment goals and rarely is it possible to accurately measure the efficacy of treatment in dealing with all the intersecting problems that clients bring into the therapy sessions.

Research into the efficacy of psychotherapy over the years has found that the most important factor is the relationship that occurs between the client and the therapist (Duncan et al., 2009; Meichenbaum, 2013; Norcross, 2009; Yalom, 2002). If the relationship is not present, then all the skills taught or symptom-reduction methodology used will be less successful. This is especially important in trauma treatment for battered women as they come into therapy with significant damage to their ability to trust that someone will not harm them. Remember, the men who treat them lovingly at some times also are the ones who hurt them at other times, usually unpredictable times for most women. Part of the therapy is to help the women learn how to predict the cycle of violence that they experience with their partner.

Meichenbaum (2013) reviewed some of the most successful trauma therapies and suggested that to build that therapeutic relationship for trauma survivors and change their behavior, it is important that psychotherapists engage in a number of actions:

1. Assess for the survivors' safety (conduct risk assessment) and ensure that basic patient needs are being met.
2. Educate the survivor about the nature and impact of trauma, PTSD, and accompanying adjustment difficulties and discuss the nature of treatment with a caring attitude.
3. Conduct assessments of the victims/survivors' presenting problems, as well as their strengths. What have the victims/survivors done to "survive" and "cope?"
4. Solicit the survivor's implicit theory about his or her presenting problems and his or her implicit theory of change. The therapist provides a cogent rationale for the treatment approach and assesses the survivor's understanding. Make the therapy process visible and transparent for the patient.
5. Alter treatment in a sensitive fashion, being responsive to cultural, developmental, and gender differences.
6. Nurture "hope" by engaging in collaborative goal setting, highlighting evidence of patient, family, cultural, and community resilience.
7. Teach intra- and interpersonal coping skills and build into such training efforts the ingredients needed to increase the likelihood of generalization and maintenance of the treatment effects.
8. Provide interventions that result in symptom relief and address the impact of comorbid disorders.
9. Encourage, challenge, cajole survivors who have been avoidant to reexperience, reexpose themselves to trauma reminders, cues, situations, and memories.
10. Teach survivors a variety of direct-action problem-solving and emotionally palliative coping skills (e.g., mindfulness activities) to the point of mastery, addressing issues of treatment nonadherence throughout.
11. Help survivors reduce the likelihood of revictimization.
12. Finally, engage survivors in developing "healing stories." (Meichenbaum, 2013, pp. 4–5, www.melissainstitute.com)

Most of the therapy techniques reviewed in the following sections do not stress the relationship between the client and the therapist although they do have many techniques that can be used to help the woman heal from the trauma symptoms. In Chapter 17, where the STEP is described, there is an emphasis on relationships while also providing information and teaching new skills. Some of the information and skills in STEP are similar to what these programs also provide.

Cognitive Behavioral Therapy (CBT)

CBT is one of the most popular psychotherapy methods used today for treatment of many different kinds of mental health issues. Based on conditioning theory, it posits that behavior can be changed by pairing a positive stimulus together with unpleasant thoughts that will change people's cognitions, which then will change how people feel about something and their behavior. It is easy to measure behavior or cognitive change in the laboratory, so many therapy theories used today that are considered "evidence based" are based on cognitive and behavioral theories. CBT is commonly used to help people eliminate the anxiety, fear, and avoidance responses from PTSD.

Twelve sessions of cognitive psychotherapy that helped people change unproductive thought patterns including stopping their ruminating about the trauma were most helpful within 4 weeks after the traumatic incident in the Shalev studies (2002). CBT that helped desensitize women's reactions to traumatic memories also worked well in relieving major PTSD symptoms. Although antidepressants did not work as well as psychotherapy during this initial phase of treatment, they may be more useful with modulating PTSD symptoms later on in combination with other medications and psychotherapy.

One of the criticisms of CBT is that the relationship between the client and the therapist is not seen as particularly important; rather, it is the elimination of undesired symptoms that is the focus. However, most trauma survivors, especially those who survive gender violence such as rape, sexual assault, harassment and exploitation, and intimate partner violence, also need to focus on relationship issues.

Trauma-Focused Cognitive Behavioral Therapy (TF-CBT)

TF-CBT is a CBT-based treatment that includes the relationship issues that are derived from experiencing trauma. Like the other CBT-based treatment techniques, there is a manualized approach to the sessions to assist in the repair of the client's relationship issues.

Prolonged Exposure Therapy (PE)

PE is a type of CBT where repeated reliving of the trauma facilitates the processing of the trauma. Clients realize that (a) reexperiencing the trauma in a safe situation reminds them that the trauma is no longer dangerous, (b) remembering the trauma is equivalent to experiencing it again, (c) anxiety does not remain indefinitely in the presence of feared situations or memories but decreases even without avoidance or escape, (d) experiencing PTSD symptoms does not lead to a loss of control.

Foa et al. (1991) suggest that traumas are usually relived with emotions, details of the event, and thoughts associated with the event. Over time the frequency and intensity of the emotional reexperiencing will decrease. However, there are often erroneous stimulus–stimulus and stimulus–response associations as well as mistaken evaluations that can be corrected by PE. The correction requires the activation of the fear structure via the introduction of the feared stimuli and the presentation of corrective information that is incompatible with the pathological elements of the fear structure.

PE treatment includes education about common reactions to trauma, breathing retraining (although similar to Briere's relaxation training, Foa teaches a special kind of breathing technique), repeated in vivo or real-life exposure to nondangerous situations that are avoided due to trauma-related fear, and imaginal exposure to trauma. The treatment is usually for 9 weeks although it can be extended for an additional 3 weeks. Research has found that beyond 12 weeks, the treatment will probably not be effective.

Briere's Trauma Triggers

Briere and Scott (2007) have developed a program that assists the therapist in helping the client recognize what her *trauma triggers* are and then reducing their emotional impact using cognitive behavioral techniques such as desensitization by building approximate hierarchies until the trigger effect is extinguished. It is important to make sure that the woman is not in a fragile emotional state when doing this work so some of this therapy is a slow reempowerment of her emotional strength and stability although it is not so described. Unlike Foa's PE, Briere has the therapist build the hierarchy for desensitization based on the client's reexperiencing of the trauma effects together with the therapist. The hierarchy may change based on trial and error. Relaxation training can be elicited using breathing techniques, imaging, or deep muscle relaxation; it does not matter which is used for the treatment to be effective. The identification of the trauma triggers is most important so as to produce the more accurate nonfeared response.

Linehan's Dialectical Behavior Therapy (DBT)

Marsha Linehan has developed the DBT approach originally to be used with those who were diagnosed with BPD and now used with trauma survivors especially those who have complex trauma. There are several modules to the treatment approach, each one being able to be used as appropriate with a client. One of the most successful modules that has been used as part of a number of other mainstream therapies is called "mindfulness." Here the client is trained to focus on the present and not dwell on the past or future. Most people require training in this type of focus as it is common for everyone, whether a trauma survivor or not, to worry about other things and not fully experience each moment. This is especially helpful for trauma survivors to teach themselves to stop worrying about things they cannot control and learn to live within the "new normal" for them.

Trauma-Focused Feminist Therapy

The application of feminist therapy for those who have experienced men's violence has been one of the most successful forms of treatment in helping women heal from abuse. The goal of feminist therapy is to empower or reempower women to take back control of their lives. An essential feature is the egalitarian relationship between the therapist and the client. Each brings certain skills to the relationship that are respected and the power between the two parties is carefully monitored by both but especially the therapist to make sure the woman is no longer coerced into doing things in her life. This requires what is termed "cognitive clarity" or the ability to think clearly and make appropriate decisions based on information available. Learning how to lower anxiety levels when they get high will reduce some of the paralysis that battered women often describe as a residual from BWS. At each step along the way, the woman and the therapist decide together what is needed next. Most important is helping the woman learn to break the psychological hold the batterer has had on her, overcoming her dependency on him to make decisions for her, and moving on with her life. This will require overcoming any isolation that has occurred during the relationship and for some women, dealing with an associated depression.

Although it is possible to enter into this type of therapy while still living together with the batterer, unless he has stopped his physical abuse and no longer needs to use his power and control over her, feminist therapy could cause further battering incidents as the woman gets stronger. Video reenactments of feminist therapy are available from various publishers to assist in learning the treatment approach.

Eye Movement Desensitization and Reprocessing

Discovered by Francine Shapiro, trauma memories that are so frightening to the woman may be dealt with using EMDR that may erase the emotional connection to the memories using bright lights or other techniques used to reprocess the brain. EMDR is usually used as an adjunct to trauma-specific psychotherapy rather than as a treatment by itself, although sometimes clients go to an EMDR-trained therapist while also in treatment elsewhere.

SPECIAL ISSUES IN TRAUMA TREATMENT

Concurrent Mental Illnesses With PTSD

There are other diagnoses that are often seen together with PTSD depending on the trauma experienced. One of the most common is *traumatic brain injury (TBI)* from injuries to the head. In domestic violence, this often occurs when the batterer punches the woman in the head or slams her head against other objects. In some women, who are held by their shoulders and shaken, there is a form of shaken-baby syndrome that impacts the brain and causes difficulties as she ages or if she is in another type of accident.

Mood Disorders

Major depressive disorder (MDD) is a mood disorder that is often seen in families where the biochemicals that facilitate the nervous system responses are impacted. MDD usually has episodes, sometimes triggered by an external event that may stop on its own even without treatment. However, each new episode is often more severe and lasts longer than the previous one. The time in between episodes may be shortened also. The most effective treatment is a combination of medication and psychotherapy.

   Dysthymic disorder is a low-grade chronic depression that some clients have where they feel the same depression symptoms at least some part of each day.

   Bipolar disorder is a mood disorder that includes both depression and manic states that often alternate with each other. Battered women with bipolar disorder may be difficult to treat as their own behavior during the manic phases can be dangerous. The batterers' responses to the woman's behavior as well as legal consequences to her behavior may cause even further problems. Bipolar disorder is treated with medication such as antidepressants and mood stabilizers as well as psychotherapy. Some people can switch from MDD to bipolar disorder when the medication triggers a manic episode so it is important to regulate the medication. Mood stabilizers can adversely affect the kidney so it is important to have regular blood tests.

   Dissociation identity disorder (DID) is a more serious form of dissociation that often occurs when someone has been severely beaten and abused as a child. It needs specific treatment in order to help heal the dissociative connections. It often is not recognized in children so treatment is delayed until adulthood. Treatment is often long term and clients need lots of support going through the healing process.

Substance Abuse Treatment

A large number of trauma survivors turn to substances for relief and then become addicted to them. Thus, special substance abuse treatment is necessary to help them learn to substitute other ways of managing their symptoms. Some clients will need residential treatment if their abuse of substances has been for a long time or if they are addicted to multiple substances. Like these other areas mentioned, it is best to have specialists involved in this treatment.

REBUILDING RESILIENCE AND WELL-BEING

As described in Chapter 14, the goal of healing from PTSD is not just a reduction of symptoms but a return to the feelings of well-being and mastery of one's own life again. Resilience to new crises and traumas is often compromised in those who have experienced PTSD. While the term has previously been used in rehabilitation psychology, and adopted in Seligman's new positive psychology paradigms, according to my friend and colleague at Nova Southeastern University's College of Psychology, psychologist Barry Nierenberg, it is important to make sure the client has developed *resilience* as a part of treatment termination.

Meichenbaum (2014) has developed a resilience checklist to help assess the components of resilience-bolstering behaviors including physical fitness, interpersonal relationships, positive emotions, cognitive flexibility, behavioral "can-do" attitude, and maintaining hope and spiritual fitness. The goal is to emphasize the positive coping strategies that individuals have developed and build upon these strengths. Reviewing their experiences with a new narrative that looks at the positive learning that has occurred and helping the individual see how those strengths can be used to create new goals that are attainable is an important area in building resilience.

Meichenbaum (2015a, 2015b) suggests survivors of sex trafficking develop SMART (specific, measurable, attainable, relevant, and timely) goals often using therapists and others to help them do so. These techniques can be used when working with battered women also, especially those who have been sexually abused. However, it is best not to introduce them too early in treatment because it can be misinterpreted as blaming the woman for the abuse rather than simply giving her new skills to make better decisions. Using some of the CBT techniques that help identify automatic thoughts and feelings, identification of triggers, and replaying old tapes can assist in building new life scripts and goals. Finally, moving toward generalizing the new thoughts and feelings with relapse prevention techniques in place can continue the progress toward well-being.

SUMMARY

Although not all battered women need psychotherapy or medication to heal from the abuse they experienced, those who do should be able to obtain appropriate and effective treatment. At present, the two therapy systems that have been found to be effective are feminist therapy and trauma therapy. These interventions can be applied in individual or group settings with or without medication or other adjunctive treatment such as EMDR. The STEP discussed elsewhere in this book is based on a combination of feminist and trauma treatment theory. Mental health treatment can take place in a variety of settings including battered woman shelters, community mental health centers or clinics, hospitals or jails, and prisons. Most important is the ability to strengthen the woman so she can get on with her life.

REFERENCES

American Psychiatric Association. (1980). *Diagnostic and statistical manual of mental disorders* (3rd ed.). Washington, DC: Author.

American Psychiatric Association. (2013). *Diagnostic and statistical manual of mental disorders* (5th ed.). Arlington, VA: American Psychiatric Publishing.

American Psychological Association. (1996). *Report from the Presidential Task Force on Violence and the Family.* Washington, DC: Author.

Briere, J. N., & Scott, C. (2007). *Principles of trauma therapy: A guide to symptoms, evaluation, and treatment.* Thousand Oaks, CA: Sage.

Brown, L. S. (1992). The feminist critique of personality disorders. In L. S. Brown & M. Ballou (Eds.), *Personality and psychopathology: Feminist reappraisals.* New York, NY: Guilford Press.

Brown, L. S. (1994). *Subversive dialogues: Theory in feminist therapy.* New York, NY: Basic Books.

Brown, L. S. (2013). *Feminist therapy.* Washington, DC: American Psychological Association.

Burgess, A. W., Baker, T., Greening, D., Hartman, C. R., Burgess, A. G., Douglas, J. E., & Halloran, R. (1997). Stalking behaviors within domestic violence. *Journal of Family Violence, 12,* 389–403.

Burgess, A. W., & Holmstrom, L. L. (1974). Rape trauma syndrome. *American Journal of Psychiatry, 131,* 981–986.

Chesler, P. (1972). *Women and madness.* Garden City, NY: Doubleday.

Courtois, C. A. (1999). *Recollections of sexual abuse: Treatment principles and guidelines.* New York, NY: W. W. Norton.

Duncan, B. L., Miller, S. D., Wampold, B. E., & Hubble, M. A. (Eds.). (2009). *The heart and soul of change: Delivering what works in therapy* (2nd ed.). Washington, DC: American Psychological Association.

Figley, C. R. (1995). *Compassion fatigue: Coping with secondary traumatic stress disorder in those who treat the traumatized.* Philadelphia, PA: Brunner/Mazel.

Foa, E. B., Rothbaum, B. O., Riggs, D. S., & Murdock, T. B. (1991). Treatment of post-traumatic stress disorder in rape victims: A comparison between cognitive-behavioral procedures and counseling. *Journal of Consulting and Clinical Psychology, 59,* 715–723.

Gold, S. N. (2000). *Not trauma alone: Therapy for child abuse survivors in family and social context.* Philadelphia, PA: Brunner-Routledge.

Herman, J. L. (1992). *Trauma and recovery.* New York, NY: Basic Books.

Harris, M., & Fallot, R. (Eds.). (2001). *Using trauma theory to design service systems: New directions for mental health services.* San Francisco, CA: Jossey-Bass.

Janoff-Bulman, R. (1985). The aftermath of victimization: Rebuilding shattered assumptions. In C. Figley (Ed.), *Trauma and its wake* (pp. 15–35). New York, NY: Brunner/Mazel.

Keane, T. M., Marshall, A. D., & Taft, C. T. (2006). Posttraumatic stress disorder: Etiology, epidemiology, and treatment outcome. *Annual Review of Clinical Psychology, 2,* 161–197.

Kolodny, E. S. (1998). Cognitive therapy for trauma-related guilt. In V. M. Follette, J. I. Ruzek, & F. R. Abueg (Eds.), *Cognitive-behavioral therapies for trauma* (pp. 124–161). New York, NY: Guilford Press.

Meichenbaum, D. (2013). *Roadmap to resilience.* Clearwater, FL: Institute Press.

Meichenbaum, D. (2014). Ways to bolster resilience in traumatized clients: Implications for psychotherapists. *Journal of Constructivist Psychology, 27*(4), 329–336.

Meichenbaum, D. (2015a, May). *Ways to bolster resilience in LGBTQ youth (lesbian, gay, bisexual, transgendered, questioning).* Paper presented at the Nineteenth Annual Conference Melissa Institute for Violence Prevention, Miami, Florida.

Meichenbaum, D. (2015b, May). *Approaches to bolster resilience in victims of human trafficking: Core tasks of interventions.* Presented at the 19th Annual Conference of the Melissa Institute for Violence Prevention and Treatment, Coral Gables, Florida.

Moore, D. M., & Pepitone-Rockwell, F. (1979). Experiences with and views about battering. In D. M. Moore (Ed.), *Battered women* (pp. 119–143). Beverly Hills, CA: Sage.

Norcross, J. (2009). The therapeutic relationship. In B. L. Duncan, S. D. Miller, B. E. Wampold, & M. A. Hubble (Eds.). *The heart and soul of change: Delivering what works in therapy* (2nd ed., pp. 113–142). Washington, DC: American Psychological Association.

Perlman, L. A., & Saakvitne, K. (1995). *Trauma and the therapist: Countertransference and vicarious traumatization in psychotherapy with incest survivors.* New York, NY: W. W. Norton.

Shalev, A. (2002, December). *From fear and horror to PTSD: What determines the longitudinal course of early PTSD responses.* Presentation at Trauma, Culture and the Brain, Los Angeles, CA.

Shapiro, F., & Forrest, M. (1997). *EMDR, the breakthrough therapy for overcoming anxiety, stress and trauma.* New York, NY: Basic Books.

Sonkin, D. J. (1995). *Counselor's guide to learning to live without violence.* Volcano, CA: Volcano Press.

Southwick, S. M., & Charney, D. S. (2012). *Resilience: The science of mastering life's greatest challenges.* New York, NY: Cambridge University Press.

van der Kolk, B. (1994). The body keeps score: Memory and the evolving psycho-biology of posttraumatic stress. *Harvard Review of Psychiatry, 1,* 253–265.

van der Kolk, B. (2015). *The body keeps the score: Brain, mind, and body in the healing of trauma.* New York, NY: Penguin Books.

Walker, L. E. (Ed.). (1984). *Women and mental health policy.* Beverly Hills, CA: Sage.

Walker, L. E. A. (1994). *Abused women and survivor therapy: A practical guide for the psychotherapist.* Washington, DC: American Psychological Association.

Walker, L. E. A. (1998). *Feminist therapy: Psychotherapy with the experts video series.* Needham Heights, MA: Allyn & Bacon.

Walker, L. E. A., & Meloy, J. R. (1998). Stalking and domestic violence. In J. R. Meloy (Ed.), *The psychology of stalking: Clinical and forensic perspectives.* San Diego, CA: Academic Press.

Wilson, J. P., Smith, W. K., & Johnson, S. K. (1985). A comparative analysis of PTSD among various survivor groups. In C. R. Figley (Ed.), *Trauma and its wake: The study and treatment of post-traumatic stress disorder* (pp. 142–172). New York, NY: Brunner/Mazel.

Yalom, I. (2002). *The gift of therapy.* New York, NY: Harper-Collins.

CHAPTER SEVENTEEN

SURVIVOR THERAPY EMPOWERMENT PROGRAM (STEP)[1]

The STEP is a carefully designed, evidence-based psychotherapeutic program that can be used to work with individuals or groups of abused women who have experienced intimate partner abuse or other forms of physical, sexual, and psychological abuse (gender violence). STEP helps women better understand how the violence they have experienced has impacted their lives and what they can do about it. As it has a psychotherapeutic focus, the program deals with how people think about what has occurred and how it affects their feelings and their behavior. Although STEP has therapeutic benefits by reducing the mental confusion and teaching tools to re-regulate emotions, all of which will change behavior, in fact it is not just psychotherapy: It also contains psychoeducation. This makes it possible to use the program in settings where confidentiality is not easily obtained, such as in jails and prisons, and for non-mental health care providers to be trained to facilitate the program.

The first edition of STEP was used in many different programs successfully. However, when we undertook to validate STEP so that it could be considered evidence based and therefore be used in settings where only evidence-based programs were used, we decided to make a few changes in the materials used with the program, not the underlying theoretical basis. We discuss how a program can be validated later in this chapter.

PRINCIPLES OF THE STEP

STEP is made up of 12 units with detailed materials that accompany each unit. Some women and places that offer the STEP groups will go through

[1]The second edition of STEP was prepared with Dr. Tara Jungersen. The validation of the program was done with Dr. Jungersen, Dr. Ryan Black, Cassandra Groth, and myself.

them 1 week at a time while others will spend a longer time on one or more of the units. Others, in settings where there is less control about how often someone attends the group will complete only some of the units and not in the usual order as presented in the program manual. Each of the STEPs is theoretically based on current feminist and trauma theory. The feminist component emphasizes the negative effect that discrimination and oppression have on a woman's life and the need to find and take back one's power to overcome these effects. The trauma component incorporates the lessons learned from the research presented in this book so that the psychological impact can be overcome, also.

Each session or STEP has three components: (a) psychoeducation: an educational section that provides information about some aspect of domestic violence and its impact on people; (b) process: a discussion section where participants talk about and process what happened to them; and (c) skill building: a section where the leader teaches the women a particular skill that may protect them and help them heal. Exercises, most of which reinforce a behavioral skill that has been taught in that session, are given out to practice the skill until the next session. Some time is spent checking in with everyone when the group begins and some time is spent in closing the group that leaves about 20 minutes for each of the three major sections in a 2-hour group session.

STEP is based on a feminist and trauma-informed model where negative affect and anxiety are specifically addressed. *Feminist theory* highlights the fact that being a woman in most societies today increases the risk of being victimized. Such victimization along with the oppression from factors other than gender, such as racism or ethnic and cultural discrimination, can cause psychological distress, but validation, emotional support, and empowerment can protect from and reverse that distress. *Trauma theory* highlights the fact that exposure to trauma/danger can cause psychological distress in healthy or clinical populations. Psychoeducation and verbal psychotherapy can reduce or ameliorate symptoms and restore health. Although resiliency may be compromised, there are psychological techniques to rebuild feelings of well-being and move toward growth.

STEP includes respect for the client and positive regard for his or her strengths. Courage, optimism about life, and support are cornerstones of how the program is delivered. There is sensitivity to both gender and multicultural issues in addition to paying attention to each person's individuality. A key to the program is to assist those participating in feeling empowered to take back control over whatever aspects of their lives is possible and to continue to grow in positive ways. We build on strengths and move toward trauma resolution and rebuilding life skills, resiliency, and a feeling of well-being. Although we use some cognitive behavioral psychological techniques in the skill-building exercises, we also pay attention to relationships. Obviously, it is easier to utilize the relationship with the therapist in individual psychotherapy to this end, but there is an attempt to use the group facilitator relationship also.

Goals

There are six major goals for the STEP:

1. Safety
2. Validation and support
3. Cognitive clarity
4. Emotional stability
5. Healing from posttraumatic stress disorder (PTSD) symptoms
6. Rebuilding resiliency and positive growth

These goals are met by the following:

- Restoring a sense of personal control that results in a sense of self-confidence
- Being aware of power dynamics at work in one's life context and strengthening relationships
- Providing validation and reducing shame and guilt from having been victimized
- Building on personal strengths by trusting one's own judgment and making good decisions
- Becoming informed about different aspects of intimate partner relationships and other gender violence, including abuser tactics
- Learning to self-regulate moods by controlling anger, depression, anxiety, using new skills
- Understanding the cycle of violence and its impact on physical and psychological health
- Expanding knowledge of alternate actions to maintain safety

Why Is It "Evidence Based?"

In the health care world today, there is a movement to try to evaluate treatment effects to see if the treatment really works as it is thought it will. Most of the time we use our clients' reports of feeling better to know that what we have done has been helpful. However, there are also specific ways to measure efficacy using certain assessment tools. Our research team that began the STEP groups in the jails, described in Chapter 14, attempted to use some of these measurements to determine how helpful the STEP groups were for the women who participated. Although the program was geared toward women who had experienced domestic violence, some of the women who self-selected to attend had been abused by family members or others. Nonetheless, they reported benefiting from the group and their assessment results confirmed their self-reports. We report some results later in this chapter.

WHAT ARE THE STEPS?

STEPs are the units that can be covered in one or more sessions.

STEP 1 Labeling, Validation of Trauma or Abuse, and Safety Planning
STEP 2 Reducing Stress and Relaxation Training
STEP 3 Cognitive Restructuring: Thinking, Feeling, and Behavior
STEP 4 Boundaries, Assertiveness, and Communication
STEP 5 Cycle of Violence and Battered Woman Syndrome
STEP 6 Trauma Triggers
STEP 7 Numbing Behaviors and Substance Abuse
STEP 8 Empathy and Emotional Re-Regulation
STEP 9 Impact of Domestic Violence and Trauma on Children
STEP 10 Legal Issues
STEP 11 Grieving and Letting Go of Old Relationships
STEP 12 Building Wellness and Resilience

Each unit has three areas that have information and materials for the facilitator should they be needed. There are charts and handouts for home exercises as most STEPs are held once a week. As mentioned earlier, if there is more discussion or information that participants want, the STEP can be repeated or broken up into sections that occur over several weeks. Table 17.1 gives an overview of each of the STEPs in STEP 2 that is currently in use.

Table 17.1 *STEP Outline*

Unit	Education	Discussion	Skill Building
1 Labeling, Validation of Trauma or Abuse, and Safety Planning	Definitions of violence	Identification of violence	Violence checklist and safety planning
2 Reducing Stress and Relaxation Training	Definitions of stress and experiencing stress	Relaxation techniques	Deep breathing and progressive relaxation
3 Cognitive Restructuring: Thinking, Feeling, and Behavior	Definitions of stalking behavior and psychological threats	Identification of negative thinking patterns	Neutralizing automatic thoughts
4 Boundaries, Assertiveness, and Communication	Definitions of passive, aggressive, and assertive communication	Asking for what you want	Assertiveness inventory
5 Cycle of Violence and Battered Woman Syndrome	Definitions of cycle of violence and battering	How to use time-outs	Identification of cycle of violence in past relationships
6 Trauma Triggers	Definitions of trauma triggers	What to expect in trauma therapy	Identification and reduction of trauma triggers
7 PTSD, Substance Abuse, and Other Trauma Triggers	Definitions of PTSD, drug, and alcohol use	Identification of PTSD symptoms	Exercise on the effects of substance use
8 Emotional Re-Regulation	Definitions of self-esteem	Learning to regulate emotions; building empathy	Self-esteem exercise
9 Impact of Violence on Children	Definitions of effects of violence on children	Rebuilding relationships with children	Examining personal history of childhood and parenting

(continued)

Table 17.1 *STEP Outline (continued)*

Unit		Education	Discussion	Skill Building
10	Legal Issues and Termination	Definitions of domestic violence legal terminology	Ending the group process and next steps	Incorporating growth and saying goodbyes
11	Grieving and Letting Go of Old Relationships	Definitions of the five stages of grief	Grieving relationship endings	Creating an ideal relationship
12	Interpersonal Relationships: Dealing With Pleasing Behaviors and Compliance Issues	Definitions of boundaries, healthy relationships, and communicating anger	How to build a healthy relationship	"What it means to be a Woman" exercise

PTSD, posttraumatic stress disorder.

STEP GROUPS IN THE JAIL OR PRISON

Conducting group therapy for battered women in jails or prisons is a difficult process that begins with trying to get permission from the command to go into the facility and present the program after it has been designed. There is a STEP 2 manual that is about to be published containing the STEPs and materials for those who are interested in conducting such groups, or contact the research team at Nova Southeastern University's College of Psychology. We had already been in our local jail collecting data for the Battered Woman Syndrome Questionnaire (BWSQ) research project reported here and some of the women and staff had asked if we could conduct groups for those who would volunteer. When we began, most of them were on a special unit that was created for women who had been abused and wanted to work on their issues while incarcerated or in substance abuse treatment units. After permission was granted, at least two psychology interns co-led the groups, on each of two jail units, one morning a week. After a few weeks, it became clear we would not be able to predict how many women would come to each session. It ranged from a low of 15 to a high of 40 at a time. Some women began the program, then were transferred to another jail or were in court hearings and could not attend for several weeks, and then came back again later on. It became clear that closed groups

Table 17.2 *Review of Protocols and Guidelines Effective in the Treatment of Female Victims of Intimate Partner Violence*

ISTSS Protocol	Kubany and Ralston (2008)	Labrador et al. (2006)	HOPE Johnson et al. (2009, 2011)	STEP Walker (2009)
1. Clear definition	+	+	+	+
2. Reliable measures	+	+	+	+
3. Blind evaluators	−	−/+	−	+
4. Team training	+	+	−	+
5. Stability treatment	+	+	+	+
6. Specific program, manualized	+	+	−	+
7. Randomization of groups	+	−/+	−	+
8. Treatment adherence	+	+	−	−
9. Data analysis	+	+	+	+

Note. Present = +, Absent = −

HOPE, Helping to Overcome PTSD through Empowerment; ISTSS, International Society for Traumatic Stress Studies; STEP, Survivor Therapy Empowerment Program.

From Caceres-Ortiz (2013). Adapted with permission.

were not possible in the jail due to the scheduling difficulties of the women, so although it was more difficult to manage, we redesigned each STEP unit to stand on its own, and the women were then able to go in and out of sessions without difficulty. As can be seen later when discussing the validation measures (Table 17.2), the efficacy was the same with open groups as with closed groups who completed the program in a sequential order.

One of the most important facts learned was the need to make sure the women do not leave the group so emotionally upset that it disrupts the rest of their routine in the jail. They were not always able to do something to distract themselves or use other defense mechanisms to deal with their emotions that they had previously learned to use outside the confined jail setting. These women had to go back to their housing, often with other inmates who were in the group, and despite the cautions about confidentiality and the rule that "whatever happens in the group, stays in the group," some women used the sensitive information to taunt and tease other women. Although we did not permit those women to return to the group if we learned of their behavior, in fact most of the participants did not disclose this information to the therapists until after the groups were over.

Many of the women we worked with also had co-occurring substance abuse disorders and had learned to numb their feelings with alcohol and other drugs. This is rarely possible in jails, so it is important to teach relaxation therapy skills or meditation so they have alternative ways of handling strong emotions. We also found that some of the women did not admit to any PTSD or battered woman syndrome (BWS) symptoms on the testing but still came to the groups. It is not known if the women simply like coming as a distraction to an otherwise boring day, if they were really battered women but not able to disclose or feel any of the emotional impact given their situation, or if they were getting something out of the groups despite not being victims of trauma or abuse.

EMPIRICAL FINDINGS FROM STEP 1

Study 1

As mentioned earlier, we used this group format with two groups in the jails. One group had volunteered for the domestic violence program, which called for 30 to 60 days in that unit, and the other group was for those who were identified as having a problem with substance abuse and also called for a 60-day stay in the substance abuse and life-skills unit. In the substance abuse unit, the program was called "life skills" and was often court ordered. The life-skills program consisted of several different "skills" training and our STEP was considered part of it, so the women were more likely to attend the group to get credit toward completion of their court-ordered program. Even so, the attendance was uneven and in neither group were there women who completed all the STEPs. This was usually due to the interference with court hearings, other programs, or early discharge back to the community or to prison.

We attempted to use a variety of psychological assessment instruments before the groups began and after they were over. However, we obtained only pretest scores for a small number of women who actually completed different STEPs. Since many of the initial participants did not remain until the end of the program, we abandoned the posttests and instead administered the Beck Anxiety Inventory (BAI) after each session. The initial BAI scores for the domestic violence group as shown in Figure 17.1 showed that almost half (43%) of the women initially did not have a

STEP in Detention Center Setting

DV Unit BAI

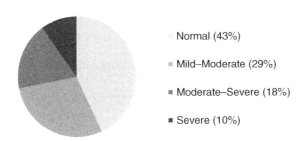

- Normal (43%)
- Mild–Moderate (29%)
- Moderate–Severe (18%)
- Severe (10%)

Figure 17.1 *Beck anxiety scores for domestic violence group pre-STEP program.*
BAI, Beck Anxiety Inventory; DV, domestic violence; STEP, Survivor Therapy Empowerment Program.

significant amount of anxiety when the group began, although almost a third (29%) of the women did have mild to moderate anxiety and another quarter of the women had moderate to severe (18%) or severe (10%) anxiety.

In the substance abuse group, even fewer had severe (5.2%) to moderate to severe (13.1%) anxiety with another fifth (20.7%) with mild to moderate anxiety and 61% reporting normal levels of anxiety on the BAI as shown in Figure 17.2.

When combining all the scores for both groups, Figure 17.3 shows the larger number of normal BAI results with a smaller number of mild to moderate, moderate to severe, and severe scores.

Using the combined groups over STEPS 1 through 9, Figure 17.4 demonstrates the reduction in anxiety scores over time. Interestingly, STEP 5 and STEP 6 show the greatest reduction, perhaps because relaxation training was then taught in STEP 5 and anger management was taught in STEP 6. We moved the relaxation training to STEP 2 in the second edition. While it might have been expected that anxiety levels would go up in STEP 6 because the women are taught the three-phase cycle of violence that will remind them of their own abuse, the reduction in anxiety remained. The rise in anxiety for STEP 8 may reflect the topic of substance abuse that is discussed there and grieving and children were the topics for STEPs 8 and 9, respectively.

The Detailed Assessment of Posttraumatic Stress (DAPS), a standardized measure of impact from one particular stressor for both domestic

STEP in Detention Center Setting

SU Unit BAI

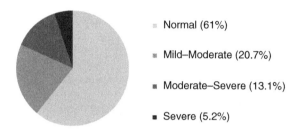

- Normal (61%)
- Mild–Moderate (20.7%)
- Moderate–Severe (13.1%)
- Severe (5.2%)

Figure 17.2 *Beck anxiety scores for substance abuse group pre-STEP program.*
BAI, Beck Anxiety Inventory; STEP, Survivor Therapy Empowerment Program; SU, substance abuse.

STEP in Detention Center Setting

DV and SU Combined BAI by Severity and Sample Size

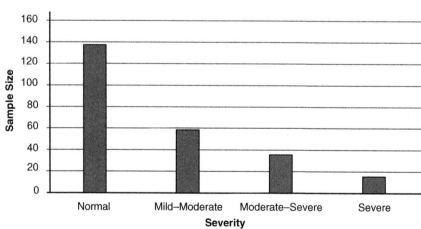

Figure 17.3 *Beck anxiety scores for both domestic violence and substance abuse groups combined.*
BAI, Beck Anxiety Inventory; DV, domestic violence; STEP, Survivor Therapy Empowerment Program; SU, substance abuse.

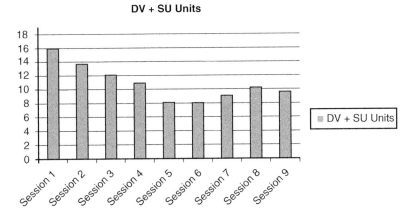

Figure 17.4 *Beck anxiety scores for both domestic violence and substance abuse groups combined after STEPs 1 through 9.*
BAI, Beck Anxiety Inventory; DV, domestic violence; STEP, Survivor Therapy Empowerment Program; SU, substance abuse.

violence and substance abuse unit participants, is shown in Figure 17.5. Here it can be seen that more women in both units experienced domestic violence and sexual abuse than other forms of trauma, although most were experienced.

Figure 17.6 indicates the specific clinical scales for both groups on the DAPS showing the small number of women who actually demonstrated statistically significant scores. As might be expected, the highest scale was substance abuse but other scales were also elevated.

The clinical consequences from interpersonal trauma in both units were also measured using the Trauma Symptom Inventory (TSI). This test assesses symptoms that are mentioned. Interestingly, the group results did not show significance (above 65) in any of the scales, although several were approaching significance as seen in Figure 17.7.

Assessment of alcohol and drug abuse for women in both groups was also done before the STEP began. Figure 17.8 shows those scales comparing both groups. As can be seen, the substance abuse group indicated more problems with abuse of substances than did the domestic violence group.

While these assessment instruments could not be used to demonstrate posttest efficacy, except for the BAI scores that were repeated at the

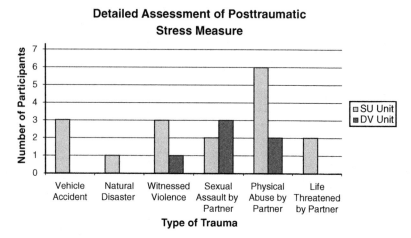

Figure 17.5 *Detailed assessment of DAPS test scores for both substance abuse and domestic violence groups in STEP.*
DV, domestic violence; SU, substance abuse.

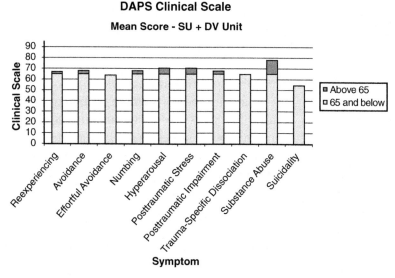

Figure 17.6 *Significant DAPS clinical scores for domestic violence and substance abuse groups.*
DAPS, Detailed Assessment of Posttraumatic Stress; DV, domestic violence; SU, substance abuse.

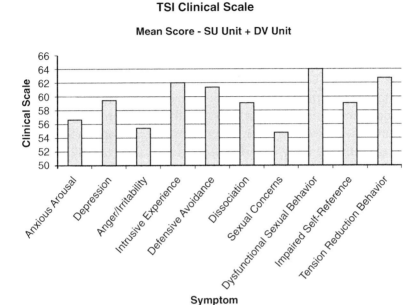

Figure 17.7 *TSI clinical scales for domestic violence and substance abuse groups.*
DV, domestic violence; SU, substance abuse; TSI, Trauma Symptom Inventory.

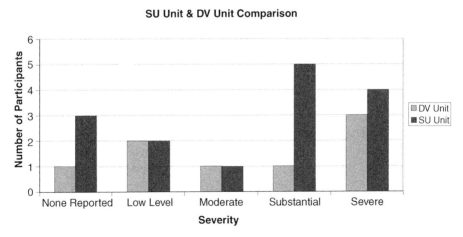

Figure 17.8 *Drug abuse screening test for substance abuse and domestic violence groups.*
DV, domestic violence; SU, substance abuse.

end of each session, they do demonstrate the ability to measure the effectiveness of the treatment program. Since some of the women will transfer from the jail groups to STEP groups in the community, we will also be better able to follow up over a period of time.

After the first analysis of the STEP, we expanded the program to new and different groups in addition to the women in the main jail. We expanded the groups that were begun in the general population in the women's jail to the men's and women's jail clinics. These were people who were found to be currently mentally ill and housed in a separate facility from those in the general population where they received counseling and medication where appropriate but no trauma-specific intervention. We also were conducting STEP groups in a state hospital setting with those found to be incompetent to proceed to trial and in a battered woman shelter population, but they were not included in either the previous or next analysis. Some modifications in content were made for the men's group but the other groups all followed the manual. In addition to BAI scores (Beck, Epstein, Brown, & Steer, 1988) being collected at the conclusion of each STEP unit, we also collected Subjective Units of Discomfort Scores (SUDS; Wolpe, 1958) pre- and postsessions and administered the trauma and substance abuse tests after the unit on the cycle of violence. Given that each woman began the program at a different STEP, we wanted to have them all gain some knowledge about their own cycle of violence before completing the trauma tests since, without that context, many of the women did not identify the symptoms accurately.

Evidence-Based Validation Study 2

Participants for this analysis were 564 men and women (49 males and 505 females) incarcerated while awaiting trial for various criminal charges in the local jail. The average age of the males was 40 years and females was 35 years. Data analysis consisted of testing for a significant (a) linear change in BAI scores across the number of sessions attended, (b) difference in mean BAI scores between the first session attended and each subsequent session, (c) mean change in SUDS before and after each session, and (d) correlation between SUDS scores and BAI scores. Finally, it was examined whether the observed change in BAI scores (both the linear effect and initial vs. subsequent sessions effect) was moderated by (dependent on) administrative site. All analyses were performed using the linear mixed modeling (LMM) procedure in SAS 9.4. Each model was parameterized to take into account within-subject correlation due to repeated measurements on each subject. Of note, according to the intervention guidelines, although all participants were invited to attend all 12 units, in fact there were fewer than 20 participants who attended more than nine units. As a result, these data from more than nine units were removed for analyses.

Analysis 1 Results

Results from the first analysis, which treated session as a continuous fixed effect variable, revealed a significant negative linear trend of anxiety scores across all sessions, $F(1, 312) = 75.56$, beta $= -1.43$, $p < .0001$, indicating that from one session to the next, BAI scores reduced by approximately 1.5 points. Results from the LMM in which session was treated as categorical fixed effect variable revealed a significant effect, $F(8, 611) = 11.44$, $p < .0001$. Post hoc pairwise comparisons demonstrated that each subsequent session had a significantly lower BAI mean score as compared to the first session ($ps < .0001$). Additional analyses showed that, after controlling for the effect of session, the mean SUDS significantly decreased from the beginning to the end of each session (mean reduction $= 5.34$), $F(1, 921) = 40.79$, $p < .0001$. Analyses also revealed a significant correlation between SUDS and BAI scores, $r = .455$, $p < .0001$. Finally, administrative site did not moderate the (a) linear trend effect on BAI scores, $F(3,339) = 0.32$, $p = .8127$, or (b) differences between initial versus subsequent sessions on BAI scores, $F(24,603) = 0.89$, $p = .6183$. Table 17.3 provides summary statistics of participants on each outcome by session number.

Descriptive analyses were conducted to determine the extent of the trauma symptomatology and substance abuse in this population. Rates of traumatic events, intimate partner violence, and substance use for STEP participants at the four administrative sites were high, similar to national trends for incarcerated populations. Of the valid profiles for participants who completed the midprogram assessments, 66% ($N = 50$) endorsed clinically significant posttraumatic stress symptoms, as measured by the TSI. TSI scores for our sample indicate that a large number of the participants scored at the clinically significant level. Of the 10 scales within the TSI, dysfunctional sexual behavior was the most highly endorsed scale

Table 17.3 *Summary Statistics on Each Outcome by Session Number*

Session #	N	Pre		Post	
		M	*SD*	**M**	*SD*
Session 1	301				
BAI		—	—	13.18	13.27
SUDS		50.81	31.22	45.66	31.52
Session 2	267				
BAI		—	—	10.84	11.94
SUDS		46.46	29.90	41.05	30.34
Session 3	179				
BAI		—	—	8.93	11.55
SUDS		45.78	28.51	38.80	28.47
Session 4	114				
BAI		—	—	8.89	10.68
SUDS		43.76	27.00	38.27	28.76
Session 5	86				
BAI		—	—	6.14	8.62
SUDS		38.77	27.51	33.11	28.00
Session 6	54				
BAI		—	—	6.17	9.94
SUDS		38.81	25.05	30.42	26.71
Session 7	41				
BAI		—	—	7.76	11.74
SUDS		32.40	24.03	27.74	25.28
Session 8	37				
BAI		—	—	5.00	6.63
SUDS		35.68	25.25	30.52	27.65
Session 9	22				
BAI		—	—	5.68	8.80
SUDS		36.65	26.00	34.71	29.00

BAI, Beck Anxiety Inventory; SUDS, Subjective Units of Discomfort.

(45% or $N = 34$), while sexual concerns (24% or $N = 18$) was the least endorsed scale. DAPS mean scores for our sample indicate that eight scales were found to be significant ($t \geq 65$): Reexperiencing, Avoidance, Effortful Avoidance, Numbing Avoidance, Posttraumatic Stress–Total, Posttraumatic Impairment, Trauma-Specific Dissociation, and Substance Abuse. Ninety-one percent ($N = 53$) endorsed a high probability of having a substance use disorder, as measured by the Substance Abuse Subtle Screening Inventory-3 (SASSI-3).

Discussion

The STEP validation study examined the development, modification, and evaluation of the STEP attended by trauma-affected individuals in detention settings. Data analyses of incarcerated women and men who have participated in the STEP in various jail settings determined significant results for our research questions. We hypothesized that participation in the STEP would result in a reduction of reported anxiety over time, as measured by the BAI, and this hypothesis was confirmed. Also confirmed was our hypothesis that participation in the STEP would result in a significant decrease between baseline anxiety scores and each postunit anxiety score, as measured by the BAI. Next, our hypothesis that participants' reported post-SUDS scores would be significantly lower than their reported pre-SUDS scores for each session, and that participants' subjective reports of anxiety would positively correlate with objective measures (e.g., SUDS and BAI) over time was confirmed. Finally, our hypothesis that anxiety score linear trends of the STEP would not differ based on administration site was also confirmed.

The results of the linear mixed models determined that there was a significant change in mean anxiety scores, between the first session and subsequent sessions ($p < .0001$), as well as a significant decrease in the linear trend of anxiety scores across all sessions ($p < .0001$) as measured by the BAI and SUDS. Therefore, program success is dose related. That is, the more sessions attended, the lower the anxiety scores.

Based on the results indicating that administrative site (e.g., life skills, mental health males) did not moderate BAI scores, the STEP appears stable across the different detention settings. STEP can be adapted to various environmental situations such as incarcerated women and men on a mental health unit as well as in general population in jails where there is minimal consistency within the groups where people are awaiting trial.

Given the descriptive analyses of the female and male participants, results indicate that the STEP may be useful in reducing trauma symptoms in a jail population where the prevalence of PTSD is highly significant. Additionally, The STEP is useful in reducing trauma symptoms and anxiety in women with comorbid substance use problems. Finally, the STEP is also helpful for men who have experienced traumatic intimate partner violence and child abuse even if they also have become perpetrators.

The STEP, which has 12 units, can be completed in as few as 12 sessions or as many more as needed, in order to cover the material for the participants. Although sessions can be completed individually or with a counselor, it has been found to be more powerful when a group format is included. Some topics, however, may need additional individual sessions, such as discussion of sexual abuse or child abuse and trafficking in some cultures. The units were designed to accompany trauma-specific or complement traditional psychotherapy for those clients who may have diagnoses other than PTSD. It is also complementary with substance abuse programs where many participants are also trauma survivors.

Limitations and Recommendations for Future Research

Due to jail proceedings and the uncontrollable nature of the criminal justice system, study participants were not considered a stable and steady population, which resulted in several threats to internal and external validity. Primarily, we utilized a sample of convenience, which did not allow for randomized sampling. A control group was not available in order to compare outcomes in a typical experimental design, although we used statistical analyses to compensate for the quasi-experimental design of the current study. Participants entered and left the study at various times throughout the program depending on when they were arrested, tried, and released, which prevented the use of a closed group format. Furthermore, even during each session, some participants may have been called out of group to see the nurse or to go to court, although this was rare as reported by the facilitators. Another limitation included the inability to complete follow-up studies of treatment adherence post-STEP completion, as the jail population disperses widely postincarceration, and may not possess the resources to access services outside the jail setting, although referrals were offered the participants who were being released back into the community. Future studies could target jail systems with a step-down monitoring program, where participants could be contacted via probation and parole connections for follow-up monitoring for treatment adherence.

Another limitation of the study is the lack of demographic variables of participants, including sexual orientation and race/ethnicity. Without these demographic variables, the applicability to ethnically, racially, and sexually diverse groups cannot be verified. Future studies could assess the efficacy of STEP across these diverse populations. Finally, our data analyses excluded factor analysis within the different instruments used in the study. In future studies, latent class analysis could be performed to uncover unique clinical profiles of incarcerated individuals using the DAPS, TSI, and SASSI-3 in order to uncover subgroups within the population.

CURRENT STATUS

After the two studies were conducted and we were convinced of the efficacy of the STEP theory and principles, revisions were made that we described earlier as STEP 2. We added more content materials for the facilitators in the manual, changed the order of some of the units to create a better flow of material, and continued the data collection. As it is 1 year since STEP 2 has been used, we intend to do another analysis within the next year to have appropriate comparisons possible.

SUMMARY

There are very few programs available for women (or men) in jails due to the difficulty in consistent attendance. Yet, it is a good time for many who are arrested and awaiting trial to begin to evaluate their life choices. Making connections between relationships where they have experienced trauma and subsequent life choices such as substance abuse and other negative behaviors may help victims of gender violence change some of these choices. The STEP is based on feminist and trauma theory and presents education about common issues for abuse victims that then can be discussed as they relate to the woman herself. She is then presented with learning new skills or reinforcing old skills that can help her make better choices in the future. In addition to the reduction in anxiety, a major component of PTSD and BWS, the women like the program and continue to attend when they can.

REFERENCES

Beck, A. T., Epstein, N., Brown, G., & Steer, R. A. (1988). An inventory for measuring clinical anxiety: Psychometric properties. *Journal of Consulting and Clinical Psychology, 56*, 893–897. http://dx.doi.org/10.1037/0022-006X.56.6.893

Caceres-Ortiz, E. (2013, August). Comparison of STEP Trauma Intervention Program with other trauma protocols. In L. E. A. Walker (Chair), *Empirically based trauma intervention (STEP) for special populations.* Symposium conducted at the APA Annual Convention, Hawaii.

Johnson, D. M., & Zlotnick, C. (2009). HOPE for battered women with PTSD in domestic violence shelters. *Professional Psychology: Research and Practice, 40*(3), 234–241.

Johnson, D. M., Zlotnick, C., & Perez, S. (2011). Cognitive behavioral treatment of PTSD in residents of battered women's shelters: Results of a randomized clinical trial. *Journal of Consulting and Clinical Psychology, 79*(4), 542–551.

Kubany, E. S., & Ralston, T. C. (2008). *Treating PTSD in battered women: A step-by-step manual for therapists & counselors.* Oakland, CA: New Harbinger.

Labrador, F. J., Fernandez-Velasco, M. D. R., & Rincon, P. (2006). Efficacy of a brief and individual participation program by posttraumatic stress disorder in female victims of domestic violence. *International Journal of Clinical and Health Psychology, 6*(3), 527–547.

Walker, L. E. A. (2009). *The battered woman syndrome* (3rd ed.). New York, NY: Springer Publishing Company.

Wolpe, J. (1958). *Psychotherapy by reciprocal inhibition.* Stanford, CA: Stanford University Press.

PART FOUR

APPLICATION OF PSYCHOLOGY TO THE LEGAL SYSTEM

CHAPTER EIGHTEEN

FALSE CONFESSIONS OF
BATTERED WOMEN[1]

Why would someone confess to a crime when he or she did not commit it? This is a question asked by many people. We know that some men have given false confessions from the work of Barry Scheck and Peter Neufield who began the Innocence Project in 1992 to help locate and exonerate those who were wrongfully convicted. To date, more than 300 individuals have been assisted by the Innocence Project and exonerated based on DNA evidence proving their innocence (Innocence Project, 2016). Although a false confession was a contributing factor in 27% of wrongful convictions, the majority of those exonerated are men. The national Innocence Project (www.innocenceproject.org) has centers in many law schools around the United States but, despite its important work, there are very few women who have been exonerated. As noted by the Innocence Project, only a limited number of cases involve biological evidence that can be scientifically tested, and this evidence is less likely to be available in crimes in which women are convicted, since the majority of DNA exoneration cases (80%) involve sexual assault (Innocence Project, 2010). Yet, estimates of up to 25% of those serving time in prison suggest that the same inappropriate policing and other techniques may have caused even more women to falsely confess.

Confessions are one of the most incriminating forms of evidence and once obtained, a conviction is almost always inevitable (Drizin & Leo, 2004). Studies have shown that the average person who serves on a jury does not believe someone would confess to something that person did not do, no matter what the evidence shows (Kassin et al., 2010). Researchers have attempted to identify additional false confession cases above and beyond those in which persons have been legally exonerated. Leo and Ofshe (1998) found 60 identified false confession cases while Drizin

[1]With gratitude for the work of Carlye Conte and Stephen Grabner who have conducted much of the research in our group on women and false confessions.

and Leo (2004) found 125 proven false confession cases. A false confession case is considered proven if no crime was committed, if it was physically impossible for the person to have committed the crime, if the real perpetrator is later found, or if scientific evidence can establish someone's innocence. Similar to the Innocence Project, the majority of identified false confession cases involved male defendants.

DARLENE GREEN

Darlene Green, an almost 80-year-old woman, had been abused by her long-time husband for at least the past 10 years after he started showing signs of dementia. Both had a long history of using alcohol in their relationship. The night before his death, he began a rant against her that lasted until she finally was able to fall asleep. When she awoke in the morning, she went into the living room, sat in her recliner, and began watching her television shows. William came in and continued the abuse. He left and came back and then, standing at the top of the chair, he held his gun against his head and screamed at her to pull the trigger and shoot him. This was not new, he had taken to threatening to shoot her and himself as his Alzheimer's disease worsened. This time, though, he pulled the trigger himself. Darlene called their adult son, Kirk, and said she killed him. He did not believe her. So she called their other son, Brad, who called the police. When the police came, Darlene told them that William had told her to do it, put the gun to his head, so she did it. Why would she tell them that she killed William when she did not do it? Further, the physical evidence such as blood splatter patterns, gun residue, and the body position all demonstrated that William had pulled the trigger himself, not Darlene.

When questioned at trial about her memory and feelings at the time of the incident, Darleen said, "I am sure now that I didn't do it . . . but I felt blame . . . that's the way it was when he was violent and abusive . . . he would go on and on about things until I finally admitted it was my fault and I was to blame."

Roland Maiuro, a Seattle psychologist, examined Darlene and wrote a report stating that it was not unusual for battered women to "step outside themselves and partially dissociate during extreme shock and later piece together events of what happened." But the trial court did not permit his testimony stating that "dissociation and altered perception of the traumatic event" was not in the definition of battered woman syndrome or part of self-defense. At 81 years of age, Darlene was convicted of man-slaughter and sentenced to 5 years in state prison.

Her appellate attorney, Lenell Nussbaum, filed an appeal stating four reasons why she should not have been tried or convicted. First, there was insufficient evidence that Darlene shot him despite her confession. Second, the trial court erred by not permitting testimony by Dr. Maiuro about posttraumatic stress disorder (PTSD) and battered woman syndrome to explain why she dissociated as part of self-defense and gave a false confession. Third, the trial court erred in not permitting her testimony about the fight before he died. And, fourth, the trial court erred in not permitting the testimony about the long history of domestic violence.

Darlene won her appeal. The appellate court reversed the trial court and ordered a new trial. Unfortunately, Darlene passed away before she could be fully exonerated. But, her case illustrates both why some battered women may confess to something they did not do and how difficult it is for judges, juries, and others to understand why they might do so.

JULIE ABNER

Julie Abner's 2-year-old daughter died in a fire that may have been set by her 5-year-old son although the courts have ruled that there was not enough evidence due to his age. During interrogation by the police, Julie confessed to setting the fire herself but since she was illiterate, she was unable to sign the confession that was orally recorded. A psychological examination found that she had the overall adaptive functioning of a 9-year-old child herself and in the bottom 2% of intellectual abilities for her age. The psychologist's testimony was not admitted at trial nor was the testimony of witnesses who heard the 5-year-old boy admitting he set the fire. Julie was found guilty of involuntary manslaughter and sentenced to 10 years in prison. Her case illustrates the difficulty with police interrogating mentally retarded people and is being appealed.

MICHELLE BYROM

Michelle Byrom, who had intentionally ingested rat poison in order to escape domestic violence, was in the hospital when her abusive husband was shot and killed. Although she was heavily medicated, she was questioned by police and eventually confessed to participating in the murder after officers suggested that her son may have been the one who shot and killed her husband. Michelle was evaluated by a psychologist who concluded that she suffered from both medical and mental health problems and had an extensive history of physical, sexual, and emotional abuse during childhood and adulthood. Despite her history and the fact that Michelle recanted her confession, she was convicted of conspiracy to commit murder. The defense failed to present any mitigating evidence during the sentencing phase, such as the extreme physical and sexual violence she was subjected to during her marriage, and Michelle was sentenced to death. The National Defense of Battered Women filed an amicus curiae on her behalf yet all of Michelle's appeals were denied. While on death row, Michelle's son began writing her letters in which he explained that he had shot his father out of rage for the years of abuse both he and his mother had suffered. A court-appointed psychologist who had evaluated Michelle's son came forward and testified during the evaluation the son had confessed to being solely responsible for his father's death. In 2014, only a few weeks before her execution date, Michelle's request for relief from her death sentence was granted and her conviction was overturned. Due to her ailing health, Michelle agreed to plead no contest to lesser charges. She was released from prison and continues to maintain her innocence.

KRISTINA EARNEST

Kristina Earnest, a 21-year-old Texas woman, and her 41-year-old boyfriend, Tommy Castro, rushed Kristina's daughter, Kati, to the emergency room. She was unresponsive. Kristina told the doctors that they found her like that floating in the bathtub. The doctors noted that Kristina had a black eye, bloody lip, and bruises and her 20-month-old son also had visible bruises. The police were called and both Kristina and Tommy were arrested for murder as Kati had died. Kristina then told the police that she took the blame because she was afraid of what Tommy would do to her and the other children. He had threatened to harm her and the others and told her what to say when they arrived at the hospital. The real story was that Kati had peed in Tommy's car that morning so he beat her with a bat and then forced her to lay down on the floor and he repeatedly stomped on her. Kati complained that her stomach hurt but Tommy would not let Kristina take her to the hospital. Kristina accepted a plea deal to testify against Tommy.

At his trial, Kristina testified that Tommy was verbally, physically, and sexually abusive to her and the children. He forced her to quit her job so she was financially dependent on him. He would control Kristina and the children's food intake, would tape the door shut when he left for work in the morning, and would "check" her to make sure she did not have sex with any of the neighbors while he was at work. He kept her sedated on medication during this time. Tommy was found guilty of felony murder and sentenced to life in prison. Kristina pled guilty to the first-degree felony offense of failure to protect her child and sentenced to 16 years in prison.

WHY DO WOMEN MAKE FALSE CONFESSIONS?

These cases illustrate some of the reasons why a woman will make a false confession to committing a criminal act when she did not do it. Darleen Green had been beaten into admitting blame for things that her husband demanded so she just repeated what he told her to say. Julie Abner was so developmentally disabled that the police were able to get her to confess to setting the house on fire when it was probably her son who recklessly did it, although the court ruled that there was not enough evidence to support those claims. Michelle Byrom was mentally ill and heavily medicated, a long-standing victim of her husband's violence, who gave a confession after learning her son killed him. She was sentenced to death and, had her son not confessed that he acted alone, she would have been killed by the state. Kristina Earnest was afraid of what her batterer would do to her and the children, so she said exactly what he told her to say until she was arrested and felt safe enough to tell the police the truth. Still, she was sentenced to 16 years in prison, a rather long sentence for being unable to protect herself and her children against a homicidal and violent man.

Together with a group of my clinical forensic psychology doctoral students, we decided to look at the problem of women's false confessions by first developing a database of 80 appellate cases where women were described as having given a false confession but most were arrested, tried, and convicted anyhow. We were surprised at the number of convictions with only the woman's confession as the evidence against her.

Not surprising, though, were the number of them who like Darlene and Kristina were battered women who were not permitted to introduce testimony about their abuse and its impact on their state of mind. We also were not surprised at the number of women like Julie and others who should have been found incompetent to stand trial due to their mental disorder or disability. In one case we read about, the woman confessed to killing her newborn baby and putting him in the dumpster after hearing about someone finding a dead baby in a dumpster on television. A long history of schizophrenia was revealed after the woman's arrest and fortunately, no charges were filed as tests proved she was never pregnant and the dead baby's DNA did not match hers.

Studies show that more than 80% of individuals taken into police custody waive their Miranda rights to remain silent and ask for a lawyer and almost two thirds of those interrogated offer a full or partial confession (Kassin, 2008; Redlich, Kulish, & Steadman, 2011; Sangero & Halpert, 2011). Research has also shown that innocent suspects may be more likely than guilty suspects to waive these rights during an interrogation, which has led researchers to propose that innocence may be a specific risk factor for false confessions (Kassin, 2012; Kassin & Norwick, 2004). Saul Kassin conducted a series of experiments in the laboratory where he found about the same percentage of people falsely confessed to doing something that happened automatically (Kassin & Kiechel, 1996). During the past 20 years a literature based on false confessions has been published in the psychology and law journals and books. The American Psychological Association (APA) has submitted several amicus curiae briefs in various legal cases reaching the appellate level, especially when expert witness testimony is not admitted due to Daubert-type challenges to the scientific research on the topic. The most recent brief was submitted in 2013 in the case of *People of the State of New York v. Adrian Thomas* (www.apa .org/about/offices/ogc/amicus/thomas.pdf). The amicus brief stated that research showed how detrimental a confession is to a defendant even when the other evidence indicates that the defendant could not have committed the crime. There is a body of information that can help laypeople understand the counterintuitive behavior of someone who confesses to something that person did not do to that person's own detriment. Further, there are specific vulnerabilities in some people that, when subjected to certain interrogation techniques, will put those people at higher risk to make false confessions. The brief does explain police interrogation techniques and tactics and certain vulnerabilities that are more likely to acquire a false confession but does not discuss all the problems specifically faced by battered women.

Reid Interrogation Technique

The Reid Interrogation Technique has been used by police departments since the 1960s and is the most commonly utilized method of interrogation in the United States (Inbau, Reid, Buckley, & Jayne, 2013). It is often considered to be a psychologically oriented and largely standardized process of exercising influence in order to gain information. It uses both positive and negative incentives to try to convince people to confess. In general, the interrogators start with a strong accusation of guilt without permitting time for objections or denial. Sometimes they also use incriminating evidence that may be real or manufactured by the police. The goal is to make the person feel trapped so they can then offer sympathy and moral justification, which normalizes and minimizes the criminal act so the person may decide a confession is the best way to get out of the situation. Saul Kassin and his colleagues at John Jay College in New York City have researched scenarios using this technique and find that so-called normal people without the high risk vulnerabilities find it difficult not to confess. Those with mental disorders and disabilities who can easily get cognitively confused are easy prey for confessions under questioning with the powerful Reid method.

Studies show that using false information or evidence is a risk factor for the average person; so is length of interrogation. The longer the interrogation lasts, the more the individual's resistance is worn down through fatigue, uncertainty, and despair, which then impairs cognitive judgment. Reviewing our database indicates that many of those who gave false confessions to police were interrogated way beyond the average 30 minutes to 2 hours found in other studies, some lasting 15 or more hours, and a few spanning over several days. Minimizing the crime is another technique that is associated with false confessions. This is often done by minimizing the moral offense of the act or blaming others for why the individual was in the particular situation. For battered women, interviewers could blame the batterer for everything that happens in a child abuse case, while minimizing the battered woman's role as failure to protect the child as something that might be expected. The subjects in experiments using these techniques show how they perceive these minimization tactics as expressions of leniency and in some studies actually can triple the rate of false confessions.

In addition to police techniques used, there are some people who are more vulnerable to influence due to their own personal factors or situations. It is suggested that youth, intellectual disability, and mental illness are individual characteristics along with two personality traits of suggestibility and compliance that can cause people to react negatively to the pressure when being interrogated (Kassin et al., 2010). Looking at our database of cases of battered women, we found several other factors including women who were covering up for someone else because of fear of further harm to themselves or others. Some of the women in our database were easily subjected to influence from authority figures, especially those whose abusers had subjected them to a long history of being told what to do and say to stop the painful ranting and raving. Others were unable to focus on long-term consequences and confessing may have served as an immediate way of getting out of a very stressful situation. Battered women, like intellectually disabled people, may more easily succumb to leading and misleading questions especially if they get approval, which they need. Others may respond with what is called an "acquiescence response bias" where they say "yes" to questions whether or not it makes sense to them.

Battered women may also respond like those with a long history of serious mental illness as their mental health issues may lower their ability to withstand the pressure of interrogation especially if they become anxious and become confused. Grabner, Hylton, Landwehr, Conte, and Walker (2015) found that trauma and abuse histories make women especially vulnerable to confess during interrogations even if they had nothing to do with the incident being questioned. They found the following reasons:

- Battered women may confess to a crime that they did not actually commit as a way to protect themselves and their children.
- Battered women may take responsibility for crimes committed by abusive partners out of fear of direct or perceived threats to themselves or their children.
- Coercive interrogation techniques may lead abused women to acquiesce to the interrogative pressure and assume a submissive role to comply with authority figures.
- Trauma histories may lead to memory disturbances and dissociative states; thus, women may not remember the entire incident, be

confused about the details, and be more susceptible to internalizing guilt and assuming responsibility for the crime.

- High rates of mental illness and comorbid substance abuse, in addition to trauma and abuse histories, may make women especially vulnerable to false confessions.

Using the database that was generated and a review of the literature, the false confession research group divided the cases into the following typology in order to try to reflect the unique experiences of women as compared to men who falsely confess.

1. *Voluntary:* The women in this category willingly and knowingly confessed to a crime they did not do with no overt external pressure or internalization of guilt. A battered woman may voluntarily confess to a crime she knows she did not commit in an attempt to escape from an abusive partner. Or women voluntarily confess to crimes they did not commit to protect a child.

2. *Voluntary internalized:* The women in this category willingly and knowingly confessed to a crime they did not do with no overt external pressure but internalized their guilt. That is to say, they really believed they were guilty at the time of their statement. Trauma-related symptomatology may lead to memory disturbances and dissociative states so that a woman may not remember the incident, be confused about the details, and be more susceptible toward internalizing the guilt and assuming responsibility for the crime. Those who were mentally ill or disabled also internalized their responsibility and confessed in an attempt to absolve themselves from feelings of grief, depression, and self-blame.

3. *Coerced internalized:* The women in this category were subjected to external pressure in the form of intense, suggestive, and persuasive interrogation leading not only to a confession but also internalization or belief in their own guilt. Women can be manipulated in ways that cause them to doubt their own recollections of events and internalize guilt for the crime. In some cases, even after their innocence is established, women who have internalized guilt may have difficulty believing that they did not commit the crime to which they confessed.

4. *Coerced compliant:* The women in this category confessed to a crime they did not do due to the external pressure but did not internalize

the guilt. They knew they were not guilty but submitted to the pressure to confess. Lengthy and coercive questioning in addition to false promises of leniency can lead a woman to confess to a crime she did not commit. Some women who are fearful and submissive may be tricked into believing that they will be able to go home once they tell the interrogator what he or she wants them to say.

5. *Coerced reactive:* The women in this group confessed to a crime they did not do as a result of external pressure from an outside entity such as an abusive partner but did not internalize the guilt. They knew they were not guilty but confessed in order to protect themselves or someone else. These cases are typical of battered women who try to protect their spouses or in some cases, to protect their children or themselves after direct threats made by their abusive partners.

WOMEN AND INNOCENCE

Gender differences exist in all areas of the criminal justice system. We describe them further in Chapter 21. Due to the difficulties in obtaining factual evidence, it is difficult to know how many women were wrongfully convicted and are currently spending time in prison. Oftentimes, women are unable to put their histories in front of the judge and jury. For example, of all the cases in which false confession expert witness testimony was proposed at trial, almost half included testimony related to trauma, domestic violence, and battered woman syndrome on the false confession (Conte, Grabner, & Walker, 2015). In most cases, the expert was not permitted to testify to abuse and trauma or to explain their behavior from that perspective.

Only five females have been exonerated (5%) of all the people exonerated by the Innocence Project. Four of the women were exonerated based on DNA evidence that proved a male codefendant's innocence; three of the four women were codefendants in the same crime. One woman was exonerated in 2015 based on DNA evidence left at the crime scene by the true male perpetrator. In the National Registry of Exonerations (2016), only 26 females have been exonerated following a false confession (11.7% of total false confession exonerations).

Yet women were three times more likely to be convicted of a crime that did not occur (63%) than were men who falsely confessed. Another gender difference for women who are wrongfully convicted is that women are two times more likely than men to be convicted of a crime involving children. Jackson and Gross (2014) found that 40% of women wrongfully convicted were for crimes involving children as compared to 22% of men. This included child homicide involving shaking baby syndrome and accidental death where 30% of women and 17% of men were wrongfully convicted and child sexual abuse where 22% of women and 11% of men were wrongfully convicted. In some of the latter convictions the women were involved in group child abuse allegations such as at a preschool or some other place where the abuse was unfounded and eventually labeled, "hysteria" although in his book, *The Witch-Hunt Narrative*, Ross Cheit (2014) scrutinizes several of these trials and questions all the data.

Analyzing the Database of Women—Initial Analysis in 2014

Proving that the cases in our database were actually false confessions has been an interesting task for our group. First, we divided the original database of cases into several demographic groups. We found that their ages ranged from 11 years old to 79 years old with nine confessing when they were still juveniles. There were no overwhelming disparities in race with half (52%) Caucasian, 17% African American, and 7.5% Hispanic. The remaining 22.5% were either identified as Asian, Native American, or other. Almost two thirds (61) were convicted of murder, nine were convicted of child physical or sexual abuse, and the remaining 10 cases were attempted murder, conspiracy to commit murder, arson, robbery, and tax fraud. The characteristics of their victims included 32 cases of children and 11 cases of significant others. Another 18 cases involved family or other relationships with 12 involving strangers or acquaintances. Only seven of the 80 cases involved no victim. It is not unusual for women to commit crimes involving those with whom they are in a relationship.

Of the 80 cases we examined, 63 went to trial and 58 were found guilty despite the evidence that their confessions were false. Charges were dropped against 12 and five pled guilty and did not go to trial. More than half of the women in our database remained incarcerated with their cases at various stages in the appellate process during our initial analysis. There were 11 whose convictions were reversed and remanded back for a new trial. Only 19 have been officially exonerated at that time. When we revised the database adding approximately 20 more cases, we went back and looked at the original 80 cases and found that fewer were still incarcerated, perhaps due to winning their appeals or other exoneration that was not fully explained in the records.

Looking at the factors that influence female confessions, we found that 39 of the original 80 women on our database reported trauma and/ or abuse; 17 reported they had developed battered woman syndrome; 62 reported mental illness, substance abuse, and/or intellectual disability, and 31 reported that threats to their children influenced their confessions. These numbers do not add to 80 as there was overlap in the different categories.

We also attempted to place the women in the various categories of the confession typology used (Conte & Grabner, 2015). Here we found that the largest numbers (62%) were those whose false confessions occurred during coerced-compliant situations and the smallest number (6%) were voluntary confessions. There were 8% who gave a voluntary confession who had internalized their guilt (voluntary internalized) while 15% who were coerced also internalized their guilt (coerced internalized). Approximately 9% confessed after being coerced by an outsider (coerced reactive). Obviously these categories were assigned based on the reported data available and might be different had we interviewed the women themselves.

The Role of Children

In approximately 40% of the cases in our database, there were reports of threats made to the woman's child (Grabner et al., 2015). Sometimes the threats were direct such as removal of her children or blaming the child for the crime. Other cases were more indirect threats such as manipulating her maternal instinct and the desire to protect the children. In domestic violence cases, there were the batterer's threats to harm the children if she did not accept blame usually for his abuse of the children. Some women reported that they confessed but knew the police would sort it out and understand that it was the man not them who hurt the child. Other women reported confessing as they believed promises that they would be allowed to go home and not send their children into foster care.

Women in our database appeared to be wrongfully convicted of child homicide when it was clear the evidence pointed to the abusive partners as the perpetrators or that no crime had actually occurred. For example, in 42% of the cases we examined, women were charged with crimes against children (Conte, Astor, Young, Grabner, & Walker, 2015). In one third of these cases, no crime had actually occurred, the most common being accidental or medically explainable deaths. Of the cases in which a crime did occur, most were committed by a different perpetrator, such as an abusive male partner. While in some cases failure to protect the child might have been a more appropriate charge, in both the homicide or sexual abuse of children cases, their false confessions seemed to seal their fates especially if an expert witness was not permitted to offer testimony to explain why they were unable to protect the children against the batterers.

THE ROLE OF EXPERT TESTIMONY

Although there were 35 cases in which expert testimony was proposed during the criminal legal proceedings, it was admitted at trial only in half (17) of the cases (Conte et al., 2015). The expert testimony was proposed in order to explain general factors related to false confessions in 14 cases, the relationship between cognitive limitations such as intellectual disability and false confessions in four cases, and the influence of trauma and abuse histories and trauma-related symptoms associated with battered woman syndrome and PTSD including dissociation, psychogenic amnesia, and confabulation in 17 cases. Expert testimony was admitted in only 11 cases. In the 35 cases where it was not admitted, the appellate court upheld the trial court in 29 cases saying that it was unnecessary to have expert witnesses as this was within the common knowledge of the jurors and would not assist the trier of fact, that the prejudicial value outweighed the probative value, or that the testimony lacked reliability. The specific reasons cited when testimony was offered to explain the relationship between false confessions and the trauma and abuse histories included a lack of general acceptance within the scientific community, the theory was not subjected to peer review and publication, the theory was novel and lacked scientific reliability, and the proposed theory had unknown error rates. Obviously the courts are inappropriately applying Daubert or Federal Rules of Evidence standards rather than allowing clinical interpretations and observations or accepting the APA amicus briefs that describe the scientific reliability and validity of the research to date.

CONCLUSIONS

The research we have been conducting on false confessions of women has pointed out the gender inequities in some of the gender-neutral and gender-specific issues in the larger body of research on false confessions. Women meet all the vulnerabilities that were found in the research with men and others including the impact of the long histories of abuse and trauma. Although APA has issued some amicus briefs discussing the scientific studies in the area, the issue of gender has not been discussed. Our research group intends to continue our work and hopefully persuade the scientific and legal communities to include the gender-based analyses to the cases of women who falsely confess to crimes they did not commit.

REFERENCES

Cheit, R. E. (2014). *The witch hunt narrative: Politics, psychology, and the sexual abuse of children.* New York, NY: Oxford University Press.

Conte, C. B., & Grabner, S. S. (2015, August). Identification of female false confession cases and creation of a database. In L. E. A. Walker & D. Shapiro (Chairs). *Women and false confessions: Broadening the typology.* Symposium conducted at the 123rd annual meeting of the American Psychological Association, Toronto, Ontario, Canada.

Conte, C. B., Astor, J. H., Young, A., Grabner, S., & Walker, L. E. A. (2015, August). *Exploring the role of child victims in female false confession cases.* Poster presented at the 123rd annual meeting of the American Psychological Association, Toronto, Ontario, Canada.

Conte, C. B., Grabner, S., & Walker, L. E. A. (2015, May). *The inadmissibility of expert witness testimony in female false confession cases.* Poster presented at the American Psychology-Law Society Annual Conference, San Diego, CA.

Drizin, S. A., & Leo, R. A. (2004). The problem of false confessions in the post-DNA world. *North Carolina Law Review, 82,* 892–1004.

Grabner, S., Hylton, T., Landwehr, A., Conte, C. B., & Walker, L. E. A. (August 2015). *Maternal instinct, threats to children, and the elicitation of false confessions.* Poster presented at the 123rd annual meeting of the American Psychological Association, Toronto, Ontario, Canada.

Inbau, F. E., Reid, J. E., Buckley, J. P., & Jayne, B. C. (2013). *Criminal interrogation and confessions* (5th ed.). Burlington, MA: Jones & Bartlett.

Innocence Project. (2010). Female exonerees represent only a few of the women who have been wrongfully convicted nationwide. Retrieved from http://

www.innocenceproject.org/news-events-exonerations/2010/female-dna
-exonerees-represent-only-a-few-of-the-women-who-have-been-wrongfully
-convicted-nationwide

Innocence Project. (2016). False confessions or admissions. Retrieved from http://
www.innocenceproject.org/causes-wrongful-conviction/false-confessions
-or-admissions

Jackson, K., & Gross, S. (2014). Female exonerees: Trends and patterns. Retrieved
from https://www.law.umich.edu/special/exoneration/Pages/Features
.Female.Exonerees.aspx

Kassin, S. M. (2008). False confessions: Causes, consequences, and implications
for reform. *Current Directions in Psychological Science, 17*(4), 249–253.

Kassin, S. M. (2012). Why confessions trump innocence. *American Psychologist,
67*(6), 431–445.

Kassin, S. M., Drizin, S. A., Grisso, T., Gudjonsson, G. H., Leo, R. A., & Redlich, A. D.
(2010). Police-induced confessions: Risk factors and recommendations. *Law
and Human Behavior, 34*(1), 3–38.

Kassin, S. M., & Kiechel, K. L. (1996). The social psychology of false confessions:
Compliance, internalization, and confabulation. *Psychological Science, 7*(3),
125–128.

Kassin, S. M., & Norwick, R. J. (2004). Why people waive their Miranda rights:
The power of innocence. *Law and Human Behavior, 28*(2), 211–221.

Leo, R. A., & Ofshe, R. J. (1998). The consequences of false confessions: Deprivations of liberty and miscarriages of justice in the age of psychological interrogation. *Journal of Criminal Law and Criminology, 88*(2), 429–496.

The National Registry of Exonerations. (2016). Exoneration detail list. Retrieved
from http://www.law.umich.edu/special/exoneration/Pages/detaillist.aspx

Redlich, A. D., Kulish, R., & Steadman, H. J. (2011). Comparing true and false
confessions among persons with serious mental illness. *Psychology, Public
Policy, and Law, 17*(3), 394–418.

Sangero, B., & Halpert, M. (2011). Proposal to reverse the view of a confession:
From key evidence requiring corroboration to corroboration for key evidence.
University of Michigan Journal of Law Reform, 44, 511.

CHAPTER NINETEEN

FAMILY COURT, CHILD CUSTODY, AND DOMESTIC VIOLENCE

There is no question that the presence of domestic violence and child maltreatment poses significant problems for the family court and child custody evaluators. I began to discuss this complex issue in an earlier chapter on children living in domestic violence homes. In fact, the largest number of complaints filed with licensing boards and malpractice insurance carriers deal with child custody evaluations. While some think this may be because there are often winners and losers in the battle for access to children, I am more inclined to believe it is because these child custody evaluators do not take the danger seriously for children exposed to intimate partner violence in their homes (Kleinman & Walker, 2015; Walker, Cummings, & Cummings, 2012). Research demonstrates the lack of knowledge of judges and child custody evaluators in protecting women and children when domestic violence and child abuse are reported as compared to battered women advocates and legal aide attorneys (Saunders, Faller, & Tolman, 2012).

An entire industry has grown up around trying to figure out the right access to children by parents of divorcing families. The state laws keep changing, trying to force parents who cannot get along with each other to cooperate in parenting their children. Despite all the new professionals added to assist the family court judges' opinions, the fact is that children from these families will rarely grow up healthy and happy when they are forced to spend parenting time with a coercive, controlling, and abusive parent, even if the abuse is not proven to be physical or sexual. It is my opinion, based on the research over these past 40 years, that if we do not fix the family courts so they better protect women and children, domestic violence will not be eradicated. Many batterers want possession of their children, like they want over their wives, which includes the right to tell them what to do, and most do not want to have to pay a fair share of child support to get their demands met. They would rather pay for child care than pay child support to the partners who have rejected them. They would rather continue to control partners through the children than to negotiate around what really are the best interests of their children. Protective mothers are hesitant to let the children go, knowing that inappropriate parenting awaits them. New organizations of mothers who have lost the right to parent their children have grown in numbers and strength during the past decade, and many are sharing their stories with legislators hoping to persuade them to change some of the laws that permit these devastating consequences for children (i.e., California Protective Parents).

Most important to change is the presumption of shared parental responsibility forcing both parents to share physical custody and decision-making responsibility around their children. While no one could disagree that parents should cooperate around the important decisions in raising children, whether they live together or are married, it is foolish to believe that batterers who demand power and control have the ability to share anything. It is also foolish to believe that an entire new industry of health care providers can force abusers to play fairly by enacting new laws requiring parenting coordinators, child custody evaluators, time-sharing coordinators, psychotherapists, court-involved therapists, and others to monitor these coerced arrangements. Ignorance about family dynamics and developmental needs of children has caused the rise of continuous litigation in this area, permitting the courts and those involved in assisting judges to continue the batterers' control over their children and partners.

IGNORANCE OR INABILITY TO PROTECT CHILDREN IN FAMILY COURT?

Why do custody evaluators have such a difficult time understanding the impact that living with an abusive parent has had on the psychological development of the child? As we have seen in this research program, the effects of abuse, maltreatment, intimidation, and bullying behaviors have on children are traumatic. They produce long-lasting effects on the children that include lower self-esteem, learning difficulties, depression, anxiety, fear, distrust, and other trauma symptoms. While not all batterers are poor fathers, research by Lundy Bancroft who served as the co-coordinator of Emerge, one of the first programs for abusive males in

Massachusetts, found that the power and coercive control needs of batterers supersede their ability to appropriately parent their children, especially when they have not worked out their anger issues against the children's mothers (Bancroft & Silverman, 2002).

Abusive behavior by the perpetrator does not begin during separation or divorce proceedings, although at times it permits children to finally disclose abuse. Rather, most children who grow up in homes where a father abuses the mother are subjected to the tension and fear that builds up before an acute battering incident, even if they are not intentionally abused themselves. Although both parents may try to hide the physical abuse from children, the bullying and intimidating behavior, the rigid rules that are set by the abuser, and the consequences for violation of any of the direct or indirect rules are often witnessed by children in these homes. It produces anxiety and fear in some and anger and resentment in others. Often, if there is more than one child in the home, the children mimic the parents' behavior with one being controlling and dominating the other. Patterson's (1982) research showed the cross-gender nature of the aggressive boys' behavior; mothers or sisters were commonly their main target.

So, what does this look like to custody evaluators as they miss the important data and place children in harm's way? In most cases, the evaluators are either ignorant of the literature on domestic violence and its impact on different members of the family or they minimize the domestic violence they do learn about. There are several ways to minimize the domestic violence that include blaming the victim for her behavior, artificially dividing domestic violence into different types of behavior and then assuming that certain types do not have negative impact, ignoring or misinterpreting signs of abuse, or alleging some factitious disorder like Munchausen by proxy or the nonexistent parental alienation syndrome or disorder.

What should the courts and custody evaluators inquire about batterers as parents according to Lundy Benjamin? First, are the power and control issues across a number of areas in the batterer's life? Does he model aggressive behavior for the children and if so, can he modify this behavior for the sake of the children? Did he become more psychologically unstable during the separation period? Did he increase his stalking and surveillance behavior and use the children to obtain information about their mother? Does he interfere with joint decision making so that decisions either do not get made without court or other interference, or the mother must give up something else to get the children's needs met? What kinds of manipulation techniques does he use and how do they impact decisions around the children? Is he using substances to cope and if so, how do they impact his safety concerns for himself and the children? For example, does he drive after drinking alcohol? Does he forget to buckle children into car seats? Does he resist giving the children prescribed medications when they are sick? Are there periods where he refuses to accept reality or to tell the truth? Does he have difficulty in accepting help or need to change his behavior? Does he cling to the image of the child he wants rather than getting to know the child he has? These are just some of the questions that need to be answered before a decision about parenting responsibilities can be answered. While not all those who fail in these skills are batterers or will harm their children, together with reports of prior domestic violence and child abuse, they make the coercive and controlling behavior even more dangerous and put the child at unnecessary risk.

Parental Alienation

Although estrangement of a child and a parent can occur during the parents' divorce, there are no empirically valid data to support the existence of syndrome of an alienated child caused by one parent's campaign of denigration of the other parent to the child. Yet, many evaluators use this theory, first proposed by psychiatrist Richard Gardner (1987), as an excuse to override the parent's wish not to continue to coparent with an abuser. Or even worse, perhaps, is to deny the so-called alienator access to the child who is given to the disliked and feared parent with no controls over that parent's behavior or parenting skills. Joan Meier among others presents compelling evidence that there is no such disorder despite the belief in its existence by family courts. It is interesting that in almost all cases the person who is blamed as an alienator parent is the mother, who may have alleged domestic violence, and the alienated parent is the father or even stepfather. Sometimes the alienated parent's family is also disliked and feared by the child, often because of refusal to believe that his family members will protect them or even because the children have witnessed members of the family being abusive themselves. It is very concerning when alienation is used as a rebuttal to charges of domestic violence or child maltreatment and no further appropriate evaluation is conducted.

Parental alienation comes from the theories of psychiatrist Richard Gardner, who initially was very involved in children's adjustment to divorce, even writing a popular book and a game called *The Boys and Girls Book of Divorce* in the 1970s, used by many child psychologists. However, something happened in the late 1980s and 1990s, where he began to suspect that allegations of child sexual abuse were being fabricated by mothers who wanted sole custody of children and thus used this as an attack against perfectly adequate fathers. He used an unvalidated assessment tool that he created to determine who was telling the truth and who was not. We discuss the difficulty of proving child sexual allegations elsewhere. After being criticized for his inaccurate and often dangerous child sexual abuse theories, Gardner went on to propose the parental alienation syndrome that he claimed was suffered by the child as a result of one parent targeting the other parent to alienate the child from the targeted parent. Again, with no empirical data to support his theories, this concept became accepted in courts all over the world and even since his own death by suicide, his proponents have carried on the battle to get some form of parental alienation accepted. Despite their failure to persuade the American Psychiatric Association to include it in the *Diagnostic and Statistical Manual of Mental Disorders* (5th ed.; *DSM-5*; American Psychiatric Association, 2013), they persist in introducing it in the family courts. My husband and colleague, psychologist David Shapiro, and I have written an article published elsewhere to refute their argument that it is even possible for alienation to cause a child to be labeled mentally ill (Walker & Shapiro, 2010).

Psychologists Leslie Drozd and Nancy Olesen in 2016 proposed what they hoped would be a compromise by developing a decision tree to help custody evaluators decide whether abuse produced alienation or actual estrangement between the child and the parent. Estranged children are those who refuse to be with a feared parent because of that parent's behavior toward the child. However, many children never get to be labeled "estranged," as they are continuously forced into parenting time with the feared and disliked parent and therefore develop what Roland Summit called "child abuse accommodation syndrome," pretending to get along during the time they were forced to spend with that parent. Protective moms tell stories about being told by judges that if they do not force their children to spend parenting time with feared and disliked parents, they will remove custody from the moms. And judges do exactly that. Many of these children who have aged out of being forced into parenting time have joined together in an organization dedicated to preventing other children from having to go through the same difficult time. Others have tried to file lawsuits against the abusive parents but have so many emotional problems that often they cannot sustain the stress of seeing the lawsuits through to the end.

In a compelling movie produced by Garland Waller, a filmmaker who is on the faculty at Boston University, called *No Way Out But One*, she chronicled the life of a mother, Holly Collins, who fled to the Netherlands with her three children, two of whom had been found abused by their father but still removed from their mother and placed in his care. After cries for help from the children fell on deaf ears in the family court, she kidnapped them, and took them to the Netherlands. After living 10 years mostly as a refugee petitioning the Dutch government for amnesty, she and the children were granted Dutch citizenship. Eventually, she was able to get the U.S. government to drop the criminal charges against her so she and all her children can live in the United States again should they choose it. Holly and her oldest daughter now travel back and forth from the Netherlands to the United States and give talks to groups of protective mothers and children. But most protective moms are not as strong as Holly Collins was and today, they could not take their children on an airplane to another country without appropriate documents, as she was able to do so many years ago.

Jenny

Jenny (this is not her real name) and her partner, Derek, had a child, although they never consistently lived in the same house together. Derek did not pay a lot of attention to the child unless he got in his way when he came to spend time with Jenny. The child became quite frightened when Derek would scream at Jenny and began his own screaming tantrums during infancy. As he grew older, Derek would punish the child while angrily screaming at both him and Jenny. When the child was 2 years old, Derek grabbed him by the arm and dislocated the child's shoulder, necessitating a trip to the hospital ER. The ER doctor made a child abuse report, child protective services became involved, and Derek was unable to contact the child or Jenny for several months until the family court heard the case. The child, who had been having difficult behavioral problems, became much calmer and easier to parent when he did not have contact with his father.

Jenny also had an easier time parenting the child during this hiatus in visitation. Although Jenny and Derek were not legally married, the dependency court transferred the case to the family court to obtain a legal dissolution of the relationship and custody and shared parenting time orders. The family court judge ordered parenting time restored to Derek, which began several years of litigation and numerous child custody evaluations, each coming to a different conclusion. Meanwhile, the child was exhibiting numerous behavioral signs and symptoms indicating he was struggling when with Derek. Jenny became more possessive of the child while Derek began demanding more time with him. Although preschool was recommended, Derek would not agree to any school Jenny chose for him. Neither parent worked so they could demand parenting time with the child. Caught in the middle, the child had no allies, and continued to decompensate. So did the parents.

Could the court have done a better job in protecting the child as well as Jenny and Derek? Probably. First, the case should have been handled as child abuse rather than a custody dispute. Second, both parents should have been ordered into psychological evaluations with an evaluator who understood the effects of domestic violence on young children. Third, the child should have been ordered into psychotherapy (probably play therapy at his young age) and an evaluation performed by someone who understood the effects of child abuse and domestic violence on children. Fourth, the change in the child's behavior when he was not with the father supported the mother's reports of inappropriate parenting behavior by the father. Fifth, this information should have been highlighted as what was proven to be in the best interests of the child. If the father continued to request parenting time, then sixth, there should be domestic violence-trained parenting therapists who could teach him appropriate parenting skills while exposing him to the child in incremental doses. The same person should work also with the mom and child together to prevent the bias that would come from having exposure only to the dad. It is not uncommon for a parenting coordinator who works only with one parent to become more attached to wanting that parent to succeed even if it is not in the best interests of the child. Some of these supervised visitation coordinators actually are untrained and have no boundaries. In one case I worked on, the visitation supervisor became infatuated with the dad who took her shopping and bought her gifts in front of the children she was hired by the court to protect.

Lilly

Lilly was a 13-year-old girl who was referred to me for psychological evaluation as her parents were in the middle of a fairly contentious divorce. Lilly's mother, Karen, walked into the television room and found her husband, Lilly's father, Charles, molesting Lilly while watching television. Horrified, she screamed out and startled both Lilly and Charles, who quickly got up and pretended not to know why Karen was so upset. Karen, who had felt disconnected from her marriage with Charles for some time, decided that this behavior was intolerable and forced Charles to leave the home, at least temporarily. Lilly had been demonstrating problematic behaviors during the past year. An "A" student, her grades went down and rather than concentrating on her homework, she would be seen just sitting and staring into space. Her hair began to fall out, she had stomachaches for which the doctor could find no cause, and she began to wear layers of clothes later revealing bruises from her father. Although Karen and Charles had not had any physically intimate contact for several years, at least not since their younger child had been born, they continued to have the outward appearance of a cohesive family, especially at their Church where Charles was a youth leader. Although Lilly did not want to spend parenting time with her father after the separation, she reluctantly went because she wanted to protect her younger brother.

Once Karen filed for divorce, the family court got involved. Karen had gotten Lilly into psychotherapy with a child psychologist who was trained to work with child abuse survivors. Although the incident was reported to child protective services, Lilly was unwilling and psychologically unable to disclose very much and the case was labeled "unfounded." Visitations that were ordered included dinners and play time at the neighborhood shopping mall. I became involved when Lilly, who had been complaining about her father paying more attention to her brother, walked away from the mall, called her mother who came to pick her up, and the father and visitation supervisor did not even know she was missing.

Karen's parents, Lilly's grandparents, contacted me and asked if I could assist in helping Karen and Lilly through the legal quagmire of family court. I agreed and after analysis of the case, suggested that they first hire a private investigator to actually see what was going on during the visitation period. When the investigator's reports came back, it was clear that Lilly's comments were accurate. Not only was the father favoring the brother, he actually was unable to make a connection with Lilly due to her anger at his betrayal of trust. As she got angrier at the father, it became clear that her anger was focused on his lying about his coming into her room at night and molesting her. He had taught her moral values to always tell the truth and she knew he was lying. This to her was worse than the physical and sexual abuse that had been going on for several years.

The second suggestion I made was for the grandparents to hire a lawyer to represent Lilly's wishes. Although children still do not have legal rights or the right to their own lawyer in family court, in fact it may be helpful for them to know that their "wishes" will be heard through their own lawyer; not a guardian-ad-litem, who must by the law represent their "best interests." Lilly, a very bright child, was delighted to have her own lawyer and felt empowered by the fact that even though she could not be in the courtroom herself, her lawyer would represent her. She knew that she might not get what she wished for, but at least she could have a voice there. In this case, the judge did permit the child's lawyer to sit and hear the case but in other cases, judges have refused. However, although her lawyer was in court along with her parents' lawyers, she could not question the witnesses, which sometimes is allowed. As there was no guardian ad litem (GAL) appointed, the court sharply limited questioning allegedly due to time limitations. Thus, the judge never did hear all the evidence and made some recommendations that were helpful for Lilly but also ordered she be in "reunification therapy" with her father when Lilly's therapist said she was ready. In some courts, judges actually order a child be removed from psychotherapy with their chosen therapist and force them to begin therapy with another therapist of the court's choosing.

All visitations were stopped with the father and, given the financial resources of this family, Charles accepted an undisclosed sum of money to give up his parental rights to Lilly and her brother, permitted them to move to another state, and both children are growing up healthy and happy. Lilly, who once she became safe, changed her name and began disclosing more and more incidents of child abuse and sexual grooming that may even have ended up with a pornography and sex-trafficking ring barely hidden from view. This family had financial resources out of the reach of the average family that goes through family court. Fortunately, we never will know what might have happened had that not been the case here.

David and Daniel

David and Daniel, ages 4 and 6, were involved in a custody dispute between their parents at the same time that a preschool teacher in another part of town was discovered to be involved with child pornography. The family court scenario was typical; the mother, who alleged domestic violence, also claimed the father was sexually abusing the boys who described the abuse with details that would be appropriate for their ages. They also talked about taking pictures with their father's friends. The family court judge listened to testimony from child abuse and domestic violence experts and decided to take custody away from their mother and give temporary custody to the father's parents. The children were upset and did not want to leave the mother. They were frightened as they had implicated the grandfather in their abuse. Apparently, the grandparents did not like the mother and were accusing her of making up lies to alienate the boys from their family. It was learned that at the very same time, in a criminal court in another part of the city, a preschool teacher had been arrested for possession of child pornography. The children's grandmother had worked at the same preschool where the teacher had been arrested, and she had been accused of failure to report a case of child abuse that had occurred several years earlier. Not surprisingly, the two cases, in two different courts, were not analyzed together to see if there was any connection between what David and Daniel were saying and what the authorities uncovered at the preschool. The big question is why not?

Witch-Hunt Narrative Trials

In the 1970s, there began several major cases of alleged child sexual abuse in child care centers that occurred across the United States. In the McMartin trial in California, where several children testified to having been abused, the perpetrators were eventually not convicted due to discrediting the testimony of the children and blaming parents for biasing them. Other major cases followed and even when convictions were obtained, like in the Kelly Michael case, they were overturned and reversed on appeal. New guidelines for questioning children, particularly young ones, doubts raised about mothers' motives for making reports, especially when consistent with domestic violence allegations, and a consistent refusal for courts and laypersons to believe the truth about so-called "upstanding" citizens' behavior all top the list for why child abuse and domestic violence continue to exist. Ross Cheit, a political scientist, wrote a detailed analysis of several of these cases in his book *The Witch-Hunt Narrative* where he showed that the truth simply may not be able to be supported given our legal system (Walker, 2015). More recently, the case of Jerry Sandusky, the Penn State University athletic coach who was accused of child abuse and molestation by now-adult survivors, gives some hope that there may be a shift in the way the criminal courts handle these cases when the abuse is not in the domestic violence families. Yet, the data tell us that over 60% of the children living in domestic violence homes are also physically and sexually abused themselves, while all could be said to be psychologically abused.

WHY WILL THE FAMILY COURTS NOT BELIEVE CHILDREN AND PROTECTIVE MOMS?

An interesting study by Robert Geffner and his colleagues in the San Diego Institute on Violence, Abuse and Trauma (IVAT) published in the December 2015 issue of the *Journal of Child Custody* surveyed perceptions and attitudes about intimate partner violence in child custody cases (Sanders, Geffner, Bucky, Ribner, & Patino, 2015). They found similar results as did others such as Dan Saunders and colleagues (2012, 2013), Davis and colleagues (2010), and Silberg and colleagues (2013). Geffner and colleagues found that the 10 custody evaluators in six different states from whom they collected qualitative data did have some knowledge about domestic violence but there was no agreement about how it should impact child custody decisions. In fact, they held beliefs that victims would make false accusations of intimate partner abuse in order to gain a legal advantage in their cases, despite Geraldine Stahly and others' research that these beliefs were more likely maintained by gender bias and are proven to be outdated.

Geffner and his colleagues suggest that confirmatory bias may help understand why custody evaluators cling to outdated and untested theories when conducting evaluations. First, the custody evaluators do not have a uniform protocol for conducting the evaluation and rarely rely on standardized tests or other assessment instruments. Second, when observing parent–child interactions during the evaluation, they may not give sufficient weight to observations consistent with abuse or again, engage in confirmatory bias; that what they know about domestic violence is not what is happening in the case. Further, several of the custody evaluators interviewed believed that parental alienation did exist while the others did not. However, those who did believe in it were adamant that it was a critical factor in deciding custody or parenting time. A structured interview can avoid such confirmatory bias as can actual assessment of the child's or parent's difficulties. Nonetheless, there are no tests to prove that a child's exposure to intimate partner violence was detrimental to the child's best interests at this time.

In the Saunders, Tolman, and Faller (2013) study, samples of family court judges and lawyers (who deal more with domestic violence cases), legal aid lawyers (who deal more with child abuse and dependency cases), child custody evaluators, and battered women advocates were shown vignettes or analogue stories of different cases that had come before the court to settle child custody disputes. They found that one of the major reasons judges, child custody evaluators, and family court lawyers do not protect women and children is that they are more likely to believe the women and children have made false allegations rather than believe legal aid and domestic violence advocates who have worked with many actual cases of child abuse and domestic violence. Even when the abuse is believed, child custody evaluators were less likely to recommend sole custody to the mother over half the time and in at least one quarter of the cases said they would be more likely to give sole custody to the father when those allegations were made. Even when the vignette reported severe domestic violence, custody evaluators still thought shared or joint legal custody was appropriate without supervised visitation.

Those favoring the offenders in the stories believed that domestic violence victims do alienate children from their fathers, that their allegations of abuse are either false or exaggerated, and that domestic violence is not important in making custody decisions. Further, they believed that victims would be likely to hurt the children if they resist coparenting. They believed that coercive controlling violence in the vignette was not important to further explore in the evaluation and that the couple would benefit from mediation. Not surprisingly, male child custody evaluators were more likely to find domestic violence allegations were false and female child custody evaluators were more likely to find that fathers are the alienators, not mothers.

Another study with similar findings occurred with a review of cases of domestic violence where there were child custody evaluations in the New York City (NYC) courts conducted by Davis, O'Sullivan, Susser, and

Fields (2010). Judge Marjory Fields has been a consistent champion for changing the family courts to better protect battered women and children, having filed the first successful class action lawsuit against the NYC courts back in the 1970s when she was still a legal aid attorney. They found that child custody reports have a profound impact on judges who make custody decisions. Judges look to the child custody evaluators to assist in assessment of the seriousness of risk of harm to children and make assumptions that the child custody evaluator does have sufficient knowledge of domestic violence and risk on which to base their recommendations. However, they found that even when the child custody evaluator had knowledge of power and control factors in domestic violence relationships, they were hesitant to apply it to giving moms the power to make the legal decisions for their children. Instead, it dooms the moms and children to continuing fights and harassment in order to simply go to summer camp, take an extra class in school, buy a new dress for a party, or skip a visitation in order to go on a much-wanted trip with a friend.

When evaluating the safety concerns that might have been put into the parenting plans, the study found that severity of physical, sexual, or psychological abuse did not appear to be considered by the custody evaluators no matter how much domestic violence knowledge they may have had. This is a critical finding because some states, such as California, keep making the domestic violence training longer for child custody evaluators without really seeing if the knowledge translates into better safety for children in their recommendations to the courts. They suggest that there needs to be more training on the power and control aspects of batterers' relationships with their partners and children, not just the facts about domestic violence. More emphasis on stereotypes, biases, and understanding the connection of controlling behavior on adverse traumatic impact over time is also needed. It is also important for custody evaluators to understand the developmental needs of children at different ages and attempt to make compromises that work for families where there are multiple children of different ages and stages of development.

I was asked to become involved in training Israeli family court judges by my good friend, retired judge Saviona Rotlevy. For several years, we would spend a week in a Moshev, far away from the courts, learning together with speakers like myself who came in from different parts of Israel. Although the lectures were extremely informative, it was the late night discussions in the lounge area where the ideas really took hold. One night we all were bussed to a battered woman's shelter in

Jerusalem where the women got to tell the judges what they thought of the family court system. One after another they got to say what they never would dare to say in court when the stakes were so high for them. The dialogue there was extraordinary with judges really listening to what the women were saying. Many of the judges admitted afterward that they never took the concerns of battered women seriously in their courtrooms. For most of them it brought what the experts were saying in the classroom alive and relevant as it applied to one woman after another. I heartily recommend that anyone who sits on the family court bench be required to spend several days in different battered woman shelters and treatment centers listening to what the women have to say to them. Child custody evaluators ought to have such real-life experiences, also. Perhaps that would help reduce their skepticism.

The Battered Woman Justice Project has provided information and materials for training in recognizing detrimental coercive controlling behavior and how it negates the needs of children especially in the area of safety, autonomy, and freedom from coercion in order to grow healthy and strong. Some of the areas that have been identified as standing in the way of promoting proper developmental growth in children even postdivorce include postseparation abuse, relentless harassment and use of bargaining to permit routine requests, problematic parenting techniques, and coercive control. It is clear that the family court model that divides up children just like it divides up property is not going to protect children and battered moms.

Leadership Council

Joyanna Silberg and her colleagues at the Leadership Council (www .leadershipcouncil.org) have studied cases where the courts gave child custody to a parent where there were allegations of child abuse. Despite the fact that there was credible evidence of abuse, the mental health worker or child custody evaluator did not believe the evidence or thought it was insufficient for the child to need protection. The judge did not protect the child and gave orders for custody or unsupervised visitation to the abuser. At a later time, when further abuse toward the child was discovered, either that judge or another judge reversed the initial rulings and ordered custody back to the protective mother. In over three quarters of these cases, the judge blamed the protective mother for the child's "false" outcries and in two thirds of them gave custody in the first time to the father despite claims of abuse. When the case came up again, 80% of judges gave sole custody to the mother. *But*, 20% still gave fathers joint custody or visitation despite the incontrovertible fact that he had abused the child. While this is a preliminary study with a small number of cases, it is frightening that despite factual evidence of abuse, judges are still giving batterers access to their children.

The most common error for child custody evaluators and judges (and some family lawyers) has been to blame the mother for "coaching" the child or "overprotecting" the child. Yet, what else can a mother do when she believes her child is being abused, often in a manner similar to how the father also abused her. But despite the fears, there are few cases of false allegations, although it may be common for some children to recant their outcries fearing the consequences of telling the family secrets. Child protection agencies suggest that around one fifth of reported cases are found to be true, although almost two thirds more are what is called "unfounded" or the evidence is insufficient to further process the case. The story of Lilly is typical of some children who cannot disclose out of fear or even improper questioning. Given protection and time, most children like Lilly eventually tell what happened to them. But, it has to be when they are comfortable, not when the courts decree it.

Most untrained mental health evaluators or detectives do not know how to question children properly. The American Professional Society Against the Abuse of Children (APSAC) has published guidelines discussed in an earlier chapter that help obtain reliable and valid information from children of various ages. It is important for those doing the questioning to be well trained and have learned to keep their emotions under control. I believe that many refuse to believe the horror of existing child abuse because they are emotionally unprepared to believe that people like themselves could be doing such terrible things to their own or other peoples' children. Thus, training is needed not only in academic knowledge but also in controlling one's own emotions.

IS THE FAMILY COURT SYSTEM BROKEN?

Several years ago, in 2012, I led a conference in Phoenix, Arizona, where we titled it, Our Broken Family Court System. The conference was underwritten by a family that had gone through what they called, "Family

Court Hell." For 2 days internationally known speakers took center stage and described both the horrors of family court when domestic violence and child abuse allegations were made and made valuable suggestions on how to make substantial changes to fix the system, if it was fixable at all. Although we invited people from various areas in the court system to attend, few judges, medical doctors, pediatricians, or psychiatrists were present. Some lawyers attended as did mental health professionals and domestic violence advocates. Interestingly, the university that had originally agreed to cosponsor the conference pulled out at the last minute after getting pressure from the local family court judges and their social work school insisting the family court was not broken. Several attorneys who worked in the local family court also refused to be speakers, again citing the pressure not to offend the judges who appointed them to cases or in whose courtrooms they had to serve their clients. Nonetheless, the conference was a success; it was both audiotaped and videotaped with speeches then used for continuing education programs. A book was published, *Our Broken Family Court System* (Walker, Cummings, & Cummings, 2012), that was sent to policy makers in local, state, and federal governments. Four years later, I have not heard of any positive legislative changes, although there are some bills pending (and hopelessly stalled) in the U.S. Congress.

One of the talks that I gave outlined what I called "Seven Deadly Sins in Family Court." They included the following:

1. The presumptions in the law have no empirical data to support them, especially the presumption that it is in the best interests of all children, including those exposed to domestic violence and child abuse, to have contact with both parents. It is also a fallacy to believe that the parent who appears the most friendly during an evaluation is actually a better parent than the parent who attempts to protect the child even to her or his own detriment.

2. Child custody evaluators, lawyers, and judges have stereotyped biases that blind them to the dangers of continued domestic violence for battered women and children who are abused by their fathers. They have not examined their own emotional reactions to behaviors surrounding domestic violence perpetrators and victims.

3. Those who make the decisions about custody and access to children do not have adequate knowledge about the developmental needs of all children at each stage and age and culture. Nor do they know

how to create parenting plans that respect these needs in the child's best interests.

4. There is ignorance about child abuse: how to assess it and how to help children who have been abused heal from the trauma. There is little respect for the dignity of the abused child and his or her perception of what has happened to him or her.

5. There is ignorance about the impact on children of living in homes where there is domestic violence, including coercive control by the abuser, postseparation abuse, fear of threats, and coercive control.

6. Children do not have legal standing in the family courts in the United States. Psychologists know that trauma survivors heal when they experience empowerment and control over their lives. Our laws around children are inconsistent. If a 14-year-old boy commits murder, he may be waived as a juvenile and tried as an adult in criminal court. A 14-year-old girl who becomes pregnant has to get her parent's permission to terminate the pregnancy but can get married to the abuser in some states to protect him from prosecution. And, if her parents are divorcing, she can be court ordered into shared parental custody with an abusive father.

7. There are few incentives for the family court system to change. There is too little funding for appeals, including rarely having actual transcripts of egregious errors during closed courtroom hearings. There is little attention by the media, and unless it is *your* family, the general public does not evidence concern.

Systemic court barriers to change so children and women are safe are many in family law. The family court system is based on fairness and what is equal for parties in the family. There is no equality or fairness in domestic violence. There is usually one perpetrator who needs to be held accountable for the abuse. While the other party may have engaged in manipulative or other disagreeable behaviors, it often has become a survival skill to protect her from the abuser's continued assaults. Equalizing her power can be accomplished by judges willing to give her legal authority to make decisions if he does not agree to what is best for their children.

Reunification of the family is not a helpful order when there has been abuse. First, the victims have to heal from the trauma, which may not be able to occur until the victims feel empowered. Forcing contact with the abuser may continue the trauma reactions as he may already have taken on the role of the "trauma trigger" so the victims cannot heal as they are being retraumatized by his presence even if he stops the abusive behavior. Friendly parent statutes that call for both parents to forgive and forget may actually increase the risk to the victims by minimizing the continuing danger that she perceives.

Many jurisdictions are so backlogged with family court cases that they cannot hear the evidence that would permit an appropriate decision. Some limit testimony to 10 or 15 minutes for each side; others split up the hearings by giving too little time to hear the case so it is postponed to the next court date that might be several months later. Still others force the attorneys and clients to sit outside and negotiate even when it is known that the battered woman is more likely to give in to something that is unfair or will not work at that time rather than continue being in legal limbo. Lack of speedy trials such as occur in criminal cases makes it difficult for parties to move on with their lives. Children are caught in the middle, either wanting to know more about their fate or being forced to break ties to existing friends and family members. Teenagers are forced into visitation plans that violate their developmental needs to spend more time with their peers rather than parenting time and many children are forced to live back and forth in two homes without having any say in the matter. Some children are being parented by stepparents who do not like them or treat them very well. Battered women have lengthy and costly removal hearings if they wish to take a new job or move to another state to start a new life. Batterers are permitted to live on the same street as their victims, continuing to harass and stalk them, in the name of fair access to the children. All are kept off balance with these rules and laws that are not based on any empirical data. The arguments that children will not grow up healthy and normal without contact with both parents are spurious; we have data from children whose parent dies or is away in the military deployment that they do just fine with one strong parent.

THERAPEUTIC JURISPRUDENCE (TJ) IN FAMILY COURT?

The concept of TJ in criminal court has been adopted by many countries around the world as a way to use the legal/court systems to help people solve their problems so they will not keep coming back before the court.

There is a clear philosophy behind these problem-solving courts that permit the judge and other personnel to find out what mental health or other issues are underlying the unwanted behavior and how it may be modified by referrals in the community. In drug court, the first such specialty court, people who were addicted to various illegal substances were given the option of attending drug rehabilitation centers or treatment groups rather than going to jail (or attending groups in jail for some). In mental health court, people who have a mental health problem could be sent for treatment rather than prison for misdemeanor and some felony crimes. In domestic violence court, batterers are given the option of attending offender-specific treatment in the community. The most recent TJ court is the veterans' court that can help veterans resolve some of their mental health or substance abuse issues that got them into difficulty with the criminal justice courts.

Why can there be not TJ family courts where the children get the chance to have a say in what happens to them? In Israel, where children's laws have been revised to give them legal rights, Tamar Morag described an experimental children's court as part of family court when parents are divorcing. As they have legal standing, they get an attorney appointed who represents their wishes even if they are not in what others might think is their best interests. Judges and mental health professionals are trained to talk with children in private and parents must give permission for them to keep the children's wishes private. Children are educated about the process of divorce and asked about their wishes about continued relationships with parents without having to choose to ally with one parent. While at first many judges were against this court, after a while it became so effective that their objections were overcome. Those judges who did not like or want to speak with children could use an advocate to inform them about the child's needs and desires. The children whose parents went through this court were found to have healed faster from trauma and divorce than those who had no role in their parents' divorce. Children of all ages were approached in age-appropriate ways. Children also had a better quality relationship with their parents, even those who initially had no contact with a parent. Perhaps most important for the legal system, the number of repeated motions to settle disputes significantly dropped in these courts.

SUMMARY

These studies show that children can be better protected and heal faster from a family court system that does not treat them as uninformed trouble makers manipulated by one or the other parent. Rather, any allegations of abuse that they make should be believed and they must be protected. The ignorance and resistance of those who currently work in the family courts suggest that the system is broken and may not be able to fix itself. Perhaps the new TJ model of children courts that empower and protect children will be helpful if adopted. Unfortunately, it will be too late for too many children around the world unless those who are child custody evaluators change their methodology to better understand the risk to children when domestic violence and child abuse are alleged.

REFERENCES

American Psychiatric Association. (2013). *Diagnostic and statistical manual of mental disorders* (5th ed.). Arlington, VA: American Psychiatric Publishing.

Bancroft, L., & Silverman, J. G. (2002). *The batterer as a parent: Addressing the impact of domestic violence on family dynamics.* Thousand Oaks, CA: Sage.

Davis, M. S., O'Sullivan, C. S., Susser, K., & Fields, M. D. (2010). *Custody evaluations when there are allegations of domestic violence: Practices, beliefs and recommendations of professional evaluators.* Retrieved from https://www.ncjrs.gov/pdffiles1/nij/grants/234465.pdf

Drozd, L., Saini, M., & Olesen, N. (2016). *Parenting plan evaluations: Applied research for the family court* (2nd ed.). New York, NY: Oxford University Press.

Gardner, R. (1987). *The parental alienation syndrome and the differentiation between fabrication and genuine child abuse.* Creskill, NJ: Creative Therapeutics.

Kleinman, T. G., & Walker, L. E. (2015). Protecting psychotherapy clients from the shadow of the law: A call for the revision of the Association of Family and Conciliation Courts (AFCC) guidelines for court-involved therapy. *Journal of Child Custody, 11*(4), 335–362.

Patterson, G. R. (1982). *Coercive family process.* Eugene, OR: Castalia Press.

Sanders, L., Geffner, R., Bucky, S., Ribner, N., & Patino, A. J. (2015). A qualitative study of child custody evaluators' beliefs and opinions. *Journal of Child Custody, 12*(3–4), 205–230.

Saunders, D. G., Faller, K. C., & Tolman, R. M. (2012). *Child custody evaluators' beliefs about domestic abuse allegations: Their relationship to evaluator demographics, background, domestic violence knowledge and custody-visitation recommendations.* Retrieved from https://www.ncjrs.gov/pdffiles1/nij/grants/238891.pdf

Saunders, D. G., Tolman, R. M., & Faller, K. C. (2013). Factors associated with child custody evaluators' recommendations in cases of intimate partner violence. *Journal of Family Psychology, 27*(3), 473–482.

Silberg, J., Dallam, S., & Samson, E. (2013). *Crisis in family court: Lessons from turned around cases.* Retrieved from http://www.protectiveparents.com/crisis-fam-court-lessons-turned-around-cases.pdf

Walker, L. E. (2015). Who is the real witch in the hunt for the truth about child sexual abuse: Review of Cheit's, The Witch-Hunt Narrative. *PsycCritiques, 60*(14). http://dx.doi.org/10.1037/a0038946

Walker, L. E. A., & Shapiro, D. L. (2010). Parental alienation disorder: Why label children with a mental disorder? *Journal of Child Custody, 7*(4), 266–286.

Walker, L. E. A., Cummings, D. M., & Cummings, N. A. (Eds.). (2012). *Our broken family court system.* Dryden, NY: Ithaca Press.

CHAPTER TWENTY

DOMESTIC VIOLENCE COURTS AND BATTERERS' TREATMENT PROGRAMS

The need for *therapeutic justice (TJ)* began to receive support within the criminal justice system as those with drug problems began to flood the system during the 1970s. Acknowledging the failure of drug programs in the jails and prisons to help inmates "just say no" as was the policy of the United States under President Ronald Reagan, residential therapeutic communities and other treatment programs began to develop across the country and in the jails and prisons. Special drug courts were designed to help identify those offenders who could benefit from them as opposed to those offenders who were also selling large quantities of drugs with or without using them themselves. So, when the criminal justice system began to deal with large numbers of domestic violence perpetrators in the 1980s, there was already a precedent for a special problem-solving court to which arrestees could be referred. Later, after domestic violence courts and drug courts had demonstrated their effectiveness, mental health courts were authorized by the U.S. Congress to defer those who were mentally ill and committed a crime into treatment rather than prison. The move to decriminalize mental illness became a cornerstone of the TJ movement.

In most large jurisdictions, the chief judges were able to set up such special criminal courts to hear and adjudicate these cases in a special domestic violence court. The policy that developed after research demonstrated its effectiveness was to remove the barriers for law enforcement to make an arrest upon the officer's determination of probable cause for domestic violence having been committed, which eliminated the need for the victim to have to sign the arrest complaint. Domestic violence was then taken off the bonding schedule so that those arrested had to spend time in jail until the next regularly scheduled court appearance. Usually this meant 24 to 48 hours although it could be longer if the person was unable to make bond. Although controversial at first, with the American Civil Liberties Union (ACLU) calling it "preventive detention," in fact this proarrest procedure became the standard protocol when a domestic violence call could result in an arrest after research determined it was successful in preventing further violence in at least some cases (Sherman & Berk, 1984).

Prosecutors identified the issue of bail as a problem for women who were arrested for committing domestic violence against their partners, as men were more likely to make bail whereas the women were typically held, especially if they were both arrested at the same time. They also found that women were intimidated by the justice system and stigmatized by the consequences, which often include having their children removed by child protective services, a record, public housing denials, loss of welfare benefits, immigration issues, and custody hearings. These issues were more salient for women as they are often the primary caretakers. Women were often coerced into treatment even if their abuse was in self-defense and confused by the system in that they did not understand the full implications of a guilty plea.

Not all courts were able to handle these cases, so the special domestic violence court was a natural outgrowth as police began to make arrests and bring defendants into the courtrooms. Vertical prosecutions were recommended so that the more dangerous abusers could be further detained and prosecuted by state attorneys trained in their identification and by judges trained to understand the dynamics and impact on victims. Victim-witness specialists were hired by many prosecutors' offices so that they could assist the victims through the difficulties of the criminal justice system. The victim-witness program actually proved to be one of the most successful in helping state attorneys win prosecutions as they could spend the time with the victims that was often difficult for the attorneys, get them used to the procedures of that particular criminal justice system, and in some cases, actually assist them in finding doctors and therapists for themselves and their children.

At the same time, agencies in the community providing services to battered women also began a court intervention program working with state attorneys and judges. For example, in Denver, Colorado, they provided assistance to the domestic violence court judges by helping the victims fill out the forms properly, assisting them in learning about their rights, educating them about the court-ordered treatment programs for which their batterers might be eligible, and explaining restraining orders. Although there has been controversy about whether a restraining order will really protect women from violent abusers, Meloy and his colleagues support the earlier studies that demonstrate obtaining a restraining order wins both the respect of the police and therefore, better protection for women who obtain them, and deterrence for some types of batterers (Meloy, Cowett, Parker, Hofland, & Friedland, 1997). In many cases, having a judge determine the facts proving domestic violence and issuing a restraining order may later assist the party in family court when protection of children during custody and visitation are at issue. All agree, however, that a restraining order itself will not stop a batterer who stalks the woman or who is obsessed with harming her. Interestingly, in communities that instituted such programs, the number of arrests have doubled, tripled, and in some even quadrupled since the inception of these policies. However, the actual number of cases where this alone deterred further violence remains small, leading most scholars to accept that it is a community-wide integrated approach that is critical and ought to include court follow-up with batterers who do not stop their abuse. More about dangerousness and risk assessments was described in Chapter 12.

DOMESTIC VIOLENCE AND PROBLEM-SOLVING COURTS

The philosophy around domestic violence has undoubtedly evolved in the past several years. Most people are in agreement that violence in the home is no longer a private matter, but a serious crime plaguing our society. This change in thinking has had implications for many entities including, but not limited to, the police and the legal system. Many states have recognized that domestic crimes need to be handled differently than nondomestic crimes in the court system. One important reason is that, unlike nondomestic crimes, these crimes are emotionally charged and involve people who have relationships, which will not necessarily end with the adjudication of the case. Thus, part of the domestic court role is to be thoughtful about and monitor the continuing relationships between the parties. Family court should adopt this role as well, but as described in Chapter 19, this rarely happens in that venue. Instead, family court judges seem to prefer becoming mediators in dispensing equity without paying attention to the danger that comes with domestic violence.

According to the U.S. Department of Justice (2005), about 22% of murders in the year 2002 were perpetrated by family members, with nearly 9% murders of a spouse, 6% murders of sons or daughters by a parent, and 7% murders by other family members. Although these statistics reflect only fatalities, family violence crimes recorded by the police in the District of Columbia and 18 states comprised 33% of all violent crimes with more than half of them between partners (U.S. Department of Justice, 2005). In addition, police receive a high percentage of repeat calls for service involving the same offenders and victims. Similarly, in New Haven, Connecticut, domestic violence accounts for approximately 30% of police calls for service and of these, 29% require repeat police calls over time, and are most dangerous for officers, victims, and children (Shaffer & Gill, 2003). In Chapter 10, the high number of murder–suicides that occur when domestic violence cases are before family court is documented.

Police calls for service of domestic issues comprise a large percentage of police activity, and the police are trained to treat them as one of the most dangerous types of calls to which police officers respond. They are also often reported by police to be the most frustrating and time-consuming. These elements may impede the attention to detail and delivery of services by police to the victims who need the services the most: battered women and children (Casey et al., 2007). In the 2000, roughly 49% of family violence crimes resulted in arrests. Most offenders (77%) were male, and nearly half of the felony assault defendants were released pending disposition of their cases. The conviction rate in family violence cases was found to be 71% as compared to 61% in nondomestic cases (Durose et al., 2005). Eighty-three percent of persons convicted of both family and nonfamily assaults were sentenced to prison or jail. Among family violence felony assaults prosecuted by the state, 68% were sentenced to jail, compared to 62% of nonfamily violence assaults. As for prison time, the U.S. Department of Justice (2005) reports that 45% of the prisoners incarcerated for family violence received sentences of more than 2 years. Furthermore, 88% of the jailed inmates convicted of family violence did not use a weapon in the assault, but 55% caused injury to their victims. In addition, 45% of these inmates had a restraining order against them at some point, and 18% had an active restraining order against them at the time of incarceration (U.S. Department of Justice 2005).

The literature is abundant in noting the negative effects on children of exposure to violence in the home as discussed in Chapters 6 and 7. For example, Marans (1998) noted that children who were chronically exposed to violence developed symptomatology that impaired their emotional, psychological, educational, and cognitive development. Also noteworthy is that in poor, urban areas where the prevalence of all types of violence is high, "there may be a natural progression from witnessing (violence) to being the victim of (violence) and then to engaging in violence" (Marans, 1996). While most scholars studying the epidemiology of domestic violence agree that it occurs in homes across all demographic groups, more people who are poor appear in domestic violence courts than those who have money.

One of the reasons that domestic violence was removed from the bonding schedule was to equalize the differences between rich and poor, influential and average citizens. In some courts, such as Denver, Colorado, and Quincy, Massachusetts, this has occurred as no one, not even a Denver Bronco player, is permitted to be released before seeing a judge. In other communities, however, poor men sit in jail for weeks while those who can pay the bond set by the court are free to go about their business and in some cases continue their abusive behavior, until their case is scheduled. Often this may be weeks or months after the incident for which they were arrested and witnesses are no longer available or at least their memories are not as sharp as if the case were prosecuted immediately. Psychologists know that learning theory tells us that the consequences must immediately follow the act or the intended punishment will not be successful in stopping the offending behavior. Yet, we persist in devising policies that work in theory but in a crowded court system are doomed to failure. Nonetheless, with all its flaws, these specialty courts appear to have a modest degree of success if only to support the victim and give her courage to better protect herself and her children.

MODELS OF DOMESTIC VIOLENCE COURTS

Individual states have developed court models that begin with the same premise: domestic cases need to be handled by a court dedicated to these complex issues. However, each state implements court protocols differently according to resources and philosophy. In addition, states vary in their definitions of what falls under the umbrella of a domestic violence offense. For example, in Connecticut, a special docket has been created with the sole purpose of hearing, monitoring, and adjudicating cases that fall under this umbrella. One judge is assigned to the docket so that the same judge sees perpetrators who later violate the court's orders. This concept is one of a vertical prosecution in the hope that having to be in front of the same judge will become a deterrent to reoffend. In addition, this court works closely with the agency that provides social services to the victims of domestic violence. So closely, in fact, that victim advocates are housed in the courthouse to allow for immediate intervention and referrals at the time of arraignment (Gill, 2006).

In another attempt to combine all cases involving one family, the courts in Hawaii tried to put both criminal and civil cases together in a unified family court. The civil cases included petitions for divorce, custody and child access disputes, and juvenile court hearings for children in these families. While the original philosophy was a good one, in practice the criminal case requirements including the defendant's constitutional right to a speedy trial, usually within 3 months, caused the civil cases to back up and the courts became so inundated with the criminal matters that they had to divide the divisions again (personal communication in 1990s, Honorable Frances Wong, Chief Judge at the time). In Miami/Dade the Unified Family Court seemed to have more success and in fact, also spurred the development of several specialized children's courts such as those that dealt with problem family and dependency court cases and a teen drug court.

One program analysis researched by Gondolf (1999) hypothesized that the rearrest rate would decrease when offenders completed a comprehensive program with extra services available to them. Four groups were analyzed: a pretrial group for a 3-month duration with additional service referrals; a 3-month postconviction group including referrals and assessments as well as a women's and a children's group; a 6-month postconviction group with referrals and assessments with women's groups; and a 9-month postconviction group that included evaluation and in-house treatment for substance abuse issues, mental health, and women's casework.

Results found differences in reassault rates only in the 9-month duration group. A significant difference was noted in severe and repeated assaults between the two 3-month programs and the 9-month program. As hypothesized, women with partners in the 9-month program reported feeling that they would not be hit again, but there were no differences between the groups in terms of feeling safer. In opposition to the hypothesis, women in the shorter-duration programs reported feeling better off than those in the longer programs. This makes sense, as the reassault rates for the men who attended 3 months of sessions were significantly lower than the 9-month group men. This difference could be attributed to the fact that the court reviewed the case at 3 months, thus serving as a deterrent to reoffend. It may be that close court monitoring and accountability can serve to decrease future violence.

Another hypothesis regarding reoffense has to do with the motivation of the individual. Dalton (2001) employed a longitudinal study design to examine whether or not men who perceived more external pressure would be more likely to complete a batterers' treatment program. This hypothesis stems from the suggestion in the literature that batterers are not intrinsically motivated to change their violent behavior, but will do so when external pressures are in place. Interviews were conducted upon entrance to one of two programs, followed by chart reviews to discern treatment progress 5 months after the interview. The hypothesis in this study was not supported, as the level of perceived external pressure did not predict program completion. This study has a possible confound in that the men who participated were the men who actually came to treatment, not the ones who were referred but did not comply. Another possible confound is in the program rule that nonpayment of treatment resulted in dismissal from the program. Also, it is important to note that neither program addressed other issues such as substance abuse and unemployment, which could also affect program attendance and success.

A study conducted by Feder and Dugan (2004) examined whether or not lower rates of violence would be found when men convicted of misdemeanor domestic violence offenses were mandated by a judge to attend either an experimental group or a control group. The experimental group consisted of 1-year probation and attendance at one of five local spouse abuse abatement programs (SAAPs), all based on the Duluth model of intervention. The control group consisted of men who received only 1-year probation. The hypothesis was that these men with a high stake in conformity, operationally defined as employment, marital status, age, and residential stability, would exhibit lower rates of repeat violence. All men were interviewed at adjudication and 6 months later; victims were interviewed at adjudication as well 6 and 12 months later. The groups were found to be similar in demographics, stake in conformity, and criminal record but the control group had a mean age 2 years younger than the experimental group. Also similar were the men's beliefs in responsibility for wife beating and attitudes regarding women's roles.

At the 6-month mark, no differences were found between both groups for use of violence: 30% self-reported using minor violence, and 8% admitted to using severe violence. Interestingly, younger men without stable residence were significantly more likely to report violent incidents. Again, with respect to stake in conformity, age and employment were significantly related to rearrest while marital status and residential stability were not. The number of months employed was significantly and inversely related to the likelihood of rearrest. Almost one quarter (24%) of men in both conditions were rearrested within the year, but the men who attended all classes were significantly less likely to be rearrested, while men who attended fewer classes were 2.5 times more likely than the control group to be arrested. This study concluded that the men who do not seem to be deterred from missing their court-mandated treatment are also not deterred from the consequences of rearrest (Feder & Dugan, 2004).

Similarly, Dobash and Dobash (2000) compared two court-mandated programs for men guilty and on probation for domestic violence with a group of similar men receiving traditional treatment such as fines, probation, and prison time. However, this study also gathered information from the female victims. The participants had similar criminal histories but the men in the program group were more likely to be employed. Evaluations were completed at three intervals: intervention time, 3 months, and again at 12 months (Times 1, 2, and 3, respectively). The program group included participation in group work with a psychoeducational approach, in that the men were provided with education about violence as a learned behavior and the need to take responsibility for their use of violence.

The group portion of the intervention was intensive in that eight stages of a "transformative process" were covered: recognition that change is possible, gaining motivation to change, consideration of costs and benefits of change, viewing the self as a subject and not an object, shifting change internally as opposed to external constraints, using words and ideas that reflect nonviolence, adopting new ways of thinking that require talking and listening to others, and learning new ways and skills for conflict resolution. This comprehensive intervention enabled men to take responsibility for their use of violence and to appreciate the fact that they made a choice to use violence.

The programs seemed to reduce men's use of violence as well as eliminate violence after several months to a year. The men were also less likely to use intimidating and controlling behaviors. Women with partners in the program groups reported a significantly better quality of life than the women with partners in the comparison group as measured by them feeling safer, a better sense of well-being, and positive improvements in their relationships. Quality-of-life changes for both men and women were more likely to be seen in men who completed the program.

Seven percent of the men in the program were rearrested at follow-up as compared to 10% of men receiving traditional sanctions. By women's reports, the men in the program group used violence significantly less in the two time periods (30% and 33%) as compared to the criminal justice group (61% and 69%). Given this difference, it was also noted that the 25% of the comparison group did remain violence free. Also noteworthy was that at Time 1, there were slight differences between the groups and violence usage compared to Times 2 and 3 where it was significant (Dobash & Dobash, 2000).

Although these studies demonstrate some efficacy for batterers' treatment programs, it is difficult to compare them because of the extreme variability from program to program. However, the results are similar to batterers' intervention programs that have been studied in the past (Holtzworth-Monroe & Stuart, 1994). Barbara Hart and her colleagues continue to find that batterers' treatment programs, despite their variability, are better at decreasing and stopping violence in combination with proarrest and prosecution policies and protection of women with the availability of shelters and other programs for women.

MODELS OF DOMESTIC VIOLENCE
TREATMENT PROGRAMS

Given the fact that the most common referral by domestic violence courts is to court-ordered treatment, the rationale behind these programs needs to be considered.

Philosophy

Early in the development of batterers' intervention programs, both a feminist and cognitive behavioral model were developed to integrate sociocultural political and individual factors. The sociocultural political model was predominantly a feminist one drawn from the victim's perspective. Historical studies showed that men were the primary users of violence against women, and that patriarchal structures in the community either perpetrated or facilitated violence against women. Institutions within the community rarely intervened to stop men from harming women. This could be due to the inequities in power and resources between men and women at the time. While on a macrolevel, men and women agreed with this analysis, as evidenced by the United Nations' findings on violence against women throughout the world, while on the microlevel, most men disagreed that such power differentials existed in their own homes.

At first men were eager to place the blame on the few violent men they knew, but when the numbers arrested became staggering, men (and some women) soon became apologists for themselves and then for their brothers, friends, and even acquaintances. Some refused to believe battered women's horrific accounts of the violence they experienced, particularly if they were in the same social class. Politicians who beat their wives were reelected even when court testimony was exposed. Filling the jails with men who beat their women left no room for the "real" criminals was the cry soon to be heard. The original zero tolerance for any types of domestic violence was soon replaced with cries demanding specifics of "how much violence was really used" or "well, he only hit her one time" and domestic violence became divided into lesser amounts that were called "domestic discord" so that consequences that disrupted the social fabric did not need to be applied. Today, fewer men who are court ordered into treatment programs actually attend them and programs that do not account for sociocultural, political, and individual uses of violence have appeared. Most egregious has been the family court where children are allowed to be with dads who continue to execute their power and control over their children and wives without any consequences (Fields, 2008). Child custody evaluators who are untrained in understanding domestic violence continue to perpetuate the myth that there are different types of domestic violence that do not impact children's development as long as they are not physically or sexually hurt themselves. Some child custody evaluators have gone so far as to suggest these families be forced into court-involved therapy programs where the goal is to make them more amenable to follow court orders even if the participants believe that the court order for shared parental responsibility will harm the children or themselves (Kleinman & Walker, 2015).

Models

There are three major models of treatment programs that are usually court ordered around the country. The first is the *Duluth model* originated in Duluth, Minnesota, and is such a well-respected model that parts of it are incorporated in most treatment programs around the world. The second model is the combination of treatment for domestic violence and mental health problems that is represented by AMEND from Denver and EMERGE from Boston. These two programs have been in existence since the 1970s and are less popular because they require greater resources such as trained therapists to conduct them. The third model comprises mental health treatment programs that are not integrated with a sociocultural feminist perspective. Although Don Dutton's treatment programs are sometimes considered part of the second model, he spends more time in individualized approaches to understand how the men's childhoods relate to current violent behavior than an integrated approach and would be considered partly in the third model. This was further described in Chapter 9 on attachment issues with intimate partners.

Does the Duluth Model Work?

The Duluth model is a psychoeducational intervention program that is based on feminist and cognitive behavioral principles. Although it is the most popular program adopted by most states and even countries around the world, it is not practiced the same from jurisdiction to jurisdiction. As has been said, more recently it has been criticized as insufficient to stop violence because it does not deal with men's individual psychological problems and rather concentrates on sociocultural underpinnings of men's attitudes toward women. Although the actual Duluth program calls for 26 weeks of intervention (Edelson, 1999), in most jurisdictions there are often 12 or fewer weeks of intervention available. Thus, assessment of efficacy is hampered by the various ways the program is implemented even though it is manualized. Even so, there is no change in either arrest rates or batterers' attitudes and behaviors in most of the studies reported based on the amount of time spent in treatment.

The AMEND program is also manualized, with 36 to 52 intervention sessions required. Judges are permitted to sentence offenders to 2-year

(104-week) interventions as well. The leaders of the program train the already licensed volunteer therapists who are then screened and trained to conduct the intervention sessions so there is uniformity in application across the state. As stated earlier, the AMEND program attempts to deal with the issues raised in the Duluth model as well as mental health issues observed or diagnosed in the batterers, all in a group format. It has a reported success rate higher than that of the Duluth programs alone.

Research Study on Efficacy of Duluth Model

The state of Florida mandates that domestic violence courts use the Duluth model. Several investigators on our project decided to try to assess its success by comparing those men who were court ordered into the program with those who were there voluntarily (Kellen, Brooks, & Walker, 2005). The records of 100 men who were in a Duluth model program during 2002 and 2003 were studied. The men were equally divided into these two groups, court ordered and volunteers for the study although they attended the program together. Five criteria were used to assess the success of participants: (a) completion of the 26-week program; (b) rearrest records; (c) posttests upon completion of the program assessing knowledge of what domestic violence is; (d) victim follow-ups; and (e) self-reports. The program was deemed to have been effective if all of the following five criteria were achieved: (a) an individual completed the 26-week program; (b) the participant was not arrested for domestic violence within 6 months following completion of the program; (c) the participant achieved a score of at least 80% on the posttest; (d) the victim reported no use of verbal, physical, or emotional violence upon completion of the program; and (e) the participant reported no use of violence at the end of the program.

Of the court-mandated individuals who enrolled in the program, 78% completed the required 26 weeks. This compares to 32% of those who enrolled voluntarily. The remaining participants had been terminated by the facilitator for failing to comply with the rules of the program. For the second criteria, 12% of those who completed the program were rearrested for domestic violence either during the program or within 6 months of their completion. Third, of those individuals who completed the program, 72% achieved a posttest score of at least 80%. The fourth criteria found that 65% of victims, with whom contact was made following their partners' completion of the program, reported that their partner was still engaging in abusive behaviors. Of these, only 10% reported physical violence and 50% of the victims reported that there had been no change in the verbal or emotional abuse experienced prior to intervention, or stated that such abuse had worsened. Upon completion of the program, 100% of the batterers denied any continued use of physical abuse, 12% admitted to verbal abuse, but stated that this was at a lesser level than prior to beginning the program.

Of those individuals who enrolled voluntarily in the program, only 32% completed the required 26 weeks, while the remaining participants dropped out of treatment prematurely. None were arrested for domestic violence either during the program or within 6 months of their completion. Of those individuals who completed the program, 84% achieved a posttest score of at least 80%. More than half (55%) of victims, with whom contact was made following their partners' completion of the program, reported that their partners were still engaging in abusive behaviors. Of these, none reported physical violence, 20% of the victims reported that there had been no change in the verbal or emotional abuse, or stated that such abuse had worsened. Upon completion of the program, 100% of the batterers denied any continued use of physical abuse, while 40% admitted to verbal abuse, but stated that this was at a lesser level than prior to beginning the program. Table 20.1 compares these two groups.

The results of the study suggested that a difference exists in efficacy of the Duluth model between those individuals who are court mandated to attend services and those who attend voluntarily. Individuals who attended services voluntarily were less likely to complete the program,

Table 20.1 *Comparison of Court Ordered and Volunteers in a Domestic Violence Treatment Program*

	Court Ordered	Volunteer
Completers	78%	32%
Rearrest	12%	0%
Score 80%+ on test	72%	84%
Victims report no abuse	65%	55%
Physical violence	10%	0%
No change or worse	50%	20%
Batterers report no abuse	100%	100%
Lower verbal abuse	12%	40%

which supports the research suggesting that the confrontational approach of this model is not supportive of men voluntarily motivated to change their behavior. Nonetheless, those who completed the program were less likely to be arrested for domestic violence. These individuals also scored higher on posttests assessing their knowledge of what domestic violence is and, according to their partners, were engaging less in abusive behaviors for which they could be rearrested although power and control issues were still reported. Interestingly, however, while fewer of their partners reported the use of abuse, these participants were more likely themselves to admit to the continued use of abuse toward their partners. Considering the high rate of denial reported in this population, this may be an important step in learning self-control of their behavior.

Efficacy of an intervention program to stop men's violence against women can be viewed both as an absolute concept and relative to an individual's previous behavior. While the Duluth model appears to have some benefits in reducing abusive behaviors, at least half of those who completed the program continued to engage in abusive behavior. While batterers were less likely to engage in physical abuse, the use of verbal and emotional abuse continued or worsened. As in most studies of batterers' intervention programs, the use of sexual abuse and coercion was not dealt with nor measured. Less than 10% of all those enrolled met all five criteria the study assessed.

Although the results of this study appear to highlight the deficiency of the Duluth model in addressing violence in domestic relationships, there are some positive outcomes and there are recommendations for future researchers to more adequately assess the efficacy of the Duluth model and for intervening with battering individuals. For instance, instead of grouping all batterers together without accounting for individual differences, it would appear beneficial according to previous research to adequately screen batterers and to classify them into their respective subgroups prior to assigning them to one treatment program, such as the Duluth model, given the assumption that different categories of batterers would benefit from various forms of intervention. For instance, battering individuals with social skills deficits may have difficulty attending to and benefiting from the group process, which constitutes the Duluth model. If such individuals are properly screened prior to treatment, time and money may be saved by not assigning such individuals to a treatment program from which they would not likely benefit.

Research Study Into Typology of Batterers

As has been written elsewhere, there are studies that suggest there are different types of batterers but each type appears to have its own classification system. Since the state of Florida mandates use of a uniform form upon which to collect data for just one type of batterer, it was decided to analyze the data on this form from a convenience sample of 700 domestic violence offenders (89% males and 11% females) who were court ordered into treatment programs during 2004 (Kellen et al., 2005). We looked at whether or not these offenders who go before the domestic violence courts had completed the Duluth model programs into which they were court ordered across the state.

Demographically, 52% of the males in the current sample actually completed the program and 49% of female participants completed the program in its entirety. This completion rate was noted to be lower than that of the previous year (57%). Of those who did not complete the program, 48% were male and 51% were female. Collectively, those participants who did not complete the program were noted to have either violated their probation, were transferred to another program, or were discharged for disruptive behavior. In terms of participant ethnicity, Caucasians and Hispanics were more likely than African Americans to complete the program. Thus, ethnic diversity variables are also important to consider when planning an intervention program for those who batter.

At the time of this analysis, 52 participants were concurrently enrolled in substance abuse treatment, and of these 50% did not complete the batterers' intervention program. This suggests that comorbid substance abuse is another important variable to consider when intervening with this population. Research suggests that most individuals who batter have substance abuse problems, although few actually receive concurrent treatment to address these difficulties. But even as these data suggest, when they do receive concurrent substance abuse treatment, early termination rates tend to be higher among batterers with comorbid substance abuse problems. Higher program completion rates were positively correlated with higher levels of academic achievement, full-time employment, formal legal relationships to the victims (i.e., married, separated, or divorced), and having children. Studies have found that of these variables, employment status is the most consistently related factor to dropping out of treatment. Batterers who maintained legal (married, separated, or divorced) relationships to their victims were also more likely to complete the program than those who were not. These findings are similar to those of Berk (1993), Sherman (1992), Sherman and Berk (1984), and Meloy et al. (1997) as reported previously.

The Duluth model appears to assume that group therapy is the best treatment modality given its current structure. However, it must be emphasized that within this model, there is a lack of focus on individual differences, psychopathology, and anger-management issues. When considering the individual characteristics of those people sent to receive batterers' intervention services, individual therapy may prove to be more beneficial for some batterers; for example, those who have themselves experienced abuse, especially childhood sexual abuse. These individuals may not feel comfortable addressing such issues in a group treatment setting, and even if they were, the Duluth treatment model does not advocate such expression of individual difficulties despite their prominence and likely contribution to battering behavior.

Some of the newer research on biological bases for violence must also be considered when decisions are being made about treatment options. Adrienne Raine and others have made convincing arguments that at least some violence, especially that committed by individuals with psychopathic tendencies, may be influenced by brain chemistry and function (Raine, 2013). Although more research is needed in this area as brain-imaging techniques become more affordable and available, it is suggested that this will be an important area to help understand why men commit more violent behavior than do women.

It must also be stressed that for some batterers, incarceration may be the only option, as no psychological intervention would work. This would likely apply to individuals who meet criteria for antisocial personality disorder, based on our clinical experience. Others who fit in this category are those who have arrest records for other crimes of violence and those who have not benefited from prior deferral into offender-specific treatment programs. These two studies from our own research program strongly suggest that a more thorough and comprehensive screening of individuals who batter is necessary to ensure that proper interventions are used that would effectively reduce recidivism and address the individual treatment needs of the batterer. Such screening and assessment could be effectively completed via the use of certain psychological tests, or items from instruments that are able to identify individuals who would be unlikely to benefit from participation in the Duluth model. For example, items from the Hare Psychopathy Checklist, Revised (PCL-R), the Spousal Assault

Risk Assessment (SARA) Guide, and the MacArthur Variables obtained from the Assessment Scale for Potential Violence (ASP-V) that assess individual psychosocial history, in addition to the presence of abuse, substance abuse, and psychopathology could prove to be quite useful for this purpose. This type of risk assessment was further described in Chapter 12.

Family Therapy

Early in the development of offender-specific treatment it was determined that group intervention was better than individual or family treatment. Far too many batterers were slick talkers and had been in individual therapy and fooled the therapists into believing they had stopped their violent behavior when in fact, they ended up rearrested and it was proved they had lied in sessions. Other group members were far better in identifying and confronting those who lied, either consciously or unconsciously. Group treatment was more economical for the courts and could be more easily monitored by the courts. It was easier to include didactic or lecture material for psychoeducational approaches in the attempt to change attitudes as well as behavior in a group than in individual therapy. Skill training was possible to accomplish in a group, also. Intuitively, family therapy seemed like it would be a good modality, especially for those couples who wished to remain together after the violence stopped. However, most family system theories call for shared responsibility of behavior in the family unit and the predominant thinking at that time as well as today is that the use of violent behavior is the total responsibility of the person who uses it and that no provocation can cause someone to use violence in the home. This message tends to get lost when exploring family dynamics in couples or family treatment. Further, most women victims lose the sense of neutrality when they have been abused. They are hypervigilant to further cues of harm and either the therapist totally supports the women or the therapist is viewed as someone who is dangerous and may either directly or inadvertently cause her to be harmed. A family therapist must support both parties in the session causing the woman to lose confidence in the therapist and therefore unable to benefit from treatment.

Another reason for not doing family therapy is the inability to meet everyone's different needs, especially after a battering incident that results in an arrest and court-ordered therapy. The victim should not be court ordered into therapy as she did nothing criminal. By including her in the court order, the judge gives the batterer the message that the abuse is a shared responsibility. She needs time to cool off and to explore her options of staying in the relationship. The batterer also needs time to cool off and think about his behavior. He knows that he has gone too far and becomes scared that the woman will terminate the relationship so he needs to find ways to persuade her to stay. A batterer usually will try sweet-talking first, but if his ability to charm and seduce her does not work, then he may escalate to threats and other reminders of his power and control over her. No matter how competent a family therapist is, the dynamics of this combination are simply too difficult to manage. Family therapy is predicated on the theory that change in one part of the system will change the family dynamics. This is true, but change could be either for better or worse. Given the intense focus of the batterer and his need to maintain control, it can be expected to change quickly for the worse. In fact, for treatment of couples with reports of domestic violence, the outcome is usually worse for one party or the other, and that party is usually the woman.

Family therapy is dangerous and can risk homicides and suicides. This is also why mediation is not a good option in trying to settle domestic violence disputes. The power imbalance between the man and woman is too pronounced to allow for a fair negotiation. Even in those couples where there is mutual violence and the power seems to be equal, it is equal only in the ability to set each other off negatively. There have been some reports of family therapy occurring after the man has been in offender-specific treatment and the woman has made the decision to stay in the relationship (Holden, Gefner, & Jouriles, 1998). In these cases, two or more therapists have been employed so that each can be a support person for their respective clients and watch for escalations of attempts to control the other party. In Milan, Italy, the Italian school of family therapy has reported conducting treatment with families reporting child abuse with each child and each parent having his or her own therapist in the therapy room with them. Obviously, training and extraordinary skills as a therapist are necessary to participate in this model.

To date, no empirical studies have been found indicating that family therapy is more effective than standard group or even individual treatment. As of 1996, the U.S. Department of Justice found that 20 states had language in their statutes actually prohibiting the use of family therapy as a treatment modality (Healy, Smith, & O'Sullivan, 1998). In some states, such as New Jersey, when a domestic violence restraining order has been issued, it is also not appropriate for forensic evaluators to see the parties together even during a child custody evaluation. In other states, mediation is routinely ordered when petitions for dissolution of marriage are filed and a type of *shuttle mediation* is recommended where the parties are in separate rooms and the mediator shuttles between the rooms bringing recommendations based on what each party desires.

DOMESTIC VIOLENCE PROGRAM STANDARDS

The Department of Justice undertook a survey of the types of programs available for domestic violence offenders throughout the United States. In their recent publication, they found:

> Obtaining current and accurate information on batterer interventions is challenging for criminal justice practitioners because programs are extremely diverse in approach and reflect a broad—and often contradictory—range of beliefs about explanations for battering as well as appropriate modes of intervention. In addition, the field is growing and diversifying in terms of the number of programs being offered, staff qualifications, and techniques used. To assist courts and probation officers in selecting suitable batterer interventions—that is—programs that emphasize victim safety and have goals consistent with those of the criminal justice system—27 states and the District of Columbia had mandated or supported the development of state-level standards or guidelines for batterer programs, and another 13 states were in the process of developing standards by 1997. However, even in states where guidelines or standards are in place, community domestic violence coalitions, the judiciary, probation officers, and other criminal justice professionals often retain considerable discretion over program accreditation and referral. Because of the complexity of the field—and the seriousness of the ongoing threat posed to battered women when offenders are mishandled—criminal justice professionals who handle domestic violence cases have increased responsibility to be knowledgeable about the content and structure of batterer programs in their jurisdictions in order to make informed choices among the interventions being offered. (Healy, Smith, & Sullivan, 1998, p. 4, emphasis deleted)

The Department of Justice suggested that all domestic violence treatment programs address the most common types of abusive behavior used by batterers (Healy, Smith, & Sullivan, 1998, p. 5). These are similar to those addressed in the Battered Woman Syndrome Questionnaire (BWSQ) research studies and include:

- *Physical violence:* Women are in the most severe danger of physical violence when they try to leave an abusive relationship: 75% of emergency room visits and calls to the police by battered women occur after separation (Stark & Flitcraft, 1983). Half the homicides resulting from domestic violence occur after separation (Langan & Innes, 1986).
- *Intimidation:* This includes looks, gestures, and actions that remind the victim of the abuser's potential for physical violence. It may also include abandoning the partner in a dangerous place.
- *Threats:* These are made to hurt the children, her family, or her pets. The batterer also may threaten to commit suicide or to cause trouble for the victim with government authorities, employers, family, or friends. Whether credible or not, threats can be as effective as taking action in deterring the victim from seeking help.
- *Isolation:* This includes controlling what the victim does or whom she sees or contacts. Isolating the victim destroys the support networks a victim usually needs to end an abusive relationship and makes her more vulnerable to the batterer's coercion.
- *Emotional abuse:* Verbal insults serve to undermine the victim's confidence, thereby discouraging her from ending the relationship.
- *Sexual abuse:* Between 33% and 46% of battered women are subjected to sexual abuse (Frieze & Browne, 1989), such as rape, unwanted sexual practices, sexual mutilation, or forced or coerced prostitution.
- *Using the children:* A recent study of batterers in Dade County found that between 30% and 50% of the batterers and victims shared children (Goldkamp, Weiland, Collins, & White, 1996). By providing for ongoing contact, joint custody enables the batterer to continue to intimidate or attack the victim, the children, or both. Some state statutes now prohibit joint custody in the event of domestic violence convictions, and recent research suggests that witnessing domestic violence has a serious long-term psychological impact on children, including increasing the children's own propensity for violence and delinquency (numerous sources).

- *Using economic control:* Examples include keeping control over all of the family's resources, including the victim's own income if she works, giving her an allowance, or forcing her to ask for money for basic necessities.
- *Using male privilege:* The batterer acts like the "master of the castle," making all-important family decisions, expecting the woman to perform all the household duties, and having the woman wait on him.

SPECIAL PROGRAMS FOR WOMEN ARRESTED FOR DOMESTIC VIOLENCE

As has been described, the majority of arrested batterers have been heterosexual men. Straus and Gelles (1990) found that men were arrested in 80% of misdemeanor cases, 85% of felony cases, and respondents in 75% of the civil actions. Even so, that leaves 20% of the misdemeanor cases, 15% of the felony cases, and 25% of the civil actions with women defendants. Among the 5% of female batterers referred to treatment programs, four distinct types of offenders have been identified by program directors, probation officers, and victim advocates according to the Department of Justice Report (Healy, Smith, & Sullivan, 1998 p. 6): (a) lesbian batterers; (b) so-called "female defendants" (battered women arrested for violent acts of self-defense); (c) angry victims who have resorted to violence to preempt further abuse; and (d) a small proportion of women batterers who have been the primary aggressors in an abusive relationship.

There are no standards for treatment programs for women arrested for domestic violence. In most cases, interventions in mixed gender groups or even in mixed groups with different types of offenders are not appropriate and may account in part for the high dropout rate for both volunteers and court-ordered women as reported in our studies mentioned previously. Also noted was that women seem to use violence differently than men in that they are usually acting in self-defense or are reacting to abuse in the relationship. Law enforcement and court action would better serve women who are arrested if they understood their violence in a contextual way and not as an isolated incident (Miller, 2001). Reports indicate that the genuinely violent woman is usually a former victim of some type of violence—child abuse, domestic violence, or sexual crimes—and often engages in violent behavior in order to deter future victimization.

SPECIAL PROGRAMS FOR LESBIAN, GAY, BISEXUAL, TRANSGENDERED, AND GENDER NONCONFORMING (LGBT)

Although there are no reliable estimates of prevalence, it is known that gay men also batter their intimate partners and are arrested (Island & Letellier, 1991). They are usually ordered into treatment programs with other heterosexual males as it is rare for there to be groups for gay male batterers. For some men, being forced to reveal their homosexuality in a group could jeopardize their jobs or security, especially in rural areas or other countries where gays do not have any civil rights. This problem has not been sufficiently addressed by the criminal justice system.

There are no special programs for lesbians in most jurisdictions where abuse occurs. If there are programs for women abusers, then those who identify as lesbian may be offered treatment there. However, this is very rare. The same is true for violence in the transgendered community, which of course, poses difficulties in where to house them if arrested. Often the transgendered and gender-nonconforming people must be placed in segregated housing if arrested to avoid jail and prison management issues with other inmates. It is more likely that their gender-identity issues will be ignored and not included in treatment decisions that may simply assign them to male or female groups. However, the danger is that many of these individuals are in greater danger of being victimized as well as being victimizers, especially if they are engaging in commercial sex where the violence rates are high.

OTHER COMMUNITY SERVICES

Although the primary referral for domestic violence offenders who choose to accept probation or withheld adjudication is to send them into offender-specific treatment programs, there have been studies to determine other community services that might also be helpful in stopping their violent behavior. The three major areas that impact the offender's use of violence include child abuse, mental illness, and substance abuse. However, it is rare that communities offer programs specializing in trauma, mental illness, and substance abuse together with domestic violence perpetrator groups. Substance abuse issues have been further discussed in Chapter

15 and mental illness with batterers has been described previously in this chapter. While issues with children have been summarized in Chapters 6 and 7, it is important to emphasize the high overlap between battering a woman and abusing a child in these homes.

Physical Abuse as a Child

Although controversial, it is a well-known belief in the social science literature that abuse gets handed down from generation to generation. Abuse begets more abuse was the theme of Straus, Gelles, and Steinmetz's (1980) seminal work in this area. More precise studies demonstrate that the generational passing down of this learned behavior is not quite as simple. Nonetheless, there is little argument that boys who are exposed to their fathers abusing their mothers are at higher risk to use violence in their own lives and if they too are abused by their fathers, that raises the risk even higher. There is also a high rate of child abuse reported by prisoners convicted of violent crimes. In fact, based on the forensic psychological evaluations of men who commit the most heinous crimes against women, it appears they have experienced some of the most violent abuse themselves.

Precisely why some men who were abused as boys go on to use violence inside and outside their homes while others do not is not really well understood. Newer trauma treatment methods, such as teaching victims to identify what may trigger their trauma reactions and cause them to reexperience the trauma as if the abuse were reoccurring when they are really not in danger, should be a critical part of any domestic violence treatment program especially if the perpetrator was also an abuse victim.

This is also an area that must be studied so that protective factors can be addressed. There are a few protective factors that are known at this time. Perhaps most important is that boys who go on to lead productive lives have good social skills and relate well to peers as well as adults. This is important as was demonstrated in Chapter 7; children who are exposed to abuse in their homes, often do not make friends easily and may be teased and bullied by other children. A second protective factor is the presence of a supportive adult in a child's life. Most often mentioned were grandmothers and teachers. Occasionally mentioned were coaches. Boys lucky enough to have Big Brother type of individualized attention were also more likely to overcome their abusive backgrounds. Not mentioned were supportive girlfriends or wives, which is very interesting as most women involved with batterers think that their loving behavior will cure them of their violent tendencies.

There exists a current debate regarding women's use of violence and how it may differ from male violence. In addition, mandatory arrest policies have resulted in the arrests of many women and there is little research on how these arrests are currently handled and should be handled by the criminal justice system. In an effort to examine the differences between male and female aggression, Henning, Jones, and Holdford (2003) conducted an exploratory analysis on both men and women who were arrested, convicted, or are currently on probation for assaulting a partner. The method included a counselor briefly meeting with the offender, a group administration of paper and pencil tests, a clinical interview, and a written evaluation for the court on information gathered. Results found that most offenders (84.2%) were African American, dating their victims, and had a mean age of 32.5, with a range from 18 to 69. Similar numbers were reported for both men and women offenders as to current living arrangements and having children in common. Women were more likely to have some college but were less likely to be working outside of the home.

Similar reports of childhood physical abuse and exposure to minor parental conflict were noted, but men were more likely to report corporal punishment by caregivers than women. Both men and women reported similar results on witnessing parental violence (25%), physical abuse (33%), high rates of parental separation, and substance abuse. Men reported having more conduct problems as children under the age of 16. They also reported significantly more treatment for substance abuse than women. Women were three times more likely to have attempted suicide and were also twice as likely to have been treated with psychotropic medications. Women were also more likely to endorse symptoms of compulsive personality, histrionic, and borderline personality disorders (95% of the women had elevated scores on one or more of the personality subscales compared to only 69.8% for men).

Women participants were twice as likely to be uncertain about continuing their relationship (29.5%–14.4%), with 39.4% planning to leave their partners. Assuming their partners are also violent, without effective information dissemination and support, these women could be at higher risk for more severe abuse. For both men and women in this study, the high rates of witnessing and experiencing abuse as children are very noteworthy and can possibly fuel further research and intervention (Henning, Jones, & Holdford, 2003).

BATTERERS WHO ABUSE THEIR OWN CHILDREN

A study interviewing child welfare workers by Shepard and Rashchick (1999) found that, although over one third of the cases referred to this child protection agency had known domestic violence issues, no formal or systematic protocol was in place. Furthermore, domestic violence was rarely mentioned in court proceedings even though 14 out of 19 cases were identified as a person being at significant risk. The other five cases were mentioned as relevant only to protective order hearings.

Workers did directly assess domestic violence in 45% of the referred cases but this was by asking at least one of three assessment questions. In 35% of the cases, the worker asked all three questions. Although most workers did ask about domestic violence, the focus was only on the victim's immediate safety needs without further probing or even providing them with additional support and information. Workers often (92%) utilized at least one domestic violence intervention. However, this included only safety issues, information on crime and calling police, and the dynamics of domestic violence. Specialized referrals, such as shelters, women's groups, written material, restraining and protective orders, services for children, and an active involvement such as arranging to check-in by phone with the client were very rarely employed.

Given the overlap of partner abuse and child abuse, child protection agencies need to have a more collaborative relationship with the other disciplines involved in domestic violence. In a study by Miller (2001), information-gathering interviews were conducted with members of several disciplines including criminal justice professionals, social service providers, directors and caseworkers of battered woman's shelters, victim service workers affiliated with the police department, probation officers, prosecutors, social workers, providers of arrested women's groups, and family court advocates. These interviews were designed to provide insight into the issues that arise from arrests for domestic violence.

Results found that not one participant believed that women were becoming more violent. They all agreed that the increase in the number of women being arrested was due to changes in police training and protocol such as mandatory arrest. A noted observation by many, either observed or heard from women, was that men manipulated and had become savvy to the criminal justice system in ways to further harm their victims. They would use this knowledge to control women particularly around issues with the children. For example, men would not accept a plea so that, at trial, the women could potentially lose their children or even end up incarcerated themselves. More examples include men inflicting wounds on themselves to have the women arrested, men calling 911 before the women could, and also, the men purposely remaining very calm when the officers arrived. The respondents also agreed that it seemed the police granted more weight to the person who called 911. There is overwhelming agreement that the police are not spending enough time to fully investigate and understand the situations into which they are called. Conversely, the police fear liability if they use their judgment.

SUMMARY

Domestic violence courts are part of the new problem-solving courts in the criminal justice system, attempting to provide referral to therapeutic services for those arrested for intimate partner violence rather than extended jail time. In some jurisdictions, batterers are eligible for deferral into domestic violence court only if they have committed a misdemeanor, while in other places there are also felony domestic violence courts. While deferral into these specialty courts is not voluntary, the defendant may be able to decide whether to go into a special offender-specific treatment program or to go forward with a trial and possible jail sentence if found guilty. New data suggest that these treatment programs are not as effective at stopping further intimate partner violence as was originally expected. This is partly due to the fact that many men who are court ordered into them do not complete the program. Nonetheless, battered women are more likely to cooperate with prosecution if they believe their partners will be able to get treatment. Police are the first responders in most of these emergency calls and although better trained to understand and intervene in domestic violence cases, it is still difficult for them to stop the violence.

REFERENCES

Berk, R. A. (1993). What the scientific evidence shows: On the average, we can do no better than arrest. In R. J. Gelles & D. R. Loeske (Eds.), *Current controversies on family violence* (pp. 323–336). Newbury Park, CA: Sage.

Casey, R. L., Berkman, M., Stover, C. S., Gill, K., Durso, S., & Marans, S. (2007). Preliminary results of a police-advocate home-visit intervention project for victims of domestic violence. *Journal of Psychological Trauma, 6*(1), 39–49.

Dalton, B. (2001). Batterer characteristics and treatment completion. *Journal of Interpersonal Violence, 16*(12), 1223–1238.

Dobash, R. E., & Dobash, R. P. (2000). Evaluating criminal justice interventions for domestic violence. *Crime and Delinquency, 46*(2), 252–270.

Durose, M. R., Harlow, C. W., Langan, P. A., Motivans, M., Rantala, R. R., & Smith, E. L. (2005). *Family violence statistics: Including statistics on strangers and acquaintances* (NCJ No. 207846). Washington, DC: Bureau of Justice Statistics.

Edleson, J. L. (1999). The overlap between child maltreatment and woman battering. *Violence Against Women, 5*(2), 134–154.

Feder, L., & Dugan, L. (2004). *Testing a court-mandated treatment program for domestic violence offenders: The Broward experiment* (NCJ No. 199729). Washington, DC: National Institute of Justice.

Fields, M. D. (2008). Getting beyond "what did she do to provoke him?". *Violence Against Women, 14*(1), 93–99.

Frieze, I. H., & Browne, A. (1989). Violence in marriage. *Crime and Justice, 11,* 163–218.

Gill, K. (2006). [Court model and procedure gathered from secretary chair position of the Greater New Haven Domestic Violence Task Force]. Unpublished raw data.

Goldkamp, J. S., Weiland, D., Collins, M., & White, M. (1996). *Role of drug and alcohol abuse in domestic violence and its treatment: Dade County's domestic violence court experiment.* Philadelphia, PA: Crime and Justice Research Institute.

Gondolf, E. W. (1999). A comparison of reassault rates in four batterer programs: Do court referral, program length and services matter? *Journal of Interpersonal Violence, 14,* 41–61.

Healy, K., Smith, C., & O'Sullivan, C. (1998). *Batterer intervention: Program approaches and criminal justice strategies* (NCJ No. 168638). Washington, DC: National Institute of Justice.

Henning, K., Jones, A., & Holdford, R. (2003). Treatment needs of women arrested for domestic violence a comparison with male offenders. *Journal of Interpersonal Violence, 18*(8), 839–856.

Holden, G. W., Geffner, R., & Jouriles, E. N. (Eds.). (1998). *Children exposed to marital violence: Theory, research, and applied issues.* Washington, DC: American Psychological Association.

Holtzworth-Monroe, A., & Stuart, G. L. (1994). Typologies of male batterers: Three subtypes and the differences among them. *Psychological Bulletin, 116,* 476–497.

Island, D., & Letellier, P. (1991). *Men who beat the men who love them: Battered gay men and domestic violence.* Binghamton, NY: Haworth Press.

Kellen, M. J., Brooks, J. S., & Walker, L. E. A. (2005, August). Batterers intervention: Typology, efficacy & treatment issues. In L. E. A. Walker (Chair), *Forensics for the independent practitioner.* Symposium conducted at the meeting of the American Psychological Association, Washington, DC.

Kleinman, T. G., & Walker, L. E. (2015). Protecting psychotherapy clients from the shadow of the law: A call for the revision of the Association of Family and Conciliation Courts (AFCC) guidelines for court-involved therapy. *Journal of Child Custody, 11*(4), 335–362.

Langan, P. A., & Innes, C. A. (1986). *Preventing domestic violence against women: Special report.* Washington, DC: Bureau of Justice Statistics.

Marans, S. (1996). Psychoanalysis on the beat: Children, police and urban trauma. In A. Solnit, P. Neubauer, S. Abrams, & A. S. Dowling (Eds.), *The psychoanalytic study of the child* (pp. 522–541). New Haven, CT: Yale University Press.

Marans, S., Berkowitz, S., & Cohen, D. (1998). Police and mental health professionals. Collaborative responses to the impact of violence on children and families. *Child and Adolescent Psychiatric Clinics of North America, 7*(3), 635–651.

Meloy, J. R., Cowett, P. Y., Parker, S. B., Hofland, B., & Friedland, A. (1997). Domestic protection orders and the prediction of subsequent criminality and violence toward protectees. *Psychotherapy: Theory, Research, Practice, Training, 34*(4), 447–458.

Miller, S. (2001). The paradox of women arrested for domestic violence. *Violence Against Women, 7*(12), 1339–1376.

Raine, A. (2013). *The anatomy of violence: The biological roots of crime.* New York, NY: Pantheon.

Shaffer, K., & Gill, K. (2003). [Crime statistics compiled from the Department of Police Service in New Haven, Connecticut, Domestic Violence Unit]. Unpublished raw data.

Shepard, M., & Rashchick, M. (1999). How child welfare workers assess and intervene around issues of domestic violence. *Child Maltreatment, 4*(2), 148–156.

Sherman, L. W. (1992). The influence of criminology on criminal law: Evaluating arrests for misdemeanor domestic violence. *Journal of Criminal Law and Criminology, 83*, 1–35.

Sherman, L. W., & Berk, R. A. (1984). The specific deterrent effects of arrest for domestic assault. *American Sociological Review, 49*, 261–272.

Stark, E., & Flitcraft, A. (1983). Social knowledge, social policy, and the abuse of women: The case against patriarchal benevolence. In D. Finkelhor, R. J. Gelles, G. Hotaling, & M. Straus (Eds.), *The dark side of families* (pp. 380–348). Beverly Hills, CA: Sage.

Straus, M., & Gelles, R. J. (1990). *Physical violence in American families: Risk factors and adaptations to violence in 8,145 families.* New Brunswick, NJ: Transaction Press.

Straus, M. A., Gelles, R. J., & Steinmetz, S. K. (1980). *Behind closed doors: Violence in the American family.* Garden City, NY: Anchor/Doubleday.

U.S. Department of Justice. (2005). *Family violence statistics including statistics on strangers and acquaintances.* Retrieved from http://www.bjs.gov/content/pub/pdf/fvs02.pdf

CHAPTER TWENTY-ONE

BATTERED WOMEN IN CRIMINAL COURT, JAIL, AND PRISON

*M*y first experience in jail occurred when I was asked to evaluate a woman who had killed her husband and claimed that she did so in self-defense. I still remember the haunting sounds of the clanging of the doors that opened to let me in once my credentials were examined. The first door opened into the *sally port,* a tiny vestibule, perhaps 6 feet by 6 feet, and it shut firmly behind me before the second door opened permitting entry into the long hallway that led to the contact rooms. My client was waiting for me by the time I got there. I must have looked as bewildered as I felt, realizing that I had no idea how to get out of there. She tried to calm me down by telling me that it was not so bad, in fact for her it was better than life with her abusive husband. That comparison has stayed with me all these years. The loss of her freedom in jail was better than the captivity she had lived with when married to her husband.

The societal institution responsible for maintaining social order that exists in almost every country is the legal system. In the United States, advocates who began working with battered women in the 1980s believed that the most important step to end threats of violence was to punish the batterer and hold him accountable for his misconduct. To do this the legal system had to be encouraged to take action whenever domestic violence was raised. In 1983, following in the successful experience of President Reagan's Task Force on Violence and Crime, the Attorney General initiated another Task Force on Violence in the Family. Lois Herrington, the assistant attorney general in charge of victim rights, was appointed the head of this investigative body and they reviewed research, other documents, and witness testimony from all over the United States concerning the problem of violence in the family. In their report, they state their conclusion: the legal system and in particular, the criminal justice part of the legal system, should deal forcefully with stopping family violence.

This signaled a major change in the attitude of the country and resulted in the criminalization of what had previously been considered private matters. Someone committing any form of violence in the family, not just where the damage was so egregious that notice and intervention could not be avoided, would be subjected to arrest and prosecution to the fullest extent of the law! Of course, the new laws were written gender neutral and so, if the police came to the home and found that the woman was assaultive, she too was arrested. These new domestic violence laws became the gateway for abuse in the home to be more clearly understood as it opened the doors that previously blocked others from knowing what was going on inside. But, it also signaled societal acceptance of imprisoning more women than ever before, even when it meant that their children would end up in state custody.

Many women report pleading guilty to domestic violence and accepting probation and a sentence to an offender-specific treatment program just so they can be released and sent home to care for their children. If they did not do so, there is danger that the children would be sent into the state child protection system. In some highly contested divorce cases, batterers have also been reporting child abuse charges against their partners (Gotbaum, 2008). It is unclear how much of this inappropriate use of the domestic violence court is due to an attempt for judges to be gender neutral or if there really is an increase in women's violence against men. However, this practice together with the arrest and prosecution of women for criminal acts, often committed under duress from abusive partners, has given us the opportunity to study women who are in jails and prisons.

Jails are the detention centers in which people are held until their crimes are adjudicated. Prisons are where people serve their sentences after they are adjudicated, either pleading guilty or being found guilty by a jury or judge. When people are arrested, they are usually able to pay a bond and be released until their case is called before a judge, but those who cannot afford to make bond or do not have anyone who is willing to put up their property as a bond in their behalf end up staying in jail after being arrested for many different types of crimes. This means that a disproportionate number of poor people remain in jail. In many places, domestic violence arrests have been taken off the bonding schedule, which means those who are arrested and charged with domestic violence must stay in jail until they go before a judge. Both women and men who are charged with domestic violence may stay in jails for long periods of time, especially in states where they may not be formally charged with a crime for several weeks.

In some areas, such as Broward County, Florida, where my students provide the Survivor Therapy Empowerment Program (STEP) to the women inmates, some are also serving short sentences for drug possession in the special program designed for those who are sentenced to drug treatment in a facility. Since there are so many people arrested with an active diagnosable mental illness, most large jails have developed clinics where they can be treated while awaiting trial. We also provide the STEP for both men and women in the clinic section, which is in addition to the other mental health services provided by the jail. We believe that the combination of mental illness and substance abuse, together with a history of trauma, requires all three types of treatment and are working to get STEP introduced in other jails where women and men are not offered trauma treatment. The recidivism rate for the mentally ill are very high and we believe that trauma-specific treatment in conjunction with the other interventions can lower it.

My colleagues Drs. James Pann, David Shapiro, and Vincent Van Hasselt and I (Walker, Pann, Shapiro, & Van Hasselt, 2016) did a study of best practices for the mentally ill in the criminal justice system and found the following:

1. No arrest and defer-to-community treatment is the best practice.
2. Community policing policy to train officers to recognize mentally ill people is needed.
3. If an arrest is made, defer immediately to mental health or other therapeutic jurisprudence (TJ) court.
4. If not possible to defer to TJ court, then place in special jail clinic.
5. Have mental health and trauma programs available in the jail.
6. Have competency restoration programs available in the jail or community.
7. Have seamless transfer to mental health programs in community when released.

WOMEN AND CRIME

There has been a growing awareness that many women currently incarcerated in jails and prisons across the country for a variety of offenses have been battered. According to the *Report of the American Psychological*

Association Presidential Task Force on Violence and the Family (American Psychological Association, 1996, p. 10), 4 million American women experience a serious assault by intimate partners during an average 12-month period. The prevalence is even higher for women who are incarcerated in jails and prisons, regardless of the type of crime committed. A special concern for women in jails and prisons is their increased likelihood to have a trauma history. Pathways for women who are incarcerated include histories of gender violence such as intimate partner abuse (Walker & Conte, in press).

As a result of women being the fastest-growing segment of the prison population, this issue deserves attention. The last decade has seen a surge in both the number and proportion of incarcerated women in the United States (Morash, Bynum, & Koons, 1998). According to a 1991 U.S. Bureau of Justice Statistics survey of state prison inmates (Morash et al., 1998), more than 43% of women inmates reported they had been physically or sexually abused prior to their prison admission. Incarcerated women report high rates of victimization, and the violence in these women's lives is often tied to the reasons they entered the criminal justice system as offenders (Browne, Miller, & Maguin, 1999). Furthermore, research shows that like the Colorado women first interviewed, many of these female prisoners were convicted and incarcerated as a result of being coerced into criminal activities by batterers.

Unfortunately, the prison system often contributes to the revictimization of women by perpetuating feelings of powerlessness and vulnerability (Bill, 1998; Walker & Conte, in press). Many prison operations include procedures that may cause vulnerable women to relive their abusive experiences, such as being routinely subject to body searches by male officers, strip searches, intrusive exploration of body parts, and examination of body cavities (Heney & Kristiansen, 1997). This is especially true for women who have been sexually assaulted or even those coerced into sexual activities against their wishes. These and other procedures contribute to the development and maintenance of posttraumatic stress disorder (PTSD) for many incarcerated women as a result of their abuse histories. Furthermore, many female inmates experience a reduced sense of self-worth, shame, and begin to think of themselves as "the kind of person" who deserves only the degradation to which they have been subjected while incarcerated. Still, others may encounter a loss of self-initiative and independence, difficulty using their own judgment, and loss of self-efficacy (Haney, 2001).

Clearly, then, the unique experiences of these women warrant special investigation, and likely require special intervention to assist them in coping with past abuse and preventing a return to abusive relationships. Few studies have attempted to explore the domestic violence histories of incarcerated women, however, and even fewer have utilized an open-ended inquiry in order to personalize these experiences.

Colorado Study

A study of the needs for victims of intimate partner violence commissioned for the Colorado legislature in the early 1990s found that over two thirds of the women in prison stated that they had been abuse victims. Estimates of up to one half of them committed the crime for which they were being punished to avoid further beatings. Forging checks to pay his bills, stealing food or other items that he denied the children, selling drugs to keep his supply filled, and hurting someone else so he did not hurt her were all acts committed under control of the batterer's threat of, or actual, violence. Some women struck back, most often with great force and usually in self-defense. Few of these women received an appropriate defense for their acts. Most listened to their attorneys' suggestions to avoid trial and plead guilty, often to a lesser negotiated plea rather than pursue a duress or diminished-capacity defense. Today psychologists who testify as expert witnesses to the psychological impact of abuse on victims' mental health functioning and current state of mind at the time of the incidents is allowed at their trials. This testimony is discussed later in this chapter.

Several other women's prisons began to organize women's self-help groups often spurred on by consultation from local battered women's task forces. Women in the Wyoming Women's prison in Evanston and Missouri's Women's Prison in Rentz sponsored conferences in the 1990s to educate themselves so as to avoid becoming victims of violence upon their release. In the Women's Correctional Institution in California, the women formed self-help groups concentrating on living more violence-free lives. Women incarcerated in the Colorado prison system begged for interventions, but the legislature was slow to appropriate the funding. Once the new prison was built, closer to Denver where psychologists could more easily volunteer their time, more programs were instituted. Women wardens who understand the special needs of their prisoners have begun to design programs that provide new opportunities in job training, education, and counseling (Schwartz, 2000). It is important for authorities to recognize that most women offenders are victims also.

In jails, where women are usually detained prior to their cases being resolved, special domestic violence units have been organized and women can volunteer to go into them rather than the general population. In some places where problem-solving courts are attempting to get mentally ill and substance-abusing women back into the community for treatment, women are able to get treatment for the impact from the trauma of having been domestic violence victims. In the next section ("Florida Study"), there is a study of the women volunteers being held in a Florida jail before the crimes they were accused of committing were adjudicated. Initially, these groups were set up for women who completed the Battered Woman Syndrome Questionnaire (BWSQ), but later on, all women in the special domestic violence units in the jail were eligible to attend the STEP groups introduced into the Broward County Detention Center in southeast Florida and further discussed in Chapter 17. As women in jail are moving in and out as their cases are being adjudicated by the courts, this program had to be adapted to jail conditions. Some of the women attending some of the group sessions did not complete the BWSQ or the group treatment even though they were also eligible to attend an outpatient group at the nearby community psychological services center.

Florida Study

The initial analysis of the BWSQ completed by 11 of the women in jail was done using qualitative rather than quantitative analysis (Tome & McMillan, 2006). Although other women began the BWSQ, it was not completed due to legal restraints mentioned previously. However, these results were consistent with others reported and give some direction to those interested in designing programs for these women.

A qualitative analysis of the female inmates' narrative accounts of battering incidents revealed three main themes consistent with the other research on battered woman syndrome: power and control, cycle of violence, and learned helplessness. These themes were prevalent in descriptions of battering in general, as well as descriptions of specific battering incidents. The analysis revealed that the inmates' partners used a variety of methods of power and control (including isolation, manipulation, degradation, and fear), and that such techniques typically increased in intensity and escalated in frequency as the relationship progressed. Similarly, the participants' experiences of learned helplessness intensified over time.

The following quotes are consistent with the themes of power and control, cycle of violence, and learned helplessness found in battered woman syndrome:

Power and Control

Of the 11 women interviewed, nine indicated that themes of power and control were common within their battering relationship. A few examples are as follows:

> "I had no freedom, no money, occasionally he let me out to go to the grocery store down the road but if I didn't return on time, he hit me badly."
> "At the beginning they're all nice [when dating], but controlling. 'Where are you, who did you go out with?' And then after I moved in they told me, 'You can't see your family, can't do this, can't do that because you're with me.' Then verbally abusive, name-calling, 'you are no good.'"
> "I had to sit beside the phone all day to answer his calls. He checked in on me all the time. I wasn't allowed to work or go anywhere without him."

Cycle of Violence

The theme of cycle of violence was found in six of the 11 interviews. These women reported the following examples in their battering relationships:

> "He hit me with an open hand a few times, and put his hands around my neck . . . he said he didn't mean it, and said he would never do it again . . . that things would change."
> "He hit me, smashed my face on the wall several times, then he apologized, bought me jewelry and swore not to do it again, but he did it over and over."

"After he stopped, he drove to a gas station to get gas. He came out of the gas station with a rose and my favorite drink. He started apologizing as usual. He always did."

Learned Helplessness

The theme of learned helplessness was found among six of the 11 women's descriptions of their battering relationships. A few examples of these descriptions are as follows:

"I felt dominated. Doomed to live life not wanting to live."
"I cannot have a good life without him, nobody would love me, or care about me, or want me, but him. I am worth nothing."
"With time I just got accustomed to the abuse."

The themes of power and control, cycle of violence, and learned helplessness were found through each victim's account of previous abuse. Findings were consistent with previous studies on battered woman syndrome. The small sample size utilized for the study limited the generalization of the results but identifies trends that can help in designing interventions to assist women in jails and prisons to heal from the traumas. Therefore, this research, which explores the dynamics of abusive relationships and female prisoners' responses to the abuse, could lead to the development of specialized treatment programs in jails and prisons, as well as community-based programs for women on probation or parole. These results may also assist women who are involved in the criminal justice system due to crimes committed upon their abusers.

RECENT STUDY

Carlye Conte and I were invited to review the issues facing battered women currently being held in jails and prisons across the United States for a chapter in a book *Gender Psychology and Justice: The Mental Health of Girls and Women in the Legal System* (Datchi & Ancis, in press). As we reviewed the history of the involvement of the criminal justice system in combating domestic violence we found some unintended consequences of the mandatory arrest and other policies adopted in the 1980s. The social and legal reforms that resulted in the criminalization of domestic violence have also resulted in the arrest of more women than ever before as described previously. As women who had experienced gender violence filled the jails and prisons, the legal system has been unprepared to provide for their needs. Often demonstrating the symptoms of PTSD and battered woman syndrome (BWS) among other mental and physical health issues, these women's needs were beyond the capabilities of the corrections system that has traditionally been underfunded and unsupportive of women. Corrections staff rarely have been trained to identify how domestic violence intersects with other forms of oppression and inequality. In fact, the entire criminal justice system has been so male dominated that it discourages women's participation. Mandatory arrest laws, for example, have resulted in dual arrests that harm rather than protect battered women. Often women plead guilty to obtain deferral into domestic violence and anger-management programs even though they have acted in self-defense, just to be able to be released to go home and prevent their children from being taken into foster care. Hirschel, Buzawa, Pattavina, and Faggiani (2007) found that the dual arrest rate is nearly two times higher than the average 2% when domestic violence arrests are mandated rather than preferred or discretionary. For some women these arrests can cause them to lose the opportunity to be a licensed health care practitioner if they are identified as the primary aggressor when they are actually acting in self-defense.

Once a woman is labeled as a violent offender, even if she acted in self-defense, she can lose access to future protection and victim assistance and she may encounter increased stigmatization and marginalization. It is simply wrong to criminalize a nonoffending woman who has been a victim of abuse, and it reduces the likelihood that she will seek assistance from the criminal justice system in the future should she need its protection. It also exacerbates her trauma symptoms and can increase her feelings of guilt, shame, powerlessness, and vulnerability.

No-drop policies are another form of legal intervention with unintended negative outcomes for the victims of domestic violence. They mandate the prosecution of individuals arrested for battering, whether or not the victim has agreed to press charges. In cases where victims have been uncooperative, the system has been known to turn against the victim sometimes even holding her in contempt of court for refusing to testify against the batterer. These cases focus on the victim and her problems rather than keeping the bright light shining on the problems with the system itself that make some victims reluctant to engage with it. For many, they are left alone to face the anger of the man who expected her to protect him rather than participate in his criminalization. Goodman and Epstein (2008) and Mallicoat (2014) describe how the legal interventions designed to protect women's safety actually can disempower survivors by taking away their choices around ramifications concerning their future lives when all they really wanted was help to stop the current violence.

Women who come in contact with the criminal justice system for the first time are often shocked at how demeaning the court personnel can be. Many staff do not hide their scorn at a woman who may go back to the batterer even after he is arrested for hurting them. Others find interactions with the judge and prosecutors frustrating especially if the rules do not permit them to tell their stories of what happened in their own words. Only facts not opinions are permitted by the witness when testifying in a legal case and it is difficult for a woman to strip the context in order to conform to these rules of evidence. Women from diverse backgrounds and those with disabilities have even more barriers to making their life experiences understood by jurors who may not be like them. Mental health practitioners and battered woman advocates are often needed to testify as expert witnesses in order to get the whole story before the court. Cross-examination may unduly revictimize the woman by trying to make the violence committed by her partner somehow be her fault. These are problems with the criminal justice system when intimate partners become involved.

As discussed in the chapter on domestic violence courts, if they follow a TJ model, it is likely they will be able to protect the victim while also providing appropriate services for the batterer to get help for his problem, rather than go off to jail or prison. However, it is important that the TJ model be utilized with those who can be helped to stop their violent behavior, something that is difficult to assess. Most domestic violence courts now give a batterer three strikes or attempts to utilize offender-specific services and then, to ensure victim safety, will no longer defer on the fourth arrest. However, in some cases, it is clear much earlier that an arrest will not deter the batterer from committing further harm to the woman or children. After one arrest in some cases, the consequences were so great that the woman knows that if there is another arrest, she will be hurt much worse. Again, she now has little or no protection from the police.

BWS EVIDENCE IN THE COURTROOM

Expert witness testimony on BWS has been permitted in the courts in the United States and many other countries for over 30 years now, although the history of its introduction demonstrated the slow legal process that occurred with case-by-case acceptance (Walker, 1989a, 1989b). I first introduced testimony in a Montana case of Miriam Grieg who shot and killed her abusive husband in the middle of an acute battering incident. After shooting the six hollow point bullets into her husband's body, Miriam ran out of their apartment, and told police to be very careful when they entered, as she was sure her husband was still alive and angry enough to shoot them. This belief in the omnipotence and invincibility of the batterer that battered women display is commonly seen in the women we have interviewed. However, these women have been unable to get the message about their desperation and belief that they will be killed by the batterer to the jurors and courts by themselves.

They need the assistance of an expert witness for several reasons. First, these women were never allowed to talk about what was happening behind their closed doors, so they were terrified to say very much even in their own defense. Second, most of the women believed that they would not be charged with murder once the police understood the danger they had faced. Third, the law allows a lay witness to testify only about facts, not opinions. However, an expert witness can talk about the woman's fears and her psychological state of mind at the time she kills the man, so that the triers of fact can make a better judgment about the level of responsibility for the woman in these cases.

Research has demonstrated that the use of BWS in court cases helps jurors make a better decision. Canadian psychologist, Regina Schuller, and her colleagues have been investigating both the impact of gender and the use of expert testimony in cases where battered women kill their abusive partners (Schuller, 1992; Schuller & Cripps, 1998; Schuller & Hastings, 1996; Schuller & Vidmar, 1992). Examining different variables, including the timing of when in the trial BWS testimony would be introduced, Schuller and her colleagues found that mock jurors were more likely to find mitigating circumstances when such testimony was introduced. Attorneys who have utilized expert testimony in defense cases have written articles published in law journals detailing how they got good results.

WOMEN'S SELF-DEFENSE CASES

Occasionally (between 10% and 15% of all homicides in the United States) a woman will kill her abuser while trying to defend herself or her children. Sometimes, she strikes back during a calm period, knowing that the tension is building toward another acute battering incident, where this time she may die. When examining the statistics, we find that more women than men are charged with first- or second-degree murder. There seems to be a sexist bias operating in which the courts find it more difficult to see justifiable or mitigating circumstances for women who kill (see Walker, 1989b, for a more complete discussion of these cases). The now classic Broverman, Broverman, Clarkson, Rosencrantz, and Vogel (1970) studies demonstrated that the kinds of behaviors and emotions expressed when committing an aggressive act will be viewed as normal for men but not for women. On the other hand, women's violence is more likely to be found excusable, if her insanity under the law can be demonstrated. Any changes in the insanity laws will probably have the greatest impact on women and other assault victims who reach a breaking point and no longer know the difference between right and wrong and/or can no longer refrain from an irresistible impulse to survive.

In most states' criminal codes, the use of self-defense is permissible if the woman can demonstrate that she had a *reasonable perception* of *imminent danger*. The definition of what a *reasonable perception* is has been the subject of debate among legal scholars—is it what a *reasonable person* or a *reasonable woman* or a *reasonable battered woman* perceives that counts? Is the *perception* an *objective* one that anyone might be expected to conclude or is it a more *subjective perception* that is based on everything the battered woman knows and has experienced? In most states, this argument has been resolved in favor of a compromise—using both objective and subjective perceptions.

Another major area that has had to be defined is, what does *imminent* mean? In some interpretations, imminent is seen as immediate. But in most jurisdictions, imminent is believed to mean *about to happen* as if on the edge of a cliff and you are about to fall off. Obviously, this is important because many battered women kill in self-defense by using what otherwise might be viewed as a preemptory strike—like getting a gun and shooting him while he is coming toward her with outstretched arms and a look in his eyes that reminds her of the last brutal beating. It would be a reasonable perception for that woman to believe that serious bodily harm or death is imminent primarily because she has been threatened with death and previously suffered serious bodily harm when he acted in the same way.

In some jurisdictions, self-defense is defined as the justifiable commission of a criminal act by using the least amount of force necessary to prevent imminent bodily harm, which needs only to be reasonably perceived as about to happen. The perception of how much force is necessary, then, must also be reasonable. Such a definition works against women because they are not socialized to use physical force, are rarely equal to a man in size, strength, or physical training, and may have learned to expect more injury with inadequate attempts to repel a man's attack. Thus, some courts, such as Washington state in 1985 in the *Kelley* case, have ruled it would be reasonable for a woman to defend herself with a deadly weapon against a man armed only with the parts of his body he learned to use as a deadly weapon. Courts also have been allowing evidence to account for the cumulative effects of repeated violence in self-defense and diminished-capacity assertions. Expert witness testimony has been admitted in many states to help explain the reasonableness of such perceptions.

One of the major changes in the criminal law is to allow battered women to present evidence of the cumulative effects of abuse in courts through the testimony of a psychologist using what the courts refer to as *BWS*. Here, the legal system uses the term "BWS" in a different way from psychologists. Psychologists use the term "BWS" like it is presented in this book—a way to talk about the psychological impact from living with domestic violence. The legal system adds to that definition a description of the dynamics of the violence, often emphasizing physical assaults and downplaying the role of psychological maltreatment and coercive control. Although some advocates do not like using "BWS" for political reasons—fearing that labeling the symptoms as a syndrome will infantilize and pathologize battered women—in fact, the legal system has thoroughly embraced the concept and uses it mostly to assist battered women in criminal and civil cases. The courts combine the entire research project under that title so that the cycle theory and learned helplessness are under the dynamics of battering relationships along with the psychological symptoms that are often seen as a result of the abuse. Despite the political implications, battered women's perceptions of imminent danger and their behavior are better understood by the lay jury when BWS is used at trial.

EXPERT TESTIMONY

Criminal Cases

As discussed in the Women's Self-Defense Cases section, presenting evidence of BWS by experts in criminal cases has been successful both in getting psychological testimony admitted in criminal and civil cases and in assisting the triers of fact as demonstrated by the research conducted by Schuller and her colleagues (Schuller, 1992). I have now testified in over 400 cases of battered women who killed their abusers in what they claimed was self-defense using the theories of BWS, learned helplessness, and the cycle of violence. In most cases, the testimony was successful in either reducing the responsibility from murder to a lesser level such as manslaughter or even not guilty because of self-defense.

Typically, a forensic psychological evaluation of the woman is performed using the BWSQ or a similar clinical interview and data from standardized tests measuring cognitive abilities and the impact from emotions on those skills. The emphasis on cognition is important since the criminal laws and levels of responsibility are based on what is in the actor's mind and how reasonable perceptions are impacted by emotions. In order to get this testimony admitted into most courts, it may be necessary to also give a clinical diagnosis. In those cases, PTSD or even major depressive or bipolar disorder may be used, not as an insanity defense, but rather, simply to show how these emotional disorders can impact the woman's state of mind and her reasonable perception of imminent danger to meet the self-defense statutes. In some states, the legislature has determined that women who assert a self-defense based on BWS must undergo a psychological evaluation by the state's doctor, similar to those who assert an insanity defense. This is unfortunate, as it mischaracterizes BWS by many uninformed mental health professionals as a mental disorder akin to an insanity excuse rather than applying it to justify why she acted as she did.

Then why use BWS at all if it may be misused by those who do not understand the dynamics of domestic violence? This question is answered because of the need to explain the often counterintuitive behavior of battered women to lay people. Although it is clear that most battered women are actually safer while living together with the batterer, given the high rates of deadly violence used by the batterer when he perceives the relationship is ending, the question that continues to be asked is: Why did the woman not leave? An explanation of the cycle of violence with its rewards coming during the third phase of the cycle helps lay people understand that the abuse is not constant and why there is a strong bond of love between the couple that is formed when things are going well. Understanding learned helplessness and its resulting belief that escape is impossible while developing more coping responses, including purchasing and using firearms for protection, is another important explanation to put before jurors.

Perhaps most important is the ability of PTSD and BWS to help the trier of fact understand that even when the actual violence is not present, the anticipation of further abuse occurs in the battered woman's mind when the batterer begins his pattern of escalating violent behavior. His behavior becomes a trigger for the traumatized woman who then reexperiences the past violence as if it was reoccurring at that moment. This is similar to what is reported by war veterans whose memories of combat are triggered by similar sounds such as a helicopter hovering above a grassy area. It is important to remember that it is the reasonable perception of imminent danger, which does not have to be accurate, but simply reasonable for the average battered woman that jurors must assess in a justification defense.

Testimony about learned helplessness can be offered by demonstrating that the seven factors that were found in the original research, associated with those who demonstrated learned helplessness from the original Seligman studies, were also present for this woman. As described in Chapter 4, those factors included:

- Abuse in the relationship occurring in a particular pattern, usually but not necessarily an identifiable cycle of violence with an escalation of the abuse
- Sexual abuse or coercion within the relationship
- Isolation, overpossessiveness, intrusiveness, and extreme jealousy by the man toward the woman
- Threats to kill the woman or other loved ones by the man. (These threats can be direct or indirect such as bragging about how he killed other people or forcing the woman, and sometimes the children, to watch as he shoots and kills family pets.)
- Psychological abuse as assessed by the Amnesty International definition of torture

- Violence correlates, including abuse toward children, pets, or other people, or destruction of objects
- Alcohol or other drug abuse

Testimony about learned helplessness from childhood factors included:

- Child experienced molestation or sexual abuse as a child
- Child was exposed to domestic violence in childhood home
- Loss of power and control experiences such as abuse, frequent moves, poverty, and shame, etc.
- Rigid sex-role socialization, including orthodox religions
- Frequent or chronic childhood illnesses

Testimony about BWS and PTSD uses the actual criteria from the *Diagnostic and Statistical Manual of Mental Disorders* (5th ed.; *DSM-5*; American Psychiatric Association, 2013) for PTSD and the three additional criteria for BWS. These included:

- Reexperiencing of trauma event(s)
- High levels of avoidance behavior and emotional numbing
- High levels of anxiety and hyperarousal
- Cognitive difficulties, including attention and concentration
- Disruption of interpersonal relationships from loss of power and control and isolation
- Distorted body image and somatic complaints
- Sexual issues

Presentation of the factors to the jury may utilize demonstrative aids to assist them in remembering all of them. Using charts with the factors first and then adding the specifics found in the evaluation of the particular woman on trial afterward is a good way to organize testimony so that the jurors and judge can follow how the diagnosis was made and conclusions were reached. This helps separate psychological testimony from the myths that it is not scientific and relies only on the examiner's opinion that is allegedly biased by the fees charged. All professionals involved with legal proceedings charge a fee, whether it is included in the salaries of those paid by the state to serve as lawyers, jurors, and expert witnesses, all of whom get paid for their time not their opinions. Forensic psychologists are trained to base their opinions on the data and use the data to educate judges and jurors who are the triers of fact. Obviously, even the best professional who is untrained in domestic violence can overlook or misunderstand important data and therefore, base his or her opinion on inadequate data.

CLEMENCY CASES

Once it became possible for battered women who killed their abusers to introduce BWS testimony by expert witnesses, it became clear that there were many women in prisons serving long sentences, even life without parole and death sentences in the United States, who never got a fair trial. In many cases they already had lost their appeals or had pled guilty at the behest of their attorneys who did not know about or wish to utilize a justification defense and therefore were not eligible to appeal their sentences. The only step left for these women was to petition the governors of their states for clemency and ask to be released earlier than their sentences required. Each state used a different standard for clemency, some utilizing strict parole boards, with others like Florida using the governor's elected cabinet officers. Ohio and Maryland both only needed the governor to make a clemency decision and in the early 1990s, the governors of those two states courageously granted clemency and released battered women who had killed their abusers in self-defense. Governor William Donald Schaefer of Maryland actually released 13 women after reviewing their histories and visiting with them in prison. Other governors soon followed suit and it is unknown exactly how many women have been released from prison. None have been known to have killed another intimate partner.

Most recently I testified at a rehearing of a case in San Jose, California, where the cases of women who did not get to present evidence of BWS or other information about the role and influence of domestic violence on the crimes for which they were sent to prison have been permitted to petition the court for a new hearing. Sonya Daniels has spent the past 20 years in prison serving a life sentence for the death of her 6-year-old son, Jory, who died of malnutrition. Both Sonya and the child were beaten by her husband Brian Daniels and frequently locked in their rooms without food for days at a time. Sonya was 15 years old when she started dating Brian and she soon became pregnant with Jory. They lived with both sets of parents who could not control Brian's abusive behavior. Her description of the domestic violence in their relationship was similar to others that have been studied. A psychologist at the time of her arrest and trial evaluated her and found she had PTSD and BWS. But, the judge at the original trial would not permit any evidence of domestic violence toward her by Brian (they were tried as codefendants) because she did not kill her husband; it was their child who died.

Sonya was vilified during that trial by prosecutors who were angry with her for failing to protect her child as a mother is supposed to do. But, without explanation of why she was incapable of protecting the child since she could not even protect herself from Brian's violence, she was found guilty of first-degree murder and sentenced to life in prison. Even today, 20 years later, the prosecutor who cross-examined me at the rehearing could not control her contempt for Sonya in her questions to me. Why did she not take the child to the hospital when he was ill? How could she not demand to buy food for the child? I tried to underscore the inability of anyone to control Brian. I described the doctors' findings of malnutrition in Sonya as well as the other children and the fact that having four pregnancies in 6 years would be difficult for anyone to manage. I gave an example that Sonya had told me about finding the door to her bedroom open rather than locked as it usually was when Brian and everyone else left the house. Sonya told of how she foraged in the garbage and found some old pieces of chicken nuggets that she ate trying to stave off her hunger. The jury never heard this testimony, only the anger from Brian's mother and family who were now raising the other children while both parents were sentenced to prison. The judge has not ruled yet, but given the prosecutor's attitude, the chances are not good that Sonya will be released anytime soon.

CIVIL LAW PERSONAL INJURY CASES

A number of the women interviewed told of filing civil lawsuits against their former husbands asking to be compensated for their physical and psychological injuries. Until fairly recently, state laws did not permit women to sue their husbands, but removal of the interspousal tort immunity has opened the way for filing such legal claims. This legal remedy has potential to raise the actual dollar cost of violence so high that men will carefully consider the consequences prior to committing an assault. It also has benefits for individual women that go beyond their recovering the actual dollars expended to heal from their attacks.

Being a plaintiff in a civil suit implies an offensive approach. Using such assertive and even aggressive behavior helps women express their anger in a socially acceptable manner at having been victimized. For many of our women, winning money was less important than the whole process of feeling as though the balance of power had changed and knowing they could control their tormentors. The civil law is a long and tedious process, and may be difficult in exposing the woman's entire life, including embarrassing things too, but many of the women stated they enjoyed learning the legal rules and watching the batterers have to conform to them. It was not seen as revenge but rather retribution for all that the men had put them through. Winning on ideological points was sometimes as therapeutic as having their financial claims prevail.

Psychologists are now giving BWS testimony in these civil courts to prove the psychological damages suffered by battered women. In New Jersey, for example, the Giovine and subsequent cases have ruled that domestic violence is a continuing tort, and therefore removed the time limit that bars some older incidents from being presented in a case. In many states, women are expected to file within 1 to 2 years of an assault. Thus, extending or removing the time limit is important because for many battered women it is not until they are out of the relationship and beginning to heal that they can start to deal with the long-term effects of abuse and put them in perspective. In New Jersey, however, the claim for damages must be filed in the same court that hears divorce actions, although it is now possible to request a jury trial that previously had been barred. The new 1994 Violence Against Women Civil Rights Act also removes the need for a time limit so that women who are barred from taking civil actions in state court may choose to use the federal laws for justice.

CIVIL RIGHTS LAW—VIOLENCE AGAINST WOMEN ACT (VAWA) OF 1994

Despite the advances made in criminal and civil areas of the law, those who wanted to stop the abuse of male violence against women advocated for a federal statute that would declare violence against women to be a civil rights violation—in other words, a violation of every woman's right to be protected under the U.S. Constitution. After several years of political lobbying efforts, the Congress passed and President Clinton signed into law the VAWA of 1994. This law did several things. By making male violence against women a civil rights complaint, it made it possible for women to file for compensatory and punitive damages against one or more abusers in federal court without having to prove the nexus between domestic violence and their personal damage from the abuse. Physical and sexual assaults of a woman were declared to pose such potential harm for the woman that it could be deemed a violation of her civil rights if the assault could be proven to have occurred. It also recognized the difficulty abuse victims have in disclosing their victimization and therefore did not place any time restrictions on when the abuse had to be reported. This was important because most state civil tort laws do have a 1- to 2-year statute of limitation that is difficult though not impossible to overcome. The statute can be tolled (stopped) if it can be proved that the woman did not have the ability to know or report what she knew. The time clock starts running again at the point she is deemed able to know what happened. Interestingly, the standard that she must prove is that the man intended to commit whatever action he took, not that he intended to harm her, which is much more difficult to prove when there is also a love bond in the relationship. Early case decisions suggested that this part of the law was going to continue to be challenged and indeed it now has been eliminated in the renewal of VAWA.

There were several other areas that this law covered in addition to the civil rights portion. One major area was in giving police departments more training and equipment so that they could better protect abused women. At the same time, police departments were instructed to make sure that they did not permit any officer who had been convicted of abuse to carry a gun or other weapon. Obviously, in the United States, it is almost impossible to remain a police officer and not carry a weapon. While this was designed to get better law enforcement protection for battered and sexually abused women, in fact it caused major difficulties for law enforcement agencies that had many officers in their departments with convictions on their records from many years earlier. Eventually, it will be easier to enforce this section of the law, as law enforcement departments learn to better screen their potential employees.

Other areas of the civil rights laws have also been used to better protect battered women. The most notable case was that of Tracey Thurman, a severely physically abused battered woman who sued the Torrington,

Connecticut, police department under the 1963 Civil Rights Act for failure to protect her constitutional rights to be free from violence and to have her safety protected by them. *Thurman v. Torrington* was filed after the police failed to protect her from a brutal beating from her abusive husband. She won over $2 million in damages in a judgment that also required the police department to change its policies and procedures to better protect all battered women. The award was significant enough to get the attention of police departments across the country and thus ended up protecting many mothers.

SUMMARY

This chapter has discussed how the criminal justice system has treated battered women over the past 40 years. While some of the new laws that were passed were intended to protect women, in fact for some it has had the opposite effect, especially those that require mandatory arrest rather than simply making arrest possible on probable cause. The gender bias, including sexism and racism, for women coming before the criminal justice system continues to make it difficult for women to seek safety and protection. Even those who commit a crime such as homicide in self-defense do not always get to present their story so the triers of fact understand. Unable to make their experiences clear in court requires that they have expert witnesses put their lives into context so their perceptions and behavior are better understood by juries and judges.

REFERENCES

American Psychiatric Association. (2013). *Diagnostic and statistical manual of mental disorders* (5th ed.). Arlington, VA: American Psychiatric Publishing.

American Psychological Association. (1996). *Report from the Presidential Task Force on Violence and the Family.* Washington, DC: Author.

Bill, L. (1998, December). The victimization and re-victimization of female offenders. *Corrections Today, 60,* 106–112.

Broverman, I. K., Broverman, D., Clarkson, F., Rosencrantz, P., & Vogel, S. (1970). Sex role stereotypes and clinical judgments of mental health. *Journal of Consulting and Clinical Psychology, 34,* 1–7.

Browne, A., Miller, B., & Maguin, E. (1999). Prevalence and severity of lifetime physical and sexual victimization among incarcerated women. *International Journal of Law and Psychiatry, 22*, 301–322.

Datchi, C. & Ancis, J. (Eds.). (in press). *Gender, psychology and justice: The mental health of women and girls in the legal system.* New York, NY: New York University Press.

Goodman, L. A., & Epstein D. (2008). The justice system response. In L. Goodman & D. Epstein (Eds.), *Listening to battered women: A survivor-centered approach to advocacy, mental health, and justice* (pp. 71–87). Washington, DC: American Psychological Association.

Gotbaum, B. (2008). *Calling in abuse: How domestic violence perpetrators are using the child welfare system to continue their abuse.* A report by Public Advocate of New York City. Retrieved from www.pubadvocate.nyc.gov

Haney, C. (2001). *The psychological impact of incarceration: Implications for post-prison adjustment.* Commissioned paper for the Department of Health and Human Services. Retrieved from http://aspe.hhs.gov/HSP/prison2home02/Haney.htm

Heney, J., & Kristiansen, C. M. (1997). An analysis of the impact of prison on women survivors of childhood sexual abuse. *Women & Therapy, 20*(4), 29–44.

Hirschel, D., Buzawa, E., Pattavina, A., & Faggiani, D. (2007). Dual arrest laws: To what extent do they influence police arrest decisions? *Journal of Criminal Law and Criminology, 98*(1), 255–298.

Mallicoat, S. L., & Ireland, C. E. (2014). *Women and crime: The essentials.* Thousand Oaks, CA: Sage.

Morash, M., Bynum, T. S., & Koons, B. A. (1998). *Women offenders: Programming needs and promising approaches.* Washington, DC: U.S. Department of Justice.

Schuller, R. A. (1992). The impact of battered woman syndrome evidence on jury decision processes. *Law and Human Behavior, 16*, 597–619.

Schuller, R. A., & Cripps, J. (1998). Expert evidence pertaining to battered women: The impact of gender of expert and timing of testimony. *Law and Human Behavior, 22*, 17–31.

Schuller, R. A., & Hastings, P. A. (1996). Trials of battered women who kill: The impact of alternative forms of expert evidence. *Law and Human Behavior, 20*, 167–187.

Schuller, R. A., & Vidmar, N. (1992). Battered woman syndrome evidence in the courtroom. *Law and Human Behavior, 16*(3), 273–291.

Schwartz, M. (2000). Methodological issues in the use of survey data for measuring and characterizing violence against women. *Violence Against Women, 6*(8), 815–838.

Tome, A., & McMillan, C. (2006). *A Review: In their own words—Domestic violence and incarcerated women.* A presentation at the annual meeting of the American Psychological Association, New Orleans, LA.

The Violence Against Women Act, 42 U.S.C. §§ 13931–14040 (1994).

Walker, L. E. (1989a). Psychology and violence against women. *American Psychologist, 44*, 695–702.

Walker, L. E. (1989b). *Terrifying love: Why battered women kill and how society responds.* New York, NY: Harper & Row.

Walker, L. E. A., & Conte, C. (in press). Vulnerabilities of survivors of domestic violence in the criminal justice system. In C. Datchi & J. Ancis (Eds.), *Gender, psychology and justice: The mental health of women and girls in the legal system.* New York: New York University Press.

Walker, L. E. A., Pann, J. M., Shapiro, D. L., & Van Hasselt, V. B. (2016). *Best practices for the mentally ill in the criminal justice system.* Cham, Switzerland: Springer.

Index

Shapiro, Francine, 423
Sheen, Charlie, 170
shell shock, 402
shock troops (rapists), 236
Siegel, Dan, 175
Silberg, Joyanna, 480
Simpson, O. J., 32, 34, 35, 239
   escalation with Nicole Brown and,
      308–309
smoking, 326
social class, battering and, 285–286
social functioning, 156. *See also*
      interpersonal functioning
social learning theory, 115. *See also*
      learning theory
sociodemographic data, 57–58, 240
somatic symptoms, 319, 339–341
Sonkin, Daniel, 177, 285, 292
SORAG. *See* Sexual Offense Risk
      Assessment Guide
Soviet collapse, 249
Spain, 57, 58, 60, 64, 69, 236, 245–248,
   359
Spanish Organic Act 1/2004 of
   December (Integrated
   Protection Measures Against
   Gender Violence), 246
spanking, 15
Spousal Assault Risk Assessment
   checklist (SARA), 293
spouse abuse abatement programs
   (SAAP), 495
SSRIs. *See* selective serotonin reuptake
   inhibitors
St. Petersburg State University, 248
stalking, 30, 210, 354
Stark, Evan, 348
STATIC 99, 297
STDs. *See* sexually transmitted
   diseases
Steinberg, Joel, 31, 146
Steinberg, Lisa, 31, 146

STEP. *See* Survivor Therapy
      Empowerment Program
Stop Violence (Russia), 249
stress
   attachment theory and, 177
   illnesses and, 323
   mind and body toll, 414
stress and coping perspective
      (Lazarus and Folkman), 117
structured clinical approaches, 296
substance abuse, 307–308, 371–395
   arrests and, 326
   BWSQ #1, 375, 384–386
   BWSQ #2, 375, 387–392
   cannabis (marijuana), 380–381
   cocaine and amphetamines, 381–382
   common themes of studies of,
      383–384
   deferral into therapeutic courts,
      372–373
   domestic violence issues of teens
      and, 131
   intervention, 394–395
   methylenedioxymethamphetamine
      (MDMA; "ecstasy"), 383
   opiates (morphine, heroin, codeine),
      379–380
   phencyclidine (PCP), 382
   role of alcohol and drug abuse in
      battered women, 392
   sedatives-hypnotics-anxiolytics
      (benzodiazepines), 378–379
   voluntary and involuntary
      intoxication, 372–373
   women's and public policy, 392–395
substance abuse treatment, combined
      with domestic violence program
      (empirical findings), 503
suicide, 303, 305–306
   murder and self-defense, 223–233
   weapons, 224
   women's intent, 512

VAWA. *See* Violence Against Women
  Act
Villavicencio, Patricia, 237, 359
violence
  adult history of abuse, 92
  alcohol abuse and, 374–378
  childhood history of abuse, 91–92,
    93, 94
  dating, 213–214
  reinforcement of, 284
  relationship between childhood
    history of abuse and adult
    experiences, 94
  sample demographics, 91
  teen, 42–43
Violence Against Women Act (1994,
    2005) civil rights act, 237, 354,
    535–537
violence in the family, 517
Violence Policy Center, 223
violence-prone personality patterns,
    281–286
  abuse in their childhood homes,
    281–283
  attachment disorders, 285
  battering history, 282
  social class and, 285–286
Violence Risk Appraisal Guide
    (VRAG), 297
visitation issues, 132–136
volunteer treatment, success of,
    501–502
VRAG. *See* Violence Risk Appraisal
    Guide

Walker, Lenore, 49, 237
  Survivor Therapy Empowerment
    Program (STEP), 40
  *Terrifying Love: Why Women Kill and
    How Society Responds,* 303
Walker Cycle Theory of Violence, 78,
    94–107

Waverly Place (Brownmiller), 31
weapons, 306
websites
  Phyllis Chesler, 31
  for prevention and intervention,
    358
wilding, 127
Witch-Hunt Narrative, The (Cheit),
    461, 477
witness tampering, 41
Woman's Inhumanity to Woman
    (Chesler), 31
women
  crime and, 519–524
  deaths and injuries due to IVP, 33
  domestic violence, 226
  false confessions
    analyzing database of 2014,
      461–462
    coerced compliant, 459–460
    coerced internalized, 459
    coerced reactive, 460
    conviction against children,
      462–463
    innocence and, 460–463
    voluntary confession to crimes,
      459
    voluntary internalized, 459
  fearful attachment style, 174
  lures with schemes for sex
    trafficking, 167–168
  murder-suicide, 223
  primary aggressors in abusive
    relationships, 509
  psychotherapy for battered women,
    39–40
  substance abuse and public policy,
    392–395
  violence toward men, 286–289
Women and Madness (Chesler), 31, 38
Women's International Zionist
    Organization (WIZO), 360